Learning and Behavior
A Psychobiological Perspective

Learning and Behavior

A Psychobiological Perspective

Lewis M. Barker
Baylor University

Macmillan College Publishing Company
New York

Maxwell Macmillan Canada
Toronto

Maxwell Macmillan International
New York   Oxford   Singapore   Sydney

Editor: Christine Cardone
Production Supervisor: Ann-Marie WongSam
Production Manager: Paul Smolenski
Text and Cover Designer: Eileen Burke
Cover Illustration: © Marjory Dressler
Photo Researcher: Diane Austin

This book was set in New Aster by The Clarinda Company
and was printed and bound by R. R. Donnelley & Sons Company.
The cover was printed by Phoenix Color Corp.

Acknowledgments and photo credits appear on pages 531–535,
which constitute a continuation of the copyright page.

Macmillan College Publishing Company
866 Third Avenue, New York, New York, 10022

Macmillan College Publishing Company is part of
the Maxwell Communication Group of Companies.

Maxwell Macmillan Canada, Inc.
1200 Eglinton Avenue East
Suite 200
Don Mills, Ontario M3C 3N1

Library of Congress Cataloging-in-Publication Data

Barker, Lewis M., 1942–
    Learning and behavior : a psychobiological perspective / Lewis M.
Barker.
      p.   cm.
    Includes bibliographical references and index.
    ISBN 0-02-305951-6
    1. Learning, Psychology of.   2. Psychobiology.   I. Title.
BF318.B37   1994
153.1′5—dc20   93-1431
                                                               CIP

Printing: 1 2 3 4 5 6 7   Year: 4 5 6 7 8 9 0

To my parents, Ronald and Sydona,
who shaped my views of love and life

Preface for Instructors

Learning and Behavior: A Psychobiological Perspective has been written as a primary text for a college-level course in learning. This book will be of interest to instructors who recognize the broad, pervasive role that learning and behavior theory currently plays in the many subfields of psychology. Several cross-field, and cross-interest integrations have been attempted here. First, the term "psychobiology" signals the merging of important concepts in biology—namely ethology, physiology, and behavioral genetics—with traditional psychological approaches to understanding the behavior of humans and other animals. I don't think that my text breaks new ground in the merging of biology and psychology, a process that has been ongoing for at least a century and a half. Certainly, the research and theoretical formulations of Pavlov and Darwin, to take two examples, have influenced contemporary psychology so much we tend to think of them as proto-psychologists. In any event, this text has a decidedly biological flavor to it.

A second cross-interest integration may make the text more palatable to instructors who prefer a main course of psychology, with a little biology on the side. This book has been specifically written for students who take a course in learning as part of their psychology major. I attempt to address their interests in applied areas of psychology by showing how laboratory experiments using animals help to account for the behavioral complexity they encounter in their everyday lives. Their issues may concern "abnormal" behavior, behavioral analysis and control, health, analyses of (free?) choice, and other complexities of human motivation. I analyze these issues from a deterministic, behavioral/biological perspective, offering a needed scientific counterbalance to the "softer" explanations they may encounter in other courses in their major.

Why another learning book? I worked with chimpanzees for several years in the 1960s, an experience that markedly shaped my views on the similarities and differences of "human" and "animal" behavior. Perhaps for this reason I have been uncomfortable with the current formulation of "learning" in most textbooks as synonymous with, and as exemplified by, "animal learning." And, although no one would ever mistake my book for a "human learning" textbook, I have nevertheless attempted to integrate consciousness, conceptual learning, thinking, language, and other cognitive activities with traditional themes and topics of animals' learning.

I think there are several good alternatives to this text, but over a 20-year period of failing to find one that my students liked—one they would actually read—I decided to write my own. As I relate to students in *their* preface, this book is designed to be thought provoking, "user friendly," and relevant to their interests. Again, my thinking is that learning is too important to be relegated to some esoteric subfield called "animal learning"—one that the majority of psychologists and students make jokes about; hence, the attempt of this textbook to integrate across fields and across the diverse interests of psychology and of psychologists. I believe that learning integrated in this fashion with traditional psychological interests will continue to be taught in Departments of Psychology in the twenty-first century.

This book has a sprinkling of engaging cartoons, boxed discussions, and footnotes. I have included them because they allow me the illusion of keeping my informal classroom voice. My major professor pointed out years ago that there's no sense talking if no one's listening. A few digressions and other surprises should reinforce page turning in the same way that an outrageous overhead will make a 50-minute class seem a little shorter. With no exceptions the boxes contain material over which a student can be tested. They might need to be reminded of that, unless your students are like mine in methodically determining if "[x] will be on the test."

In lieu of walking you through the textbook organization, I recommend that you first browse through the Contents and Chapter 1 for an overview. Each chapter ends with a Summary, followed by Discussion Questions. Reading some of these Discussion Questions will give you both a feel for the material in that chapter as well as something of the tone and level of discourse of the text. Finally, as this book was written primarily for students taking their first learning course, you might also want to read their preface to help you decide if my book fills the bill.

Deciding to write a textbook is presumptuous. Actually writing it is both tedious and humbling. Christine Cardone, Executive Editor at Macmillan, shared my initial vision. Her emotional support and technical expertise got me going and kept me on track. Her colleagues at Macmillan, Ann-Marie WongSam and Paul Smolenski, and the copyeditor, Andrew Schwartz, made it happen. Excellent reviewers—Stephen F. Davis, Emporia State University; Joseph Farley, Indiana University; David K. Hogberg, Albion College; and Wayne Sjoberg, Northern Arizona University—shaped the manuscript, and my good friends and colleagues, Mike Best, John Flynn, Chuck Weaver, and Jim Patton, provided critical, personal, mirrors for many of my ideas. Baylor University supported these efforts by affording me a sabbatical. A faculty writing group under the direction of Professor Tom Hanks worked with me on various portions of this text over a period of several years. My parents and extended family, my wife Beverly, and daughters Kristen, Melinda, Kira, and Jane are at one and the same time my sources of energy, and the "reasons" I enjoy living. You will meet some of them in this book.

Preface for Students

Psychology approaches several crossroads as it enters the twenty-first century. On the one hand, the realm of applied clinical psychology has captured the majority interests of psychology students and professional psychologists alike. And for good reason. Is there anything more intriguing than the varieties and nuances of abnormal human behavior? Psychology has a long, proud tradition of training professionals to help people live happier, more productive lives.

On the other hand, basic research by behavioral neuroscientists during the past century has provided tremendous insight into the mind and human behavior. For example, we now know that pleasure and pain have neurochemical substrates and that specialization of the left and right cerebral hemispheres, under some circumstances, makes literally true the saying that "the left hand does not know what the right hand is doing." A small portion of one hemisphere even allows us to talk about it!

You, the student, stand at these crossroads. Some of you want to become researchers. Others want to learn basic psychological science and apply it to your chosen profession in clinical or industrial psychology. Yet the "hard science" side of psychology and biology is neither well integrated nor readily accessible to many students who lack a good background in the basic sciences. Compounding the problem, all of us are caught up in an information explosion that spans an incredible gap; from the molecular studies of genetics, hormones, and neurotransmitters, to brain-behavior relationships, to the more molar behavioral concerns of short- and long-term memory phenomena, eating disorders, and social development. In a word, there is too much to know, and not enough time to learn it all.

Understanding Elephants. What to do, what to do? What I have attempted here is to integrate traditional areas of academic psychology and biology with the concerns of applied psychology at a level appropriate for a first course in *learning*. The benefits of integration should be self-evident. Human behavior is multidimensional, but the unique focus of each research area in biology and psychology reveals only a small portion of the action. Imagine scientists with different interests who agree to restrict their examination of an elephant by dividing the animal into one-inch cubes. No matter how thorough a job they do in analyzing their cube, understanding the elephant will only come about by an integration of their individual findings. Recognize also that such an integration can come about only when the particulars of each individual cube are underplayed; shifting the focus to a higher level allows the elephant to assume its synthetic form and shape.

Integration is an important component of science in general, and of learning theory in particular. Due to the tensions that exist within specialties, however (i.e., between psychology and biology, between clinical and experimental psychology, between human and animal learning, etc.), the risk is that each specialty area will be leery of being short-changed by such an effort. After all, advances in *research* are primarily made by analyzing one-inch cubes, not elephants. Research scientists, therefore, have a different focus than do students and textbook writers. In the process of examining and integrating the most important one-inch cubes in this text, I try to never lose sight of the elephant.

Psychobiology?   The title of this book, *Learning and Behavior: A Psychobiological Perspective,* speaks both to the tensions in modern psychology and to my attempt at integration across fields. *Psychobiology* is neither traditional psychology nor traditional biology. Rather, it is the interdisciplinary study of learning, motivation, and behavior that draws upon and attempts to integrate observations and experiments in, among other sciences, psychology, ethology, physiology, and genetics. My working premise is that a psychobiological approach addresses the complexities of human behavior better than either psychology or biology alone.

Is the study of learning and behavior theory truly at a crossroads of modern psychology? Yes, because the questions society expects psychologists to address concern human nature and human motivation. And inquiries into human motivation—the "why" questions—rely upon both behavioral *and* biological analyses for their answers. Many psychology texts in "learning" emphasize only animals and how they learn. My text keeps the focus upon humans and the many ways in which scientific experiments help us better understand *human* behavior.

Who Am I? What Am I Doing Here?   How specifically does psychobiology address questions of human motivation? Let us look at this issue more closely by considering the following questions: "Why am I taking a course in learning?" "Why do I care so much what person X thinks about me?" "Am I really going crazy, or does it only seem that way?" "Why would I rather watch television than study?" One thing all these questions have in common is that they reflect *individual differences* in motivation. Each of us has learned to behave in unique ways. Compare your answers to these questions with those of a friend or family member. Because each person is motivated differently, it is highly unlikely that any two people would answer these questions in the same way. Individual differences are testimony to the vagaries and inconsistencies of human nature as well as to differences in the parents, schools, churches, and friends that have influenced our thinking. No wonder studying human behavior is so interesting!

Relevance to Applied Psychology. Granted that a psychobiological perspective makes sense in the academic realm, you may still wonder about its application to the interests of a counselor or clinical psychologist. I make the case in this text that learning and behavior theory are essential elements in the preparation of students and professionals who have applied interests. To understand a person, or to help someone, you must know what motivates that person. You must know something of his or her early learning history and environment—that is, the determinants of how that person behaves and thinks as well as how he or she experiences emotions. To the extent that the pathology you see in a patient is the result of aversively conditioned emotional responses, or of having learned maladaptive patterns of interpersonal behavior, one of your goals is to help that patient relearn more adaptive modes of behavior.

The operative terms here are "learn" and "relearn." A psychobiological approach to understanding human behavior is particularly applicable in the area of health psychology. Eating disorders, asthma, and phobias, to take three diverse examples, are best understood and treated by recognizing their inherent biological and psychological components. Indeed, most health problems are "psychobiological." Applications of learning and behavior theory from a psychobiological perspective are integrated in examples throughout the text, including an entire chapter devoted to behavioral medicine (Chapter 8).

Human or Animal Learning? I wrote this textbook as much to help you understand your unique human behavior as to bring together diverse areas of interest within psychology. Permit me to personalize this statement further. Although I have been involved in animal experimentation for 30 years, my primary passion has always been to better understand the *human* condition. For this reason I have made no attempt to exhaustively cover the tens of thousands of experiments that have been accomplished in the field of "animal learning." The more selective coverage of animal learning in this text (i.e., Chapters 4–7 and 10) reflects my personal biases—namely, an overriding belief that humans are the most interesting animals of all.

The point of animal experiments should be relevant to and further our understanding of humans. By focusing upon *animal* and not human learning and behavior, we run the risk of underemphasizing insights into human behavior that such experimentation has afforded us over the past century. For example, some textbooks treat the subject of *comparative animal language* outside of the framework of human language. This seems almost ludicrous to me because, as I develop the argument in Chapter 10, a strong case can be made that humans are the only animals who use language.

What Do Students Want?   Another reason this text has assumed its present form is because of my classroom experiences over the past 20 years. Psychology majors want to study a specialty area such as learning in a way that both complements and extends their existing understanding of human behavior. I have, therefore, attempted to write a book *about* students as much as for students, *about* issues that concern students rather than about esoteric experiments in animal learning.

Learning Is Not a Grim and Serious Business.   A course in learning and behavior theory can be among the most grim, formal, and esoteric experiences you will ever encounter in a college classroom. Over the years my students have convinced me, however, that it doesn't have to be that way. Students can "learn about learning" without being bored to tears. As a result, and not wanting to be guilty of producing "another stuffy textbook," I have written one that may err on the side of being too informal. If, however, I have been successful in writing a book that is "user friendly," and relevant to student interests as well as thought provoking, I will accept the criticism of being "too informal."

I enjoy teaching and writing. My decision to write a textbook acknowledges both interests. I wish I could tell you that my attempts at humor in this text are conscious efforts to "teach better." This is not the case, however, either in my classroom or in this textbook. Rather, there exists more than a little zaniness in my world view, which tends to creep into my prose—especially in the more informal discussion questions that follow each chapter. Such an admission constitutes neither an apology nor a warning; rather, it is a recognition that, on occasion, you may find yourself smiling, or you may merely be bewildered. Either response is appropriate—to my prose, and to the human condition.

Paraphrasing a Hindu expression, "If the journey is not what you expected, don't be surprised."

———————————

Psychology is at a crossroads, and you are faced with many choices early in your academic career. This text is merely one path to explore. I hope you find your journey both enjoyable and profitable. And keep an eye out for the elephants.

Brief Contents

Detailed Contents

Chapter 3   Experimental Methodology and Associative Theory in the Behavioral Sciences   69

Chapter 5   Complexities of Conditioning   165

Chapter 6   Instrumental Learning   217

Chapter 7   Reinforcement and Punishment

Chapter 8   **Applications of Learning**   **341**

Chapter 9   Choice Behavior   401

1

Issues in Learning and Behavior

I.   Introduction

What Is Learning?

This is a book about how humans and other animals learn. For present purposes, **learning**[1] is defined as *a more or less permanent change in behavior resulting from personal experiences in your environment.* Learning is defined as a change in behavior (as opposed to a change in thinking, or to an alteration in the way the brain works—to name but two alternative definitions). Why? Because *behavior* is more easily observed. We can typically see and readily measure changes in behavior. By contrast, even though we assume that learning causes changes in the brain, the science of the neurochemistry of learning and memory is in its infancy.

As for thinking? Thinking is different from learning. Certainly thinking results from learning. Much of what we learn in life, however, only marginally involves thinking. Later in this chapter we will return to the relationship of "thinking" to "learning."

What Is Behavior?

Behavior is what you do, the ways you act, how you respond to your environment. Much of your behavior has been learned, but behavior change by itself is not "learning." Your behavior is affected by other means as well as by learning. Drugs can change behavior, but typically the alteration is temporary, and behavior returns to normal. By contrast, learning is relatively permanent. A child's fatigue, as every parent knows, can drastically alter his or her behavior. A night's rest restores behavior to normal. By contrast, once a child has learned the alphabet, under most circumstances the change in his or her behavior does not go away.

Your patterns of behavior in part are determined by the expression of your **genes** in ways scientists are only now beginning to understand. A toddler does not *learn* to walk or to babble. Rather, these behaviors appear during the course of development, and each is an indication of the *genetic endowment* each person inherits at conception.

A summary statement: An animal's genetic endowment provides inherited tendencies, but in the course of a lifetime *what* is learned, and *how*, determines that animal's unique behavioral tendencies. (The reader may notice that all arguments thus far are applicable to animals in general, not just to humans.)

---

[1]Boldfaced terms will appear in a glossary at the end of each chapter and in an appendix to the text.

Genes and Environment. Few readers would disagree with the observation that most of their behavior is the result of their personal interactions with a distinctive **environment.** Without any personal knowledge of each other, both you and I can deduce that we have learned a great deal in classroom settings. You, for example, are reading this written text. Without extensive educational experience humans cannot understand written language.

Another way of saying this is that there appears to be nothing in the human **genotype** (the sum of your genetic endowment) that has specifically prepared you to read and to write. To speak, yes. Almost all humans speak even when raised in widely varying and less than optimal environments. But as every schoolchild knows, learning to read and write requires much more effort than talking. Most humans talk; only highly organized environmental experiences afford us the ability to read and to write.

As a student you have learned to make mathematical computations and to think logically as well as to read and write. *Learn* is the operative word. Human infants cannot read, write, or do math, nor do they engage in rational processes. If you had lived in any of a number of third world countries, you might be illiterate. If you had had deficient educational opportunities in this country, not only would you be unable to read this text, your very capacity to reason and to think would be altered, possibly impaired.

The Realm of Behavior

Other assumptions about your behavior follow: Each of you has learned to like certain foods, songs, books, people—and to dislike others. Had you been raised in a different environment, presumably you would prefer other foods, songs, books, and people. For example, your choice of a best friend is likely to be a person presently sharing your local, immediate environment. Think of those you know who recently have gotten engaged or married. More than likely they met at school, or work, or in an apartment complex. That is, they shared the same environment. Had one or the other been in a different location they likely would have become involved with someone else. Environment shapes behavior.

Most people in our culture have learned to drive an automobile, to operate a television, a VCR, a microwave oven, and other electronic appliances. The same cannot be said for other cultures. Even within a culture, learning experiences can vary from generation to generation. My grandfather never learned to operate a VCR. Likewise, I haven't a clue how to shoe a horse.

Depending upon your unique *learning history,* you may already know how to dance and to ice skate, and many of you are able to play soccer, the guitar, and the piano. You have *learned* to shop, to cook, to sing, and to sew, as well as to be coy, and to control your temper—or not! Your thinking when expressed as language is *behavior.* Returning to an earlier distinction: Thinking reflects what you have learned, but you have learned many things without conscious thought. In summary, your behavior is what you do, the ways you act upon your environment.

Evidence mounts, to take another example, that in many cases we learn how to be sick and we learn how to be well. Many of us have learned how to "get our way" in our immediate environment. Another way of saying this, we will see in Chapter 7, is that we have learned how to attain *reinforcers* and also how to avoid *punishing* situations. Can more important lessons be learned than these? Arguably not, since these activities define the successful negotiation of our environments, our happiness, and our well-being.

Unconscious Processes.   Especially in our human interactions, we are not always aware when we have learned something, or exactly what it is we have learned. For example, the playground bully says ". . . I taught him a lesson he will never forget." The nature of the lesson is elusive. What *is* learned as a result of physical punishment, or when we argue, or when you persuade someone to do it your way? Quite often, verbalizing what it is that has been learned is difficult.

Likewise, can you think of behaviors you (or your roommate, or a family member) have learned that do not involve conscious thought? Swimming, dancing, and playing a musical instrument after a period of inactivity reflect behaviors previously learned and not forgotten. You may not be aware of how your body "remembers" what to do, and probably you can't even verbalize what it is that you are doing. You have forgotten the details that were important when you were initially learning, the result being that many of your previously learned experiences have become unconscious processes.

The importance of observations of unconscious processes in learning is twofold: First, newborn humans and other animals learn many things despite their lower level of consciousness relative to adult humans. Another way of saying this is that human consciousness does not seem to be necessary for many demonstrations of learning. Second, both emotions and skilled behavior can be easily conditioned in humans independent of language and the rational processes language affords. "Book learning" accounts for only a small (but important) portion of all the things we learn in our lifetimes.

Learning and Behavior: A Psychobiological Approach

Your human ability to learn widely varying tasks during a lifetime complements other behavioral tendencies you inherited at conception. The research of psychologists and other behavioral scientists enhances our understanding of the interplay of these innate and learned behaviors.

What is a "psychobiological approach" to learning and behavior? **Psychobiology** is the interdisciplinary science of brain-behavior, or mind-body, interactions. Psychobiologists recognize that learning and memory processes—indeed, all phenomena of the human and animal mind—are the end result of the interplay of genetically unique organisms behaving within their environments. To understand how animals learn, you must understand both the nature of the animal and the immediate environment with which it interacts.

That sounds good, but you may be asking, "What does it mean to 'understand' the nature of an animal?" The answer, unfortunately, is not simple. To fully understand an animal (such as yourself) you would need to know its evolutionary history, its biology, psychology, and sociology. How does the brain work? How do endocrine glands influence behavior? What does it eat? These "body" aspects in turn are related to questions of survival. What is its life cycle? In the niche it occupies, how does the animal's brain/behavior solve problems of reproduction and care of offspring? And, using the term consciousness in the human sense, to what extent is the animal *conscious* of itself and of its surroundings.

A psychobiological approach to learning and behavior, then, is an examination of *how* and *why* animals learn *what* they do. Our undertaking becomes especially ambitious given that you and I are among the "animals" whose behavior we are trying to understand.

Learning and Behavior Contrasted

As we have just seen, "behavior" is a term that encompasses both learned (acquired) and innate (instinctive) components. Were you to make a list of behaviors acquired in your lifetime, more than likely you would consider only a few of them to be either "innate" or "instinctive." In comparison with simpler animals, human behavior is especially variable. Evidence the multitude of cultural variations among humans. For this very reason the science of psychology focuses upon a systematic analysis of individual differences: i.e., what *you* have learned and how *you* have learned over the course of your lifetime. Particular experiences have shaped you to be "you," and yet other experiences have made them "them."

What Makes You, You?   Would it be fair to say that unless one knows your unique history—that is, all that you have experienced since conception, one really doesn't know *you?* **Learning theory** is an attempt to account for how your behavior has been shaped by your immediate environment—the people, places, relationships, and events you have experienced. What stimuli impinged upon you, and what effect did they have? What were the outcomes of your unique encounters with your unique environment? Certain events have greater impact than others, including, as we will see in later chapters, stimuli that reward and punish, and stimuli that allow you predictability and control over your environment.

Take, for example, language. Most readers of this text first heard the unique sounds of the English language—an environment that influenced but did not totally determine language behavior. Obviously this environment does not produce language behavior among infrahumans.[2] Your unique human genetic make-up allowed you to be receptive to and to learn from a language environment. So, *what* you learned in part has been determined by your human genotype. A tentative first conclusion: Learning theory by itself cannot account for language or any other acquired behavior. The role of learning in language acquisition is further pursued in Chapter 10.

Behavior Theory

By contrast, **behavior theory** encompasses the interplay of genes and environment (Halliday & Slater, 1983; Plomin, 1990).[3] As we have noted, your total genetic endowment—that which you received from biological parents at conception—defines your *genotype*. The combination of these innate tendencies *plus* the learned personal behaviors acquired in your lifetime determines your unique physical and psychological nature—your **phenotype.** Your genotype is the theoretical you, the potential "you" at the moment of conception. Your phenotype is the *real* you resulting from the special environment your genotype encountered. Another way of saying this: Phenotypes are genotypes expressed in environment.

You think and behave differently from your family, friends, and unknown others (a) because of your basic nature and (b) because you have had unique experiences. Each of us has been raised in a unique environment.

Nature and Nurture. Learning is the "nurture" in the "nature-nurture argument." Learning is the "environment" in questions relat-

---

[2]*Infrahuman* is a convenient term denoting animals other than humans. Using the term *animal* in our culture connotes a significant division between "humans" and "animals."

[3]*Behavior theory* should not be confused with *behaviorism* as defined by John B. Watson, B. F. Skinner, and others (see Chapter 6). As we will see, **behaviorism** embodies an extreme environmental determinism that, for the most part, ignores genetic differences in behavior.

ing the role of environment to gene expression. Let us take as an example the feeding behavior of titmice (various species of birds) native to England. Some individual birds of the species have been observed to remove the paper caps and to eat the cream from the tops of bottles of home-delivered milk (Fisher & Hinde, 1949). Neither this nor any other species evolved in an **ecological niche** (i.e., an immediate environment) containing bottles of milk as a food source. Such feeding behavior, therefore, is not instinctive ("instincts" will be discussed in the next chapter). These birds have, however, inherited eyes, motivational systems of hunger, a manipulative beak, etc., which support feeding in a variety of environments. Therefore, we can safely conclude that in their lifetime birds learn their exploitation of drinking cow's milk from bottles. (A simplified behavioral analysis: The cream reward keeps the birds returning to the next milk bottle. We will explore examples such as these in more detail in later chapters.)

Question: Can you think of a scenario in which a bird for the very first time picks the paper cap off the top of a bottle and drinks the cream? Hint: Do birds ever peck at nonfood objects? In Chapter 6 we will discover that feeding patterns sometimes emerge at inappropriate times and disrupt trained animal acts in circuses.

Is the foregoing feeding example similar to our earlier discussion of reading and writing language? Neither reading nor writing is instinctive. Nevertheless, we use visual, auditory, and motor systems that are inherited, and that serve other functions, to get the job done.

Questions of how and what each species learns are crucial to our understanding of both why individual animals behave differently one from another and why such profound cultural differences exist among *Homo sapiens*. In summary, living organisms have unique natures and unique nurtures.

Behavior Theory Is All-Encompassing. Modern *behavior theory* is more encompassing than *learning theory*. Think about it. A "theory of behavior"—a theory ostensibly aimed at understanding why humans behave as they do—would encompass all of personality theory (normal and abnormal), motivation theory, learning theory, ethology, behavioral genetics, anthropology, neurophysiology, sociology, and other relevant enterprises. Why? Because each of these ways of studying human behavior adds to an understanding of human complexity.

Learning theories help us to understand why humans behave as they do. In and of themselves, however, learning theories do not provide complete accounts of behavior. In the next section we will briefly look at examples of complex human behaviors that learning *cannot* account for.

Analysis of Complex Human Behavior

IQ: Innate or Learned?   Genetic components of schizophrenia, alcoholism, manic depression, and intelligence, among other complex behaviors, have been reported (Plomin, 1990). One measure of "intelligent behavior" in humans is quantified by tests yielding an "intelligence quotient," or IQ. With respect to "intelligent behavior," mounting evidence has persuaded behavioral scientists that both "genes" and "environment" are important determinants. Another way of saying this is that "learning" and "environment" each provide an incomplete account of intelligent behavior.

How do we know this? The method is rather simple. **Monozygotic** (one egg) twins have identical genotypes. Such twins separated at birth encounter different environments, hence, different learning experiences, throughout their respective lifetimes. Nevertheless, their IQ scores remain remarkably close together in comparison with non-monozygotic twins sharing a common environment but having different genotypes at conception (i.e., **dizygotic,** or two-egg, twins).

We can conclude that genetics, rather than environment, better accounts for much of the observed variance (i.e., differences) of IQ scores of monozygotic twins raised apart (Bouchard, Lykken, McGue, Segal, & Tellegen, 1990). Learning theory alone *cannot* account for individual differences in intelligence test scores of monozygotic twins. In this and other studies, specific environmental interventions *do* affect intelligence scores in the short term. Project Head Start and other educational experiences allow children to score higher on the IQ test.

Interestingly enough, the Bouchard et al. (1990) study found that genetics better accounts for observed differences among *adult* monozygotic (MZ) twins. IQ scores of adult MZ twins showed *less* variance than *child* MZ twins, even though the effect of cumulative environmental differences over the years would lead to the opposite prediction.

Can we conclude from this study that genetics, and not learning experiences, accounts for *intelligent behavior* as measured by standard IQ tests? Not really. A simple thought experiment will suffice. Prior to age two (i.e., before verbal development is completed), maroon monozygotic twin "A" on a deserted island containing food and water, but with no other human company. Hence, no language, and no books. At age 50, retrieve her, and compare her IQ scores with those of her middle-class, college-educated identical twin sister "B." You can predict the outcome. In this instance environment determines the measured differences in intelligence.

The point is that no such animal as "pure" learning or "pure" genetics exists. Phenotypic behavior contains both elements, inextricably intertwined. One goal of this text: The analysis of these component elements of behavior.

A Rationale for Studying Learning

Why study learning? If behavior theory is more all-encompassing than learning theory, why is learning emphasized throughout this text? One answer has already been given: Behavioral scientists at present do not know enough to interrelate all of personality theory, all of behavioral genetics, all of neurochemistry, etc. As we approach the twenty-first century, therefore, our behavior theory is woefully incomplete.

And so we openly acknowledge what we do not know, and we concentrate on what we do know. After nearly 100 years of laboratory study, we know a great deal about the realm of learning and about applications of learning theory to the study of behavior. *Learning*, then, will be our focus, even though an all-encompassing behavior theory remains one of our goals.

II. Underlying Issues in Learning and Behavior Theory

Animal Learning versus Human Cognition and Memory

The foregoing discussion of human intelligence raises an issue frequently met during the many years I have taught courses in learning. Once students realize that the evidence underlying learning theory comes primarily from laboratory experiments using animals, questions—and challenges—arise. Why study rats, pigeons, and dogs to find out how humans learn? Doesn't the fact that I can speak, that I can reason—and that animals can't—make animal learning experiments both irrelevant and inapplicable to humans?

Let us separate the issues raised by these questions:

1. Humans and Other Animals Compared. First, how are humans the same and how do they differ from other animals? *Which* other animals? What do we know of the genetic structure of different animals? Of their brains compared with ours? Of their behavior patterns compared with ours? These questions are entertained primarily in Chapter 2 and again in Chapter 10.

2. Individual Differences. Second, do all *humans* learn in a like manner? For example, is it reasonable to assume that human neonates (newborns) and severely mentally retarded adults learn as other humans do, or as other nonverbal animals do? Likewise, do "smart" humans learn differently from the less well endowed? Have you shared a classroom with the "learning disabled"? If so, did they learn differently from you? Do your friends who are more mechanically (or musically, or mathematically) inclined learn these skills differently from you?

These questions are variations on the theme of *individual differences* in learning, and questions regarding individual differences will be entertained throughout the text. In general, the focus of learning in the 1990s is *not* on accounting for individual differences. The reason for this is that, exceptions notwithstanding, *basic* learning processes appear to be applicable to all vertebrates, which would include all humans, regardless of age, gender, and ethnicity. *Complex* learning processes, as well as species-specific differences in learning, are exceptions to these general rules.

3. Animal Intelligence.   What evidence should we accept to support or refute claims of so-called animal intelligence? Do we know if animals are capable of thinking, or if they are able to reason? (You might want to try out these questions on your pet dog, cat, or goldfish.) As we will see in Chapter 10, a number of chimpanzees, for example, have been taught American Sign Language (ASL) and other ways to communicate with humans. Now that they have language, do they use it? For example, we might ask if chimpanzees with admittedly primitive language skills learn other tasks differently from chimps lacking these communication skills. One conclusion we will reach is that humans are *not* the only animals capable of both conceptual learning and thinking, broadly defined.

Problems of Extrapolation

Another issue raised by experiments in this book is the problem of the **extrapolation** of (i.e., of applying) experimental results from the laboratory to real life. How relevant can "artificial" findings be to everyday living? Can results from one experiment (let us say, an analysis of how one learns to play the guitar) be applied to another experiment (i.e., learning how to tie shoes, or to program a computer)?

Do you remember the other type of extrapolation encountered earlier? How do we compare learning in one species of animal (rats learning a maze) with another (pigeons learning a maze)? From a monkey learning the concept of "odd and even" (in Chapter 10) to a human learning to discriminate and label round and oval objects (in Chapter 5)?

There are no easy answers here; arguments for and against extrapolation of experimental findings will appear throughout the text. The student should realize that the stakes in successfully answering these questions are high. If behavioral scientists are successful, then the goal of discovering *general principles* (as has been the case in chemistry and physics) *of learning and behavior* may be achieved; the science of behavioral analysis furthered. The alternative is not too exciting—the mere cataloguing of what each species is or is not capable of learning, with no general principles. Some may find such catalogues interesting, but not I. Here we will search for general principles.

Scientific and Nonscientific Views of Humans

Yet another issue raised by the study of learning is that of *scientific versus nonscientific* approaches to an understanding of the human mind and human behavior. Three hundred fifty years ago Rene Descartes divided the psychological world of humans and animals into two realms; one which is shared—reflexes and instinct—the other, voluntary behavior, which Descartes restricted to humans. In this Cartesian view, animals are reflexive machines and humans are purposive; humans can act voluntarily.

Large segments of our Western culture remain both prescientific and Cartesian in outlook. Ignorance about the human mind preserves its mystery, and many individuals in cultures around the world are invested in a prescientific view of humankind. Some contemporary religious thinkers, for example, continue to assert human preeminence over (as well as distinctiveness from) the "animal world."

Special Creation or Continuity? Students' questions reflect our culture's understanding of what it means to be "human." For example, fully 80 percent of Americans espouse a belief in the "special creation" of humans as distinct from other animals. The ideas developed by Charles Darwin and other scientists, which focus upon biological and psychological continuities of humans with other animals, are not universally taught in America's public schools. This situation is untenable for students and scientists alike. As long as humans are considered to be mysteriously different from other life forms, a science of human behavior is not possible.

Some of you may think that human beings cannot or should not be studied scientifically. If so, the present study of animal learning and behavior may seem like an esoteric exercise in trivial research findings. I sincerely hope this is not the case. Science alone does not have all the answers about humans and their place in the universe, but scientifically formulated questions and experimental methodologies can further such understanding. Box 1.1 highlights three individuals who in challenging us to think differently about ourselves helped bring about a scientific conception of human experience.

This text accepts the challenge of trying to analyze and understand the human mind from within a scientific framework. You may be sur-

BOX 1.1

Three Intellectual Giants in Psychobiology

What *is* a scientific understanding of human experience? Ask 10 people and get 10 answers. Most would agree that such a view would encompass mainstream findings and theory in chemistry and physics, including a *Big Bang* origin of the matter in the universe. Focusing more upon the existence of life, and that which constitutes *human nature*, here I offer my three candidates for "most influential thinkers," namely, Charles Darwin, Ivan Pavlov, and Sigmund Freud.

We will meet Darwin (in the next chapter) and Pavlov (in Chapters 4 and 5) in more detail. Here I simply point out the similarities and differences among these three individuals. All were born in nineteenth-century Europe, and all had biological interests. While none were psychologists per se, each profoundly influenced modern conceptions of the human mind and behavior. Darwin addressed our phyletic and behavioral continuities with other animals; Pavlov showed us that we shared with other animals both common reflexes and common processes of conditioning those reflexes; and Freud pointed out to us that while we were not always conscious of what we had learned during our lifetime, the adult's mind was continuous with and was in part determined by childhood experiences. Hence, all were materialists who espoused various forms of biological determinism.

All three individuals addressed mental as well as physical aspects of human experience. For this reason they can be retrospectively characterized as *psychobiologists*.

prised to find that behavioral scientists now have answers to questions about humans and other animals that Descartes did not know enough to ask. The challenge to view humans from a scientific perspective begins here and continues through each of the following chapters.

Psychology of "Learning" and "Cognition" Compared

Thinking, memorizing, reasoning, reading, knowing. These terms comprise the vocabulary and psychological constructs of *cognitive psychology* and the study of **cognition.** Historically, "learning psychologists" have been concerned with laboratory experiments on animals. By contrast, cognitive psychologists tend to view learning as the acquisition of, and retrieval from, human memory as interpreted within an "information processing" model of psychology.

Concepts of learning and memory are obviously related. Can you think of an instance of learning that does not presuppose memory, or vice versa? Seldom, however, do they seem to interact in the minds of psychologists! Separate research journals report experiments on "animal learning" and "human memory." Different courses, using distinctive textbooks on "learning" or "cognition" (or "memory") are offered in our colleges and universities by psychologists with vastly different research interests.

"Learning" or "Thinking"? For the sake of argument, and questions of evolution and psychological continuity among animals aside for the moment, let us accept the assumption that humans are sufficiently different from animals that separate rules, or principles, may guide their learning. Let us listen to one of many students over the years who doubts that animal learning experiments mirror her own learning experiences in the classroom:

> I sit here, listening to you, trying to make sense, thinking, comparing, contrasting, trying to understand. Then I go to the library and read, read, read . . . trying to learn the material in the textbook. Some of it I memorize.
>
> My dog cannot do what I do; it does not learn in the same way. What good does it do to study animal learning experiments if animals don't think like I do?

These are excellent observations, and you may likewise be entertaining similar reservations. But consider the following: This student's comments imply (a) that she fully understands the realms of human learning and cognition, and (b) that she intuitively knows that human learning is distinct from infrahuman learning and cognition.[4] Unfortunately, *behavioral scientists* do not presently know enough to make these judgments. Since we don't have all the answers, isn't it preferable to adopt their strategy of (a) looking at the evidence, (b) noting that the evidence is incomplete, and (c) coming to some tentative conclusion that may change as more data are gathered. The hard part for both scientists and students alike is to be content with less than perfect answers to such complex questions. We must learn to be patient and accept the fact that more is unknown than known about human and animal minds.

Animals Have Minds? Some evidence that bears on the "animal mind" may surprise you. Many lines of converging evidence presented in this text comprise tentative answers/hypotheses regarding

---

[4]Note that the issue of psychological continuities among species can be legitimately raised even if one does *not* espouse a belief in "special creation."

learning and cognition. For example, humans and animals alike engage in "timing" behaviors; likewise, both make similar *choices* when presented with similar alternatives. Humans and animals both learn *concepts*, and knowledge of their respective learning histories allow us to predict which choices they will make from among given alternatives. Many species, not just humans, learn concepts. And not unlike humans, a number of animal species pass on knowledge from generation to generation.

Let us suspend judgment for the present, then, and return to these questions later in the text. My hope is that you, like the other student who raised these questions, will have a better idea of just how complex the questions are, even if the answers are less than satisfying. For now, consider the following questions: What evidence would convince you that animals can tell time? That animals can think? That animals can make decisions? That animals can behave in a voluntary fashion?

Human Cognition.   Animals reason and learn some tasks in a manner resembling humans. Animals make choices, think, and otherwise behave in quite complex ways reflecting sophisticated psychological properties. Human language, however, provides us with conceptual tools that far exceed infrahuman cognitive capabilities.

Another answer to students who have concerns about applicability and extrapolation of animal learning to their own lives, therefore, is to recommend the study of "learning" and of "cognition" as somewhat independent endeavors. In the same way that psychology and sociology are distinct though related disciplines, human cognition can be studied independently from animal learning. We will return to these issues in Chapter 10. The reader is referred to any of a number of excellent textbooks that deal with language, reasoning, imagery, and other aspects of human cognition.

Psychology of Learning and Clinical Psychology

Many undergraduate majors studying psychology in American colleges and universities have professional aspirations. Their goal is to go to graduate school and then through course work, practicums, and internships to become licensed—as clinical psychologists, as social workers, as professional counselors, or in other applied occupations. More often than not these career-oriented students do not see the relevance of courses in animal learning (or, for that matter, courses in perception, physiology, or cognitive or quantitative psychology!). Rather, the "applied" courses (personality, testing, and abnormal, social, and developmental psychology) are viewed by most students as the relevant preprofessional curriculum.

Allow me to suggest a different perspective. The study of animal learning is *critically* important to the practice of clinical psychology. The bulk of patients seeking therapy have emotional- and cognitive-based "life-style disorders." Most were *not* born that way. Many are presently dysfunctional because of a myriad of *aversive learning experiences*. As we will see in examples throughout this text, aversive conditioning is rapid, powerful, and long-lasting under a variety of circumstances in differing environments. Our understanding of phobic and panic disorders, posttraumatic stress disorders (PTSD), reactive depression, eating disorders, educational problems, sexual disorders, marital disorders, and psychophysiological disorders, to name but a few, is dependent upon theories of *learned* behavior.

Likewise, therapeutic regimens for these and other disorders are by and large laboratory based. By that I mean that associative models used in behavioral and cognitive-behavioral therapy are predicated upon, and substantiated by, laboratory animal research. In summary, students with aspirations in clinical psychology are well served by learning the empirical research basis for their chosen discipline.

Psychology of Learning and Parenting Skills

Many students are attracted to a psychology major because they seek a better understanding of themselves, and of friends and family members. Who am I? Why do I think, feel, and act as I do? To return to an earlier theme, such questions can be addressed by a multifaceted behavior theory—including genetics, learning, sociology, etc. In many respects, each course in a psychology curriculum addresses one or more aspects of a broad "theory" (or "theories") of behavior.

Integral to a comprehensive theory of behavior is learning, and the analysis of learned behavior such theory affords. Beginning with your genetic endowment, you subsequently have learned to be who and what you presently are. You are the sum total of your environmental experiences. Significant others have guided you (or not), reinforced and punished you (or not), arranged formal learning opportunities in schools, camps, churches (or not).

Many of you will become parents during your lifetime and will be faced with making decisions about how you will rear your children. What do you want from them and for them, and how will you arrange their environment to maximize attaining your mutual goals?

Throughout this text you will be exposed to outcomes of experiments that reflect the results of environmental manipulations on animals, including humans. No guarantees, but your children might profit from your study of behavioral analysis in this text. At a minimum you will likely be more self-analytical about your parenting role.

Interim Summary

The study of animal learning and behavior can help us better understand how humans learn and think. Likewise, many of the techniques used by cognitive psychologists to study human memory involve problem solving, list learning, and procedural memory, to name but a few methods. Interpreting the results of these human experiments makes use of *associative models* (as will be seen in the next chapter) that are based upon the study of laboratory animals. The point is that both animal learning and human cognitive approaches are complementary, and that learning and memory theories for both animals and humans *are* increasingly interdependent.

The psychology of learning also has an applied dimension. We better understand how to educate our children, why some might have eating disorders and others a chemical dependency, and how each of us can learn to be sick and learn to be well. By applying learning theory to our skilled performances, our use of language, our emotional and rational behaviors—both dysfunctional and normal—we attain insight and the power to change behavior.

III. Learning and Behavior: A Preview

Evolution and Behavior

Where did we come from? What nature of creature am I? In Chapter 2 the role of learning in behavior theory is examined within the context of Darwin's theory of evolution and related issues of behavioral genetics and sociobiology. Some questions to guide your reading:

- In what ways are humans like and in what ways are they unlike other animals? What is instinct? Do humans have instincts? Do you behave instinctively?
- We return to questions of extrapolation. What is the theoretical basis for research using animal models of human behavior? Can relatively simple associative models profitably be used to analyze the complex organization of human brains?
- What is ethology? How do bees and birds learn to navigate over long distances? How do psychologists' experiments (that investigate animal learning and behavior) differ in theory and method from those of ethologists?

Methodology

A statement to the effect that the study of animal learning is a "scientific" area of psychology will come as no surprise to the reader. Certain agreed upon rules and procedures have been developed, which allow researchers to standardize experimental procedures and to communicate their findings with each other. As a result, a number of standard methodologies have emerged during the past 100 years of experimentation.

Methodological issues are explored in detail in Chapter 3, where a number of questions, including the following, are raised and answered:

- Is learning "real"? How can "it" be measured?
- What constitutes a scientific approach to the study of learning? How are learning experiments conducted?
- What are the strengths and weaknesses of a stimulus-response approach to the study of behavior?

Theoretical Approaches to Learning

Two main "connectionist" theories of learning, classical conditioning and instrumental learning, are introduced in Chapters 4 and 6, respectively. These two approaches constitute the "meat," or basic science, of animal learning. Among the questions considered:

- Why are there *two* theories? What methodological differences underlie them? How are these approaches the same, and how do they differ?
- In what way is learning "law-like"? What constitutes the "laws of learning"?
- Do the conditioning processes described in these chapters apply to humans? What is the evidence?
- Can animal models *really* account for skilled human performance— playing the piano, for example?

Complex Conditioning

Classical conditioning studies over the past 90 years have progressed well beyond Ivan Pavlov's demonstration that dogs can be trained to salivate to the sound of a bell. Indeed, conditioning of human behavior is the norm rather than the exception. Chapter 5 pursues puzzling intricacies of associative theory.

Contemporary conditioning experiments often involve complex stimulus arrangements. In part this programmed complexity is an attempt to mirror behavior in the real world. The outcomes of these experiments often give us several kinds of information—how stimuli in complexes become associated; how the brain perceives stimuli, affecting their association; and how contextual conditioning occurs in the "real world." Consider these questions:

- Why are some things easier to learn than others? Why do so many students have a math phobia, but not a music phobia?
- How do children learn when and where it is okay to use profanity, and when and where such language is inappropriate?
- Why do different people have different fears? How applicable are the "laws of learning" to real-life situations?
- Why does conditioning sometimes fail?

Carrots and Sticks

Psychobiology, the science of mind-body interactions, is exemplified by questions of how and why reinforcers (carrots) and punishers (sticks) control behavior. The role of motivation in learning is pursued in Chapters 6 and 7, where the following questions will be addressed:

- What is hedonism? Are *all* animals, including humans, hedonistic?
- Why is it that the most memorable things in life are most often associated with pleasure and pain?
- Are rewards and punishments universal? If so, why do humans differ so much in their likes and dislikes?
- Which is better in controlling behavior, rewards or punishment?
- Can learning occur in the absence of rewards and punishments?

Physiology and Behavior

Still skeptical that the study of rats, pigeons, and other guinea pigs can tell you anything about your own behavior? Chapter 8 is designed to make a believer of you. The application of basic principles of conditioning and learning to human physiology and health is in its infancy, but it is nevertheless exciting. Consider the following:

- How can your immune system be conditioned? Can asthma? If so, can you learn to be sick? Can you learn to be healthy?
- What is the role of learning in the etiology of psychosomatic (mind-body) disorders?
- Is becoming angry a conditioned response? Is falling in love a conditioned response?
- Is drug effectiveness more dependent upon pharmacology or psychology? To what extent do the reinforcing properties of alcohol and cocaine control behavior?
- How does learning affect your eating patterns? Can learning principles be applied to *understand* abnormal eating and drinking behaviors? To *change* abnormal eating and drinking behaviors?

Choice Behavior

Behavioral scientists approach their study of human behavior from a philosophical position known as **determinism.** Determinists assert that behavior is caused by genetics (biological determinism) and environmental influences (environmental determinism).

Whether or not you consider yourself a "free agent," animals and humans behave as though they make choices. To what extent are they voluntary? That is, what is the role of *volition* in choice behavior?

Chapter 9 presents an analysis of research into the determinants of choice behavior. Among other interesting issues are the extent to which this animal research informs "economic theory" governing human behavior.

- Are humans and other animals free to make choices, or, as B. F. Skinner has argued, are our alleged choices shaped and determined by the environment?
- Are you an unwitting component of a market economy? Do advertisers know more about you than you do?
- What laws, or rules, govern choice behavior?

Language and Thought

We come full circle in Chapter 10, again raising such cognitive issues as insight, thinking, and language behavior in humans and animals. Three questions guide our examination of cognitive issues:

- What higher order processes do animals (pigeons, monkeys, chimpanzees) exhibit?
- To what extent are such cognitive processes in humans and animals understood as extensions of basic associative theory?
- What psychological properties are unique to humans?

Summary

1. Learning is defined as a relatively permanent change in observable behavior that results from experience.

2. Behavior is (a) what you do, (b) how you act, and (c) the way you respond to your environment. Individual differences among humans have been learned.

3. A psychobiological approach to learning and behavior recognizes that both genes and environment affect both the learning process and observable behavior. That is, behavior is best understood as the end result of genetically predisposed organisms interacting with the environment they encounter in living their lives.

4. A psychobiological approach to learning and behavior is characterized by interdisciplinary study of biology (especially evolution, behavioral genetics, ethology, physiology) and psychology.

5. Learning theory attempts to account for behavior that is determined by immediate, local environments, such as those found in field and laboratory studies of infrahumans, and in homes, classrooms, and other environments of humans.

6. Behavior theory includes both genetic and environmental components; i.e., behavior theory can be thought of as a nature/nurture analysis of behavior.

7. Issues in learning include questions regarding the universality of "laws of learning," the extrapolation of the results of animal experiments to humans; humans as objects of scientific study; the influence of human language and cognition on conditioning; the role of volition and choice in learning; and individual differences in learning.

8. Learning theory derived from animal models can be applied to an understanding of psychopathology; to parenting skills and child development; to the learning of skilled behavior (i.e., playing a musical instrument); and to health issues such as obesity and chemical dependency.

Discussion Questions

1. My mother says that there are some things we will never know about people, and other things we should not even try to find out. I love my mother, and I respect her opinions. But as a scientist I respectfully disagree with her, and I think that an experimental analysis of human behavior is both desirable and possible. Do you think that human beings cannot or should not be studied scientifically? How do you feel about being "an object of study"?

2. You will likely find your future in your present. That is, your local, immediate environment of home/apartment, school/work will in part determine your present and future friends, career, etc. In a nutshell, that is all that is meant by the phase *environment shapes behavior*. I give my children a lot of freedom, but I encourage them to "stay in school" rather than to "go to work." What likely reasons other than "completing their education" contribute to my concern for where they spend their time?

3. Do you agree with the assertion that "book learning" accounts for only a small

(but important) portion of all the things we learn in our lifetimes? If you disagree, are you prepared to explain to millions of illiterate humans how little they have learned in their lifetimes?

4. An accomplished pianist was asked how she came to play the piano so well. She replied that ". . . she chose her parents well." Have you contemplated your genetic endowment? Your early environmental experiences? Or do you think you are a free agent who can choose to make your own way in life irrespective of your specific nature and nurture? We will return to these questions in later chapters.

5. *"But what is the correct answer?"* I share the exasperation of students who ask questions that aren't yet answerable. (And as a psychology professor, I am well aware that there are more of those kinds of questions than any other!) Consider the risks, however, of not being able to live with tentative conclusions . . . the inability to live with indecision. How do you respond to someone who always has the "right" answer to your every question? Something of an anomaly, isn't it?

Society considers *people who have all the answers* to be less educated than people who say *"I'm not sure . . . possibly this is the answer, based upon this evidence."*

Glossary

Behavior The way in which an animal acts or responds within the environment.

Behaviorism An extreme environmental determinism, which ignores genetic influences and attempts to account for individual differences in an animal's behavior in terms of the effects of rewards or punishment.

Behavior Theory An analysis of the way in which animals act or respond with environments as encompassing the interplay of genes and environment.

Cognition The acts of perceiving, thinking, knowing, and remembering.

Determinism The philosophical position that behavior is caused by the joint actions of genes (i.e., biological determinism) and environmental influences (i.e., environmental determinism).

Dizygotic Developed from two zygotes; fraternal, or two-egg, twins. Dizygotic twins have different genotypes.

Ecological niche The place of an animal or plant in nature; the interrelatedness of plants and animals with their local environments.

Environment The sum total of conditions and influences affecting the growth and development of living things, including air, water, soil, other plants and animals, etc.

Extrapolation The real-world application of experimental results found in field and laboratory experimentation (typically conducted with animals) to the human condition.

Gene Comprised of DNA (deoxyribonucleic acid), a gene is a part of a chromosome that, during the reproductive process, influences the inheritance and development of characteristics in the offspring.

Genotype The sum total of an organism's genetic information.

Learning A relatively permanent change in observable behavior that results from experience within the environment.

Learning Theory The proposition that a limited number of general principles of learning can account for much of the observed variability in animal behavior.

Monozygotic Developed from a single zygote; identical, or one-egg, twins. Monozygotic twins have identical genotypes.

Phenotype A phenotype is a genotype as expressed in environment; i.e., an individual organism as defined by its appearance, and not by its genetic constitution or hereditary potential.

Psychobiology An interdisciplinary approach to questions of physiology, learning, and behavior that draws upon and attempts to integrate observations and experiments in, among other sciences, psychology, ethology, physiology, and genetics.

2

Evolution and the Study of Behavior

FIGURE 2.1

An understanding of Charles Darwin's theory of **evolution** is critical to an understanding of behavior in general, and to learning and memory processes in particular. At an intuitive level the logic and rationale for incorporating evolutionary theory into a textbook on learning may not be apparent. Consider, however, that "learning" and "behavior" are the activities of living creatures, and, further, that evolution is *the* major scientific theory that addresses the meaning of "life."

Evolutionary theory provides both an account of the *origin* of life forms as well as a rationale for and understanding of basic processes of biological and behavioral *motivation*. In other words, *where* we came from, and *why* we live the way we do. Let us begin by considering learning and behavior in two broad categories of life, plants and animals.

I.   Evolution

Plants

"Live and learn" is a common figure of speech. Living and learning are not synonymous, however. Not all life forms learn. Few would disagree with the statement that plants do not learn, remember, or for that matter, even *behave* much! What plants "do" is respond in curious and highly interesting ways to certain physical features in their immediate environment. The manner in which plants do this superficially resembles *reflexive* behavior in animals (see Chapter 4). For example, the tendency for some plants to open leaves in sunlight, and to orient roots "down" and stems "up," are forms of tropistic behavior, or **tropisms.**

Tropisms are movement adjustments that simple organisms make in response to changes in the environment. Since most plants are *sessile* (attached, relatively unmoving), they are capable of making only minor, usually local, movements. Compared to animals, plants sense their environment poorly and move very little. Lacking sensory and motor neurons, synapses, and a central nervous system, plant behavior is *not* characterized by learning and memory processes. (See Box 2.1, however, for a curious example of "memory" (?) in plants.)

Animals

Now contrast the foregoing behavior of plants with that of animals. The animal kingdom is "full of life." Animals move (cf. "animation"). Because they move, animals encounter much more variation in their environment. Among other "things" they encounter are other animals (see Figure 2.2). Behavior of increasing *complexity* and *variability* is required to cope with the constantly changing environment encountered through movement. To test this theory, compare the amount of "environment" you would experience sitting for five minutes with walking around (or driving) for five minutes.

The Role of Learning in Animal Behavior

The behavior of animals is characterized by the ability to profit from encounters with the environment. That is, animals can *learn*. They form memories. The range of responses in animals is considerably beyond that of the "blind" tropisms of plants: Animals are able to *adjust their reactions on the basis of the outcomes of previous actions*. Another way of saying this is that animals are able to learn that certain features of the environment are more often than not associated with other features of the environment.

For example, bears can *remember* that buzzing gold and black insects with stingers also predict the nearby presence of honey. Humans and other land-dwelling vertebrates learn about and form *memories* of the environments they inhabit. For example, I have a *memory* of this particular stretch of muddy river. Last year I *learned* that this river floods over there when it rains; now I *remember* that it can be crossed where it narrows, by the large cottonwood tree.

What I have learned in my past experiences with this river will help me survive future encounters in this area. That is, my ability to

BOX 2.1

Can Plants Remember?

A group of French scientists have recently proposed that plants have "memory-like" processes (Thellier, Desbiez, Champagnat, & Kergosien, 1982). What is their evidence? First, they stick a pin four times into the mid-rib of one of the two symmetrical cotyledons (primary leaves) of a young plant. Five minutes later they cut off both leaves. (The young plant will readily survive this treatment, and nothing will happen for several weeks if the plant is left alone.)

Thirteen days after both leaves have been removed, the top of the now bare plant is "decapitated." This treatment normally induces the leaf buds (axillary buds) to put out another set of leaves within about five days. What they found, however, was that the plant more often than not put out only one new leaf. Apparently the expected symmetry of two-leaf output had been broken by the leaf-pricking treatment, even though only five minutes had elapsed between leaf pricking and the removal of both leaves.

During this five-minute interval, the investigators reasoned, the signal of "leaf pricking" was in some way or another transmitted through the leaf to the stem of the plant. The stem then "remembered" this treatment over the next thirteen days.

According to these researchers, the transmission of the "pin prick" information involves both rapid cellular exchanges of K^+ as well as the transmission of waves of electrical depolarization. They suggest that while plants lack central nervous systems, and therefore cannot be expected to learn and remember in the same manner as animals, "they seem to possess at least some of the basic cellular mechanisms whose evolution has led to the development of the nervous system in animals."

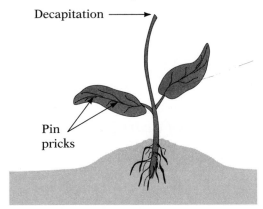

learn and to remember is **adaptive.** Such learning is neither frivolous nor random—rather, it tracks the environment. Learning very often promotes survival and enhances future opportunities to reproduce. Indeed, the argument has been made by many that in comparison with other animals, intelligence—which includes the ability to learn and to remember—is *the* most adaptive characteristic of human beings.

To summarize, unlike sessile organisms, moving animals can and do make complex behavioral adjustments based upon prior learning experiences. Very often such learning promotes the animal's survival.

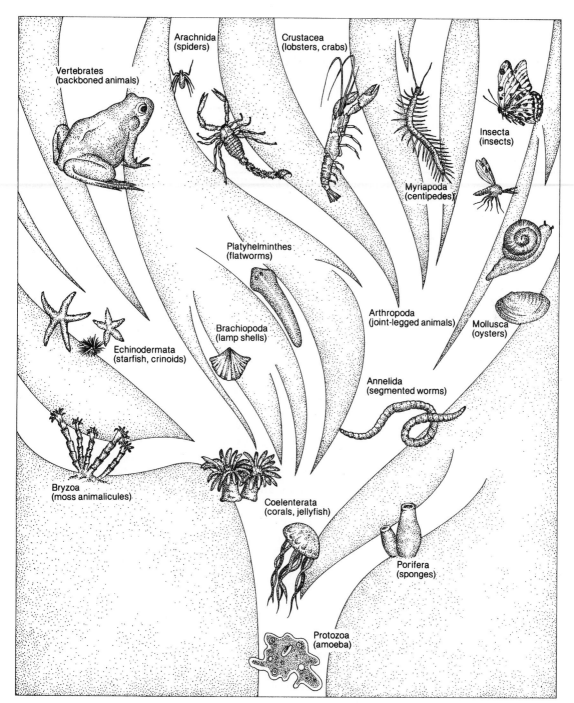

FIGURE 2.2 The Animal Kingdom

While the study of animal learning is focused upon vertebrates, enough research has been accomplished on various representatives of the animal kingdom to justify the blanket statement that "all animals are capable of learning." The same *cannot* be said for plants.

Complex Animals and Learning: A Preview

Some animals have more simple behavior patterns than others. As a general rule, animals with simpler nervous systems exhibit less complex behavior—behavior that is less amenable to change by learning experiences. For example, the common housefly feeds reflexively (read "automatically") when taste cells on the fly's legs are stimulated, causing its proboscis (trunklike mouth) to lower (Dethier, 1978). Chickens, however, must *learn* how to eat. They initially peck at both grain and sand indiscriminately. Grain but not sand satisfies their hunger, and the chicks eventually learn to peck the grain and to not peck the sand (Hogan, 1977).

Should one surmise, therefore, that the housefly is born "knowing" what to eat? This is not a simple question. Humans cannot experience what a housefly "knows," since human brains do not allow the same qualities of mental life as that afforded by housefly brains. For present purposes let us simply say that feeding behavior in the housefly is reflexive, and that the role of learning in behavioral expression varies considerably among species.

What *is* clear is that learning and memory formation play an increasingly important role in the behavior of *complex* animals, as opposed to the tropisms and reflexes of plants and simpler animals. Why is the behavior of animals so variable? How did it come to be this way? Our focus here *is* on animals, and we might ask why some animals survive perfectly well by reflex, while others must *learn* life's lessons. Further, we might challenge the notion that learning is *adaptive*. Always adaptive? If so, why is "maladaptive behavior" so often the end result—especially among humans? In Chapter 8 we will consider maladaptive behavior in some detail.

Let us begin by more carefully examining the concept of **adaptation.** Adaptation refers to an alteration in an animal's structure or function that promotes survival and that gives the animal a reproductive advantage. Asking questions about adaptation across generations brings us to the theory of evolution.

Darwin's Theory of Evolution

We turn to Charles Darwin's theory of evolution for the purpose of addressing behavioral processes of motivation and adaptation. To help direct your reading of this section on evolution, let us first consider the following questions:

- How are humans and animals related?
- What is "instinctive" behavior in animals?
- Do humans have instincts?

- What laws govern how and why each species behaves, learns, and remembers?
- Do humans follow the same laws of learning and behavior as other animals?

Let us begin by examining evolution historically and then as it relates to behavior theory.

Charles Darwin (see Figure 2.3) proposed a theory of organic evolution in his book *On the Origin of Species by Means of Natural Selection,* first published in 1859. Social and scientific controversy regarding his theory has characterized the ensuing 130-plus years. The biological and social sciences have incorporated Darwin's basic ideas of adaptation and **continuity of species** into their respective accounts of life. At the same time, many highly educated individuals—and a majority of the lay public—have either rejected Darwin's theory or "revised" critical details of the theory to better accommodate their cultural/religious views. Indeed, a 1991 Gallup poll revealed that about half of all Americans think that God created the universe and humans within the past 10,000 years. An additional 40 percent believe that God directed evolution to specifically create humans.

Evolutionary Theory and Culture.   Many people are uncomfortable with the position taken by Darwin and modern evolutionists that humans have a biological nature that is physically related to other animals. And, of course, for even more individuals, the very suggestion that *psychological* continuities might exist between humans and animals is considered preposterous.

Why is evolutionary theory so controversial? Sigmund Freud, writing in *Civilization and Its Discontents,* suggests that *scientific thinking* is the culprit:

> Humanity has in course of time had to endure from the hands of science two great outrages upon its naive selflove. The first was when it realized that our earth was not the center of the universe, but only a speck in a world system of a magnitude hardly conceivable. . . . The second was when biological research robbed man of his particular privilege of having been specially created, and relegated him to a descent from the animal world.

The importance of evolutionary theory for modern psychology cannot be understated. Contemporary theories of both learning and behavior—the focus of this text—are predicated on evolutionary considerations. As we have noted, *all* organisms have a biological nature that allows them to learn in a predictable fashion. Psychobiologists work from the assumption that the human mind and human behav-

FIGURE 2.3

Charles Darwin (1809–1882) is one of the most influential and controversial individuals in our species' intellectual history. His concept of the origin and meaning of life provides *the* unifying theoretical framework for the biological and behavioral sciences. (Photo courtesy of National Portrait Gallery, London) ior can be understood best by examining evidence from both nature (biology) and nurture (the study of environment and behavior).

Part of the problem of acceptance of Darwin's "theory" may be that it actually encompasses a number of distinct component theories (Mayr, 1991). Each component theory will be discussed in turn here.

Neo-Evolutionary Theory.   Modern evolutionary theory (cf. neo-evolutionary theory) is a synthesis of Darwin's theory with the more recent science of **genetics.** Four concepts that define current evolutionary theory (theories?), and that relate to learning and behavior theory, will be covered here: **heredity, variability, reproduction,** and **natural selection.**

Heredity

The most obvious feature of life forms is physical—how plants and animals appear. Early taxonomies (groupings, or arrangements) were primarily based upon the physical features of plants and animals. At its most basic, the term *heredity* refers to the fact that chickens reproduce chickens, and humans, humans—that there is a transmission of like structure, of physical form, through sexual reproduction. Offspring resemble parents.

The basic unit of the process of heredity is the *gene,* and readers are referred to any of a number of modern biology books to fathom the complexities of gene functioning. The concept of how genes might evolve is also beyond the scope of this text (see Lewontin, 1983). For present purposes, human genes are the mechanism for making the next generation of humans, and chicken genes make chickens.

Related concepts of *genotype, phenotype,* and *heritability* will help us better understand the term heredity. A **genotype** is defined as the basic combination of genes that defines a species. The concept of genotype is often confused with that of **phenotype.** A phenotype is the genotype as expressed in the environment. Your genotype is the potential "you" at conception; the physical you, at conception through the present, is an example of a phenotype.

Phenotypes of the same genotype (as in "identical" twins) typically vary because of differing environments in which the genotype is expressed. For present purposes, we can consider that phenotypes learn and form memories following interactions with environments. Therefore, "learning" can be considered a *phenotypical character* of an organism's behavior.

Heritability.   One approach to questions of "instinctive" versus "learned" behavior is to try to divide a given behavior into component parts. **Heritability** is a mathematical concept that attempts to partition biological, behavioral, or psychological phenotypical characters into genetic or environmental components. On the assumption that genes and environment (a) are uncorrelated and (b) can be added, observed differences between individuals varying on a phenotypical character (for example, differences in learning rate) can be expressed as

$$V_t = V_g + V_e + V_m,$$

where V is a measure of the observed variance, or differences (for example, difference in learning rate among individuals); t = total differences; g = genetic differences, e = differences due to environment, and m = measurement error.

Heritability may vary between zero and one (0.0 to 1.0); behavioral characters with measured values approaching 1.0 are defined as highly heritable; mostly environmental determinants of a behavioral character would have heritability nearer to zero. Returning to the question of whether human intelligence is "learned" or "inherited" (research on this question was discussed in Chapter 1), heritability values of 0.70 have been reported for measures of intelligence (Bouchard, Lykken, McGue, Segal, & Tellegen, 1990). As mentioned in Chapter 1, significant heritability values for schizophrenia, alcoholism, manic depression, and other complex behavioral patterns have also been found (Plomin, 1990).

Given the foregoing observation that the phenotype and, more specifically, phenotypical behavior are influenced during interactions with the environment, is it also possible for the environment to influence the *genotype?* The answer is yes . . . and no. An understanding of "how yes" and "how no" will clarify the complex relationships of genotype, phenotype, heredity, and behavior.

Lamarckian Inheritance.   The noted French naturalist Jean Baptiste Lamarck (1744–1849) proposed a theory of evolution different from (and preceding) Darwin's theory. Lamarck believed that the environment caused changes in the genotype (even though the specific term and modern concept of genotype was developed many years later). **Lamarckian evolution** asserted that a continuous process of gradual modification of structure across generations was made possible by slight changes that occurred during an animal's lifetime. Lamarck believed that the next generation profited from the transmission of these *acquired characteristics.*

One ramification of this view is that children would benefit from the musical, or mathematical, or bowling abilities of their parents who patiently perfected these skills during their lifetime. What a great idea! Unfortunately (or, fortunately, for the children of murderers, car thieves, and other undesirables), evidence supporting the theory of Lamarckian evolution is lacking. Rather, the next generation's genotypes are relatively well protected from environmental influence. Specifically, the genes in sperm and eggs are *not* affected by the minute biochemical changes in the brain that are known to underlie memory and other experiences acquired during a lifetime. Therefore, the only environment that *can* influence one's genes (genes that produce the next generation's genotypes) during the course of one's lifetime consists of certain chromosome-damaging drugs, high levels of ionizing radiation, and other known *mutagens* responsible for genetic mutations.

Human Inheritance

Does your school work come as easily for you as it does for your roommate? For your brothers and sisters? Obviously not all humans are equal in their ability to learn and to memorize. Why are there individual differences?

Evolutionary theory and genetics can be brought to a more personal level (literally) when students begin to consider their own human identity. As an individual you have both a unique and a shared inheritance. You are unique because of the one-of-a-kind **DNA** contributed by your mother and by your father. DNA is deoxyribonucleic acid, a complex protein structure containing all genetic instructions. Your behavior in part is determined by the DNA you received from each parent.

Genetic History Extends Beyond Parents.   Each of your parents likewise was created by a unique combination of approximately 20,000 genes on each of 23 chromosomes from each of *their* mothers and fathers. And so on. The "and so on's" become intriguing! Your "shared inheritance" refers to the process of genetic transmission—a process that has been ongoing in *Homo sapiens* for 100,000 or more years. (See Box 2.2.)

Prehistoric Minds.   *Homo sapiens'* brain 100,000 years ago was probably not radically different from yours and mine (Stringer & Andrews, 1988). Is it presumptuous to speculate that our male and female predecessors enjoyed similar levels of sensory experiences and aspects of consciousness as we do at present?

Little is known about the presence of language beyond about 10,000 years ago, nor about other aspects of the mental life of men and women in prehistoric times.[1] *Cranial endocasts* (rubber castings taken from the inside of skulls, which allow estimates of brain size

---

[1]For an intriguing commentary on language development and hemispheric specialization in prototypical hominids, see Corballis (1989).

BOX 2.2

What Is a "Relative"?

You are genetically unique, but you also share with all other humans common genetic material. Each of us had the same parents sometime in the past; i.e., a *common ancestor*. Regardless of racial origin, each of us shares common parents—a great, great, great . . . great grandmother and grandfather.

An example: A popular account recently asserted that more than 500,000 individuals in the United States are related to British royalty. By itself this figure is meaningless; the number of "relatives" a person has is determined by the genetic distance one is from a "common ancestor." The figure 500,000 includes all those individuals who were one-tenth cousins or closer in relationship. Obviously if we counted every person who was a cousin one-twentieth removed, the number of "royal" relatives would increase.

Many European-derived Americans take great pride in having had ancestors in the American Revolutionary War (approximately 10 generations). Some are "Mayflower stock" (approximately 15 generations). Yet other individuals delight in tracing their ancestry over 1000 years, roughly 50 generations, or more. (I now know three people who claim to be a distant relative of Charlemagne!) The foregoing lineages do not even begin to convey the immense period of time your direct human ancestors have been walking the earth—approximately 5000 *generations* of consorting *Homo sapiens*.

and shape) suggest few differences during the past 100,000 years, however. With the possible exception of elaborations of language (allowing higher levels of cognition?), our ancestors probably lived, learned, laughed, and loved much as we currently do.

Beyond *200,000* years ago? Evolutionary theory is based upon the assumption of continuity *among* species as well as relatedness *within* species. That is to say, humans have common ancestors with *all* life forms. Understandably, we are most interested in humans, and microbiological findings continue to elaborate upon our origins. Estimates of human lineage have been made using mitochondrial DNA ($_m$DNA) techniques. Though these models are tentative (Hedges, Kuman, Tamura, & Stoneking, 1991), researchers postulate a common origin of African women, a "mother of Africa," designated "Eve," who lived approximately 200,000 years ago (Vigilant, Stoneking, Harpending, Hawkes, & Wilson, 1991).

Humans' closest *living* relative? The chimpanzee, with whom we share a common ancestor, living approximately seven million years ago. How apelike are humans? See Box 2.3 for some comparisons.

BOX 2.3

Chimpanzees: So Close, and Yet So Far Away

DNA, deoxyribonucleic acid, makes up the complex molecules from which each gene is constructed. Fifteen years ago scientists Charles Sibley and John Alquist took chimpanzee DNA and human DNA, separated the double helix of each into two strands, and allowed one strand from each species to recombine. Then they measured the resulting match of the DNA of one species to the other. Their technique resulted in a 98 percent match of the DNA of humans and chimpanzees, and a 97 percent match of human DNA with mountain gorilla DNA. Humans diverged from chimpanzees about 7 million years ago, they estimated, and humans from gorillas about 10 million years ago.

More recent estimates? *Ninety-nine* percent of the DNA of humans is common with that of the chimpanzee. According to Washburn and Moore (1974, pp. 11–13): "Man and chimpanzee proved to be as (genetically) close as sheep and goat, two species that had always been regarded as very close. Man and chimpanzee are more closely related than horse and donkey, cape buffalo and water buffalo, cat and lion, or dog and fox."

The chimpanzee has a brain size of only 450 cubic centimeters (cc) compared with humans' large, 1350 cc brain. Nevertheless, it is a trifle discomforting to realize that human civilization is dependent upon only 1 percent of our "essence."

Human Nature

Let us shift our focus from individual differences among humans to similarities. Given our genetic relationships with other primates, the observation that all *humans* are related should come as no surprise. This shared inheritance is the physical basis for "human nature"—the tendency for humans to behave like humans and less like other species of animals.

"Human nature," which has produced human culture, has three components: our collective **phylogenetic history** (history of life on earth); our collective **ontogenetic histories** (where an individual's ontogeny is defined as the sum total of life experiences from conception to death); and our **written history** (cumulative oral and written experiences of ontogenetic histories; cf. Sagan's (1977) "extra-genetic history").

Of course, it follows that there is also "tiger nature," "pigeon nature," "bee nature," etc. Each member of a species shares common genetic material and common inherited behavior patterns. Indeed,

(a)

FIGURE 2.4 Phylogenetic Relationships

(a) In addition to fish and amphibians, the other three classes of vertebrates are mammals, birds, and reptiles. Most learning theory is aimed at discovering associative processes common to all vertebrates. (From Wallace, 1979)

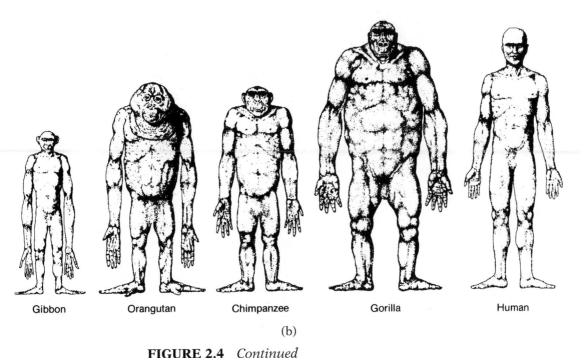

Gibbon   Orangutan   Chimpanzee   Gorilla   Human

(b)

FIGURE 2.4 *Continued*

(b) The extant primates with all hair removed, showing proportions of adult apes, drawn to the same scale. (From Strickberger, 1990)

common genetic material and common behavior patterns define the term *species.*

Do aspects of human behavior also resemble the behavior of other species of animals? Some, obviously, more than others. We behave more like other primates than chickens because we share more genetic material with primates (see Figure 2.4). Likewise, in many particulars we behave more like rats, dogs, and cats than like chickens or trout. Humans, rats, dogs, cats, and monkeys are mammals, and as such share certain common, yet important, psychobiological characteristics.

Summary of Heredity.   To summarize, heredity refers to the transmission of physical structure from one generation to the next. A new genotype is formed at conception. The proportion of a phenotypical character, such as learning, which can be attributed to the genotype can be estimated by mathematically measuring the character's heritability. Each individual's genotype is determined at conception; the phenotype changes during a lifetime, but not the genotype. Changes in the phenotype, such as learned behavior, do not change the genotype, and therefore such changes cannot be inherited by the next generation.

Evidence from paleontology, comparative anatomy, and DNA matching techniques reveals that humans share common genetic ancestry with each other, and with other living animals. "Human nature" differs from that of other animals because humans have unique phylogenetic, ontogenetic, and written histories.

Let us return again to individual differences. We dress differently; we prefer certain kinds of music (and foods, and people) over others. Another aspect of Darwin's theory allows insight into these differences.

Variability

The second major concept defining evolutionary theory is that of *variability*. When genetic material is transmitted through sexual reproduction from a parent generation to offspring, *differences* in structure are introduced. Unless you have an identical twin, you are an individual genetically different from all others. We need not concern ourselves here with the mechanisms of variability; the science of genetics points to both *mutation* and events during cell *meiosis* as contributing factors. Mutation is a permanent, random chemical change in the DNA molecule. Meiosis refers to the fact that during fertilization human males and females each contribute 23 chromosomes to produce offspring with 46 chromosomes.

Many have observed that "variety" makes life interesting. According to Darwin, variety makes life possible. For it is the slight differences introduced from generation to generation that determine the course of evolution. Variability in part determines which individual organisms survive and which do not. Why? Because some of the differences are advantageous to living and others are not.

The significance of the concept of variability in Darwin's theory, therefore, is that some genotypes in interaction with environment (i.e., phenotypes) are more viable than others.

Reproduction

Oftentimes in discussing Darwin's theory *reproduction* is minimized. But heredity and variability are genetic mechanisms that can only be expressed as the result of a reproductive act. In politics and the world of business, power lies with those who control the money. In biology, the name of the game is "who produces (reproduces) the next generation?"

Indeed, the reproductive urge appears to be central to the adult life of most animal species. We do not find it surprising that literally *billions* of dollars are spent annually by humans for perfumes and other odorants, the apparent purpose of which is to enhance opportunities for, and otherwise maximize, encounters that may lead to sexual reproduction (Stoddart, 1990). Nor does anyone find it surprising when a student passes on a study session for the opportunity to spend time with a potential mate.

Most psychologists view sex as a primary reinforcer and incentive (see Chapter 7 for a full discussion). Freud and Jung asserted that sexual energy, and an innate "life force," respectively, were prime human motivators. What do you think? Is most (all?) of your motivation derived from the more primal motivations of sexual pleasure, that is, of your "selfish gene" (cf. Dawkins, 1976). Before even considering the concepts of reward and of reinforcement, would you suspect that the opportunity to engage in sexual behavior would be high on a list of satisfying events?

Natural Selection

Both heredity and variability can be accounted for by the science of genetics. Even in the absence of a theory of genetics, in Darwin's time animal breeders selectively bred dogs and horses for specified phenotypical characters—color, size, temperament, etc. Changes introduced from generation to generation were accomplished by human-directed, or *artificial*, selection.

Darwin postulated that similar selection factors occurred from one generation to the next under *natural* rather than artificial circumstances. He and others noted that as a general rule too many offspring are reproduced in the course of a breeding lifetime, and that typically there are insufficient resources to accommodate the abundance of new lives. Therefore, competition ensues for limited resources. The prize of winning this competition for nature's resources is life, and the opportunity to be around long enough to reproduce. The cost of losing is death, or lessened opportunities to successfully produce the next generation.

Darwin's theory of *natural selection* is as prone to misinterpretation as it is insightful and controversial. Essentially, he proposed that each species is best understood as a unique solution to specific problems of survival. Some individuals are better able than others to overcome the environmental obstacles they face in day-to-day living. Such obstacles, or impediments to survival, are called **selective pressures.** Not only might some birds have better *protective coloration* (i.e., camouflage), to take a popular example, but they may also learn more quickly than others. That is, some individuals may be bigger, stronger, and faster, and some others may be slower but smarter. The environment blindly "selects" behavioral characters (such as rapid learning) in the same way it selects adaptively colored individuals.

Protective coloration, rapid learning, and other behavioral adaptations facilitate survival for "lucky" individuals (Gould, 1989). When environmental conditions change between generations (i.e., if and when selective pressures change), some individuals live and some die—the luck of the draw. Yet others among the varying offspring that *do* survive will have more of a reproductive advantage in reproducing *their* offspring—in which case, *nature* again selects the more advantageous characteristics to be reproduced.

Interim Summary

The end result of evolution is a world populated by unique living organisms. So disparate in appearance and behavior are these plants and animals that Darwin's allegation that all are related, indeed, are *continuous* forms of life, seems bizarre.

Darwin's theory continues to be vital even as it is modified (see Box 2.4). Nevertheless, his conceptual framework has been remarkably successful in accounting for seemingly contradictory (and certainly puzzling) features of life on earth. The sexual nature of animals is self-evident. Heredity successfully accounts for similarity and continuity; variability accounts for dissimilarity and diversity. And, depending upon the nature of the environmental pressures, natural selection accounts for the historical progression of certain living forms and the exclusion of others. Little evidence supports the view that present conditions differ substantially from times past when the fossil record was accumulating. And there is no good reason to suspect that humans are other than another end product of these processes.

Preview. Current theories of learning take into account both general and highly specialized features of living organisms. The behavior of many animal species reflects their genetic similarity. We humans in fact appear to learn some behaviors in the same manner that rats and pigeons do—that is, some behavior seems to be governed by *general processes*. At the same time dissimilarity and diversity among life forms are apparent, and **species-specific behaviors** reflect unique evolutionary strategies in meeting environmental obstacles. Taken together, the theoretical approaches of *general processes* and *species-specific behaviors* help us to understand learning, the most adaptive of all behavior processes (Halliday & Slater, 1983).

In the next section the findings of those scientists who focus their study upon species-specific behaviors will be considered.

BOX 2.4

Stephen J. Gould: Contemporary Evolutionist

Stephen J. Gould has made accessible the complexities of Darwin's theory in a popular series of essays and books (*The Panda's Thumb, Ever Since Darwin, The Flamingo's Smile*, etc.). More recently, in *Wonderful Life: The Burgess Shale and the Nature of History* (New York: W. W. Norton, 1989), Gould challenges existing taxonomies such as those depicted in Figure 2.2. The "tree of life" conception of diversification of species, he argues, is belied by the fossil record of early life forms. Rather, he argues, random destruction of early life forms by cataclysmic environmental insults (impacts with asteroids, for example) largely determined which phyla survived and which were killed off—accidents that in large measure caused the present similarities and disparities of life forms. Blind luck, Gould argues, accounts for more of the variance than does Darwin's theory of "natural selection" in producing variety. Gould's arguments challenge neither Darwin's theory of continuity of life forms, nor the role of natural selection in speciation; rather, they reinforce Dar-win's view that nature is blind in providing obstacles to survival, and that all extant (living, as opposed to extinct) creatures could tell interesting tales of how they got here.

II. Study of Behavior in the Field and in the Laboratory

You may question why a behavioral scientist must be an "evolutionist" in order to analyze behavior experimentally. Is an evolutionary perspective essential if one merely wants to study and characterize the learning and memory processes of humans? . . . or of dogs, or any other particular species? This question focuses upon particular research strategies taken by behavioral researchers both in the field (i.e., where animals normally live) and in the laboratory (where animals can be brought for study).

For a variety of reasons, most behavioral scientists are specialized and study the psychological processes of only a single species. And, in the area of learning, that species is typically *not Homo sapiens.*

The **Black Box** *Approach*

Students almost invariably ask why dogs, or rats, or pigeons are studied in the laboratory if the researcher is interested in human learning and memory processes. One answer is that each of these species can be considered interchangeable "black boxes" in which stimuli go in one end, and responses come out the other end (see Figure 3.1, p. 75). For some researchers what might be inside the "black box" is often of less interest than whether there are similarities in differing species' responses to stimuli going in the box.

One assumption underlying this black box approach is that the behavioral processes under study *are* the same (or are similar) from species to species. We will have much more to say about this viewpoint later. Yet other researchers justify the study of a particular species of animal, such as kangaroo rats, or Japanese quail, or honey bees, because they are interested in the peculiarities of that *particular* species' behavior. *Homo sapiens,* after all, is only one of thousands of species whose behavior we do not understand! The point is that there are legitimate reasons to study the behavior of *all* animals.

Research Strategies

Obviously not all behavioral scientists agree upon what constitutes the most appropriate research strategy. There are certainly those who would disagree with the position taken here that a *comparative* perspective based upon evolutionary theory is critical in developing theories of learning and memory. For example, among experimental psychologists, *behaviorists,* taking their lead from B. F. Skinner (see Chapter 6) have been highly successful in describing and analyzing animal behavior from a laboratory-based, black box, stimulus-response perspective. Because most contemporary behaviorists are also evolutionists, the disagreement in research approach is *not* about discontinuity of species or other aspects of evolutionary theory.

In the next section we will examine the diverse research strategies taken by behavioral scientists who work from an evolutionary perspective. Some conduct field research (ethologists), and some do laboratory research (comparative psychologists), and yet others a combination of the two (various other specialty fields will be noted).

Although these fields have distinct histories, their methods and theoretical orientations often overlap. In particular, the relationship of ethology to comparative psychology constitutes a long and controversial history. The interested reader is directed to Jaynes, 1969; Hodos and Campbell, 1969; Gottlieb, 1984; Galef, 1984; and Domjan, 1987a,b.

We begin with classic ethology.

III. Ethology

Ethologists study the role of learning within the context of species-specific behaviors—how animals behave within their naturally occurring *ecological niches*. Citing examples of free-ranging behavior among these animals (as opposed to laboratory observation and manipulation of animal behavior), the ethologist proposes that behavior is lawful and best understood as *instinctive*. Particular behaviors are considered to be evolutionary adaptations that implement survival strategies. Classical European ethologists, therefore, heartily disagreed with the laboratory approach to animal behavior taken by American psychologists.

Consummatory Behaviors

Classical ethologists focused their studies on several species of birds, and only occasionally on a mammal. Among birds' behavioral repertoires are behaviors indispensable for survival: feeding, courting, reproducing, caretaking of offspring, etc. Collectively these behaviors are called **consummatory behaviors.** The concept of *consummatory behaviors* is often confused with feeding or ingestional behavior. The manner in which ethologists use the term is in the broader sense of *behaviors necessary for survival.*

Behavior as Adaptation

How does one explain the remarkable diversity of animal behavior observed in nature? Ethologists suggest that we first ask what *selective pressures* are currently operative in the niche the animal occupies. Second, what selective pressures must have been present in the animal's evolutionary past? Then, ethologists ask how a particular behavioral pattern has helped the animal overcome a specific problem presented by the environment.

Ethologists argue that an animal's behavior (no matter how remarkable and seemingly uninterpretable) can be best accounted for by knowing the function of that particular behavior—that is, how the behavior helps the animal adapt to its niche requirements. Indeed, ultimately, the behavior is the *adaptation*. Behavior, therefore, is *purposive*. And the ultimate purpose of behavior is to survive and to reproduce.

Ethological Methods

The first step in any scientific study is systematic observation. Through patience, training, and perseverance, ethologists have given us a more meaningful understanding and appreciation of the diversity and adaptiveness of animal behavior. The ethologists' most noteworthy successes can be attributed to their skilled observation of naturally occurring behaviors in a select few animals.

The second step of the ethologist is to systematically isolate the *independent variables* (stimuli in the environment) that are presumed to be responsible for eliciting the behavior under observation. (See the next chapter for a full discussion of independent and dependent variables.) One example is the analysis of the phenomenon of **imprinting.**

Imprinting.   Nobel prize winner Konrad Lorenz found that geese behave in a peculiar manner if they are exposed to abnormal environments during a few critical hours shortly after hatching. If during this time period goslings view a moving human (instead of a moving mother goose), for the remainder of their lives they tend to treat humans as geese. At maturity, they even court and attempt to mate with humans (see Box 2.5). Lorenz called this phenomenon imprinting, which is now considered to be a special type of rapid, long-lasting learning.

Instincts

Many ethologists and laypersons continue to use the term **instinct** to describe patterns of behavior common to a species. Another usage of the term *instinct* refers to the motivation underlying consummatory behaviors.

Instinct is both a useful and a slippery term. At its worst the term is tautologically circular. Why do squirrels bury nuts? Squirrels bury nuts because this behavior has "survival value." A "survival instinct" ensures a "fit" with the niche into which the animal was born. According to this argument, those squirrel-like creatures in the past who did not *instinctively* bury nuts (or successfully engage in other consummatory behaviors) died. How do we know this? Because (completing the circle) the ones that are alive bury nuts.

BOX 2.5

Critical Periods in Geese

With childlike curiosity, Konrad Lorenz played with hatchling geese and recorded his valuable observations. He and other European ethologists identified critical variables in the gosling's behavioral development, including the phenomenon of *imprinting*.

Imprinting occurs only during a few critical posthatching hours, known as the **critical period.** For the "following" behavior depicted in the photo (and alluded to in the text), the object (i.e., Lorenz) must be observed to move during the critical period. If the moving object is seen at 1–2 days of age, for example, rather than a few hours after hatching, the moving object would have no greater effect than any other kind of visual stimulus on the bird's subsequent behavior. Imprinting to moving objects is an example of a *species-specific behavior* in that only a few species of birds exhibit this particular behavior (Lorenz, 1938). Other species also display behaviors specific to their particular niche requirements.

Likewise, chickens (are motivated to) scratch to secure food. The scratching behavior is adaptive—is instrumental for survival. More often than not, these kinds of behaviors appear in animals naturally, meaning without elaborate training.

Fixed Action Patterns

Modern ethologists have recast the concept of instinct as **fixed action patterns (FAPs).** To qualify as an FAP a behavioral sequence must meet four specific criteria (Moltz, 1963). First, the behavior must be *stereotyped*—it occurs in the same way each time. Second, once begun this behavioral sequence should be difficult to disrupt and should *continue to completion.* A third characteristic of FAPs is that once completed, some time must pass (i.e., there must be a *latent period*) before the FAP will again occur. Finally, an FAP must be *innate,* or unlearned. That is, the animal must perform the full integrated behavioral sequence of the FAP upon first encountering the eliciting stimuli. An excellent example of an FAP is the analysis of egg-retrieving responses of the graylag goose (Lorenz & Tinbergen, 1938; see Box 2.6).

Sign Stimuli. A fixed action pattern is defined as a programmed sequence of behaviors that is triggered by specifiable environmental stimuli, called **sign stimuli.** An underlying brain mechanism called an **innate releasing mechanism,** or **IRM,** is hypothesized to be particularly receptive to these stimuli. The IRM is the "lock" to which the sign stimulus "key" has been perfectly tailored. Encountering a particular stimulus unlocks the neural mechanism, causing release of the fixed action pattern. (Compare this analysis of FAPs with the description of reflexive feeding in flies on p. 28.)

Except for the *complexity* of motor behavior exhibited by the geese (see the box on Dr. Nancy Dess later in this chapter), in many particulars fixed action patterns resemble behavioral *reflexes.* The concept of reflexes (physiological, behavioral, and conditioned) is discussed in detail in Chapter 4 (see Table 4.1). Reflexes, it will be seen, are modifiable in interaction with the environment, while FAPs are not. Nevertheless, we may consider FAPs to be "reflex-like," and the concept of FAPs a more sophisticated analysis of the slippery term *instinct.*

Classical ethology has spawned a variety of research approaches, which include neuroethology and sociobiology. These modern disciplines also emphasize the evolutionary determinants of behavior—specifically, how brain mechanisms and behavior reflect past selective pressures. How do the brain and behavior of an animal function to enhance adaptive fitness? In the following section we will begin to ex-

BOX 2.6

"Smart" Birds or "Smart" Genes?

It is not uncommon for an egg to slip from under a brooding female Graylag goose and roll a few feet from the nest. Upon noticing this the goose will get up and approach the egg. The initial sighting of, and approach reaction to, the egg is called an *appetitive behavior*. This appetitive behavior is modifiable; it is followed by a *fixed action pattern* (FAP), which, by definition, is not.

The egg is the *sign stimulus* (or *sign-releasing stimulus*—see text). The FAP consists of the goose placing the upper surface of her bill against the far side of the egg and systematically scooping it into the nest. If all goes well, the egg will be retrieved and the goose will sit on it. If the egg rolls off to the side once the retrieval sequence begins, however, something interesting occurs. The bird often simply continues the sequence to completion; she inefficiently scoops the area where the egg *should* be, waddles back into her nest, and assumes her position on an imaginary egg.

The more frequently the egg rolls out, the less vigorous the retrieval response. If the egg stays in the nest (where it belongs) for a long period of time, the goose may well wind up retrieving an imaginary one anyway! In other words, she may perform the FAP in a *vacuum* (Lorenz's term) without the relevant sign stimulus provided by the egg.

Furthermore, a particularly vigorous retrieval response can be elicited by an oversize egg—even an egg (in the form of a bowling ball) that is so big that the goose is unable to get her bill over it. Finally, fulfilling the requirements necessary to be classified as a FAP, a brooding goose will react in this fashion to a "wandering egg" the first time it is encountered.

amine this question by taking a brief look at these and other animal behavior disciplines. Our focus will remain upon laboratory-based research.

IV. Comparative Psychology and Other Behavioral Approaches

Types of Behavioral Scientists

Behavioral scientists in departments of psychology in the United States and Europe (a) who teach courses in learning and (b) who do laboratory research with animals have any of a number of possible titles. When asked, some will say they are simply *psychologists,* or *experimental psychologists;* others may call themselves *comparative psychologists.* Many would say their research area is *animal learning.* Yet others may variously identify themselves as *biopsychologists, psychobiologists, neuroscientists,* or *behavioral neuroscientists.*

If breeding animals and the systematic identification of one or more genetic components of learning characterizes their research, psychologists (and biologists) might describe their field as *behavioral genetics.* Researchers trying to find the neurobiological basis of a learned behavior that has a strong biological component (i.e., a species-specific behavior such as birdsong, or navigation—to be described later) might identify their field as *neuroethology. Sociobiology* is the realm of yet other researchers who use evolutionary theory to account for the origins of social behavior of animals.

The foregoing profusion of labels is not exhaustive, nor are the research areas mentioned mutually exclusive. Researchers and the general public alike have every right to be confused! The up side of this situation is that both subtle and substantive differences in the education of scientists interested in studying animal behavior from an evolutionary perspective have produced a healthy, productive research climate during the past 100 years. An excellent history of Darwin's influence on approaches to the study of mind and behavior can be found in Boakes (1984).

Comparative Psychology

Comparative psychology is the study of the behavior of various species of animals for the express purpose of identifying similarities and differences among them. From the beginning of written history we have lived with domesticated animals. Since then, probably almost every cat and dog owner has at one time or another wondered what his or her pet thought about. The first comparative psychologists interested in animal behavior were no different. What, they wondered, was the nature of animal minds?[2]

One obvious clue to an animal's mind was the fact that animals showed evidence of *learning*. They readily learn where and when food is presented, how to get around in their surroundings, to respond to signals and cues, etc. Understandably, *animal learning* became the focus of a number of these early scientists.

Compared with *feral* (wild) animals, the niche of *domesticated animals* contains human beings. Animals reared in environments containing humans learn different behaviors in comparison with nondomesticated animals. Feral animal niches, for example, better allow for the appearance of FAPs and other *species-specific* behaviors.

Role of Environment in Controlling Behavior.

Studying domesticated animals raises other issues. How could a domesticated animal's *environment* be arranged so as to better *control* its behavior? Such focus differed from the strategy of noninterventive observations of feral animals by ethologists. Obviously the manipulation and control of animal behavior is best accomplished in an artificial laboratory environment. Note, however, that Konrad Lorenz (Box 2.5) also gained control over his domesticated goslings' *following behavior* by his presence in their environment during a *critical period*.

Individual Differences Versus Species-Typical Behavior.

Comparative psychologists brought the question of *following behavior* into the laboratory, and they showed that individual birds could be trained to behave differently depending upon which particular environment they encountered. That is, you could control the behavior of *individuals* within a species by differentially manipulating the environment. At the same time, researchers gained a better understanding of species-typical behavior by analyzing how the environment (of the animals' natural niche, and of the laboratory niche) controlled the expression of the "following" behavior. The issue of behavioral control will be addressed in detail in Chapter 6.

Historically, comparative psychologists have concentrated their research on just a few species of animals—rats, cats, dogs, pigeons,

[2]Domjan (1987b) has identified the earliest scientists who specifically contributed to the field of comparative psychology as Charles Darwin (*The Descent of Man*, 1871); George Romanes (*Animal Intelligence*, 1884); C. Lloyd Morgan (*An Introduction to Comparative Psychology*, 1894); and Margaret Washburn, (*The Animal Mind: A Textbook of Comparative Psychology*, 1908).

monkeys, and humans. (Note that all have been domesticated for hundreds of years in various cultures.) One criticism of comparative psychologists has been that their selection of these specific animals for comparison with one another does not make good sense from an evolutionary perspective (Hodos & Campbell, 1969). The reasoning was that the phylogenetic relationships among these animals made little sense if comparative psychologists were attempting to discover *the evolution of learning*. Why? Because we did not evolve from a simple progression of rat to monkey to human.

Certainly this argument has merit. But what if the behavior of animals with larger brains *does* become "more organized" and "more versatile . . . due to enhanced perceptual, cognitive, learning, social, and/or motor skills" (Gottlieb, 1984, p. 454). There is, Gottlieb argues, a logic, and an implicit theory, both in the range of animals selected for study and in the evolutionary strategy employed by comparative psychologists.

The selection of both species of research animal and type of behavior studied continues to divide ethologists and comparative psychologists (Domjan, 1987b). A further rationale for "rat research" will be presented in the concluding section of this chapter.

Behavioral Genetics

Genetic components of psychological and behavioral functioning have been known (and studied) for many years, especially in the breeding of domesticated animals, and, more recently, from human studies. Findings in the field of **behavioral genetics** are peripheral to the learning emphasis of this text; students interested in the heritability of behavior can find many recent books in this field. An example of representative research can be found in Table 2.1, which lists *heritability estimates* of a number of psychological traits important for guide dogs for the blind (Goddard & Beilharz, 1983; see Mackenzie, Oltenacu, & Houpt, 1986, for a review of canine behavioral genetics).

As discussed in Chapter 1, many types of human mental disorders (schizophrenia, manic depression, etc.) and "normal" attributes of mind such as temperament and intelligence have been shown to have a heritable component (see Loehlin, Willerman, & Horn, 1988, for a review). Our future understanding of complex human behavior awaits the synthesis of behavioral genetics with theories of environmentally determined (i.e., learned) behavior (Plomin, 1990).

TABLE 2.1   Heritability Estimates for
Psychological Characteristics of a
Particular Breed of Dog

Trait	Heritability
Nervousness	0.58
Suspicion	0.10
Concentration	0.28
Willingness	0.22
Distraction	0.08
Dog distraction	0.27
Nose distraction	0.00
Sound-shy	0.14
Hearing sensitivity	0.00
Body sensitivity	0.33

Data from Goddard and Beilharz (1983) as cited in
Mackenzie, Oltenacu, and Houpt (1986).

Sociobiology and Behavioral Ecology

Complex human and animal *social* interactions have been analyzed from within evolutionary perspectives. The models and concepts of **sociobiology** (Wilson, 1975) have generated both excitement and controversy. Sociobiological theory at present lacks a compelling data base for vertebrates. Nevertheless, sociobiological thinking, and related research in **behavioral ecology** (Hinde, 1981), has contributed to the theoretical orientation of behavioral scientists attempting to understand how behavior interacts with and affects the evolutionary process.

Attempts to synthesize contemporary theories of human motivation and behavior with sociobiology (Barash, 1979, 1982; Dawkins, 1976) have been criticized on grounds that each and every behavioral feature and motivation cannot and should not be considered as representing an evolutionary adaptation (Lewontin, 1977; Gould & Lewontin, 1979). Nevertheless, sociobiological thinking permeates many contemporary psychological theories; Dawkins's (1976) provocative book is highly recommended reading.

Why Birds Sing: A Neuroethological Analysis

Our current understanding of birdsong illustrates the interplay of traditional ethology with that of comparative learning and behavioral neuroscience—an interdisciplinary merger called **neuroethology.**

Neuroethologists bring to their study of behavior an interest in both the underlying brain mechanisms mediating the behavior in question and the extent to which consummatory behaviors are modified by environment. Whereas classical ethologists focused upon *fixed* patterns of behavior, neuroethologists study how "fixed" patterns can be altered by learning.

Role of the Neuroendocrine System. Two areas of the brains of songbirds when damaged prevent the appearance of song. In normal male birds, the size of these brain areas is determined by testosterone; if castrated, the size of these brain areas diminishes, and the male bird no longer sings. In addition, testosterone injected into female birds induces the relevant brain areas to grow, and nonsinging females begin to sing (Nottebohm, 1980).

Each species of bird has its own song. Males hearing recorded birdsong during a *critical period* (20–60 days of age, depending upon species) will, upon maturity several months later, begin to sing the dialect they heard during the critical period. If they hear nothing during this period, they do not develop song (Marler & Peters, 1988).

Role of Reward and Punishment in Song Production. How effective is the male bird's song at getting females to copulate? The study of cowbird song reveals several interesting anomalies. Male birds raised in isolation (called isolates) develop slightly different songs, which prove to be more effective in both attracting and successfully copulating with females. Males reared together have "normal song," which is relatively less successful in attracting females. When the isolates sing their smooth song within earshot of these socially grouped males, however, the isolates are attacked and driven off, thereby reducing their opportunities to copulate with females (West & King, 1980). Here we can see the effects of a rewarding (successful copulation) and punishing environment shaping the cowbird-specific behavior.

Psychobiologists and Ethologists Compared

To simplify the matter let us refer to two types of behavioral scientists, psychobiologists and ethologists. Ethologists observe a particular species' behavior in the natural environment (i.e., in "nature"). For this reason ethologists study *species-specific behavior.* Psychobiologists typically bring a number of different animals into laboratories to conduct behavioral experiments, often studying how these different animals learn the same task. They ask questions about *general process learning.*

In no small measure, differing methodologies account for many of the conceptual differences between ethology and psychobiology. Psychobiologists who study learning prefer the more tightly controlled, contrived, artificial setting of the laboratory. Many of the species-specific tendencies that might otherwise intrude into an investigation of "pure" association formation are neutralized in the laboratory. In turn, the laboratory environment allows the researcher to seek general processes across species and situations, including consummatory behaviors studied by ethologists (Domjan, 1983).

Species-Specific Defense Reactions.   Many contemporary studies of animal learning blend the foregoing distinctions between ethology and comparative psychology. Consider, for example, laboratory research into innately organized behavior in mammals, which has some similarities to FAPs described in birds (Bolles, 1972). An experimental psychologist, Bolles noted that rats respond to aversive stimulation in predictable, characteristic ways. For example, when given painful electric shock they jump and run; in the presence of moving stimuli they initially freeze, then run. By contrast, pigeons flap their wings and fly when shocked rather than jumping and running.

Can animals *learn* new responses, rather than merely default to innately organized behavior? Yes, but at a significant cost in time and energy. For example, rats required to press a bar to avoid electric shock took thousands of trials, and not all of the rats learned the task (D'Amato & Schiff, 1964). Running in response to pain takes no training.

Bolles called these innately patterned responses **species-specific defense reactions (SSDRs),** because the order in which such defensive behaviors occur is invariant both for the particular environmental stimulus encountered and for each species of animal.

Thought question: Do humans have innately organized SSDRs in the face of adversity?

Cross-Disciplinary Behavioral Research.   A great deal of contemporary research in animal learning reflects an interest in understanding *innately organized behavior* as distinct from, but influenced by, local environments. From the preceding examples it should be obvious that most observed patterns of behavior are combinations of innately organized and newly learned responses. Dr. Nancy Dess is a contemporary researcher who integrates ethological, physiological, and behavioral approaches with traditional animal learning approaches. She and her colleagues are currently using laboratory animal models to study the effects of emotionality on ingestive behavior (Dess, 1991) and upon respiratory distress (Dess & Soltysik, 1989, 1993).

FOCUS ON RESEARCH 2.1

Dr. Nancy Dess

Studying the "Emotional Flow"

Dr. Nancy Dess, Department of Psychology, Occidental College, Los Angeles, California

"Humans are animals. Though unique in some very important ways, we are, along with other mammals, caught up in a visceral, emotional flow of events. I am intrigued by the primitive underpinnings of mammalian behavior: hedonic and response production systems and their modification by simple learning processes. My research currently concerns ingestion, fear, and learning. Taken together, these processes occupy a substantial part of most mammals' waking life. Studying how they interact in the lab will help us understand the general organization of mammalian behavior and perhaps some particular problems of our species, such as emotional and eating disorders."

Personality Differences Among Psychologists and Ethologists?

As we have seen, the question of why ethologists and comparative psychologists study animal learning in different ways has many answers. Let me suggest yet another. Many individual psychologists have personalities and temperaments that differ from more biologically oriented ethologists. Many psychologists by interest and training are ultimately more concerned with an understanding of the *human* mind and *human* behavior than are classical ethologists. For example, I personally consider humans to be the most interesting animals of all. Humans provide the reference points to which I compare the behavior of all *other* animals. Not all researchers interested in "animal behavior" share this anthropocentric (human-centered) view.

Discussion Question: What does *your* professor consider to be the appropriate domain of those interested in "animal behavior"?

Animal Models

Psychobiologists often use **animal models** in their quest to better understand the behavior of *humans*. Examples of animal models? The search for the determinants of alcoholism, or the formation of

TABLE 2.2 Two Methods of Studying Behavior

Psychological Approaches	*Ethological Approaches*
1. Focus on individual differences within a species/across species	1. Focus upon species-typical behavior across species
2. Interest in general processes among vertebrates	2. Interest in species-specific behaviors
3. Study domestic animals under laboratory conditions	3. Study feral animals within (natural) ecological niche
4. Interventive manipulation of behavior	4. Unobtrusive observations of behavior
5. Human manipulation and control of animal behavior	5. Observation of animal in niche; no interest in behavior control
6. Use of animal models; extrapolation to human behavior; tests of general theories	6. Animals do not "model" behavior; little/no interest in extrapolation to human condition or testing "general" models
7. Ultimate focus is human species and human behavior	7. Focus on nonhuman animal behavior

learned food aversions (both discussed in Chapter 8). The largest use of *animal models* by psychologists is found throughout the remainder of this text—namely, the use of laboratory animals to test associative theory and other general process learning theories that are deemed applicable to all animals, including humans.

By contrast, the primary interest of ethologists seems to be the in-depth understanding of a particular (nonhuman) species' animal behavior. The application of animal research to better understand human behavior and/or to test general theories sets psychologists apart from classical ethologists.

Interim Summary

Table 2.2 summarizes the major differences between psychological and classical ethological approaches to the study of behavior.

V. Psychobiologists' Quest for General Processes and a Science of Behavior

Lever-pressing responses by rats and key pressing by pigeons in controlled laboratory environments seem at first blush to be only minimally related to any "natural" behavior of these animals. Indeed, that something quite fundamental and basic might be discovered about the learning process—independent of the animal's niche behaviors—was one reason B. F. Skinner (1959) developed his now famous experimental chamber, called the *Skinner Box.*

Skinner thought it to be unlikely that any FAPs, SSDRs, or other rat-specific or pigeon-specific behavior would interfere with an analysis of the manner in which responses might be learned in the laboratory. "Pure" association formation has proven to be an elusive goal, however. Skinner's position that most responses by animals in his chambers are "arbitrary behaviors" is incorrect. In recent years, almost all animal responses have been shown to be heavily influenced by species-specific factors (as we will see in Chapter 6). Nevertheless, we have learned a great deal about behavior from laboratory studies.

Is There a Best Approach to the Study of Behavior?   Perhaps. Both ethological and laboratory methods are "best" in furthering our understanding of extremely complicated behavioral processes of adaptation and learning. Both ethology and psychology have learned from the shortcomings of the other, and a modern synthesis incorporates method and theory from both approaches (Halliday & Slater, 1983; Gould & Marler, 1987). Ethologists recognize the role of learning in adaptation—as illustrated by the research highlighted in the box on Dr. Nancy Dess—and psychobiologists increasingly incorporate both ecological and phylogenetic considerations into their experiments and subsequent theory development. There is no reason to suspect that this merger will not continue in the future.

How Basic Is General Process Learning Theory?

Some tentative integrative statements: First, learning is a very basic, fundamental process that has been around for a long time—even by evolutionary time-scale standards. Nonassociative learning processes (discussed in the next chapter) are found in all extant vertebrates and most invertebrates. Simple sensitization and habituation processes, for example, modify an animal's responsiveness to stimuli. As we shall see, such changes in basic reflexes are mediated by relatively permanent changes in memory, and qualify, therefore, as learning phenomena.

Certainly a science of behavior built upon general features of learning and behavior among vertebrates is emerging. But other problems remain. Let us look at a few.

Why White Rats?

White Rats, Brown Rats, and Other Feathered Creatures.   Many psychologists continue to use white mice or rats, or pigeons, in laboratory studies of learning. We have seen that ethologists (and some psychologists) object to these laboratory experiments. Why do so many psychobiologists continue to use so few species in learning experiments?

Two opinions regarding the use of white rats in psychology have emerged during the past 80 years; namely, rats are/are not worthy of study. On one hand, white rats remain *the most commonly used* laboratory animals (and experimental subjects) in learning research. From this observation it can be concluded that at least one large group of scientists continues to think their use is justified. Indeed, the majority of experiments cited in this text used white rats as subjects.

Most students, many ethologists, and some psychologists, however, decry the use of these "loathsome" creatures because they are convinced that no good will come from their study—except the dubious goal of better understanding the behavior of white rats (see Box 2.7). "The proper study of mankind is man" (and of womankind, woman?)—so the saying goes (and as modified). Indeed, a comparison of the mental mechanisms and capacities of white rats and humans is no contest. (The size of the rat's brain can be approximated by measuring from the top joint to the tip of your little finger.)

BOX 2.7

Snarks, Boojums, and Other Imaginary Animals

The general public views the experimental psychologists' use of white rats in behavioral research with bemused bewilderment. Some criticism has even come from other experimental psychologists. Dr. Frank Beach, for example, in 1950 wrote a strong critique entitled "The Snark Was a Boojum." The terms referred to imaginary animals; Beach chided psychologists for extrapolating the results of findings of a very few species to all other animals, in essence treating them as interchangeable. The cartoon accompanying the article communicates Beach's concern that comparative psychology was not truly "comparative," and

that the study of many species would be necessary to arrive at general principles of behavior.

Are White Rats Degenerate?   Arguments against using animals in psychobiological research take many forms. (Some "animal rights" activists would outlaw all animal research on grounds of cruelty. At the risk of oversimplifying complex issues, the benefits accruing from the responsible use of animals in medical and neuroscience research would seem to outweigh the negatives.) White rats capture most of the general criticism. For example, citing the unusual breeding history of white lab rats, Lockard (1969) asserted that albino rats were deviant from creatures "naturally" evolved on this planet. Regarding the removal of selective pressures from albinos, replaced in turn by artificial selection for "gentleness," Lockard asserts that white rats became "degenerate"—so degenerate they could not at present exist outside of environmentally controlled laboratories.

Serious allegations, indeed. If it is improper to study white rats, 90 years of behavioral investigation and the time and talents of many

Mouse in information booth in maze. From *The New Yorker,* March 16, 1981, p. 47. Drawing by Chas. Addams; © 1981 The New Yorker Magazine, Inc.

FIGURE 2.5

"It's a rather interesting phenomenon. Every time I press this lever, that graduate student breathes a sigh of relief."

From *Omni Magazine*, November 1990, p. 128. Drawing by Thomas Cheney. Reprinted courtesy *Omni Magazine* © 1990.

Frank and Ernest by Bob Thaves. Reprinted by permission of United Media.

FIGURE 2.5 *Continued*

researchers have been tragically wasted. And if white rat usage was a problem over 20 years ago, when Lockard proposed his argument, the situation has only worsened. Rats and mice dominate the laboratory animal world.

History of White Rats.   In part, scientists continue to use white rats for the simple reason that they have been successfully used in the past. A researcher named Small (1901) first used them in tests of "mental processes" (see Figure 2.5). Successive generations of graduate students became researchers who also adopted rats as laboratory subjects.

White laboratory rats continue to be used because they are hardy, fecund, and relatively cheap. *Fecundity* refers to reproductive capability. White rats are fecund; they have large litters throughout their normal lifetime, allowing many researchers to breed their own research subjects. Large litters are quite a feat for a species alleged to be on the brink of self-destruction through "degeneracy"! Rats (and mice) are used because they are small, require minimal facilities and support personnel, and are resistant to infection. They are social (they *are* mammals!) and can be group housed at little risk to life and limb. A rat's life span (indeed that of all rodents) is relatively short compared with other mammals. They have, therefore, been exploited in neonatal studies, studies of aging, and other investigations involving life-span development.

Using White Rats Breeds Success.   Just how successfully white rats have been used in laboratory investigations is often overlooked by their critics. Since so many scientists in diverse disciplines use them, we know more about rat and mouse anatomy, physiology, and behavior than any mammal other than humans.

Behavioral measurements of white rats satisfy many of the methodological requirements of science. That is, white rats behave similarly, predictably, in similar situations. Observations on them are replicable, indicating an underlying stability and orderliness in their physiology and behavior. The behavioral data collected on them are, therefore, not capricious.

Are White Rats "Normal"?   Back to the question of "degeneracy." In comparisons of the behavior of an albino rat with ***Rattus norvegicus,*** the wild stock from which it was derived, quantitative rather than qualitative differences are found. For example, comparisons of food neophobia (wariness of novel foods) (Mitchell, 1976), of taste preference behavior (Shumake, Thompson, & Caudill, 1971), of burrowing behavior in climatic extremes (Boice, 1977), and of learning (Eibl-Eibesfeldt, 1970; Boice, 1973) reveal no major differences among strains of rats, including albinos.

As a result of nine decades of experimentation we know a lot about the brain and behavior of mice and rats. While grossly less complex than a human brain, the rat's brain has proven to be sufficiently complex so as to keep several generations, and many thousands of scientists, busy. As the study of sweet peas and Drosophilia (a fruit fly) have allowed scientists better understanding of the general mechanisms of genetics, the white rat is revealing to us knowledge of both brain-behavior relationships and generalized mammalian learning and memory processes.

Would Brown Rats Be Any Better? Psychobiologists who study learning assert that they are interested in "general processes." Given that white rats are not substantially different from brown rats,[3] one may inquire as to whether *brown* rats are sufficiently representative of "generalized mammals." That is, are rats "general" enough for the study of general process learning?

Although the argument is not an easy one to make, rats in fact are primitive, nonspecialized mammals. That is, if one were to select from extant mammals a species that is somewhat prototypic of all mammals, rats are not a bad choice. The opossum may be considered a better representative of the common ancestor of mammals, but for many of the reasons cited rats are a much better laboratory subject.

Comparison of Representative Brains

But wait, you may say. Learning takes place in the brain. The size of my human brain can be approximated by placing my two closed fists together. And the rat brain is no larger than the tip of my finger? How can these two brains be compared for learning capabilities? More importantly, why assume that these brains learn *anything* in the same manner?

Vertebrate Plan. Many researchers have studied the brains of representative species of vertebrates. Two comparison outcomes are noted here, beginning with observations by C. Judson Herrick. Common features of brain organization, which Herrick (1948) called the **vertebrate plan,** reflect the evolutionary relatedness and continuity of vertebrates. Humans have in common with other vertebrates a spinal cord containing similarly organized sensory and motor nerves, a medulla (brain stem), 12 cranial nerves and their attendant motor and sensory nuclei, a hypothalamus, and a thalamus. This not-so-

---

[3]*Brown* is used here simply to denote the color of *Rattus norvegicus* as it occurs in its nonlaboratory ecological niche. A more accurate term is *agouti,* the mixture of brown, tan, white, and black hair found in deer, field mice, squirrels, etc.

simple bilateral organization provides the underlying neuroanatomical basis for a stimulus-response (S-R) psychology common to all vertebrates.

Reptilian Brain. Further brain organization common to all vertebrates can be seen in Figure 2.6. MacLean (1970, 1977) describes "reptilian" features of the human brain common to all vertebrates, which are overlain by "old mammalian" and "new mammalian" features. Higher cognitive processes of humans, McLean argues, are among the functions of the cerebral hemispheres ("new mammalian").

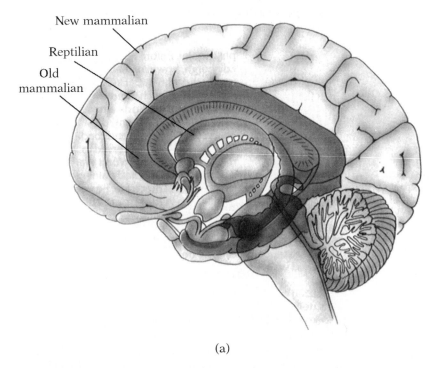

(a)

FIGURE 2.6 Common Brain Features Yield Common Learning Processes
_____

(a) The human brain as conceptualized by MacLean (1977) consists of a primitive "reptilian" brain, overlain successively by "old" and "new" mammalian brains. In more recently evolved mammals, the increase in forebrain, especially the cerebral hemispheres, is called corticalization.

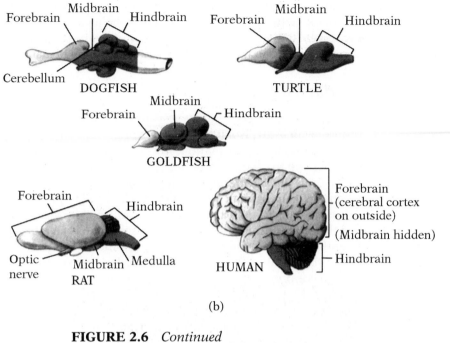

(b)

FIGURE 2.6   *Continued*
_____

(b) Note the three major divisions of hindbrain, midbrain, and forebrain in representative vertebrate brains (not to scale). (After Kalat, 1984.)

Conclusions from Brain Comparisons

Rats, birds, monkeys, and humans certainly have "old mammalian brain" structures, conform to a "vertebrate plan," and possess other features of physiological organization, including common neurotransmitters and neuroendocrine systems. The rat's brain may be only as big as the tip of your finger, but its organization is sufficiently complex to allow it to process information and to readily learn from interactions in its environment.

Species-specific behaviors are often accounted for by reference to special brain structures. For example, perhaps the visual tectum of some goslings (lacking in others) promoted better *following behavior.* Behaviors learned by *general processes* also have an underlying anatomical and physiological basis.

In summary, both similarities in behavior *(general processes)* and *(species)* differences in behavior can in part be accounted for by brain structure and other anatomical/physiological bases. Anatomical and physiological *similarities* among species lend some justification to the previously mentioned *black box* approach to the study of behavior. Results of research into basic behavioral and physiological processes in rats can be extrapolated with caution to other mammals, and with somewhat more caution to *all* vertebrates.

Interim Summary

Behavioral scientists conduct research on only a few species of vertebrates, which are isolated in laboratories. They discover and report laws of association formation and behavioral change, which may be extrapolated to other vertebrates. Processes of learning and memory of white rats, pigeons, monkeys, dogs, and humans are commonly studied in the laboratory within a framework of general process learning.

Behavioral scientists assume that all life forms are continuous; i.e., they are evolved from a common source. Extant life forms are differentiated by millions of years, during which time speciation has produced the peculiarities of each class, order, and species. All mammals share a common, quite recent genetic closeness. Rats, mice, or any of a number of species of mammals can be studied to provide insight into "generalized mammalian behavior," including that of humans.

The basics of association formation are apparently so old, moreover, that all that may be needed for study is a representative vertebrate. That is, fishes, amphibians, reptiles, birds, and mammals all appear to have sufficiently adequate central nervous systems to support most nonassociative and many associative learning processes. Medical researchers use "generalizable" features of hearts, kidneys, and reproductive and respiratory systems of laboratory animals as models for corresponding functions in humans. Psychologists and neuroscientists likewise study the brains and behavior of laboratory animals to construct models of general processes.

Finally, behavioral scientists are aware of species-specific behaviors; they know that species are *not interchangeable*, nor are their behavioral processes identical. Results from one species can be extrapolated to another, however, with the same precautions that are entailed when the behavior of one individual is studied and extrapolated to another individual of the same species.

Conclusion? The laboratory study of animal learning and behavior *is* well grounded in evolutionary theory, genetics, anatomy, and physiology.

Summary

1. Concepts of learning and behavior in both the biological and behavioral sciences have been contrasted, and an attempt made to integrate findings from diverse methodologies.

2. The ability to learn new behaviors

complements more innately organized behaviors. Hence, learning is adaptive.

3. Behavior theory, more so than learning theory, recognizes the importance of heredity.

4. Regarding learning and behavior theory, biological science approaches consist of analyses of the phylogenetic determinants of behavior, of evolutionary processes, of genetics (especially behavioral genetics), and of comparative physiology, including comparative brain structure.

5. Darwin's theory of evolution provides an understanding of continuity among species as well as the basis for such concepts as species-specific behavior, instinct, motivation, and learning as adaptation.

6. Behavioral scientists are most concerned with an animal's ontogenetic history—especially how environment influences behavior—while biologists, especially ethologists, are concerned with how species are adapted to their environmental niches.

7. Behavioral scientists concentrate more upon environmentally determined individual differences within species, and typically they study a single species (such as rats) in laboratory settings.

8. Emphasis upon biology (by ethologists) or upon environment (by psychobiologists) in analyzing behavior is now a matter of degree, not of kind.

9. A synthesis of hereditary and environmental determinants of behavior is one goal of this text. That such a synthesis is both desirable and possible has also been proposed by both ethologists and psychobiologists.

10. General psychological processes exist across species in part due to similarities of brain and other physiological measures.

11. Rats and other laboratory animals are appropriate animal models for general behavioral studies. What different animals learn is highly variable; the process by which they learn has many features in common.

12. The study of learning processes and the development of behavioral theory are well grounded in evolutionary theory, genetics, anatomy, and physiology, and they are the proper domain of psychology and behavioral neuroscience.

Discussion Questions

1. Are cats smarter than mice? If you answered yes, now ask yourself why there are so many mice in the world.

2. Is sleep a FAP according to Moltz's four criteria?

3. When I was about 13 years old I became fascinated with female breasts, and since then have discovered that I was not alone. Why age 13, and why the near universal interest in female breasts?

4. The history of our species is a short, recent one. Our human brains are essentially mammalian, and they differ little from other primates'. In particular, except for size the human brain is remarkably similar to the chimpanzee brain. Assume that a goal of neuroscience is the complete understanding of the human mind and behavior. What are the implications of the fact that our brains have been nonhuman far longer than they have been human?

5. Given our nonhuman ancestry, perhaps we are *too* cautious in extrapolating findings from research on animals to ourselves. Is it possible that we *underes-*

timate animal intelligence and *overestimate* human intelligence? Can you think of examples that do *not* involve Lassie? (We will return to questions of extrapolation in Chapter 8, and to the comparison of minds in humans and animals in Chapter 10.)

Glossary

Adaptation   Any characteristic that improves an organism's chances of transmitting its genes to the next generation.

Adaptive   Describing a characteristic or behavior that enhances survival.

Animal Model   The use of animals in research that bears upon the human condition. Example: An animal model of alcohol addiction.

Behavioral Ecology   The study of interrelationships among organisms and their environments focusing upon the development of survival behaviors—feeding, reproduction, social organization, etc.

Behavioral Genetics   The study of the interaction of environment and patterns of inheritance in expressed behavior.

Comparative Psychology   The study of animal behavior, stressing both similarities and species-specific differences.

Consummatory Behaviors   (Ethology) Innate, genetically determined "survival" behaviors, including fixed action patterns, which determine species-specific patterns of feeding, courting, reproduction, social interactions, etc.

Continuity of Species   (Darwin)   The theory that all living organisms are evolutionary adaptations of earlier life forms and, therefore, are all genetically related.

Critical Period   (Ethology)   A specific time period (usually early in an animal's development) when an animal is particularly sensitive to certain features in the environment. Exposure to such *sign stimuli* "releases" genetically determined behavioral responses. (Cf. *imprinting; sign stimulus.*)

DNA (deoxyribonucleic acid)   A complex molecule that composes the chromosomes and is the primary genetic material in (most) organisms.

Evolution   Changes taking place in the genetic makeup of populations. *Darwinian,* or *neo-Darwinian, evolution* is a complex theory (comprised of many subtheories) proposed to account for the history of life on earth.

Fixed Action Pattern (FAP) (Ethology)   A fixed series of movements ordered in time and space and triggered by an environmental stimulus. FAPs are species-typical, and once initiated, proceed through sequence to completion.

Genetics   The study of patterns of heredity and variations in plants and animals.

Genotype   The genetic constitution of an individual organism.

Heredity   The genetic transmission of characteristics from one generation to the next.

Heritability   The fraction of the total phenotypic variance that is accounted for by genetic variation.

Imprinting (Ethology)   A genetically programmed aspect of behavior change involving the rapid development of a response to a specific stimulus at a particular stage of development. (Cf. *critical period; innate releasing mechanism.*)

Innate Releasing Mechanism (IRM) (Ethology) A postulated neural mechanism that, when stimulated by a *sign-releasing stimulus,* triggers an innately organized motor program. (Cf. *critical period; sign stimulus.*)

Instinct Innately organized behavior.

Lamarckian Evolution The theory that genetic changes in populations (i.e., evolution) can occur through the inheritance of characters acquired during a lifetime.

Natural Selection (Darwin) An aspect of the theory of evolution that stresses the reproductive advantage of certain offspring suited to their environment over others not suited. Darwin argued that environment (i.e., nature) selects those individuals who will reproduce the next generation depending upon their relative fitness. Animals not able to overcome these *selection pressures* drop out of the gene pool. (Cf. *selective pressure.*)

Neuroethology The study of the relationship between the nervous system and consummatory behaviors.

Ontogenetic History A history of an animal's entire development—from fertilization through death.

Phenotype The physical expression of features in an individual animal that results from the interaction of its genotype with the environment.

Phylogenetic History The entire evolutionary history of a specific taxonomic group of organisms. Collectively, the natural history of life on earth.

Rattus Norvegicus (Norway rat) The genus and species designation for the wild Norway rat, whose descendants are the most commonly used laboratory rat.

Reproduction The behavioral and physiological means by which animals produce offspring.

Selective Pressure Any feature of an environment that allows one phenotype to have reproductive advantage over another.

Sign Stimulus (Ethology) A specific environmental stimulus that triggers innately organized behaviors. (Cf. *fixed action pattern; innate releasing mechanism.*)

Sociobiology The study of the genetic determinants of social behavior.

Species-Specific Defense Reaction (SSDR) An innately organized hierarchy of defense behaviors elicited by signals indicating potential danger.

Species-Specific Behaviors Innate perceptual and response patterns typical of a species.

Tropism A differential growth movement in a plant away from or toward a directional stimulus.

Variability (Darwin) An aspect of the theory of evolution that describes the role played by the wide range of genetic variation (i.e., variability) within a species. Genetic variance is the raw material upon which natural selection works. (Cf. *natural selection; selective pressure.*)

Vertebrate Plan The observed similarities in brain structure among all vertebrates, characterized by their common bilaterality, cranial nerves, thalamus, medulla, etc.

Written History The transmission of cultural knowledge; a cumulative record of the ontogenetic histories of many individuals that provides the basis for *civilization,* which is an invention unique to *Homo sapiens.*

3

Experimental Methodology and Associative Theory in the Behavioral Sciences

I. Introduction: The Quest for a Science of Learning

History of Science

Science is one of the more complex (and curious) activities in which humans engage. Those of us who enjoy Western culture take for granted the various methods by which science is accomplished, the knowledge attained by science, and the technology made possible by these findings. Others, however, may ignore, devalue, and even reject scientific thinking. Various kinds of artistic and religious experience, for example, provide a type of *knowledge* that is independent of scientific criteria. One premise of this text is that human behavior and human experience are *best* understood from a scientific perspective.

Those who study the history of science and scientific thinking find precursors of "modern" science in Greek philosophers who lived several thousand years ago. These mathematicians, astronomers, logicians, and inventors—to name but a few of the behavioral activities of *natural philosophers*—formulated problems and discovered a variety of philosophical tools. The activity of these ancient philosophers found fruition in modern Western European scientific thinking, which dates from the seventeenth century. Our present focus is upon the behavioral sciences, arguably only about 150 years old. Behavioral studies on laboratory animals have only a 100-year history.

Generations of students have found the activities of psychologists working with animals in laboratories to be a curious enterprise, indeed. As we saw in the preceding chapter, "What are you trying to prove?" and "What can we learn about humans from the study of rats?" are legitimate questions. And laboratory approaches to understanding behavior were asserted to provide insights that naturalistic observation alone cannot provide. In this chapter a rationale for behavioral studies from a scientific perspective will be made explicit.

The Science of Learning. A behavioral scientist's activities in the laboratory can be divided into two parts. First, a decision is made as to *what* will be studied, followed by the question of *how* the investigation will proceed. In the same way that our understanding of *any* phenomenon is dependent upon the perspective from which we view it, the results of learning experiments are directly influenced by the way in which the experiment is performed—i.e., the method used. For this reason it is important at the outset to understand some of the underlying theory and methods used to investigate learning and behavior—in real life, and in the laboratory.

Learning as a Hypothetical Construct

Learning is defined as *a relatively enduring change in behavior resulting from particular kinds of experiences.* Unfortunately, it is presently impossible to directly observe the learning process. We simply cannot crawl into the minds of the people (or, for that matter, the minds of much simpler animals) and actually see or feel or hear learning. The process is unobservable.

How is it possible to have a science of learning if learning is unobservable? Processes such as "learning" are not unusual in psychology—consider, for example, other terms such as *memory, motivation, fear,* and *intelligence.* These concepts describing processes of the mind are generally referred to as **hypothetical constructs.** "Intelligence," for example, is assumed to exist but cannot be observed directly. (It is not even clear what it means to suggest "it" *could* be observed directly, other than to assert that "it" is comprised of patterns of neural activity.)

Hypothetical is perhaps a poor term, because it implies that processes such as learning and intelligence are nonexistent, or even imaginary. Nothing could be further from the truth. As every schoolchild knows, memory and intelligence are routinely measured as *performance on paper and pencil tests.*

Behavioral scientists *define* intelligence as performance on an IQ (or other kind of) test. Intelligence so defined is an **operational definition**—literally, defined according to the operations that measure the presumptive process. Typically, arguments to the effect that IQ tests do not measure "real" intelligence are disagreements concerning operational definitions. Such arguments run the risk of **reification,** of asserting the existence of a presumptive process independent of evidence for that process. The futility of asserting that "intelligence cannot be measured" should be apparent.

In summary, hypothetical constructs are inferred from certain patterns of behavior. In psychology, the most commonly used evidence for learning are changes in performance, or behavior, resulting from specific, identifiable experiences. The learning process is real—as defined and measured behaviorally.

Does another reality of learning exist at the anatomical and physiological level? Is learning better defined as changes in the brain resulting from experience? Yes, and no, respectively. The arguments will be developed in what follows.

"Hard Science" and Psychology

The psychology of learning is characterized as a science—that is, as a systematic, objective, analytical enterprise. It is instructive to compare what behavioral scientists do relative to other scientists.

Biologists, chemists, and physicists, for example, sometimes object to the subject matter of psychology. How can one study learning (or motivation, or memory, etc.) they ask, when these processes are unobservable? After all, the primary goal of a science is to observe and analyze objectively the various phenomena of nature. Are not physical phenomena, such as the chemical reactions of basic biological processes, more susceptible to the objective methods of scientific analysis? Would it perhaps be better to be looking for the biochemical determinants of the learning process, and not merely analyzing the behaving animal?

Obviously behavioral scientists and ethologists alike think not. But let us analyze the argument. What are the consequences of reducing the learning process to concrete physical or chemical entities? The argument is called reductionism.

Reductionism

As you well know, the world is described by several kinds of language. Artists and musicians and priests certainly see the world in different terms from engineers and politicians. Within the world of science there also exist different *levels of analysis.*

At best a communality of purpose and spirit exists among scientists. Their activities vary widely. Some scientists do their investigations at a **molar level,** on which the behavior of whole, intact organisms is studied. Others attempt to understand some aspect of behavior by determining which parts of the brain (anatomy) or which chemicals (biochemistry) are involved when a particular behavior occurs. They are pursuing a more **molecular level** of analysis. The tendency to explain a phenomenon by reference to a more molecular level of analysis, such as biochemistry, is called **reductionism.**

Chicken Example. Let us take as an example a scientist wanting to understand the sand-eating behavior of a newly hatched chicken. Young chicks do in fact ingest sand. As far as it is known there are no more nutritive advantages for sand-eating chickens than there are for sand-eating kids.

Over a period of time sand eating drops out. And when given a choice between food and sand, edibles such as seeds are increasingly consumed. It appears that young chicks must learn to develop a complex discrimination between grains of sand and similarly shaped seeds. Indeed, through clever, painstaking research, just such a learning analysis has been accomplished (Hogan, 1977).

Now it is certain that there are biochemical changes occurring in the brain of the chick as it learns the sand-seed discrimination. Moreover, as researchers proceed to tell us *which* biochemicals change, *when*, and *how*, our understanding of the sand-seed discrimination will be enhanced. But also recognize that a complete knowledge of these biochemical changes does not in and of itself constitute anything approaching a complete explanation of the sand-seed behavioral discrimination.

It is, after all, the *behavior* of the creature for which we are attempting to account. How does the animal interact with the environment? Why does it respond as it does, etc.?

To the extent that a biochemical analysis clarifies a behavior, additional explanatory function is attained. In no way, however, does the biochemical analysis constitute a *better* explanation of the phenomenon in comparison with the molar analysis of learning as described by Hogan. Together, the molar and molecular analyses provide a more complete understanding than either alone.

Summary Statement Concerning Reductionism. Molar analyses of a behavior are appropriate and necessary for a complete understanding of that behavior. Reductionism constitutes neither better explanation nor better science.

Content and Method Compared

Science can be roughly divided into two components—*methodology* (how and what is done in an experiment) and *content* (what is found out). Students typically hate "methodological considerations." ("I don't care who did what, when, or how! All I want to know is *what was found out!*") Unfortunately, content cannot neatly be separated from methodology. Indeed, as just argued, more often than not methodology determines content.

An Example: Sleep Research. The job of the behavioral scientist can be simply divided into two parts: first, deciding upon *what* is to be studied, and then deciding upon *how* to study it. Consider, for example, sleep research. Let us imagine a sleep study in which the methodology is limited to watching a person's behavior from sun down to sun up, and recording activity, tosses and turns, perhaps a verbal report of a dream upon awakening, etc. This method would give us a veridical (truthful, accurate), but limited, understanding and perspective of one of the more fascinating aspects of our lives.

Various scientific methodologies (and some nonscientific approaches, such as Jungian dream analysis) have added other dimensions to our understanding of sleep and dreams during this century. For example, a psychoanalytic perspective might focus on the latent and manifest sexual content of someone's dreams, and relate such findings to id-ego interactions during that person's waking hours.

Recording electrodes might be attached to the scalp during sleep, and sleep stages monitored (i.e., electrophysiological measures).

Alternatively, we might compare the sleep patterns of vertebrates—of prey animals and of predators—and note the longer, deeper sleep enjoyed by the latter. These patterns relate to questions of evolutionary adaptation (i.e., the comparative method). Finally, we could note the changes in serotonin levels during dreams and other sleep stages, and develop hypotheses concerning the physiological restorative function of sleep (i.e., the biochemical method).

Note that each experimental methodology allows us only partial insight into the nature of sleep. Likewise, different methodologies used to investigate "learning" provide multiple perspectives of this process.

Perhaps to the extent that learning methodologies are successful in mimicking "real-life" learning situations, laboratory studies are interesting in their own right. It is certainly true that individual investigators develop and become expert in a particular methodology, often because of "real-life" interests and applications.

Psychological Experiments in Laboratories

Most of the psychological experiments you will encounter in this text are designed to investigate cause-and-effect relationships. Certain precise experiences or manipulations are imposed on groups of experimental subjects. Then, effects of these treatments are assessed in tests specifically designed to measure one or more aspects of the changed behavior.

As discussed in Chapter 2, ethologists typically study animal behavior in the field (within an animal's ecological niche). Laboratory manipulation of important variables supplements field research (Gould & Marler, 1987). Therefore, the most complete explanations of behavior incorporate both systematic observation in naturalistic contexts as well as control and manipulation of variables afforded by laboratory study.

Laboratory studies in the behavioral sciences—in areas of learning and memory in particular—have common features. Indeed, experiments on rats and college students more often than not use a similar scientific method.

The Effects of Study on Language Learning.   Consider, for example, an experiment using college students as subjects who are allowed to study Spanish language vocabulary for several minutes. Sometime later the subjects are asked to recall these words in a test for retention. Referring to the "black box" in Figure 3.1, note that the *words* may be considered to be the **stimulus variables** (i.e., the experimental manipulation imposed on the subjects). And the degree of reten-

Stimulus ⟶ ⟶ Response

FIGURE 3.1   The Black Box Approach to Behavior

In the **black box** model of behavior, stimuli impinge upon an animal, and the animal responds. The S-R relationships can be investigated regardless of what happens inside the animal, either physiologically or psychologically. Behaviorists attempted to build a science of behavior using this approach.

tion—the number of words recalled, or the percentage of the list retained—is the **response variable.** This response, or behavioral measure—specifically, the number of words recalled—is the evidence that learning has occurred in a subject. (Yes, when college professors test their students, they consider the students' responses to be indicants of how much has been learned!) For students familiar with scientific methodology, stimulus and response variables are also known as *independent and dependent variables* (see below).

Learning-Performance Distinction

Note that behavioral scientists measure "performance," and they infer learning from performance. As we have noted, learning and memory formation are "invisible" processes. We infer such processes based upon the changes in performance that *can* be measured. The difference between what is actually measured and that which is inferred is known as the **learning-performance distinction.**[1]

It should be apparent in the preceding example that if zero words are recalled, no "learning" has occurred (at least as measured *operationally* in this experiment). Likewise, if 10 words from the list are recalled, better "learning" is inferred than if 5 words are recalled, and so forth.

Stimulus, Response, and Intervening Variables

In this example, you can see the sequence of events typical of *all* psychological experiments. Response variables are systematically related to preceding stimulus variables, rendering the process of "learning" into an observable event. The *cause* is the stimulus variable imposed on the experimental subjects, and the *effect* is reflected in the re-

[1]The learning-performance distinction as well as many other methodological considerations in this chapter were elaborated by Clark L. Hull, whose learning theory we will study in Chapter 7.

sponse measure selected by the experimenter. *Learning* in laboratory animals, then, is operationally defined by changes in behavior that can be related to manipulations of the environment. When behavioral scientists are able to make reliable, law-like statements that relate responses to preceding stimulus conditions, *learning* assumes the status of an "intervening variable." The behavioral scientist identifies as the **intervening variable** the psychological process occurring inside the black box. These intervening variables presumably mediate the cause-and-effect relationship between the experience and the behavior.

At the risk of confusing the reader, Freudian concepts such as ego and id are considered to be *hypothetical constructs* rather than intervening variables. For these "soft" constructs to be considered intervening variables, the manipulation of specific stimulus variables would have to be shown to be systematically related to changes in response measures used to define "ego" and "id." Such research has not been accomplished. By contrast, learning is shown to change systematically with the manipulation of stimulus variables. For this reason, learning is considered to be an *intervening variable* rather than a hypothetical construct.

II.   Scientific Method[2]

Independent and Dependent Variables

In all learning experiments—indeed, in all psychological experiments—the goal is to identify the cause-and-effect relationship under investigation. The treatment, or manipulation, of stimulus variables imposed by the experimenter on the experimental subject is referred to as the **independent variable.** In the previous example, the list of Spanish words is the independent variable.

In all experiments the experimental manipulation is called the *treatment,* and the group of subjects that receive the experimental manipulation—the *independent variable*—is known as the **treatment group.** Typically these subjects are compared with other group(s) of subjects given a *control* treatment. **Control groups,** therefore, are exposed to all conditions in the experiment that the treatment group experiences, but *not* to the independent variable.

The response used to assess the treatment effects of the independent variable is known as the **dependent variable.** The measure of retention of Spanish words, then, constitutes the dependent variable in the previous example. The dependent variable is so named because the response outcome *depends upon* the treatment.

[2]Readers who already have a good understanding of basic scientific methods and terminology may prefer to merely review or skim this section.

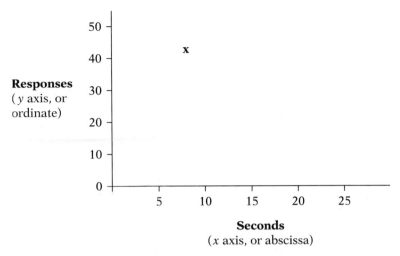

FIGURE 3.2 Visualizing Experimental Results on Graphs

X-Y axes are used to plot two variables simultaneously. In this example, the passage of time is depicted on the *x* axis, and up to 50 responses can be plotted along the *y* axis. Can you verbalize what "point *x*" represents?

Graphs

Flip through the text and notice the graphs and their word descriptions: *rate of lever pressing, number of avoidance responses, time, percent recall, amount of saccharin consumed, latency, magnitude of conditioned response,* etc. Graphs allow scientists to efficiently represent the outcome of an experiment, or, oftentimes, graphs provide a convenient visual summary of a set of experiments. A few rules will allow you, with practice, to interpret graphs readily, to make your reading easier, and to absorb complex information more efficiently.[3]

As you can see in Figure 3.2, two lines, or axes, frame a graph. One is horizontal and one is vertical. Of interest is the manner in which the psychological experiment is represented on these axes. The vertical axis, also known as the *ordinate,* usually contains some representation of the response, or behavioral measure. In other words, the dependent variable is plotted along this dimension (see Figure 3.2). Likewise, the horizontal axis, or *abscissa,* typically reflects some measure of an independent variable in the experiment. For example, you might see a representation of each treatment group, or a pre-post

---

[3]Probably because humans have a great deal of cortex devoted to interpreting visual information, and considerably less devoted to the analysis of language, we are better able to understand pictures than words.

condition, or a trial-by-trial account of an experiment, or often, *time* is the variable reflected on the *x* axis.

Relationships between stimuli and responses can be easily represented on *x* and *y* axes. For example, among the graphs of learning you will encounter in this text are *curves* of responding. In these cases, the number of responses (such as pressing a lever) is represented relative to the passage of time. A response curve is depicted in Figure 3.3.

Functional Relationships

Recall that one goal of behavioral science is to uncover orderly relationships between stimuli and responses. Figure 3.3 depicts a **functional relationship** between response output and the passage of time. What inference about learning *might* you make from the performance graph in Figure 3.3? That an animal has *learned* to respond? Maybe, maybe not. The performance relationship is measurable, and it certainly exists as plotted. To conclude, however, that an animal has learned this response, you would need to know additional details about the reasons why the performance changes as it does.

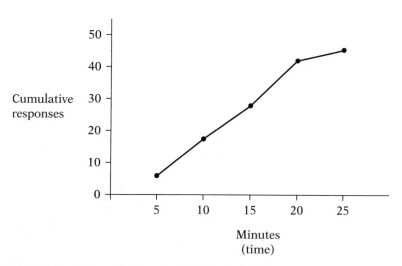

FIGURE 3.3   A Cumulative Response Curve

Cumulative means that responses are added, or accumulated during successive time periods. For example, the responses made during the second five-minute period are added to the responses made during the first five minutes and plotted at the 10-minute point. Note the orderly, mathematically definable, *functional relationship* between responding and the passage of time. Approximately how many responses have occurred after 15 minutes?

Another example of the kinds of graphs you will encounter is the *bar graph*. In the bar graph depicted in Figure 3.4, the *y* axis reflects the behavioral measure of relevance and the *x* axis plots each treatment group. (You will have the opportunity to interpret this bar graph a little later in the text.)

Both kinds of graphs—bar graphs and response curves—will be encountered throughout your text. The more quickly you master this shorthand manner of visualizing experimental outcomes, the better you will become at interpreting learning phenomena.

What Constitutes an Experiment?

Groups receiving experimental treatments are compared with control groups in order to determine if an effect was found. You may wonder what the control group was in the foregoing "experiment," which measured the recall of foreign words. There was none. The example given was not truly an experiment!

Hypotheses.   An experiment involves **hypothesis** testing. For example, one might have a **working hypothesis** that more Spanish words

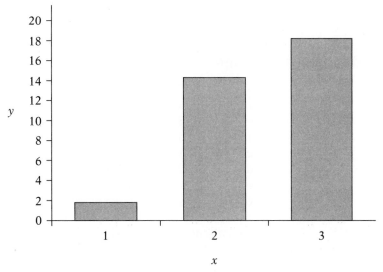

FIGURE 3.4 A Bar Graph

In the bar graph depicted, responses are plotted along the *y* axis as a function of conditions 1, 2, and 3, plotted along the *x* axis. Note the general form: *Any* responses can be plotted as a function of *any* stimulus conditions.

will be recalled if a person studies more (which was implied, but not specified, in the example). Note that a working hypothesis is a simple statement of what you expect to happen if you run an experiment. Let us set up the experiment more appropriately:

Identify 30 students enrolled in a first-year Spanish course. Each student is given the same list of 20 Spanish words to study. Next, divide the 30 students into three groups numbering *(n)* 10 students in each group (i.e., $n = 10$/group).

Group 1 studies for 60 seconds (enough to read the list one time). Then they are allowed to read a novel of their choosing for 59 minutes. Note that from the beginning of the treatment 60 minutes have elapsed.

Group 2 studies the Spanish words for 15 minutes and then reads a novel of their choice for 45 minutes.

Group 3 studies the Spanish words for 60 minutes.

Twenty-four hours later the students are given the English equivalents of the 20 words, and they are asked to make the Spanish translations. The mean number of correct responses is computed for each group. The results are displayed in Figure 3.4. Can you identify the treatment group(s) and the control group(s)? By interpreting the graph can you verbalize the results before reading further? Another way of asking this question is as follows: Can you label the x axis, the y axis, and the *functional relationship* that is depicted?

Experimental Design

Note that the independent variable in this experiment, the amount of time each group is allowed to study, is displayed along the x axis as a *category* (1, 2, or 3), or, variously, as a treatment condition (1, 2, or 3). Each category comprises one level of the independent variable. Note also that the experimenter chooses, or selects, the levels, or **parameters**, of the independent variable. In this and many experiments you will encounter, identified as **between-groups designs,** researchers create comparison groups by varying parameters of the independent variable. The idea is to test the hypothesis that a systematic relationship exists between the independent variable and the dependent variable. In this experiment, that amount of study (1 minute, 15 minutes, or 60 minutes) influences the number of Spanish words recalled in a later test.

By contrast, a **within-groups design** compares a pretreatment measure of the dependent variable with a posttreatment measure *in the same subjects*. For example, the investigator might give the 20 Spanish words to all three groups before allowing them to study. Their performance would constitute a pre-test (or a *baseline*) from which to measure the effects of the treatment. After studying the Spanish words for 1, 15, or 60 minutes they would then take a post-test. The post-test performance of each group would be compared with the respective pre-test performance—hence, a *within-groups* design.

Look at Figure 3.4 once again. What parameter of the independent variable was manipulated?[4] Note that the dependent variable plotted on the y axis is the number of Spanish words recalled during the test. The mean values plotted are 1.8, 14.3, and 18.2 words, respectively, for Groups 1, 2, and 3.

Statistical Analysis.   These experimental results could be subjected to a statistical analysis to see if the **null hypothesis** could be rejected. The null hypothesis in this experiment is that the three groups do not differ from each other. That is, that the results observed in Figure 3.4 would have occurred even if study time had been equal for the three groups. Yet another way of stating this counterintuitive argument (i.e., the null hypothesis) is that the amount of time spent studying had nothing to do with the number of successful Spanish translations.

A statistical procedure called an ANOVA (analysis of variance) of these data would compare both the means and the variance (distributions of recalled words) of the three groups. The size of the mean differences in Figure 3.4 is sufficiently large that the results of the ANOVA would likely allow us to reject the null hypothesis. A statistically significant difference among the groups would allow us to conclude that the "amount of time studying the Spanish words" was *causally related* to the recall performance of these words. We can now accept the working hypothesis. From the performance of these students, we can infer that "study" (practice? familiarity?) is related to the learning process.

Control Groups.   A question asked earlier has not been addressed. Which of these three groups, if any, is the *control* group? Technically, none of the three is a control group. Had we used the within-subjects design, the pre-test condition for all three groups could be identified as a "control" condition. That is, because "time spent studying" was the independent variable, the pre-test constituted performance in the absence of (prior to) the independent variable.

Does this mean that the between-groups experiment depicted in Figure 3.4 is meaningless because there was no identifiable control group? Not necessarily. The pattern of results (i.e., the functional relationship depicted in the figure) allows the researcher to *infer* the performance expected from *zero minutes of study* (i.e., the complete

---

[4]The parameter of *time*—the amount of time students were allowed to study the Spanish words—was manipulated.

absence of the independent variable). The functional relationship suggests (as one would intuitively predict) that English-speaking humans do not know Spanish vocabulary words unless they spend some time studying.

Interim Summary

1. Molar behavior can be studied scientifically.
2. Explanations of behavior in physiological or chemical terms are not better, nor are they more scientific.
3. Learning is an inference that can be made from observations of an animal's performance behavior.
4. A simple analysis of learning employs a black box model in which a response can be systematically related to incoming stimuli.
5. Learning experiments manipulate treatment conditions, or independent variables, and measure dependent variables (usually some form of a behavioral response).
6. Experiments are designed in which treatment groups are compared with control groups. The conditions of the control group are made as close to identical as possible to the treatment group, except that the independent variable is not manipulated in the control group.
7. Working hypotheses about the causes of learned behavior may be tested in experiments, in which terms are operationally defined, treatment and control conditions are compared, and null hypotheses can be tested with statistics.
8. One outcome of successful experiments is the identification of functional relationships where responses are related to antecedent stimulus conditions.

III.   Stimulus and Response: The Behavioral Analysis of Association

Modern learning theory is a form of *philosophical associationism*. The theory of associationism can be traced to the writings of seventeenth-century philosophers now known as the *British Empiricists*—John Locke, Thomas Hobbes, George Berkeley, and others. Our ideas, wrote Locke, result from the association of simple sensory events. These "raw sensations" became associated to produce complex associations:

> All the ideas we have of particular distinct sorts of substances, are nothing but several combinations of simple ideas. . . . It is by such combinations of simple ideas, and nothing else, that we (mentally) represent particular sorts of substances to ourselves. . . .

. . . . Thus, the idea of the sun—what is it but an aggregate of those several simple ideas—bright, hot roundish, having a constant regular motion, (etc.).

(John Locke, *An Essay Concerning Human Understanding*, 1690)

The British Empiricists, also known as Associationists, did not do experiments in laboratories. Nevertheless, many of their ideas about **associationism** (cf. association formation) have proven to be remarkably insightful. Modern scientists retain the basic approach of these philosophers, operationally defining simple learning as the association of two or more sensory experiences.

Empiricism.   A second debt owed to the British Associationists is their assumption that a primary source of knowledge about the world comes from (is based upon) *experience* with the world. Hence, knowledge is *empirical*, which means *guided by observation*. Modern science uses empirical methods; laboratory study involves seeing, hearing, and otherwise observing, testing, and measuring. **Empiricism** is the main method (and philosophy) that distinguishes science from other ways humans can get knowledge about the world (cf. "intuitionism," which has no real-world referents).

Four Tenets of Association Theory

From the British Associationists and subsequent findings of researchers, modern association theory may be summarized as follows:

1. *Temporal Contiguity.* The process of association formation is integrally dependent upon **temporal contiguity.** That is, for stimulus events to be associated, they must occur close together in time. (How close is close enough we will explore later.) You did not learn what "WATCH OUT!" means by experiencing a near miss with an 18-wheeler 30 minutes after someone yelled at you. Vertebrate nervous systems readily make associations when stimuli sensed by them occur closely together in time.

2. *Intensity.* The **intensity** of two sensory experiences influences the process of association formation (more intense stimuli being more readily associable). We will see in Chapter 5 that large rewards (or punishments) influence the rate of learning more than smaller amounts. In addition, for reasons not well understood, louder sounds and brighter lights (as advertisers know only too well) are associated more quickly, and the learning lasts longer, than less intense stimuli.

3. *Frequency.* The **frequency** of occurrence of stimuli strengthens their association. Readers who have used flash cards to learn

math facts or to learn another language are well aware that mastery depends upon study. The more frequently you go through the cards (i.e., more trials), the better the material is associated/learned.

4. *Similarity.* **Similarity** of experiences influences their associability; some events "belong" together—i.e., are more easily associated than others. For example, suppose while listening to unfamiliar exotic music (a novel sound) you eat half of an unfamiliar exotic fruit (a novel taste), and half an hour later you become nauseous and vomit. Would you attribute the sickness to the novel sound or to the novel taste? That is, would you be more likely to associate sickness with taste or sound? Why? We will explore several hypotheses "why" at a later point. Not all stimuli are equally associable, and their "similarity" (or belongingness, or the way in which the brain is organized) presumably has something to do with this phenomenon.

Association Theory: Example and Analysis

With these principles in mind, try, as John Locke might, to analyze the following scenario involving the experiences of a small child:

> While riding in a car with her father through a north Florida thunderstorm, a four-year-old child experiences bright flashes of lightning and rumbling thunder. For 10 minutes, thunder follows lightning in rapid succession. Then the storm begins to dissipate.
> "Where is the thunder?" the child asks.
> Distracted, the father ponders how to explain the physics of thunder and lightning to a four-year-old.
> Far off in the distance where the storm has moved another flash brightens the dark sky.
> Again the youngster asks, "Where'd the thunder go?"
> At this point the father realizes that the child could still see the flashes, but the low growl of thunder was too distant to be heard.[5]

Learning About Causality. The child has apparently learned a lightning-thunder (or thunder-lightning) association. She now has an "idea" that a storm is composed of rain, thunder, and lightning (in the same way that Locke's idea of sun was warm, red, and round). In this four-year-old's perceptual world, however, **causality** was probably *not* inferred from her observations. Due to the nature of thunderstorms, thunder sometimes seems to precede and sometimes to follow lightning. It is highly likely that the child learned that thunder and lightning were highly correlated, but had yet to learn that lightning *causes* thunder. That is, she most likely had *not* learned that lightning is the

---

[5]In 1971 this incident happened as described. An early reader of this textbook thought the example was too contrived to be believable. You be the judge.

antecedent condition, or *cause,* of the thunder.[6] Having learned the thunder-lightning/lightning-thunder association, the absence of thunder was puzzling. Her still-not-quite-predictable world has become even less so.

Two-Stage Theory of Association

From this example we can see that associative theory has two distinct stages. In stage one, two stimuli are perceived in such a way that one stimulus does not reliably precede the other. A simple association is formed, and the stimuli are perceived simply as being *correlated.* After a number of trials (cf. *frequency* of association, in the preceding) in which one stimulus is perceived as always preceding the second stimulus, a more complex association is learned. The first stimulus is perceived to cause the second. As will be discussed in more detail in the next chapter, the simple association is said to occur by *contiguity,* the more complex association by *contingency.*

Association Theory and S-R Theory. Behavioral science begins when the methods of laboratory research are added to philosophical theorizing. The raw sensory experiences of John Locke become the psychologist's *stimuli* (singular is stimul*us*). Since "ideas" are difficult to measure, the scientist instead concentrates upon relating the organism's response to an incoming stimulus—both of which are measurable. Association theory easily becomes translated into the S-R (stimulus-response) theory of the laboratory.

More often than not such analyses do not make reference to what is happening "inside" the organism—for example, the changes taking place in the brain as learning occurs and as memories are formed. It is for this reason that S-R Psychology is also known as a "black box" approach to understanding behavior.

Nonassociative Learning

Is it intuitively obvious that "association formation" is more complicated than simply "sensing" stimuli? Let us first consider, then, what happens when thunder and lightning stimuli impinge separately upon our nervous systems.

---

[6]Careful observation over a number of trials with a nearby storm *might* allow human observers to detect the fact that thunder is contingent upon (invariably follows) lightning strikes. Unless one learns about (and remembers) the physics of lightning and thunder in a science class, however, many adult humans will *not* know that a lightning strike *causes* thunder by heating and expanding air molecules, which "thunder" upon contraction.

The stimulus events that the four-year-old experienced can be depicted in a 2×2 table of possible outcomes of association or nonassociation (see Figure 3.5). The stimulus event of lightning (S_1) occurs or not. The second stimulus event (S_2), thunder, also may or may not occur.

Habituation

Direct your attention for a moment to these **single-stimulus effects.** First consider "silent" lightning strikes many miles away. The child might initially see this display, orient (direct attention) to it, and perhaps respond by making a verbal inquiry. Over a period of time, faraway lightning by itself would elicit less responsiveness from the child. This reduced responsiveness of an organism to repeated stimulation is called **habituation.**

Habituation is a basic property of behaving organisms. Stimuli that by themselves are not too meaningful tend to be ignored. Habituation is the most basic form of learning—that is, learning not to respond to repetitious, meaningless stimuli. Other examples of habituation include not hearing the ticks of a clock, not feeling the clothes you are wearing, and not seeing the page numbers as you read through this book—until your attention is directed to these stimuli.

Habituation is typically considered to be an example of **nonasso-**

S_2 - **Thunder**

	Present	Absent
Present	a	b
Absent	c	d

S_1 - **Lightning**

FIGURE 3.5   An Association Matrix

The joint occurrence of S_1 and S_2 occupies the upper left cell, labeled "a." Either stimulus may occur alone; e.g., cell "c," thunder alone, or cell "b," lightning alone. Note that stimulus *association* occurs only in cell a; the effect of either stimulus by itself (cells b & c) is called a *nonassociative* effect. Cell "d" indicates the absence of both stimulus events. Cell d can be labeled "context" in that stimulus events always occur against a *background of ambient conditions,* or **context**. In the example given, wind and rain, the moving automobile, the radio, and voices would comprise some of the context against which thunder and lightning might be experienced.

ciative learning.[7] Each of us is exposed to thousands of stimuli (auditory, visual, cutaneous, chemical, etc.) each minute. Fortunately, we cannot possibly attend to all of them. Only the most critical, meaningful stimuli that *demand* attention get our attention. The other stimuli *must* fade into the background stimulus conditions (cell "d," Figure 3.5) or we would constantly be in sensory overload.

Habituation is the process that allows this fading to occur. In a sense, we are learning what *not* to respond to, what *not* to attend to . . . and this seems to be a perfectly reasonable usage of the term "learning." Single-stimulus events that are repeatedly encountered become relatively permanently "habituated." Such stimuli, for example, can less readily be used to form new associations, a phenomenon called *latent inhibition*, discussed in the next chapter.

Habituation Is Not Receptor Adaptation. The process of habituation is often confused with the more peripheral processes of receptor adaptation and receptor fatigue. For example, rods and cones become less sensitive to light stimulation immediately after they are exposed to light, and hair cells in the cochlea following sound stimulation likewise have refractory periods during which their response is inhibited. In the absence of further stimulation, these sensory adaption processes typically recover within a few seconds to a few minutes. By contrast, habituated responses may remain so for days, weeks, or months.

Remember the distinction made earlier between "learning" and "performance"? We infer learning from performance, but not all changes in performance constitute learning. The present example of sensory adaption is an excellent example of performance changes (i.e., reduced sensitivity to sights and sounds) that do not constitute learning.

How "General" Is Habituation? We have begun to entertain arguments to the effect that learning is a *general process*. A general process allows one to make meaningful behavioral comparisons across widely divergent species and in a variety of learning situations. For example, if we were to compare the effects of rhythmically stroking the "arm" of a starfish and the arm of a human infant (i.e., an invertebrate and a vertebrate), the initial reflexive movements of the "arms" of both species diminish following repeated stimulation. In both instances we would say that the response *habituated*, although the mechanisms underlying these responses differ markedly because of the highly dissimilar nervous systems involved (see Box 3.1).

---

[7]An alternative view, that habituation is an *associative* phenomenon, will be presented in Chapter 5.

BOX 3.1

Habituation: A General Behavioral Phenomenon

Most general process arguments you will encounter presuppose a common underlying neural mechanism. *Habituation*, however, is a behavioral phenomenon that apparently can be accomplished by many different types of nervous systems. Note in the figure the similarity of the time course of decreased responsiveness to repeated stimulation in spinal rats, normal rats, and adult humans (Lehner, 1941).

(a) Withdrawal response decreased for tail-pinched rats after 13 trials in the first "habituation cycle." (These rats had transected spinal cords, thereby eliminating the brain's control over the habituation response.) Fifteen seconds later, the same tail-pinch stimulus habituated in seven trials (second habituation cycle). By the sixth cycle, habituation was accomplished in two trials.

(b) "Startle," or jerking, reflex to a loud sound habituates more slowly in intact rats, compared with the tail-pinch reflex in spinal rats. Again, the interval between blocks of rapidly repeated stimulations is 15 seconds. Note that half as many stimulations (approximately 15) are sufficient to habituate the response in the second cycle, compared with 30 stimulations in the first cycle.

(c) Note the same pattern of habituation of the abdominal reflex of adult humans, again with 15 seconds between each block of response habituation.

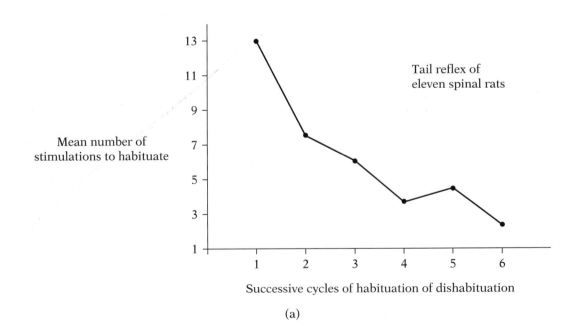

Tail reflex of eleven spinal rats

Mean number of stimulations to habituate

Successive cycles of habituation of dishabituation

(a)

BOX 3.1

Continued

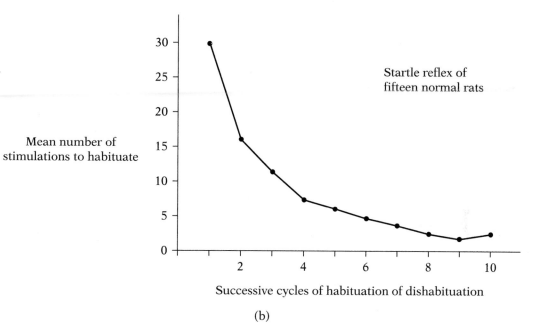

(b)

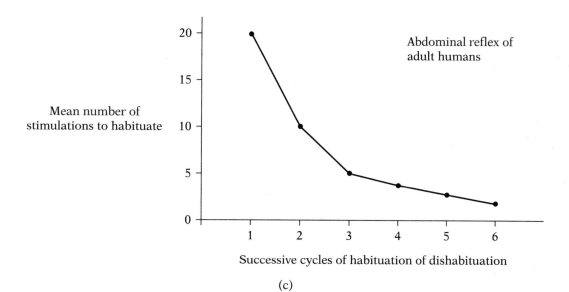

(c)

Perhaps we should not be surprised at the similar outcomes of habituation experiments displayed in Box 3.1. Apparently there are no exceptions to the generality of nonassociative processes throughout the animal kingdom. Razran (1971) cites the similarity of patterns of habituation in a variety of responses in planaria, worms, snails, goldfish, frogs, turtles, birds, and humans.

Sensitization

Repetitive stimulation does not invariably lead to reduced responsiveness by the organism. Had the four-year-old in the previous example experienced lightning flashes up close (again, for the sake of the argument, in the absence of thunder), as opposed to relatively benign displays at the horizon, it is probable that a somewhat different outcome would have ensued. Intense visual, auditory, cutaneous, and chemical stimuli do not habituate readily. In fact, oftentimes one or more presentations of a powerful stimulus have the opposite effect. Rather than reduced responsiveness, the organism tends to become yet more activated when the stimulus is presented again—a phenomenon called **sensitization.**

Habituation and Sensitization Compared

To reiterate, some responses to repetitive stimuli tend to habituate, and others tend to sensitize. Both processes occur in all species of animals (Peeke & Petrinoviche, 1984). As a general rule, responses to regularly occurring presentations of stimuli of low to moderate intensity tend to habituate (Thompson & Spencer, 1966). Moderate to high intensity stimuli tend to sensitize the organism. To give you some idea of the complications that can arise in assessing nonassociative effects, consider the following experiment by Davis (1974). He compared the effects of presenting a loud noise (110 dB) lasting only a fraction of a second to two groups of rats differing only in the level of background noise in their experimental chamber. The two groups had background noises of 60 dB (relatively quiet) and 80 dB (relatively loud), respectively. Davis measured the rats' startle response to aperiodic presentations of the loud, 110-dB noise. The startle response decreased over trials in the group with low background noise, but it increased in the group with the high background noise. That is, the same 110-dB stimulus had two opposing effects—habituation and sensitization, respectively!

Nervous systems are constantly being attuned to the environment in which they interact. The stimulus effects of lightning and thunder are good examples of the nonassociative processes of sensitization and habituation. A sharp crack of thunder sensitizes four-year-olds and adults alike. After one or more bone-jarring stimulus events, one's "nerves" are on edge, and other noises tend to elicit a greater-than-normal response. We await, we anticipate, the next crack of thunder. Such is the nature of sensitization. Not so the gentle rumbling of distant thunder. In fact, low-intensity, rhythmic stimulation (such as petting a cat) has a calming effect (on both the stroker and the strokee!).

Sensitization can produce a relatively permanent change in a person's behavior. For several years after the lightning incident, for example, the four-year-old in question was aroused at the first approach of thunderstorms. Her memory of close lightning strikes remains with her and has sensitized her to that particular class of auditory stimulus events. Perhaps this is the stuff phobias are made of? We will address this question in Chapter 8.

Analysis of Nonassociative Learning

The foregoing examples readily illustrate the importance of the concepts of habituation and sensitization for understanding important changes in response patterns. There is irony in the fact that all psychologists cannot agree upon the importance of single-stimulus events—even to the point that some theorists ignore nonassociative phenomena and do not consider them to be instances of learning. Why is this so? How has "learning" come to be defined as "due to association" and single-stimulus effects relegated to psychophysics and physiological psychology? Answers to these questions are not simple. Consider the following arguments.

Post hoc **Analyses of Nonassociative Effects.** Ideally scientists would like to be able to predict in advance the nature and direction of the outcome of an experimental treatment. Take habituation. A scientist interested in investigating habituation would like to be able to select a stimulus, present it to the organism a few times, and measure the process of response diminution. Unfortunately, our experimental psychologist may find that the response outcome is in the nonpredicted direction. That is to say, one of *enhanced* rather than diminished responsiveness. And to complicate the matter, another test subject, or the same test subject on another day, might give a different result.

All too often in studying nonassociative processes one is restricted to *post hoc* analyses of the presumptive process. The experiment is done, results recorded, and then a hypothesis is formed. Not good science!

This loss of predictability retards the scientist's search for law-like relationships. It may be for this reason that not many psychologists specialize in the study of nonassociative learning, and, as a result, less is known about these processes than is known about the laws of association between two stimuli. A curious situation, indeed!

Example of Learned Helplessness.   Even general rules concerning the nature of stimuli that typically lead to habituation or to sensitization do not always hold. A case in point is the phenomenon known as **learned helplessness.** Learned helplessness is a condition described by Seligman and Maier (1967) in which an animal fails to respond in an adaptive fashion to avoid a painful experience. Experimentally, a dog or rat in an experimental chamber is administered one or two very intense electric shocks. One would expect the organism to be sensitized, to respond vigorously to even mild electric shock in the future. Yet in fact there is an overall *reduction* in responsiveness to subsequent electric shocks, characteristic of habituation. Why? Probably because the shocks were too intense! So, very low-intensity shocks habituate; medium to high level shocks sensitize; and *very* high-intensity shocks again produce a reduction in responsiveness that resembles habituation. Single-stimulus effects are difficult to conceptualize, and difficult to investigate in the laboratory. The learned helplessness phenomenon is currently a model underlying some forms of human psychopathology, a topic we will return to in Chapter 8.

To summarize, it is problematic predicting whether certain independent variables will act to sensitize, to habituate, or to have some other effect. The organism's response depends critically upon the nature of the physical stimulus, the species under study, and the organism's prior history with the stimulus in question.

Stimuli: Simple? Complex?

In their search for general process laws, behavioral scientists find it convenient to refer to diverse environmental events as "stimuli" or "stimulus events." A child's crying sounds are stimulus events, as is a flashing light, an M&M® candy, a ringing bell, a spoken word, a lover's caress, and a lightning display! This is not to say that seeing is the same as hearing, smelling, tasting, and feeling. Rather, what is important is the recognition that perceptible stimulus events have some common properties, both acting alone and in associative combination. And "learning" is the science of ascertaining these common properties of stimulus events, making generalizations about them, and ultimately predicting the results of their joint stimulation.

"Simple" Stimuli.   Within each sensory modality a stimulus can be conveniently arranged along a simple-to-complex continuum. A single note on a piano (or better yet, a pure tone) is a simple stimulus, whereas a chord, or combination of single notes, or a spoken word is a more complex auditory stimulus. "Simple" and "complex" refer both to the physical nature of the stimulus and to the measurable effect of the stimulus upon the organism. In the most simple cases only a few auditory nerve fibers fire, activating only a few parts of the brain, while many more nerve fibers and more parts of the brain are involved as stimulus complexity increases. Using this brain activity, humans and animals in psychophysical experiments can reliably judge stimuli and place them on a continuum from simple to complex.

"Complex" Stimuli. A corresponding psychological complexity, or richness, accompanies the more complex stimulus. Combinations of chords, such as in a musical melody, produce complex auditory stimulation experienced over longer periods of time.[8]

Stimulus Complexity and Nonassociative Effects

Back to the question at hand. Suffice it to say that all stimuli are not equal in effect. Rather, *the nonassociative effects of complex stimuli produce response patterns that differ from those of simple stimuli.*

Consider, for example, the stimulus effects of a drug such as amphetamine. Depending upon dosage, method of administration, and many other variables, amphetamine is relatively long lasting and affects a variety of physiological systems. Obviously this "stimulus" is much different from, for example, Pavlov's "ringing bell." The latter is a relatively simple auditory stimulus acting upon the auditory nerve and auditory portions of the brain.

We can therefore expect more complex nonassociative effects (sensitization and habituation) as well as more complex associative effects when the stimulus being used is a drug rather than a simple tone. Repeated exposure to drugs can lead to *tolerance* and *addiction* in some cases, and sensitization-like responses to others. These "drug effects" often entail a learning component (see p. 362), but even acting alone, unpaired with other stimuli, drug effects cannot be simply described by reference to habituation and sensitization phenomena found using simple stimuli.

The remaining chapters of this text are concerned with questions of associative learning. Indeed, many learning theorists consider

---

[8]Who among us has not experienced the complexities and intricacies of feeling (e.g., emotional responses) accompanying the perception of such complex stimulus events as a musical symphony . . . a sunset with its myriad colors . . . the subtleties of a gourmet meal? Is it perhaps stretching the term to consider these examples "stimulus events"? Probably! Certainly the responses defy analysis.

nonassociative phenomena relatively unimportant. But one need not be a scientist to note the inherent survival value of sensitization, habituation, and other single-stimulus effects. As noted in Chapter 2, fixed action patterns (FAPs) are often released by a single stimulus, called a *sign stimulus*. One example of an interpretation of the complex responses elicited by such a stimulus is that the goose's visual brain is preprogrammed to be sensitive to movement at a critical period of development. Neurons subserving vision are tuned to whatever moving stimulus is experienced, and the following behavior is tied to subsequent activation of these neurons.

The point here is that the degree of "complexity" of a stimulus can be *learned through experience.* Although stimuli can and do vary in physical complexity, even a simple stimulus can be made complex by experience. Such processes presumably are part of the "operating equipment" present at birth. Simple processes such as sensitization and habituation presumably require only the most primitive of nervous systems, since forms of both responses are seen in all animals (see Box 3.1).

Adaptiveness of Sensitization and Habituation.   What is the adaptive significance of sensitization and habituation processes? Consider the following: Living organisms that are either "drowsy" or "wired" are at less than their optimal arousal level for coping with environmental demands. In large measure a learned balance of habituation and sensitization is critical for functional awareness. Potentially important stimuli are better perceived against a background of habituated stimuli, and for a period of time following a "stronger" stimulus, the nervous system displays a greater than normal sensitivity.

Behavior Analysis in the Laboratory

Psychologists have not always been concerned with the systematic analysis of learned and innate components of behavior. Nor, for that matter, do all contemporary psychologists concern themselves with ethological interpretations of behavior. As recently as 70 years ago psychology was a subset of the department of philosophy in many universities, and only those interested in animal behavior per se had biological training. (And, of course, at that time there was no such animal as a *clinical* psychologist.)

American Behaviorism.   In 1913, a psychologist by the name of John B. Watson (1879–1958) consciously worked to establish an objective science of unconscious behavior. In his paper, *Psychology As the Behaviorist Views It,* Watson (1919) noted the shortcomings of existing philosophical approaches to psychology. He criticized the *struc-*

turalists (an early field of psychology) because he distrusted their method of **introspection.** When asked why he disdained introspection, Watson replied that people often distort or even lie about what they are perceiving or thinking. The experimenter cannot be sure when humans are giving accurate verbal reports. (Is it possible the same criticism could be applied to human interpretations of infrahuman behavior?) Watson also singled out Sigmund Freud for criticism. He felt that Freud had failed in his attempt to explore the complexities of the human mind within a scientific framework.

Russian Reflexology. During this same time period Ivan Pavlov in Russia was independently arriving at a philosophical position similar to Watson's. As we will see in the next chapter, Pavlov studied both reflexive and conditioned reflexive (learned) behavior. Both Watson and Pavlov encouraged their students to conceive of behavior as a "mirror of the mind"; that is, psychological processes such as learning are to be inferred from measures of behavioral performance.

Several generations of contemporary learning theorists were influenced by Watson, Pavlov, and others. Learning was to be studied as an observable change in *behavior* rather than as a mental process. Modern learning theory follows the lead of these early behaviorists. Ultimately, however, the elusive constructs we call "learning" and "memory" will be understood from a variety of perspectives—including those of ethology, psychology, and biology.

Assumptions Underlying General Process Learning Theory

The modern extension of traditional associationism is called **general process learning theory.** A primary assumption of this position is that a set of laws exists that can adequately describe the learning process. A goal of many contemporary scientists who do learning experiments is to identify these laws as systematically and objectively as possible.

What assumptions underlie this approach?

1. *Behavioral Flexibility.* At the outset, most behavioral scientists acknowledge the importance of learning in the development of behavior. Biological influences on behavior are not ignored, but learning is viewed as the primary source of identifiable behavioral variability. Another way of stating this is that instinctive behavior is important, but that which is of most interest in both human and animal behavior comes about through both nonassociative and associative learning processes.

2. *Laboratory Analysis.* Most scientists agree that a laboratory is the best place to investigate and to understand behavioral processes

such as learning. Why? (a) Laboratories allow for more careful measurement of the learning process than do observations made in natural settings. (b) *Manipulation* of variables in laboratories allows for the use of control procedures.

3. *Logical Analysis.* Control procedures in turn allow the experimenter to deduce with confidence the *necessary* and *sufficient* conditions for learning. For example, is temporal contiguity necessary for learning to occur? If not, is it a sufficient condition? A logical analysis of these questions requires scientists to control the experimental environment in which learning occurs.

Included is the necessity of controlling various nonlearning effects, or **confounded variables.** In the absence of specific control procedures, many experiences (such as light-dark cycles, changes in diet and sleep, age of organism, to name a few confounded variables) contribute to changes in behavior that are easily mistaken for learning effects.

4. *Lawfulness of Learning.* A further assumption of behavioral scientists is that behavior is not capricious, accidental, or random. Rather, it changes in predictable ways. A simple example: You get mad and kick at a jammed door—and break a toe. More than likely you will not repeat that behavior. Why not? Because *most animals* change their behavior rather than continuing to induce painful outcomes. Most animals respond to rewards and punishments in predictable ways.

Scientists also assume that the various phenomena of learning are reproducible—that they can be demonstrated in other laboratories under similar sets of circumstances. Both replicability and predictability of outcome, therefore, illustrate what is meant by the lawfulness of learning.

5. *Generality of Learning.* General process learning theory implies that many of the phenomena of learning are both *general across species* and *transituational.* "General processes" can be observed under comparable sets of conditions in a variety of species. The biological and behavioral continuities offered by Darwin's evolutionary theory provide the conceptual basis for assuming common psychological processes.[9] *Transituational* means that the same stimuli conform in a law-like (read, predictable) manner at different times, in different experiments, and in different laboratories. When, as we will see in Chapter 5 (p. 201 ff), species differences in learning emerge,

---

[9]Invertebrate neurons for all intents and purposes are like vertebrate neurons. Common processes such as habituation and sensitization are in part due to the functioning of individual neurons. Moreover, all vertebrates have similarities of nervous system functioning (forebrain, midbrain, hindbrain, cranial nerves, etc.) that underlie common processes of learning. Similarities and differences in nervous system structure will be noted as animal learning experiments are presented throughout the text.

and certain stimuli are seen to enter into association more readily than others, general process assumptions will be severely challenged.

Interim Summary

1. Seventeenth-century philosophers now known as the British Associationists proposed that knowledge was derived through the association of sensory stimuli.
2. Four tenets, or rules, proposed by the British Associationists that govern the formation of associations are (a) temporal contiguity, (b) frequency, (c) intensity, and (d) similarity (or belongingness) of stimuli.
3. A two-stage theory of association posits that events are first perceived as being correlated, and secondly interpreted as being causally related.
4. Nonassociative learning is the concept that single stimuli can produce relatively permanent effects, known as habituation and sensitization.
5. Habituation refers to a relatively permanent reduced responsiveness following repeated stimulation with low-intensity stimuli.
6. Sensitization is the term used to identify increased responsiveness for a time period following a relatively intense stimulus.
7. Stimuli can be characterized as lying along a dimension from (physically/perceptually) simple to (physically/perceptually) complex. In addition, simple stimuli have less effect (both associative and nonassociative) on animals than do complex stimuli.
8. Nonassociative effects such as sensitization and habituation are behaviorally adaptive.
9. Researchers identified as behaviorists focus upon observable behavior change rather than introspective reports in their study of learning.
10. Assumptions underlying *general process learning theory:* More of behavior is learned behavior than genetically determined behavior; laboratory analyses of behavior are preferred to classical ethological study; learning is both lawful and general.
11. To the extent that the assumptions in (10) are true, the quest for *general* laws of learning becomes a legitimate enterprise.

IV. Ethological and Laboratory Analyses: A Summary Comparison

Two theoretical views of what the proper study of behavior should entail have been presented in the previous and present chapters. Experimental psychologists' general process learning theory proposes common ways in which species learn and remember. In contrast, ethologists emphasize each species' unique behavioral adaptations to environmental problems of survival.

Both positions are meaningful, and both are credible. By focusing upon differences in adaptation among species, ethologists run the risk of overlooking general processes of learning and memory. Psychologists, on the other hand, are open to the criticism of studying processes that have no relevance to survival in natural settings, and of proposing too-general laws of learning.

Two important distinctions can be made between the ethological and behavioral positions. Ethology is a branch of biology that (a) is species oriented and (b) approaches behavior primarily in a nonassociative manner. Ethologists find that in some species, in some situations, a single-stimulus event can markedly alter behavior. The general process viewpoint is primarily concerned with associative processes presumed to be general to almost all species.

Ethology studies the particulars of development in the life histories of selected species. General process theory is concerned with associations made in a variety of situations by any animal at any time in life.

Ethology recognizes that natural selection and niche requirements are important determinants of behavior. General process theory posits that all life forms have common problems of survival, and that solutions to these problems are often common ones, presumably because they are solved by similar brain processes.

Single-Stimulus Effects in Ethology and in Associative Theory

Look back to Figure 3.5 and note the upper left hand cell (cell "a"), representing *associative* effects. Most present day investigations of learning and of memory are associative in nature. This is not to say that the effects of single stimuli acting upon organisms are considered unimportant. As we saw earlier, habituation and sensitization are among the most important phenomena of single-stimulus effects on organisms.

In addition, ethological studies indicate that certain complex stimuli, called sign stimuli, can have unusually large effects on behavior. Relatively few of the stimuli animals encounter in their lifetime are sign stimuli, however. This is especially true for those complex animals (such as humans) that move freely throughout wide, ever-changing niches. Complex animals that move freely throughout wide, ever-changing niches solve many of their problems by learning to associate and remember the stimuli they encounter, and by the reinforcing and punishing consequences of their behavior.

Ethology is not the only science that historically has directed its attention to the nonassociative effects of stimuli. Indeed, psychologists who study processes of *sensation* and *perception* are very much interested in single-stimulus effects in humans and other animals. The discipline of *psychophysics* has been successful in measuring response characteristics to a variety of stimuli. Yet other behavioral and biological scientists have traced physical stimuli through our sensory systems and throughout the central nervous system. *Physiological psychologists* and those in *neuroscience* investigate the effects of complex stimuli such as foods, drugs, spoken words, etc., acting upon the body.

Implicit Assumptions of Psychologists

Throughout these first three chapters I have attempted to answer questions asked by students in their first course in learning. Too often academic psychologists (and probably most professors) fail to recognize the tremendous burden of assumptions they carry into their classrooms. We forget how many years we have had to become used to our way of looking at the world.

Why do psychologists think about "learning" the way they do? Why do psychologists insist upon using an animal model to investigate learning? Why not think about animal behavior the way ethologists do?

As discussed in detail in Chapter 2, the point is well taken. In studying animal behavior as it relates to survival, ethological research has *ecological validity*. Ironically, the case can be made that there is *too much* ecological validity in what they do! Risking the wrath of fellow scientists, I am less interested in the behavior of muskrats or bees than that of humans.

Perhaps, as detailed in Table 2.2, the one great unspoken distinction between ethological and psychological approaches to the study of behavior is that different kinds of people were attracted to each discipline. Ethologists have primary interests in natural history and field biology. Arguably, classical ethologists were less interested in human behavior because of their focus of study upon a single, nonhuman species.

The primary interests of most psychologists, by contrast, ultimately concern the human mind and human behavior. Is it not reasonable that psychologists would propose learning theories based upon nonhuman animals, but generalizable to human beings? Certainly Pavlov (1927), Thorndike (1932), Watson (1924), Tolman (1932), Hull (1943), and Skinner (1938), to name just a few prominent learning theorists, did just that.

When in Chapters 8–10 you find that applied learning theory informs the human condition, that the results of learning experiments that used a variety of animals tell us a great deal about the human mind and human behavior, do not be surprised. That is what psychologists had in mind the whole time.

. . .

And that is what Ivan Pavlov, the great Russian physiologist, had in mind when he investigated "psychic secretions" in dogs. We turn to his work in the next chapter.

Cartoon by R. L. Zamorano

"Pavlov. . . Pavlov. . . That name rings a bell."

FIGURE 3.6

Summary

1. Although other kinds of experience and knowledge inform the human condition, human behavior and human experience are *best* understood from a scientific perspective. The study of learning is a major component of the scientific analysis of human behavior.

2. Learning is a hypothetical construct. Like other psychological constructs—intelligence, memory, and personality—learning is inferred from observations of behavior. Learning can be distinguished, then, from performance.

3. Learning can be analyzed and explained at several levels of analysis. Explaining learning by reference to biochemical changes in the brain is reductionistic.

4. Learning is conceptualized within an associative framework and is studied by empirical methods.

5. Learning is studied in laboratories using scientific methods. Stimulus and response variables (independent and dependent variables, respectively) can be graphed, and functional relationships noted.

6. Hypotheses about the learning process are frequently tested in animal experiments. Like other scientific experiments, treatment groups are compared with control groups, and statistical analyses allow null hypotheses to be disconfirmed.

7. Learning via association occurs in (at least) two stages; animals first seem to learn that stimulus events are correlated, secondly that one event is causally related to the second event.

8. Animals also learn nonassociatively (and adaptively) through single-stimulus processes of habituation and sensitization.

9. Stimulus events being associated during learning range along a continuum from simple to complex. Rules of association and nonassociative effects will vary as a function of stimulus complexity.

10. General process learning theory focuses upon features of association formation, and nonassociative effects, common to all animals.

11. Classical ethologists focus upon single-stimulus effects and less upon associative theory common to all animals.

Discussion Questions

1. B. F. Skinner justified the black box approach to understanding learning in two ways: (a) ca. 1950 not enough physiology was known to worry about what went on inside the brain (i.e., the black box) during the learning process; and (b) a stimulus-response analysis was sufficient to experimentally analyze behavior, even if the underlying physiology *were* known.

In responding to the following questions, assume that the physiological mechanisms underlying learning are now known: (a) Would a behavioral analysis of learning any longer be necessary? (b) Can you make the case that a black box approach might still yield valuable information?

2. Freud reified the concepts of id, ego, unconscious, etc. What does the reification of "the unconscious" mean? Do IQ tests measure "intelligence"? Why or why not?

3. The opposite of *reductionism* is *emergence*. Can you think of an example in which a neuroscientist uses emergence (rather than reductionism) to "explain," for example, the biochemical called beta-endorphin?

4. The learning-performance distinction can be illustrated with an old (and not especially funny) joke. It seems that a "scientist" was able to demonstrate not only that a flea hears but also that it could learn and remember what it heard—with its right hind leg. First, the scientist demonstrated that the flea was trained to jump every time it heard a loud sound—when he made a loud sound, the flea jumped. Then, he cut off the flea's legs one by one. When only the right hind leg remained, the loud sound still made the flea jump (almost) straight up. Finally, the flea's last leg was removed; the flea no longer jumped to the sound. Conclusion? Obviously, the flea no longer remembers that the sound is the cue to jump. Why? Because learning and memory had to be located in the flea's right hind leg.

   In disagreeing with this conclusion, demonstrate that you understand the learning-performance distinction.

5. Recently I asked several hundred students about thunder and lightning, and I found that more than half did not remember the physics they had learned in elementary and secondary schools (see footnote 6). Most thought that thunder and lightning occurred simultaneously, and that lightning only seemed to occur before thunder "because light travels faster than sound in air." Why do you think that more people remembered the physics of "sound and light transmission in air" rather than the physics of "lightning heats air, which causes thunder when the expanded air molecules collapse"? Do one or more of the *British Associationists'* four rules (i.e., contiguity, intensity, frequency, and similarity) help to explain this misattribution of causality? Hint: Which of the foregoing two rules of physics have you heard the most often?

6. The "Coolidge effect" (Carlson, 1992) refers to the fact that males of some (most?) species of mammals and birds respond with more interest to new sexual partners than to familiar partners (i.e., ones they had copulated with in the immediately preceding time period). Is this an example of habituation? Can you identify in this example a learning-performance distinction?

7. In Box 3.1, successive blocks of habituation and "rehabituation" eventually produce near-zero responding. Imagine you are the human subject whose responses are depicted in the lower figure, and you no longer respond to the stimulation after the sixth block of trials. What do you think would happen if you were to be stimulated the next day, or a week later? Is it likely your "fully habituated" response would return? In the next chapter, we discuss a similar phenomenon called *spontaneous recovery*.

Glossary

Antecedent Condition   In a causal relationship, that condition which precedes, and causes an event to occur.

Associationism   Basic learning defined as the association of two or more sensory experiences. (Cf. association formation.)

Between-Groups Design   The design of an experiment in which the effect of manipulating an independent variable (i.e., the treatment group) is compared with a control group not having any effect from the independent variable. (Cf. *within-groups design.*)

Black Box A model of investigating causal relations that focuses upon the relationship of input to output variables, and that ignores intervening variables hidden within the "black box."

Causality The relationship of cause and effect. A goal of science is to investigate *why* events occur, on the assumption that nothing can happen without a cause.

Confounded Variables Changes in a dependent variable may be mistakenly attributed to the independent variable under study and may be really due to other *(confounding)* variables. Example: The study of how a drug affects activity may be *confounded* by normal changes in activity during a 24-hour cycle.

Context The immediate environment, background, attendant circumstances, or conditions.

Control Group A comparison group for a treatment group. In an experiment, a group of subjects exposed to all conditions that the treatment group experiences, but *not* to the independent variable.

Dependent Variable In an experiment, the treatment effects of an independent variable are measured by measuring changes in the *dependent variable.* In the behavioral sciences, most dependent variables are changes in behavior. Example: A drug (independent variable) *caused* increased activity (dependent variable).

Empiricism The primary method (and philosophy) of *observation* and *experimentation* that distinguishes science from other ways humans can get knowledge about the world. (Cf. "intuitionism," which has no real-world referents.)

Frequency *(associative theory)* The observation that associations are strengthened through repetition; that the number of times two stimuli occur together strengthens their association.

Functional Relationship An orderly relationship existing between stimulus and response. Example: Higher drug doses cause higher levels of activity.

General Process Learning Theory The theory that common anatomical and physiological features among animals (i.e., genetic similarity producing similar brains, immune systems, digestive systems, etc.) provide the mechanisms by which animals perceive, associate, and learn to respond in similar ways.

Habituation The reduced responsiveness of an organism to repeated stimulation.

Hypothesis A hunch, or idea, or theory that is formally tested in an experiment.

Hypothetical Construct The conceptualization of an alleged process of the mind to account for various aspects of personality, memory, motivation, perception, intelligence, etc. (Cf. *intervening variable.*)

Independent Variable In an experiment, the experimenter manipulates the *independent variable* to see how it affects the dependent variable. The independent variable is seen as the cause, and the effect is how it changes the dependent variable. Example: A drug (independent variable) *caused* increased activity (dependent variable)

Intensity *(associative theory)* The observation that the association of two stimuli is influenced by the intensity with which the stimuli are perceived. More intense stimuli are more associable.

Intervening Variable Processes of the mind, such as learning, memory, motivation, etc., are such variables, inferred from observations of behavior. When "learning," for example, is operationally defined and studied by experimentation, it is conceptualized as an *intervening variable* that bridges the gap between measurable *stimulus* and *response variables*. (Cf. *hypothetical construct.*)

Introspection Looking within. Analyzing the "contents" of mind by verbal descriptions of perceptions, thoughts, memories, etc.

Learned Helplessness The results of a *learned helplessness treatment* in which an animal is prevented from escaping intensely painful stimuli. Subsequently, the animal fails to respond in an adaptive fashion by escaping a painful experience when allowed the opportunity. The animal is said to have *learned* to be *helpless*.

Learning-Performance Distinction The difference between what is actually measured (performance) and that which is inferred from the performance (learning).

Molar Level In research, investigations of the behavior of whole, intact organisms. (Contrast with *molecular level.*)

Molecular Level In research, investigations of behavior by determining which parts of the brain (anatomy) or which biochemicals are involved concomitant with the behavior. (Contrast with *molar level.*)

Nonassociative Learning Relatively permanent changes in behavior that result from an animal experiencing a particular stimulus. *Sensitization* and *habituation* are two examples. (Cf. associative learning.)

Null Hypothesis In an experiment, a researcher compares the results of a treatment condition with a control group. The *null hypothesis* is that there are *no* differences between these two groups. Rejecting the null hypothesis (using a statistical analysis) leads to the conclusion that the two groups in fact differ, and that the treatment effect caused this difference.

Operational Definition A definition of a term or concept that refers to the operations that measure the presumptive process. Example: Intelligence is that which IQ tests measure.

Parameter In an experiment, the various levels that an independent variable can assume are referred to as the *parameters* of that variable. Example: The parameters of a drug treatment are low, medium, and high dosages.

Reductionism Explaining a phenomenon by reference to a more molecular analysis (i.e., a biochemical level) is to *reduce* the level of analysis—hence, *reductionism*. Reductionism is the primary means of scientific explanation.

Reification Asserting the existence of a presumptive process independent of evidence for that process. Example: Intelligence is *there*, awaiting its measurement.

Response Variable The measured response in a behavioral experiment is called the *response variable*. (In chemistry, the "response variable" is typically called a *reaction*.) In the behavioral sciences, the response variable is typically some measure of behavioral change.

Sensitization If, after experiencing a stimulus, an animal tends to become *more* activated when the stimulus is presented again, the animal is said to be *sensitized*. This increased responsiveness, or *sensitization*, is considered to be a form of nonassociative learning.

Similarity (*associative theory*) The associability of two stimuli is strengthened if they are in some way *similar* to each other or if they are perceived as "belonging" together.

Single-Stimulus Effect *(associative theory)* Behavioral change due to the action of a single stimulus, as opposed to the asociation of two or more stimuli. (see *nonassociative learning; sensitization; habituation.*)

Stimulus Variable   The experimental manipulation imposed on a subject in an experiment is the *stimulus variable,* or independent variable. Stimulus variables impinge upon animals, causing responses (see *black box*).

Temporal Contiguity *(associative theory)* Two or more events closely related together in time are said to be temporally contiguous.

Treatment Group   In all experiments the experimental manipulation is called the *treatment,* and the group of subjects that receive the experimental manipulation—the independent variable—is called the *treatment group.*

Within-Groups Design   The design of an experiment in which a pretreatment measure of the dependent variable is compared with a posttreatment measure *in the same subjects.* (Cf. *between-groups design.*)

Working Hypothesis   A simple statement of what is expected to happen in an experiment. Example: A low dose of drug X will have less effect on activity than a high dose of drug X.

4

Reflexes and Simple Conditioning

I. Reflexes

An animal is born with innate, unlearned response tendencies. These responses, called **reflexes,** occur involuntarily whenever the animal encounters specific stimuli in the environment called *eliciting stimuli.* Reflexes are more complex than tropisms and simpler than *fixed action patterns (FAPs),* both discussed in Chapter 2. We now turn to the reflex and to reflexive behavior for three reasons: (a) because reflexes are of interest to ethologists, physiologists, and psychologists alike; (b) because reflexes provide the basis for simple Pavlovian conditioning; and (c) because both reflexes and *conditioned* reflexes are important in understanding many of the complexities of human behavior.

A number of diverse reflexes and reflexlike behaviors are listed in Table 4.1. The survival value of each is self-evident. A human infant, for example, will draw up arms and legs reflexively in response to a sudden, loud noise, or a loss of equilibrium—a response known as the *Moro reflex.* Further disturbance will elicit crying. Noise, the eliciting

TABLE 4.1 Types of Reflexes

Eliciting Stimulus *(Source: Environment, Darwin's "Nature")*	*Reflex* *(Source: DNA's Programmed Response)*
1. "Motor" (touch) reflexes	
Patellar tap ⟶	Knee jerk
Pressure on the ⟶ surface of the eye	Eye blink
2. Light and sound reflexes	
Loud noise, loss of equilibrium ⟶	Moro reflex
Decrease/increase ⟶ in light intensity	Dilation/constriction of the pupil
3. Temperature reflexes	
Increase in body temperature ⟶	Sweating
Localized intense heat (burn) ⟶	Blister
Match burn on arm ⟶	Arm withdrawal
Sudden drop in body temperature ⟶	Goosebumps
4. Feeding/ingestional reflexes	
Taste of food ⟶	Salivation
Taste of sour lemon ⟶	Salivation
Finger, food in throat ⟶	Gag reflex
Ingestion of toxin ⟶	Nausea, loss of appetite, vomiting
Salt loss ⟶	Aldosterone release
5. Immune system reflexes	
Cedar pollen ⟶	Histamine release
Antigens ⟶	T-lymphocyte release

stimulus, triggers the reflexive-like response, crying, which in turn triggers the infant's caretaker to action. Thus, reflexes, like FAPs, are, without exception, considered to be adaptive. Most of the reflexes listed in Table 4.1 are retained into adulthood.

Note that the stimulus in the simple stimulus-response (S-R) framework of the reflex can be directly tied to the environment—Darwin's "nature." Each response reflects the operation of an organism's inherited anatomy and physiology as it encounters the environment. Indeed, the environment is the *source* of reflexive behavior in that the environment places a *selective pressure* on evolving animals. Animals with reflexive tendencies were selected over those lacking such tendencies.

Sherringtonian Reflexes

Not all reflexes have the underlying anatomical simplicity of the patellar (knee-jerk), or of the eye-blink reflex. These two well-known reflexes are characterized by identifiable *sensory neurons* synapsing upon identifiable *motor neurons*. Typically, one or more *interneurons* separate the direct sensory and motor component. For the patellar (knee-jerk) and eye-blink reflex, the synapses occur in the spinal cord and medulla, respectively. Sensory-to-motor nerve activation completes what is known as a *reflex arc*.[1]

The motor component of the reflex was identified by Sherrington (1906) as the "final common pathway." Due to his observations such simple reflexes are often called **Sherringtonian reflexes.**

Look, however, at other reflexes listed in categories three through five in Table 4.1. "Sweating" and "salivation" are glandular responses, not skeletal muscle contractions, yet by convention both are considered "reflexive."

But what about blister formation to burns? Remember that in the patellar reflex, motor neurons comprise the "final common pathway" causing the lower leg to jerk when the patella is tapped. What is the "final common pathway" that directs *histamine* release and extracellular fluids, which are secreted around cells that have been injured? And what of nausea and vomiting in response to toxins?

The Poison-Illness Reflex

Assuredly these latter responses are more complex behaviorally and neurologically than the eye-blink and patellar reflexes. Take, for example, sickness or nausea. Many environmental toxins and poisons

---

[1]Kalat (1992) provides an excellent, readable review of the physiology of reflexes, of sensory and motor nerves, and of the physiochemical events that take place at synapse.

are sensed by neurons comprising the *area postrema*. Also known as the *chemical trigger zone*, or *CTZ*, the area postrema lies in the back part of the brain, just underneath the cerebellum. It is known that neurons from the CTZ project to a portion of the *solitary nucleus* (another group of neurons found in the medulla, or brain stem). Next to the solitary nucleus in the medulla can be found neurons of the *vagus* nerve that project to the esophagus and stomach. Activating the motor portion of the vagus nerve can result in "gagging" and reverse peristalsis of the esophagus—vomiting. A poison-illness "reflex," then, is described by the following sequence: environmental toxins → CTZ → solitary n. → vagus nerve → nausea/vomiting.

Extending the Concept of Reflex

For present purposes, let us simply observe that all reflexes are not Sherringtonian, and that the underlying physiology of poisoning, of immune system functioning, of temperature regulation, of fluid and electrolyte regulation, etc., though more complex, can be conceptualized as basically reflexlike in nature.

Such unlearned responses serve to protect the newborn and adult organism alike against any number of environmental dangers. This arsenal of reflexes, however, falls woefully short of the complex responses (e.g., running, shouting, climbing) and the chains of responses (stalking prey, escaping predators, fighting, eating and drinking, communicating) that an animal requires for survival. These seemingly more "voluntary" responses are acquired through learning.

Hardwiring versus Plasticity.   Reflexes are primarily studied by physiologists. The brain organization underlying reflexive behavior is fairly well understood. Innately organized sensory and motor nerves are often referred to as the brain's "hardwiring." By contrast, modification of brain physiology (which is presumed to underlie learned behavior) is often referred to as the brain's "plasticity." Our working assumption is that complex behavior is mediated by both "hardwired" and more "plastic" brain functioning.

Interim Summary

1. Reflexes are unlearned responses to environmental stimuli. Reflexive behavior can be best understood as involuntary, adaptive responses that have evolved because they promote survival and enhance reproductive success.
2. Reflexes have sensory and motor nerve components, which mediate a reflex arc when elicited by the appropriate environmental stimulus. The patellar and eye-blink reflexes are often called Sher-

ringtonian reflexes because only a few interneurons precede the motor component, also known as the final common pathway.

3. More complex reflexive-like tendencies such as immune system functioning, and the physiology of ingestion, involve more brain—more interneurons and less easily specifiable sensory and motor components.

4. Reflexes are considered to be hardwired, and learned behaviors presumably involve a modification of these inherited response tendencies.

II. Pavlov's Salivary Conditioning

Experiments that we now refer to as **Pavlovian conditioning** (also known as classical conditioning) were first reported at the turn of this century by a Russian physiologist, Ivan Pavlov. His main work in this area, *Conditioned Reflexes,* was published in 1927.

Pavlov's research and that of his associates originally focused upon the digestive process in dogs. In the course of his physiological studies he described the **salivary reflex;** that is, he carefully measured the amount of salivation caused by precisely measured amounts of food placed on the dog's tongue. Not too interesting, perhaps, but these and other studies in digestion earned Ivan Pavlov a Nobel Prize in 1906.

Pavlov's other observations that we continue to study *are* more interesting. He noted that salivation occurred not only as a reflexive response when food was placed in the animal's mouth, but also just prior to actual ingestion—almost as if the animal "anticipated" eating. He called this phenomenon **psychic secretion** because salivation occurred without "real-world" food—that is, without the appropriate eliciting stimulus. Reflexes were not supposed to work this way. Could he understand the dog's higher mental faculties by investigating the role of the dog's cerebral hemispheres as new associations to the salivary reflex were learned? Pavlov took a chance and devoted 30 years of his life to a thorough examination of this question (Pavlov, 1927).

Association of Bell and Food.   On closer examination of the phenomenon, Pavlov found that the mere sight of food preparation was sufficient to produce salivation in his dogs. Because the sight and taste of food were always *paired in time,* Pavlov reasoned that the animal had learned through the **association** of sight and taste to salivate to a broad range of stimuli. Figure 4.1 shows a dog in a conditioning apparatus that Pavlov used to study how these associations were formed.

FIGURE 4.1   Inside Pavlov's Laboratory

Pavlov and his colleagues trained dogs to stand in a harnesslike apparatus during experimental sessions. During an experiment the dog would be isolated and could only see and hear the sights and sounds presented by the researchers. Food was placed on the animal's tongue, and salivation was collected and measured by a mechanical apparatus not depicted in the photograph. The dogs were well cared for, and Pavlov's lab set high standards for animal experimentation.

Pavlov tested his hypothesis by pairing the sound of a bell[2] with the taste of food. He noted that the dog pricked up its ears and turned its head to the source of the bell's sound, but did *not* salivate. This **orienting reflex** to the bell differed from the salivary reflex to the food. After a number of paired presentations with food, the bell's sound elicited salivation even before food was tasted—a process Pavlov called *conditioning*.

His analysis of this phenomenon follows:

> It seems obvious that the whole activity of the organism should conform to definite laws. If the animal were not in exact correspondence with its environment, it would, sooner or later, cease to exist. To give a biological example: if, instead of being attracted to food, the animal were repelled by it, or if instead of running from fire the animal threw itself into the fire, then it would quickly perish. The animal must respond to changes in the environment in such a manner that its responsive activity is directed towards the preservation of its existence (Pavlov, 1927/1960, pp. 7–8).

[2]In addition to an electronic bell, Pavlov used the sounds of a metronome and "bubbling water," various pictures, vibration, etc. in pairings with food. For ease of illustration most examples given will refer to a "bell."

Questions of adaptation aside, on the face of it Pavlov's description of conditioning sounds like an esoteric laboratory exercise. Present day behavioral scientists are not especially interested in the digestive processes of dogs, nor, for that matter, in the lever-pressing or maze-running abilities of rats. But we continue to study behavior in experiments such as these because the results of these experiments are applicable to human conditioning.

Our present interest, then, is in how these early laboratory experiments inform the process by which basic learning occurs in all species in a variety of situations. The general form of research discussed throughout this chapter involves taking any inborn reflex and controlling that reflex by replacing the original eliciting stimulus with a new, arbitrary stimulus.

Are simple conditioning processes determining factors in human behavioral repertoires? Certainly. Consider, for example, the many domestic creatures who inhabit kitchens, for whom the rattling of a box of milk bones or the lid of the cookie jar is sufficient to cause both orienting responses and conditioned salivation. For most of us, the mere mention of a thick, juicy steak or chicken fajitas sizzling over a bed of hot charcoal will often have the same effect. But not for vegetarians. Why is that? A perfume may bring to mind a particular individual and may cause your stomach to flip-flop. Why is that?

Similarly, running toward an icy lake will raise goosebumps. The sight of a fast approaching dust cloud (or fist) will produce an eye blink—over and above the reflex elicited by touching the cornea. The appearance of a green sheen on a slice of turkey elicits a disgust response in adults but not in very young children. Why is that?

Sherrington's reflexes can be modified by experience. The environment comes to control reflexes in new ways. Thought experiment: Given what you now know about how Pavlov brought the salivary reflex under the control of a neutral stimulus (i.e., the bell), can you describe how it might be possible to condition a person to be disgusted at the sight of green meat? Or to sneeze when he or she merely *sees* a cat?

Elements of Pavlovian Conditioning

Simplicity in theory and method may not guarantee scientific success, but in part we recognize Pavlov's research 90 years after the fact because only four basic components (two stimuli, one response, and time) are involved. Let us now consider **excitatory conditioning,** as initially construed and demonstrated by Pavlov (see Figure 4.2). More specifically, the following preparation is an example of **appetitive conditioning,** in that Pavlov elaborated a conditioned response to a food stimulus (cf. *appetite*).

1. Before the initiation of training procedures:

$$\text{US (taste)} \xrightarrow{\text{(elicits)}} \text{UR (reflexive salivation)}$$

$$\text{CS (bell)} \xrightarrow{\hspace{1.5cm}} \text{OR (orienting response)}$$
    (no effect on salivation)

2. First paired presentation of US and CS:

$$\text{CS (bell)} + \text{US (taste)} \xrightarrow{\hspace{1.5cm}} \text{UR (salivation)}$$

3. After 5–9 paired presentations of CS with US:

$$\text{CS (bell)} + \text{US (taste)} \xrightarrow{\hspace{1.5cm}} \text{UR (unconditioned salivatio}$$
    $$+$$
    $$\xrightarrow{\hspace{1.5cm}} \text{CR (conditioned salivation)}$$

4. Test presentation of the CS alone:

$$\text{CS (bell)} \xrightarrow{\hspace{1.5cm}} \text{CR (conditioned salivation)}$$

FIGURE 4.2   Pavlovian Conditioning Procedure

Two of the four components you already know—the unlearned *stimulus* and the *response* that form the salivary reflex. These unlearned components were labeled by Pavlov the **unconditioned stimulus (US)** and the **unconditioned response (UR),** respectively. For Pavlov's dogs the taste of *food* is the unconditioned stimulus, which automatically elicits the reflexive response of *salivation,* the unconditioned response.

To this basic reflex is added a learned, or conditioned, component. A stimulus (e.g., bell, whistle, metronome) to which a new response is learned is called the **conditioned stimulus (CS),** and the learned response (e.g., salivation to the bell) is called the **conditioned response (CR).** Before training, the bell has no special effect on the animal's appetitive behavior. That is to say, the bell initially is a *neutral stimulus* with respect to the salivation response.

As noted, the bell *does* produce an *orienting response*—that is, the dog makes head and ear adjustments in localizing the source of the sound. Recall that the four basic elements of conditioning are the CS and US, the CR, and the time interval relating these two stimuli. The *orienting response (OR)* is not considered "basic" (a) because it rapidly changes with repeated trials; (b) because during conditioning the experimenter's focus shifts to the conditioned response; and (c) because changes in the OR are considered to be nonassociative, whereas Pavlovian conditioning is associative.

After repeated pairings of the CS (bell) with the US (taste of food), the bell acquires the capacity to produce the learned, or conditioned, response of salivation.

A Typical Pavlovian Conditioning Experiment

Let us conduct an idealized experiment along the lines that Pavlov reported. Our experiment can be characterized as appetitive *excitatory* conditioning (*inhibitory* conditioning will be discussed later). Let us first set the CS, US, and time interval parameters. Recall from Chapter 3 that the specification of intensity, frequency, and duration of stimuli are *parameters* of the stimulus. As we shall see, conditioning outcomes are critically dependent upon stimulus parameters.

Conditioning Parameters. Let the CS be a 500 Hz frequency tone sounded at 70 dB loudness for 10 seconds duration. Let the US be 5 gm of meat powder dropped onto the animal's tongue, with a **CS-US interval** of 30 seconds. By convention, the *CS-US interval* is measured from stimulus onset to stimulus onset, in the present example from the first sound of the tone to the first taste of the meat.

Next, let us set the **intertrial interval** at three minutes, where a **trial** consists of a CS-US pairing, and the *intertrial interval* the amount of time between pairings. Now let us condition the dog for 10 trials, and then stop to assess how much conditioning has taken place.

To summarize our hypothetical experiment, the stimulus parameters are:

CS = 10.0 s, 500 Hz tone at 70 dB
US = 5.0 gm meat powder
CS-US interval = 30.0 s
Intertrial interval = 3.0 min
Trials: n (number) = 10

Measuring Conditioning. How do we know if and when conditioning is completed? The researcher can only measure changes in salivation if he or she has some idea how much dogs will salivate in the first place. Since an animal salivates when food is placed on its tongue, Pavlov was able to measure both *un*conditioned salivation (i.e., salivation to the food alone) as well as conditioned salivation when the tone was sounded (see Figure 4.2).

The first measure of salivation in the presence of the tone, prior to conditioning, is called a **baseline** measure of salivation. The baseline measure answers the question, how much saliva flows normally? That is, where does the animal start from? The second measure of salivation to the tone occurs after conditioning trials are completed, during **experimental extinction;** i.e., measuring salivation to the tone in the absence of the food after conditioning trials are completed.

In our experiment let us measure the total amount of saliva during a 10-second tone CS and, say, for 20 seconds following the tone (total = 30 seconds). We will measure salivation to the tone before the first trial (i.e., before conditioning) to establish a baseline of salivation, and again on every fifth trial thereafter.

Conditioning Results. The results of our hypothetical experiment are shown in Figure 4.3. Plotted on the ordinate (i.e., the *y* axis) is the amount of saliva measured when the tone is sounded before conditioning and on the first, fifth, tenth, fifteenth, and twentieth trials (plotted on the *x* axis, or *abscissa*). Note in the figure that unconditioned salivation is high on *all* conditioning trials (open squares) due to the reflexive response of salivation when food is placed on the dog's tongue. Figure 4.3b plots only the conditioned responses to the tone in the absence of food as measured before conditioning, and on the fifth, tenth, fifteenth, and twentieth trials.

How Can We Conclude That Conditioning Has Occurred?

In Figure 4.3a how do we know that the change in salivation on test trials 5, 10, 15, and 20 reflects conditioning? Might not salivation have occurred even if the tone had not been sounded, or if the tone *had* been sounded and no food presented? Another possibility that should be ruled out: Sounding a tone for 30 seconds every three minutes might drive the dog nuts, thereby increasing salivation, as in a "mad dog"!

Control Groups. What is needed for us to conclude that conditioning is due to stimulus-stimulus association, i.e., to a *treatment effect*, and not to some other nonassociative phenomenon, are control groups (refer to the association matrix, Figure 3.5, p. 86). Recall that several nonassociative control groups are possible. A **habituation control group** receives only the CS, and a **sensitization control group** receives only the US. (Control groups are often referred to as *sham-treatment groups*. Some researchers call the sensitization control group a *pseudoconditioning control*.)

Rescorla (1967) also suggested the inclusion of a **random control group** in which the CS and US are both presented but never together in time. Random control groups preclude association of the

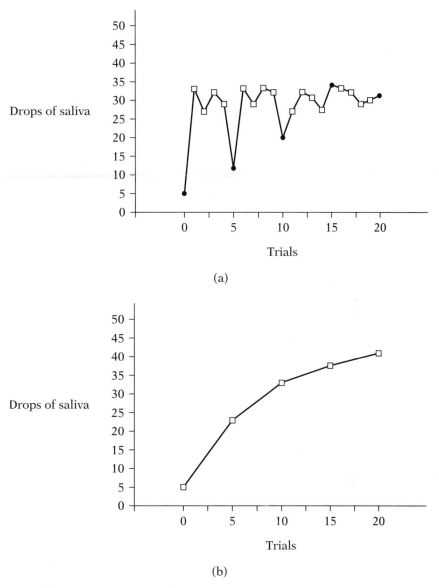

FIGURE 4.3 Two Depictions of the Growth of Association

(a) The tone is presented without food on trials 0 (zero) 5, 10, 15, and 20 (dark circles). Trial zero, before conditioning, is our baseline measure of salivation for this dog. The remaining trials are *conditioning trials* (squares) in which salivation is measured *after food has been placed on the dog's tongue*. (Would acquisition of the conditioned response be accomplished more quickly if the dog had been reinforced on all trials?) (b) Typical plot of an acquisition function. Note that this figure does *not* show salivation on all the conditioning trials as is displayed in (a).

CS and US by not allowing them to be associated together during the same time interval.

Pavlov's "control group" was a *within-subjects control* during pretesting; the dog's baseline salivation was assessed in the absence of either the CS or US (refer to cell "d" in the association matrix, Figure 3.5, p. 86).

For present purposes, in this idealized experiment let us train three additional dogs, one for each of three conditions: an habituation control, a sensitization control, and a random control. (Thought question: Why would more than one animal per group be conditioned in a "real" experiment using the between-subjects control groups described here?)

Displaying Results.   The results of our hypothetical experiment are presented in Figure 4.4. Note that the four groups during preconditioning do not differ (Conditioning Trial Zero) on the left side of the graph. The four groups do begin to vary in amount of conditioned salivation as conditioning proceeds. Note that after 5 and again after 10 and 15 conditioning trials the only group that differs from the other groups is the one in which the CS and US are associated together in time. We can conclude that the *association* of the stimuli, not their mere presence, accounts for the measured differences.

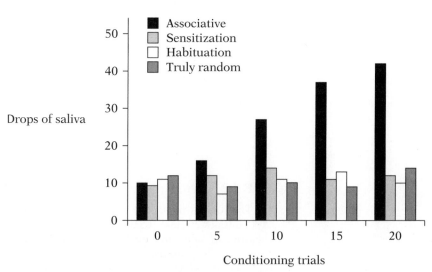

FIGURE 4.4   Commonly Used Control Groups

Control groups used in typical conditioning experiments. Note the growth of association in the treatment group but not in the habituation, sensitization, or random control groups. See text for additional details.

As a general rule, it is both costly and time consuming to run all possible control groups in every experiment. The random control group alone is usually sufficient to assess treatment effects.

Experimental Extinction and Spontaneous Recovery

If, after conditioning, the CS continues to be presented without the US, the conditioned response diminishes. This procedure is called experimental **extinction,** and the decline in the conditioned response is called an **extinction gradient,** or **extinction curve** (see Figure 4.5). In the example we have been considering, salivation during *experimental extinction* comprises our measure of conditioning.

Theories of Extinction.   Why does extinction occur? Two possibilities are offered. First, the intentional "unpairing" of the two stimuli

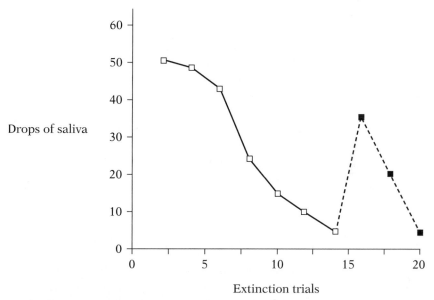

FIGURE 4.5   Extinction and Spontaneous Recovery

A salivatory response to a CS has been previously conditioned. When on extinction trials 1–14 the CS continues to be presented but food is no longer forthcoming, the drops of saliva decline over trials (open squares). If time is allowed to pass (i.e., the animal is returned to its home cage overnight) and experimental extinction trials resume the next day (dotted lines), the animal salivates more than would be expected, a phenomenon called *spontaneous recovery* (dark squares).

might be seen as breaking the learned association between the CS and the US. A more plausible approach, however, is to highlight the similarities between *habituation* and *extinction*. In both instances, responses diminish to repeatedly presented stimuli. It may be that one function of the US is to prevent habituation to the CS. When the US is removed (as is the case during extinction), the CS merely habituates. In the next chapter we will return to a further examination of the interplay of associative and nonassociative factors under the topic of *latent inhibition*.

Learning Is Measured in Extinction.   With few exceptions, in most experiments *conditioning is measured during extinction trials*. How much of the basic reflex will occur when the CS, and not the US, is presented to the animal? What has the animal learned about the CS?

As we will see in the following sections, the rate of extinction of the conditioned response is dependent upon many conditioning variables, including the nature of the CS and US and the number of previous conditioning trials. As a general rule, the conditioned response will last longer, and the rate of extinction will be slower, following many as opposed to a few conditioning trials.

Spontaneous Recovery.   Suppose the conditioned response has extinguished to the level depicted on the fifteenth extinction trial (solid lines in Figure 4.5). If, instead of conducting the sixteenth trial in that session, the dog is removed from the conditioning laboratory and is returned to its home cage, and then is brought back *the next day* for the sixteenth trial, another outcome is measured (dashed lines). The level of extinction is not as great after the 24-hour interruption in consecutive extinction trials. As can be seen in Figure 4.5, the conditioned salivary response on the sixteenth trial is stronger than it would have been without the 24-hour interruption.

This reappearance of conditioning following a delay in the extinction process is called **spontaneous recovery.** Pavlov argued that normal extinction is hastened by a process he called **internal inhibition;** such inhibition, which he likened to the dog's frustration at not receiving its expected food, dissipates with the passage of time, allowing the true extinction rate to be seen.

We will explore more on inhibition later.

Appetitive and Defense (Aversive) Conditioning

As noted in the preceding discussion, *appetitive* refers to conditioning that takes advantage of a dog's appetite. Some of Pavlov's experiments used a sour solution instead of food as the unconditioned stimulus. Dogs salivate unconditionally to sour tastes as they do to tasty food. You might want to try dripping lemon juice on your tongue to see if you salivate. (You will.) If you have a good imagination, just the thought of dripping lemon juice on your tongue will cause you to salivate.[3]

By contrast with food-based appetitive conditioning, Pavlov used the term **defense conditioning** to describe experiments that used sour solutions placed on the tongue (or electric shock to condition a leg-withdrawal reflex, or other aversive forms of stimulation) as the unconditioned stimulus. Conditioning experiments using aversive stimuli (as opposed to a food stimulus) are now referred to as **aversive conditioning.**

In the next section you will be introduced to three contemporary *aversive* conditioning procedures: eyelid conditioning, conditioned suppression (cf. fear conditioning), and taste aversion conditioning.

III.   Contemporary Conditioning Methods: An Introduction

Note again the variety of physiological reflexes outlined in Table 4.1. Appetitive conditioning experiments that take advantage of the salivary reflex comprise many of the examples in this chapter. At present, however, few appetitive conditioning experiments with dogs continue to be conducted. Rather, methodologies taking advantage of three *other* reflexes have been developed within American behavioral laboratories. The total amount of empirical research using contemporary methods far exceeds the number of experiments conducted by Pavlov and others who investigated the salivary reflex.

A brief introduction to these alternative methodologies follows. Note that all are examples of aversive conditioning.

Rabbit and Human Eye-Blink Conditioning

A puff of air to a human's or restrained rabbit's eye will elicit a reflexive blinking response (see Figure 4.6). When a tone (CS) is presented immediately prior to the air puff (US), a human or rabbit can be conditioned to blink to the sound of the tone. A number of investigators have used this classical preparation for many years, and a range of questions concerning associative theory have been addressed (Gormezano, Kehoe, & Marshall, 1983).

Two examples of the outcome of conditioning eye-blink respons-

---

[3]"Thinking" that produces reflexive responses sounds suspiciously like Pavlov's "psychic reflexes." Throughout this text we will be confronted with the fact that *thoughts* and *words* acquire conditioned stimulus properties.

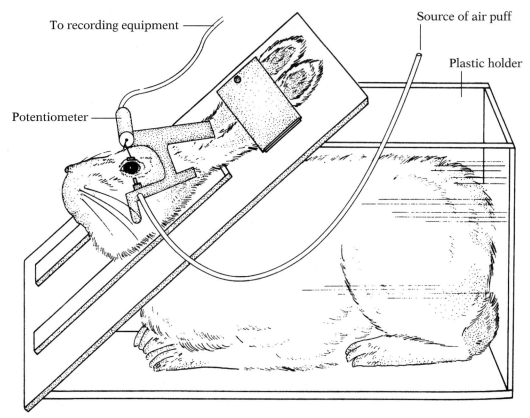

To recording equipment

Source of air puff

Plastic holder

Potentiometer

FIGURE 4.6 A Rabbit Eye-Blink Conditioning Apparatus

Rabbit eye-blink conditioning is accomplished by more-or-less comfortably immobilizing the rabbit so that flashes of light, or brief tones, can be paired with a mild air puff to the rabbit's eye. The eye blink is measured and recorded by an electronic sensing apparatus. (From Domjan and Burkhard, 1988.)

es in rabbits and humans can be found in Figure 4.7. Rabbit conditioning is shown in Figure 4.7a. The percentage of conditioned responses (out of 82 conditioning trials per day) is plotted for eight acquisition days. Note the relative lack of conditioning in the early trials, and the regular growth of responding (as indicated by the percentage of conditioned responses on each day) throughout the 600-plus trial acquisition period.

Figure 4.7b shows the outcomes of conditioning eye-blink responses of humans (Hartman & Grant, 1960). Students were paid to be attached to an apparatus not unlike the one shown in Figure 4.6. In different treatment groups the tone CS was always followed by an

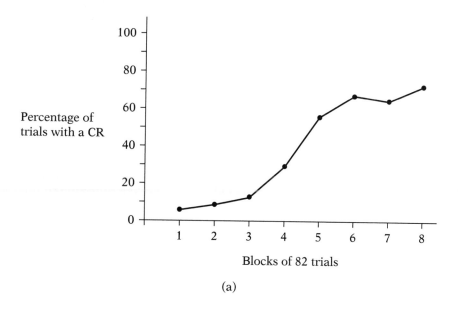

Percentage of trials with a CR

Blocks of 82 trials

(a)

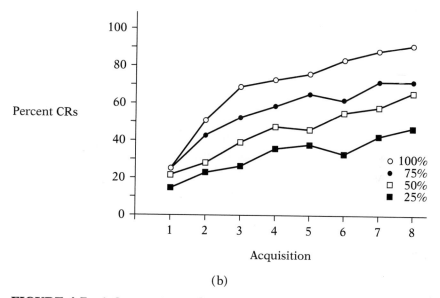

Percent CRs

Acquisition

○ 100%
● 75%
□ 50%
■ 25%

(b)

FIGURE 4.7 A Comparison of Human and Rabbit Eyelid Conditioning

(a) The increase in percentage of conditioned eye-blink responses in rabbits is plotted as a function of training days. (See text.) (b) Four groups of humans received 40 pairings of a light (CS) followed by an air puff (US) to the eye. Group 25% received 120 additional CSs without USs; Group 50% received an additional 40 CSs, and Group 75% received an additional 14 CSs. Note that conditioning was degraded to the extent that the CS was presented in the absence of the US (From Hartman and Grant, 1960).

air puff US (Group 100%), and the results were compared with treatment groups that received extra CSs (i.e., Groups 75%, 50%, and 25%, respectively).[4]

For present purposes simply note the growth of the acquisition of the conditioned response over 40 CS-US trials.

Salivary and Eye-Blink Conditioning Compared.   Comparing Figures 4.7a and b, note that the form of the acquisition curves is similar to that depicted for salivary conditioning in dogs (cf. Figures 4.3 and 4.4). Both rabbits and humans require many more trials to condition an eye-blink response, however. Dogs required 5 to 9 trials, humans 15 to 40 trials, and rabbits several hundred trials. What is going on? Why does eye-blink conditioning require more trials than salivary conditioning? And why do rabbits require hundreds more trials than humans? Let us find out more about the determinants of conditioning before attempting to answer these questions.

Fear Conditioning

Any of a number of intense environmental stimuli produce pain or fear-inducing responses in animals. For example, loud noises, electric shocks, and sudden loss of support disrupt normal homeostatic functioning in animals. Such stimuli induce changes in the *autonomic nervous system,* which in turn activates them to action. When a normally neutral stimulus (such as a tone CS) is repeatedly paired with a disruptive stimulus (such as an electric shock US), conditioning is usually the result. An example of fear conditioning in humans can be found in Box 4.1.

One way to measure a **conditioned emotional response** in the laboratory is to sound a tone (CS) that has been paired with electric shock (US) while a rat is pressing a lever to obtain food (Estes & Skinner, 1941). The intensity of the shock is adjusted just high enough to cause the rat to momentarily stop the lever-pressing response. After a number of tone-shock pairings the rat learns (is conditioned) to interrupt lever pressing when the tone is sounded.

Because the lever-pressing response is disrupted in the presence of the tone, this method is called **conditioned suppression.** The conditioned suppression technique is one of the most popular methods used in the contemporary study of Pavlovian conditioning. A conditioned suppression experiment and the results of fear conditioning in the laboratory can be found in Figure 4.8, p. 131.

---

[4]"Extra" CSs were presented but *not* followed by a US. A full discussion of the rationale for this experiment can be found on p. 138.

BOX 4.1

An Unusual Example of Fear Conditioning

During the 1960s I was one of a number of paid U.S. Air Force volunteers who rode an "impact sled." In some of this research, airmen tested space suits that eventually were worn by Apollo astronauts. Would the suits tear on impact, or would critical helmet fittings fail during take-offs, landings, EVAs (space walks), moon walks, etc? Strapped for money, we volunteered to be strapped to a sled that was propelled along rails. Impacts were varied to simulate the various angles and *g* forces astronauts would experience in emergency situations. (Notice the bent nose and lips in this photo, taken with high-speed film at the point of impact.)

A 40-second countdown preceded the sled acceleration and final impact. During this 40 seconds, a European-style emergency vehicle horn ("dee doo, dee doo") reverberated throughout the test site. This distinctive signal accompanied the anticipation and high autonomic nervous system arousal of being strapped to a sled soon to be slammed into a barrier. To this day emergency vehicles in Paris and London cause heart palpitations and sphincter-control problems for at least one of these now aging airmen. The sound of helicopters presents yet more serious problems for Vietnam veterans— a theme we will return to in Chapter 8.

Taste Aversion Conditioning

Several thousand experiments on a variety of animals over the past 30 years has made **taste aversion conditioning** another popular method of studying Pavlovian conditioning (see Riley & Tuck, 1985, for a bibliography of these experiments). In animal experiments, rats are allowed to drink a normally preferred flavor (the CS) and then are made sick by giving them an illness-inducing toxin (the US). Conditioned taste aversions to the target flavor result. That is, in comparison with control rats not made sick, the conditioned rats no longer prefer the target flavor (Garcia, Kimeldorf, & Koelling, 1955).

Humans have an intuitive grasp of this kind of conditioning because in our lifetimes many of us have become sick after eating or drinking. Often a particular flavor or food item is tagged as the culprit. A personal vignette: At the age of six I became sick after eating fresh pineapple. I disliked pineapple for many years afterward, and even today I remember the incident all too vividly. Ilene Bernstein is attempting to understand eating disorders in children who are undergoing treatment for cancer by applying taste aversion conditioning concepts. Her research is highlighted below.

FOCUS ON RESEARCH 4.1

Dr. Ilene Bernstein

Tumor Anorexia: Application of an Animal Model

Dr. Ilene Bernstein, Department of Psychology, University of Washington, Seattle

"My early work in the area of taste aversions and cancer indicated that food aversions arise not only as a consequence of chemotherapy treatment but also as a consequence of the disease itself. Using an animal model, our findings suggested that aversions which develop as a result of the association of tumor growth with consumption of specific foods were causally related to the depressions of food intake and body weight known as tumor anorexia. These observations led me to ask whether food aversion acquisition involves . . . classical conditioning. Thus, a taste previously paired with nausea could, upon reexposure, be capable of triggering an illness or nausea response. My current work explores the hypothesis that conditioned illness triggered by food stimuli plays a mediating role in the development of anorexia symptoms. Relevant publications are Bernstein and Borson (1986) and Meachum and Bernstein (1990)."

One-Trial Learning.   Interestingly, an alleged shortcoming of the taste aversion conditioning procedure is that humans and animals learn aversions *too* quickly—oftentimes in a single trial. Such rapid learning presents problems for contingency theories of acquisition in which the animal is assumed to learn by computing the probability of a US given the presentation of a CS (see the next section). The taste aversion conditioning methodology remains popular, however, and has provided behavioral scientists with, among other information, factors that control eating and drinking (Chapter 8, p. 379ff) as well as informing associative conditioning theory. The "problem" presented by one-trial conditioning studies will be addressed in this chapter and again in Chapter 5.

Conditioned Immune Suppression.   Taste aversion conditioning is now an important animal learning methodology that is allowing new insight into immune system functioning (Husband, 1992). In Chapter 8 we will explore in detail such experiments as conducted by Ader (1985) and others.

Interim Summary

Eye-blink conditioning in which tones and lights (CSs) signal an aversive air puff to the eye is typically conducted on rabbits. After conditioning, the CSs can evoke a reflexive eye blink. In conditioned suppression, tones and lights (CS) are paired with electric shock (the US), and conditioning is measured by the degree to which the tone and light CSs suppress lever-pressing responses in rats. Conditioned taste aversions are studied in rats, humans, and other animals. Flavors (the CS) are paired with toxins (the US), and conditioned responses take the form of learned aversions to the formerly preferred flavors.

Eye-blink conditioning, conditioned suppression, and conditioned taste aversions are three of the most widely used contemporary conditioning methods by which Pavlovian conditioning continues to be studied.[5] The reader is advised to become familiar with the basic terminology and procedures employed in each method. The experimental results of each procedure will be used interchangeably to build a general theory of conditioning.

Table 4.2 summarizes the contemporary conditioning methods discussed in this section and compares each with Pavlov's appetitive and defense salivary conditioning preparations.

---

[5]A fourth method called autoshaping will be discussed in Chapter 6. Autoshaping contains both classical and instrumental components, as well as species-specific tendencies.

TABLE 4.2 Comparison of Contemporary Conditioning Methodologies

Name of Procedure *(Subject)*	*US*	*UR*	*CS*	*CR*
Pavlov's appetitive salivary conditioning (dogs)	Food	Salivation	Bell, metronome, pictures, cutaneous stimuli	Salivation
Pavlov's defense (aversive) conditioning (dogs)	Sour flavor	Salivation	Bell, metronome, pictures, cutaneous stimuli	Salivation
Rabbit eyelid conditioning (rabbits, humans)	Air puff to eye	Eye-blink flash	Tone, light	Eye blink
Conditioned suppression (conditoned fear) (rats, pigeons)	Electric Shock	Stops lever-pressing response	Tone, light flash	Stop lever-pressing response
Conditioned taste aversion (rats, humans)	Toxin	Sickness, loss of appetite	Flavored fluid	Loss of appetite

IV. Variables That Affect Conditioning

Pavlov was interested in discovering what events, or variables, control the conditioning process. Why did some of his dogs learn more quickly than others? Why were some CSs more effective in producing conditioned salivation than others? Why is it that conditioning tends to persist (last longer) following conditioning procedure "A" compared with procedure "B"?

Resistance-to-Extinction

For example, Pavlov noted that his dogs would not only salivate more after 20 conditioning trials than 10 trials, but also that the conditioned response lasted longer in extinction. That is, there is more **re- sistance-to-extinction** of the conditioned response after more trials have been accomplished compared with extinction after only a few trials. We will find that resistance-to-extinction is one of the more important ways in which we can compare conditioning outcomes.

Five Rules of Conditioning

Let us begin by listing five rules that Pavlov and other experimenters have discovered that govern how associations are formed:

1. Number of trials rule
2. CS intensity rule
3. US intensity rule
4. CS-US interval rule
5. CS-US, or US-CS sequencing rule

1. *Number of Trials Rule.* Pavlov was the first laboratory scientist to measure how conditioning improves as more trials are conducted. In Figure 4.3 note that more salivation is evident on the fifteenth trial than on the fifth or the tenth trial. As a general rule, *the magnitude and persistence of the conditioned response are directly related to the number of conditioning trials.*

Intuitively obvious though it may be, *why* more than one trial is typically necessary for conditioning is a matter of speculation. It is sometimes the case that only one trial is necessary for conditioning to occur. The questions of "how many trials?" and "why more than one trial?" will be raised at a number of places in both this chapter and the next.

In addition to the number of trials in which the dog was conditioned, Pavlov found three other interrelated factors that lead to *faster acquisition* of the conditioned response, as well as greater *resistance-to-extinction.* Collectively, these next three rules for predicting conditioning outcomes are known as Pavlov's **law of strength** (where strength refers to the magnitude, or amount, of conditioning).

2. *CS Intensity Rule.* If a louder bell is used (i.e., a stronger, more intense CS), the dog conditions faster and the training lasts longer. This finding is not as intuitively obvious as is the "number of trials" variable. Perhaps it is the case that Pavlov is better able to capture the dog's attention during conditioning by using a louder bell. For whatever reason, we know from this and other experiments that *attentional factors* are as important in conditioning as they are in other learning situations. For example, most of us must pay attention to what we are reading if we want to learn and remember the material. One theory is that the CS "signals" that the next few seconds (minutes?) are important . . . that is, that something important is about to happen. More intense signals also activate more of the nervous system, which may in some way enhance the associative process.

3. *US Intensity Rule.* If more food is used in the conditioning situation (i.e., a more intense US is used), dogs condition more rapidly and the training lasts longer. From this and other experiments we know that the magnitude of a food reward is an important variable in conditioning. A related variable is the quality of the reward; tastier foods also lead to better conditioning than nontasty foods.

Magnitude of *punishment* is also an important variable in *aversive* conditioning. Stronger poisons condition greater food aversions, and higher intensities of shock produce more rapid acquisition and longer lasting conditioned fear responses (see Focus on Research 4.2, later in this chapter).

4. *CS-US Interval Rule.* When the interval between the bell and the food is short (i.e., when the CS-US interval is only a second or two), dogs condition faster and the training persists longer over time than would be the case if the bell and food were separated in time. That is, *contiguity* of stimuli in time, or **temporal contiguity,** is an important factor in conditioning. Likewise, the tone-to-shock interval in conditioned suppression is an important variable in learning fear responses. As predicted, the longer the interval between tone and shock during conditioning, the less conditioning is likely to occur.

Law of Strength.   As noted earlier, these last three rules of conditioning are collectively known as Pavlov's *law of strength.* Such rules governing conditioning outcomes are not really "laws" comparable to "Henry's Law," or "Boyle's Law" in chemistry. Rather, the law of strength is better understood as a series of three, interrelated functional relationships that summarize the outcomes of three separate experiments. Pavlovian conditioning has three variables (i.e., CS, US, and CS-US interval). Holding any two constant and systematically manipulating the other one has a predictable outcome. Knowing this, experimenters can adjust stimulus parameters to better predict experimental results.

Extended discussion of the law of strength can be found in Gray (1964) and in Razran (1971). Tests of the law of strength by Kamin (1965) using the conditioned suppression methodology are detailed in Figure 4.8. Next we further consider the all-important factors of time and stimulus sequencing in determining the outcomes of conditioning procedures.

5. *CS-US or US-CS sequencing.* The fifth rule of Pavlovian conditioning is that the *sequencing of stimuli in time determines the nature, or direction, of the response to be learned.* Let us do another thought experiment. Assume you are a rat trapped in an experimental test chamber. Every time you hear a tone, five seconds later you receive a brief

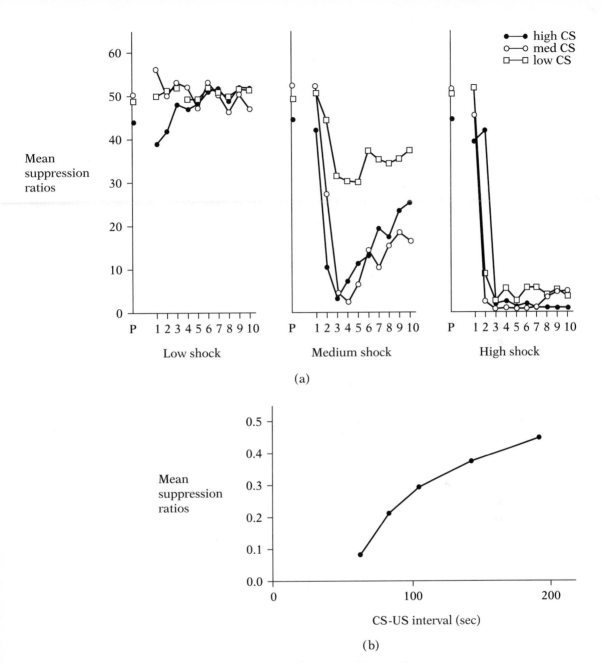

FIGURE 4.8 Testing the *Law of Strength*

Conditioned suppression tests of Pavlov's law of strength are reported by Annau and Kamin (1961). (a) Note that increasing CS intensity (low, medium, and high) and US intensity (left, middle, and right panels, respectively) led to both faster acquisition and lower suppression ratios. (b) In the lower panel (redrawn from Kamin, 1965), suppression ratios are plotted as a function of the interval between a 1.5-second tone CS and a brief electric shock US. Data are means for acquisition days two through five.

electric shock. More than likely, after 10 trials you would use the tone to prepare yourself for the shock—perhaps by adjusting your posture—to minimize the effects of the shock. (In fact, rats do just that.)

Now imagine a slightly different conditioning situation: You are first shocked, and then five seconds later you hear the brief tone. The tone no longer predicts the shock; rather, the shock predicts the tone. The tone predicts a safe period of time during which no shocks will occur (i.e., the intertrial interval). Question: Would your responses to the tone differ in the two instances? Obviously, yes. Just as the tone acquires fear-inducing properties in the first situation, in the second situation, after 10 conditioning trials you can begin to relax when you hear the tone. The tone predicts that the ordeal is over.

What have we learned from our thought experiment? That merely knowing the first four rules of conditioning described in the preceding section did not allow us to predict the experimental outcome. Note that the only thing that differs in the two situations is the *sequencing* of the stimuli. Even with full knowledge of the number of trials, and holding constant both tone and shock intensity, and the time interval connecting the stimuli, two very different response outcomes were learned.

Interim Summary

To summarize, five main factors determine the *rate* of acquisition of conditioning, the *magnitude* of the conditioned response, and the *persistence* of conditioning as measured by resistance-to-extinction. Rule 1 is that the number of conditioning trials determines how much conditioning occurs. Rules 2, 3, and 4 comprise Pavlov's *law of strength,* which states that when other factors are held constant, the magnitude of a conditioned response varies as direct functions of CS and US intensity, and as an inverse function of the CS-US interval. Rule 5 states that the direction of stimuli sequenced in time (which stimulus comes first) determines the nature, or direction, of the response to be learned.

Yet other dimensions of stimuli that play an important role in conditioning are *qualitative* parameters (whether the stimuli are sights, sounds, foods, etc.) and other *quantitative* parameters (including *how long* a stimulus lasts). More will be said about these latter variables in the next chapter, which deals with more complex conditioning situations.

Temporal Factors in Conditioning

Our foregoing thought experiment did not begin to exhaust the many possible ways in which two stimuli can be related in time. Several of the more important of these *temporal relationships* between the CS and US are diagrammed in Figure 4.9. This type of diagram emphasizes the quantitative parameters of *onset, duration,* and *offset* of the stimuli, as well as their relationship to each other in time. Not depicted are yet other dimensions of stimuli that play an important role in conditioning: *quantitative* parameters such as stimulus intensity (brighter, quieter, etc.), and *qualitative* parameters such as sight, sound, taste, etc. The latter will be discussed in the next chapter.

For reasons at present not understood, the time relationship linking the conditioned and unconditioned stimuli is one of the most important of the laws of strength just discussed. That is, having specified earlier the necessity of *temporal contiguity* between two stimulus events in order for conditioning to occur, complications immediately arise. As we will see, just because two stimuli are contiguous in time, such a stimulus arrangement does not always lead to their association.

Forward and Trace Conditioning. Let us begin by more formally defining the now familiar instances of Pavlovian conditioning that have already been introduced—namely, **forward conditioning** and

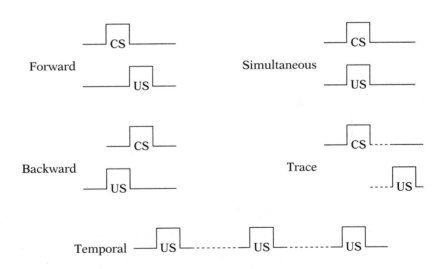

FIGURE 4.9 Five Temporal Patterns of Pavlovian Conditioning

In Pavlovian conditioning, stimulus events with measurable onsets, durations, and offsets are arranged in time. *CS* stands for *conditioned stimulus; US* for *unconditioned stimulus.* Note that in temporal conditioning the US events are presented on a regular schedule without an explicit CS. The passage of time becomes the CS, and dogs reliably salivate prior to the presentation of the food stimulus.

trace conditioning. In *forward conditioning* the CS onset precedes the US onset, and both stimuli overlap somewhat in time. Compare the stimulus arrangements of both types of conditioning in Figure 4.9. Note that *trace conditioning* is a special example of forward conditioning in which both the CS onset *and offset* precedes the US onset. Both kinds of conditioning are typical experiments described by Pavlov and others in this chapter.

Remember that Pavlov's law of strength describes how conditioning diminishes if, in the trace conditioning method, the CS and US are separated from each other in time. Hence, in trace conditioning there are limits as to how much gap can exist between the CS and US.[6] For example, imagine being the dog that is conditioned with a (tone) CS → (food) US. The tone sounds for 10 seconds, and the food is presented 30 seconds from the tone's onset (hence the CS-US interval is 30 seconds). After a number of trace-conditioning trials you would likely learn a conditioned salivary response. If, however, the CS-US interval were 30 *minutes* rather than 30 seconds, you would most likely *not* be conditioned to salivate to the tone.

Simultaneous and Embedded Conditioning. You would be mistaken if you were led to conclude from this example that conditioning results when stimuli are contiguous (close together in time), and does *not* result when stimuli are far removed in time. As can be seen in Figure 4.9, among the most contiguous of stimulus relationships is one called **simultaneous conditioning.** Note that in *simultaneous conditioning* the CS and US have identical onsets, durations, and offsets. Ironically, if the conditioning involves relatively brief conditioned stimuli (tones and lights lasting only a second) paired with short duration unconditioned stimuli (a tiny amount of food, or a brief electric shock), very little conditioning occurs, even after many trials (Pavlov, 1927; Kamin, 1965). Apparently, strict contiguity of stimuli is *not* a sufficient condition for association to occur.

Embedded conditioning is a variation of simultaneous conditioning in which the onset and offset of one of the stimulus elements occurs *in the middle* of the other element (Heth, 1976; see also Figure 4.9). Embedded conditioning situations often involve the pairing of longer duration stimuli. For example, in taste aversion conditioning a flavor of several minutes' duration might be experienced in the middle of an illness episode lasting several hours. The flavor (CS) can be said to be *embedded* in illness (US). Conditioning flavor aversions *does* occur in these situations (Barker, Suarez, & Grey, 1974).

[6]Historically, the term "trace" in *trace conditioning* refers to a "memory trace" theory. In this theory when the conditioned stimulus is presented, it is conceptualized as being loaded into memory. At stimulus offset, it persists as a memory trace just long enough to be associated with the US when *it* is presented.

The differentiation of embedded conditioning from simultaneous conditioning is important for another reason. Outside of the laboratory, timing arrangements encountered by animals are not as neat as those arranged by laboratory researchers. Most stimuli encountered in natural contexts are of longer duration than 1.0 seconds, and the relationship of these stimuli with other stimuli often varies across trials. Yet conditioning occurs despite the lack of precision in timing. The embedded conditioning category includes (but is not restricted to) conditioning situations using drugs as stimuli, ingestional stimuli, and other long-duration stimulus complexes.

Backward Conditioning.   In **backward conditioning,** the US onset precedes the CS onset. The outcome of this temporal sequencing confused even Pavlov! Again, contiguity predicts that stimulus association should occur, and it does. The *direction* of conditioning, however, is less predictable. That is, many such stimulus arrangements produce what is called *inhibitory* conditioning, the *opposite* of excitatory conditioning, especially after many conditioning trials have been conducted.

As was discussed in the section on stimulus sequencing, in forward conditioning with dogs, for example, the animal salivates to the tone CS. In backward conditioning the dog suppresses salivation to the tone. In conditioned suppression experiments with rats, tone-shock (forward) sequences condition fear responses, while shock-tone (backward) sequences condition "safety" responses. We will have much more to say about excitatory and inhibitory conditioning later in this chapter.

Temporal Conditioning.   **Temporal conditioning** is unusual in that other than the passage of time, the CS is unspecified. Pavlov noted that following regularly spaced placements of food on the dog's tongue, salivation eventually began to occur just prior to food delivery.

Pavlov's observation is an important one. Time schedules are principal ways in which civilized humans organize events and responses in their world, and the passage of time can and does act as a signal to control these responses. We often eat at 12:00 noon *because* it is 12:00 noon, whether we are hungry or not. Moreover, in laboratory experiments the passage of time can be a confounding factor. That is, animals (like humans) may anticipate when certain treatments are likely to occur, and adjust their responses accordingly. Another way of saying this is that "time of day" and "time between treatments" provide animals with important contextual cues that affect their responses. These cues must be taken into account in the interpretation of treatment effects.

Interim Summary

1. Time arrangements connecting stimuli determine their associability and the direction of the conditioned response.
2. *Forward* and (short) *trace* arrangements are the best for conditioning most stimuli.
3. Simultaneous *and* embedded timing relationships work for some intense, long-duration stimuli but typically *not* for brief stimuli.
4. The conditioned response following a few *backward* conditioning trials *may* produce excitatory conditioning, but after many more trials *usually* produces inhibitory conditioning.
5. Finally, *temporal conditioning* results from regularly scheduled unconditioned stimuli; the passage of time can act as a conditioned stimulus.

V. Theories of Association Formation

To this point, Pavlovian conditioning has been labeled, described, and defined, but not explained. That is, a *theory of conditioning* has not been presented. For good reason. No matter how simplistic (and, by way of hindsight, intuitively obvious) Pavlovian conditioning may seem to be, contemporary theories of conditioning remain incomplete. That is to say, existing theories are neither exhaustive nor mutually exclusive. Nor is there agreement about whether the theory should be at the level of either brain functioning or of observable behavior.

In the remainder of this chapter several theoretical considerations are presented. Some you will be familiar with, and others are presented to extend your thinking about what form brain-based and behavioral theories of conditioning might take.

Information Processing Approach. Pavlov's law of strength described how associative conditioning could be degraded by separating the CS and US in time. Implicit in this formulation is the "theory" that association formation depends upon perceived *contiguity* of stimuli; hence, we *should* expect that trace conditioning produces poorer conditioning due to less association of stimulus elements. Contiguity theory, unfortunately, does not account for a number of experimental findings.

In the following section, contingency theory will be discussed as an alternative to contiguity theory. Implicit in the comparison of these two theories is the notion that humans and other animals process incoming sensory information. The comparison of contiguity and contingency theories, therefore, can be conceptualized as *information processing* theories.

Contiguity and Contingency

One component of Pavlov's law of strength is that contiguous stimuli, that is, stimuli occurring close together in time, are more apt to become associated than those separated by a longer time interval. One problem with this statement is that "simultaneous," "embedded," and "backward" pairings are all contiguous, but they do not become associated as well as "forward" and short "trace" pairings (see Figure 4.9). Therefore, a **contiguity theory of association** cannot alone account for the way in which associations have been observed to form.

By contrast, a **contingency theory of association** focuses upon the *information* value of one stimulus preceding and thereby *signaling* a second stimulus. Contingency theory, therefore, highlights two aspects of what an animal learns during conditioning: (a) the predictability of the US by the CS and (b) the *sequencing* of the CS and US. We begin with an analysis of the many contingent relationships possible between the CS and the US.

CS-US Contingencies. Let us call Pavlov's conditioned stimulus S_1 and the unconditioned stimulus, S_2. A *contingent* relationship between these two stimuli refers to their degree of relatedness to each other. For example, if the contingency between S_1 and S_2 is perfect, then the probability of S_2 given the occurrence of S_1 is equal to one. Symbolically (where "p" means "probability"),

$$p(S_2/S_1) = 1.0. \qquad (4.1)$$

This equation reads "the probability of S_2 given S_1 is equal to 1.0." In Pavlov's basic experiment, the food (US) is preceded by the tone (CS) each and every time; the contingency is 1.0.

Note that this perfect relationship between the CS and the US can be altered in several ways. For example, the CS can be presented to the animal in the absence of the US:

$$p(S_2/S_1) = 0.0; \qquad (4.2)$$

or the US can be presented to the animal in the absence of the CS:

$$p(S_2/ \text{ no } S_1) = 1.0. \qquad (4.3)$$

Positive Contingencies. Yet other combinations are possible. In Pavlov's traditional experiments, for example, there was always a perfect *positive contingency* between the CS and the US. That is, the US was always presented with the CS (Eq. 4.1) and was never presented in the absence of the CS (Eq. 4.3). What would be the outcome of an experiment in which the US did not always follow the CS?

Figure 4.7b (p. 123) shows the results of a human eye-blink conditioning experiment in which the percentage of CSs followed by USs was varied. In one group (labeled "25%"), a brief light CS was followed by an air-puff US on 40 occasions; on 120 other occasions the CS was not followed by the US. Compare both the rate of acquisition and the asymptotic performance of this group with one that received a CS followed by a US on all 160 occasions. Conditioning is better in the latter group. We can conclude that a perfect positive contingency produces better conditioning than when the contingency is degraded.

Likewise, in conditioned suppression experiments by Rescorla (1968) the probability of the US (a brief electric shock) given the CS (a brief tone) was varied from 0.0 to 1.0 in different groups of rats. He found that associations formed more readily as the probability of the US given the CS approached 1.0. That is, the tone became a fear-inducing stimulus when it reliably predicted electric shock. Moreover, Rescorla found that S_1 *had to predict* S_2 *more than half the time for conditioning to occur,* or

$$p(S_2/S_1) > 0.5. \tag{4.4}$$

But didn't we just see that humans learned an eye-blink response when only 25 percent of the CSs were followed by USs (Figure 4.7b)? Does this finding differ from Rescorla's results? Rescorla presented the same number of CS events and US events in his rat experiment; merely the number of CSs that were followed by USs varied between groups. His finding was that for conditioning to occur, at least half the CSs had to be followed by USs. In the Hartman and Grant (1960) human eye-blink conditioning data presented in Figure 4.7b, 120 additional CSs were presented the subjects in the "25% Group" (i.e., 40/160), or

$$p(S_1/S_2) = 0.25. \tag{4.5}$$

But the probability of the *US* being preceded by a CS was 100% (i.e., 40/40), or

$$p(S_2/S_1) = 1.0. \tag{4.6}$$

Comparing (4.4) with (4.6), one can see that the contingency of US given a CS was 0.5 and 1.0, respectively; hence the likelihood of conditioning was excellent in both studies.

Negative Contingencies. What happens in "backward" conditioning experiments? Interestingly, contingency theory predicts that if the US reliably *precedes* the CS, when the CS occurs it now predicts a time period during which no US will occur. These *negative contingencies* are as informative to the animal as positive contingencies. If, for example, a shock US reliably is *followed* by a tone CS, the tone predicts a safe period (i.e., one in which no shock will occur).

Note that learning does occur when negative contingencies are employed; however, *what* is learned differs from pairing the same stimuli in a positive contingency. In the present example, tone followed by shock (a positive contingency) produces excitatory conditioning; shock followed by tone (a negative contingency) produces inhibitory conditioning. As described earlier, the tone predicts a safe period in which no shock occurs.

But the story is even more complicated than this. During the first few conditioning trials of a negative shock-tone contingency, the animal learns a fear response (excitatory conditioning) to the tone. Only after many more trials does the animal learn that the tone is signaling a safe period (Heth, 1976). The learning literature is sprinkled with similar reports of excitatory backward conditioning since Pavlov's reports in 1927 (see Spetch, Wilkie, & Pinel, 1981, for a review).

Note that contingency theory accounts for association formation in both forward and trace conditioning experiments. Likewise, contingency theory predicts the absence of conditioning in a "simultaneous" or "embedded" design (see Figure 4.9). In both stimulus arrangements the conditioned stimulus (S_1) does not precede, and therefore does not predict, the unconditioned stimulus (S_2).

Contiguity and Contingency Theories Compared

Both contingency and contiguity theories of association formation are necessary to account for the conditioning examples we have considered to this point. Contingency theory can better account for the fact that a very slight delay between the CS onset and the US onset (delay and trace procedures) produces much better conditioning than if the stimulus onsets are simultaneous. In both delay and trace procedures a relatively neutral stimulus *predicts* a biologically more meaningful stimulus.

Contingency theory also predicts that conditioning is *not* the inevitable outcome of pairing two stimuli, as follows: (a) if enough USs are presented in the absence of the CS, for example, the ones that *are* paired with the CS do not form associations as readily; and (b) simultaneous and backward procedures, both lacking US predictability by the CS, typically produce less excitatory conditioning.

Neither theory is especially informative for some conditioning examples: Instances of one-trial conditioning are not accounted for especially well by either contingency *or* contiguity theory. Consider, for example, the many reports of one-trial, long-delay taste aversion conditioning in humans (Bernstein, 1978) and rats (Smith & Roll, 1967). First, stimulus contiguity is violated if tasting a flavor and getting ill are separated by several hours. In addition, an animal cannot learn much about the contingent relationships of two stimuli after only one trial!

Necessity of Contiguity.   Contiguity of stimuli remains a necessary condition for association formation. Consider the following thought experiment using a conditioned suppression methodology: What would you predict to be the outcome of presenting a five-second duration tone to a rat in an experimental chamber, and *five hours later* delivering a one-second electric shock? Even if this pairing were to continue for 20 days, where $p(S_2/S_1) = 1.0$, an association of tone with shock would be unlikely (see Figure 4.10).

Conclusion? Every example of conditioning by "contingency" is confounded by the contiguity of the stimuli involved. If the two stimuli in a contingent relationship are too far removed in time from each other, no association will occur.

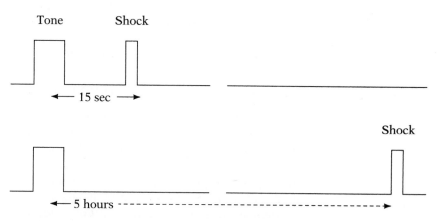

FIGURE 4.10   Contiguity Is Necessary for Contingency

The top group receives 20 trials consisting of a five-second duration tone followed 15 seconds later by a one-second electric shock. The bottom group experiences the same stimuli. The shock, however, is presented not 15 seconds, but rather five hours later. Note that over 20 trials both groups enjoy the same contingency:

$$p(S_2/S_1) = 1.0.$$

Conditioning is a highly likely outcome for contiguous stimuli (top), and highly unlikely for contingent but noncontiguous stimuli (bottom).

TABLE 4.3 A Comparison of Contiguity and Contingency Theories

Contiguity

Arguments for:
1. Two stimuli presented closer together are better associated than two presented further apart.
2. Simultaneous and embedded stimuli can be associated together.
3. Backward excitatory conditioning can result from negative contingencies.

Arguments against:
1. Contiguous stimuli are associated less if contingent relationship is degraded.
2. Direction of stimulus sequencing should not affect conditioning.

Contingency

Arguments for:
1. Positive contingencies produce excitatory conditioning, and negative contingencies often produce inhibitory conditioning.

Arguments against:
1. Contingent stimuli must be close together to be associated.
2. All demonstrations of simultaneous, embedded, and backward excitatory conditioning argue against contingency theory.

Interim Summary

Two theories of association formation can be conceptualized as information processing models. Contiguity theory merely states that when two stimuli are presented together in time, they are likely to be perceived as belonging together by the animal. Contingency theory stresses that animals process the sequencing of two stimuli, such that the first stimulus predicts the occurrence of the second stimulus.

A comparison of arguments both supporting and refuting each position is found in Table 4.3.

Three additional theoretical formulations that attempt to account for basic phenomena of conditioning will be presented next—namely, the theoretical position of Robert Rescorla and his colleagues (Rescorla, 1967; Rescorla & Wagner, 1972); the *comparator hypothesis* of Ralph Miller and colleagues (Miller & Matzel, 1988); and Gregory Razran's *dominance-contiguity theory* (Razran, 1957, 1971).

Rescorla–Wagner Model

The information processing approaches that have been described allow us to make valuable generalizations about the basic nature of association formation. Another approach is to attempt to model how humans and animals actually learn.

Learning English-Spanish Associations. Consider, for example, using flip cards to memorize English language equivalents of Spanish words. This task can be conceptualized as learning by association. The word *amarillo* is associated with *yellow* (which was associated with the sensation of seeing yellow earlier in the English speaker's life). Two items learned in this manner are called *paired associates*.

One question that can be asked concerns the growth of association. Can we measure the association of *amarillo* with *yellow* as the student uses the flip cards, where each encounter with the *amarillo-yellow* card constitutes one trial? Let us assume that it takes 10 trials to learn the association. Would you predict that most of the learning occurred in the first few trials, the middle trials, the last few trials, or in equal amounts on each trial?

The **Rescorla–Wagner model** addresses this and many other questions regarding the growth of associations (Rescorla & Wagner, 1972; Wagner & Rescorla, 1972). Before seeing their solution, let us first look at three graphs of the question that has been posed.

Modeling the Growth of Association. Three alternative models of the growth of association with each conditioning trial are presented in Figure 4.11. In parts (a) and (b) the association of the CS and the US grows either at a faster rate (Figure 4.11a) or at a constant rate (Figure 4.11b) with each successive pairing of CS and US. That is, if you had predicted that most of the flip card learning had occurred in

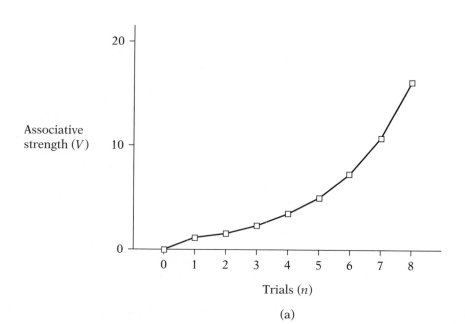

(a)

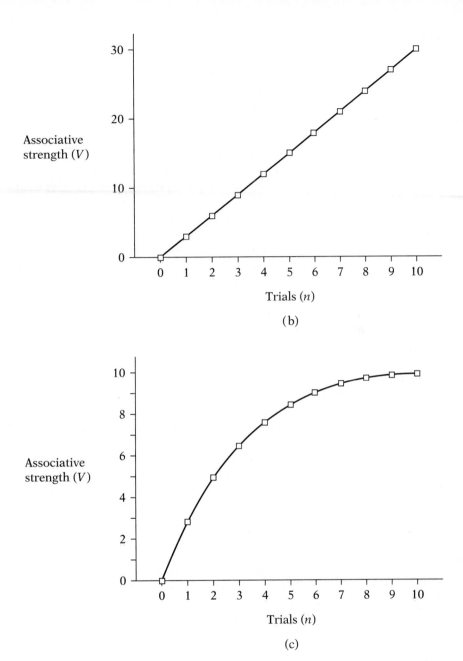

FIGURE 4.11 Three Alternatives of Associative Growth

Three alternative models of the growth of association are compared. In (a), each successive trial contributes a greater amount of associability; in (b), an equal amount of association. Note that for (a) and (b) there are no upper limits to the degree of association between stimuli. In (c) each successive trial contributes less, resulting in the negatively accelerated learning curve typical of most (but not all) conditioning experiments.

the last of the 10 trials, the graph in part (a) depicts this model. If you predicted that associations are learned in equal amounts on each trial, the graph in part (b) depicts this model.

Both Figure 4.11a and Figure 4.11b have *intuitive* appeal (which means that they feel right—the models jive with what it feels like when you are memorizing a list of words). These intuitively appealing notions about the growth of association do not accord with the facts, however. Figure 4.11c better models the real world. Compare the idealized learning curve in Figure 4.11c with the acquisition functions of salivation (Figure 4.3) and of fear conditioning using the conditioned suppression methodology described in Focus on Research 4.2 and depicted in Figure 4.8.

In both graphs in Figure 4.8, *most of the associative learning occurs during the first few pairings;* in the last few trials very little is added to the strength of the association. Mathematical equations of both the growth of association and of the shape of extinction functions have been proposed by two Yale psychologists, Allan Wagner and Robert Rescorla. The Rescorla–Wagner model states that

$$\Delta V_n = \mathring{a} \beta (\lambda - V_n). \tag{4.7}$$

The left side of the equation defines how a conditioning trial changes the strength of association: "Δ" refers to "the change in," V_n refers to the amount of learned association that exists at the beginning of trial n. The equation reads as follows: "The growth of association (learning change in each trial)" is determined by ("equals") CS and US parameters ($\mathring{a}$ and β, respectively) times a quantity

$$\lambda - V_n \tag{4.8}$$

where λ (lambda) represents the maximum amount of conditioning possible in this experiment, and V_n represents how much conditioning has already occurred.

Equation (4.7) is actually quite simple even for those of us not mathematically inclined. It states:

The amount of association that occurs on any trial is determined by the maximum learning (association) possible (λ), minus how much has already been learned (V_n), taking into consideration the nature of the CSs and US ($\mathring{a}$ and β, respectively) that are being associated.

Referring back to the curve depicted in Figure 4.11c, let us work through the equation with an example. Note that ΔV_1 (the change from trial 1) is greater than ΔV_2 (the change from trial 2), and that

ΔV_3 (the change from trial 3) is less than ΔV_2. Assume that the maximum conditioning λ has a value of 5. Entering the value of V_1, and $\lambda = 5$ into the Rescorla–Wagner equation,

$$\Delta V_1 = \mathring{a}\beta(\lambda - V_1) \tag{4.9}$$

and ignoring for the moment the CS and US parameters,

$$\Delta V_1 = 5 - 2; \tag{4.10}$$

solving the equation,

$$\Delta V_1 = 3. \tag{4.11}$$

Again referring back to the curve depicted in Figure 4.11c, now solve the equations for the values ΔV_2, and ΔV_3,:

$$\Delta V_2 = 5 - 3 = 2; \tag{4.12}$$

$$\Delta V_3 = 5 - 3.5 = 1.5. \tag{4.13}$$

Comparing the values determined in Eq. (4.11) with Eqs. (4.12) and (4.13), you can see that 3.0 units of association were gained on the first trial, 2.0 on the second, and 1.5 on the third. More "units of association," therefore, were learned in earlier trials than in later trials.

We can now make the prediction that more flip card learning of paired associates (English and Spanish words) takes place on earlier trials than on later trials.

Salience

Does the Rescorla–Wagner model allow researchers to predict how many trials will be necessary to effect conditioning? No. Only the form of the acquisition function is predicted; the rate of acquisition is determined by $\mathring{a}$ and β, values representing the **salience** of the CS and US, respectively.

Salience is a descriptive rather than an explanatory term. The salience of a stimulus refers to its relative associability. Take as an example the following statement in which the term is used: "The flavor stimulus was more *salient* than the tone stimulus." The only way to interpret the statement is to assume that an experiment was conducted, and the flavor stimulus conditioned either more quickly (in fewer trials) or to a higher level than did the tone stimulus. Hence, the flavor was more salient than the tone *under these conditions, in this experiment.*

The concept of salience—indeed, the Rescorla–Wagner model—should sound familiar to the reader. A number of the five rules of conditioning discussed earlier in this chapter are conceptualized mathematically in the Rescorla-Wagner model. For example, the growth of association over conditioning trials is implicit in Rule 1 (p. 129). In addition, Pavlov's law of strength (Rules 2 and 3) states that more intense CSs and USs enter into association more readily and lead to better conditioning. CS and US intensity, then, are two parameters of salience that Rescorla and Wagner plugged into their equation.

What about Rule 3 (relating to the role of the CS-US interval in conditioning) and Rule 5 (concerning the direction of the conditioned response when S_1-S_2 sequencing is reversed)? Rule 3 is not specifically addressed in the model. Increasing the CS-US interval, however, would slow the growth of associative strength in a predictable manner. As was discussed earlier, the initial association in US-CS (backward) pairings is excitatory, only later becoming inhibitory.

Limits of the Rescorla–Wagner Model. The Rescorla–Wagner model does not make predictions concerning the *backward sequencing* of stimuli. What the Rescorla–Wagner model *does* do is make interesting predictions about the phenomena of *blocking, overshadowing,* and some instances of *conditioned inhibition,* all of which are dealt with in Chapter 5. Indeed, associative learning theory since Pavlov has in large measure been defined by the research and theory of Robert Rescorla and his colleagues (see Focus on Research 4.2).

Interim Summary

The Rescorla–Wagner model is a relatively straightforward prediction about the growth of association between a conditioned stimulus and an unconditioned stimulus presented together in a forward sequence. The model asserts that there is an asymptotic level (a limit) of associative strength, which is approached with each conditioning trial. Further, the model of the growth of the association best resembles that depicted in Figure 4.11c in that more associative strength accrues on earlier rather than later conditioning trials. Certain parameters of the CS and US as well as the number of trials influence the rate of growth of the associative function. CS and US parameters that lead to more rapid growth of association are described as being more *salient* stimuli.

The model intuitively predicts that stimulus intensity and many trials produce conditioning. It does not address either the role of contiguity (or contingency) or changes that may result from reversing the CS-US sequence. The Rescorla–Wagner model predicts the way in which associations can be *blocked, overshadowed,* and *inhibited,* as discussed in the next chapter.

FOCUS ON RESEARCH 4.2

Dr. Robert Rescorla

Simple Animals, but Complex Processing

Dr. Robert Rescorla, Department of Psychology, University of Pennsylvania, Philadelphia

"My research interests focus on elementary learning processes, particularly associative learning. Much of my earlier work concerned how animals learn relations among events in the environment, as exemplified by Pavlovian conditioning. More recently, I have been concerned with the organism's learning of relations between its own behavior and the consequences of that behavior, as exemplified in instrumental learning (see Rescorla, 1990a; 1990b).

"In both cases, the goal of the analysis is to understand the way in which organisms represent the richness of the environment. The striking thing is that even relatively simple animals seem to have an amazingly complex representation of the world. The trick for the scientist is to expose how the organism develops that representation using only simple associative mechanisms."

Miller's Comparator Hypothesis

In a typical conditioning situation, the experimenter specifies one stimulus as the CS, and the association of that CS with a given US is tested. In theory, all other stimuli that comprise the context for the CS are also present, and they are also being conditioned by the US. Ralph Miller and his colleagues have proposed that the animal *compares* what happens to it in the presence of the CS with what happens to it the rest of the time it is in the experimental situation: the *comparator hypothesis* (Miller & Matzel, 1988, 1989). The comparator hypothesis makes the following three assumptions about the nature of associations that are made during conditioning trials:

1. Associations are learned between the target CS and the US.
2. Associations are learned between the target CS and the context CSs within which the target is embedded (cf. *sensory preconditioning*).
3. Associations are learned between the US and various CSs comprising the context of the experimental situation.

As we saw earlier, if during excitatory conditioning the target CS is *always* accompanied by a US, more conditioning accrues to the CS than if the US is presented alone on a portion of the trials. In the former situation, the comparison of the events during the CS (i.e., US always present) stands out more than in the latter situation (i.e., US sometimes present with CS, sometimes present with context). The comparator hypothesis, then, simply states that in comparison with other potential CSs that comprise the context of a conditioning experiment, an animal is conditioned to respond to a specific CS when that stimulus takes more of the associative strength of the US.

The comparator hypothesis accurately predicts the results of experiments in which contextual cues are altered following conditioning. For example, if after conditioning the contextual cues are first *extinguished* before measuring the conditioned response to the target CS, a greater response to the target CS is seen (Hallam, Matzel, Sloat, & Miller, 1990). This means that the contextual cues took some of the associative strength during conditioning to the target CS. In summary, the comparator hypothesis accurately describes a number of performance parameters affecting both the acquisition and extinction of conditioned responses.

Razran's Dominance-Contiguity Theory

In addition to maintaining his own program of animal research, Gregory Razran read and translated Russian experiments for 30 years following Pavlov's death. His book *Mind in Evolution* (1971) presents an evolutionary schema in which animals learn at different conceptual levels depending upon their brain development. In this respect his book anticipates a number of the major themes of this one, written more than two decades later.

Razran (1957, 1972) shifted the theoretical focus of Pavlovian conditioning from that of association between *stimuli* to association of *responses* to those stimuli. In **Razran's dominance-contiguity theory,** afferent neural activity (i.e., sensory nerves signaling events in the environment to the brain) underlies each conditioning experiment. The CS and US produce the "R_o" (his abbreviation for the orienting response to the CS) and the UR, respectively. The association is made between the R_o and the UR via unspecified *neural activation* (Razran, 1972).

According to Razran, *contiguity is necessary but not sufficient for conditioning.* In each conditioning situation the neural events must occur close in time, and for conditioning to occur, two conditions typically are met: R_o slightly precedes the UR, and the UR *dominates* R_o. By "dominate" Razran refers to both the quantity and quality of the unmeasured neural activity that underlies the UR (see Box 4.2).

BOX 4.2

Razran's Models of Neural Activity

Razran (1971) proposes that associations take place between "R_o," the unmeasured (but measurable) afferent neural activity activated by the CS, and neural events similarly activated by the US. Such hypothetical neural events are indicated in the figure. In Razran's *dominance-contiguity theory*, two combinations of neural activity must be present for association to occur: *contiguity* (indicated as shaded overlap of neural activity in both the "forward" (a) and "trace" (b) depictions), and *dominance* of the first by the succeeding neural activity.

The lack of contiguity of afferent neural activity precludes associability ("nonassociation," part c). Failures of backward conditioning can be accounted for by the *first* stimulus being too intense (part d). Razran suggests that some experimental arrangements of stimuli allow for both "simultaneous" and "backward" (part e) conditioning when the intensities of both stimuli are moderate, and their afferent neural activity is relatively "matched." One way to think of this is that both stimuli on such occasions have "US-like" properties.

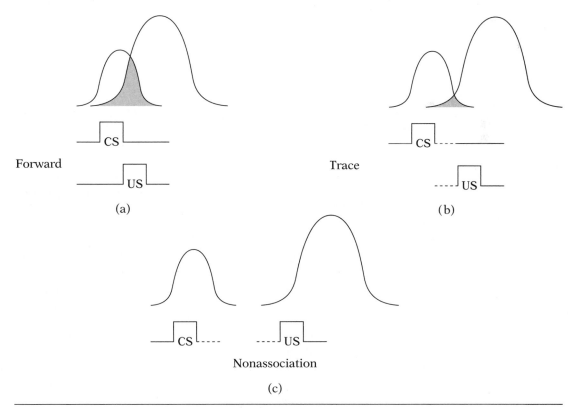

Forward

(a)

Trace

(b)

Nonassociation

(c)

BOX 4.2 *continued*

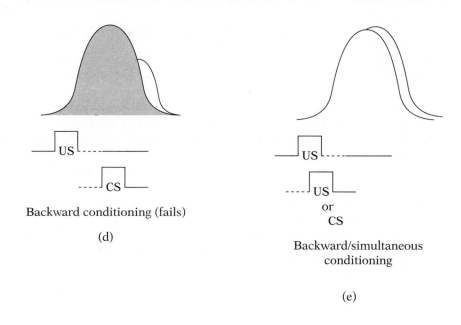

Backward conditioning (fails)

(d)

Backward/simultaneous
conditioning

(e)

Excitatory backward conditioning can occur in Razran's model by postulating that the second stimulus in the sequence (whether a CS or US) merely be the "dominating stimulus" of the pair. For example, if a weak US were used as the first stimulus and were paired with a strong "CS" as the second stimulus, associative conditioning could result. In some unspecified way, the brain would apparently "sort out" which was the "CS" and which was the "US."

Criticism of Dominance-Contiguity Theory.   Razran uses unmeasured nervous activity to speculate about the outcomes of various behavioral manipulations. As such, the "theory" is more of an assertion about untestable hypotheses than an organized account of our laboratory observations. In addition, Razran's theory is *post hoc;* only in the most general way can predictions about conditioning outcomes be made before the fact. Finally, the circumstances of many (most?) experiments do not allow researchers to specify in a meaningful way either the magnitudes, the onsets, durations, or offsets of neural responses to stimuli. Given this constraint, tests of dominance-contiguity theory become impossible.

Why bother discussing a theory that is difficult to test? One reason is that Razran's logic that associations ultimately involve *neural responses* to stimuli seems irrefutable. In addition, he shifts the focus of association theory back to the *nature* of stimuli being associated—to both their *innate* and *acquired* meaningfulness. Rather than one stimulus merely signaling the occurrence of another, Razran asks how their relative strengths and weaknesses in having an impact upon an animal's senses enter into and determine the nature of the association. Finally, simultaneous and excitatory backward conditioning phenomena are often overlooked (disregarded?) by most theorists, and Razran attempts to account for conditioning of stimuli not amenable to a contingency analysis. Any theory that addresses a difficult area is better than one that merely ignores problematic data.

US-US and Bidirectional Conditioning

Other theorists have also addressed alternatives to the traditional Pavlovian view of association formation (Solomon, 1977; Gormezano & Tait, 1976). They build upon Razran's focus upon the brain's response to intense USs. Rather than the role reversal of CS and US proposed by Razran, both of these theoretical positions posit that two USs may enter into association; i.e., *US-US conditioning.* For example, Solomon (1977) interprets the rapid, one-trial acquisition of flavor aversions as being the result of a flavor *US* (rather than a flavor CS) entering into association with a toxin (illness-producing) US.

In addition, Gormezano and Tait (1976) cite Russian literature and some of their own research to develop a theory of *bidirectional conditioning.* They propose that conditioned responses develop concurrently both to the first and to the second stimulus presented the animal during conditioning. That is, *all stimulus pairings* produce both forward, and to a lesser degree, backward associations. They point out that researchers never measure the backward associations that may have formed to the US, merely the conditioned responses that have formed to the CS.

Very little empirical evidence exists to support the theory of bidirectional conditioning. Pavlov never mentioned what the dog's ears did, when, after bell-food conditioning, he merely fed the dog. Question: Why would this observation be relevant to a theory of bidirectional conditioning?

Neural Theories of Conditioning

Razran's dominance-contiguity theory of how (hypothetical) neural responses become associated during conditioning raises the question of what *is* known about brain mechanisms underlying conditioning.

Mention was made in Chapter 2 of research conducted on *Aplysia*, a tiny marine invertebrate. The chemical events at synapse in sensory and motor neurons subserving a gill-withdrawal reflex have been studied by Kandel and his associates (Kandel & Schwartz, 1982; Carew, Hawkins, & Kandel, 1983). Nonassociative learning (sensitization and habituation) can be observed in Aplysia's responses to tactile and electric shock stimulation. These behavioral changes are mediated by changes in the ion channels that provide gates for potassium and calcium ions. Such gates allow ions to cross the membranes of neurons subserving Aplysia's cutaneous senses. Similar membrane changes can be seen following conditioning-like procedures that yield a conditioned gill withdrawal (Carew et al., 1983).

It is likely, however, that "conditioning" the few neurons found in Aplysia is different from the neuronal changes subserving associative conditioning in vertebrate brains. Why? By contrast the brains of dogs, rabbits, and humans are both enormous and highly organized (see Box 4.3). Such brains allow a richness of sensitivity to environmental change, of perceptual knowledge of environment enhanced and mediated by memory, and of plasticity of responsiveness unknown to and unknowable by Aplysia's brain. Neuronal models for classical conditioning of vertebrates (Klopf, 1988); for conditioned taste aversions (Chambers, 1990); and for eyelid conditioning have been proposed (for a review, see Thompson, 1986; for representative research, see Sears & Steinmetz, 1991).

Long-Term Potentiation. A profitable line of research into the neural substrates of learning is **long-term potentiation (LTP).** Neurons rapidly stimulated for a brief time show potentiation effects lasting for days and even weeks (Bliss & Lomo, 1973). Stimulating several axons simultaneously produces more LTP than if only one neuron is stimulated, raising the possibility of long-lasting associative effects between neurons (Kelso, Ganong, & Brown, 1986).

Is LTP a likely mechanism underlying associative learning in vertebrates? Perhaps, perhaps not. Extrapolating the measured effects of LTP on one or two "cooperating" neurons to the probable integration of thousands of CNS neurons in associative learning is a tremendous leap.

Neural Basis of Eye-Blink Conditioning. An object lesson in humility for those who seek the neurophysiological basis of learning and memory is provided by Thompson (1986). Most neuroscientists in this century assumed as did Pavlov that the cerebral hemispheres mediated learning. Neurons in a discrete area of the cerebellum (called the *lateral interpositus nucleus*), however, have been found to underlie the tone–air puff conditioning of the rabbit's nictitating membrane (McCormick & Thompson, 1984).

BOX 4.3

Peeking Inside the Black Box: Spotski's Brain

Salivary conditioning in dogs is initiated by nerve pathways in the brain. The salivary reflex begins with stimulation of the dog's taste nerves, primarily the *chorda tympani* (branch of Cranial Nerve VII), which synapses in the *Solitary nucleus* in the medulla (brain stem). Interneurons from the solitary nucleus synapse in the adjacent *salivatory nucleus,* also in the medulla, completing a Sherrington-like reflex of salivation. For sights and sounds to activate the salivatory nucleus, both the thalamus and cortex of the brain must become involved. For sights, the *optic nerve, lateral geniculate nucleus (LGN), striate cortex,* and other areas subserving vision can come to elicit the reflex. For sounds, the cochlear nucleus (and other nuclei) in the medulla, *medial geniculate nucleus (MGN),* and primary and secondary projection areas of *auditory cortex* are involved.

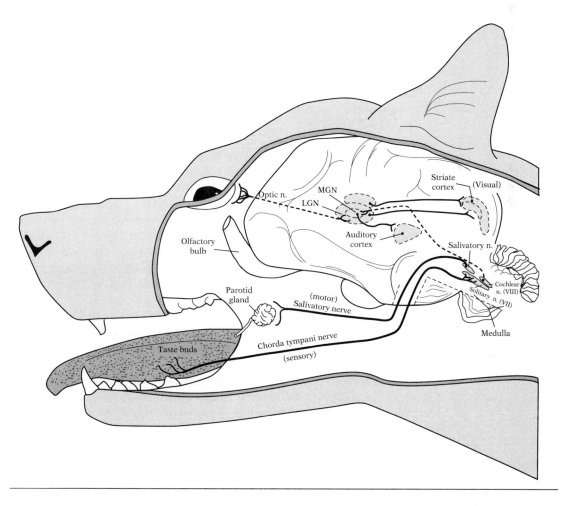

One implication of Richard F. Thompson's research is that "Pavlovian conditioning" may not be centrally represented as such. Rather, certain brain areas will underlie taste aversion learning, other areas will be dedicated to eye-blink conditioning, and appetitive and defense conditioning, though behaviorally similar, may have quite different anatomical loci.

VI.   Conditioning and Perception

When an optometrist asks which of two lenses makes your visual world appear more clearly, or when an audiologist asks you to press a button when you no longer hear a sound, your responses communicate your personal sensory experiences. The study of how your responses are related to incoming physical stimuli is called *psychophysics*.

In the same manner, measuring a dog's responses to systematically presented stimuli allows insight into its perceptual world. The results of Pavlovian conditioning experiments have provided important windows into the nature of the minds of infants (nonverbal humans) and other animals.

Because a dog initially salivates to food placed on the tongue and does not salivate to a ringing bell, we can infer that the dog *discriminates* between auditory and taste/smell sensitivity. When, during the course of training, his dogs began to salivate to the sight of the white lab coats worn by technicians, Pavlov concluded that the dog's visual world differed from its auditory world.

Pavlov (1927) described the portions of the dog's brain responsible for the different senses as "analyzers." In his late nineteenth century understanding of brain functioning, the sound of the bell was perceived by the dog's "auditory analyzer," a picture by the "visual analyzer," touch by a "cutaneous analyzer," etc. Vision, audition, touch, taste, and smell among other senses define how animals discriminate their environment, and conditioning was viewed as a way to get one of these analyzers to signal another.

Likewise, Pavlov found that his dogs responded to similar stimuli in a similar manner. For example, a tone of 500 Hz heard by dogs (and humans) sounds more similar to a tone of 512 Hz than to one of 530 Hz.

How do we know that? For humans this is an easy experiment. Because we have learned to use language to track the environment (words denoting concepts such as "greater than," "more than," "equal to," etc. are learned early in life), we can simply ask humans, "which of these two stimuli are more alike?" German psychophysicists did these experiments over 100 years ago.

Generalization

But what about dogs and other animals? What do their psychophysical functions look like? Using Pavlovian methods across a variety of animals, researchers have measured sensory functions and found that vertebrate nervous systems track the environment in a similar way to humans'. The method? First condition a dog to respond to a 500-Hz tone, then measure salivation to various tones of differing frequencies. You would find indeed that responses *track* the stimuli. That is, dogs respond most to the original CS (500 Hz), next most to closely related stimuli (for example, 490 and 510 Hz), and least to highly dissimilar stimuli (for example, 400 and 600 Hz). This tendency of animals to respond similarly to like stimuli is called **generalization.**

Discrimination

Pavlov reported an experiment that demonstrates the process of generalization and the related process of discrimination. He used a **conditioned discrimination** procedure (see Figure 4.12). A black circle served as the conditioned stimulus. After the dog reliably salivated in the presence of the circle (CS_1), an ellipse (CS_2) was substituted. At first the dog salivated to CS_2, thereby demonstrating *generalization.* We can infer that the ellipse and the circle were perceived as similar by the dog.

Conditioning Discriminations. The circle (CS_1) continues to be paired with food. On alternate trials the ellipse (CS_2) is shown to the dog, but it is *never* followed by food. By convention we designate "CS with food" as **CS^+ trials** and "CS without food" as **CS^- trials** (read "CS plus" and "CS minus").

In the present example, the circle is a CS^+ trial and the ellipse is a CS^- trial. A *conditioned discrimination* is said to develop when the dog reliably salivates to CS^+ but not to CS^-. Note that in the present experiment the dog had to overcome an innate tendency to *generalize* from the circle to the ellipse.

Generalization and conditioned discriminations are readily measured in all contemporary conditioning methodologies. We shall return to these phenomena in Chapter 6 when the concept of *stimulus control* is introduced. A thought experiment: Assume that you became very, very sick after eating fresh pineapple. Would you be likely to eat pineapple sherbet during the next few days?[7] Why or why not?

---

[7]My conditioned aversion to the taste of pineapple generalized to pineapple-flavored preserves, pineapple-flavored Life Savers®, and *all* citrus fruit flavors of sherbet.

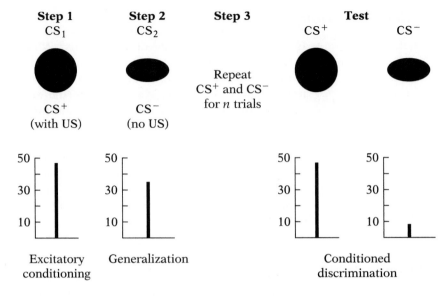

FIGURE 4.12   Generalization and Conditioned Discrimination

> The relationship of generalization to conditioned discrimination. In Step 1, a circle (the CS) is paired with food (the US) until salivation reliably occurs (excitatory conditioning). In Step 2, an ellipse rather than the circle is shown to the dog. The amount of salivation to the ellipse is more than would be expected in an unconditioned animal (not shown), but is less than to the circle CS. Salivation to the ellipse shows *generalization* from the circle. After repeated trials of circle-food, ellipse-no food, generalization disappears, and a conditioned discrimination of the circle and the ellipse is the result. As we will see in Chapter 5, the ellipse also acquires inhibitory properties.

Importance of Generalization and Discrimination

One goal of this text is to account for human behavior in the context of inherited and learned tendencies. The importance of the concept of generalization is that we can account for responses to stimuli that have never been experienced first hand. Learning one response to a particular situation generalizes to others. Our language reflects these properties, which are characteristic of all animal nervous systems. Following a particular experience (such as getting a traffic ticket in a school zone), we "learn" about similar situations never before encountered. Not only do I slow down in that particular school zone, I slow down in *all* school zones. That is, my learned response *generalizes* to other school zones, hospital zones, etc. I exhibit highly adaptive behavior, predicted from a limited but meaningful experience.

Likewise, if, after a bad experience with catfish at my favorite restaurant but a delightful experience with flounder, I can discriminate (differentiate) between the two stimuli, and not make the mistake of overgeneralization to all fish. The end result is that previous conditioning trials, limited in number that they are, through the processes of generalization and discrimination allow us to respond adaptively to new environments.

Summary

1. Animals are born both with relatively simple response tendencies, Sherringtonian reflexes, as well as more complex reflexlike behaviors such as immune system, brain, and endocrine system functioning.

2. Reflexive behavior can be modified by environmental experience using simple conditioning procedures developed by Ivan Pavlov and others. Reflexes, reflexive-like behaviors, and conditioned responses are adaptive in meeting niche requirements.

3. Reflexes readily enter into association with other stimuli in the environment and can be conditioned in a predictable manner. The predictability of conditioning presumably reflects both the lawfulness of physical stimuli in the environment and the underlying nature of the nervous system, which evolved in interaction with this environment.

4. Pavlovian salivary conditioning involves modification of the food-saliva reflex by pairing neutral sights and sounds (conditioned stimuli, or CSs) with food (unconditioned stimulus, or US) so that CSs produce the conditioned response (CR) of salivation.

5. Contemporary conditioning methodologies include (but are not restricted to) the following:

a. Eye-blink conditioning in rabbits and humans (CSs = tones; and air puffs to the cornea as USs)

b. Conditioned suppression (also known as conditioned fear responses) in rats (CSs = tones or lights; USs = electric shock)

c. Conditioned taste aversions in humans and rats (CSs = flavors; USs = toxins)

6. Five rules of conditioning are evidence of the lawfulness of association formation. Amount of conditioning is predicted by (1) number of trials; (2) and (3) CS and US intensity; (4) the time interval between CS and US; and (5) the sequence of stimulus events (either CS preceding US, or US preceding CS). Rules 2, 3, and 4 are collectively known as Pavlov's law of strength.

7. Experimental extinction is a measure of conditioning. In extinction the conditioned response is measured when the CS is presented in the absence of the US. The strength of association is measured by resistance-to-extinction. Following extinction, recovery of the conditioned response to a higher level is known as spontaneous recovery.

8. Contiguity and contingency theories of conditioning can be compared and contrasted. Contiguity refers to association of two stimuli occurring close together in time. Contingency refers to the probability that a given US is preceded by a CS, a value that varies between 0.0 and 1.0. The sequence of two stimuli is stressed, in which a first stimulus predicts (or not) the occurrence of a second stimulus.

9. Temporal contiguity is a necessary but not sufficient condition for association to occur. While some conditioning procedures (such as conditioned suppression) are amenable to a contingency analysis, contingency of stimuli is neither necessary nor sufficient for the associative conditioning process. Contingency accounts of conditioning are *always* confounded by contiguity of stimuli.

10. In addition to information processing models of contiguity and contingency, theories of association formation include the Rescorla–Wagner model, Razran's dominance-contiguity theory, and various neural models.

11. The Rescorla-Wagner model mathematically describes the growth of associative potential with each successive conditioning trial. The formula, $\Delta V_n = \mathring{a}\beta(\lambda - V_n)$, includes a role for CS ($\mathring{a}$) and US (β) salience (relative conditionability), the limit of conditioning (λ) and the number of conditioning trials (n) in the growth of associative potential (V).

12. Ralph Miller's comparator hypothesis posits that animals in conditioning situations compare what is happening to them in the presence of the CS with what is happening to them in the absence of the CS. Conditioning is said to occur when the US is reliably predicted by the CS, and, by comparison, when the US is not reliably predicted by other contextual cues.

14. Razran's dominance-contiguity theory stresses that the association that forms during conditioning takes place in the brain and is largely determined by the interaction of neural responses to the stimuli. For conditioning to occur, the neural response to the second of the two incoming stimuli must (in some unspecified way) dominate the neural response to the first stimulus.

15. At present the analysis of neural responses during conditioning does not provide an adequate theory of conditioning. Several diverse, promising methodologies involve simple-system approaches (measurement of individual neurons in the invertebrate Aplysia) and vertebrate research including both long-term potentiation (LTP) and cerebellar units.

16. Generalization and discrimination are perceptual processes that can be inferred in animals by measuring their responses to stimuli during and following conditioning. Responses generalize to similar stimuli, while similar stimuli can be discriminated by conditioning procedures.

Discussion Questions

1. Manual stimulation of the genitals typically produces sexual arousal. Erotic daydreams can also produce sexual arousal. Can you identify unconditioned and conditioned reflexes in this example?

2. For years *digitalis* has been used pharmacologically to stimulate the heart's pumping action, thereby increasing cardiac output. A typical daily dosage maintains a fairly constant level of digitalis in blood serum. Often patients maintained on this drug suffer both nausea and appetite suppression (anorexia), which physicians and pharmacologists alike treat as "side effects" of the drug's action. Can you make the case that some of the appetite disturbances might be learned?

3. To explain often means to be able to *verbalize the contingencies*—as in "I get a headache [*effect*] when my blood sugar

drops [*cause*]," or "I took an aspirin [*cause*] and my headache went away within the hour [*effect*]." But many medicines used in chronic conditions act over long periods of time. Among the reasons that physicians, pharmacologists, and patients alike think of "side effects" rather than "conditioning effects" when taking drugs is that a "conditioning trial" is less easily specified outside of a laboratory setting. For example, an elderly patient who feels bad all the time is less likely to attribute "feeling bad" to a single pill taken daily, even if that pill is responsible for chronic discomfort.

Now frame the foregoing in terms of the attribution of causality within *contingency* and *contiguity* frameworks. Is it obvious that contingency arguments *demand* discrete trials, and that conditioning over a longer time period is likely due to association by contiguity?

4. Flashing red or blue lights in rear-view mirrors reliably elicit fear responses in most people in our culture. Identify conditioning situations that have produced yet other fear-eliciting stimuli in your life.

5. Are you sometimes anxious without knowing why? Is it possible that there are fear-eliciting stimuli of which you are not conscious? Of which you are not aware? Of which you cannot verbalize the contingencies?

6. Compared with the occasional observer, sports fanatics enjoy athletic contests at a different level. In knowing the intricacies and nuances of the game, including the players and the win-loss records, fanatics can be characterized as more discriminating observers. Given the relationship between *generalization* and *discrimination*, how would you characterize the occasional observer? What experiences enhance the fanatic's *discrimination* abilities? Why is a 3-2 pitch "not just another pitch"?

7. Is it likely that a human suffering cortical damage in an automobile accident would no longer be able to be classically conditioned? Why or why not?

Glossary

Appetitive Conditioning (Pavlov) Food-based Pavlovian conditioning (cf. appetite).

Association The relationship (connection, union) that results when two or more stimuli are paired together in time.

Aversive Conditioning Conditioning experiments using aversive unconditioned stimuli (as opposed to an appetitive food stimulus). Three contemporary *aversive* conditioning procedures are eye-blink conditioning, conditioned suppression, and taste aversion conditioning, employing aversive air puffs to the eye, electric shock, and toxins, respectively.

Backward Conditioning (Pavlov) A conditioning procedure in which the onset of the unconditioned stimulus precedes the onset of the conditioned stimulus. Both inhibitory conditioning (often) and excitatory conditioning (rarely) can result from backwards pairings of US and CS. (Also referred to as a *negative contingency* between the CS and the US.)

Baseline The preexperimental, or normal level of a measured response. The baseline often constitutes the control condition to which the effects of an experimental treatment are compared.

Classical Conditioning (see *Pavlovian conditioning*)

Conditioned Discrimination A procedure used to train an animal to discriminate and respond differently to two different stimuli. One stimulus (CS⁺) is reliably paired with an unconditioned stimulus, and on alternating trials, another stimulus (CS⁻) is not paired with the US. The animal learns to respond to CS⁺ and to not respond to CS⁻, thereby demonstrating that it can *discriminate* one from the other. (Cf. *generalization,* in which an animal responds in a *similar* manner to different stimuli.)

Conditioned Emotional Response The outcome of an experimental treatment in which emotional responses are conditioned to neutral (non–emotion-inducing) stimuli. (cf. fear conditioning; *conditioned suppression*).

Conditioned Response (CR) (Cf. Pavlov's conditioned reflex) Following pairings of a neutral stimulus (i.e., the CS) with an unconditioned stimulus, a new response, called a *conditioned response,* is learned to CS. Salivation to the sound of a bell is an example of a conditioned response.

Conditioned Stimulus (CS) (Pavlov) Following pairings with an unconditioned stimulus (i.e., food), a stimulus such as the sound of a bell can come to control a new response such as salivation. The bell's sound is initially "neutral"—it doesn't make the animal salivate. The bell is called a *conditioned stimulus* when, after conditioning with food, the animal salivates to the sound of the bell.

Conditioned Suppression A laboratory technique used to measure aversive (fear) conditioning. A neutral stimulus is paired with electric shock while an animal is lever pressing for food. Following tone-shock conditioning, the tone disrupts (suppresses) lever pressing, allowing the experimenter to easily quantify the amount of fear conditioning the animal has experienced.

Contiguity Theory of Association The theory that stimulus-stimulus associations occur because the animal perceives the two stimuli close together (cf. contiguous) in time.

Contingency Theory of Association The theory that stimulus-stimulus associations occur because the animal perceives the relationship, or pattern, or sequence, of one stimulus preceding and *signaling* the occurrence of a second stimulus.

CS⁺ and CS⁻ Trials In a conditioned discrimination procedure, an animal is taught to discriminate between two different CSs by pairing one with food (called *CS⁺* trials) and the other CS without food (called *CS⁻* trials). Following training, the animal responds in extinction to CS⁺ but not to CS⁻. CS⁺ trials yield excitatory conditioning, and CS⁻ trials, inhibitory conditioning.

CS-US Interval During conditioning, the CS and the US are related to each other by time. By convention, the *CS-US interval* is measured from the onset of the conditioned stimulus to the onset of the unconditioned stimulus.

Defense Conditioning (Pavlov) In contrast to his food-based appetitive conditioning experiments, Pavlov used the term *defense conditioning* to describe experiments that used aversive unconditioned stimuli (i.e., sour solutions placed on the tongue; electric shock to condition a leg-withdrawal reflex, etc.). Experiments using aversive USs are now referred to as *aversive conditioning.*

Embedded Conditioning A variation of simultaneous conditioning in which the onset and offset of either the CS or US occurs during (i.e., *embedded in the middle of*) presentation of the other element. Embedded conditioning situations often involve the pairing of long-duration stimuli, such as flavors experienced during meals, sensory events during drug effects, etc.

Excitatory Conditioning (Pavlov) "Normal" forward conditioning in which a CS is paired with a US, and the conditioned response resembles the unconditioned response.

Extinction (Experimental Extinction) (Pavlov) Following conditioning, when the CS continues to be presented without the US, the conditioned response diminishes. The conditioned response is said to *extinguish*, and the procedure is called *extinction*, or *experimental extinction*. When, after instrumental conditioning, a response is no longer reinforced or punished, the response tends to *extinguish* to its preconditioning, or baseline, level. This treatment is also called extinction.

Extinction Curve (or **Extinction Gradient**) During extinction, a plot of the magnitude of the conditioned response as a function of extinction trials is called an *extinction curve* (or *extinction gradient*). In a typical extinction curve, response magnitude diminishes to preconditioning levels.

Forward Conditioning (Pavlov) In forward conditioning the CS onset precedes the US onset, and both stimuli overlap somewhat in time. Forward conditioning is the most common form of "normal" excitatory conditioning; an example is a bell CS followed immediately by a food US.

Generalization The tendency of animals to both perceive *(stimulus generalization)* and to respond *(response general-*

ization) in a similar manner to stimuli that share common properties.

Habituation Control Group A nonassociative control group that is presented only the CS during conditioning. The manner in which this group responds to the CS following conditioning provides a basis for comparison with the association formed in a CS-US treatment group.

Internal Inhibition (Pavlov) A term Pavlov used to account for the loss of a conditioned response during an extinction procedure. Spontaneous recovery was interpreted by Pavlov as evidence for an active process of *internal* inhibition (i.e., within the dog), as opposed to the disruptive effects of an *external* inhibitor (i.e., a stimulus occurring external to the dog).

Intertrial Interval The elapsed time between conditioning trials in a conditioning experiment.

Law of Strength (Pavlov) Three interrelated factors that account for the *strength* (or magnitude) of a conditioned response are the intensity of the CS, the intensity of the US, and a close interstimulus interval between the CS and US.

Long-Term Potentiation (LTP) Neurons rapidly stimulated for a brief time show *potentiation* (increased responsiveness) lasting for days and even weeks. LTP may mediate associative effects between neurons.

Orienting Reflex (Pavlov) When a CS such as a tone is first sounded, a dog will prick up its ears and turns its head, locating the source of the sound. Pavlov labeled this response an *orienting reflex*.

Pavlovian Conditioning An experimental procedure in which a basic *reflex*, consisting of an *unconditioned stimu-*

lus *(US)* and an *unconditioned response (UR),* is paired in time with a neutral stimulus (called the *conditioned stimulus, CS*). After several pairings, the CS by itself can elicit components of the original reflex, called the *conditioned response (CR).* (Also called *conditioning,* and *classical conditioning.*)

Psychic Secretion (Pavlov) Pavlov's term for salivation attributable to psychological factors—the dog's thoughts, memories, expectations, prior learning, etc.—rather than due to a physiological reflex.

Random Control Group A nonassociative control group in which the CS and US are both presented separately, never together, in time.

Razran's Dominance-Contiguity Theory A modification of Pavlov's basic theory of conditioning that (a) focused upon the associability of an animal's *responses* to CSs and USs, rather than the stimuli; (b) stressed the role of contiguity over contingency; and (c) postulated that the second of two stimulus events must "dominate" the first for association to occur.

Reflex An innate, involuntarily response an animal makes to a specific stimulus in the environment. Iris closure in response to sudden bright light is an example.

Rescorla–Wagner Model Rescorla and Wagner modeled the growth of association during conditioning (a) by quantifying the effects of using stimuli of different novelty and salience; (b) by predicting and quantifying the greater growth of associative potential in early training trials; and (c) by predicting and quantifying the effects of extinction and blocking procedures.

Resistance-to-Extinction Comparing the number of extinction trials necessary for a conditioned response to extinguish provides an indirect measure of the amount of conditioning that has occurred. As a general rule, greater *resistance-to-extinction* is found following many conditioning trials as compared with a few conditioning trials.

Salience A descriptive (not explanatory) term, the *salience* of a stimulus refers to its relative associability. More *salient* stimuli are more easily conditioned.

Salivary Reflex Food placed on a dog's tongue elicits reflexive salivation.

Sensitization Control Group A nonassociative control group exposed only to the US during conditioning. The manner in which this group responds to the CS following conditioning provides a basis for comparison with the association formed in a CS-US treatment group. The *sensitization* control group is sometimes called a *pseudoconditioning* control.

Sherringtonian Reflex A reflex characterized by an identifiable *sensory neuron* synapsing upon an identifiable *interneuron* and *motor neuron.*

Simultaneous Conditioning (Pavlov) The CS and US have identical onsets, durations, and offsets in simultaneous conditioning. Very little conditioning results in these trials.

Spontaneous Recovery (Pavlov) The reappearance of a higher level of conditioned response following a delay in the extinction process.

Taste Aversion Conditioning A method of studying aversive Pavlovian conditioning in which rats are allowed to drink a flavored solution (the CS) and then are made sick by giving them an illness-inducing toxin (the US). Conditioned taste aversions to the target flavor result from one or a few pairings.

Temporal Conditioning (Pavlov)   A varia- tion of conditioning in which dogs are presented food at regular intervals. After many such trials, salivation is found to occur just prior to food ad- ministration. Pavlov interpreted these results by postulating that the inter- food time interval had acquired condi- tioned stimulus properties, and that the salivation was a conditioned response.

Temporal Contiguity   Two or more events closely related together in time are said to be temporally contiguous.

Trace Conditioning (Pavlov)   *Trace condi- tioning* is a special example of forward conditioning in which both the CS onset *and offset* precede the US onset. Historically, the term "trace" refers to a hypothetical memory trace that re- mains after the termination of the stimulus.

Trial   A *trial* consists of a CS-US pairing.

Unconditioned Response (UR)   (Pavlov) The reflexive response to an uncondi- tioned stimulus (the US). Salivation is the unconditioned response to food.

Unconditioned Stimulus (US) (Pavlov)   A stimulus that innately, involuntarily, elicits a reflexive response (i.e., the UR). Food is an unconditioned stimu- lus that elicits reflexive salivation.

5

Complexities of Conditioning

I. Introduction

Learning in Natural Environments and in Laboratories

Many learning experiments on caged animals appear to lack in **ecological validity.** To be ecologically valid an experiment should ask an animal to learn a task that is likely to be encountered in the animal's ecological niche. Learning about foods, the location of predators, and to use language are examples of ecologically valid tasks.

Association of Simple and Complex Stimuli.   In Chapter 2 we learned that questions of ecological validity were more a concern of ethologists than comparative psychologists. How can we best understand animal behavior in natural environments? Too often, ethologists argue, the precision that laboratory researchers achieve by using carefully timed sequences of bells and whistles, flashing lights, tiny food rewards, and brief electric shocks limits the real-life applicability of experimental results.

But laboratory researchers are placed in a Catch-22 situation by this criticism. Why? Because scientific analysis suffers as more variables are left uncontrolled. When animals are confronted with complex stimulus situations in laboratories, similar to what they might encounter in a "natural" environment, their responses become more multidimensional and less predictable.

Another issue raised in Chapter 2 concerned the problem of extrapolation of results attained from laboratory research. Given the differing evolutionary histories of animals, and the different niches they occupied, was it reasonable to think about "learning" as a general process shared by all species. Does research on learning processes in rats have any relevance for dogs, or vice versa, and do you really think research on either animal has anything to do with humans?

One question that will be addressed in this chapter, then, concerns the adequacy of the animal conditioning models described in Chapter 4:

> *Question 1. Can a relatively simple associative theory (such as Pavlovian conditioning) account for how humans and animals learn ecologically valid tasks in the laboratory as well as in natural environments?*

Naive Animals.   In addition to questions of ecological validity and stimulus complexity, laboratory studies are typically short term in nature. Most experiments encountered so far, in this and in succeeding chapters, use naive animals in short-term learning experiments. By naive, researchers mean that animals employed in a given learning experiment are inexperienced and have not been "used" before.[1]

Learning Influences Learning.   Why do experimenters typically use naive laboratory animals? Because what an animal has previously learned is presumed to bias the results of the next experiment. The animal's responses being measured now may not be solely attributed to the independent variables in this treatment condition, but rather to a combination (cf. interaction) of the present and previous treatment conditions.

The problem of how prior learning affects subsequent learning has practical implications. College algebra teachers, for example, are often heard decrying the methods by which their college students were taught algebra while in high school. What students previously learned, they argue, often interferes with the student's performance in college classrooms. Furthermore, given the variation of high school learning experiences students bring to college, it difficult to judge the effectiveness, for example, of two classroom methodologies, such as comparing an algebra lecture method with an interactive computerized tutorial. Some students may be better prepared through prior learning to do better under one or the other "new" methods.

Obviously, what is called for is research that addresses how prior learning affects new learning. Many of the experiments described in this chapter provide answers to the knotty question of "prior experience."

> *Question 2. Can the many ways in which prior learning affects present learning be investigated in the laboratory using a relatively simple associative methodology such as Pavlovian conditioning?*

Why is this an important question? If it turns out that laboratory analyses of behavior are merely esoteric exercises—games that researchers play to test meaningless theories—ultimately, no matter how interesting the experiments may be, such research is worthless. Questions of ecological validity and behavioral complexity present very real problems for laboratory analyses of learning and behavior. As we will see, psychologists and other neuroscientists have been

---

[1]After naive animals have been used in experiments they are often called "dirty" animals. Where this vernacular came from is unclear. One possibility is that the mind of a naive animal that is to be used in a learning experiment can be considered a *tabula rasa* (John Locke's "blank slate") upon which experience "writes." Once used in an experiment, the slate is dirty, as in "dirty blackboard."

most clever in designing meaningful laboratory studies that accurately model complex human behavior.

Chapter Preview

Introducing Complexity into the Laboratory. This chapter attempts to address the foregoing criticisms of laboratory research by noting what happens when complexity is introduced into conditioning experiments. What happens when prior learning experiences *are* allowed to interact with current learning situations? Is all predictability lost, and with it the possibility of a scientific analysis of behavior? Is it indeed the case that a scientific analysis of two learning methodologies in a college algebra classroom is not possible because students have had a myriad of prior learning experiences?

As we saw in Chapter 4, simple conditioned responses may result when one CS enters into association with one US. It is in fact the case, however, that environments seldom present us with such solitary, "simple" stimulus events. Does predictability disappear when several stimuli are placed in contiguous or contingent arrangements? When "natural" stimuli are used? When the duration of the CS and US is varied from fractions of a second to minutes and even hours? When a stimulus is one the animal is already familiar with?

> *Question 3. Is it possible to mirror in the laboratory the complexity presented by "nature"? To deconstruct nature into simple stimulus elements, accomplish associative experiments, analyze results, and then reconstruct and synthesize the complex behavior of animals (humans) going about their business of living in their niches?*

Many experiments presented in this chapter adopt this strategy. The environmental *context* in which experiments are conducted in *laboratories* can be understood as the laboratory animal's ecological niche. This niche, or context, includes home-cage housing, feeding schedules, laboratory light/dark cycles, experimental chambers, prior learning experiences, and interactions with human caretakers *as well as stimulus-response interactions* during the brief time an experiment is being conducted.

Human learning also occurs in contexts of classrooms, automobiles, televisions, meals, and interactions with other humans. That is, a human's ecological niche is in many ways as artificial as that of a laboratory animal (see Richter, 1942). Research begun by Pavlov and continued by others indeed addresses the complexity of human and animal behavior in laboratory environments. We shall see that *latent* and *conditioned inhibition, blocking, overshadowing, higher-order conditioning,* and *potentiation* are among the many possible outcomes of these stimulus-response interactions in complex laboratory environments.

Failures of Conditioning?   The concluding section of this chapter is concerned with apparent failures of conditioning theory. Why do animals learn some responses after a single experience and yet fail to learn others after many trials? Sound familiar? How is it possible that humans are able to remember a face over a period of many years even after a brief meeting, while an acquaintance's name may escape you even as you interact! Why is it that we can conjure up a face by merely hearing the person's voice on the phone, yet have such a hard time making name-face associations?

As we saw in Chapter 4, rats and humans can learn flavor-illness associations in one trial; dogs can learn bell-food associations in about seven trials; and yet rabbits and humans require dozens (in some cases hundreds) of eye-blink conditioning trials. Why? How?

> *Question 4. Why are certain stimuli and certain responses in certain animals conditioned relatively easily, and why do others apparently fail to be conditioned?*

Analysis of Complex Conditioning: An Ecologically Valid Example. Resolution of these so-called "failures" of conditioning will ultimately help us to better understand the lawfulness of associative learning. Can learning theory help us understand complex human behavior? Let us look at the example given in Box 5.1.

We will come back to this taste aversion conditioning example for further analysis. You may want to re-read the vignette and review the questions again before continuing. It is likely that you already have several hypotheses for Tracy's, Candace's, and Carlos's behavior, and you may even want to take a minute to jot down in the margins your best guesses for their differences.

Analyzing the complexities of their behavior will be made possible by applying results of laboratory animal experiments. Unless you already have a good background in learning theory, you will probably be surprised by the range and sophistication of arguments that can be brought to bear on their human behavior, based upon laboratory animal experiments. By the end of the chapter you will have a better idea why Candace, Tracy, and Carlos learned, remembered, and behaved as they did.

Let us get on with it.

BOX 5.1

Conditioning Food Aversions

Three years ago, Candace and Tracy, identical twins living in a rural part of Nebraska, came to Miami, Florida, to visit their cousin Carlos. All three had previously eaten pepperoni pizza and were hungry for it, so Carlos took them to his favorite restaurant, *Momma Rollo's*. Neither Candace nor Tracy had eaten at Momma Rollo's before this occasion.

In addition to the pepperoni pizza, Candace and Carlos each ordered a can of Dr. Spicey®, while Tracy drank only water. Since Dr. Spicey® was unavailable in rural Nebraska, neither Candace nor Tracy had ever before experienced its distinctive taste. All ate three slices of the pepperoni pizza.

Hours later, the twins became sick, including both nausea and vomiting. Carlos felt okay, and a phone call home confirmed that the twins' mother was sick. Because Carlos did not get sick, and their mother was, Candace and Tracy reluctantly concluded that their meal at Momma Rollo's did *not* make them sick, and that they probably had a stomach virus brought with them from Nebraska.

After this incident the following changes in their behavior were noted:

1. For several months after returning to Nebraska neither Candace nor Tracy had any desire to eat pizza. Why?*

---

* You probably know the answer to this question already, since taste aversion conditioning was discussed in Chapter 4. Other experiments presented in this chapter will help you answer the remaining questions.

2. Carlos returned to Momma Rollo's three weeks later and ate pepperoni pizza. Why the difference between Carlos's and the twins' behavior?

3. (Assume that prior to their experience at Momma Rollo's the twins had identical taste preferences.) After several months elapsed the twins begin to eat pizza again. Candace orders a cheese topping only, and Tracy, a sausage pizza. Why did neither order pepperoni? What is your hypothesis as to why Candace ordered a cheese topping rather than sausage?

4. Two days after the illness incident (while still in Florida) Tracy drank a Dr. Spicey® at Tom's apartment and loved it. Candace still dislikes the taste of Dr. Spicey® three years later. Why the difference?

5. After the illness incident Candace dislikes Dr. Spicey® more than she dislikes pepperoni pizza. Why the difference?

6. Candace and Tracy visit Carlos one year after the illness episode. Candace says she will eat pizza but would rather not go back to Momma Rollo's; Tracy also says she will eat pizza, and, furthermore, she is indifferent about the choice of restaurant. Why do the twins respond to Momma Rollo's restaurant differently after one year?

7. Candace says "just mentioning 'Dr. Spicey®' or seeing the Dr. Spicey® can makes me ill." Why?

II. Learning and Relearning: Effects of Prior Experience on Conditioning New Responses

Latent Inhibition

Pavlov was the first experimenter to observe that a *novel* CS more readily entered into association with an unconditioned stimulus than did a *familiar* CS. That is, he found that if a dog had previously heard a bell, whistle, or metronome of a particular timbre and intensity before the stimulus was used as a conditioned stimulus in pairings with food, the dog required more CS-US trials to acquire a conditioned response. Novel stimuli condition more easily than familiar stimuli.

A systematic demonstration that familiar stimuli condition less readily than novel stimuli was made by Lubow, who called the phenomenon **latent inhibition** (Lubow & Moore, 1959; Lubow, 1989). Many demonstrations of latent inhibition, also known as the **CS preexposure effect,** now exist. Familiar stimuli have less *associative potential* than novel stimuli in the same way that more intense CSs and USs have greater associative potential than weaker CSs and USs. The latent inhibition effect is diagrammed in Figure 5.1.

Similar differences are also found to exist between novel and familiar unconditioned stimuli (cf. **US preexposure effect,** Randich &

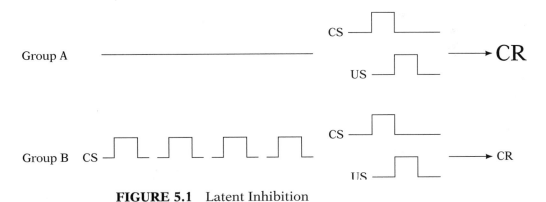

FIGURE 5.1   Latent Inhibition

If a conditioned stimulus (such as a tone) is presented several times before it is paired with an unconditioned stimulus (for example, food) in a conditioning situation (B), the conditioned response (salivation) is less than if the conditioned stimulus was novel (A). The same design (not shown) substituting the US as the preexposed stimulus would yield similar results following conditioning.

LoLordo, 1979). That is, if an animal is exposed to a drug, an electric shock, or a food reinforcement prior to using these stimuli in conditioning a novel CS, less association of that CS with the US occurs.

Why Are Familiar Stimuli Less Easily Conditioned? Hypotheses abound as to why familiar stimuli are less readily conditioned than novel stimuli. The question is an important one. With apologies to Pavlov, the adage "you can't teach an old dog new tricks" comes to mind. Probably the saying refers more to "being set in one's ways" than it does with the inability of an aging brain to learn new tasks. Prior experience *does* influence later learning, and the latent inhibition phenomenon may be the most elementary demonstration of this point.

Nonassociative Theories of Latent Inhibition. Students often confuse *habituation* with *latent inhibition,* and for good reason. The two phenomena are similar. Habituation refers to response diminution following repeated presentations of a stimulus; latent inhibition refers to lowered associability when a familiar stimulus is used in conditioning. The orienting response is diminished in both cases; humans and animals so habituated appear to pay less attention to the familiar stimulus.

One theory proposed to account for the latent inhibition effect, then, is *nonassociative.* Stimuli that have become habituated, and that capture less attention during conditioning, are less associable than novel stimuli to which attention is directed.

The habituation hypothesis has a particularly difficult time accounting for the *US preexposure effect*. By definition, USs are less susceptible to habituation, and are more "attention getting" than are CSs. And yet, preexposed USs (including even electric shock; Baker & Mackintosh, 1977) do not work as well as novel USs in conditioning. Both CS and US preexposure effects seem to be better accounted for by associative theories.

Associative Theories of Latent Inhibition

In addition to the nonassociative theory involving reduced attention-capturing properties of familiar stimuli, two associative theories of latent inhibition have been proposed:

1. *Interference Theory of Latent Inhibition.* In this theory, presenting the CS alone allows the CS to become associated with background contextual cues, thereby effectively becoming part of (merging with) the context. The signal-to-noise ratio of the CS is diminished; the now familiar CS is less a signal and more a part of

the background, reducing its associative potential (Wagner, 1976). These prior associations of the CS with other contextual cues are presumed to interfere with the formation of new associations.

2. *Learned Irrelevance Theory of Latent Inhibition.* A second associative theory also posits that associations are made when the CS is presented alone, prior to conditioning with a US. The animal learns that the CS does not predict anything new; hence, an "association" is made between the CS and "nothing new." According to this theory the CS becomes irrelevant (Baker & Mackintosh, 1977; Kalat, 1977) to an information processing animal.

Comparing Theories of Latent Inhibition. Closer to the truth would be a revised saying that "it is *more difficult* to teach an old dog new tricks." Older animals (do not forget humans) typically have been exposed to more environments, have encountered more stimuli, and have made more associations—you have both experienced more and learned more now compared with 10 years ago.

In Chapter 2, habituation was characterized (a) as being nonassociative, and (b) as a "theory" that accounted for a large proportion of your environmentally determined behavior (i.e., "learning" that most of the stimuli you sense in your immediate environment can be ignored). The phenomenon of latent inhibition may be an even more likely explanation for what we learn (and do not learn) during the course of our lifetimes. Let us compare the theories of habituation and latent inhibition by way of an example.

Algebra, Algebra, and More Algebra. The first day of class in a new school. You are awash in a sea of new faces, new desks, smells, and sounds. You are alert. You are excited. You are processing your environment at an incredible rate (many orienting responses to rapidly changing stimuli). If you are a new student in a new country, the amount of new information may be overwhelming.

The college classroom context in which you find yourself is composed of a combination of new and old experiences. That is, classrooms have features in common with most institutional buildings. In this classroom, you may notice windows (if most other classrooms you have sat in did not have them) or not notice windows (if most other classrooms you have experienced *did* have them). Padded seats noticed, or not. Amphitheater noticed, or not. The signaling strength of any stimulus in this new classroom is related to its novelty as well as to its intensity.

This new algebra classroom signals other previously learned associations as well. You experienced failure in a high school algebra class that shared many features: "Algebra" written on the blackboard, formulas, a textbook with the word "Algebra" written on it, and other students who by their verbal and nonverbal behavior expressed the anxiety you now feel. The instructor writes on the board a "familiar" equation:

$$y = ax + b.$$

You recognize the equation as one you have seen before but were unable to master in a previous class. Your heart sinks, as does your performance.

Skip to the end of the semester. You now realize that only with great difficulty were you able to understand *this* equation, $y = ax + b$, though you readily learned several novel equations (ones that you had not previously seen). Why? Which of the following theories best accounts for your behavior?

Habituation Hypothesis.   According to the habituation hypothesis you would be less likely to learn new associations to familiar stimuli because familiar stimuli are attended to less than novel stimuli. (I doubt it. Evidence to the contrary would be the sinking feeling you had when *that* equation was written on the board. No lack of orienting response there!) Rather, the evidence presented here leads to the conclusion that the difficulty of forming new associations to the equation $y = ax + b$ was *not* due to habituation to the stimulus.

Learned Irrelevance Hypothesis.   According to the learned irrelevance hypothesis, you had more trouble learning $y = ax + b$ because the equation had been previously associated with other events and no longer predicted anything new when reencountered in the college classroom. Hardly! We have already determined that you associated the formula $y = ax + b$ with anxiety and feelings of failure. Nothing irrelevant about *this* particular equation. In this example the learned irrelevance hypothesis does not apply.[2]

Associative Interference Hypothesis.   The clue to understanding how prior associations with a stimulus can influence new associations with that stimulus is readily evident in this example. Stimuli in previous algebra classrooms shared common contextual features with the equation $y = ax + b$. Presumably, the equation, blackboards, textbooks, and anxiety became associated together (we will see how, later). The "new" classroom is a complex CS eliciting both anxiety and "feelings of failure." The new teacher's job, moreover, is to somehow explicate the latently inhibited "$y = ax + b$" stimulus from the "math phobia stimulus

---

[2]You could make the case that for some individuals $y = ax + b$ is both familiar and is "irrelevant" in the sense that the student verbalizes no interest in math; i.e., "math is irrelevant to what I want to do with my life." The *learned irrelevance hypothesis* does not address this cognitive usage of the term *irrelevance*.

context" in which it occurs. Until that is done, new associations to the equation will be learned only with great difficulty. (More will be said about the formation and treatment of phobias in Chapter 8.)

In summary, the extent to which you had difficulty making new associations to the equation $y = ax + b$ can be attributed to two prior associations: (a) the equation "merged" into (became associated with other features of) the contextual background, in effect, becoming part of it, and (b) the equation was conditioned through association with an aversive state of anxiety and other emotional stimuli relating to failed expectations.

Are you able to apply what you have learned about *latent inhibition?* In Box 5.1 (question 5) you are asked to provide a hypothesis to account for the fact that Candace dislikes Dr. Spicey® more than she dislikes pepperoni pizza after a sickness experience. Reread the account of conditioning, and see if you can relate latent inhibition to Candace's observed behavior. Again, for future reference you might want to jot down your hypothesis in the margin.

Sensory Preconditioning

In the foregoing example the observant reader may have wondered how blackboards, the word "algebra," formulas, textbooks, and faces can become associated together in a college classroom. All are stimuli, but where is the *unconditioned* stimulus (such as food, electric shock, illness-inducing toxin, etc.) that we have noted in all previous examples of conditioning? How can CSs become associated with each other in the absence of USs? Is a CS_1-CS_2 association possible?

One honest answer is that our theories of association are not adequate in providing an answer to this question. In fact, we typically measure CS-CS associations only indirectly. One method called **sensory preconditioning** is outlined in Figure 5.2.

In Figure 5.2 note that prior to conditioning with an unconditioned stimulus (which is depicted in the middle panels for both Groups A and B) conditioned stimuli are presented together (Group A) or separately (Group B). CS_1 is then conditioned to a US in both groups, and CS_2 is tested in extinction in both groups (right panel). CS_2 yields a conditioned response only in Group A, animals that had experienced CS_1 and CS_2 together in time.

The importance of sensory preconditioning lies in the fact that we can understand "background context" as a stimulus complex of associated elements—associated because these stimuli are experienced together. The reader is referred to Figure 3.5, cell d, on p. 86. When we attempt to condition a CS with a CS, a CS with a US, or a US with a US, the contextual background, held together in associative fashion, is always present.

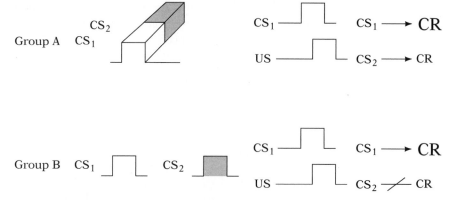

FIGURE 5.2   Sensory Preconditioning

Prior exposure to CS_1 and CS_2 *simultaneously presented together* (Group A, left panel) produces a CR to both CS_1 and CS_2 (right panel) after CS_1 alone is conditioned with a US (middle panel). Compare with Control Group B, in which CS_1 and CS_2 are first presented *separate from each other* (left panel). In this case, conditioning CS_1 does *not* produce a CR to CS_2 (right panel). Why is the CR larger to CS_1 than to CS_2 in Group A? Example: Let CS_1 = the equation $y = ax + b$; CS_2 = the blackboard; US = a punishing stimulus (such as the teacher's saying "wrong")—or simply not understanding what is going on when other students apparently do. Any combination of these US events produces the stress of failure, associated with the stimulus complex of equation, blackboard, "school," etc.

Returning to the algebra classroom example, it is unlikely that a student can ever "start over" or follow an instructor's advice to "forget everything you have learned [meaning 'mislearned'] before." Too many contextual stimuli with prior negative associations are always present to wipe the slate clean and start over. Relearning is, of course, possible; from what we have learned in Chapter 4, one form of remediation would be to extinguish aversive conditioned responses by presenting the stimuli ("$y = ax + b$," the blackboard, etc.) without the negative USs. That is, to extinguish the emotional responses that were previously conditioned.

Pavlov's Second Signal System

How can the word "algebra" come to evoke anxiety? Pavlov described how words can become conditioned stimuli and can come to control conditioned responses. He called "words as CSs" the **second signal system** (Pavlov, 1927).

Pavlov reasoned that all words derive their meaning by *association* with signals from the environment. For example, seeing an apple is a signal, which, in his terminology, stimulates the animal's "visual analyzer." The visual representation of the apple is a signal of the real-world apple, one level of reality removed. Attaching the word "apple" to the visual signal of the apple is accomplished by the second signal system. The word "apple" is yet another level of reality removed from the real-world apple.

The apple is real. "Seeing" the apple is the first signal of the real apple. Naming the apple "apple" is the second signal of the apple—hence, the *second signal system*.

Pavlov further avowed that conditioning in the second signal system was no different from standard conditioning—all the rules governing the formation of conditioned responses applied equally to language. That is, a parent interacting with a child who is learning to talk typically presents to the child objects, relations, actions, etc., and names them in close temporal contiguity—"apple" for apple, "water" for water, "hot" for a heated object, etc. More often than not repetitions of word-with-object (i.e., trials) are necessary. Additionally, more intense stimuli lead to more rapid learning; the direction of stimulus presentation is important, etc. (you may want to review the "rules of conditioning" in Chapter 4).

Pavlov's observations are important for a number of reasons. Humans make only about 40 phonemic sounds, but language patterns using these sounds vary widely across cultures. Languages as spoken sounds are meaningful only to the extent that particular sounds are associated with the environment through the process of Pavlovian conditioning.

The nature of the word-object or word-activity associations determines the meaning of the word. "Algebra" has a different meaning to a mathematician than to a failing student. The word "algebra" produces different conditioned responses for the *A* and the *F* student. For a small child, no associations to the word "algebra" have formed. But most small children come to know the meaning of "good" and "no" early in their language environment.

How do "good" and "no" acquire motivating properties? And why do some students have a sinking feeling when they merely look at their algebra textbook?

Higher-Order Conditioning

In the college classroom example we have been examining, blackboards, formulas, textbooks, and the student's anxiety were identified as stimuli that had become associated together. "Anxiety" and "fear" are not neutral stimuli but are obviously an integral part of "math phobia." Given that algebra-related stimuli are initially neutral, by what process can students form fear associations to them?

In Chapter 4 we saw that when a tone is paired with an electric shock in rats (and, in Box 4.1, when a "dee doo" sound is associated with a nasty sled ride), the auditory stimulus comes to produce a *conditioned emotion response (CER)*. Another name for a CER is a *conditioned fear response*. In the college classroom, "fear of failure" is best understood as a conditioned response (CR). Can we account for how a conditioned fear response can in turn be used to condition associations with new CSs?

The process of **higher-order conditioning** was initially described by Pavlov. The procedures differ, but the outcome of higher-order conditioning resembles sensory preconditioning in one respect; both are associative conditioning processes in which there is no unconditioned stimulus.

Remember Pavlov's distinction between the stimuli he called CSs and those he labeled as USs; the latter are "biologically meaningful" to the animal (i.e., food, water, pain, etc.). In *higher-order conditioning* the end result is to take an arbitrary stimulus, such as a sound, and show that it has acquired unconditioned stimulus properties.

A three-step process illustrating two levels of higher-order conditioning is presented in Figure 5.3. Pavlov (1927) describes an experiment in which a dog is conditioned in Step 1 to salivate to the sound of a metronome [CS_1] in pairings with food (the US). Then, in Step 2, for 10 trials, "a black square [CS_2] is held in front of the dog for ten seconds, and after an interval of fifteen seconds the metronome is sounded during thirty seconds."

On the tenth trial Pavlov reported that the dog salivated 5.5 drops to the black square, compared with a range of 9.5 to 13.5 drops of conditioned salivation to the sound of the metronome. Note that the black square had never been directly associated with food, yet a response had been conditioned to it. Pavlov called this phenomenon **second-order conditioning** (Pavlov, 1927, p. 34).

Interestingly enough, Pavlov reports that he was able to accomplish *third-order conditioning* (see Step 3, Figure 5.3) only when he conditioned his dogs with an electric shock US. That is, he could not use the food-based conditioned response to the black square to condition yet a third stimulus. (Apparently the conditioned response established by a food reward was not powerful enough?)

Pavlov then reports the results of experiments by Dr. Foursikov, another researcher in his laboratory. First, Foursikov elaborated a leg-withdrawal conditioned response (CS = touching the hind paw, US = briefly shocking the front paw, CR = withdrawing the front paw when the hind paw is touched). He then presented the sound of bub-

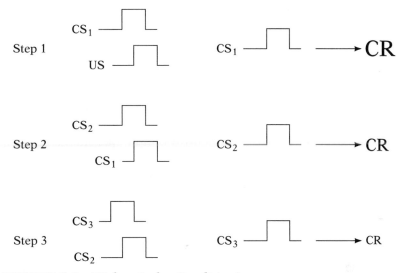

FIGURE 5.3 Higher-Order Conditioning

A stimulus associated with the US in Step 1 acquires US-like properties. Note that even in the absence of a US in Steps 2 and 3, conditioning nevertheless occurs due to these US-like properties.

bling water (CS_2), followed by touching the hind paw (CS_1). Second-order conditioned was noted. Finally, Foursikov presented a tone (CS_3), which he paired with the sound of bubbling water (CS_2). After a number of pairings CS_3 (the tone), when sounded alone, would produce the conditioned response of paw withdrawal (Step 3, Figure 5.3). Such "conditioning of the third order" along with the more common second-order conditioning are collectively known as higher-order conditioning.

The significance of higher-order conditioning is twofold; first, it provides a process by which associative conditioning can occur in the absence of an unconditioned stimulus, and second, it further demonstrates that prior conditioning experiences can continue to have a persisting influence on the present. Once neutral stimuli are conditioned, they can in turn be used to condition other responses.

Let us continue with the language example. Most humans inhabit language-rich environments. As we saw previously, language attains meaning through associative processes. Let us look at the possibilities presented by the higher-order conditioning of language. Referring back to Step 1 in Figure 5.3, let CS_1 be the word "no" and the "biologically meaningful" US be a stimulus complex represented by a parental figure. The parental figure's voice (intonation, intensity, etc.)

or the parent's withdrawal of affection (or physical punishment, or a "time-out," etc.) is each a potentially aversive US that enters into association with the word "no." In Step 1, then, the word "no" acquires punishing/fear-inducing properties not unlike those acquired by the tone in tone-shock conditioning.

CS_1, the word "no," can now be used in association with other neutral stimuli in second-order conditioning during Step 2.[3] The conditioned emotional responses associated with the word "no" can now attach to other neutral stimuli. Back in the classroom, the word "algebra" can be seen to have been conditioned by failure through the process of higher-order conditioning. "No," "wrong," and "incorrect" with attendant conditioned emotional responses have become associated with the formulas and equations found in a book labeled "Algebra."

Test your understanding of this section. First read Box 5.2. Then see if you can incorporate Pavlov's *second signal system* conditioning, the process of *higher-order conditioning*, and *generalization* to show how failure experiences in an algebra classroom might contribute to problems in other school subjects.

Overshadowing

When an animal is conditioned, both the CS and the context (background stimulus conditions) in which the CS is presented become associated with the US. The CS competes successfully with the context to capture most of the associative potential of the US for reasons already discussed—namely, the context is latently inhibited, and the CS intensity allows this signal to emerge from background stimulus conditions.

What would happen if two novel CSs were presented simultaneously? Would both become conditioned, or would only one be attended to, the other merging into the background? Pavlov and others have done these experiments. The basic design is shown in Figure 5.4. As can be seen in the figure, the result of conditioning the two stimuli simultaneously is compared with the results of conditioning each stimulus separately. In the example given, CS_1 competes with and captures more of the associative potential of the US than does CS_2. When both are conditioned together and tested separately (Group A in Figure 5.4), the CR to CS_1 is larger than the CR to CS_2. The procedure is called **overshadowing** (Pavlov, 1927, pp. 269ff). CS_1 is said to *overshadow* CS_2. Because CS_1 is more easily conditioned than CS_2, CS_1 is also said to be more *salient* than CS_2.

---

[3]Among other stimuli that can be conditioned by the word "no" are other words, such as "don't," "wrong," "incorrect," "stop," etc.

BOX 5.2

Symbols of Value

Is money an important part of your ecological niche? A fistful of $100 bills gets the attention of most of us. What about ¥100 (Japanese yen) or £100 (English pounds)? Obviously the value of any given currency is relative to the values of other currencies. If you have specific knowledge of exchange rates (where the value of one currency is *associated* with the value of other currencies), you may already know whether $100 is more or less than £100 or ¥100. (£100 = approximately $150; ¥100 = approximately 7¢.)

How does money attain "value"? Aside from international macroeconomic considerations that fine tune each currency's value, a $1 bill is a CS (a symbolic token) that has been associated with "biologically meaningful" events (USs) in one's niche. As a child you learned the value of money by its association with candy, toys, and clothes, and later with food, beverages, perfume and other cosmetics, companionship, music, shelter, tuition, automobiles, and other stimuli and activities that can be purchased in our culture.

As we will see in Chapter 7, *secondary reinforcers* attain value through Pavlov's process of *higher-order conditioning*. Money is one of the most important *secondary reinforcers* (language is the most important?) that governs our behavior. Just talking about money makes me salivate. Can you identify any "conditioning of the third order" in your past? And, using the concept of higher-order conditioning, can you describe why someone might "fall in love with a car"? Why do *you* feel the way you do about the following artificial symbols?

HIV+   BMW   ☩

"Oh, not bad. The light comes on, I press the bar, they write me a check. How about you?"

From The New Yorker, May 3, 1993, p. 79. Drawing by Cheney; © 1993 The New Yorker Magazine, Inc.

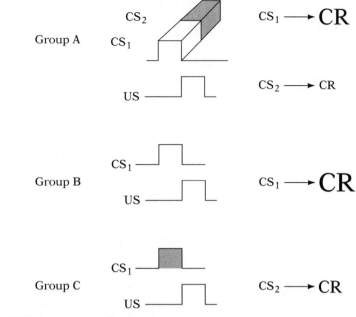

FIGURE 5.4   Overshadowing

In Group A, both CS_1 and CS_2 are conditioned; CS_1 overshadows CS_2 because the CR is larger to CS_1 than to CS_2. Note that when CS_1 and CS_2 are conditioned separately (Groups B and C, respectively), the CRs are greater to both stimuli than when they are conditioned concurrently. In Group A, only a fixed amount of US associative strength is shared with both CSs; hence the CRs are less than when they are conditioned separately.

When two or more CSs are presented simultaneously, which stimulus will overshadow and which will be overshadowed is best predicted by Pavlov's law of strength; the most intense stimulus captures most of the associative potential of the US. As noted, *between* stimulus modalities—vision, audition, taste, smell, etc.—species differences may play an important role in *which* stimuli overshadow, and *which* get overshadowed. Pavlov (1927), for example, reported that in salivary conditioning, dogs associated food (the US) better with auditory than visual CSs (i.e., sounds rather than sights were more easily learned).

Equating stimulus intensity across modalities is problematic, making it difficult to judge whether any given auditory stimulus is more intense than a given visual stimulus. We will return to this question, and the possibility of cross-modality differences in overshadowing, later in this chapter.

Potentiation

Overshadowing is a demonstration that not all stimuli are equally associable with a given US. If two flavor stimuli (for example, a pepperoni pizza and Dr. Spicey®) were tasted during the same meal, it is likely one would overshadow the other in association with an aversive event. But flavors have other unique properties not shared by other stimuli. For reasons that are not readily apparent, when a flavor stimulus is simultaneously presented to an animal with another stimulus (a sight, sound, or odor, for example), **potentiation** rather than *overshadowing* is the outcome. Potentiation means that the sight, sound, or odor is conditioned *better* than it would have been if conditioned alone (see Figure 5.5).

Experiments by Mark Bouton and his colleagues (Bouton, Dunlap, & Swartzentruber, 1987) and by Dr. Michael Best and his colleagues reveal the special power of flavors to potentiate the conditioning of background environments during training procedures (see Focus on Research 5.1).

Return with me to Momma Rollo's. Many flavors were experienced there, and some were conditioned aversively. Did any of the fla-

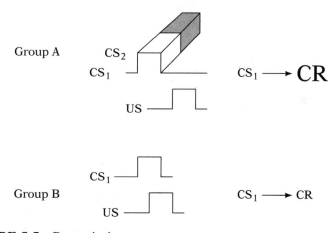

FIGURE 5.5 Potentiation

When either a simple stimulus CS_1 or a stimulus compound (such as the sights and sounds making up your friend's apartment) is conditioned simultaneously with a flavor stimulus (CS_2), conditioning to CS_1 is facilitated. (Compare the CR in Group B with that of Group A. Note: CS_2 *must* be a flavor.) Getting sick after *eating* in your friend's apartment is more likely to produce an *apartment aversion* than merely getting sick there without eating.

FOCUS ON RESEARCH 5.1

Dr. Michael R. Best

"I'll Never Go Back There . . . ."

Dr. Michael R. Best, Department of Psychology, Southern Methodist University, Dallas

"We have known for years that the sights, sounds, and smells of environments can be associated with illness produced by drugs and toxins. G. Andrew Mickley and I conducted some of the first experiments demonstrating this in Phillip Best's lab at the University of Virginia. Subsequently (and with considerable difficulty, I might add) we eventually published them (Best, Best, & Mickley, 1973).

"Since that time it has become clear to everyone working in animal learning that environmental contexts can be connected with sickness. Perhaps ironically, we now know that tastes can even enhance or *potentiate* the association of the environment with illness.

"Rats that drink a novel saccharin flavor in a distinctive environment and are then poisoned are less likely to consume familiar, nonaversive fluids (including water) in that conditioning environment—even though the rats never got sick after drinking them there (Best, Brown, & Sowell, 1984; Best & Meachum, 1986). It is therefore not surprising to find that you may be reluctant to eat at a restaurant if you become sick shortly thereafter. In these cases, it isn't just the food. It is also the location and other attendant stimuli to which you have been conditioned which motivate your decision.

"Although decisions about what you put in your mouth each day are possibly the most important you make, apparently you also keep track of *where* you eat and drink."

---

vors potentiate the conditioning of other stimuli? Hint: Can you come up with a hypothesis for why Candace was more hesitant to return to Momma Rollo's than Tracy was (see Box 5.1, question 6, p. 170), based upon the phenomenon of *potentiation?*

Blocking

We have seen that stimulus intensity best predicts which stimulus will overshadow and which will be overshadowed when both are paired with a US. What would happen if CS_1 were familiar and CS_2 were novel? Would CS_2 overshadow CS_1, or vice versa?

In an earlier section we learned that the theory of latent inhibition addresses the question of why familiar stimuli are less conditionable than novel stimuli. Familiar stimuli are apparently less associable in a subsequent pairing with a US because familiar stimuli have already become associated with other stimuli. Our prediction is, therefore, that a novel stimulus will overshadow a familiar stimulus when both are presented simultaneously.

Let us test this hypothesis by first conditioning an association to CS_1, and then simultaneously presenting CS_1 with a novel CS_2 in an overshadowing design, as shown in Figure 5.6. Kamin (1968), for example, used a conditioned suppression design in which he first conditioned rats to fear a tone (CS_1) using electric shock (US). Then Kamin simultaneously presented the tone with a novel light (CS_2), followed by electric shock. Remember that our prediction is that the novel light will capture most of the associative strength of the shock (US).

The results may surprise you. We predicted that a novel stimulus would overshadow the familiar stimulus. Kamin found, however, just the opposite. The surprising result is that prior conditioning to CS_1 *blocks* conditioning to CS_2. The procedure is a *blocking* design, and the counterintuitive phenomenon is called **blocking** (Kamin, 1968, 1969).

Why did the novel light fail to be conditioned? One hypothesis is that the novel light is a *redundant* stimulus, not useful in predicting

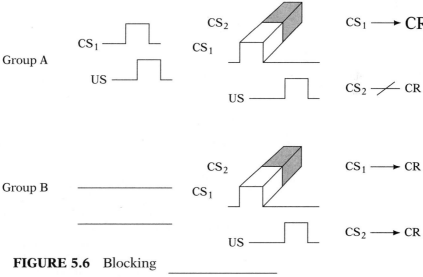

FIGURE 5.6   Blocking _____

Prior conditioning to CS_1 (Group A, left-hand panel) can block association to CS_2 (right-hand panel) after both CS_1 and CS_2 are conditioned in a compound (middle panel). Note that CRs to both CS_1 and CS_2 are learned in the absence of blocking (Group B), and further, that neither stimulus overshadows the other during conditioning in Group B.

the occurrence of electric shock. That is, the tone already predicts shock, and the rat may simply ignore the light when it occurs.

Let us return to the algebra classroom. The college teacher says that she will use a different (new) method to help you learn a familiar (previously conditioned) mathematical equation. For the sake of the argument, let us assume that the previous CS (the equation in question) was aversively conditioned by association with anxiety-inducing stimuli ("wrong," "no," "incorrect," a grade of "D," etc.). Given Kamin's findings about blocking, what is your prediction concerning the success of "new" conditioning? One more reason why it is difficult for an old dog to learn new tricks (see Figure 5.7).

THE FAR SIDE   By GARY LARSON

High above the hushed crowd, Rex tried to remain focused. Still, he couldn't shake one nagging thought: He was an old dog and this was a new trick.

FIGURE 5.7   Teaching an Old Dog New Tricks

Interim Summary

1. Familiar stimuli are less easily conditioned than novel stimuli, a phenomenon known as *latent inhibition*.
2. Both associative and nonassociative theories of latent inhibition can be compared, including habituation, interference, and learned irrelevance theories. An associative interference hypothesis was entertained as best accounting for the phenomenon of latent inhibition.
3. *Sensory preconditioning* describes a procedure demonstrating that CSs can become associated with each other *prior* to an association with a US. Such associations are measured indirectly by observing the transfer of associative effects from one CS to another following conditioning of one of the CSs with a US.
4. *Higher-order conditioning* is a procedure in which the transfer of associative strength from one CS to another occurs after a CS has previously entered into association with a US. The CS acquires US-like properties and can condition another CS.
5. *Overshadowing* results when two CSs simultaneously enter into association with a US; the one CS acquiring more associative strength (i.e., the one that conditions the better of the two) is said to overshadow the other CS. The overshadowing stimulus is said to be more *salient* than the overshadowed stimulus.
6. *Potentiation* describes a phenomenon in which the presence of one CS (a taste) allows a second CS to acquire more associative strength in a pairing with a US than it would have had it been presented alone. Sights, sounds, and odor stimuli are *potentiated* when accompanied by taste stimuli.
7. If a CS (CS_1) has already entered into association with a US, and CS_1 is then presented simultaneously with CS_2, followed by a US, CS_2 does not acquire associative strength (i.e., does not condition). CS_1 is said to have *blocked* CS_2. Such *blocking* may be complete or partial.

III. Inhibitory Conditioning

The foregoing phenomena of latent inhibition, sensory preconditioning, higher-order conditioning, potentiation, and blocking reveal the extent to which prior learning experiences can affect the conditioning of new responses. *Conditioned inhibition* is the last and one of the most important of this set of phenomena. But before conditioned inhibition is discussed, usage of the term "inhibition" will be clarified.

You have already been exposed to numerous concepts in which the terms "inhibitory" and "inhibition" have been used. For example, at several points in Chapter 4, "inhibitory conditioning" was identified as the outcome of *backward conditioning* procedures. A backward conditioning procedure yields a *negative contingency*, and the result is that performance of the conditioned response is opposite in direction relative to the unconditioned response. For example, if tone-shock sequences (i.e., forward, excitatory conditioning) predict conditioned fear, shock-tone sequences (backward, inhibitory conditioning) produce conditioned "safety." Excitatory conditioning produces more salivation in Pavlov's dogs, and inhibitory conditioning produces less-than-normal salivation. Excitatory and inhibitory conditioning resulting from forward and backward conditioning procedures is diagrammed in Figure 5.8. CSs that result from one or the other procedure are renamed **conditioned excitors** and **conditioned inhibitors,** respectively.

Pavlov's Internal and External Inhibition

The term *inhibition* was also used in two other concepts identified by Pavlov. **Internal inhibition** was proposed to explain *spontaneous recovery* following extinction. Remember that spontaneous recovery is measured while a conditioned response is in the process of being extinguished. If the animal is rested during this process, a larger than expected conditioned response follows the rest period (see Figure 4.5).

Pavlov understood the phenomenon to mean that active psychological properties of the dog were contributing to the diminishing CR—that is, that extinction involved *both* the loss of the excitatory conditioned response (passive) and an active *inhibitory* process that suppressed the excitatory process. This inhibitory process (frustration at not getting food?) would apparently diminish if the spacing between extinction trials was lengthened (allowing the frustration to dissipate?).

Pavlov's "External" Inhibition.   Why did Pavlov use the term *internal* inhibition? Two reasons. First, he had already identified as **external inhibition** the temporary disruption in conditioned salivation that occurs when a dog's attention is distracted during conditioning. Second, he assumed that the process emanated from within the animal.

To understand this latter phenomenon, place yourself in the dog's position—hung up on a sling in a conditioning chamber in a controlled laboratory environment. The background context against which the tone CS and food US are delivered is now predictable (latently inhibited). In the last two days you have been conditioned to salivate to the sound of the tone (CS⁺) and to not salivate to the sound of bubbling water (CS⁻). On this, your fifth CS⁺ trial of the day, the 30-second tone has been sounding for about five seconds when Igor,

Pavlov's clumsy assistant, blunders in, slamming the door behind him. Your salivation goes to zero as you orient ears and head to locate this distracting sound.

Pavlov's notation in your training log is that the reduced salivation on trial five was attributed to external factors, that the door slam *externally inhibited* the salivation response. After waiting a minute or

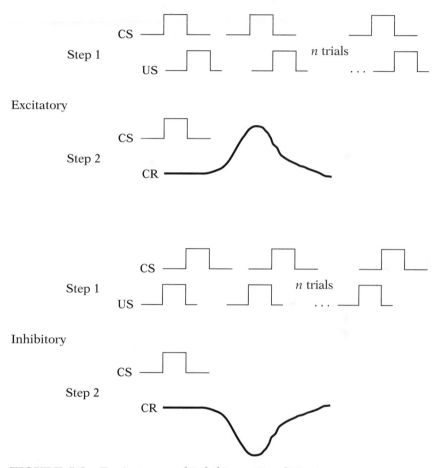

FIGURE 5.8   Excitatory and Inhibitory Conditioning

A comparison of excitatory (forward) and inhibitory (backward) conditioning. Note that the conditioned response following inhibitory conditioning is opposite in direction to the conditioned (and unconditioned) response following excitatory conditioning. In Step 2, the CS has become either an *excitor* (top) or an *inhibitor* (bottom).

so, trials are resumed, and your conditioned salivatory responses return to normal.

What Accounts for "Inhibition"?

Conditioned inhibition on the surface appears to be no more than the mirror image of conditioned excitation (see Figure 5.8), in that the conditioned response changes direction when the CS-US relationship is reversed. Conditioned inhibition is more complex than conditioned excitation, however, because inhibition requires an *excitatory context* in which to be expressed (Rescorla, 1969, 1985). Excitation must both precede and set the stage for inhibition. That is, demonstrations of conditioned inhibition require

1. That the animal has a prior history of conditioned excitation
2. That the animal be in an excitatory state when the inhibitory CS is present

Explaining Internal Inhibition. Let us briefly review Pavlov's demonstration of internal inhibition to see if these criteria are met. First, the dog is conditioned in an excitatory manner (CS = tone followed by US = food). Now, during extinction, the tone is presented, setting up an excitatory state. Trial after trial, food is *not* forthcoming in the presence of the tone; the extended passage of time (without food) becomes an inhibitory stimulus.

A human application: In our culture motorists have a conditioning history in which a red traffic light means "stop and wait." In other words, a red light sets up an expectancy to respond in a certain way. If the signal does not change in a fixed length of time, however, we ignore the red light, assuming it is broken, and "go." Here as in Pavlov's laboratory the inhibitory context is also *the passage of time,* conditioned by our prior (excitatory conditioning) experiences. The long time delay can be interpreted as an *inhibitory stimulus* that has signal value only in relation to prior excitatory conditioning at shorter intervals.

How about Pavlov's phenomenon of *external* inhibition? Remember that Igor slammed the door during an acquisition trial in which the tone CS provided an excitatory context. The door slam violates the animal's expectancy, thereby acting as a stimulus that inhibited the conditioned response.

Pavlov's internal and external inhibition are temporary phenomena; both dissipate with the passage of relative brief periods of time. They are best understood, therefore, as nonassociative in nature. By contrast, both *latent inhibition* and *conditioned inhibition* are long-lasting associative phenomena.

Table 5.1 summarizes the various uses of the term *inhibition.*

TABLE 5.1 Types of Inhibition

Phenomenon	Description of Phenomenon	Process
External inhibition	Temporary disruption of conditioned response due to presentation of extraneous stimulus	Nonassociative
Internal inhibition	Unobservable process alleged to occur during extinction of conditioned response; dissipates with time, as evidenced by spontaneous recovery	Nonassociative (?)
Latent inhibition	Reduced associability of familiar stimuli relative to novel stimuli	Associative
Conditioned inhibition	A state opposite to that of conditioned excitation; a process that produces a stimulus with conditioned inhibitory properties	Associative

Conditioned Inhibition

Four methods have been used to produce **conditioned inhibition** (i.e., *negative contingencies, induction, conditioned discrimination,* and *inhibition of delay*). In addition, two commonly used tests to measure inhibition indirectly are *summation* and *retardation*. We will cover each in turn.

Both the *negative contingencies* and *conditioned discrimination* method were introduced and briefly discussed in Chapter 4; let us briefly review both to see how conditioned inhibition is produced and why inhibition is important.

Negative, or US-CS, Contingencies Procedure

In an earlier discussion of backward conditioning using the CER procedure (see Chapter 4, p. 139), we learned that Heth (1976) conditioned rats by exposing them to 60 US-CS (i.e., backwards, or shocktone) pairings. A backward pairing sets up a **negative contingency** of CS and US. By measuring their rate of lever-pressing responses, Heth inferred that first the rats feared the tone, and that later the tone had become a safety signal. (Remember that rats ostensibly fearing the tone suppress their lever-pressing responses during the tone, and rats treating the tone as a safety signal increase their rate of response.)

Given what we now have learned about conditioned inhibition, the reader should not be surprised at Heth's (1976) finding that *excitatory* (fear) conditioning to the tone preceded the appearance of *inhibitory* (safety) conditioning. You be the rat, trapped again in the scientist's box. If at the beginning of the experiment tones and shocks were introduced into your environment—no matter which came first—wouldn't you be fearful? Only later, after quite a few conditioning trials in which you were first shocked, then heard the tone, would you interpret the tone as a signal that no shocks were forthcoming for a given time period—i.e., a "safe period." Heth found that even after 20 trials the rats feared the tone; inhibitory conditioning (accelerated response in the presence of the tone) took 60 trials.

Is it obvious that the tone became a safety signal only in the context of fear? That merely presenting the tone without shock would not make the tone a safety signal?

Inhibitory Conditioning of Flavors. In a standard taste aversion conditioning experiment, rats first drink a flavored fluid and are then make sick by exposure to an illness-inducing agent such as a drug or toxin. Flavor-illness contingencies make rats (and humans) no longer like the flavor in question. What if we reversed the contingency? Made the animal sick, then afterwards allowed it to drink a novel flavor? The rat comes to prefer the flavor it tastes while presumably recovering from the illness—a phenomenon known as the *medicine effect* (Green & Garcia, 1971).

Is the flavor initially aversive, only later becoming preferred, as is the case in other measures of inhibitory conditioning? Yes. Rats tasting a coffee flavor find it aversive after two illness-flavor (i.e., backward conditioning) trials, but show a preference for the flavor after eight such trials (Barker & Weaver, 1991).

Note that in both examples an initial excitatory conditioning component (fear of tone and avoidance of flavor, respectively) is followed by the development of conditioned inhibition (tone = safety signal, and flavor is preferred, respectively).

Conditioned Discrimination Procedure

Another method used to condition inhibition was encountered earlier in a discussion of Pavlov's conditioned discrimination procedure. Recall that Pavlov first conditioned a response to a circle. The circle (CS⁺) became an excitor. Then, on alternating trials, Pavlov presented the figure of an ellipse to the dog; the ellipse (CS⁻) was not paired with food. (The procedure is diagrammed in Figure 4.12, p. 156.)

Pavlov found a surprising result in the foregoing experiment. When he forced the animal to make finer and finer discriminations between a circle and an almost circular ellipse, the discrimination broke down. And so, apparently, did the dog. In Pavlov's words:

> At the same time the whole behavior of the animal underwent an abrupt change. The hitherto quiet dog began to squeal in its stand, kept wriggling about, tore off with its teeth the apparatus for mechanical stimulation of the skin, and bit through the tubes connecting the animal's room with the observer, a behavior which never happened before . . . the animal now barked violently . . . in short, it displayed all the symptoms of acute neurosis (for several weeks). (Pavlov, 1927, p. 291)

Conditioned inhibitors have been produced from a variety of other conditioned discrimination procedures (Hearst, 1972). We can be confident that Pavlov was essentially correct in assuming that the interaction of powerful excitatory and inhibitory processes were responsible for the dog's aberrant behavior. Not reinforcing the ellipse was an extinction procedure, and presumably *all* extinction procedures are stressful.[4] It is highly likely that conditioned inhibitors, among their other effects, produce measurable stress responses in the form of stress hormones (Dantzer, Arnone, & Mormede, 1980).

Induction Method

Presents. Presents. Presents. The facial expression of young Nancy reveals all too clearly her disappointment on opening her next present, the book *Black Beauty.* Her father is equally dismayed that he has apparently been unsuccessful in instilling good manners in Nancy. How can she be so unappreciative of this beautiful book? (Not to mention her lack of common courtesy in not hiding her displeasure.) After all, she likes horses. And she likes to read. Why the adverse reaction to the book?

Indeed, why is it the case that normally well-behaved children—and adults—all too often look a gift horse in the mouth and find it lacking?

The answer may be found by applying the results of experiments on inhibition conditioned by the **induction method** (illustrated in Figure 5.9). Let us examine the animal model before returning to the

---

[4]Ever been in a situation in which someone you cared for put you on extinction by withholding reinforcement? (Not talking with you on the phone. Not returning your "hello.") Can you identify the CSs during which extinction occurs? Now address the question, is extinction stressful?

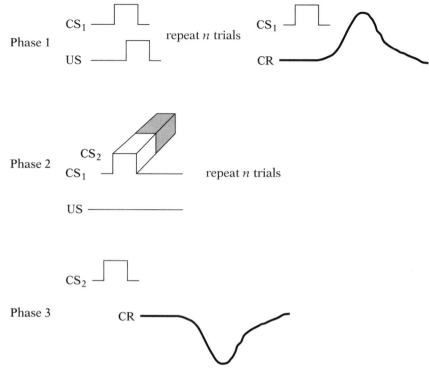

FIGURE 5.9   Conditioned Inhibition—Induction Procedure

After having been made excitatory in Phase 1, CS_1 is presented in compound with CS_2 in Phase 2. Notice that the compound is presented without the US during Phase 2. In Phase 3 CS_2 is demonstrated to have acquired inhibitory properties.

example. An excitatory context is first created (in Phase 1, Figure 5.9) by normal excitatory conditioning—say a fear response to a tone, as measured in a conditioned suppression experiment using rats. In Phase 2, the tone—now a conditioned excitor—is presented in conjunction with a neutral stimulus, such as a light, and the rat is *not* shocked. Finally, the light is tested alone; the animal's response to the light is opposite to that of the tone.

In the *induction method,* then, an excitatory stimulus (the tone) creates the context that makes the light become an inhibitory stimulus.

Returning to the birthday party. Did I mention that before opening *Black Beauty,* the first present that Nancy unwrapped was a small color television for her bedroom? Let the television be an excitor, setting up an excitatory state in the form of expectations in young Nancy. Let the book *Black Beauty* be a neutral stimulus that occurs during the excitatory state. Are the conditions right for the book to become a conditioned inhibitor? If so, what effect will the book have on Nancy's excitatory state?

What should you do, as a representative of the next generation of parents, to ensure that *your* child will not be a monster at her own party?[5]

Inhibition of Delay Procedures

Remember being stuck at the traffic light that would not change, and after waiting through two cycles, deciding the light was broken? After inhibiting your response, you used the passage of time as a cue to respond by pressing the accelerator. In that example, the time delay was identified as a *conditioned inhibitor* when added to the red light, the excitor. The red light (excitor) controlled your "foot-on-the-brake" response. The combination of the excitor and "time passing" (inhibitor) produced the "go" response, opposite to the "stop" response to the red light alone.

An experiment by Pavlov helps us to understand the concept of **inhibition of delay,** and the role that time delays play in inhibition. Figure 5.10 shows the results of measuring when a dog salivates to a tactile CS during conditioning over a 30-second delay. After many conditioning trials, salivation is *inhibited* during the first part of the interval; salivation now occurs *just before* delivery of food (highly adaptive, in that salivation helps the animal begin the digestive process). If the experiment tells us nothing else, we can infer that dogs, like humans, can sense the passage of time.

How do we know that salivation is being *actively inhibited* during the initial 15-second period? Pavlov used two lines of evidence to argue his case. First, he noted that many of his dogs became drowsy—some even fell asleep—during conditioning over long delays. The reduced attentiveness and alertness was an observable consequence of active inhibition. Second, Pavlov ran a test in which he introduced another stimulus—the sound of a metronome—during the 30-second tactile stimulus. As can be seen in Figure 5.10, the metronome-plus-tactile stimulus (open squares) *released* the process

---

[5](a) not celebrate birthdays;
  (b) celebrate birthdays, but not give gifts;
  (c) punish the child by taking back any gift the child is not thankful for;
  *(d) arrange for your child to open the gifts in an ascending order of perceived value (i.e., save the best for last).

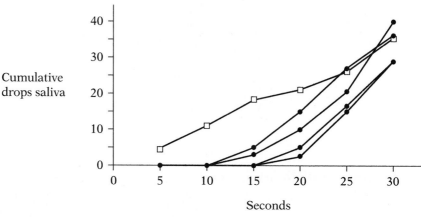

FIGURE 5.10   Inhibition of Delay

A dog is conditioned to salivate to a 30-second tactile stimulus. Pavlov (1927, p. 93) then measured salivation during the 30-second period on four occasions (circles). Note that the dog does not salivate an equal amount throughout the 30-second period; rather, salivation is inhibited during the first 15 seconds, a phenomenon Pavlov called *inhibition of delay*. On a fifth trial Pavlov added a metronome's sound to the tactile stimulus and measured salivation (open squares). Note that the metronome had the effect of *disinhibiting* the inhibited salivation to the tactile stimulus, as evidenced by salivation throughout the entire 30-second period.

of inhibition, causing the dog to again salivate throughout the 30-second interval. Pavlov called the process "inhibition of inhibition" (awkward), or **disinhibition** (better). The metronome is a *disinhibitor*.

Can you think of any instance in which you become drowsy if you have to wait a fixed period of time before being rewarded? Let us make the waiting period 50 minutes. Anything come to mind? Can you make the case that a boring lecture is one in which there are no disinhibitors?

Still stuck back at the red light? Perhaps your mind has wandered (become drowsy during the wait?) and you have not noticed that the light has changed to green. A honking horn is a pretty fair disinhibitor, isn't it?

Indirect Methods of Measuring Conditioned Inhibition

Four methods that produce conditioned inhibition have been presented: *negative contingencies, induction, conditioned discrimination,* and *inhibition of delay*. These procedures are important because they demonstrate the subtleties and interactions of excitatory and inhibitory processes during conditioning. Animals learn to increase or decrease response tendencies, depending upon prior conditioning, and upon the context of the present conditioning experiment. Two *indirect* methods of measuring conditioned inhibition, *summation* and *retardation*, are discussed next. Why are they important? Because they provide demonstration experiments that inhibitors and excitors combine algebraically to modulate behavior (Rescorla, 1971).

Summation Test.   As the name implies, the **summation test** refers to a procedure in which CS_2 (a conditioned inhibitor) is presented with (added to) CS_1 (a conditioned excitor).

Excitatory and inhibitory conditioning are initially accomplished separately (as indicated in Figure 5.8). As in the previous example, a tone CS is conditioned by presenting the tone, followed by shock (i.e., excitatory conditioning), producing conditioned *suppression* of lever pressing. On another day a light CS is *preceded* by an electric shock US (i.e., a negative contingency that produces inhibitory conditioning). This latter procedure produces *enhanced* responding.

What would you predict would happen if, after this training, on yet another day *excitor* and *inhibitor* are presented simultaneously? The procedure and results are outlined in Figure 5.11.

Note first in Figure 5.11 that adding the light (CS_2) to the excitatory conditioned tone (CS_1) produces *less* suppression than would be expected in response to the tone alone. The CR to the combined stimuli indicates that the CR to each stimulus were algebraically summed. In the conditioned suppression example, adding the light *diminishes* the ability of the excitor to suppress lever-pressing responses (Solomon, Brennan, & Moore, 1974).

The experimenter must control for the possibility that *any* stimulus might interfere with an excitatory conditioned response, not just one that was conditioned in an inhibitory manner. (Remember the slamming door in Pavlov's external inhibition phenomenon, and what it did to the dog's excitatory conditioned response?) A control group in which the light is made familiar prior to adding it to the tone is shown in Figure 5.11. Note that the control group sees the light the same number of times as the treatment group, but that for the treatment group the light is a conditioned inhibitor.

Merely presenting the light with the tone does not produce summation as it did with the treatment group. Can you figure out why, in the control group, the familiar light did *not* externally inhibit the tone in the same way that a slamming door inhibited the dog's conditioned salivatory response?[6]

---

[6]The key is that the light was made familiar (loss of orienting response) in the present example. Therefore, when presented along with the tone, the light presumably captured little of the animal's attention.

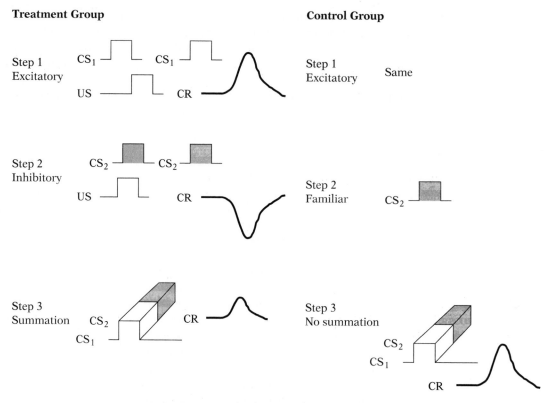

FIGURE 5.11 Summation Test

Excitors and inhibitors apparently sum (algebraically) when both are presented together (Step 3, left figure). See text for further discussion.

The speed at which you drive a car in traffic is an illustration of the summation of excitatory and inhibitory elements. You approach a green traffic signal in a 35-mph zone. What stimulus elements contribute to your selected speed? It is raining (inhibitor), the traffic is flowing smoothly (excitor), a police car is adjacent (inhibitor), you are late for an appointment (excitor), you hear a siren (major inhibitor), your rear-view mirror is clear (major excitor), etc.

Retardation Test. A final procedure that allows experimenters to indirectly measure conditioned inhibition is called the **retardation test.** Simply put, once a stimulus has been made a conditioned inhibitor, it is more difficult to turn that stimulus into an excitor. Let us use as an example flavor preference and aversion conditioning, as outlined in Figure 5.12. First condition a preference to a flavor using

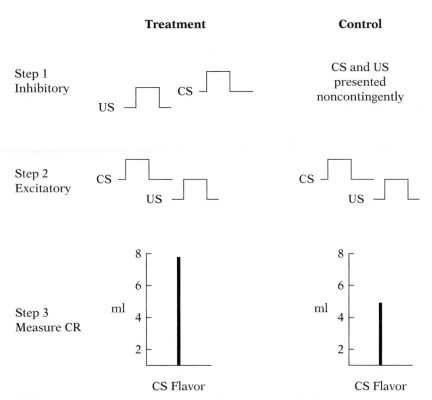

FIGURE 5.12 Retardation Test of Conditioned Inhibition

In the figure more aversion to the flavor is conditioned in the control group (5-ml intake) than the inhibitory treatment group (~8-ml intake). Why? Because following inhibitory training in Step 1, an inhibitory flavor is less easily conditioned when now used as an excitor (Treatment Steps 2 and 3) relative to an equally familiar flavor (Control). Hence, the inhibitory treatment "retarded" the excitatory aversive conditioning. Note: Greater excitatory conditioned taste aversion is reflected by *lower* intake values.

a negative contingency (cf. the *medicine effect*). That is, in Step 1 (Figure 5.12) an illness experience (US) is always followed by a flavor CS, eventually making the flavor a conditioned inhibitor. In Step 2, the same flavor is now paired with illness in an excitatory framework. Can a conditioned inhibitor be made into a conditioned excitor? As we will see in the next paragraph, only with difficulty.

The results of this retardation treatment are compared with a control group in Figure 5.12. The control group experiences both the flavor and the illness but not in a contingent (or contiguous) way.

Then the flavor is made a conditioned excitor in Step 2, the same as in the retardation treatment (i.e., the flavor is made aversive by having the rat experience sickness *after* tasting the flavor). Note in Figure 5.12, Step 3, that after conditioning, the control group dislikes the flavor more (consumes fewer milliliters of the flavor in a test) than does the treatment group.

Conclusion: The treatment group was *retarded* in acquiring an aversion to a flavor that was previously conditioned in an inhibitory manner. A conditioned inhibitor can become a conditioned excitor, but more trials are required relative to a control group.

Interim Summary

A summary of the various ways by which inhibitors are conditioned and the indirect tests for conditioned inhibition are presented in Table 5.2.

TABLE 5.2   Conditioned Inhibition

Methods of Production	
Method	*Description*
Negative contingency	A procedure that produces a conditioned response opposite in direction to the unconditioned response (e.g., if fear is the excitatory CR, safety is the inhibitory CR).
Conditioned discrimination	A procedure in which CS_1 is conditioned as an excitor (CS^+), and then CS_2 is presented without food; CS_2 becomes a conditioned inhibitor.
Induction procedure	A neutral stimulus is added to an excitatory CS in extinction; the neutral stimulus acquires inhibitory properties.
Inhibition of delay	During a long CS extinction trial, a response to the CS is delayed (inhibited) until the end of the interval; time is the conditioned inhibitor.
Indirect Methods of Testing	
Retardation procedure	An inhibitory conditioned stimulus is slower to acquire excitatory properties during reconditioning.
Summation procedure	An inhibitory conditioned stimulus when placed in compound with a novel CS slows excitatory conditioning to the novel CS.

At the beginning of this chapter a number of questions were posed concerning both the ecological validity and extrapolation of results of conditioning experiments on animals in laboratories. Ultimately you, the reader, must be the judge of these issues. From your reading so far, have you derived any insight into your personal behavior:

- In classrooms (bored and sleepy, waiting for the bell, or hopeless in the face of algebra)?
- In your reaction to gifts?
- In automobiles (how fast you drive, or drowsy while waiting at red lights)?
- In your personal interactions with others?
- In your attitudes toward foods and restaurants?
- In the effects language has on you, and how your words may motivate others?

Given what you have learned so far, do you think associative models of learning tested in laboratories using dogs and rats are relevant to other animals, including humans?

IV. Learning as a General Process, or Species-Specific Learning?

Two views of behavior were presented in Chapter 2. On one hand, ethologists were seen to focus upon phyletic relationships among animals, and species differences of animals living within distinctive ethological niches. Animals appear to behave in highly adaptive ways; animals engage in those behaviors which promote their individual lives, which lead to reproducing the next generation, and (among birds and mammals) which help in taking care of offspring.

Comparative psychologists and other neuroscientists who study behavior focus more on behavioral *plasticity*. How do relatively large-brained vertebrates respond to changes in their immediate environment? How do they learn and remember from their interactions with their environment?

A suggestion was made in Chapter 2 that psychologists focus upon plasticity in behavior (rather than upon fixed action patterns, critical periods, and consummatory behaviors) because their ultimate goals are different from those of ethologists. Historically, psychologists' *primary* interests lie in understanding the mind of the creature with the most variable behavior of all, *Homo sapiens*. In addition to studying the behavior of a *particular* animal in the laboratory, laboratory animals become a convenient means to test theories and *to model human learning and memory processes* as well. Hence the interest throughout this chapter in applying the results of animal experiments to real-life human situations. Indeed, Chapter 8 in its entirety is devoted to applications of animal learning experiments and theory to the human condition.

Reexamination of Issues.   In this concluding section we will reexamine several issues raised earlier. Are there species differences in learning? Does each animal bring "prior learning experiences" in the form of genetically coded behavior and innate reaction patterns to each new experiment in the laboratory? Is *general process learning theory* sufficient to account for almost all instances of animal learning? And finally, why are certain stimuli and certain responses in certain animals conditioned relatively easily, and why do others apparently fail to be conditioned?

Can Any Stimulus Become a Conditioned Stimulus?

We start with a question about whether the laboratory is a valid ecological niche in which to study learning. One question raised about laboratory research has to do with the use of "artificial" stimuli in conditioning animals. Where can electric shock be found in nature? Or, for that matter, carefully timed bells, whistles, and metronomes?

Given the divergent evolutionary histories of animals, and the different niches they presently occupy, is it reasonable to think that *any* stimulus is arbitrarily interchangeable with another? If some animals rely primarily upon taste and smell to negotiate their niche, for example, isn't it reasonable to expect that they would learn differently using these stimuli than, for example, a visual or an auditory stimulus? Can "learning" measured in laboratories using arbitrary stimuli and arbitrary responses (lever pressing?) ever reflect real-life learning?

Pavlov's Assertion: "Yes."   After studying the issue for 30 years, Pavlov's conclusion was as follows:

> We must now take some account of the agencies which can be transformed into conditioned stimuli. This is not so easy a problem as appears at first sight. Of course to give a general answer is very simple; *any agent in nature which acts on any adequate receptor apparatus of an organism can be made into a conditioned stimulus for that organism.* This general statement, however needs both amplification and restriction. (Pavlov, 1927, p. 38; my italics)

Among the "amplifications and restrictions" were pages and pages of experiments with dogs in which *particular* stimuli selected to be CSs conditioned either with ease or with difficulty. The *law of strength* held for a wide range of stimulus intensities, but if a stimulus was *too* intense, it could not effectively be used as a CS. Another troubling example is that of *temporal conditioning*—the mere passage of time (for which there is no apparent "receptor apparatus"!) can become an effective conditioned stimulus.

In yet other experiments he found that the *cessation* of a stimulus could become a conditioned stimulus. In Pavlov's words:

> A metronome is sounded continuously in the experimental laboratory when the dog is brought in. The sound of the metronome is now cut out, and immediately an unconditioned stimulus, say food or a rejectable substance, is introduced. After several repetitions of this procedure it is found that the disappearance of the sound has become the stimulus to a new conditioned reflex. (Pavlov, 1927, p. 39)

Growth of General Process Learning Theory

Laboratory researchers took Pavlov at his word, and by the mid-1960s had developed a *general process learning* philosophy that made the following assumptions:

1. The choice of research animal was relatively arbitrary
2. The choice of stimuli used in experiments was relatively arbitrary
3. The choice of reflexes and type of responses by which to measure learning was relatively arbitrary

From many different laboratories had come results with a variety of animals in different conditioning situations that seemed to support a general process approach to learning. Some of these experiments are presented in Table 5.3.

In Table 5.3 note both the similarities and the differences in these experiments. For example, four different species (albeit all mammals) were used: dogs, a human infant, rats, and rabbits. Three sounds (a metronome, white noise, a pure tone) and one visual stimulus (the sight of a moving white rat) were used as CSs. Four different USs (three aversive, one appetitive) were used: electric shock, a loud clang, an air puff, and food. CSs were a half-second to two minutes in duration; USs ranged from less than a second to a few seconds in duration. Interestingly enough, the number of trials to accomplish conditioning (with the exception of eye-blink conditioning) ranged from five to nine trials even in these highly diverse situations.

TABLE 5.3   General Process Learning: A Comparison of Conditioning Parameters

Researcher (Subject)	CS (Duration)	US (Duration)	CS-US Interval	Number of Trials
Pavlov (1927) (dog)	Metronome (30 s)	Food (~10 s)	30 s	5–9
Watson and Rayner (1920) (human)	White rat (~5 s)	Loud clang (~2 s)	~2–3 s	7
Kamin (1965) (rat)	81-dB white noise (2.0 min)	0.85-mA shock (0.5 s)	3.0 min	6–8
Gormezano (1965) (rabbit)	800-hz tone, 72 dB (0.6 s)	Air puff (0.5 s)	0.5 s	~200

The basis of a *general process* position, then, is that conditioning outcomes are predictable in a variety of animals, and in a variety of stimulus situations. And, for whatever reasons that eye-blink conditionings take longer, the end result is the same.

Challenge to General Process Learning Theory

And then several new experiments were published—one in 1955, others in the mid-1960s, that did not seem to fit general process learning theory. Let us take a closer look at them.

Ionizing Radiation as an Unconditioned Stimulus. For many years following World War II the United States government supported research into the biological effects of ionizing radiation. Among its other effects, ionizing radiation had been demonstrated to disrupt eating and drinking patterns. An important paper published in the journal *Science* suggested that some of the disruption was conditioned (Garcia, Kimeldorf, & Koelling, 1955).

If so, the conditioning was unlike anything Pavlov had previously reported. Rats had been allowed to drink a 0.1% saccharin solution during a six-hour low-level ionizing radiation exposure (i.e., an *embedded* design). Several days later these rats' preference for saccharin was tested; after the radiation exposure the rats now avoided the saccharin.

Over the next several weeks the rats drank increasing amounts of the saccharin solution, relative to water. Garcia and his colleagues' analysis was that the saccharin had functioned as a CS during the radiation exposure, and the radiation acted as an unconditioned stimulus; and the aversion to saccharin was interpreted as a conditioned response. The CR (aversion to saccharin) extinguished over the next few weeks as inferred from the rats' increasing acceptance of the saccharin-flavored water.

The Garcia et al. (1955) finding raised several problems for traditional learning theory:

1. The CS and the US each lasted six hours rather than a few seconds or minutes.
2. Conditioning was accomplished in one trial.
3. Stimulus *contiguity was apparently unnecessary:* Assuming that the rats tasted saccharin early in the six-hour interval, and that the response to radiation (radiation sickness?) occurred some time *after* the six-hour interval, the taste-to-illness interval could be interpreted to be more than six hours in duration.

Such rapid, one-trial, long-delay learning was unprecedented. Was it unique? Was it outside the pale of general process theory? Many thought so.

The "Bright, Noisy, Tasty Water" Experiment

After a number of rejections by the editors of journals of animal learning research, John Garcia finally published the results of another controversial experiment that provided further insight into his first paper (Garcia & Koelling, 1966). Their "bright, noisy, tasty water" experiment is now considered a classic.

Rats were placed in an experimental chamber and allowed to lick a tube containing water. By adding saccharin, the water could be made "tasty." Every time the animal licked the water tube, an electric circuit was completed that briefly flashed a ("bright") light in the rat's environment. The same circuit also produced a brief clicking noise—hence, the water had bright, noisy, and tasty (as well as wet) conditioned stimulus properties.

Half the rats were trained to drink the bright, noisy, tasty water, after which they were exposed to ionizing radiation (the US). The other half were punished by being exposed to a brief electric shock after licking the fluid for a short time.

To test whether the audio-visual (bright, noisy) or the taste component of the water conditioned best with the electric shock or with the radiation US, the bright, noisy, tasty water was separated into component parts during extinction tests. Rats had a choice of drinking either bright, noisy water or tasty water. The results are shown in Figure 5.13.

	Radiation	Electric shock
Bright, noisy water	No conditioning	Aversive conditioning
Tasty water	Aversive conditioning	No conditioning

FIGURE 5.13   The Bright, Noisy, Tasty Water Experiment

The results of Garcia and Koelling's (1966) "bright, noisy, tasty water experiment" are summarized in the 2 × 2 matrix of two CSs (bright, noisy water or tasty water) and two USs (radiation or electric shock). Notice that not all CSs were conditioned with all USs. Garcia's conceptual schema of two conditioning systems—telereceptors (eyes, ears) with cutaneous stimuli (skin pain), and gustatory stimuli (taste) with visceral stimuli (gut pain)—was proposed by Garcia, Hankins, and Rusiniak (1974).

In the bright, noisy, tasty water experiment, rats associated the audio-visual components of the compound stimulus with electric shock, and the taste component with the radiation exposure. Garcia and Koelling (1966) interpreted these results to mean that not all stimuli were capable of entering into association; rather, that there was **stimulus specificity in conditioning.** Taste and sickness were easily associated together, Garcia argued, because rats were evolutionarily prepared to associate flavors with the normal consequences of eating. Likewise, the sights and sounds of predators were more likely to be conditioned with pain rather than with gut sickness. This experiment, he argued, provided evidence for two different learning systems: a telereceptor-cutaneous system, and a gustatory-visceral system (see Figure 5.13).

A number of methodological problems in Garcia and Koelling's experiment clouded interpretation of their results. A replication of the bright, noisy, tasty water experiment by Domjan and Wilson (1972) using a between-groups design, however, both simplified the methods and clarified the theoretical issues. For this reason, their experiment rather than Garcia's will be the basis for further discussion.

In most particulars Garcia's "bright, noisy, tasty water findings" were replicated by Domjan and Wilson (1972); the taste stimulus was conditioned with sickness (lithium chloride was used to induce sickness, rather than a radiation stimulus), but again the taste cue was not associated with electric shock. Likewise, a "pulsed buzzer" was associated with electric shock, but not with lithium-induced sickness (Domjan & Wilson, 1972).

Preparedness

Several other learning theorists agreed with Garcia's analysis (i.e., Seligman, 1970; Rozin & Kalat, 1971). These theorists broadened the evolutionary argument. In developing a theory of **preparedness,** these theorists argued that certain animals are (evolutionarily) *prepared* to readily make some associations and are *unprepared*, or even *contraprepared*, to make others:

> What an organism learns in the laboratory or in his natural habitat is the result not only of the contingencies which he faces and has faced in his past but also of the contingencies which his species faced before him—its evolutionary history and genetic outcome. (Rozin & Kalat, 1971)

Preparedness and Neophobia

The rapid learning about flavors found in experiments by John Garcia and others complements other species-specific behavioral tendencies in rats, which together facilitate their success at securing food. Rats display **neophobia** *(fear of new)* when they confront unfamiliar flavors (tastes and smells) of foods and fluids.[7] Their innately organized feeding behavior prepares even hungry rats to approach new foods cautiously. Rats sniff, retreat, approach, sniff and nibble (taste), and retreat. On their next approach they sniff, nibble, and ingest a small amount (the exact amount depending upon hunger, and the taste, smell, and temperature characteristics of the food). After minimal ingestion again they retreat. On subsequent encounters they eat increasingly more (Domjan, 1977). One theory is that if rats experience no immediate ill effects of what they ate, they will shortly return to eat more.

Given this innate wariness, or *bait-shyness*, about new foods, complemented by the rat's ability to form flavor-illness associations in only one trial, it is easy to see why "rats as pests" are so difficult to poison (Rzoska, 1953). Let us look more closely at the "number of trials to learn" evidence for preparedness.

---

[7]Including, of course, rug rats. Neophobic tendencies in humans are so strong that children attribute Draconian motivations to parents who attempt to introduce new foods. Indeed, more than one of my children, even at 10 years of age, have accused me of trying to poison them.

Preparedness and Number of Trials

Garcia used the "number of trials to learn" metric to support evolutionary arguments; for example, learning taste aversions in one trial constitutes evidence of preparedness in learning. The brains of animals that learn certain behaviors in one trial have been selected for through the evolutionary process. Animals possessing brain structures that were able to learn rapidly about poisoned food sources lived; those that did not, died. Why? Because more than one poisoning trial increases the likelihood of a fatal encounter with poison.

Contraprepared and Unprepared Learning

Pavlov's dogs, the argument continues, took five to nine trials to learn about the relationship of sights and sounds with foods. They were **unprepared** or, at best, neutral regarding these stimuli; the intermediate number of trials necessary for conditioning to occur is evidence for their unpreparedness. Using similar reasoning, rabbits and humans are apparently **contraprepared** to learn about sights and sounds that predict air puffs to the cornea of the eye. Such conditioning is unlikely (read not *ever* likely) to happen in *any* animal's ecological niche. That such conditioning can occur at all, even if it takes hundreds of trials, attests to the inherent plasticity of mammalian brains.

Birds Associate Color, Not Taste, with Poison?   Given the diversity of life forms and of the niches they occupy, what predictions can be made concerning cross-species comparisons? One prediction is that such comparisons need be made with care. Unless animals occupy very similar niches, the preparedness argument goes, one should not expect them to associate stimuli in the same way.

Birds, for example, which conduct visual rather than olfactory searches for food, and which make ingestional decisions more upon what something *looks* like than how it tastes, should learn better about foods using visual rather than taste cues (i.e., the reverse of rats).

This hypothesis was tested by Wilcoxson, Dragoin, and Kral (1971). They allowed both laboratory rats and Japanese quail to drink blue (food coloring) in sour (slightly acidic) water, and then poisoned the animals with a drug called cyclophosphamide. The entire procedure was accomplished in one trial. As in the bright, noisy, tasty water experiment, the compound CS was separated during extinction testing. The rats and quail were tested with a choice of drinking either blue or sour water. Rats, they reported, chose blue and declined the sour water. Quail rejected the blue-colored water but drank the sour water.

Again, these results constitute evidence for *stimulus specificity in conditioning.* The quail and rats were evolutionarily *prepared* to make these selective associations.

Interim Summary

The foregoing experiments present problems for general process learning theory on several counts: First, one-trial learning over very long delays is possible for taste paired with illness-inducing stimuli. Second, specific stimuli appear to enter into association, and others not, depending upon species of animal.

The preparedness challenge to general process theory is an important one, because most humans consider themselves to be *truly* unique among species. If special rules of association formation are found to hold for some species, it must certainly be the case that learning accomplished by humans will be found to be the most different of all. Let us take a further look at these issues.

Analysis of Conditioning Failures

Why did rats fail to associate the audio-visual stimulus with the radiation stimulus? Is the rat really unable to make flavor–electric shock associations in the bright, noisy, tasty water experiment? Why are quail apparently unable to form a sour taste–sickness association? Let us take a closer look at the conditioning failures noted in these two experiments. Conditioning parameters used in these experiments are summarized in Table 5.4.

Compare the procedures in Table 5.4 with those in Table 5.3. Note in Table 5.4 the one glaring difference in these experiments with conditioning *failures;* namely, that only *one* conditioning trial

TABLE 5.4   Conditioning Failures?

Researcher	CS (Duration)	US (Quantity, Duration)	CS-US Interval	Number of Trials
Domjan and Wilson (1972)	Pulsed buzzer (35 s)	Lithium chloride (~20 ml/kg, ip)	35 s	3
	0.2% saccharin (35 s)	Electric shock (140 V, 0.5 s)	35 s	3
Wilcoxson, Dragoin, and Kral (1971)	Blue water (30 min)	Cytoxan® (66 mg/kg)	30 min	1

(Wilcoxson et al., 1971) and *three* conditioning trials (Domjan & Wilson, 1972) were conducted. The most parsimonious argument that can be presented for these conditioning "failures," then, is that not enough conditioning trials were conducted.

Is it easier to condition a taste with illness in rats, and a visual cue with illness in Japanese quail? Apparently so. Is it *possible* to condition a taste with illness in quail, and visual cues with illness in rats? The answer for quail is *probably* "yes," and for rats, *definitely* "yes" (see the box on Michael Best's experiments, p. 184).

Among birds there appear to be species differences. Hawks, for example, apparently *require* taste cues to make visual associations. Hawks poisoned after eating black mice only learned *not* to eat them if the mice were also made bitter flavored; only after the black-bitter-poison association was made did they quit eating black mice and continue eating white mice (Brett, Hankins, & Garcia, 1976).[8]

Taste-shock Associations.   Given the findings that visual cues *can* be associated with poisons, is there comparable evidence that *taste* can be associated with electric shock? Yes. An interesting experiment reported by Krane and Wagner (1975) indicated that an important variable in taste-shock conditioning was to delay the shock. Saccharin has a relatively long-lasting aftertaste. Krane and Wagner compared taste-shock conditioning at various intervals and found associations formed only if the taste's duration did not extend past delivery of the electric shock.[9]

Analysis of Preparedness Conditioning

The foregoing conditioning "failures" were accounted for by simply noting that stimulus-stimulus associations cannot be expected to form in one to three trials. Were associations found to be *impossible* after many trials, perhaps the specificity in conditioning position could be considered a more serious threat to a general process learning position.

But, you may argue, taste aversions *do* form in one trial over long CS-US delays. Doesn't that observation by itself violate general process learning theory? Maybe, maybe not. Consider the following arguments:

---

[8]Why did the taste cue allow the hawk to begin to associate the visual cue with poison? (Why was Candace reluctant to return to Mamma Rollo's?) See Focus on Research 5.1.

[9]A student once suggested that if the electric shock were made intense enough, it presumably would take on some of the same characteristics of an "illness-inducing agent," e.g., nausea. Why is this an important observation?

1. Within a sensory modality, both intensity and duration effects are important factors in conditioning (see Pavlov's *law of strength*).
2. Although, beginning with Pavlov, many have tried, no one has yet solved the problem of equating stimulus intensities *across* modalities.
3. Regarding "tastes" and "poisons," general process learning theory predicts that both intensity and duration effects are important factors that predict ease of conditioning.
4. Most demonstrations of one-trial taste aversion conditioning over delays of several hours have used very intense taste stimuli; i.e., strong solutions consumed for several minutes (Smith and Roll, 1967) or hours (Garcia et al., 1955), followed by long-lasting illnesses induced by radiation or lithium (Barker & Smith, 1974).

Preparedness, or Stimulus Intensity Effects?   If taste aversion conditioning parameters are altered so that they more closely resemble *other* general process procedures (i.e., such as are found in Table 5.3), preparedness appears to go away. That is, one-trial conditioning over a 30-minute delay becomes impossible if a *very brief* flavor (lasting only a few seconds) is paired with a tiny amount of toxin (presumably producing only a mild illness). Conditioned aversion to the taste grows slowly as a function of trials using these stimulus parameters (Monroe & Barker, 1979).

Interim Summary

Animals not only bring specialized sensory and motor apparatus to the laboratory, but also an associative apparatus that has a long and specialized evolutionary history. Each animal's nervous system apparently makes certain contingencies easier to learn than others, in that, as Pavlov first noted, some stimuli are conditioned in a few trials, and others require many trials.

Role of Stimulus Salience in Conditioning.   The number of trials it takes for a stimulus to become a CS defines the *salience* of that stimulus. Among other variables, the best predictor of salience is stimulus intensity. As a general rule, more intense stimuli are more salient in that they require fewer trials to be associated. That stimulus intensity is the best predictor of stimulus salience seems to be invariant across species.

Role of Stimulus Specificity in Conditioning.   Evidence for stimulus specificity in conditioning across species is not as compelling as evidence for stimulus intensity in conditioning across species. For example, Pavlov noted that his dogs associated sounds better than visual stimuli with food during excitatory conditioning, and sights better than sounds with food during (inhibitory) conditioning over a delay. But the general rule he formulated still holds—namely, that any stimulus can be made into a conditioned stimulus.

Preparedness arguments are hindered by the experimenter's inability to equate stimulus intensity across modalities. Rather than invoke preparedness arguments, a more cautious conclusion regarding the *bright, noisy, tasty water experiment* is that for reasons not understood at present, rats (and other animals) associate some stimuli more easily than others.

Summary

1. Conditioning procedures accomplished in laboratories that build and elaborate upon Pavlov's simple associative model can account for increasingly complex behavior.

2. A number of procedures have been developed to measure the effects of prior experience on subsequent learning, including latent inhibition, sensory preconditioning, higher-order conditioning, overshadowing, potentiation, blocking, and inhibitory conditioning.

3. Compared with novel stimuli, conditioned responses to familiar stimuli take longer to develop—a phenomenon called latent inhibition.

4. Two CSs can become associated together without the benefit of an unconditioned stimulus. If one of the two CSs is then made a conditioned excitor, the other when tested shows conditioned excitor properties.

5. When, through prior association with a US, a CS (CS_1) becomes an excitor, pairing a neutral stimulus (CS_2) with the CS_1 makes CS_2 an excitor also. This phenomenon is called higher-order conditioning, and it is the basis for secondary reinforcement.

6. When two CSs are simultaneously conditioned, one is typically conditioned better than the other. One CS is therefore said to overshadow the other CS. The overshadowing stimulus is also said to be the more salient of the two CSs.

7. If taste is added to an exteroceptive CS (i.e., an audio-visual CS) in a conditioning situation, the exteroceptive CS conditions better. Taste is said to potentiate the conditioning of nontaste cues.

8. If CS_1 is first conditioned to be an excitor, and it is then put in a compound with CS_2 and both are then conditioned with a US, CS_2 does *not* become an excitor. CS_1 is said to have blocked CS_2, and the procedure is called blocking.

9. In addition to latent inhibition, Pavlov identified internal inhibition, external inhibition, and conditioned inhibition. In all examples of inhibition, or inhibitory conditioning, the CR is opposite in direction from the CR to excitatory conditioning.

10. Conditioned inhibitors can be produced by four methods: (a) by negative, or US-CS contingencies; (b) in a conditioned discrimination procedure, a CS^- becomes an inhibitor in contrast with CS^+ excitor; (c) by the induction method, where a neutral CS becomes an inhibitor after having been simultaneously paired with an excitor in extinction; and (d) through an inhibition of delay procedure, in which the early portion of a long-duration CS becomes inhibitory.

11. Two *indirect* methods of measuring

conditioned inhibition are the summation test and the retardation test. Inhibitors and excitors algebraically sum when added together in extinction. When inhibitors are put into an excitatory conditioning context, the acquisition of excitation is slowed (retarded).

12. Almost all stimuli can be made into conditioned stimuli, but both stimulus intensity and stimulus quality affect the ease of stimulus associability.

13. A number of experiments demonstrate that some stimulus-stimulus associations are easy and others are difficult; i.e., that there is stimulus specificity of association.

14. Preparedness theory argues that some animals are evolutionarily predisposed to make some associations, and to learn some tasks, more easily than others. If many trials are required for learning, the animal is said to be contraprepared; for an intermediate number of trials, the animal is unprepared.

15. Rapid learning about the consequences of ingestion is aided by innately organized feeding behavior. Neophobia toward new foods and reduced neophobia with continued exposure to them minimize poisonings.

16. Flavors are easily associated with illness-inducing toxins and less easily associated with electric shock. With optimal stimulus parameters, flavors and toxin effects can become associated in one trial over a several hour delay.

17. Matching shock intensity with illness intensity, and intensity and duration of taste stimuli with audio-visual stimuli, is problematic. Until experiments that better equate stimulus intensity and number of conditioning trials are accomplished, appealing to preparedness arguments to account for different conditioning outcomes are confounded by procedural differences.

18. General process learning remains the best theory to account for observed plasticity in animal behavior, including complex human behavior.

Discussion Questions

1. Eating foods in pizza parlors, studying algebraic equations in college classrooms, and monitoring emotional expressions while opening gifts at birthday parties were among the many examples of human behavior analyzed from the perspective of animal laboratory-based learning theory. How do these examples bear on questions of *ecological validity* raised in the first sentence of this chapter and Question 1 on p. 186?

2. Why is it so important to investigate the effect that prior learning experiences have on new learning?

3. What do you suppose Dr. Spicey® tastes like? Do you remember the learning concept introduced in Chapter 4 that might help you account for the fact that you know what a fictitious drink tastes like?

4. A reader of this text thought that I had overstated the power of taste aversion conditioning. Specifically, he said that he shared with me an aversion to pineapple, but he did not get sick at the thought of it. Furthermore, he doubted that the sight of the can of Dr. Spicey® (Box 5.1) would make a person ill. What do you think? Is the thought of an aversive learning experience sufficient to produce a conditioned response?

5. Don't you just love it that American idiom embodies animal learning theory as well as human behavior? Based upon what you have learned in this chapter,

what evidence can you bring to bear to dispute the saying that *you can't teach an old dog new tricks* while at the same time acknowledging the wisdom of the saying? How about *practice makes perfect?* Also, in what way are professors who are *so boring they put me to sleep* like Pavlov's dogs (see the section on inhibition of delay)? If I belabor this issue, I risk making you *sick to your stomach*—but it might be suggested this is not really possible (see the immediately preceding discussion question). Come up with some other examples of idioms that reflect learning principles, and send them to me. (If, when revising this text, I include your example, you will be acknowledged.)

6. Some people cannot study with the television on, or in the presence of other distracting sounds, while other students cannot study in a room that is too quiet. Pavlov and his successors were interested in individual differences such as these, and you can read about them in a book entitled *Pavlov's Typology* by J. A. B. Gray (1964). Can you use Pavlov's con-

cept of *external inhibition* to account for the psychological dimension of *noise,* where noise is *unwanted sound?*

7. I recently wrecked my car because I could not release my foot from the accelerator. A wild dog in a rural environment was attempting to get in the passenger-side door, and I was attempting to get my family and myself out of danger. My superexcitatory state seemed to prevent me (a) from taking my foot off the gas and (b) placing it on the brake. I crashed into another car.

   Can you help explain to my insurance company what went wrong in terms of excitatory and inhibitory processes controlling my erratic driving behavior?

8. Chapter 10 deals in part with language behavior. Given what you know about the concept of preparedness, can you make a guess which of the following aspects of language behavior is (are) *prepared,* and which is (are) *unprepared?* Babbling? Speaking? Reading? Writing? Spelling? Which should take the most trials to learn?

Glossary

Blocking   When, following conditioning to CS_1, CS_1 is then put into a compound with CS_2, attempts to condition CS_2 in the compound fail. The phenomenon is called *blocking* (or, sometimes, "Kamin blocking" after the researcher who designed the procedure and described the phenomenon). One hypothesis is that CS_2 is blocked because it is a *redundant* stimulus; i.e., not useful in predicting the occurrence of the US.

Conditioned Excitor   A descriptive term for the CS after it has been conditioned in a forward, or excitatory, manner. The CS acquires excitatory properties;

for example, the excitor can be used "as a US" in higher-order conditioning.

Conditioned Inhibition   The usual result of "backward" procedures (cf. *negative contingency*), conditioned inhibition is the opposite of conditioned excitation. Example: If *fear* is the conditioned (excitatory) response, *safety,* or *elation,* is the conditioned inhibitory response.

Conditioned Inhibitor   A descriptive term for the CS after it has been conditioned in a backward, or inhibitory, manner. The CS acquires inhibitory properties; for example, the inhibitor can retard the conditioning of another stimulus.

Contraprepared The opposite of a prepared, or easily conditioned, response. When associations between two stimuli, or a stimulus and a response, require many trials to learn, an animal is said to be *contraprepared* for association.

CS Preexposure Effect Preexposed, or familiar, conditioned stimuli require more trials to become associated with a given US than do novel conditioned stimuli. The reduced associability of familiar stimuli is also known as *latent inhibition*.

Disinhibition (Pavlov) An extraneous stimulus that disrupts the ongoing effects of an inhibitory stimulus, typically allowing a release of excitation, is called a *disinhibiting stimulus,* and the process is called *disinhibition.* Example: the effect of a loud noise on a drowsy state.

Ecological Validity In animal experiments, requiring an animal to learn a task that is likely to be encountered in the real world. Learning about foods is an *ecologically valid* task; learning to maintain balance on a hind paw while inebriated is of questionable ecological validity.

External Inhibition (Pavlov) Temporarily disrupting the ongoing process of conditioned excitation by introducing an extraneous stimulus. The extraneous stimulus acts as a distractor, a temporary inhibitory stimulus.

Higher-Order Conditioning (Pavlov) The process by which an arbitrary (conditioned) stimulus (CS_1) acquires unconditioned stimulus properties. CS_1 is first paired with a US. Following conditioning, CS_1 is then paired with yet another arbitrary stimulus (CS_2). CS_2 acquires US properties through the process called *higher-order conditioning.*

Induction Method An excitatory stimulus (such as a tone) is paired with shock. When another stimulus (such as a light) is paired with the tone, and the pair is not shocked, the tone "induces" the light to become an inhibitory, or "safe," stimulus. The procedure is called the *induction method* of conditioned inhibition.

Inhibition of Delay (Pavlov) The passage of time can produce an inhibitory process. Responding is suppressed, or inhibited, during the first part of regularly spaced intervals. An extraneous stimulus can disinhibit this *inhibition of delay.*

Internal Inhibition (Pavlov) Proposed by Pavlov as a counterpart to external inhibition. A process alleged to account for spontaneous recovery (following inhibition produced by extinction).

Latent Inhibition Preexposed, or familiar, conditioned stimuli require more trials to become associated with a given US than do novel conditioned stimuli. A preexposed CS thus is said to be *latently inhibited.* Reduced associability of familiar stimuli is also known as the *CS-preexposure effect.*

Negative Contingency A backward pairing sets up a *negative contingency* of CS and US. By contrast, a forward pairing sets up a positive contingency. Negative contingencies often result in the formation of conditioned inhibition, rarely in conditioned excitation.

Neophobia A behavioral tendency to approach new objects cautiously (literally, *fear of the new*). When applied to rats and humans responding to unfamiliar foods, their innate feeding tendencies are to cautiously approach and sniff before tasting, to be generally finicky.

Overshadowing When two CSs are conditioned at the same time, the usual result is that one CS acquires more associative strength than the other. This result is called *overshadowing*, in which one CS is said to overshadow the other CS.

Potentiation When a flavor stimulus (CS_1) is simultaneously conditioned with any other conditioned stimulus (i.e., CS_2), CS_2 is conditioned better than it would have been if merely conditioned by itself. The flavor stimulus is said to *potentiate* the conditioning of CS_2.

Preparedness The argument that animals are (evolutionarily) prepared to readily make associations between certain stimuli, and between some stimuli and certain responses, because such rapid learning enhances fitness.

Retardation Test A procedure that allows indirect measurement of conditioned inhibition. A stimulus is first made a conditioned inhibitor, and it is then conditioned as an excitor. The acquisition of conditioned excitation is retarded when a conditioned inhibitor is used, relative to a neutral stimulus.

Second-Order Conditioning (Pavlov) The first step, and the lowest level, of higher-order conditioning. After CS_1 has been paired with a US, CS_1 is then paired with CS_2—called conditioning of the second order. CS_2 acquires US properties through the process called higher-order conditioning.

Second Signal System (Pavlov) Words are arbitrary auditory (i.e., spoken) and visual (i.e., written) signals that are associated with real-world sensory impressions, such as "red sun" and "cold water." *Red sun* and *cold water* are the first signals of the real world. Words are symbols that represent these raw sensory experiences. Words are one level of abstraction removed from the world they represent—in Pavlov's terms, words are the signal of signals; hence, the *second signal system*.

Sensory Preconditioning A method used to measure CS-CS associations. In the first step, two conditioned stimuli (CS_1 and CS_2) are repeatedly paired together. CS_1 is then conditioned to a US, after which CS_2 is tested as if it had been conditioned. In sensory preconditioning, CS_2 shows (indirect) evidence of conditioning through its prior association with CS_1.

Stimulus Specificity in Conditioning Genetically determined (prepared) brain structures allow rapid learning of certain (specific) stimuli, and make the learning of other associations more difficult. Example: Garcia's telereceptor-cutaneous and gustatory-visceral conditioning systems. (Cf. *preparedness*.)

Summation Test A procedure that allows indirect measurement of conditioned inhibition. Following conditioning of CS_2 (a conditioned inhibitor) and CS_1 (a conditioned excitor), when presented together in extinction CS_1 and CS_2 will algebraically combine, or sum, such both the excitatory and inhibitory response are lessened.

Unprepared The theory that while some learning is *prepared* (i.e., learned in one or only a few trials), and other learning is *contraprepared* to be associated (i.e., many, many trials to learn); yet other stimuli and responses are *unprepared*, i.e., are relatively neutral in their associability (requiring an intermediate number of trials).

US Preexposure Effect Preexposed, or familiar, unconditioned stimuli require more trials to become associated with a given CS than do novel unconditioned stimuli. (cf. *CS preexposure effect*). Example: Exposing an animal to an electric shock before conditioning makes the electric shock a less effective unconditioned stimulus.

6

Instrumental Learning

I. Introduction

Until now the lens we have used to study learning has focused narrowly. In Chapters 4 and 5 we examined basic ways in which animals make associations between stimuli—namely, through the process of Pavlovian conditioning. In Pavlovian conditioning environmental stimuli impinge upon animals. In turn, animals respond in reflexive ways. Ultimately, through a process called conditioning, modified reflexes may result from these reflexive interactions with the environment.

In describing Pavlovian conditioning as "the modification of basic reflexes," we relegate animals to automatons—highly interesting but nevertheless robotlike creatures programmed to respond in certain ways. We are not robots, but a great deal of evidence suggests that, indeed, we are programmed to respond in identifiable patterns. Our reflexes and other innately disposed behavior patterns have evolved in ways that guarantee matches with environments we are likely to encounter during our lifetimes. That is, our reflexes are adaptive, and their modification, no matter how mechanical the process may be, also tends to increase our fitness with respect to the environment.

Is All Behavior Reflexive? But animals are not just reflexive machines. Animals engage in a variety of behaviors that seem to be initiated from within (internal environment—the brain) rather than from without (the external environment). Humans and other complex animals seem to exhibit volition and will; they seem to engage in spontaneous voluntary behavior as well as involuntary reflexive behavior.[1]

As we saw in Chapter 1, people behave in a variety of idiosyncratic ways. Genetic arguments aside for the moment, the very existence of individual differences is best interpreted as resulting from particular learning experiences. Individuals like particular foods, songs, books, people—and dislike others. We drive automobiles, operate televisions and VCRs, dance, play soccer and guitars, and use language. Some of us excel, some are average, and yet others never quite get the hang of these learned behaviors. We can account for the many observed differences in human behavior by analyzing the *learning histories* of individuals.

In this chapter, then, we begin to expand the study of learning by considering changes in such *nonreflexive* behaviors. How do animals learn as they move around in and act upon the environments they occupy? That is, when they *do* something, as opposed to having something done to them? Such behavior that acts upon the environment has been called *instrumental* behavior, as in "Carl's driving skills were *instrumental* in getting him to Miami safely," and "Wyomia's polite demeanor is *instrumental* in getting her teacher's attention." Not restricted to the modification of innately determined behavior, the learning of instrumental behavior allows us to construct "new" behavioral units.

II.   Instrumental and Thorndikean Conditioning

Acquiring and modifying "voluntary" or nonreflexive behavior has historically been called **instrumental learning,** or **instrumental conditioning.** E. L. Thorndike (1898) was among the first of behavioral scientists to describe how laboratory animals learn to make instrumental responses. Hence, another name for instrumental learning is **Thorndikean conditioning** (or **Thorndikean learning**).[2]

A question we will pursue throughout this chapter and the next is the extent to which classical conditioning and instrumental conditioning result from different processes. As a first consideration, however, note that reflexive and instrumental behaviors more often than not work together in concert. Thus, a woman caught walking in a dust storm will both blink as the swirling cloud approaches her face (a reflexive response) and turn her head, pull her hat brim lower, and

---

[1]Questions regarding "voluntary" and "involuntary" behavior will be asked throughout this chapter and again in Chapter 9. For present purposes, based upon common language usage, accept the distinction as meaningful.

[2]In conventional usage, *instrumental conditioning* is often contrasted with *classical conditioning*, and, likewise, comparisons are made between *Pavlovian* and *Thorndikean* conditioning.

wrap a scarf about her face (all **instrumental responses**) to avoid the full brunt of the blast. Her eye-blink response is acquired through Pavlovian conditioning (taking advantage of a reflex), while the instrumental responses of bowing her head and of making other shielding gestures are learned through instrumental conditioning (by escaping the punishment of blowing dust).

Shooting Free Throws.   Another example: We learn to aim a basketball shot toward a hoop by taking advantage of sensory-motor reflexes as well as by making skeletal-muscle adjustments. The eye involuntarily accommodates (the lens becomes thinner) while viewing the moving ball as it approaches the hoop. We shift weight, make minor adjustments in body posture via skeletal muscle flexion and extension, and perhaps change our timing for the next shot. Some of these adjustments are under conscious control, while others are not. If the next shot is successful, the previous posture (comprised of both reflexive and voluntary components) is reproduced (successfully or not) on succeeding shots.

As we will see, instrumental conditioning of new behaviors, such as making a successful hook shot, is strengthened or weakened depending upon whether the basket goes through the hoop (i.e., is *reinforced*) or not.

Stimulus Contingencies and Response Contingencies

Instrumental conditioning differs from classical conditioning in a number of ways. One distinction already described, that of contrasting "reflexes" with "voluntary behavior," is not as simple as it seems, primarily because not everyone agrees upon what constitutes "voluntary behavior." A distinction between classical and instrumental conditioning that can be agreed upon has to do with the requirement of a **response contingency** in instrumental conditioning.

Tail Wagging and Saliva Flow.   Recall that during Pavlovian salivary conditioning an experimenter arranges stimulus elements to be presented to the dog. Spotski is given food on a certain schedule in relation to a ringing bell. Spotski does not have to make any particular response in order to attain the food. Another way of saying this is that a stimulus-stimulus (i.e., CS-US) contingency is in effect in Pavlovian conditioning.

Salivation is measured as the reflexive response to the US and as the conditioned reflex to the CS. But dogs invariably make other responses during Pavlovian conditioning. For example, they look around, they wag their tails, and they pant when they are about to be fed. Are these other responses reflexive? Are they voluntary or involuntary?

What if the experimenter arranged conditions such that Spotski was *required* to wag his tail, or otherwise to "beg" for his food? That is, rather than merely pairing a ringing bell with food (a stimulus-stimulus contingency), the experimenter required tail wagging before giving food to the dog (a response-stimulus contingency)? An experimenter requiring a tail wag has set up an instrumental contingency between tail wagging and food.

Would tail wagging increase under these circumstances? Would salivation also increase?

S-S versus R-S Conditioning.   A shorthand designation for a Pavlovian (bell-food) contingency is stimulus-stimulus, or **S-S conditioning.** A Thorndikean contingency requiring a response before presenting food (such as tail wag—food) is called response-stimulus, or **R-S conditioning.** The most straightforward distinction that can be made between Pavlovian and Thorndikean conditioning is the S-S versus R-S contingency.

Why is this distinction important? What does it matter if an experimenter requires a dog to wag its tail for food (R-S contingency) rather than merely pair the food with the sound of a bell (S-S contingency)? The example may appear trivial, but let us consider the *range of behaviors* that may be conditioned using either S-S or R-S contingencies.

Instead of having the dog wag its tail, let us require it to climb stairs; or to sit quietly "on command"; or to "point" a bird while hunting; or to race other dogs around a track; or to sniff out explosives hidden in airport luggage. Do such accomplishments seem on the surface to be more complicated, more impressive, than being conditioned to salivate to the sound of a bell? Why? What is the difference?

Knowing what you now know, could you train a dog to accomplish these instrumental behaviors?

Range of Possible Responses.   One answer to the question of differences between S-S and R-S conditioning is that *what* animals can learn by S-S contingencies is limited to the range of reflexive responses the animal can make. That is, only inborn response tendencies can be conditioned. By contrast, using their skeletal muscles, animals make a wide range of responses while physically moving within their niche. Risking oversimplification, we say that to successfully operate in their environment requires the integration of both sensory and motor aspects of the animal's brain and body. Relative to reflexive responding, animal behavior becomes both more complicated and more interesting as it operates upon a much wider environment.

Smelling her perfume may elicit an orienting response (i.e., elicited behavior), but getting up the nerve to act on it (i.e., voluntary behavior) is another matter. But that is getting ahead of the story, because not everyone is agreed upon just how different are these two types of response tendencies. Let us next look at an experiment that studied the consequences of animals behaving in relatively simple environments.

Thorndike's Experiments

In his famous "puzzle box" studies, Thorndike (1898) constructed an experimental chamber with a latching door that could be opened by animals trapped inside (see Box 6.1). Hungry cats placed in the box for the first time, for example, "moved." Their movement included scratching, climbing, and bumping against the walls in a frenzied reaction both to the confinement and to the sight and smell of food available just outside the box. Eventually, by chance movement, the animal might bump against or claw a latching mechanism, releasing the door, allowing escape from the box.

Some time later when the cat was returned to the puzzle box for a second and third trial, it took less time to successfully locate and operate the latch. Eventually, after many more trials, upon being put in the box the cat performed the specific behavior required to unlatch the door without hesitation. Thorndike's measure of learning, then, was "time to escape from the puzzle box as a function of trials" (see Box 6.1).

Thorndike also observed dogs and chickens operating in different box environments. He then formulated basic general principles of instrumental learning, so named because the animals' responses were "instrumental" in escaping the box.

Thorndike's Law of Effect

Thorndike postulated an elementary principle governing all behavior, namely, the **law of effect.** The *law of effect* simply states that a *response that is followed by a pleasant consequence will tend to be repeated and a response followed by an unpleasant consequence will tend to decrease in frequency.* He called such pleasant and unpleasant consequences, respectively, **"satisfiers"** and **"annoyers."** Instrumental movements (responses) that led to the hungry cat's escape through an open door and to food (both pleasant consequences) tended, in Thorndike's terms, to be "stamped in." ["Stamping in" can be likened to "writing" on John Locke's *tabula rasa* (blank slate); both are metaphors for hypothesized changes in the brain when learning occurs.] Unsuccessful movements by the cat (i.e., those that did not allow escape, thereby maintaining both hunger and the annoying confinement) tended to drop out. The end result of the law of effect? Successful responses increase, and unsuccessful responses decrease;

BOX 6.1

Thorndike's Puzzle Boxes

Edward L. Thorndike (1874–1949) confined cats, dogs, and chickens in a variety of boxes to study their associative processes. Some boxes were easier to escape from than others. Pictured is box "K" in which a lever had to be depressed and a rope pulled to unlock the door. Another (box "Z") required that a cat make a response selected by Thorndike—such a scratching its belly—which cued Thorndike to open the door and allow the cat to escape to its food. Thorndike found that the arbitrarily selected scratching response "degraded" over a period of time to the point the cat merely made swiping motions at its underside, rather than effectively scratching itself. Later in this chapter you will see that Marion and Keller Breland, who trained circus animals to perform crowd-pleasing instrumental tasks, provided theoretical insight into the nature of these "response degradations." (From Thorndike, 1898.)

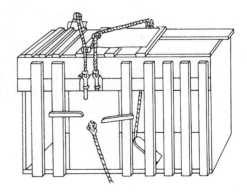

animals learn to be more efficient and more effective in operating upon the environment.

Hedonism.   Another way to describe the law of effect is to note that all organisms are born with hedonistic tendencies; it is both adaptive and "normal" for us to seek pleasure and to avoid pain. Note that Thorndike neither discovered nor invented the law of effect; rather, he recognized the importance of this commonly known general rule governing behavior.[3]

In a discipline for which exceptions to the rule are the rule, **hedonism** is best understood as a psychobiological law. Most animals, most of the time, engage in behaviors that produce pleasure and discontinue behaviors that produce pain.

Among the best understood incentives for hedonistic tendencies are the taste and olfactory components of palatable foods (Bolles, 1991). Following Thorndike's use of the puzzle box, many thousands of laboratory animals have been conditioned and have learned instrumental responses based upon food rewards. (The aversive control of behavior in laboratory animals—typically through the use of "annoyers" such as electric shock—will be discussed in Chapter 7.)

The Psychobiological Law of Effect

Combine Thorndike's original conception of the law of effect with that of hedonism as an evolutionary behavioral tendency, add the results of nearly 100 years of laboratory animal experimentation, and the resulting "psychobiological" *law of effect* occupies a unique position in contemporary learning theory.

General Process Learning Theory.   The law of effect is a deceptively simple concept. Asserting that "satisfiers" increase and that "annoyers" decrease the probability of occurrence of *all* preceding behaviors, in *all* animals, however, covers a lot of ground! The law of effect complements classical conditioning in providing support for a *general process learning theory*, described in the preceding two chapters.

Both hedonism and the law of effect are firmly grounded in biology. Each can be accounted for as evolutionary adaptations. Risking a tautology, most pleasurable activities in life promote fitness, survival, and reproduction. Food, shelter, and mating (Thorndike's "satisfiers") are all pleasurable and adaptive, while the opposite is true of "annoyers" in the form of hunger, pain, and adverse climate. For most animals in their ecological niches, therefore, the very behaviors they engage in are instrumental in producing food, in securing shelter and mates, and in avoiding predators, toxins, and reproductive extinction. In summary, the law of effect embodies adaptive responses to selective pressures.

[3]My grandmother (and hers) understood and applied basic *carrot and stick* psychology without the benefit of exposure to Thorndike's theory. Carrots (dangled in front) and sticks (applied to the rear) were traditionally used as incentives to motivate donkeys to move in accordance with their human owner's wishes.

BOX 6.2

Thinking Good Thoughts and Making Good Choices

Why do reinforcers reinforce? Why does the presentation of food to a hungry animal (or water to a thirsty animal) allow responses that preceded these reinforcers to be so readily learned and repeated on future occasions? D. C. Dennett (1975), in an article entitled "Why the Law of Effect Will Not Go Away," argues that the role of reinforcement is to "select" behaviors and responses much the same way that the environment in Darwin's theory of natural selection "chooses" which organisms are to live and which will die.

According to Dennett, those animals in past times who were not sensitive to "positive reinforcers" or "punishers" (i.e., those aspects of the environment which promote survival) have gone extinct. Therefore, all extant animals were selected to obey the *law of effect*.

Dennett further argues that "good ideas" are also selected by the same general mechanism. In response to a complicated stimulus environment (i.e., one in which simple reflexive responses are not elicited), all humans *generate* hypotheses, or ideas. The generation of such hypotheses is accomplished by brain structures that have also been selected through evolution; some genotypes underlying some brain structures are better than others at generating likely hypotheses. Intelligent humans *select* those ideas which provide the most optimal consequences (in the same way reinforcement selects appropriate responses). Therefore, according to Dennett, a Darwinian *natural* selection of intelligent behavior, mediated by the law of effect, ensues.

In light of Dennett's arguments, under what conditions is behavior "maladaptive"? Does the law of effect provide an ethic of "right" and "wrong"?

Dennett (1975) has beautifully described both the adaptive nature of hedonism and the law of effect. His argument for the inevitability of the law of effect, and his outline of a theory of human cognitive behavior based upon these innate response tendencies, can be found in Box 6.2.

Determinism and the Law of Effect

How well does the law of effect account for human learning and behavior? Again, the reader must ultimately be the judge. Most of us are vaguely aware that "the environment" at a minimum influences our behavior, even if we might disagree that it *determines* our behavior. Indeed, as we shall see, differences in philosophy and in learning theories hinge on this very distinction.

A position of *hard determinism* asserts that all human behavior can be accounted for by combining **biological determinism** with **environmental determinism.** A *biological determinist* asserts that genes expressed in a given environment severely limit (prohibit) alternative response outcomes. Hardwired, reflexive behavior, FAPs, instincts, etc., are examples of biologically determined behavior. Such behaviors are typically seen as being more or less "involuntary."

An *environmental determinist* asserts that choice is delimited by reinforcement and punishment contingencies (i.e., the *law of strength*). In Thorndike's terms, such learned behavior is (involuntarily) "stamped in" by satisfiers.

A hard determinist position, then, proposes that humans and other animals do not have "free choice." John B. Watson and B. F. Skinner are famous advocates of a hard determinist position (see what follows). By contrast, a philosophy of *soft determinism* asserts that both genes and environments influence but do not determine human behavior. Genes and environment limit response alternatives, but do not prohibit choice (i.e., voluntary behavior) from among these alternatives.

To test your understanding of the distinction between hard and soft determinism, review Dennett's position in Box 6.2. Is Dennett a hard or soft determinist?[4]

John B. Watson's Behaviorism

One of the first psychologists to espouse a position of hard environmental determinism was also one of the more amazing characters in the history of psychology (see Box 6.3). John B. Watson's belief that human behavior is directly, inevitably determined by the environment is evident in his famous statement announcing a philosophy he called **behaviorism:**

> Give me a dozen healthy infants, well-formed, and my own specified world to bring them up in and I'll guarantee to take anyone at random and train him to become any type of specialist I might select—doctor, lawyer, artist, merchant-chief, and yes, even beggar-man and thief, regardless of his talents, penchants, tendencies, abilities, vocations, and race of his ancestors. (Watson, 1924)

The term *behaviorism* is unfortunate; *environmentalism* is better. Why? Because genetic predispositions are ignored in Watson's theory, and a general theory of behavior must include both innate and environmental components (see Chapter 1, Footnote 3, p. 6).

[4]hard

BOX 6.3

John B. Watson and the History of Behaviorism

John B. Watson during his student days at Furman University, circa 1899.

In his book *Mechanical Man: John Broadus Watson and the Beginnings of Behaviorism*, Kerry W. Buckley asserts that Watson's *behaviorism* played a major role in the modernization of American society. At the turn of the century Watson left the South Carolina farm where he had been reared in poverty. After taking his doctorate at the University of Chicago, he moved to Johns Hopkins University, where, within a few short years, he founded the *behaviorist movement* and became one of America's most influential psychologists.

At the pinnacle of his academic career, Watson and his graduate student, Rosalie Rayner, published the "Little Albert" experiment in which an eleven-month-old child was classically conditioned to fear a white rat. Their point? Not unlike other animals, Watson argued, humans are buffeted by instinct on the one hand and an all-controlling environment on the other. We are programmed throughout our childhood. According to Watson, human minds, consciousness, and will are illusions.

John B. Watson's academic career came to an abrupt end in 1920. Forced to resign, Watson headed for a more lucrative job with the J. Walter Thompson advertising agency. There Watson promoted his behaviorist philosophy to a far wider audience than would have been the case had he remained a university professor. Together the Watsons wrote popular magazine articles, published books, and gave radio interviews, on, among other topics, their (sometimes bizarre) philosophy of child rearing. Fathers should be remote and inaccessible, they asserted. And even mothers should severely limit the amount of affection they give their children. Buckley points out that the behaviorist philosophy fit well with the emerging urban culture of the Roaring Twenties. A review of *Watson's Behaviorism*, published in 1924, by the *New York Times* considered it "perhaps the most important book ever written."

While we may be generous and forgive Watson's trumpeting of environment over biology (due, presumably, to a relative paucity of evidence for behavioral genetics in 1920), the fact is that he offered little experimental evidence to support even his environmental claims. As we will see in more detail in Chapter 8, Watson's laboratory investigations bearing on the foregoing assertion consisted of one published paper—the results of conditioning one fear response in one child (Watson & Rayner, 1920).

Nevertheless, John B. Watson's influence was profound. Behaviorism dominated academic psychology for the next 40 years, and in addition it influenced both American educators and popular culture (Buckley, 1989). Among those Watson influenced was a young experimental psychologist just embarking upon a 50-year research career. Burrhus Frederic Skinner (1904–1990) and his many students were successful in accomplishing laboratory research upon which a formal experimental analysis of learned behavior could be built.

Interim Summary

1. Behavior has both reflexive and nonreflexive (voluntary and involuntary) components.
2. Nonreflexive behavior can be modified by a process called *instrumental conditioning,* or *instrumental learning.* Also known as *Thorndikean conditioning,* instrumental conditioning complements *classical conditioning* (the modification of reflexive behavior).
3. Researchers conditioning animals by Pavlovian, or *S-S,* procedures arrange *stimulus contingencies:* A CS is followed by a US. Researchers conditioning animals by Thorndikean, or *R-S,* procedures arrange *response contingencies:* A response is followed by a positive reinforcer or a punishing stimulus.
4. E. L. Thorndike proposed that behavior is modifiable by the *law of effect:* Responses followed by *satisfiers* will be repeated and responses followed by *annoyers* will not.
5. The psychobiological *law of effect* asserts that the hedonistic experience of pleasure and of pain avoidance (a) selects or reinforces behavior and (b) constitutes an evolutionary selective pressure.
6. Instrumental learning based upon the law of effect addresses how *all* animals learn in all circumstances, and it is therefore a *general process learning theory.*
7. John B. Watson's philosophy of *behaviorism* espouses a hard environmental *determinism* in which the expression of behavior is controlled by reinforcers and punishers.

III.   Operant Conditioning

As a graduate student B. F. Skinner objected to the way animal learning experiments were conducted in the laboratory. By the 1930s rats in mazes were in and Thorndike's puzzle boxes were out. Rats were placed in runways and given food rewards for their successful negotiation of right and left turns. How many trials did it take before the rat made no errors such as turning right when it was supposed to turn left? How many seconds did the rat take to get from the start box to the goal box, on the first trial and on the last trial?

By his own account Skinner decided to automate the runway procedure (see Figure 6.1). First he attached a feeder to the runway; the weight of the moving rat was *instrumental* in tilting the runway, mechanically activating the feeder. Skinner eventually did away with the runway altogether. He next simplified the apparatus to where the rat merely pushed open a door to get food:

> The behavior of the rat in pushing open the door . . . was obviously learned, but its status as part of the final performance was not clear. It seemed wise to add an initial conditioned response connected with ingestion in a quite arbitrary way. I chose the first device which came to hand—a horizontal bar or lever placed where it could be conveniently depressed by the rat to close a switch which operated a (feeder). (Skinner, 1959, p. 366)

The Experimental Environment

With the invention of what became known as a **Skinner Box,** Skinner's research strategy for many years focused upon an analysis of how food rewards influenced key pecking by pigeons and lever pressing by rats and other animals. The primary dependent variables that can be measured in this experimental environment are (a) rate of lever pressing; (b) control of response patterning under different conditions of reinforcement; and (c) "choice" behavior (in boxes with more than one response key).

Skinner's Research Strategy.   Skinner was aware of the criticism of ethologists regarding the study of animal behavior in laboratories, and he was sensitive to the ethologists concept of innately organized behavior (Skinner, 1966). How did he justify his use of the conditioning-box methodology?

1. Skinner intentionally removed animals from their natural environments to better identify and isolate independent variables controlling the animal's responses.

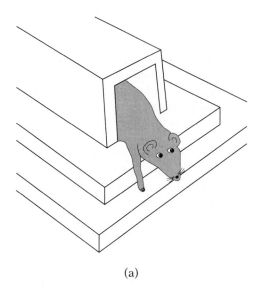

(a)

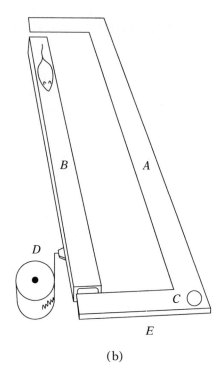

(b)

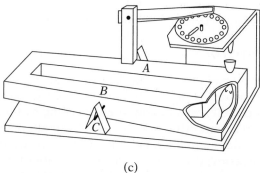

(c)

FIGURE 6.1 The Evolution of the Skinner Box

B. F. Skinner describes the evolution of the Skinner Box in a tongue-in-cheek article decrying formal scientific method (Skinner, 1959). He points out two instrumental factors in his career. First, the role of serendipity—finding something you are not looking for, and pursuing it. Second, he claims that personal laziness (which was *not* characteristic of him) led him to design the Skinner Box to automate the collection of data rather than continue the labor-intensive use of runways (a), of circular runways (b), and of a circular runway with an automated feeding device (c). (From Skinner, 1959.)

2. Skinner intentionally selected arbitrary responses (key pecking and lever pressing) that were presumably not akin to FAPs or other biologically prepared responses (Skinner, 1963).
3. Skinner designed a convenient, economical, and reliable way to automate stimulus delivery and to measure animal responses, thereby assuring a standardized methodology that investigators could adopt in laboratories around the world. They did.

The Skinner Box.   Let us take a closer look at B. F. Skinner and his Skinner Box (see Figure 6.2). The small chamber consists of four walls, a ceiling, and a grid floor. From one wall a lever (called a *manipulandum*—plural is *manipulanda*) protrudes. A rat or other small mammal is trained to press the lever. Depressing the lever activates an electrical switch, allowing responses to be recorded. In another version of the chamber, the manipulandum is a back-lit panel, or lighted key. Positioned on the wall at an optimal height for a pigeon to peck, the key is also connected to a microswitch allowing the pigeon's responses to be electrically recorded. Food or water can be delivered into a small container attached to the wall for the rats. For pigeons, a "grain hopper" from which food can be pecked is made available for a few seconds.

The chamber may also be fitted with a speaker over which background masking noise (or any other auditory stimulus) can be introduced, and with lights for both illumination and signaling purposes. Finally, aversive control of behavior can be investigated by applying electric current to the grid floor.

The Study of Operant Conditioning

How did Skinner begin the experimental analysis of behavior? Starting in the 1930s and continuing for 50 years, Skinner and his many students systematically studied **operant conditioning** in the experimental chambers described in the foregoing.

Operant Responses.   First, Skinner defined the response by which he would analyze behavior. He defined an **operant** as any response that "operated" upon the environment (cf. instrumental response). Because a lever-pressing response is an easily repeated operant, Skinner's **free operant** method can be contrasted with the **discrete trial** methods characteristic of other types of behavioral analysis. Pavlovian conditioning, escaping from a puzzle box, and negotiating a maze each have a discrete beginning, duration, and end—a sequence called a *trial*. By contrast, in operant conditioning one lever-pressing response is *not* called a trial. Rather, learning is measured during periods, or sessions, of lever pressing typically lasting 30 to 60 minutes.

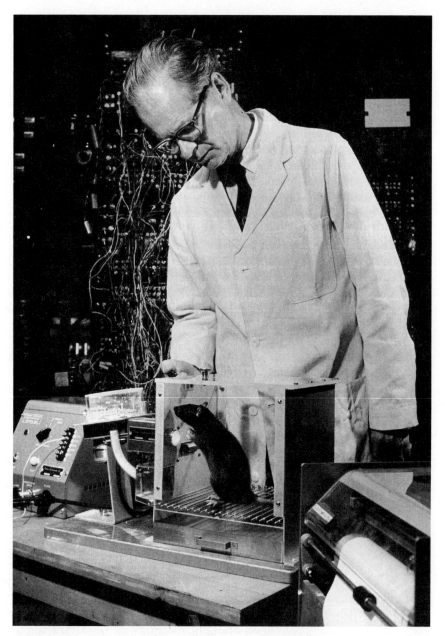

FIGURE 6.2   Burrhus Fredric Skinner, 1904–1990.

Operant conditioning is best understood as a variant of instrumental learning that presents a unique methodology and specialized terminology to experimentally analyze behavior.

Operant Methodology in Action

The power of the law of effect can be seen in operantly conditioning a naive rat to lever press or a pigeon to key peck. For example, a hungry rat when placed in the chamber will explore the new environment for several minutes by sniffing, rearing on its hind legs, and touching objects with its front paws.

The rat's exploratory behavior appears to be both voluntary and purposive, rather than reflexive. For this reason, the rat's behavior is said to be emitted, rather than elicited. We explored examples of **elicited behavior,** such as reflexive salivation, in earlier chapters; food placed on the dog's tongue involuntarily *elicited* a salivation response. By contrast, instrumental responses—including arbitrary operants such as pressing a lever—are examples of what Skinner called **emitted behavior.**

Operant Levels.   Every emitted behavior has a *baseline,* or **operant level** of occurrence. For example, the rat's likelihood of sniffing floors and walls upon first entering the box is high; deftly depressing the lever in the box, low. Operant conditioning, then, involves selecting a low-level operant and through reinforcement making the target response more probable.

Magazine Training.   During the rat's initial exploration the experimenter initiates the first phase of training, called **magazine training.** Approaches to the food cup (cf. "magazine," where military provisions are kept) are *reinforced* when the rat finds food in the cup. That is, behavior is reinforced by providing food immediately following the desired response. The food is called a **positive reinforcer** (cf. Thorndike's "satisfiers").

Secondary Reinforcers.   What has the rat learned up to now? *Where* the food is located. While the rat is eating from the cup the electrical feeder is activated by the experimenter, delivering more food to the cup. The feeder noise may initially produce a startle response in the rat. The startle response quickly disappears, however, presumably because in a few trials the sound of the electrically activated feeder becomes a *conditioned stimulus* signaling food. Furthermore, after the feeder sound has been paired several times with food delivery, the feeder sound becomes a **secondary reinforcer** via the process of higher-order conditioning (discussed in Chapter 5). We shall return to the secondary reinforcing effects of the feeder.

What has the rat or pigeon learned up to this point? *Where* the food is located, and *when* food becomes available (i.e., when food is delivered to the food cup, as signaled by the feeder's sound).

Shaping Behavior

At the end of training, the experimenter will reinforce only the **target response** (or *target behavior*), in this instance, a lever-pressing or key-pecking response. Shortly after magazine training, however, the rat initially is reinforced for merely approaching the manipulandum (lever), conveniently located next to the food cup. This intermediate procedure is necessary because the rat has yet to learn the target behavior. For example, should the animal retreat to the rear of the cage and then turn its head back in the direction of the lever, or make any movement toward the lever, the orientation behavior is reinforced by delivery of food. Next, only the intermediate behavior of approaching and touching the lever is reinforced.

The foregoing method of training responses that are approximately like the target behavior is called **shaping** by **successive approximation.** Eventually, only the target response (i.e., lever pressing) will earn the food reward. The process by which selected operants are altered by the application of positive reinforcers is called **positive reinforcement.**

Thought question: Can you verbalize the difference between the concept of *positive reinforcement* and a *positive reinforcer?*

Putting It All Together.   What has the rat or pigeon learned? *Where* the food is located, *when* food is delivered to the food cup, and most importantly, the response contingency—*which* operant response is associated with the positive reinforcer, food.

Measuring Operant Responses

As we have seen, B. F. Skinner quickly discovered that programming reinforcements and measuring animal responses are difficult and tedious to accomplish without automatic equipment (Skinner, 1959). Let us look more closely at how operant behavior is measured.

Cumulative Records.   At present, computer-controlled equipment is used to connect the animal with its programmed environment (see Figure 6.2). A popular and relatively simple way to visualize behavioral effects of reinforcement is to use an instrument called a *cumulative recorder,* a device that generates a **cumulative record.**

The operation of a cumulative recorder is quite simple. Paper is unrolled onto a drum (see Figure 6.3), and ink-writing pens (fixed in

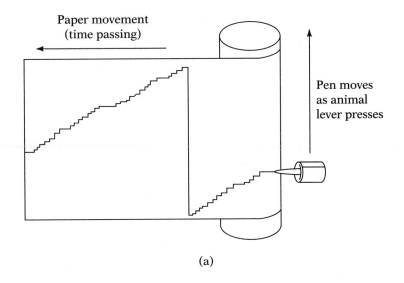

Paper movement
(time passing)

Pen moves
as animal
lever presses

(a)

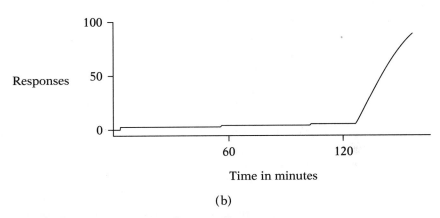

Responses

100

50

0

60   120

Time in minutes

(b)

FIGURE 6.3   Measuring Operant Responses

Operant responses distributed in time are easily visualized on a *cumulative recorder* (a). A motor turns the drum of the instrument, pulling the paper through at a constant speed. A pen resting on the paper writes on the passing paper. When the animal makes a lever-pressing or key-pecking response, a ratchet moves the pen sideways. In (a), then, the passage of time is indicated by the direction of the moving paper, and responses by sideways pen movements. In (b), only a few responses have been made in the first two hours, as indicated by the flat line indicating the passage of time. You can see several sideways excursions of the pen during the first two hours, and the rapid increase in lever pressing after two hours (after Skinner, 1938).

position) resting against the drum write on the paper as it is rolled beneath them at a constant rate.

First, note how responses are plotted as time unfolds. An inked line is made horizontally (*x* axis) with the passage of time. The pen is also connected to a pulley. Each lever press sends the pen up, vertically, one notch. If the lever is not depressed, the line continues horizontally. Lever presses (vertical) are therefore displayed with the passage of time (horizontal). The rate of lever pressing (number of responses per unit time) is revealed by the *slope* of the ink-drawn line. Note the slope of the lines in Figure 6.3.

Finally, a cumulative record can be programmed to show when food reinforcement occurs. Little slashes, or ticks, can be programmed on the response line, as indicated at the arrows in Figure 6.4 (see p. 240). The cumulative record is a visual shorthand allowing the experimenter to quickly and surely analyze the effects of reinforcement on operant behavior.

The Home Environment as a Skinner Box

Can human behavior be shaped? Is it possible to adopt both Skinner's methodology and his terminology to experimentally analyze how human behavior can be both acquired and subsequently modified?

In his earliest writings B. F. Skinner asserted that human behavior could be systematically changed by the judicious application of reinforcement and punishment. For example, his famous utopian novel, *Walden Two* (Skinner, 1948) created a carefully controlled environment in which humans lived. Adult "planners" and "programmers" shaped appropriate behaviors in both children and adults by the judicious application of reinforcement. Likewise, the programmers modified inefficient, (or incorrect, or maladaptive) behaviors either by extinction or punishment, or by rewarding alternative behaviors.

Questions of whether human behavior can be controlled, and *how*, will be entertained later in this chapter and again in Chapters 8 and 10. At that time we will analyze Skinner's hard determinist assertion that behavior is controlled by environmental stimuli.

Are there similarities in the methods by which humans, rats, and pigeons acquire new patterns of responding in Skinner boxes and home environments? Let us look at a few examples:

A Game of "Hot and Cold."   A favorite game children (and some adults) play resembles experimenters with their rats. The task of the person that is selected to be "it" is to determine a target behavior—to find a particular object that has been hidden, or to guess a secret word. The experimenter(s) *shapes* the behavior (moving around in the environment or guessing categories of words) by saying "you're hot" for getting close or "you're cold" for inappropriate responses. For example, if a marble has been hidden in a vase on a shelf, movements toward that side of the room would be reinforced with the words "you're getting hot." Likewise, adults lead small children to Easter eggs by *successive approximation*. The words "hot" and "cold" can be construed as *secondary* reinforcers and punishers (see Chapter 5, Pavlov's *second signal system*, regarding how words acquire meaning).

Thought question 1: Depending upon the child's age and other circumstances, might one get better performance if M&M's® candy was used in place of the words "you're hot"?

Thought question 2: Assume you are "it" and in place of eggs you are competing with other participants to hunt down a limited number of hidden $100 bills. You can select your own "guide" to shape your search behavior. Your choices are an excellent algebra teacher with a great deal of common sense, a highly successful basketball coach, or a nerd "rat runner." Each has 15 years experience in their professions. Your choice is . . . ?

Training Rats and Children.   More often than not we underestimate the power of operant conditioning and the lessons that can be learned by its study. Prospective parents might profit by first training laboratory animals under the supervision of a behaviorist. Two things would very quickly become evident: first, how powerful are reinforcement and the law of effect; and second, how easy it is to screw up an animal's (and a child's) behavior. Let us look at two examples.

A behavioral expert can efficiently train bar-pressing responses of animals in well less than an hour. Without appropriate attention to detail, novices may be ineffective in shaping skilled rat behavior even after many hours of training, and some may never get the hang of it. Even a skilled animal trainer can sometimes end up with behavior different from what was envisioned. For example, a graduate student once asked me to look at a rat that had been shaped to depress a lever for food reinforcement. The rat was lying on its back, under the lever, and pulling on the lever as if it were doing chin-ups. When I asked him how in the world he had managed to train such a complicated behavior pattern, he confessed that he had stepped out of the room for a few hours and left the rat to its own devices. Apparently, the rat had been reinforced several times while in that position; extensive retraining was necessary to get the rat up off the floor.

Another example: All of us have seen parents with their "out of control" children in grocery stores. Behavioral experts recognize that it is the parent, not the child, who has lost **behavioral control.** When the term *behavioral control* is used in this formal sense, it refers to the reinforcement and punishment contingencies in operation at the time a behavior is being exhibited. In this usage, behavioral control is not equivalent to "parents disciplining their children." For example, the same parent whose commonsense approach precludes "bribing a child to do something" will inadvertently perpetuate an undesirable behavior by buying candy for the child after the tenth annoying "pleeeezzz." Achieving behavioral control in child rearing is expedited by a knowledge of operant conditioning. Playing *"hot and cold"* works. Nonsystematic observations of grandma's *carrot and stick* psychology, however, does little to further the scientific analysis of behavior pursued by Thorndike, Watson, and Skinner. Let us return to the more formal analyses of behavior afforded by Skinner.

Interim Summary

1. B. F. Skinner's research strategy was to pick an arbitrary response (which he called an *operant*) and to analyze how reinforcement modified and controlled that response.
2. Skinner and his students measured the operant responses of lever pressing and key pecking in an experimental chamber called a Skinner Box.
3. The sequence of training operant responses is (a) to measure the baseline, or *operant level,* prior to reinforcement; (b) to initiate *magazine training* in which the sound of a feeder becomes associated with the *positive reinforcer* of food; (c) to *shape* responses similar to the *target response* by the method of *successive approximation;* and (d) to finally reinforce only the target response.
4. Skinner boxes are computer programmed to present stimuli to the animal and to measure the animal's operant responses. Lever-pressing responses can be displayed on cumulative records.
5. Operant conditioning can be extended to behaviors outside of the Skinner Box.

IV. Schedules of Reinforcement

Recall that Skinner opted to analyze behavior using both rate and patterning of lever-pressing responses as his dependent variables. Among his many findings are that peculiar, highly distinctive patterns of lever pressing result when animals are subjected to different **schedules of reinforcement.** Obviously, behavioral scientists are interested in how reinforcement produces patterns of behavior more complex than lever pressing. Before exploring the application of reinforcement theory to complex human behavior, let us examine the effects of scheduling reinforcement on lever pressing.

Continuous Reinforcement

Continuous reinforcement (abbreviated **CRF**) is important in the acquisition of many operant responses. CRF means that each emitted response produces a positive reinforcement. Simply stated, animals appear to learn an "if-then" contingency: *if* I turn left in the maze, or *if* I peck the key, *then* a food pellet (or drink of water) magically appears.

The acquisition of this new pattern of lever-pressing behavior proceeds in a predictable manner. Not unlike the acquisition of a Pavlovian conditioning response, CRF schedules during acquisition characteristically produce *positively accelerated* patterns of response. A positively accelerated slope merely means that as time passes increasingly more responses are made, and less time is taken between responses. After training, bar pressing proceeds at a rate dictated by how rapidly the animal eats (or drinks) the positive reinforcer.

By contrast, if, early in training, each response is not reinforced, more time is required to achieve steady lever-pressing responses. Many types of intermittent, or partial, reinforcement schedules have been studied. A few examples follow.

Partial, or Intermittent, Reinforcement

In contrast to continuous reinforcement, **partial reinforcement,** or **intermittent reinforcement,** schedules have three main characteristics: (a) they result in *slower acquisition* of stable responding; (b) partial reinforcement schedules produce *more responses* in a session of fixed duration (presumably because reinforcement occurs aperiodically, slowing down the ingestive process); and (3) partial reinforcement produces *greater* **resistance-to-extinction** when reinforcement is no longer forthcoming (see what follows).

Four schedules of reinforcement have been most intensively studied: fixed ratio (FR), variable ratio (VR), fixed interval (FI), and variable interval (VI). Figure 6.4 shows cumulative records generated by these various schedules of reinforcement.

Fixed-Ratio Schedules

In a **fixed-ratio (FR) schedule,** reinforcement is contingent upon the completion of a fixed number of operants, such as lever-pressing responses. For example, if every tenth response is reinforced, the schedule is designated *FR-10*. The animal can bar press quickly or slowly in making the 10 responses. In a given session more positive reinforcers can be earned if the animal presses the lever faster.

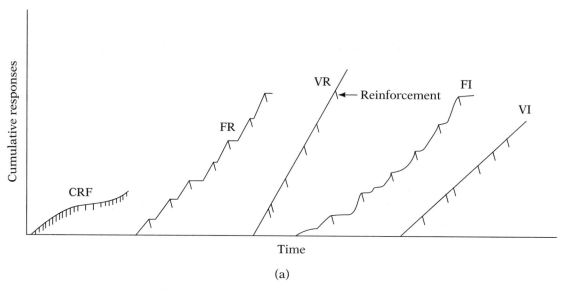

FIGURE 6.4   Cumulative Records of Common Schedules of Reinforcement

(a) Cumulative records of CRF (continuous reinforcement), FI (fixed-interval), FR (fixed-ratio), VR (variable-ratio), and VI (variable-interval) schedules of reinforcement. The steepness (slope) of the each line reflects the *rate* of response. Notice that while the VR produces a higher rate of response than the VI, both schedules produce straighter lines than CRF, FR, and FI schedules—indicating more stable, evenly spaced responding. When the reinforcing frequencies of VI and VR schedules are equated, the rate of responding on the VR schedule might be 2–4 times higher than on the VI. The reasons are (1) that "pausing" decreases the frequency of reinforcement on the VR more than it does on the VI, and (2) animals are apparently sensitive to relationship of their work (rate of responding) to their pay (rate of reinforcement). "Work for pay" will be further discussed in Chapter 9.

The Postreinforcement Pause on FR Schedules.   When the ratio of unreinforced to reinforced responses is relatively small (such as when every fifth response is reinforced, i.e., a FR-5), fairly high rates of evenly spaced responses result. Responding resumes shortly after the animal eats (or drinks) the positive reinforcement. As the ratio becomes larger (e.g., FR-100, every one-hundredth response produces a positive reinforcer), the response that produces food is typically followed by a long pause, called the **postreinforcement pause.**

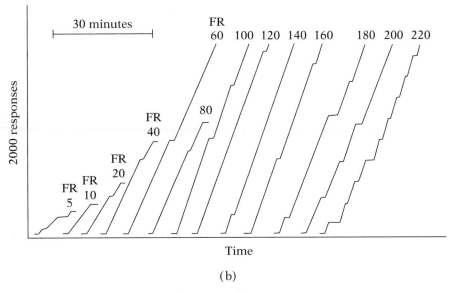

(b)

FIGURE 6.4 (continued)

(b) Cumulative records of increasing FR requirements from a single rat. Fewer responses are made on the FR-5, FR-10, FR-20, and FR-40 schedules because the rat receives more food relative to responses, gets full, and quits responding. Notice on the highest ratios (FR-180, FR-200, and FR-220) the postreinforcement pause is greater, as indicated by the straight horizontal segments following reinforcement. (Part (b) from Collier, Hirsch, & Hamlin, 1972.)

Let us compare the behavior of pigeon "A" pecking on a FR-10 and pigeon "B" pecking on a FR-100 schedule. Assume that the positive reinforcer for both pigeons is "five seconds access to a grain hopper full of food." Pigeon "A" on a FR-10 schedule may resume responding within a second or two after eating. Pigeon "B" responding on an FR-100 schedule may not resume responding immediately after eating the food; rather, it may wait an additional 10–15 seconds or more. The duration of the pause before responding resumes is directly related to the size of the ratio.[5]

[5]"Postreinforcement pauses" are seen in everyday life in a variety of situations, and bear little resemblance to lever pressing and the presence or absence of food. For example, longer periods of study and daily class attendance are usual responses immediately prior to an exam. What pattern of behavior is typically found in the class period following an exam? Another example: We seldom hear from politicians until just before election time. Why then? What is the "availability of reinforcement" in both examples?

Variable-Ratio Schedules

As is the case with *fixed-ratio* schedules of reinforcement, the **variable-ratio (VR) schedule** requires a specified number of responses before the reinforcer is delivered. A rat responding on a VR-10, for example, is reinforced, on the average, for every tenth response. But the number of responses required for a particular positive reinforcer varies during the work session. Computer programs determine that the rat is reinforced after 1 or 2 responses or after 15 or 20 responses; on a VR-10 their average during a work session is 10 responses.

The *postreinforcement pauses* seen for animals working on fixed-ratio schedules of reinforcement are longer than those seen when variable-ratio schedules are in effect. Why? Put yourself in the rat's place. Can you first come up with a *cognitive hypothesis* involving "expectancies"? Again, this time as a hungry rat, can you come up with a *behavioral hypothesis* of maximizing your responses to get the most reinforcers per unit time?

Lacking the postreinforcement pause, VR schedules generally produce high, steady rates of operant responding (cf. Figure 6.4). Can you think of an example of human behavior that resembles that of rats working on a VR schedule of reinforcement? If you owned a gambling casino in Las Vegas, and you could program the slot machines that your customers would play, what payoff schedules (reinforcement schedules) would you use to maximize your profits? CRF? FR-50? VR-50?

Fixed-Interval Schedules

An animal on a **fixed-interval (FI) schedule** is reinforced for its first response following a specified *time interval.* Another way of saying this is that *interval* schedules of reinforcement make the positive reinforcer available after a programmed amount of time passes. Interval schedules, therefore, are contrasted with fixed- or variable-ratio schedules in which reinforcement is dependent upon amount and rate of work, irrespective of time.

For example, in a fixed-interval 60-second schedule of reinforcement (abbreviated *FI-60*), the first response after 60 seconds has elapsed is reinforced. (The interval is measured from the time of delivery of the preceding reinforced response.) Note that even though a time contingency has been added, the delivery of the food reinforcement is still *response* contingent.

You be the hungry pigeon. Would you rather earn food for the first response you make after 10 seconds (FI-10) or for the first response you make after 45 seconds (FI-45)? After experiencing these two payoff schedules for several sessions, would you respond the same on each? That is, can you predict what your postreinforcement pause would look like on these two FI schedules? Think about it. After receiving a food pellet, what are your chances of getting another one any time soon? Better on the FI-10. On the other schedule, 45 seconds must elapse before food is available again.

Scalloping.   For that reason fixed-interval schedules of many seconds duration typically produce cumulative curves showing a zero or near-zero response rate immediately following reinforcement and a gradual increase in rate as the end of the fixed interval approaches. A distinctive pattern called *scalloping* appears on the cumulative record (see Figure 6.4). These "scallops" begin to appear following extensive training on longer VI schedules. Can you visualize the shape of the respective scallops on FI-30 and FI-120 schedules of reinforcement?

Do we see scallops in human behavior? For example, do employees work harder on payday than on other days? Why or why not? Under what conditions might they? A remarkable example of the patterning of responses leading to the self-administration of morphine on an FI schedule is described in Box 6.4.

Variable-Interval Schedules

In a **variable-interval (VI) schedule,** rather than being fixed, the interval of time between positive reinforcer availability varies from a few to many seconds. Compare a FI-45 with a VI-45. A computer-generated VI-45 second schedule might deliver response-contingent reinforcement after 1 or after 100 seconds. In a given work session the interreinforcement interval *averages* 45 seconds.

What is the effect of scheduling reinforcement availability such that it *averages* 45 seconds rather than being *exactly* 45 seconds? Again, the postreinforcement pause is eliminated. Both variable-interval (VI) and variable-ratio (VR) schedules (see Figure 6.4) have little postreinforcement pause, while both long fixed-ratio (FR) and long fixed-interval (FI) schedules do. Why? Because in both "variable" schedules reinforcement is possible with the very next response following the last reinforced response.

Stable Responding.   Indeed, the passage of time rather than the number of responses determines the availability of reinforcement. As a result VI schedules produce highly stable, moment to moment operant responses throughout a given work session. VRs and FRs produce the highest rates of responding; the variable-interval (VI) schedule produces the most evenly spaced, or stable, rate of responding. Another way of describing the effects of VI schedules is to note that they produce the least variation in interresponse intervals.

BOX 6.4

Self-Administering Addictive Drugs

While visiting a friend in his hospital room where he was recovering from surgery, I had the opportunity to observe him self-administering morphine to control pain. The morphine was dispensed by an automated pump through an indwelling intravenous catheter. Both the amount of morphine available and the interval of time between administrations were predetermined by his physician. My friend could administer the morphine to himself by pressing a button once every two hours (i.e., delivery of the drug was response-contingent on a FI-2.0 hour schedule of reinforcement).

By watching his wristwatch this patient learned to accurately time the two-hour interval. After a number of such trials, his response pattern emerged clearly and predictably. As the two-hour period wound down, his button-pressing responses increased in frequency. During the final 30 seconds (as best he could estimate by his wristwatch) responses were made every few seconds until morphine was administered. A clear scalloping pattern had emerged.

Was this response pattern inevitable? Other drug studies investigating the use of morphine to control pain (Melzac, 1990) report individual differences in drug-seeking (cf. *sensation-seeking*) behavior. Not all individuals crave the pleasurable effects of morphine; rather, their behavior (including verbal reports) indicates that they fear the addictive properties of morphine. Although they experience pain, these individuals do not self-administer the drug as just described even when placed on the same schedule of reinforcement.

VI and VR Schedules of Reinforcement in Everyday Life

Assume that reinforcement maintains patterns of behavior, and that positive reinforcers can be identified in our daily lives. We have already seen two examples of the outcomes of scheduling reinforcement on human behavior—how people continue to play slot machines with little payoff (VR schedules) and (at least in one individual) how the periodic availability of morphine determined a distinctive pattern of responses. Let us look at one or two other examples.

For most people, courteous behavior is typically ignored and only occasionally reinforced. Drivers reducing their speed to allow other cars to merge into traffic or to make left-hand turns in front of them, for example, only on rare occasions get a smile or wave acknowledging (reinforcing) their behavior.[6]

[6]Yes, it is likely that courteous drivers also incur fewer "fender benders" and that their driving behavior is maintained as much by negative reinforcement (discussed in Chapter 7) as by positive reinforcement.

Maintaining Behavior over Long Periods.   More typically, all forms of courteous behavior are "in extinction"—that is, are not being reinforced. Can you make the case that "courteous behavior" is being maintained on an aperiodic schedule of reinforcement? Could you effectively argue that response-contingent reinforcement (public acknowledgment of courteous behavior) is more time dependent (i.e., on a VI schedule)? Or is it more rate dependent (i.e., on a VR schedule)?

Consider an elementary school teacher. As part of her lesson plan a third grade teacher contracts to make two to three response-contingent positive comments per week to each student during classroom activities. How would you characterize this schedule of reinforcement?

Surprising Reinforcers.   Especially in the absence of continuous reinforcement, responding can be maintained at high levels on partial reinforcement schedules. Why is this so? One aspect characteristic of variable schedules of reinforcement that may increase their power to reinforce and thereby maintain behavior is that each aperiodic reinforcement is unexpected—that is, is surprising (Kamin, 1969; Rescorla & Wagner, 1972; Terry & Wagner, 1975). Unexpected events capture attention. The response that produces an unexpected positive reinforcement stands out more than the rest ("What did I do to deserve *this?!*"). The occasional reinforcement therefore selects from a welter of ongoing behavior a particular instance and makes it noteworthy. ("A little reinforcement can go a long way!")

As students progress from elementary to secondary schools to college, parents and teachers alike pay less daily attention to both courteous behavior and scholastic performance. Tests and course grades at fixed intervals serve as opportunities for reinforcement. Yet these opportunities are only loosely attached to complex behaviors such as reading, writing, comprehending, memorizing, etc., which characterize academic performance. Only rarely does one hear "good answer!" in the college classroom.

Achieving internalized standards and goals at aperiodical intervals are the reinforcing events that replace more overt reinforcers in the external environment. Overt reinforcers do not disappear, however, as is evidenced by the incentive value of BMWs and other positive reinforcers—positive reinforcers that occur only a finite number of times in one's life (see Box 5.2, p. 181).

Extinction and the Partial Reinforcement Effect

Back in the Skinner Box. We saw earlier that CRF (continuous reinforcement) produces the fastest acquisition of stable responding. For this reason, when training animals (including humans) on any schedule of reinforcement, the experimenter typically begins with CRF.

After lever pressing occurs reliably, the animal is shifted to the target schedule.

If the response requirements of the target schedule are high (such as FR-100 or VR-50), or if the interval between reinforcements is long (such as FI-60 or VI-30), the experimenter typically "weans" the animal from continuous reinforcement to (low) ratio schedules. For example, an FR-2 or FR-3 gradually introduces the partial reinforcement contingencies to the animal; going from CRF to FR-100 would likely be unsuccessful because of the phenomenon of experimental extinction.

Pavlovian and Thorndikean Extinction Compared.   The concept of experimental extinction was introduced in Chapter 4. Remember what happened to Spotski's conditioned salivary response when the bell kept ringing but food was not forthcoming? The conditioned response of salivation extinguished.

A similar process is evident in operant conditioning. Instrumental responses (operants) that are being maintained by reinforcement undergo *extinction* when they are no longer reinforced with food. Extinguished responses never return completely to baseline (i.e., to pre-conditioning operant levels), but within a given session, lever-pressing stops.

Resistance-to-Extinction.   It should be obvious, then, why an experimenter must "wean" animals from CRF to more demanding target schedules of reinforcement. Animals with a continuous-reinforcement history will soon stop responding; i.e., they will extinguish when reinforcement is not forthcoming. Animals maintained on CRF show little *resistance-to-extinction*. By contrast, animals with a history of responding for long periods of time in the absence of reinforcement (i.e., FR-100, VR-50, FI-60, VI-45, etc.) are highly resistant to extinction.

Remember from our study of Pavlovian conditioning that resistance-to-extinction is an important measure of the success of conditioning. Typically, resistance-to-extinction increases (a) with more conditioning trials, (b) with more optimal conditioning parameters, and (c) with more "prepared" responses (see Chapter 4, p. 129, and Chapter 5, p. 208).

Here, however, we have something of a conundrum. Partial reinforcement by definition results in fewer reinforced responses. How can partial reinforcement (maintained by fewer reinforced responses) result in better conditioning than continuous reinforcement as measured by resistance-to-extinction?

The Partial Reinforcement Effect.   The tendency for animals maintained on partial reinforcement schedules to be highly resistant to extinction is called the **partial reinforcement effect,** or **PRE.** The PRE addresses both intuitive and counterintuitive observations about learned behavior. We might start by asking if what the rat learned during acquisition is being reflected in extinction. For example, during acquisition training, and for the extended period of time the animal experiences partial reinforcement while lever pressing, many responses are not reinforced. It may be that when the animal is then put on an extinction schedule, it cannot tell the difference. Therefore, it continues to respond longer than an animal trained and maintained on continuous reinforcement.

Again the best insight into the phenomenon is to ask you, the reader, to be the rat. For example, describe your behavior the last time you put a quarter into a telephone or a vending machine and came up blank. Zero. Quarter gone. No reinforcement.

Frustration Theory.   Amsel (1958) points out that following a history of continuous reinforcement, one consequence of extinction is a state of negative emotions such as frustration. Amsel's **frustration theory** also includes the cognitive component alluded to in the foregoing; one can only be frustrated if one has *expectations* concerning what the consequences of responding *should* be. By this analysis, past candy bars vended, successful telephone connections, and food pellets delivered on a continuous basis set up predictable expectations of what should happen "the next time." Now, imagine living in Italy, where local phone systems are unpredictable at best. In using public phones there over the years, you lost many coins. That is, your telephoning operants were never consistently reinforced. Sometimes you connected on the first coin; other time you had to try several times (and lose coins) before connections were made.

In which phone system would you be more likely to continue feeding your coins—the Italian system, in which you have a history of nonreinforcement, or a highly reliable phone system in which most all responses had been reliably reinforced? In which system would nonreinforcement be more frustrating? Given this understanding, can you explain why Italians are surprised when Americans "become angry at telephones."

Let us return to the Las Vegas casino where you control the payoff schedules in your slot machines. Now that you know how to maximize resistance-to-extinction, how might you go about minimizing the frustration of nonreinforcement in your customers? Can you conceptualize a trade-off between customer frustration and customer satisfaction? What are the optimal conditions guaranteeing that you, the owner, maximize profits?

To summarize, different expectations are set up when animals are trained on partial reinforcement and continuous reinforcement.

If trained on partial reinforcement, the animal may not even become aware of the difference when it is put into an extinction period. By contrast, the animal trained on continuous reinforcement is immediately aware of the absence of reinforcement, and it will stop responding sooner. Frustration results from thwarted expectations.

Extinction on Cumulative Records.   Extinction as measured on a cumulative record is easy to detect. Remember that each lever press sends the line up, vertically, a notch. If the lever is not pressed, the cumulative record continues horizontally (to the right, as indicated by the line at the pen in Figure 6.3). Therefore, when the rat or pigeon quits responding—as in an extinction phase of training—the plot continues horizontally rather than returning to point zero.

Work and Efficiency

Continuous reinforcement, and FR and VR schedules of reinforcement, allow animals to adjust their work output to determine the amount of food they can receive in a given session. Generally speaking, the harder the animal works (the more lever presses the animal makes per unit time), the more food is forthcoming. A fair analogy is the factory worker who does "piece work" in which the more units produced (for example, dresses in a clothing factory), the more money earned. Within a work session, however, local rate of responding is unimportant. For example, workers may be considered less efficient for working slowly on completing a dress, but nonetheless they receive full pay for completed items.

How can local rates of responding be controlled? That is, can more precise timing of responses be generated by manipulation of reinforcement schedules?

DRH and DRL Schedules of Reinforcement

Two schedules of reinforcement *are* designed to *reinforce local rates of responding*. A **differential reinforcement of high rate** of responding **(DRH)** schedule reinforces bursts of lever pressing. A computer program monitors local rates of lever pressing and defines the response contingencies. A burst, for example, may be defined as 5 or more lever presses by a rat (or 10 or more pecks by a pigeon on a lighted key) in a two-second time period. Only when the target level of responding is reached is a food reinforcer made available.

Instead of speed, what if the desired target behavior is very slow, accurately timed responding? A researcher might use a **DRL** schedule of reinforcement, where DRL stands for **differential reinforcement of low rate** of responding. For example, an animal on a DRL-30 sec-

BOX 6.5

Training Monkeys to Be Patient

While stationed at an USAF research laboratory in the mid-1960s, I had the opportunity to train Rhesus monkeys on a DRL schedule of reinforcement. Eventually the monkeys were to be administered an experimental drug that, among other effects, was likely to impair their timing behavior. I selected a DRL-15 second schedule of reinforcement to help assess the drug's effects. On the DRL-15 schedule, a monkey withholds a lever-pressing response for 15 seconds, allowing a clock to time out. The next response thereafter rewards the monkey with a sugar pellet.

How do you train animals to be patient? Reinforcement by definition tends to *increase* the rate of response, which in this case resets the clock, preventing further reinforcement!

With the first animal I carefully followed a progression of time intervals leading up to 15 seconds. After establishing responding to CRF, on successive days I put the monkey on a DRL-3, then a DRL-5, then a DRL-10 schedule of reinforcement. Progress was slow, because each time the schedule was changed the monkey responded too much, delaying

reinforcement and increasing vocalized frustration.

I accepted the advice of another psychologist who suggested that in training the next naive animal, I first establish minimal responding on CRF, set the timer on DRL-15 seconds, and walk away. His reasoning was that too-fast responding would extinguish, but that spontaneous recovery of responding would be immediately reinforced. The monkey's behavior? Initially, and predictably, a burst of responding following reinforcement, then many minutes of not responding, followed by a (spontaneous recovery) response that produced reinforcement. Ultimately this schedule produced a patient animal.

How efficient do Rhesus monkeys become after many hours practice on a DRL-15? Unbelievably so. In one representative session, Rhesus #079 produced interresponse latencies (time between responses) measured to the hundredth of a second, as follows: 15.04; 15.08; 15.02; 15.04; 15.04; 14.97 (not reinforced); 15.14; 15.07, 15.04, and so on, with no further misses during a four-minute session.

---

ond schedule must wait a minimum of 30 seconds before a response will produce reinforcement. Each response made before 30 seconds has elapsed resets a clock, and the animal must wait an *additional* 30 seconds before reinforcement is again available. The training and terminal performance of Rhesus monkeys on a DRL schedule of reinforcement are discussed in Box 6.5.

Of what practical use are schedules of reinforcement that by their operation produce fine control over local rates of response? Absolutely none that I can think of.[7]

Analysis of Schedules of Reinforcement

Why have we spent so much time on schedules of reinforcement? Why should we care how a pigeon or rat responds when reinforcement is scheduled contingent upon time and rate of lever pressing? Consider the following arguments. First, these laboratory investigations have produced a body of findings that has considerable application to the human condition. Humans in fact respond as predicted by these studies. Not all humans, not all of the time, but for a wide variety of human behaviors, reinforcement, especially partial reinforcement, determines patterns of responding—be it morphine administration, gambling behavior, piano playing, using machinery, or being courteous to one another.

Perhaps a more important point is one that both Skinner and Watson were preoccupied with—namely, the prediction and control of human behavior. These studies of laboratory animals demonstrate the power of reinforcement, and as we will see in the next chapter, of punishment, to manipulate and control behavior. Now there are only so many things one can do with a lever, and so we should not be surprised that the focus to this point has been upon the *rate and patterning of responding* on the lever. While one might criticize the narrowing of behavior demanded by the Skinner Box, at the same time one must recognized the power of prediction and elegance of behavioral control afforded by this methodology. It is to the issue of behavioral control that we turn in the next section.

Interim Summary

1. *Schedules of reinforcement* describe the manner in which reinforcement delivery is patterned, or scheduled, following operant responses.
2. The delivery of reinforcement for each response is called *continuous reinforcement,* or *CRF.* If each response is not reinforced, the animal is said to be on a *partial,* or *intermittent, reinforcement schedule.*

---

[7]Actually, a lot. For example, all behavior requiring rhythm and pacing—*all* skilled movement requiring precise local control over rate of response, including the artist's brush strokes, playing a piano, and reading and writing. Observe two people having a conversation, and note the subtle cues controlling speaking and listening. Can you reconstruct the likely reinforcement history of individuals who lack conversational skills—who have not learned when to inhibit responding?

3. Schedules delivering reinforcement based upon the *number of responses* an animal makes are called ratio schedules, including fixed-ratio (FR) and variable-ratio (VR) schedules.

4. Schedules delivering reinforcement based upon *time* between reinforcement are called interval schedules. These include fixed-interval (FI) and variable-interval (VI) schedules.

5. An animal's behavior on different schedules of reinforcement can be compared with respect to acquisition and with respect to patterning of responses, including bursts (i.e., DRH), pauses (i.e., DRL), stability, and resistance-to-extinction.

6. In general, longer FI and FR schedules produce postreinforcement pauses; FI schedules produce scalloping patterns; VI schedules produce stable responding; and ratio schedules produce faster responding.

7. CRF extinguishes quickly, and partial reinforcement schedules are resistant to extinction, which is called the partial reinforcement effect (PRE).

8. Differential reinforcement of high (DRH) and low (DRL) schedules of reinforcement control the fast rates of responding, and the withholding of responses, respectively.

9. Schedules of reinforcement have numerous real-life applications.

V. Issues of Behavioral Control

Let us return to the supermarket. The whining is nonstop as you stand in line waiting to be checked out. You join other uncomfortable shoppers watching the battle of wills. Every time mom says "no, you can't have it," little Joey's hand in the candy counter clutches his choice more tightly. He turns up the volume: "Why not?" he whines. "I want this one. Pleeeease . . .? You said if I was good. . . ."

After several more iterations, mom's "no, and that's final!" is followed by loud crying. Mom counters with "if you'll be a good boy and not cry, you can have it, but this is the last time." Joey nods contritely, quits crying, and tears open the wrapper. Both mother and son (and everyone within earshot) appear content.

Let us begin our analysis of this behavioral encounter by answering the following question:

1. In the scenario just described:
    (a) Is mom controlling Joey's behavior?
    (b) Is Joey controlling mom's behavior?
    (c) Are both (a) and (b) correct?
    (d) Is neither person in control of the other?
    (e) Are both out of control?

Who's in Charge, Here?   Answers (d) and (e) are both appealing. As a figure-of-speech answer, (e) seems to be self-evident, but it is incorrect when we analyze the problem as a behaviorist world.

The problem is one of semantics. A behaviorist analyzes behavior in terms of control issues, thereby using the word "control" somewhat differently than the lay public. For a behaviorist, *all* behavior is controlled, or determined, by environment. Therefore, mom is controlling Joey, and Joey is controlling mom. Answer (c) covers all the possibilities.

In what way is mom controlling Joey, and Joey controlling mom? Can you identify the reinforcement contingencies at work in this example? At a minimum is it possible that Joey's persistence in responding is being maintained by some sort of partial reinforcement schedule?

The Concept of Behavioral Control

The manner in which the environment comes to control human and animal behavior has been a continuing theme in B. F. Skinner's writings.[8] His behaviorist philosophy, like John B. Watson's, is an extreme form of *environmental determinism*.

The method of behaviorism is to identify and analyze the way in which environmental stimuli exert control over an animal's behavior. The success of the method is measured (a) by the manipulation and control over ongoing behavior via reinforcement and (b) by the ability to predict which behavior will next occur, given a knowledge of past reinforcement history.

A formal definition of *stimulus control* will be discussed later. For present purposes, an organism's behavior is said to be under control at that point in training when an experimenter can make highly accurate, reliable predictions that a particular response will occur in a particular situation. Before analyzing mom and Joey, let us again detour by the Skinner Box.

Controlling Operant Behavior.   Why does a pigeon peck a lighted key, or a rat press a lever? The obvious answer is to obtain food. And with a few exceptions, this commonsense analysis is essentially correct.[9] Stimulus cues of hunger motivate an animal to move instrumentally, seeking food within its ecological niche. Prior learning in the Skinner Box now allows specific responses to operate on the environment, that is, to be instrumental, in securing food.

---

[8]*The Behavior of Organisms* (1938); *Walden Two* (1948); *Verbal Behavior* (1957); *Beyond Freedom and Dignity* (1971).
[9]But see the phenomenon of autoshaping, p. 269.

Stimuli in Skinner Boxes. Placing trained, hungry animals in a Skinner Box, therefore, provides the occasion for specific operants to occur. The sights, sounds, and smells of the box are environmental stimuli (i.e., the context) that *control* the specific response of bar pressing. Changing the sights, sounds, and smells comprising the stimulus complex in which the bar-pressing operant was initially learned (perhaps moving the manipulandum to a different wall, or changing the flavor of the food reward) will disrupt the operant response. In this way we see that *environmental context* is a major controlling factor in whether or not an operant response will occur.

The importance of context in the control and prediction of behavior is currently being investigated using a number of methodologies (see Bouton, 1984, 1991; Miller & Schactman, 1985). An oversimplified way of appreciating the relevance of these experiments is to imagine that you first learned to drive over a one-year period of time in the same car. Now you are transferred to a different car that has all the same operating features (steering wheel, brake and gas pedals, shifter, etc.), but the sights, sounds, and smells differ (i.e., the context differs). Your driving ability (operant responses) would differ because of these contextual differences.

Getting Control of Responses. An easier way to demonstrate how a stimulus in the animal's environment can come to control operant responding is to arrange for a specific stimulus to be present when a response-food contingency is in effect. For example, the rat or bird can be trained to bar press or key peck when the house lights are on, and to not make these operant responses when the house lights are off. How? By having a response-food contingency in effect only when the houselights are on. When the house lights are turned off, the manipulandum is electrically disconnected from the feeder mechanism. Under these circumstances, the operants are no longer instrumental in securing food; the response-food contingency has been broken.

After several sessions of lights on/responses produce food, and lights off/responses do *not* produce food, the animal soon learns to respond in the presence of the lights, and to not respond in darkness. (The opposite can also be trained, where responses in the dark are reinforced, but not those made in the light.)

Discriminative and Negative Discriminative Stimuli. Skinner called a stimulus (such as a house light) signaling that response-food contingencies were in effect a **discriminative stimulus** (abbreviated **S**$^\mathbf{d}$, and pronounced "s"-"d"). Therefore, *discriminative stimuli (S^d's)* set occasions in which trained operant responses become highly probable; S^d's control high rates of operant responding because the responses are reinforced. Conversely, a stimulus that signals that response-food contingencies are *not* in effect is called a **negative discriminative stimulus** (abbreviated S^Δ and pronounced "s"-"delta"). There being no payoff for such responses, they drop out.

Stimulus Control.   We are now able to formally define the stimulus control of behavior. When trained animals reliably make operant responses in the presence of S^d's and do *not* respond in the presence of S^Δ's, the animal is said to be under **stimulus control.** In a Skinner Box environment, an S^d (such as a 500-Hz tone) sets the occasion for a high rate of response, and an S^Δ (no tone, or perhaps a tone of a different frequency) sets the occasion for a low rate of response. Responses in the presence of the S^d are reinforced, but not in the presence of the S^Δ.

Losing Stimulus Control.   Note that this S^d-S^Δ discrimination is not unlike Pavlov's CS^+-CS^- conditioned discrimination procedure (see Figure 4.12, p. 156). Pavlov trained dogs to salivate in the presence of a circle, and to *not* salivate to an ellipse. The difference is that S^d's control *operant* responding and CS^+'s control *reflexive* responding.

Recall that when Pavlov forced a discrimination between a circle and an ellipse that was beyond the dog's capacity of visual resolution, the dog began to salivate to both stimuli indiscriminately. In Skinner's terms, Pavlov had "lost stimulus control" over the animal. Likewise, after successfully training an S^d-S^Δ discrimination, if for whatever reason operant responses are no longer reliably controlled by the S^d and S^Δ, the trainer (or parent) is said to have lost stimulus control.

Red and Green Traffic Lights.   As an example, if you reliably stop your automobile at a red light, and go on green, Skinner would say that you are under stimulus control. The red and green traffic lights are S^d's that control the operant responses of foot pressure on the brake, and foot pressure on the accelerator, respectively. The same red and green traffic lights are S^Δ's for foot pressure off the accelerator, and foot pressure off the brake, respectively (that is, to *not* press the accelerator or brake, respectively).

The stimulus control properties of red and green lights on driving an automobile are relatively simple. Can you identify the control characteristics of the yellow caution light? See Box 6.6 for some help.

Generalization and Stimulus Control

Traffic lights in Mexico control the behavior of Americans who drive there. The reds and greens are often of different hues, and the positions of the signals may vary (i.e., reversed, so that a green "go" light is on top of a standard, and the red "stop" light is below).

BOX 6.6

Behavioral Analysis of Free Will

As we will see in Chapter 10, Tolman (1932) believed that both a formal psychology of learning and a relatively complete understanding of human behavior would result from the laboratory study of the behavior of a rat at a choice point in a maze. That is, if we could predict 100 percent of the time when a rat would turn left or right (or, presumably, around), at any point in time, our scientific understanding of behavior would be complete.

The merits of Tolman's arguments aside for the moment, let us attempt to analyze our "choices" when confronted with the appearance of a yellow caution light while driving an automobile. Are both operant and reflexive responses under stimulus control? Can we shed light upon the enigma of "voluntary" behavior when the light turns yellow?

Operating an automobile can be described as a complex sequence of operant responses. The accelerator, brake, clutch, turn signals, and steering wheel are among the manipulanda necessary for successful operation. Stimuli controlling the operants in driving include visually detected movements of other cars and of the speedometer as well as the traffic control signs and signals.

Recall how bewildering driving was on the first few occasions! The operants of steering, braking, and controlling the clutch and accelerator—all at the same time—had to be coordinated with a flux of signals from the environment. Some of us even had dear old dad.

And now you encounter a dreaded *yellow* light. How fast am I going? How long until I arrive at the intersection? To brake, or not to brake—*that* is the question. The S^d's controlling the braking operant include speed of travel, distance to intersection, performance of brakes, road surface conditions (wet or dry), presence of police, past accidents, driving record, duration of the yellow light, presence of parents in car, alcohol (or other drugs) affecting performance, etc.

It is easy to overlook the Pavlovian conditioned reflexive responses that occur when the light turns yellow (not to be confused with the autonomic nervous system arousal of seeing flashing blue and red lights in your rear-view mirror). The dilation of your pupils is one indication of heightened activity in the reticular activating system (RAS) and increased sympathetic nervous system activity.

Do you begin braking or increase your rate of speed? If it makes you feel any better, you can continue to believe you have a choice in the matter.

We take for granted that learning in one situation applies to others. In Chapter 4 the concept of *generalization* was introduced to account for such transfer of learning effects. After Pavlov had trained a dog to salivate to a tone of 1500 Hz, he found that it would also respond to tones of 1490 and 1510 Hz, presumably because the tones sounded similar to the dog.

Stimulus Generalization Gradient. Experiments using operant conditioning methodology have demonstrated similar findings. In a classic study (Guttman & Kalish, 1956), pigeons were reinforced with food on a VI schedule when they pecked at a key back-lit with, for example, a yellow light (the yellow light's wavelength was 580 nanometers (nm)).[10] After training, the wavelength of light was changed on successive test trials, and the number of responses to a variety of wavelengths around the original wavelength were measured. (During the test trials only the responses to one wavelength were reinforced; the VI schedule kept the pigeons responding during extinction as the S^d was changed to other wavelengths.)

As you might expect, more responses were made to the most similar wavelengths, and the fewest responses to the most different (most easily discriminated) wavelengths. This orderly pattern of responses is called a **stimulus generalization gradient** (see Figure 6.5).

The Guttman and Kalish (1956) experiment addresses previously raised questions concerning the *ecological validity* of laboratory investigations. Let us look at the real-world applicability of these findings.

Invariant Stimuli? One criticism of laboratory research concerns the nature of stimuli used in experiments. Seldom is a "pure" stimulus repeatedly presented and consistently reinforced in the real world. In the present case, the visual stimulus that sets the occasion for response contingent food availability was an invariant 580-nm "yellow" in a laboratory setting. In nonlaboratory niches, one could argue, a predator sees form and movement as well as color in locating prey. The color may change as the prey moves. Movement also guarantees different patterns on the predator's retina from moment to moment. Does the learning that occurs under these stimulus conditions resemble learning using static stimuli in the laboratory?

The Guttman and Kalish (1956) findings demonstrate that a stimulus does not have to be perfectly reproduced on each occasion in order to control responding. Presumably, views of shapes and movements that differ from those initially reinforced also come to control responses. Generalization across varying stimuli produces meaningful, predictable patterns of responses.

---

[10]Recognize that the "yellow" experienced by humans is likely to be perceived differently by pigeon brains.

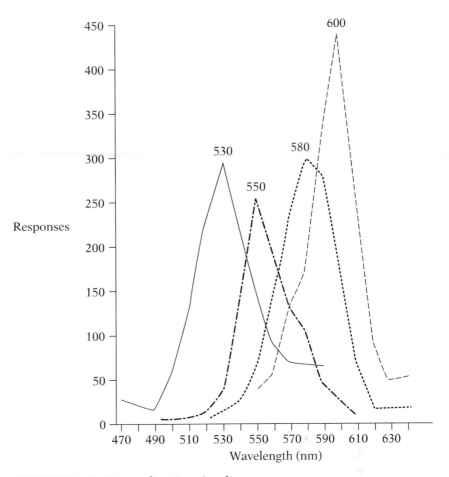

FIGURE 6.5 Generalization Gradients

Pigeons were food reinforced to peck at back-lit disks illuminated with wavelengths of either 530, 550, 580, or 600 nanometers (to humans these wavelengths appear green, greenish yellow, yellowish orange, and red, respectively). Each bird was then put on extinction, and pecking responses to the wavelength it was trained with and immediately neighboring wavelengths were measured. Each pigeon's pecking responses distributed around the peak of the original training wavelength. The pattern of responses is called a generalization gradient. (After Guttman & Kalish, 1956.)

Stimulus Control of Reinforced
and Nonreinforced Responses

Let us analyze a small child learning her multiplication tables in terms of stimulus control: discriminative stimuli (S^d's, the multiplication problems) control responses (answers), which are reinforced (correct) or not (incorrect). This real-world example points out a methodological problem with Guttman and Kalish's (1956) training procedure. In most examples of learned behavior (especially of skilled performance), the subject learns which responses are reinforced and at the same time which are *not* reinforced. "Four times four = sixteen" (correct); "four times four = fifteen" (incorrect). Shooting the basketball "this way" is reinforced; shooting the ball "that way" is not reinforced.

By way of contrast, Guttman and Kalish's pigeons did not initially learn that nonyellow stimuli were S^Δ's. That is, during training, the birds only saw one stimulus at 580 nm, the S^d, which was always reinforced. What would happen if the pigeon initially learns that one stimulus is associated with reinforcement and that another is not? That is, what is the effect of initially learning S^d-S^Δ discriminations on subsequent patterns of generalization? In the real world, does it matter if children also learn that "$4 \times 4 \neq 15$," or is it enough that they merely learn that "$4 \times 4 = 16$?"

Role of Nonreinforced Responses.   Recall that Pavlov's dog learned to salivate to a circle (CS^+) and to not salivate to an ellipse (CS^-). In investigating the role of S^Δ in S^d-S^Δ discriminations, the question that Hanson (1959) asked his pigeons was related both to Guttman and Kalish's (1956) and to Pavlov's findings. Specifically, what differences result when a correct response is trained in the presence of one stimulus (the S^d), versus training the correct responses in the context of both reinforced and nonreinforced stimuli (i.e., an S^d-S^Δ discrimination)?

In a design similar to that used by Guttman and Kalish (1954), Hanson (1959) used the following three treatment conditions to answer questions about the role of the S^Δ during training:

Group 1: S^d = 550 nm; S^Δ = 590 nm (S^d-S^Δ difference = 40 nm)
Group 2: S^d = 550 nm; S^Δ = 555 nm (S^d-S^Δ difference = 5 nm)
Group 3: S^d = 550 nm; no S^Δ (S^d-S^Δ difference = ∞)

Note that all three groups of pigeons were trained with the same reinforced stimulus, a light of 550 nm. They differed by having a very similar S^Δ condition (i.e., 555 nm); a dissimilar S^Δ condition (i.e., 590 nm); or no S^Δ during training.

Stimulus Generalization of Operant Responses.   After training, all pigeons were tested for stimulus generalization. Pigeons in Group 3 produced a familiar generalization gradient around 550 nm (see Figure 6.6) quite similar to that found by Guttman and Kalish (1956; cf. Figure 6.5). Note that the peak of responding is precisely at 550 nm, the reinforced wavelength.

Of interest in Figure 6.6, however, are the generalization gradients of the pigeons in which S^d-S^Δ discriminations had been trained. Even though pigeons in all three groups were reinforced for responding to an S^d of the same wavelength, all three generalization gradients were found to differ.

Peak Shift.   First, note that the generalization gradients of both groups trained with S^d-S^Δ discriminations are *shifted to the left*. The

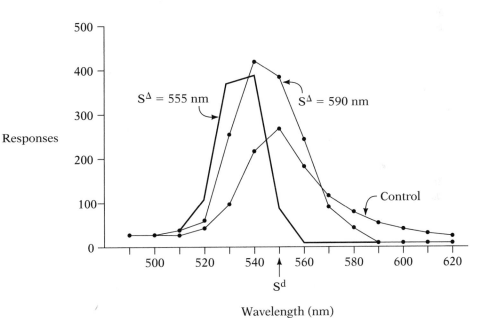

FIGURE 6.6   The Peak Shift Phenomenon

Three groups of pigeons were food reinforced to peck at a back-lit key (wavelength = 550 nanometers), the S^d condition. One of the three groups was also trained with an S^Δ = 555 nm, another with S^Δ = 590 nm, and the third group with no S^Δ (a control condition). The generalization gradients for all three groups responding to S^d = 550 nm, in extinction, are plotted. Note the gradients are shifted to the left of the peak wavelength of 550 nm. (From Hanson, 1959.)

peaks of their generalization gradients are to the left of the 550-nm wavelength.

A question immediately arises: Why should pigeons make more responses to wavelengths of light for which their responses had never been reinforced? And, perhaps more importantly, why should the peak of responding be shifted *further* when, during training, the S^Δ is closer to the S^d? (Note that the peak of responding by Group 2 is shifted further than the peak response of Group 1.) This phenomenon is called **peak shift.** The peak of responding to the S^d is shifted away from the S^Δ experienced during training. Peak shift provides a clue to the role of the S^Δ in S^d-S^Δ discrimination learning.

A second difference that arises during S^d-S^Δ discrimination training is that the generalization gradients are narrower than the S^d-only group (see Figure 6.6). Third, when the S^Δ = 555 nm (only 5 nm different from S^d = 550 nm) the generalization gradient is narrower than when S^Δ = 590 nm (40 nm different from S^d = 550 nm).

To summarize, after S^d-S^Δ discrimination training, (a) the shift in peak response is greater and (b) the generalization gradient is narrower if the S^Δ was more similar to the S^d.

S^d-S^Δ *Training Sharpens Discriminations.*

What is the importance of these findings? First, the presence of a nonreinforced stimulus, the S^Δ, appears to *sharpen* the discrimination of the reinforced stimulus. Furthermore, the closer the stimulus characteristics are of the reinforced to the nonreinforced stimulus, the more *discriminable* are the two stimuli. It is as if the bird is forced to pay more attention to the exact attributes of a stimulus that provide information about reinforcement. *Four times four* is not fifteen, and *three times four* is not sixteen; only the exact stimulus, *"four times four,"* is reinforced by the exact response, *"sixteen."* Likewise, when playing the piano, a G7 major chord *is* different from a G7 chord. Only by repeatedly comparing two stimuli having highly similar attributes can one distinguish, for example, that one red wine is slightly better than another.

Second, something rather than nothing is learned when a stimulus is not reinforced in the training context of a related stimulus that is reinforced. In Hanson's (1959) research, the presence of a nonreinforced wavelength during training changed the bird's response tendencies to all other wavelengths. Another way of saying this is that what the bird learned in the presence of the nonreinforced stimulus was measurable, but only indirectly. The effect could only be assessed in the presence of other stimuli.

The Inhibitory Nature of S^Δ *Training.*

The necessity of measuring the effects of nonreinforced stimuli indirectly by the peak shift phenomenon is reminiscent of Pavlovian conditioned inhibition. Remember that conditioned inhibition was also measured indirectly via summation and retardation tests, and then only in the presence of a conditioned excitor (for a review, see Chapter 5, p. 196ff). In the present situation, the S^d can be construed as an excitor and the S^Δ as an inhibitor. The peak response to the excitatory S^d is shifted, indirectly reflecting the role of S^Δ. Can the responses to S^Δ also generalize in the same way that responses to S^d generalize? Yes, *inhibitory* generalization gradients have been reported by Honig, Boneau, Burstein, and Pennypacker (1963).

Controlling Human Verbal Behavior

You may or may not be impressed with the behaviorist's analysis of your behavior at the choice point of a yellow traffic signal. More than likely you conceptualize human behavior as being far more complicated than a mere succession of operants controlled by discriminative stimuli. What role, for example, does language and thought play in controlling behavior?

As we will see in Chapter 10, our use of language (and the thought processes language allows) *does* make human behavior different from animal behavior. But, as Skinner and others have pointed out, language usage can also be analyzed from a behavioral perspective (Skinner, 1957).

Back to the supermarket. We left mom and Joey exchanging words at the checkout counter. At that time mom was characterized as being in control of Joey's behavior, and Joey, mom's. Can we bring the behaviorist concept of stimulus control to each person's behavior, including their verbal behavior?

Discriminated Operants.   The bright candy wrappers are CSs that have been associated with the appetitive chocolate USs they contain. In addition to these learned associations, Joey's past reinforcement history includes a sequence of operant behaviors that have been positively reinforced.

"Reaching for candy" is a **discriminated operant,** which reflects the stimulus control the candy has over Joey's behavior. That is, on previous occasions in this part of the Skinner Box, these particular operants (reaching, grabbing, removing wrapper) have produced response-contingent reinforcement.

Mutual Control in Human Interactions.   Mom and her language are part of this stimulus complex. Her words on past occasions were S^d's controlling Joey's behavior. How so? In past encounters mom's words "no, you can't have it" were part of the stimulus complex in the presence of which Joey's operant behavior was ultimately reinforced

TABLE 6.1   Who's in Control?

S^d's Controlling Behavior	Discriminated Operants
Joey	
Supermarket stimuli	Orient; search for candy
Sight of candy	(a) Approach candy; (b) reach for candy; (c) "Mom, I want this piece" (verbal behavior).
"No, you can't have it."	Louder vocalizations
"O.K., but this is the last time."	Tear off wrapper and eat candy
Mom	
Sight of Joey moving toward candy	"No candy" (verbal behavior).
Joey says "please."	"No, you can't have it."
Louder vocalizations; others staring.	"O.K. but this is the last time."
Joey eats candy.	Mom resumes shopping.

by the candy. The word "no" in this stimulus context is an S^d for Joey to turn up the volume of his cry, and to hold onto the candy even more tightly. Why? Because that response in this context produced reinforcement in the past.

In turn, Joey's vocalizations (and the caustic looks of other shoppers) are the S^d's for mom to respond verbally "if you'll be a good boy and not cry, you can have the candy . . . but this is the last time." Joey stops crying, which reinforces mom's verbal behavior, just as it did the last time. (As we will see in the next chapter, stopping an aversive event is an example of *negative reinforcement*.) Table 6.1 summarizes both the S^d's and the discriminated operant responses characterizing this human interaction.

Three points are emphasized from the foregoing example:

1. Words can and do function as discriminative stimuli.
2. Speaking words (using language) can be understood as an operant behavior, which, like any other operant, can result in reinforcement or punishment.
3. In all human interactions, the operant responses of one individual have stimulus properties that set the occasion for operant respons-

es of the other person. From this example it is easy to see how Joey's behavior is controlling mom's, and vice versa.[11]

Complex Behavior as Chained Operants

Another point to be made from Table 6.1 is that seemingly complex human interactions can be analyzed into simpler behavioral sequences that are "chained" together. In these **stimulus-response chains,** each response has stimulus features that control the next response. Thus, Joey's verbal response "please" is the stimulus for mom's "no, you can't have it."

The concept of **chained operants** also allows us to analyze Joey's behavior in terms of discriminative stimuli, operant responses, and reinforcement: He sees candy at distance (S^d); approaches candy (operant); sees candy up close (S^d); reaches for candy (operant); sensory input as fingers touch candy (S^d); candy is picked up (operant); candy in hand is stimulus (S^d); for "Mom, I want this piece" (verbal operant). Joey puts the candy in his mouth and bites off a piece (operants). The taste of candy (positive reinforcer) reinforces all preceding operants.

Thought question: Can you describe student-teacher interactions in the classroom in terms of stimulus-response chains? What are the discriminative stimuli controlling the behavior of student and teacher? Hint: Identify the operant responses of both students and teachers. Note the stimulus characteristics of students' operants that control the teacher, and vice versa. For starters, you may want to analyze eye contact, pauses in lecture, students' yawning, responses to hands raised, etc.

Behavioral Analysis of "Volition" and "Will"

Earlier, mom and Joey's interaction was described as a "battle of wills." John B. Watson and B. F. Skinner objected to the use of language such as "volition" and "will" to describe presumed intrapsychic events. Watson denied the premise of human consciousness, and Skinner merely ignored it. Both thought that analyses of observed behavior were more productive—that explaining behavior was best accomplished by reference to past reinforcement histories, rather than hypothetical personality characteristics.

What do you, the reader think? Which terminology lends itself best to a scientific analysis of human behavior? What, if anything, is added to an understanding of Joey's behavior by describing him as a

---

[11]A clinical example that profits from this analysis is the co-dependency relationship of human couples.

"strong-willed individual"? In this instance, might not the label be inappropriate, given that Joey's mother is controlling his behavior?

Sequence of Learning Complex Chains

Complex sequences of operant behavior are learned with difficulty. Remember learning to swim, to ride a bike, or to painstakingly print the alphabet? Pianists take many years to learn hand and finger movements, and they practice intensely for months for recitals. In all these examples, operants must be performed in sequence. What do we know about how these sequences are learned? Our theory is good, but empirical examples are limited. Let us analyze the simple example of a of a small child learning to tie shoes (see Box 6.7).[12]

Rules for Learning Chains

Note in the example in Box 6.7 that each operant can only be performed if the preceding operant has been successfully accomplished. Whether it be driving a car, writing your name, tying your shoe, or whistling a tune, all complex chains require the successful completion of individual operants.

In working with children, parents, teachers, and coaches should be sensitive to differences in sensory-motor development (do not ask fingers to do what they are not capable of doing). To expedite learning, parents should simplify the shoe-tying task for their child as follows:

1. Separate each component response, and have the child practice each operant separately.
2. Reinforce each component operant separately.
3. Initially reinforce the child for accomplishing the simple operants.
4. After the child is capable of accomplishing each component operant, practice each operant in the reverse order of the shoe-lacing sequence.

Errors in Mazes.   Why the *reverse* order? An analysis of the errors of rats learning mazes indicates that they make fewer errors at the end of the chains than at the beginning (Hull, 1932). That is, the last response (for example, a *left turn* before entering the goal box) that produces reinforcement is learned first, then the next to last response, the third from last response, etc. For this reason, after practice with all operants involved in lacing shoes, the child should be helped up to step 7 (see Box 6.7), then allowed to accomplish the last part of step 7 with minimal guidance. Step 7 is reinforced. After several trials, allow

---

[12]Parents know that tying shoes is far from simple for a child. This example is from Domjan and Burkhard (1988).

BOX 6.7

Learning to Tie Shoelaces

Ready. Set. Tie your laces. Visualize the task requirements as they are briefly described here (or better, lace a shoe as you read the following descriptions):

1. With shoe on foot, both laces are visually located and each is picked up with the forefinger and thumb of each hand (several operants).
2. Left and right laces are passed to the opposite hand as both laces are pulled across the top of the shoe (several operants).
3. The left lace in the right hand is looped over the right lace in left hand, and the right forefinger pulls the lace through; both laces are pulled until snug (several operants).
4. Next, the left-hand lace is held tightly with the heel of cupped left hand, freeing the left forefinger, around which the right lace can be looped (several operants).
5. This loop is grasped by the thumb and forefinger of the right hand, freeing the left hand to grab the lace on the left side and wind it counterclockwise around the looped lace on the right (several difficult operants).
6. Maintaining lace tension with left hand, the right forefinger is lifted and is used to hook the nonlooped lace on the left side and pull it back through the first loop (several operants—this is the really hard part for novice lacers).
7. The left thumb and forefinger grab the loop formed by the right forefinger. The free right thumb and forefinger grasp the right loop. The two loops are pulled away from each other, tightening the knot (several operants —much difficulty).

The foregoing sequence of operants is reinforced two ways: (a) by the success of making a two-loop knot that holds together for at least a few steps; and (more importantly) (b) the love and admiration of parental caretakers for successful completion of this task.

Piece of cake.

---

the child to work alone on steps 6 and 7. These two operants will be chained together by the terminal reinforcement (as well as by the verbal reinforcement of the caretaker at each step).

Interim Summary

1. Behavior control is a concept that certain stimuli in the environment (called *discriminative stimuli,* or S^d's) become associated with reinforced responses, while other stimuli (called *negative discriminative stimuli,* or S^Δ's) are not associated with reinforced responses.

2. The animal is said to be under *stimulus control* if, after S^d-S^Δ training, the response reliably occurs to the S^d but not to the S^Δ (i.e., the discriminative stimulus controls the response).

3. If one stimulus also controls the response to another, the second response is said to have *generalized* to the second stimulus, which lies along a *stimulus generalization gradient*.

4. S^d-S^Δ training sharpens discrimination of the $S^{d.}$ The presence of the S^Δ causes the response (which normally peaks to the S^d) to shift in a direction opposite the S^Δ (i.e., the *peak shift* phenomenon).

5. Human interactions, including verbal behavior, can be analyzed from the perspective of reinforced operant responding under stimulus control.

6. Learning complex behaviors can be analyzed as the acquisition of simple operant responses being chained together.

VI. Instinctive Behavior and Operant Conditioning

To this point we have contrasted Skinner's analysis of how reinforcement can modify emitted behavior with Pavlov's conditioning of innate reflexes. Both are examples of learning. But, as conceptualized in Chapter 2, and as implied by the name of this book, *behavior* is more than learning. Behavioral analysis involves the interplay of species-specific behavior and learning and instrumental behavior.

Recall that Skinner assumed that lever pressing by rats and key pecking by pigeons were relatively arbitrary "operants." That is, the responses were neutral with respect to the ingestive behaviors involved in eating the positive reinforcement.

Why did Skinner think that the distinction between "arbitrary responses" and "innate feeding responses" was an important one? Simply because the range of possible behaviors that can be "arbitrarily" conditioned is greater than innately organized responses. Humans in fact write poetry, and they play the piano as well as basketball. None of these behaviors evolved in response to selective pressures, and none are as important as the *consummatory behaviors* discussed in Chapter 2. A fortunate few can make a living playing games and musical instruments, but eating, drinking, courting, mating, and taking care of offspring are essential both in maintaining individual life as well as ensuring the continuity of species.

Is Key Pecking Arbitrary?   Skinner and others have recognized that a great deal of behavior exhibited by humans and other animals does not appear to be innately organized nor otherwise reflexive. To investigate how "arbitrary behavior" is learned, therefore, requires an arbitrary "operant" that is not innately organized. Lever pressing and key pecking seemed to fit the bill. Surely, the positioning of neck muscles and the postures of pigeons pecking at back-lit keys are unrelated to eating food and drinking water.

But look closely at the photos in Figure 6.7. A pigeon is reinforced with food for pecking at a back-lit key (bottom photos), and reinforced with water for pecking at a key (top photos). The difference is obvious. Water-reinforced pecking responses produce closed-mouthed drinking postures (top), and food-reinforced pecking responses model those made by pigeons eating grain (Jenkins & Moore, 1973). At least in this instance, the operant is not as arbitrary as Skinner hoped.

FIGURE 6.7 Birds' Beaks: Eating and Drinking Positions

Pigeons peck keys differently depending upon whether they are food (bottom row) or water (top row) reinforced. Apparently, open beaks are for picking up grain, and closed beaks for drinking. The response topography is not as arbitrary as Skinner thought "operant responding" should be. (From Jenkins & Moore, 1973; photos courtesy of Dr. Herbert Jenkins.)

Preparedness and Instrumental Behavior

Should we be surprised that an analysis of operant responses reveals a certain degree of "innate" organization? Certainly not. Skinner's assertion that instrumental responses are "emitted" does not obviate the fact that animals have evolved to behave in specific ways as a function of the niches they occupied over many years (Skinner, 1966).

Evidence for innately organized behavior has been presented earlier: In Chapter 2 we examined various examples of *species-specific behaviors,* and in Chapter 5 we studied the concepts of *preparedness* and *stimulus specificity* in the conditioning of responses. What else can we find out about the interactions of instinctive behavior and operantly conditioned responses? We begin with an example of complex human courtship behavior.

Human Courtship Patterns.   Have you ever found yourself wandering back to a place where you had a chance encounter with a "hot" guy or gal? Imagine that one day you are driving around, and see this magnificent person whose smile may or may not be for you. Over the next few days you begin to go out of your way in an attempt to locate Person "X." For the sake of argument, let us consider this complex behavior of "I'm attracted to you and want to see you/please notice me" a form of innately organized human courtship behavior.

Let us assume two things: first, that merely seeing "X" is a positive reinforcer, and second, that your presence has no effect on whether or not "X" appears. You learn that "X" can be seen at precisely 8:15 A.M. and 5:30 P.M. You continue to check at other times even though you are seldom reinforced. As a matter of fact, you shower, change your clothes, and brush your hair before driving by at various times during the day and night. To your embarrassment, you find yourself parking nearby on the off chance . . .

Further assume that this person finds out about you, considers you a pest (who is this strange person always smiling at me?) and without your knowledge begins to punish your behavior. Noticing your ever-present car, a different entrance and exit to the apartment complex is used. No reinforcement for this strange person.

Aware that you no longer see this person with the same frequency, you nevertheless continue your pattern of behavior. Unaware that your behavior keeps you from seeing this person as often as you might, you nonetheless manage to encounter your "satisfier" at least some of the time.

How can we account for this pattern of behavior? What maintains your persistence? Recognizing that much of our sexual behavior defies rational analysis, should we suspect that some innate patterns of human courtship behavior are involved? Is it possible that associative reinforcement theory may also help explain what is going on?

Let us begin our analysis by observing a pigeon in a (marginally) similar situation.

Autoshaping and Automaintenance

Place a pigeon in a Skinner Box and on the average of once a minute light the bird's pecking key for eight seconds. After eight seconds, turn off the light and raise the grain hopper to allow the hungry pigeon to eat for several seconds. Simple enough. All the bird has to do is walk over to the grain hopper when it notices the light is on, wait for the food reinforcer to appear a few seconds later, and then eat. This procedure resembles classical conditioning: The light is the CS and the food is the US, and no response contingency is required. (Compare: "X's" apartment is the CS; the sight of "X" is the US; and no response on your part is required to make "X" appear.)

Of the 36 birds trained in this manner by Brown and Jenkins (1968), *all* of them began to peck at the lighted key, even though pecking had nothing to do either with the light coming on or the food becoming available. Note that these researchers did not use the method of successive approximation to shape the naive birds' key-pecking behavior. Rather, they set automatic timers for the lights to come on and food to be delivered, and then they walked away. Hence, the Brown and Jenkins (1968) training procedure came to be known as **autoshaping** (also called **sign tracking**).

Analysis of Autoshaping. On the surface autoshaping appears to be procedurally more like classical conditioning than instrumental conditioning. The initial key-pecking response, however, is problematic. Food elicits reflexive salivation. Why does the light induce pecking behavior? The size of the back-lit key is presumably too large to elicit generalized feeding responses (see Hogan, 1973). Since the bird does not confuse the spot of light with food, most researchers concur that a simple light-food Pavlovian association is learned quite quickly. Because food and the light appear together in time, the pigeon begins to peck the light "as if" it were food.

Thought question: Would you predict that "X's" apartment complex becomes "hot" by its association with "X"? Is our hero "courting" the apartment complex as well as "courting" the person?

Automaintenance. Why does the pigeon continue pecking the key? Probably because the unnecessary pecking is being reinforced both by the food (primary reinforcer) and by the light (a secondary reinforcer established by higher-order conditioning). First, and most importantly, for the pecking response to continue, the availability of food must be positively correlated with the light being on. That is, pigeons will *not* peck at lighted keys if food is predicted less than 50 percent of the time that the light is on (Gamzu & Williams, 1971, 1973). Moreover, if grain availability continues to be associated with the light, pigeons maintain their (unnecessary) key-pecking responses indefinitely. Gamzu and Schwartz (1973) called this phenomenon **automaintenance.**

What else is known about the phenomena of autoshaping and automaintenance? Perhaps the most striking finding is that pigeons seem to be relatively insensitive to the consequences of their key-pecking responses. This is quite ironic. Reinforcement theory demands that animals be exquisitely sensitive to the consequences of their responses, and, indeed, the subtle patternings of key pecking and bar pressing in response to the various schedules of reinforcement described previously attest to such sensitivity. But if the experimenter changes the reinforcement rules for pigeons on automaintenance schedules, another surprising finding emerges.

"Maladaptive" Key-Pecking Responses?   Suppose that key pecking *delays* reinforcement. That is, arrange the contingency such that key pecks to the lighted key turn the light off and are not reinforced with food. (Note in this arrangement that both the *primary* and *secondary reinforcer* have been removed.) If the bird makes no key-pecking responses while the light is on, food *is* forthcoming. Therefore, it pays the bird to not key peck, because key pecking is punished by not getting the expected food reinforcement. Even after several hundred such trials, this procedure, called *negative automaintenance,* results in birds continuing to peck the lighted key about one-third of the time (Williams & Williams, 1969). And for this one-third of the time they miss out on being fed.

The nonreinforced key-pecking behavior seen on negative automaintenance schedules is troublesome. Such behavior seems to be both maladaptive (expending energy without payoff) and contrary to the *law of effect* (engaging in behavior that delays reinforcement).

But is it?

Significance of Autoshaping and Automaintenance

What is the theoretical significance of autoshaping and automaintenance phenomena? These experimental results require us to analyze behavior within both innate and "arbitrary" categories, and to see how each is affected by positive reinforcers. We begin with a question: Why do pigeons continue to expend energy to key peck in these situations? If we can answer this question, we may gain some insight into the human courtship pattern described earlier.

Pigeons Know How to Peck.   First, the pigeons. Pigeons know how to peck at back-lit keys without special training, and, as seen in Figure 6.7, their pecking responses reflect innately organized behavior patterns for eating and drinking. Innately organized feeding responses of birds are not restricted to pecking; mature hens, for example, visually search for food, peck at a variety of nonfood objects, make clucking noises to their chicks, and pick up and drop pieces of food near their chicks (Wickler, 1972).

Even though laboratory researchers are only interested in "operant key-pecking responses," pigeons have no alternative but to bring their species-specific behaviors into laboratory settings. In addition to key pecks, cocking the head and visually orienting to a lighted key, predictive of food, are also reinforced. We can safely conclude that autoshaping and automaintenance procedures result in the partial reinforcement of a variety of innately organized feeding responses (see Timberlake & Grant, 1975).

Reinforcement of Innate Feeding Responses.   Pecking responses of hungry pigeons are neither arbitrary nor trivial. Success in finding and ingesting food helps define their adaptive fitness. Recall that during automaintenance, when more than half of pigeon key-pecking responses went unreinforced, the pigeons would stop pecking the lighted key. Thus, these pigeons were adaptively responding to reinforcement contingencies. Likewise, Williams and Williams (1969) reported that during a negative automaintenance procedure, about one-third of the pigeons key-pecking responses were "wasted." The focus on unreinforced responses clouds the fact that *two-thirds* of all key pecks were (partially) reinforced with food.

Furthermore, "wasted" or "inefficient" pecking at a lighted key has parallels with other niche behaviors that are *not* considered maladaptive. Birds peck for other reasons than to secure food. While most pecking responses do result in food ingestion, other pecking responses—at nonfood objects, and dropping food near offspring are two examples—do not result in food ingestion. It may be that when all pecking responses are considered within the bird's niche, producing food two-thirds of the time may be *very* efficient.

Pigeon's Light Becomes Secondary Reinforcer.   In the Skinner Box, visual orientation and nonfood pecking responses are components of these innately organized feeding patterns, which are *also* reinforced by food. Because of the light/food association, the light becomes a secondary reinforcer. Both the appearance of the light and the partial reinforcement with food appear to maintain these component behaviors (orientation and pecking) indefinitely.

Conclusion? The behavior of a pigeon on an automaintenance schedule in a Skinner Box is neither maladaptive nor contrary to the law of effect. Indeed, predictions derived from associative reinforcement theory complement innate feeding behavior analyses. Together these theories provide an adequate account of the observed pecking behavior.

Automaintenance of Human Courtship Patterns.   The outcome of feeding strategies may determine life or death. Likewise, courting patterns of sexually mature humans that bear upon reproductive success are neither arbitrary or trivial. To the extent we were successful in analyzing the pigeon's feeding behavior, can we identify innate behavior patterns, reinforced responses, and their interactions in our example of human courtship behavior?

Needless to say, human courting behavior appears to be far more complicated than the manner in which pigeons secure food. But common elements can be identified. Both feeding and courting require a visual search. (Where is the positive reinforcer located?) Both require locomotor responses (approach behaviors) and other instrumental responses (preening?) necessary to secure the reinforcer.

Driving by "X's" apartment can be likened to the pigeon's orienting responses to the light. Both the apartment complex and the light have something to do with reinforcement (i.e., both have been previously associated with reinforcement).

Pecking is a component behavior of an innately organized feeding response. *Grooming* and "notice me" behaviors are components of innately organized human courting responses. While on automaintenance, pecks at a lighted key are not instrumental in producing food. Likewise, grooming and "notice me" behaviors are not instrumental in producing "X." In both cases, however, these innately organized behaviors are being maintained by partial reinforcement (i.e., both responses are associated with food and "X's" appearance, respectively).

Under certain conditions, both pecking responses and "notice me" behaviors may be punished. Food reinforcement can be made contingent upon not pecking, and "X" can disappear contingent upon your persistent responses. Both pigeon and human responses will continue, however, as long as some reinforcement is ultimately forthcoming (i.e., persistence pays).

Thought question: Does pigeon behavior on an automaintenance schedule successfully model the example of human courtship behavior? Why or why not?

Let us look at other ways in which reinforcement theory can modify innate predispositions to respond, and vice versa.

Misbehavior of Organisms

Marion and Keller Breland were students of B. F. Skinner who applied behavioral methodologies developed in laboratory research with pigeons and rats to other animals. Chickens, pigs, raccoons, and other animals were trained to perform cute circus acts for side shows.

If you have trained animals to do tricks, you already know how difficult it is to achieve a consistent and reliable performance. In 1960 the Brelands wrote *The Misbehavior of Organisms,* a book describing their animal training difficulties.[13] Their book is important, because it calls for nothing less than a modification of the law of effect.

Among their other trained animal acts, pigs and raccoons were reinforced for response chains that ended with a "coin" being deposited in a "bank." For example, a raccoon would work to earn a coin, and it would then pick it up and drop it into the "bank." Depositing the coin was the operant response that resulted in food reinforcement.

Failure of the Law of Effect?   The *law of effect* predicts that reinforced operant behavior such as "dropping a coin" would be learned efficiently. After a sufficient number of trials, the hungry animal should rapidly and effectively perform the operant and eat the food reinforcer. Many of the Brelands' trained animals did something else, however. Instead of depositing the coin, they played with it, delaying reinforcement.

Listen to the Brelands describe a raccoon required to drop *two* coins in the bank to secure reinforcement: "Not only [would] he not let go of the coins, but he spent seconds, even minutes, rubbing them together . . . and dipping them into the [bank]. . . . The rubbing behavior became worse as time went on, in spite of non-reinforcement" (Breland & Breland, 1960).

Likewise, pigs would repeatedly push coins along the floor with their snouts (cf."rooting behavior") rather than deposit them in the bank as they had been trained to do. Observations of the pigs' "rooting" behavior corroborated that of raccoons' "washing" behavior in two ways; namely, both patterns of behavior delayed reinforcement, and both patterns of behavior became worse with repeated trials.

Do you recognize parallels in the behavior patterns of these pigs and raccoons with previously encountered pigeons on automaintenance schedules?

Instinctive Drift.   How did the Brelands explain such instances of "misbehavior"? First, they reasoned that in their respective niches, raccoons routinely wash their food before eating, and pigs routinely root with their snouts. These innate patterns of feeding appear to intrude upon newly learned, highly arbitrary operants maintained by food reinforcement. The Brelands' term **instinctive drift** captures two of the most important aspects of the "misbehavior" they ob-

---

[13]The title is a parody of Skinner's *The Behavior of Organisms* (1938).

served; namely, that arbitrarily established responses erode (drift) in the face of more innately organized behavior (instinct).

Comparing Instinctive Drift and Preparedness.   In Chapter 5 we saw that rats have an innate tendency to be wary of novel foods, a phenomenon called *neophobia*. A rat's phobic response to new foods appears to complement its rapid (evolutionarily prepared) learning of flavor-toxin associations. By contrast, the Brelands' formulation of *instinctive drift* suggests that rather than working together, innate feeding patterns can also *conflict* with the learning of new associations. To the extent instinctive drift works against prepared learning, it would seem to be an example of *contraprepared* learning. Let us look more closely at details of the Brelands' experiments.

What Controls Instinctive Drift?

What would happen, if, instead of using small coins, food reinforcement were made contingent upon the operant response of rolling a large, heavy bowling ball into the bank? Or if reinforcement were contingent upon the operant response of pushing a wheelbarrow through a door in the bank? Would you expect to see instinctive drift in these circumstances? Or is it likely that instinctive drift is restricted to instances in which components of the animal's normal feeding niche are incorporated into the "arbitrary" operant?

The question being asked is whether the raccoon and pig are treating the coin as a *substitute* for food in the same way pigeons pecked the light "as if" it were food. Consider that the coin, or token, is a conditioned stimulus associated with the unconditioned stimulus of food (see Wolfe, 1934, for an account of chimps hoarding tokens that had been associated with food reinforcement). Note that these coins are also similar in size to the foods eaten by raccoons and pigs. After many trials, feeding responses may have become associated with the sight of the coin, and responses to the coins may have generalized from their responses to foods (Timberlake, Wahl, & King, 1982). Such a theory of **stimulus substitution** was proposed initially by Pavlov (1927).

Associations can be made between a wheelbarrow and food, but can bowling balls and wheelbarrows also be *substitutes* for food? To the extent these objects fall outside the stimulus generalization gradient of "food objects," substitution is highly unlikely. If they were on the generalization gradient, we would expect to see raccoons attempting to "wash" bowling balls, and pigs "root" at wheelbarrows.

(You would likely attach positive feelings to "X's" apartment complex by association; but since it is off the generalization gradient, you would not "court" it. On the other hand, you *might* wash "X's" car.)

Reconciling "Misbehavior" and the Law of Effect

To what extent does the "misbehavior of organisms" argue against the generality of the law of effect? Let us summarize an analysis of the issues:

Issues

1. Pigeons and the Brelands' pigs and raccoons engaged in behavior that delayed the food-reinforced terminal response (key pecking; dropping the coins).
2. The pigs and raccoons began to treat the coins as food as evidenced by "rooting" and "washing" the coins, respectively. (It is less likely the pigeons substituted the light for food, because the light is presumably off the generalization gradient.)
3. The Brelands alleged that the law of effect was violated by animals engaging in behavior that delayed reinforcement.

Analysis

1. By their association with food, the tokens (coins) had become *secondary reinforcers* for the Brelands' animals, in the same way the light became a secondary reinforcer for the pigeons.
2. The size and shape of the coins generalized from the stimulus dimensions of these animals' food; hence, these animals *substituted* their innate responses to foods to the coins.
3. Washing and rooting behaviors elicited by the foodlike coins were reinforced by the coins via secondary reinforcement.
4. As predicted by the law of effect, the observed "misbehavior" is being maintained by both primary and secondary reinforcement.

Behavior of Hungry Animals.   Both the Brelands' observations and the automaintenance phenomenon illustrate the complexities of behavioral analysis. Innate response tendencies and reinforcement principles interact in intricate ways to cloud even a "simple" key-pecking response. Among others, Shettleworth (1975) continues to study the behavioral complexities of hungry animals.

Interim Summary

1. Contrary to B. F. Skinner's assertion that a pigeon's key peck is an "arbitrary" response, several lines of evidence reveal pecking to be a niche-specific feeding behavior.
2. *Autoshaping* and *automaintenance* describe pigeon-in-the-box methodologies that apparently produce nonreinforced responding.
3. In autoshaping, aperiodic presentation of a lighted key followed by food (a Pavlovian stimulus-stimulus contingency) produces unnec-

essary pecking at the lighted key. If food is paired with the light on at least half of the occasions the key is lit, key-pecking responses will be maintained indefinitely (automaintenance).

4. Key-pecking in the absence of a food reinforcement contingency occurs because (a) species-specific key pecking is emitted for reasons other than feeding; (b) the global feeding response involves orientation and approach behaviors (such as to the lighted key) as well as pecking behaviors; (c) the lighted key has become a secondary reinforcer (due to pairings with food) that reinforces both approach and pecking; and (d) responding is maintained by partial reinforcement with food (primary reinforcer).

5. The Brelands' trained circus acts and reported what they believed to be *misbehavior of organisms* vis-à-vis the failure of the law of effect.

6. Because the Brelands' pigs and raccoons delayed the food-reinforced terminal response of "dropping coins," and instead "washed" and "rooted" them, the animals' behavior was said to be influenced by *instinctive drift*.

7. Analysis of the "misbehaving" animals revealed them to be under the control of the coins for two reasons: (a) the coins were on the food's reinforcer generalization gradient, and (b) they had also become secondary reinforcers that maintained the "washing" and "rooting" behavior.

8. Human courting behavior and pigeon feeding behavior were both analyzed from the perspective of how reinforced behavior interacts with innate response tendencies.

Preview: Reinforcement and Punishment

Throughout these first six chapters two themes have recurred—namely, the power of associative theory to account for learned behavior, and the ways in which these learned associations interact with and modify innately organized behavior. Pavlovian and Thorndikean conditioning represent our modern conceptions of associative learning, and both require "biologically meaningful" stimuli for learning to occur. That is, we have already noted that Pavlov's *unconditioned stimuli* and Skinner's *reinforcers* are very often food, and that "responses" produce "stimuli," which are available for association with food; similar underlying processes of association are assumed to exist in both forms of learning.

In this and preceding chapters we have also noted more similarities than differences in these two versions of associative theory. For example, from both S-S and R-S perspectives similar rules of acquisition, generalization, discrimination, and resistance-to-extinction govern learning. Both Pavlov and Thorndike also thought that associations were similar in outcome whether the "biologically meaningful" stimulus was appetitive/aversive or satisfying/annoying, respectively. Is this truly the case? Does it matter if we raise our children using punishment in place of reward? Are pleasure and pain equally effective in allowing us to modify our more innately organized behavior?

In the next chapter we will look more closely at Pavlov's *USs*, Thorndike's *satisfiers* and *annoyers,* and Skinner's *positive* and *negative reinforcers* and *punishers.* One question we will try to answer is why, each in its own way, do pain and pleasure control so much of our behavior?

Summary

1. In instrumental learning a response is learned or modified when it is followed by a positive reinforcer or a punishing stimulus.

2. E. L. Thorndike's law of effect states that responses followed by satisfiers (Skinner's positive reinforcers) will increase in frequency, and responses followed by annoyers (Skinner's punishers) will decrease in frequency.

3. The law of effect "works" because animals are hedonistic. Reinforcement typically selects adaptive responses.

4. John B. Watson and B. F. Skinner's behaviorism is best understood as a strict environmental determinism. In this philosophy voluntary behavior is nonexistent, because reinforced behavior is brought under stimulus control.

5. B. F. Skinner's operant conditioning method experimentally analyzes behavior in terms of how reinforcement contingencies control response tendencies. Operant behavior in the laboratory is analyzed in computer-programmed Skinner Boxes that present stimuli and measure the animal's responses.

6. Control of responding is analyzed by measuring the effects of schedules of reinforcement on responding, including continuous reinforcement (CRF) and partial, or intermittent, reinforcement.

7. Partial reinforcement schedules include fixed-ratio (FR); variable-ratio (VR); fixed-interval (FI); variable-interval (VI); and differential reinforcement of high (DRH) and low (DRL) schedules of reinforcement.

8. Longer FI and FR schedules produce postreinforcement pauses; FI schedules produce scalloping patterns; VI schedules produce stable responding; ratio and DRH schedules produce faster responding; and the DRL schedule teaches withholding of responses (patience).

9. CRF extinguishes quickly, and by comparison partial reinforcement schedules are resistant to extinction. The partial reinforcement effect (PRE) points out the roles of frustration and surprise in the maintenance of behavior.

10. Behavior control addresses questions of voluntary and involuntary behavior. An animal is said to be under stimulus control if a response reliably occurs in the presence of one but not another stimulus.

11. A discriminative stimulus (S^d) sets the occasion for reinforced responses; a negative discriminative stimulus (S^Δ) predicts nonreinforcement. S^d-S^Δ discrimination training sharpens discrimination of the S^d. The peak shift phenomenon is evidence that the S^Δ condition acquires an inhibitory influence on behavior.

12. Reinforcement theory and the analysis of stimulus control enhance our understanding of various aspects of human verbal behavior, of how complex behaviors are learned, and of how social interactions are maintained.

13. B. F. Skinner's "emitted operants" reflect inborn response tendencies.

14. Autoshaping and automaintenance entail procedures that include both Pavlovian and Thorndikean conditioning components.

15. In automaintenance, pigeons peck lighted keys due to both inborn response tendencies (i.e., behaviors appropriate to their feeding niches) and because their key approach and key pecking is reinforced by a secondary reinforcer (the lighted key) and partial reinforcement with food, respectively.

16. Marion and Keller Breland reported instances of the misbehavior of organisms, which they though violated the law of effect, and which they proposed were due to instinctive drift. The "misbehavior" was analyzed in terms of both innate feeding niche behaviors, and the secondary and primary reinforcing stimuli maintaining the behavior.

17. Human courting behavior was analyzed from the perspective of how reinforced behavior interacts with innate response tendencies.

Discussion Questions

1. Skinner's distinction between elicited and emitted behavior is controversial. Remember his observation that when a hungry rat is placed in a Skinner Box it will explore the new environment for several minutes by sniffing, rearing on its hind legs, and touching objects with its front paws. A familiar environment does not elicit such behavior. Would a hungry rat behave differently in such a situation as one just fed? Why does such behavior occur in a novel environment? Is such behavior elicited or emitted (or both)? Is it reflexive? Is it adaptive?

2. In an earlier discussion concerning the partial reinforcement effect (PRE), you were asked about the relationship between customer frustration and customer satisfaction. How is the optimal fee for service determined that maximizes customer satisfaction and your profit? Given Amsel's frustration theory,

can you make the case for "the customer is always right"?

3. Assume that your boss pays you and your roommate $10 for an hour of performing a telephone survey, and that the money is distributed to each of you in equal increments, but irregularly throughout the hour, contingent upon both of you making phone calls. You earn your $10 during the hour at a rate that depends upon how many phone calls you make in that hour, as distributed on a *variable-ratio* schedule. Your roommate is paid at *variable intervals* throughout the hour, also contingent upon a phone call (i.e., a variable-interval schedule). While you both make $10, you must work at a high rate to earn yours, while all your roommate has to do is to "dial regularly" during the hour to earn the same amount. Is it any wonder, comparing the cumulative records for VR and VI schedules or reinforcement in Figure 6.4a, that while both VR and VI schedules generate steady responding, VR schedules generate much higher rates of response than VIs? Why do plant workers complain about the speed of the assembly line? To increase a worker's output, can you think up an alternative to speeding up the assembly line?

4. Consider the following dialogue:

Student: Among other demonstrations of my *freedom to choose*, Dr. Skinner, are the very clothes I selected to wear this morning.

Skinner: Were you free to wear your roommate's clothes?

Student: No. But I'm free to choose to wear anything I own.

Skinner: So some people have more freedom to choose than others because they have more alternatives— either more resources to buy clothes, or less scruples about wearing the clothes of others?

Student: I suppose so, but that is not the point. I am free to choose to wear anything I own.

Skinner: Did you choose to wear your clean clothes or your stylish clothes as opposed to your dirty or nonstylish clothes?

Student: Of course. That was my choice. However, I could choose to wear dirty or nonstylish clothes.

Skinner: Why did you choose to wear clean, stylish clothes? [The dialogue continues.]

Can you hypothesize an early family environment making the "choice" of wearing clean clothes more likely? Could advertisers condition you to choose other stylish clothes? Can you also hypothesize environmental determinants of a student who "rebels" and "chooses" to wear dirty, nonstylish clothes?

5. Remember learning to ride a bike? Can you identify chained, component operants of this acquired skill? If someone helped you to learn, did he or she use successive approximation?

6. We trained the professor of our graduate learning class to write only at the very top of the blackboard, an uncomfortable position that he could reach only by stretching. He never knew what we were up to. We took advantage of his behavior of writing on the board while at the same time attempting to make eye contact with students. Before class we got together, made two little marks on each side of the blackboard about one-third down from the top, and only reinforced the professor when he wrote above but not below the imaginary line connecting our marks. What is reinforcing to a professor? Eye contact. Expressions of interest in students' eyes. When he wrote below the line, we looked away. When he wrote above the line, we smiled, nodded sagely, and paid rapt attention. By successive approximation we inched him up, class by class. After several weeks he was on his tiptoes.

Get together with other students before class and . . .

7. My major professor was James C. Smith of Florida State University. Among the many valuable things I learned from him was his analysis of *behavioral control* in the classroom. It only seems, he argued, that teachers are in control of their students. *Good* teachers are as much *controlled by* their students as they are *in control* in the classroom. What do you think Smith means by his analysis? Taking your clue from what our class did to our learning professor in question 6, can you make the case that good teachers always respond to the reinforcement and punishment contingencies to which they are exposed?

8. Those of you who have been horseback riding know what happens at the end of your ride when you and your horse are on the way back to the stable. It takes off like a shot. Can you analyze the horse's behavior in terms of stimulus control? Instinctive drift? Reinforcement contingencies?

9. Cigarettes kill more people than heroin or cocaine. Should we make cigarettes illegal, or continue to let people choose to smoke? AIDS kills people. Should people with AIDS be allowed to engage in behavior that spreads the disease, or should their behavior be restricted by law? How much behavior control should "society" be allowed to exercise in "the land of the free"?

Glossary

Annoyers   Thorndike's law of effect proposed that when unpleasant stimuli, which he called *annoyers,* followed a response, the response would less likely be made thereafter (cf. punisher).

Automaintenance   Pigeons that have a history of being fed in the presence of a lighted key will unnecessarily peck at the light even though their pecking response has no effect on when food is made available. The maintenance of pigeons continuing to respond under these conditions is called *automaintenance.*

Autoshaping   An untrained pigeon is placed in a Skinner Box, and food is presented in the presence of a lighted key. Without specific training, the bird will begin to peck at the lighted key, a procedure (and phenomenon) that is called *autoshaping* (and also called *sign tracking*).

Behavioral Control   The past and present reinforcement and punishment contingencies that determine the expression of a behavior.

Behaviorism   A philosophical position espousing an extreme environmental determinism. The assertion that human and animal behavior is directly, inevitably determined and controlled by the reinforcing and punishing contingencies of the local environment. (John B. Watson and B. F. Skinner are two famous proponents of behaviorism.)

Biological Determinism   The philosophical position that behavior is caused by the immutable action of genes. (Cf. *environmental determinism.*)

Chained Operants   A behavioral sequence analyzed in terms of a succession of discriminative stimuli that set the occasions for operant responses, eventually leading to reinforcement. (Cf. *stimulus-response chains.*)

Continuous Reinforcement (CRF)   A schedule of reinforcement in which each emitted response produces a positive reinforcement.

CRF   See *continuous reinforcement.*

Cumulative Record   A visual record of responses and reinforcement patterns in time generated by an ink-writing instrument called a *cumulative recorder.*

Differential Reinforcement of High Rates (DRH)   A schedule of reinforcement designed to reinforce bursts of operant responding. (Example: The tenth response within a five-second time period would be reinforced.)

Differential Reinforcement of Low Rates (DRL)   A schedule of reinforcement designed to reinforce timed pauses between operant responses. (Example: The first response after five seconds of nonresponding would be reinforced.)

Discrete Trial   A method of testing an animal's response on a given trial, such as placing it in a runway, or presenting a stimulus requiring a single response (cf. *free operant* method).

Discriminated Operant   A particular operant response under stimulus control. (Example: Removing the wrapper [S^d] from a stick of gum [reinforcer].)

Discriminative Stimulus (S^d)   A stimulus that signals that a particular response-reinforcement contingency is in effect, therefore setting occasions during which operant response become highly probably.

Elicited Behavior   Reflexive, or otherwise innately organized behavior, sometimes characterized as *involuntary* behavior (cf. Skinner's distinction of *elicited* and *emitted* behavior).

Emitted Behavior   Instrumental responses, sometimes characterized as *voluntary* behavior, that are not readily tied to specific eliciting stimuli (cf. Skinner's distinction of *elicited* and *emitted* behavior).

Environmental Determinism   The philosophical position that behavior is caused (determined) by environmental influences. (Cf. *behaviorism; biological determinism.*)

FI   See *fixed-interval schedule.*

Fixed-Interval (FI) Schedule   A schedule of reinforcement in which an animal is reinforced for its first response following a specified *time interval* from the preceding reinforcer.

Fixed-Ratio (FR) Schedule   A schedule of reinforcement in which reinforcement is contingent upon the completion of a fixed number of operant responses.

FR   See *fixed-ratio schedule.*

Free Operant   An easy, repeatable operant response, such as a lever press. (Contrast with tasks requiring *discrete trials*.)

Frustration Theory   (Amsel)   Following a history of continuous reinforcement, the theory that an extinction procedure produces a state of negative emotions such as frustration.

Hedonism   A philosophical position to the effect that the sole motivation of humans and other animals is to seek pleasure and to avoid pain.

Instinctive Drift   (Breland)   The theory that arbitrarily established responses erode (drift) in the face of more innately organized (instinctive) behavior.

Instrumental Conditioning   See *instrumental learning.*

Instrumental Learning   (Thorndike)   Acquiring and modifying so-called "voluntary," emitted, or otherwise nonreflexive behavior by the application of reinforcers or punishers. (Cf. *Pavlovian conditioning; operant conditioning*)

Instrumental Response   Voluntary, nonreflexive responses that act upon the environment in a meaningful, or instrumental, fashion.

Intermittent Reinforcement   See *partial reinforcement.*

Law of Effect   (Thorndike)   An elementary principle, postulated by Thorndike to govern *all* behavior, which simply states that a response that is followed by a pleasant consequence will tend to be repeated and a response followed by an unpleasant consequence will tend to decrease in frequency.

Magazine Training   An initial stage of operant conditioning in which approaches to the food cup (or magazine) are *reinforced* when the animal finds food there, and somewhat later, when the sound of the food delivery mechanism becomes associated with food delivery.

Negative Discriminative Stimulus (S$^\Delta$) A stimulus that signals that response-food contingencies are *not* in effect. Responding in the presence of this stimulus is not reinforced.

Operant (or operant response) (Skinner) A designated response, such as a lever press, that effectively *operates* upon the environment. (Cf. *instrumental response*.)

Operant Conditioning (Skinner) A variant of instrumental conditioning defined by B. F. Skinner. (See *instrumental conditioning*.)

Operant Level (Skinner) An existing baseline rate of a response as measured prior to the administration of reinforcement and punishment contingencies (cf. *baseline* or *free-operant level*).

Partial Reinforcement Any reinforcement situation other than continuous reinforcement. Also called *intermittent reinforcement*.

Partial Reinforcement Effect (PRE) The tendency for animals maintained on partial reinforcement schedules to be highly resistant to extinction.

Peak Shift Following S^d/S$^\Delta$ discrimination training of two wavelengths, the peak response of the generalization gradient to the target S^d is shifted in a direction opposite to (away from) the S$^\Delta$ wavelength.

Positive Reinforcement The process by which the application of a reinforcer contingent upon a desired response increases the frequency of that response.

Positive Reinforcer Any stimulus (such as food) delivered to an animal immediately following a designated response that leads to an increase in the frequen-

cy of that response is called a positive reinforcer. (Cf. Thorndike's *"satisfiers."*)

Postreinforcement Pause A break in responding following delivery of a reinforcer. Longer pauses are seen for higher FR schedules than for lower FR schedules (i.e., for FR-100 vs. FR-10), and very *short* postreinforcement pauses are typically found using VI and VR schedules of reinforcement.

Reinforcement See *positive reinforcement* and *negative reinforcement* (Chapter 7).

Resistance-to-Extinction The number of extinction trials necessary for a conditioned response to extinguish; an indirect measure of the amount of conditioning that has occurred. Greater *resistance-to-extinction* is found following many conditioning trials compared with a few conditioning trials in Pavlovian conditioning, and following partial rather than continuous reinforcement in instrumental conditioning.

Response Contingency In instrumental conditioning, making a reinforcer or punisher contingent upon a specified response. No such requirement exists for Pavlovian conditioning.

R-S Conditioning In instrumental conditioning, a response is required prior to presentation of a food stimulus. Hence, instrumental conditioning is sometimes referred to as response-stimulus, or *R-S conditioning*. (Contrast with *S-S* or *Pavlovian conditioning*.)

Satisfiers Thorndike's law of effect proposed that if pleasant stimuli, which he called *satisfiers*, followed a response, the response would more likely to occur thereafter. (Cf. *positive reinforcer*.)

Schedules of Reinforcement The experimenter specifies rules that govern the relationship of reinforcing events to an animal's responses. Example: In *contin-*

uous reinforcement the rule is that each response is reinforced. Other schedules include fixed ratios, variable intervals, etc.

Secondary Reinforcers Neutral stimuli that acquire reinforcing properties via the process of higher-order conditioning are called *secondary,* or conditioned, reinforcers. An example is money.

Shaping A training system that involves the selective reinforcement of responses that approximate the target behavior. The process by which increasingly stringent response requirements are placed on the animal, eventuating in reinforcement only for successful completion of the target response (i.e., a lever press), is called *shaping by successive approximation.*

Sign Tracking See *autoshaping.*

Skinner Box An experimental environment consisting of a small box containing one or more (a) levers or response keys, (b) lights/speakers, and (c) feeding/watering devices used in animal learning experiments (named for B. F. Skinner).

S-S Conditioning In Pavlovian conditioning, a stimulus is paired with another stimulus (such as food). Hence, Pavlovian conditioning is sometimes referred to as stimulus-stimulus, or *S-S conditioning.* (Contrast with *R-S* or *instrumental conditioning.)*

Stimulus Control Trained humans and animals that reliably make operant responses in the presence of S^d's and do not respond in the presence of S^Δ's are said to be under *stimulus control.*

Stimulus Generalization Gradient Following training to a target stimulus, a pattern of responses to similar stimuli, in which more responses are made to the most similar, and the fewest responses are made to stimuli most different from the target.

Stimulus-Response Chains The theory that in learning to perform a sequence of responses (such as left and right turns in a maze), each response may acquire stimulus properties that cue the next response. (Cf. *chained operants.)*

Stimulus Substitution (Pavlov) The theory that in the course of conditioning, animals come to consider the conditioned stimulus to be a "substitute" for the unconditioned stimulus. (Example: Chimpanzees who hoard tokens associated with prior food reinforcement.)

Successive Approximation See *shaping.*

Target Response The instrumental or operant response that, when executed, is reinforced.

Thorndikean Conditioning See *instrumental learning.*

Thorndikean Learning See *instrumental learning.*

Variable-Interval (VI) Schedule A schedule of reinforcement in which an animal is reinforced for its first response following a *variable interval* of time from the preceding reinforcer. Example: An animal on a VI-60 is reinforced at varying time periods averaging 60 seconds from the preceding reinforcement.

Variable-Ratio (VR) Schedule A schedule of reinforcement in which delivery of a reinforcer is contingent upon the completion of a variable number of operant responses from the preceding reinforcement. Example: An animal responding on a VR-10 is reinforced for different numbers of responses, their average being 10.

VI See *variable-interval schedule.*

VR See *variable-ratio schedule*

7

Reinforcement and Punishment

I.   Introduction

In previous chapters we have seen that learned changes in behavior result from stimulus-stimulus associations *(Pavlovian conditioning)* and response-stimulus associations *(instrumental learning)*. Furthermore, we have seen that in both conditioning procedures, learning occurs when the consequences of a behavior are either *satisfying* (i.e., tasty food, a smile) or are *annoying* (i.e., a painful electric shock, a disproving glance). The similarities of procedures and results in both systems suggest that both processes are related. And, as we will see, brain mechanisms appear to be common to both kinds of learning.

Up to now, the question of *why* associations are formed in both Pavlovian and instrumental conditioning has been raised only informally. In the present chapter, *theories* of reinforcement, of punishment, of avoidance behavior, and other questions of *motivation* will be entertained. Our goal is to develop a theory that integrates reinforcement and punishment in both Pavlovian conditioning and instrumental learning—a mighty tall order.

Atheoretical Behaviorists   Why devote an entire chapter to theories of reinforcement and punishment? B. F. Skinner, for example, espoused the well-known and highly influential *behaviorist* position that such theories were unnecessary for the development of a science of behavior (Skinner, 1950). Responding in part to Clark L. Hull's "drive theory" of behavior, which postulated many intervening variables

(Hull, 1943, 1952—see below), Skinner countered that a quantified *description* of how reinforcement and punishment controlled behavior in carefully conducted experiments was sufficient to develop a science of behavior.

An "atheoretical" behaviorist position may have been defensible at the time it was espoused. And the lack of an overall organizing theory did not impede the conduct of literally thousands of experiments directed at discovering the determinants of behavior. The results of decades of research, however (almost 100 years, going back to Pavlov's first experiments), now permit—and perhaps demand—attempts to formulate theory rather than continue to merely describe instances of learning and motivation.

As was discussed in Chapter 1, a "Grand Theory of Behavior" that would encompass and integrate diverse findings in behavioral genetics, neuroscience, psychology, etc., has not yet been achieved. Although Clark L. Hull outlined the problem 50 years ago (Hull, 1943), no one has been quite so ambitious since. After reviewing traditional theories of reinforcement and punishment, in this chapter we will merely try to organize and integrate a number of contemporary theories that address different aspects of learning and motivation.

Learning and Motivation.   Our understanding of how learning affects behavior seems to be intimately connected to our understanding of what *motivates* our behavior. When in this chapter we begin to focus on concepts of reward and punishment, and on *incentives,* we enter the realm of motivated behavior. Questions as to *what* we learn and *how* we learn shift ever so subtly to *why* we learn what we do. Consider the following:

> "Beat me, beat me!" said the masochist.
> "No!" said the sadist.

Maladaptive learned behavior intrigues us all. How is it that pain can become pleasure, and inflicting pain can give some people so much pleasure? One way to address this question is to ask *why* some events bring us pleasure and others are so annoying.

Reinforcers and Reinforcement.   The process of *reinforcement* and the class of stimuli known as *reinforcers* are of sufficient complexity and of such importance that both demand extensive analysis. What is reinforcement? What determines whether a given stimulus is a reinforcer? What do food, sex, water, some drugs, and electrical stimulation of the *medial forebrain bundle* (see what follows) of the brain have in common? Why is association formation and memory acquisition so dependent upon the special properties of these diverse stimuli?

More interesting questions cannot be asked than those which concern the wellsprings of human motivation and behavior. In courts of law and in personal relationships, such questions as "what motivated you to leave him?" and "why did you try to kill yourself?" and "will you still love me?" command every ounce of our attention. These questions go to the very heart of human nature. And it is to questions of motivated behavior that we now turn.

II. Traditional Theories of Reinforcement and Punishment

A Review of Pavlov, Thorndike, Skinner, and Hull

For almost 100 years learning theorists have struggled with the complexities presented by the fact that humans and other animals not only are born with, but also in the course of their lifetimes acquire, motivated behaviors. We have studied three such systems up to this point, and here we will here review the theories underlying them.

Pavlov's Theory

Pavlov (1927) focused upon "biologically meaningful stimuli" in the environment that produce reflexes in animals. He observed that both humans and dogs struggled against confinement and hypothesized that all animals have a "freedom reflex." He identified "appetitive" USs such as food, and aversive ("defensive") USs such as sour fluid placed on the tongue. Both of these stimuli produce reflexive salivation in dogs and humans. Pavlov also studied the aversive motivating properties of electric shock, which elicited leg-flexion reflexes. He found that the latter entered into association with neutral conditioned stimuli in the same manner as observed in appetitive conditioning. Pavlov's "theory," then, is a biological statement:

1. Animals are "motivated" to survive.
2. Reflexes are physiological adaptations that promote survival.
3. Neutral stimuli paired with these innate reflexes alter the brain's connections, so that conditioned reflexes may eventually occur to formerly neutral stimuli.
4. More often than not the conditioned reflexes are also adaptive in that they promote well-being and survival.

Thorndike's Theory

Yet another of these early formulations of human motivation was that of Thorndike (1898, 1932). Recall from Chapter 6 that he labeled stimuli in the environment based upon their perceived effect; i.e., some stimuli are *satisfiers*, others are *annoyers*, and yet others are neutral. Recall that his animal subjects were motivated to get out of puzzle boxes presumably because they found confinement (innately) *annoying*. Escape from confinement was (innately) *satisfying*. The satisfaction associated with escape, in Thorndike's way of looking at the world, had the effect of *stamping in* the immediately preceding instrumental escape responses. Learning, therefore, was motivated by innately satisfying events, and by escape or avoidance of innately dissatisfying events. The learned responses, as governed by the *law of effect*, were the inevitable results of associations with satisfiers and annoyers. Thorndike's law of effect is summarized in Figure 7.1.

Pavlov and Thorndike Compared. Is it obvious that Thorndike's perspective is similar to that of Pavlov? For both, the satisfactions of appetite and freedom are in opposition to the annoyances of aversive events. And for both, positive and negative events support parallel systems for learning new responses. Differences? Pavlov studied physiological reflexes, and Thorndike, instrumental responses. While the similarities may seem to outweigh the differences, consider that

		Stimulus	
		Satisfier	Annoyer
Response	Produces	Stamp in preceding response	Stamp out preceding response
	Removes	Stamp out preceding response	Stamp in preceding response

FIGURE 7.1   Diagram of the Law of Effect

In Thorndike's *law of effect*, instrumental responses that produce or remove Thorndike's *satisfiers* and *annoyers* either *stamp in* or *stamp out* behavior, respectively.

the organization of this textbook in part emphasizes their differences: Pavlov's methods and results (Chapters 4–5) are considered separately from those of Thorndike and Skinner (Chapter 6). In this chapter and the next, similarities rather than differences will be emphasized. Before examining these similarities, let us first review B. F. Skinner's contributions to a theory of motivated human behavior.

Skinner's Theory

B. F. Skinner (1950) insisted that his position on questions of reinforcement, learning, and motivated human behavior was *atheoretical*, a most interesting theoretical position to take! As a strict behaviorist (and following the lead of John B. Watson), Skinner proposed that questions relating to motivation were both unnecessary and undesirable. For example, in Skinner's view the very term "learning" was a *hypothetical construct* inferred from changes in an animal's performance (see the discussion on p. 71). To say that an animal is *motivated* to learn and now has a *memory* for what it has *learned* does not, in Skinner's view, add anything to the observation that the animal's behavior changed as the result of experiences a, b, and c. (Note that these italicized terms are *intervening variables*.) The description of the performance change based upon the operations of the experiment (cf. *operational definitions*) constitutes a sufficient explanation for the behavioral change. For the strict behaviorist, the use of terms such as *motivation, incentive, learning,* and *memory* adds nothing. These terms allude to unobservable events, and each is an additional step removed from the reality of the observations of performance changes.

Skinner's Definitions of Reinforcement and Punishment. B. F. Skinner's "atheoretical position" had the intended effect of making behavioral analysis more rigorous and "scientific." As noted in Chapter 6, most behavioral scientists at present follow his lead in operationally defining reinforcers and punishers according to the effect each has upon the preceding response. A *reinforcer* is therefore defined as any stimulus whose application following a response has the effect of increasing the probability of that response. Though awkard to state, this operational definition serves to differentiate a "reinforcing stimulus" from Thorndike's requirement that the stimulus be "pleasing." How so?

Are All Reinforcers, "Rewards"? With their respective concepts of *unconditioned stimuli* and *satisfiers,* both Pavlov and Thorndike clearly had in mind that such stimuli *innately* elicited pleasure. That is, pleasure-producing properties were inherent in the stimulus. B. F. Skinner, by way of contrast, makes no such requirement. If the effect of the stimulus is to increase the rate of emission of the preceding response, by definition the stimulus is a *reinforcer,* and the process is called *reinforcement.*[1] From Thorndike's perspective, all rewards (such as candy) are reinforcers; but for Skinner, a reinforcer need not be a reward.

The same distinctions hold for aversive stimuli. For Pavlov and Thorndike, such stimuli were *inherently* aversive. By contrast, Skinner also defined punishment operationally. If the effect of the stimulus is to decrease the rate of emission of the preceding response, by definition the stimulus is a **punisher,** and the process is called **punishment.**

Removing or Preventing Satisfiers and Annoyers. Skinner also pointed out that responses can also have the effect of removing a stimulus, or preventing a stimulus from occurring. Obviously, withholding one of Thorndike's satisfiers is punishment; parents more often punish teenagers by *preventing* them from driving a car or watching television than by spanking or applying some other aversive stimulus. Likewise, withholding one of Thorndike's annoyers can be a reinforcing event (it feels good when you stop hitting yourself in the head).

Later in this chapter we will look at evidence for both assertions as to the reinforcing and punishing effects of withholding aversive stimuli (Section IV) and withholding rewarding stimuli (Section V), respectively. We merely note here that these concepts, too, will be operationally defined. A descriptive summary of the way in which responses can be strengthened or weakened by the effects they have in producing or preventing either positive and negative environmental stimuli is presented in Figure 7.2. You may want to compare Figures 7.1 and 7.2 to see how B. F. Skinner elaborated upon Thorndike's simple conception of the law of effect.

Clark L. Hull's Drive Theory of Behavior

Given that Figure 7.2 accurately summarizes behavioral definitions of reinforcement and punishment, and noting that these definitions provide our *zeitgeist,* you might wonder what is to be gained by looking at Clark L. Hull's theoretical system—a system that is for the most part ignored by contemporary learning theorists. Recall that Skinner's experimental analysis of behavior restricts observations and theory to that which can be measured—stimuli impinging upon and responses emanating from the organism (see Figure 3.1). This *black box* approach has served us well. Why did Hull intentionally put "made-up" intervening variables inside the black box?

---

[1]Yes, this is a circular definition. "Why is a given stimulus reinforcing? Because by increasing the rate of the preceding response, it acts as a reinforcer." In a later discussion we will find a way out of this circularity by noting other defining properties shared by all reinforcers.

Effect of Stimulus on Preceding Response

	Probability, or rate of response ↑	Probability, or rate of response ↓
Response **produces** stimulus	Process is *Reinforcement* Stimulus is a *Reinforcer*	Process is *Punishment* Stimulus is a *Punisher*
Response **prevents** stimulus	Process is *Negative Reinforcement* Absence of stimulus is a *Negative Reinforcer*	Process is *Punishment* Absence of stimulus is a *Punisher*

FIGURE 7.2 Diagram of Reinforcement and Punishment

Summary of B. F. Skinner's operationally defined concepts of *reinforcement* and *punishment,* and the operational labeling of *reinforcers* and *punishers.* See text for discussion.

Hull's Neobehaviorism. Clark L. Hull was dissatisfied with a limiting S-R behavioral approach. In his view, animal behavior was better characterized as a complex of physiological *drives* and *need states,* which could in part be met through learning experiences. Furthermore, as he wrote in *Principles of Behavior* (1943), learning was "driven" (motivated) by the necessity of meeting these physiological demands. Hull proposed a **drive theory** of behavior as an alternative to descriptive behaviorism (Hull, 1943, 1952).

S-O-R Theory. Hull self-consciously described himself as a *neobehaviorist* to contrast his position with that of other behaviorists. Strict behaviorists, he thought, failed both in their lack of formal theoretical analysis and in their tendency to ignore crucial details of behavior. Hull developed *methodological objectivism* more sharply. He deviated from a pure S-R orientation by specifically including *intervening variables.* Hence, his position is characterized not as S-R, but rather as **S-O-R theory,** where "O" stands for such *organismic variables* as thirst and hunger. Given our knowledge of physiology (even in 1943!), he queried, why continue to treat the organism as a black box? Obviously his reasoning is even more valid today.[2]

Drive Reduction Theory.   Following Pavlov's lead, Hull emphasized physiological variables critical for survival. Skinner did not. Skinner's 1938 book was entitled *The Behavior of Organisms*, but "behavior" was confined to descriptions of operant responses. Taking his lead from John B. Watson, Skinner was content to concentrate on the *environmental* control of behavior. In adopting a position of *environmental determinism*, Skinner minimized biological determinants of behavior (Skinner, 1957).

By contrast, Hull's behavioral theory proceeded from the assumption that learning was intimately tied to physiology. Innately determined homeostatic mechanisms allowed organisms to survive. Food and water deprivation set up conditions of specific physiological *needs*, and these needs were translated into motivated behavior by specific **drive states.** When these *drives* resulted in behavior that fulfilled the specific *needs*, restoring the organism's homeostatic balance, the drive was said to be *reduced*—hence, **drive reduction theory.** "Reducing" drives has the effect of reinforcing instrumental behaviors.

Hull's System of Quantification.   Clark L. Hull's (1952) efforts represent a monumental attempt to construct a theory of learning built upon observations of behavior, from which are derived corollaries, postulates, and theorems. His *drive reduction theory of learning* was stated in the form of a mathematical equation:

$$_sE_R = {}_sH_R \times D \times V \times K - (I_R + {}_sI_R). \qquad (7.1)$$

Though imposing, in reality Eq. (7.1) is not that difficult to understand. While we are not going to elaborate all of the intervening variables he postulated, we can begin by noting that the terms in the equation are merely being added, subtracted, or multiplied.

---

[2]Arguably even B. F. Skinner would have agreed with this analysis at the end of his career. In one of his last articles he wrote: "Behavior analysts leave what is inside the black box to those who have the instruments and methods needed to study it properly. There are two unavoidable gaps in any behavioral account: one between the stimulating action of the environment and the response of the organism, and one between consequences and the resulting change in behavior. Only brain science can fill those gaps. In doing so it completes the account; it doesn't not give a different account of the same thing. Human behavior will eventually be explained (as it can only be explained) by the cooperative action of ethology, brain science, and behavior analysis. (Skinner, 1989, p. 18)

What is Hull attempting to model with this equation? The notation "$_sE_R$" refers to *reaction potential*—a probability that the *performance* of a learned behavioral response (R) has the potential *(E)* to occur under certain stimulus conditions (S). In other words, Hull is attempting to write a learning equation that will predict the probability of a learned response in a given situation — such as how quickly a rat can learn a maze.

What factors are important in how rapidly a rat learns to negotiate straight alley and T-shaped runways? Among the variables included in Hull's equation are $_sH_R$ *(habit strength,* or how much has already been *learned), D (drive), V (stimulus intensity dynamism—*a variable akin to intensity effects in Pavlov's *law of strength), K (incentive motivation—*both innate and acquired), I_R *(reactive inhibition —*a variable that included fatigue effects), and $_sI_R$ *(conditioned inhibition).* These variables are in turn operationally defined; for example, *drive* is defined in terms of "hours of food or water deprivation." The quality and amount of a reinforcer in part determines the degree of **incentive motivation** underlying behavior. Larger amounts of food provide greater (primary, or innate) incentive for hungry animals.

Acquired Incentives. Stimuli paired with innate incentives such as food and water become **acquired incentives.** For example, a distinctively colored goal box, or the muscle cues associated with a left-turn entry into the goal box, acquire reinforcing properties. Acquired incentives in Hull's theory are secondary reinforcers in Skinner's system. Presumably both are acquired by the process of higher-order conditioning as described by Pavlov. Hull's system models negatively accelerated learning curves similar to those predicted by the Rescorla–Wagner model (see p. 141). That is, the increment of $_sH_R$ (habit strength) that accrues with each reinforced trial is a fraction of the amount remaining to be learned. Hull's theory further predicts that the upper limit of learning tends to be at a maximum when need reduction is greatest (i.e., when incentive motivation is highest), and when the delay between response and reinforcement is short.

Finally, can you look at the equation and determine why Hull is described as a drive reduction theorist? Note that without *drive* (in the equation, let *D* = 0), there can be no reinforcement, and, hence, the right side of the equation when multiplied by zero has the value zero. Solving the equation when *D* = 0, $_sE_R$ also is zero.

Drive-Stimulus Reduction Theory

We have seen that Hull initially conceived of both reinforcement (and punishment) as being mediated through *drive reduction.* Because of a simple experiment reported by Sheffield and Roby (1950), Hull modified his position and endorsed a theory of **drive-stimulus reduction.**

Recall that if any of the terms in Hull's equation go to zero, no learning should occur. Sheffield and Roby (1950) demonstrated that satiated (nonhungry) rats could learn an instrumental response when nonnutritive saccharin was used as a reinforcer. In this experiment a hunger drive was not reduced; apparently, the stimulus properties of saccharin were a sufficient incentive for learning to occur. Hull reasoned that reducing the drive caused by *this* stimulus was reinforcing; hence the (unfortunate) name, *drive-stimulus reduction.*

Stimulation or Satiation Is Reinforcing.   Once the implications of Sheffield and Roby's simple demonstration sunk in, other examples of non–drive-reducing reinforcement appeared in the literature. The concept of reinforcement changed rapidly. For example, Sheffield and his colleagues next demonstrated that rather than reducing a drive, engaging in a behavior that presumably *increased* a drive (or at least increased the level of excitement) could also act as a reinforcer. In these experiments male rats learned to run quickly to a female in estrous and to engage in copulatory behavior. Drive reduction theory predicts that achieving orgasm would *reduce* the sex drive; the resulting reinforcing effects would enable the rat to effectively learn the preceding instrumental behaviors. In this experiment, however, the rats were separated *before* achieving orgasm. The male rats learned despite the lack of drive reduction, presumably because sexual excitement was itself reinforcing (Sheffield, Wulff, & Backer, 1951).

Analysis of Hull's Theory.   By his recognition of the complexity of behavior, by his insights that differentiated *learning* variables from *performance* variables, and by his *hypothetico-deductive model* of how data can be used to generate a formal theory of behavior, Hull had a profound impact on both behavior analysis and learning and behavior theory. Although drive theory was found wanting, both drive reduction theory and the prominent role played by acquired incentives remain as his legacy. Hull's theory was both premature and too ambitious; but in that he attempted to integrate biological and psychological variables into a general theory of behavior, the approach was not misguided.

Equation (7.1) does *not* serve the function that Hull envisioned, because it does not allow us to predict the course of learned behavior in other than the most general terms. Nevertheless, his overall approach to a theory of learning is more timely than Skinner's atheoretical position. Why? Because contemporary investigations in behavioral neuroscience proceed from adaptive-evolutionary premises and use integrated physiological and behavioral methodologies. Modern neuroscience is more in tune with Hull's theory in that purely descriptive behaviorism is too limiting. In the next section we turn to physiological observations and behavioral data that have expanded the concept of reinforcement beyond the formulations of Pavlov, Thorndike, Skinner, and Hull.

Interim Summary

1. Pavlov hypothized that biologically meaningful stimuli elicit survival-promoting reflexes. Examples include innate responses to food and withdrawal from aversive stimuli. New behaviors, also typically adaptive, can be learned by the association of these reflexes with neutral stimuli.
2. Thorndike proposed the *law of effect*, a simple statement that responses followed by a satisfying state tend to increase, and responses followed by an aversive state ("annoyers") tend to decrease in frequency.
3. B. F. Skinner defined *reinforcement* as the process of strengthening a responses (increasing the probability of response) by the application of a reinforcer. He further defined a *reinforcer* (in a circular manner) as any stimulus that increased the rate of the preceding response.
4. Clark L. Hull's drive reduction theory of behavior is a formal model theory involving data gathered from behavioral observations, and the derivation of corollaries, postulates, and theorems. Hull attempted to predict performance in a learning task by specifying physiological and psychological variables within the black box (i.e., a S-O-R model rather than a S-R model). Physiological needs induced drives, which when reduced (satisfied) reinforced behavior.
5. Drive-stimulus reduction theory was proposed to account for observations that some effective reinforcers not only failed to reduce drive, but sometimes induced behavior. Drinking a saccharin-flavored solution empty of calories is an example of a reinforcing event that does not reduce a hunger drive.

III. Contemporary Theories of Reinforcement

Primary and Secondary Reinforcement Revisited

We should not be too surprised by the fact that both nonnutritive (but good tasting) saccharin and sexual foreplay can act as reinforcers in both rats and humans. Many activities we engage in are pleasurable in spite of the fact our survival does not depend upon them. We ski, flirt, ride bicycles, take pleasure-inducing drugs, play (pianos, soccer, Nintendo®), read, worship, swim, sweet talk, watch television, spend hours cooking gourmet meals, high five, listen to CDs, celebrate holidays, tell jokes, sunbathe, talk on telephones, soak in a tub, brush hair, and rub backs. (What an impressive list! Let us modify an earlier statement to suggest that *most* activities humans engage in are pleasurable in spite of the fact our immediate survival does not depend upon them.)

Which of the foregoing behaviors and events are innately reinforcing, which are acquired, and which include both components?[3] Because Hull recognized the concept of **acquired motivation,** perhaps he can be faulted for requiring all motivation to be drive reducing in the first place. All the foregoing activities give pleasure, but most do not involve drive reduction.

In fact, the satisfaction of *social approval* may be among the items at the top of the list of effective reinforcers for both children and adults. A theory of social reinforcement has been proposed to account for modeling behavior of children (Bandura, 1977). For present purposes, *social reinforcement theory* can be understood as the application of a specific subset of learned secondary reinforcers (including smiling, paying attention, saying "good," etc.) to reinforce certain human behaviors.

Let us raise the possibility that almost *all* the preceding behaviors that humans engage in are being maintained by a common process of reinforcement. Certainly "pleasure" seems to be common to these examples. What is the nature of this alleged "common reinforcer" if it is other than pleasure? We must look inside the black box for an answer.

Inside the Black Box: The Brain's Basis for Reinforcement

Serendipity. Over and above being a pleasant sounding word, "serendipity" plays an important role in the conduct of science. The word was coined by Horace Walpole to describe a mythical faculty possessed by scientists that allowed them to make important discoveries—by accident. Others have noted that a successful discovery is often best attributed to "being in the right place at the right time." Indeed, B. F. Skinner, in eschewing the role of theory in his research, asserted that *serendipity* (including equipment breakdowns!) better accounted for both the direction and the successes of his behavioral discoveries (Skinner, 1959). As it turns out, serendipity also played a crucial role in a classic experiment that opened a window in the black box, allowing for the first time a look at the brain's mechanisms of reinforcement (Olds & Milner, 1954).

Electrical Stimulation of the Brain. Two psychologists, James Olds and Peter Milner, had implanted electrodes into areas near the hypo-

---

[3]As we saw in Chapter 6, the process by which secondary reinforcers can be derived from primary reinforcers involves Pavlov's higher-order conditioning. You may want to test yourself on the distinctions among primary, secondary, and mixed reinforcers by sorting the foregoing list of behaviors into these three categories.

thalamus of rats. They were in the process of assessing the effects of **electrical stimulation of the brain (ESB)** of a conscious, free-ranging rat by passing minute amounts of electric current through an implanted electrode. By chance, Olds and Milner noted that some of the rats seemed to return to the particular place in the open field apparatus where they had received the ESB on previous trials. The researchers had prepared minds (i.e., they were in the right place at the right time); they recognized that the ESB in these rats seemed to be acting as a reinforcer, and that the rats were learning an instrumental response because of the ESB (Olds & Milner, 1954).

To test their hypothesis, they programmed a Skinner Box in a way that made ESB contingent upon lever pressing. If ESB was really a reinforcer and acted the same as food and water in deprived rats, they reasoned, then rats should press the lever to secure ESB (Olds, 1962). Their hypothesis proved correct. ESB passed through certain electrode placements near the hypothalamus acted as a reinforcer in that rats would "self-stimulate" by pressing a lever that delivered ESB (see Figure 7.3).

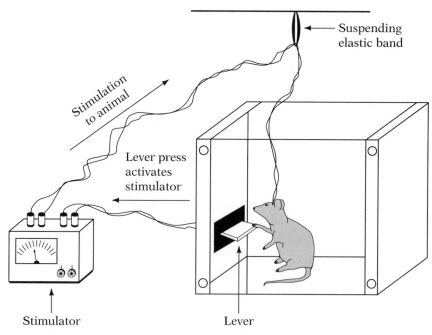

FIGURE 7.3   Electrical Stimulation of the Brain

Rats increase the rate of lever pressing when each lever press delivers electrical stimulation to a rewarding site in its brain.

Interim Summary

In the 40 years since Olds and Milner's original observations, neuro-science research has illuminated the brain basis for reinforcement to a level that goes well beyond the scope of this book (see Pinel, 1993, for a readable overview). A summary of some of the more important findings of this diverse research follows:

1. ESB has been demonstrated to have reinforcing properties for all species tested, including humans (Heath, 1963).
2. A factor common to many successful electrode placements (i.e., those which yield reinforcing effects) is that a structure called the *medial forebrain bundle (MFB)* is activated (Stein, 1969). (The MFB is a *limbic system pathway* that courses through portions of the hy-pothalamus.) More recent research has indicated that stimulation of the *mesotelencephalic dopamine system* plays a crucial role in ESB (Phillips & Fibiger, 1989). Other brain structures than the MFB and other neurotransmitters than dopamine have been impli-cated in the reinforcing effects of ESB.
3. ESB can have motivational effects as well as reinforcing effects. That is, rats that are neither food, water, nor sex deprived can nev-ertheless be in induced to eat or drink (Valenstein, Cox, & Kakolewski, 1967), or to initiate sexual behaviors (Caggiula & Hoebel, 1966) when ESB is delivered in the presence of food, water, or a sexual partner, respectively.
4. The foregoing ESB-induced behaviors are called *stimulus-bound behaviors*. The electrode sites that produce stimulus-bound behav-ior can also be shown to reinforce instrumental responding (Grat-ton & Wise, 1988). One implication of this finding is that *engaging in certain behaviors can be reinforcing*. As we will see in a later sec-tion in this chapter, the opportunity to engage in behavior forms the basis of Premack's (1962) concept of reinforcement.

Comparison of ESB with Traditional Reinforcers

How effective is ESB? How does ESB (from a positive electrode placement—one that "works") compare with a traditional reinforcer such as food? One way to answer this question is to arrange for rats to choose between one of two levers—pressing one produces ESB re-inforcement; pressing the other produces food. Such an experiment was conducted during daily, one-hour trials (Routtenberg & Lindy, 1965). The rats chose ESB reinforcement. Since the one-hour period was the only time rats were allowed to eat during the course of this experiment, by choosing ESB they died of starvation within a few days.

FI-10 Schedules Using ESB or Food Reinforcement. Another demonstration of the relative effectiveness of food and ESB reinforcement can be found in an elegant experiment by Anderson, Ferland, and Williams (1992). Because this experiment provides both a review of material learned in the previous chapter and illustrates several new concepts as well, we will look closely at their methods. Rats were first trained on an FR-10 schedule for food reinforcement until stable responding ensued throughout a 90-second time period. Each FR-10 segment (signaled by S^d = light) alternated with 30 seconds of forced nonresponding. Nonresponding was accomplished by a DRL-30 second requirement (S^d = tone) in which a response would reset a timer for an additional 30 seconds, further delaying access to food available on the FR-10 schedule of reinforcement. The S^d signaling food availability on the FR-10 was the secondary reinforcer maintaining the DRL schedule. As can be seen in Figure 7.4, after many sessions of responding on alternating FR-10, DRL-30 second schedules of reinforcement, a representative rat's rate of response was high on the FR-10, and low on the DRL-30.

Anderson et al. (1992) then began alternating two kinds of reinforcement available on the FI segments: namely, food and ESB (electrical stimulation of the MFB). The same S^d was used for both the food and ESB schedules, and the DRL-30 second segment now separated these two reinforced schedules. The way in which this rat responded on alternating FI segments with either food or ESB reinforcement allowed for a continuing comparison of their relative effectiveness. First, note in Figure 7.4a that following the first occasion ESB was made available, the pattern of (non)responding on the DRL was disrupted. Electrical stimulation of the brain on the FI segment seemed to carry over into the following DRL segment, during which the rat was no longer able to inhibit its responding. Remember that responding on the DRL resets the timer, delaying entry into the next food-reinforced segment. At this point we do not know if the ESB has merely induced (excited) the bar pressing, or if the ESB has acted as a different kind of reinforcer and changed the pattern of responding during extinction.

Negative Contrast. After several more iterations of FI, DRL, ESB, DRL, etc., a new phenomenon emerges. By the fourth session (Figure 7.4b), the rat's bar pressing for food virtually stops. At the same time, by not responding on the DRL segment, the rat does not delay entry into the FI segment for ESB. And once in the FI segment maintained by ESB reinforcement, the rat rapidly bar presses for ESB. Having experienced both forms of reinforcement, apparently food reinforcement is now perceived as less reinforcing to the rat— a phenomenon called **negative contrast.** Negative contrast is an

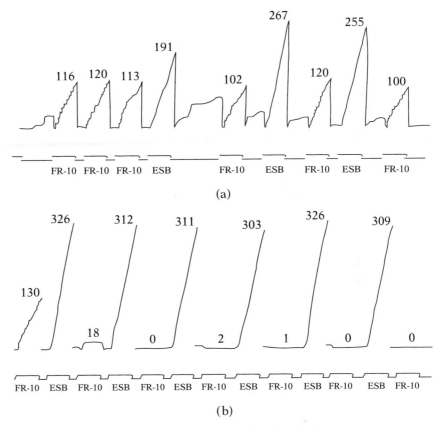

FIGURE 7.4 Rats Prefer ESB to Food—Absolutely!

Rats are trained to bar press on multiple schedules of reinforcement, beginning with FR-10 for food, alternating with DRL-30 (not labeled) for the first three segments (a). The DRL-30 was reinforced by reentry into the FR-10 segment. Then (fourth cycle from left), for the first time the rat's FR-10 was reinforced with ESB rather than food. Note how the rat responds at a higher rate, and continues lever pressing through the DRL portion of the schedule, thereby resetting the timer, delaying reentry to the FR-10 portion of the schedule. The bottom panel (b) depicts responding four sessions later. Note that the hungry rat stops responding entirely for food while continuing to bar press at a high rate for ESB stimulation. Numbers reflect responses during each segment.

example of **behavioral contrast,** or *incentive contrast,* in which reinforcement and punishment effects are determined in part by the context in which they are delivered (see Flaherty, 1982, 1991, for reviews). In this study, we can use evidence of negative contrast to conclude that ESB is a more powerful reinforcer than food.

Choosing Between Two Reinforcers. While the results of the Anderson et al. (1992) and Routtenberg and Lindy (1965) studies attest to the power and efficacy of ESB as a reinforcer, they also raise questions concerning reinforcers and adaptiveness. Rats who died because they chose the pleasures of ESB reinforcement over food (Routtenberg & Lindy, 1965) might invite a sermon about the evils of hedonism or the perils of succumbing to immediate gratification. An alternative is to pose two serious questions: (a) about the relationship of reinforcement to adaptive and maladaptive behavior, and (b) about the relative value of two reinforcing events at a given moment in time.

Most examples of the effects of reinforcement on behavior are adaptive, which is why the *law of effect* is so pervasive (see Box 6.2 in which Dennett, 1975, outlines the argument that reinforcement selects behavior in an analogous manner to the role natural selection plays in evolutionary theory). Ironically, we take for granted that humans often behave maladaptively; it is an interesting commentary that we are truly surprised when other animals seem to behave so. The fact that humans are the only animals who exhibit masochistic and sadistic behavior does not rule out the possibility that infrahumans can exhibit maladaptive behavior. Another example of seemingly maladaptive animal behavior and a further examination of the relationship of the law of effect to maladaptive behavior can be found in Box 7.1.

ESB in Humans. Watching rats respond to electrical stimulation of brain sites that supported lever pressing, James Olds thought they looked as if they were "enjoying" the ESB. Humans who have experienced ESB in similar areas of the brain report that the sensation is generally pleasurable, although one, unable to achieve orgasm no matter how often he pressed the button to stimulate himself, reported being frustrated (Heath, 1963). Such self-reports, coupled with the effect ESB has on animals in learning experiments, forces the conclusion that the sensations produced by ESB can be thought of as highly pleasurable Thorndikean "satisfiers."

Integrating Brain Mechanisms with Reinforcement Theory

What are the implications of the finding that vertebrate brains have "reinforcement" areas, which, when stimulated, can either induce or reinforce behaviors? In the first place, recall that Hull's *drive theory* had to be modified to a *drive-stimulus theory* because of research showing that both nonnutritive saccharin and nonorgasmic sex had reinforcing properties. Both instances are arguably pleasurable. The reported effects of recreational drugs such as cocaine and marijuana

BOX 7.1

Reinforcers and Maladaptive Behavior?

The Routtenberg and Lindy (1965) finding that rats chose the pleasures of ESB reinforcement over food parallels an experiment in which adrenalectomized rats had a daily one-hour choice between a salt solution and a sucrose solution. Because adrenalectomized rats do not secrete aldosterone, they excrete too much salt. Unless salt is replaced, these rats will die within about 10 days. When given the opportunity to select the life-affording salt solution, some (but not all) adrenalectomized rats will instead drink the sucrose solution and die of salt depletion (Harriman, 1955).

In the two experiments being compared, both the sucrose and ESB were *more reinforcing* than the salt solution and food, respectively. *Why?* Using Skinner's definition, sucrose and ESB were more reinforcing because each stimulus better controlled the animals' responses in the two-choice situation. But also by definition, selecting sucrose and ESB appears to be *maladaptive* because each behavior resulted in death. How can we account for this apparent violation of the law of effect?

What is reinforcing for normal rats? Normal rats prefer sucrose solutions to salt solutions, presumably because "sweet" predicts calories within the feeding niches in which rats evolved (Richter, 1942). Furthermore, in normal rats, a host of physiological mechanisms serve to conserve salt; destruction of the adrenal glands is certainly a rare, most likely lethal, event. Finally, except in laboratories, rats feed throughout the night-

time, not during one hour in the middle of the day.

Conclusion? It is normal for rats to select sucrose over salt. To expect otherwise in one-hour feeding period merely because a rat's adrenal glands have been removed is wishful thinking. Rats have been naturally selected to be sensitive to calories, but not to survive removal of their adrenal glands. The fact that several rats *did* choose salt over sucrose is more an example of the remarkable redundancy of salt-conserving mechanisms than it is *maladaptive* behavior on the part of those who selected sucrose.

Is ESB "like" food? So much for salt and sucrose. Why was ESB selected over food in the Routtenberg and Lindy (1965) experiment? Again, the one-hour daily feeding periods demand tremendous feeding plasticity on the part of the rat. The question is why a starving rat would select ESB (which presumably it has little experience with) over eating food (an innately predisposed behavior). One suggestion is that the sensations attendant with ESB are both highly pleasurable and in some sense "reminiscent" of the pleasures of eating palatable foods (Pfaffman, 1960). In this scenario, lacking the cognitive abilities of humans to talk about "what the sensation of ESB *is like*," rats might simply confuse ESB sensations with eating sensations.

Another possibility: Perhaps ESB is more pleasurable than eating tasty food because ESB elicits more palatable feeding sensations than the real-food alternative. For example, the ESB might pro-

BOX 7.1

Continued

duce a chocolate-chip cookie sensation, compared with the bland Purina rat chow alternative. Is there data that would support such a bizarre interpretation? Emphatically yes. As we will see in Chapter 8, many humans report a preference for the pleasures of a cocaine high over that of sexual orgasm. Our understanding of this phenomenon is that the cocaine molecule is a more or less perfect key to activate locks on the endorphin receptor mechanism. And, as was noted, it is likely that ESB also works on these same receptor mechanisms (Phillips & Fibiger, 1989).

We have a lot to learn about brain mechanisms underlying reinforcement. The artificial stimulation of drugs, ESB, and perhaps the "normal" stimulation of other very powerful reinforcers and punishers (cf. posttraumatic stress disorders, p. 385) can apparently override the correspondence normally seen between adaptive behavior and the law of effect.

---

can be added to the list. We can now hypothesize that these activities and perhaps *most* other pleasurable activities are reinforcing because they involve activation of the MFB (see Milner, 1976, for a discussion) and of the *mesotelencephalic dopamine system*. Given that activation of these areas both induces and reinforces behavior, the necessary and sufficient conditions for reinforcement seem to be the activation of these and other brain areas. At least for humans, if a stimulus, event, or activity is described as producing pleasure, it probably involves specific structures such as the MFB and the mesotelencephalic dopamine system, and it is highly likely to act as a reinforcer. We will return to these ideas in Chapter 8 when we look at the addictive properties of such potent reinforcers as alcohol, morphine, cocaine, and other drugs.

Premack's Theory of Reinforcement

David Premack (1962) deemphasized both concepts of reinforcement through *drive reduction* and through *drive-stimulus reduction*. He instead proposed that engaging in "pleasurable activities" (i.e., those that presumably stimulate the foregoing brain areas) was the reinforcing event. He then designed experiments to demonstrate that all behavioral activities were not equally reinforcing; rather, certain behaviors were more or less reinforcing at different times within an individual.

Prior to Premack the reinforcer was conceptualized as an application of a stimulus event; Pavlov's *unconditioned stimulus,* Thorndike's *satisfier,* and Hull's need-satisfying food are examples. In Hull's *reaction potential equation,* food was a separate variable. The reinforcement value of food was determined by the quality and quantity of the food itself. Premack set out to demonstrate that the reinforcing effects of food could not be separated from the behavior of eating the food. That is, both the eating behavior and the food occurred during the reinforcement event, and for Premack, *eating* the food, rather than the food itself, was the reinforcing event.

Drinking and Running Rats.   How did Premack demonstrate these ideas? In an early experiment, he deprived rats of water for 23 hours, and then measured how much time they spent either drinking water or running in a running wheel (Premack, 1962). (Running in a running wheel is reinforcing to caged rats in the same way that most physical activities are reinforcing to humans confined in prison.) On another day he allowed rats unlimited access to water in their home cages, and he measured how much time they spent running or drinking in a one-hour test session. Under these latter conditions, rats predictably spent more time running than drinking during the test hour.

The Premack Principle.   Having established these baselines of behavioral activity, Premack then demonstrated that under certain conditions running would reinforce drinking behavior. How? Running was made more probable during the one-hour test session by both restricting running and allowing the rat to drink unrestricted quantities during the preceding 23 hours. When running was more probable, he showed that rats would engage in "overdrinking" behavior (drink even though they were not thirsty) if the drinking behavior was reinforced by the opportunity to run in a wheel. In a series of similar experiments Premack and his students found that the more probable of two responses would always reinforce the less probable response, a relationship now known as the **Premack principle.** Note that this reinforcement relationship is *reversible.* Restrict drinking or eating (as is normally done in most animal learning experiments), and eating and drinking will reinforce most other behaviors. Why? Because in a given testing session, *most other behaviors are less likely to occur* than is eating (if the animal is hungry) or drinking (if the animal is thirsty).

Eating Candy or Playing Pinball.   In a clever experiment, Premack (1965) and his students demonstrated that more probable behaviors will reinforce less probable behaviors in children. First, the investigators measured two behavioral baselines for each child in the study;

given the choice of playing a pinball machine or of eating candy, which activity does each child choose over the other? Having established that some children preferred candy over pinball, and vice versa, Premack then determined under what conditions candy would reinforce pinball playing and under what conditions pinball playing would reinforce candy eating. Remember that the Premack principle predicts that playing pinball would reinforce candy eating only for those children who preferred pinball to candy during the baseline measurement (and that eating candy would reinforce pinball playing only for those children who preferred eating candy to playing pinball during the baseline measurement). These predictions held true (Premack, 1965). And, as you might expect, the less probable behavior would not reinforce the more probable behavior, even though both were pleasurable.

Analysis of Premack's Principle. At the time Premack was proposing his theory, "reinforcers" were "things" that behavior produced or avoided, and the process of reinforcement was the effect that such "things" had upon the preceding responses. By extending the concept of reinforcement to "the opportunity to engage in [pleasurable] behavior," and by providing a method that demonstrated that reinforcement relationships were reversible as conditions changed, Premack shifted the focus of analysis away from "things," and back to behavior. The Premack principle remains just one of many ways to conceptualize reinforcement, however. Consider the following criticisms:

1. Reinforcers do not go away merely because one chooses to measure "engaging in behavior." When rats "engage in drinking behavior," rats drink *water*. Likewise, children eat *candy*. Put bitter quinine in water and candy, and the behaviors involved in their consumption cease. The point is that the process of reinforcement in part is determined by properties of "things," and the behavior being measured is determined by these properties.

2. Running in a running wheel, playing pinball, skiing, and riding bicycles are reinforcing events that presumably share with candy and water the activation of pleasure-giving brain sites. One does not need the Premack principle to account for the pleasure derived from engaging in certain behaviors.

3. That "engaging in reinforcing behavior" varies during the course of the day, or, for that matter, in the course of a lifetime, is not surprising. All traditional theories of reinforcement recognize that the reinforcing properties of food and water are conditional upon hunger and thirst, respectively. Among 15-year-olds in our culture, to take another example, the opportunity to drive a car is a high-probability behavior and taking out the trash is a low-probability behavior.

New drivers will move mountains of trash for a spin around the block. After driving for a year or so, however, the suggestion that "I'll let you drive around the block if you take out the trash for me" does not seem like such a good deal. Likewise, given the alternative of purchasing either a new car or a face-lift, the choice can be expected to vary as a function of a person's age, sex, etc.

Is Reinforcement Necessary for Learning?

We have seen that Premack joins other reinforcement theorists in stressing that the incentive value of reinforcers changes from hour to hour and throughout a lifetime. Not all theorists would be comfortable, though, with Premack's view that the opportunity to run in a running wheel or to play pinball was reinforcing. Why? Because there is no specifiable reinforcing "event" in these examples as there is in "drinking behavior." Nor would traditionalists be especially comfortable with an analysis suggesting that reinforcement is the (hypothetical) stimulation of pleasure-producing areas in the brain. After all, there is no escaping the circularity of arguing for the presence of a reinforcing event just because the behavior changed "as if" a reinforcing event occurred.

How Do Rats Learn to Run Mazes? This problem of accounting for behavioral change that "looks like learning" under conditions in which a specific reinforcer is absent has a long history. A classic study by Tolman and Honzik (1930b) studied the role of reward in how rats learned their way through a complex maze that had over a dozen choice points prior to arrival in a "goal box." On each trial, the number of errors (reversals in the runways and entries into blind alleys) were counted along the way to the goal box. Once there, one group of rats was rewarded by eating food placed in the goal box, and, for the first 10 trials, two other groups were simply removed and put back in their home cages without being fed. The prediction of traditional reinforcement theorists is that the food reinforcement would allow one group to learn the maze more quickly than the other two. And, as can be seen in Figure 7.5, for the first 10 trials the number of errors decreased by over 60 percent for the food-reinforced group. Notice, however, that even in the absence of a food reward, the other two groups also showed a 35 percent improvement in error rate.

In addition to the obvious question concerning the role of food reinforcement in learning, several more basic questions are raised by the Tolman and Honzik (1930b) experiment. In order of behavioral complexity: (a) Why do rats move in a maze? (b) Why do rats find their way to the goal boxes in mazes? and (c) Why do rats reduce the number of wrong turns on their way to the goal box in a maze?

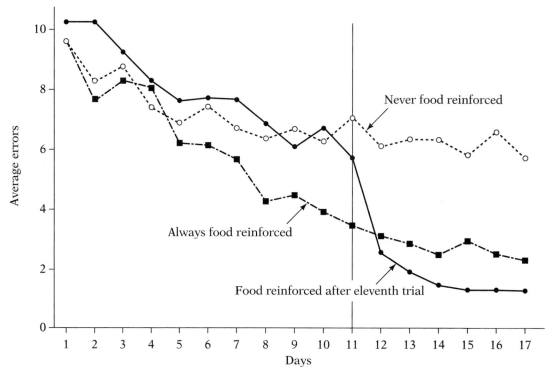

FIGURE 7.5 Tolman's Latent Learning Experiment

In Tolman and Honzik's *latent learning* experiment, the performance of a group of rats that were "never food reinforced" is compared with a group that were "food reinforced after [the] eleventh trial." Note the latter group's rapid improvement in performance relative to a third group, which were "always food reinforced," evidence for the phenomenon of latent learning. (From Tolman & Honzik, 1930b.)

Species-Specific Foraging Behavior. We can only make educated guesses as to a rat's motivation. Here we note that food deprivation increases movement in rats; increasing movement is adaptive, in that active rats are more likely to encounter food than inactive rats. So, the fact that all groups in the Tolman and Honzik (1930b) experiment were food deprived provides each rat the basic motivation to forage within a novel environment. The answer to the second question is not unrelated to the first; rats also have species-specific foraging tendencies that allow them to rapidly and efficiently "map" the environment they traverse (see Olton & Samuelson, 1976; Olton, Collison, & Werz,

1977; and the discussion on p. 445). These *cognitive maps* allow rats to become increasingly efficient at getting to the goal box. Once there, one of two events takes place: either they are fed (which is reinforcing), or they are removed from a place in which there is no food to a place where there is food (also reinforcing). The better performance of rats finding food in the goal box suggests that food is *more* reinforcing than merely being removed from the goal box and placed in a home cage in which the rat has a history of being fed.

Latent Learning

The second part of Tolman and Honzik's (1930b) experiment is not so easily explained, however. Note in Figure 7.5 that on the eleventh trial, after traversing the maze, one group of rats that had never been food reinforced now found food in the goal box. The effect of this single food-reinforced trial was dramatic, for on the very next trial these rats' performance equaled that of rats who had been food reinforced from the beginning (see Figure 7.5). The remaining group of rats (which never experienced food reward in the goal box) continued to make the same number of errors as before. Tolman reasoned that the dramatic improvement in one trial reflected a change in *performance* rather than *learning;* that is, he assumed that all groups had learned the maze more or less equally after 10 trials. According to Tolman, experiencing the maze in the absence of food reinforcement was sufficient for learning to occur; adding food reward merely increased the animal's performance. Tolman used the term **latent learning** to describe the learning that occurred in the absence of food reward.

Interpreting "Latent Learning."   Even Tolman admitted to the possibility of some form of weak, nonfood reinforcement being responsible for the improved performance of all rats over the first 10 trials. How do we now interpret the relatively more rapid learning of the rats that were food reinforced beginning on the eleventh trial? These rats experienced the following cumulative reinforcement: (a) learning where food *wasn't* while foraging on trials 1–10; (2) being taken out of a nonfood environment and placed in a home cage, which had acquired secondary reinforcing properties; and (3) after trial 10, discovering food in the goal box.

So much for the latent learning of this group. How about the food-reinforced group? During trials 1–10 the food-reinforced rats learned where food wasn't (early part of maze) and where it was (end of maze). Both the latent learning group and the food-reinforced group of rats, then, had a sufficient number of foraging trials to map the maze. The addition of the food incentive determined their terminal level of performance.[4]

A traditional interpretation of Tolman and Honzik's (1930b) concept of latent learning, then, is that learning can occur in the absence of *food* reinforcement, and also that other sources of reinforcement cannot be ruled out. Why are there fewer errors across the first few trials for all groups in Figure 7.5? Making fewer errors means that the rat arrives at the goal box sooner, either to eat food (reinforced group) or to be taken out of the goal box and returned to the home cage more quickly (the other two groups). Animals in the nonfood reward groups had a history of being fed in the home cage and a history of never being fed in the maze; therefore, the home cage would have more secondary-reinforcing cues associated with it.

Latent Learning or Foraging?   An alternative interpretation of Tolman and Honzik's experiment stresses the rats' innate behavioral predispositions: Making fewer errors in a maze makes a rat more efficient in that it expends less energy in locating the source(s) of food. Innate feeding tendencies are further played out in differentially reinforcing environments—i.e., food found in the goal box, or food found in the home cage. In this view, hungry rats are disposed to systematic foraging, and these foraging experiences, whether successful or not in finding food in the maze, are remembered (Olton & Samuelson, 1976; Olton et al., 1977).

Purposive Behavior.   Ironically, Tolman would be in complete agreement with this "alternative" interpretation in that he was among the first learning psychologists to propose that behavior is *purposive* (Tolman, 1932).[5] In Tolman's view, rats ran "in order to" secure food incentives, rather than food acting to mechanically *stamp in* faster running speeds. For this and other reasons, as we will see again in Chapter 10, Tolman is one of the first animal learning theorists who attributed *cognitive processes* to infrahumans.

---

[4]The reader should not assume that the terminal performance of the two food-rewarded groups differed significantly merely because the mean number of errors of one group was less than the mean number of errors of the other (cf. Figure 7.5). Also, the terminal level of performance theoretically could be shifted by either increasing or decreasing the rat's hunger level, by increasing or decreasing the palatability of the food reinforcer, etc.

[5]Recall that B. F. Skinner was aware of Tolman's experiments and agreed with Tolman that rats brought innate tendencies into the laboratory. Skinner stopped using alleys and mazes and designed an arbitrary operant response, lever pressing, to study the effects of reinforcement. His reasoning was that rats might have evolved to forage, but not to lever press. Lever pressing, therefore, was a more arbitrary response, and, free from innate behavioral tendencies, the effects of reinforcement on such a response could more easily be determined.

Reinforcing Innate Feeding Tendencies in Humans.   Let us move from hungry rats seeking food in a maze to a human neonate seeking food from her immediate environment. Are there similarities? A human baby innately roots when hungry. Environmental stimulation (tactile stimulation around her mouth) provides feedback as to her progress in finding a food source. (Not here. Not there. What's that smell? Here it is!) Sweet, warm milk from a nipple is a powerful primary reinforcer that both elicits and then reinforces the consummatory behaviors of sucking and swallowing. The sweet milk likely stimulates pleasure-producing neurons in the brain, as does the *drive reduction* of hunger being satisfied. That learning occurs, and that memories of this learned behavior are formed, is evidenced by the increased efficiency of older, more "experienced" nursers.

Interim Summary

1. Reinforcers as either "pleasing events" or "engaging in pleasing behaviors" appear to have common brain bases; current candidates are the *medial forebrain bundle* and the *mesotelencephalic dopamine system.*
2. A contemporary theory of (brain) reinforcement is based upon studies using electrical stimulation of the brain (ESB) in traditional learning situations and observations regarding addictive drugs such as crack cocaine.
3. Premack's theory of reinforcement focuses upon *behaving* rather than on reinforcers as pleasing stimuli. The *Premack principle* states that more probable behaviors will reinforce less probable behaviors, and that this reinforcement relationship is reversible.
4. Tolman studied the role that reinforcement plays in how rats learn to run mazes. He found evidence that food reinforcement was not necessary for learning, a phenomenon he called *latent learning.*
5. An alternative interpretation of the latent learning experiment is that rats engage in species-specific foraging behavior. Successful foraging involves reinforcement at any of a number of the various stages of foraging, including, but not restricted to, the attainment of food.

Looking Ahead

Incredibly, up to now we have restricted discussion of theories of reinforcement to only the top left-hand cell of Figure 7.2. We have seen that learning occurs when our responses produce events that make us feel good. Let us now look at the many instances of behavior in which our responses make us feel good—by preventing bad things from happening.

IV. Negative Reinforcement

Students and researchers (Kimble, 1992) alike dislike Skinner's terminology of "negative reinforcement" for much the same reason that no one enjoys reading a sentence in which "alike" and "dislike" appear side by side. "Negative reinforcement" seems to be an oxymoron. If reinforcement is a process that *increases* the rate of response, then *negative* reinforcement should *decrease* it. But, by convention, procedures that decrease the rate of response are called punishment (see the right-hand side of Figure 7.2).

Perhaps in a later edition I will do battle to simplify learning terminology. But for present purposes, students should simply memorize the traditional distinction between the concepts of negative reinforcement and punishment: Reinforcement *of any kind*, including **negative reinforcement,** increases the rate of the preceding response, and punishment of any kind decreases the same. Let us take a closer look at a number of procedures that are used to study the concept of negative reinforcement.

Negative Reinforcement, Escape, and Avoidance

Imagine being trapped barefooted in a dimly illuminated Skinner Box with a steel grid floor and a lever sticking out of one wall. Unable to escape, and just as you decide to relax and make the best of it, you feel electric shock on the soles of your feet. Aroused, you begin hopping around, and you accidentally bump up against the lever. The shock is turned off. About the time you start to relax, the scenario repeats itself. Again, by hitting the lever you escape the shock. The third time the shock occurs, you make a beeline for the lever, hit it, and terminate the shock.

(By Jove, I think I've got it! This lever, my response, and electric shock seem to be associated together. Can I verbalize the contingencies after a few trials? It seems that my lever-pressing response allows me to escape, or remove myself, from the punishing stimulus called electric shock. Whether I can verbalize it or not, I think I'll hang around this lever.)

Escape and Avoidance Procedures. An experiment such as this was accomplished with rats by Murray Sidman (1953). Not only did Sidman's rats learn an **escape procedure,** that is, they learned to make a response that terminated an aversive stimulus, but with additional training another behavior emerged. Sidman reprogrammed his apparatus such that a lever-pressing response would both terminate a shock and also delay the onset of the next shock. Not surprisingly, in this **avoidance procedure** the rats eventually learned to respond *before* the onset of the shock, thereby avoiding the shock altogether. After several sessions, rats lever pressing on this unsignaled **Sidman avoidance** task soon begin to respond at relatively high rates. *Sidman avoidance* is also known as *free-operant avoidance* because to avoid shock the operant responses must be repeated by the animal during a work session. In this procedure, Sidman's rats learn to make avoidance responses to aversive stimuli by the process of *negative reinforcement* (see Figure 7.2).

Determinants of Avoidance Response Rates

Sidman avoidance is "unsignaled" in that only the lever and other cues of the Skinner Box set the occasion for the lever-pressing response. Since levers and electric shocks do not exist in the rat's world outside of the Skinner Box, in reality the box and the lever are highly distinctive signals. The rat has no way of knowing that a "distinctive" cue is important to the experimenter! The point is that we should not make too much of any alleged differences between unsignaled and the signaled avoidance tasks discussed in the next section.

Role of Shock Intensity.   What other stimuli control responding in a Sidman avoidance task? Certainly the intensity of shock the animal experiences will influence its rate of response. An occasional low-intensity shock would presumably be tolerated better than one of higher intensity. Predictably, lever-pressing response rates vary as a direct function of shock intensity (see Theios, Lynch, & Lowe, 1966, for relevant experiments). But a shock level too high is likely to condition the passivity of *learned helplessness* rather than avoidance responses (see p. 92 and p. 387).

Role of Time's Passage.   In the unsignaled Sidman avoidance task the animal must respond at least often enough to avoid shock. That they learn this schedule (and learn it well—see Box 7.2, following) attests to the ability of rats, dogs, monkeys, and humans to effectively use the passage of time as a cue. Earlier we saw that Pavlov reliably conditioned salivary responses in dogs using only regularly spaced food USs and no CS (see *temporal conditioning*, Figure 4.9, p. 133). Furthermore, as described in Box 6.5 (p. 249), monkeys also exhibit an exquisite sense of timing of their lever-pressing responses on a DRL schedule. Regularly spaced responses on a Sidman avoidance schedule can be similarly interpreted as reflecting the rat's very precise sense of time.

Discrete-Trial Avoidance Schedules

When a *specific* discriminative stimulus is added to the experimental environment, even more precise stimulus control of avoidance responding can be achieved. For example, a *signaled **discrete trial*** avoidance procedure was reported by Solomon and Wynne (1953). They placed a dog in a **shuttle-box,** and when a tone was sounded escape/avoidance contingencies were put into effect. During each discrete trial, signaled by a tone, the dog was allowed to first *escape* and with further training to *avoid* electric shock when it jumped across a barrier dividing one compartment of the shuttle-box from the other. The dog soon learned to avoid electric shock entirely by jumping from one compartment to the other at the onset of the tone, a task known as **shuttle-avoidance.**

The use of discriminative stimuli (S^ds) to control responding allows different types of avoidance schedules to be combined. Box 7.2 describes two types of concurrent avoidance behavior trained in monkeys to each of three different S^ds.

Analyzing Avoidance Learning by Humans. In the previous chapter we analyzed ways in which traffic signals exercised control over our driving behavior. Think about collisions in intersections as events to be avoided. Can you verbalize parallels between pushing a key on a performance panel (the example in Box 7.2), or jumping a barrier in a shuttle-box, and hitting the brakes as your automobile approaches an intersection? What are the discriminative stimuli (S^ds) controlling each of these responses? What motivates each response?

Assuming that you could train someone to "hit the brakes," and that you could explain how such signaled, discrete trial avoidance behavior illustrates the concept of *negative reinforcement,* are you ready for a more challenging task? Explain the following two examples of avoidance learning in humans: Small children learning to play soccer often turn their heads and bodies when an opposing player kicks the ball in their direction. What motivates this behavior? Finally, both skiing and riding a bicycle require a person to make small behavioral adjustments collectively known as "maintaining your balance." After learning both skilled acts, (a) why do people seldom fall, and (b) under what conditions do they fall? Hint: You might want to consider both skiing and riding a bicycle as *free operants.*

Where Is the Reinforcement in "Negative" Reinforcement?

Referring once again to Figure 7.2, note that in the lower left cell the process of *negative reinforcement* is accomplished in the *absence* of a reinforcing stimulus. The question learning theorists have raised for

BOX 7.2

High Performance Motivated by Avoidance Schedules

In simulations of the performance requirements of astronauts in spacecraft, chimpanzees were trained on signaled Sidman avoidance and other discrete avoidance schedules (Koestler & Barker, 1965). A work session sequence involved both appetitive and aversive schedules of reinforcement. Why use aversive schedules? Because both appetite and appetitively based performance are hindered under conditions of high stress, including, for example, stressful drug effects (Dews, 1958) and temporary suffocation following loss of breathable atmosphere (Koestler & Barker, 1965).

A red light above one lever was the discriminative stimulus (S^d) for the *Sidman avoidance* task. When the red light was on, lever pressing delayed (avoided) electric shock (a). Both the response-to-shock interval *(r-s interval)*, and the shock-to-shock interval *(s-s interval)* were set at five seconds. That is, the chimpanzee had to make one response every five seconds (r-s interval = five seconds) to avoid electric shock. If it did not respond, it received a one-second shock every five seconds (s-s interval = five seconds) throughout the work session.

Discriminative stimuli (S^d's) for the **discrete avoidance** tasks were back-lit stimulus-response keys on the animal's performance panel. Each was illuminated in turn for one second. After one second the light terminated, and electric shock was applied to the sole of the foot. The shock could be avoided if the chimpanzee pushed the key (depressing a microswitch) before one second elapsed. A tone served as the S^d for another unlit key, which, when depressed within one second, allowed the shock to be avoided (b).

Even with the low levels of electric shock used in these studies, chimpanzees rarely failed to respond to the negative reinforcement contingencies. Most performed flawlessly session after session, day after day, without receiving an electric shock.

As a historical note, this experiment could no longer be accomplished. For ethical reasons, chimpanzees are no longer subjected to restraints (such as being confined to sitting in a chair) nor subjected to electric shock or most other invasive insults.

(a)

(b)

half a century is how the *absence* of a stimulus can reinforce behavior (Mowrer & Lamoreaux, 1942; Mowrer, 1960). Interestingly, when we consider specific examples of the phenomenon, negative reinforcement does not seem to be counterintuitive. For example, after sufficient avoidance training, people can ride bicycles for years on end without ever falling. We are initially motivated to keep our balance because it hurts to fall down. When asked the question: "Why are you skiing so cautiously?" the predictable answer is "Because I don't want to fall." We cannot ask rats, monkeys, and dogs why they keep responding even though they are no longer being shocked, but we can put ourselves in their place, and their behavior seems reasonable enough.

What Persists Following Aversive Training?   We accept the foregoing statements regarding our motivation underlying avoidance behavior because we suspect that at least some aspect of the reinforcer is never totally absent. Rather the negative reinforcer is present in the form of a memory. For example, we *remember* the pain of falling off bikes and skis. When a skier says "I ski slowly because I don't want to fall," is it possible that we are not hearing a dispassionate statement of fact, but rather a disguised *fear* (or wariness) of falling. Perhaps the lessons learned during avoidance training remain with us in terms of memories of a painful experience, translated into *fear* that it might again recur.

Two-Process Theory of Avoidance

Such an analysis, known as **two-factor theory,** was first proposed by Mowrer (1947, 1960). According to this theory, the two factors underlying avoidance behavior are Pavlovian-conditioned emotional behavior and instrumentally conditioned motor (skeletal) responses. Two-factor theory posits that fear is conditioned first, and separately from instrumentally reinforced avoidance responses. Fear is classically conditioned by the pairing of pain with stimuli in the avoidance training environment. The stimuli may be easily specified, such as the presence of a lever in a Skinner Box, or a tone or color that signals shock-induced pain is imminent. Or the conditioned stimuli can be more subtle, such as the sensations of losing balance afforded by our vestibular apparatus, which, along with skis and bikes, have been associated with the pain of falling down.

After the fear response is conditioned, according to two-factor theory, the second step involves conditioning instrumental responses (such as lever pressing or jumping a barrier to avoid shock, or maintaining one's balance by turning a handlebar). Mowrer assumed that conditioned fear was present at all times during avoidance training. The (negative) reinforcement for such instrumental responses, he asserted, was the termination of the fear response. He reasoned that alleviation of fear is a positive experience, and that it is this positive experience that acts as the reinforcer for the preceding instrumental response.

Evaluation of the Two-Process Theory of Avoidance

Are people who ride bikes, who ski, and who study their books to avoid failing classes really motivated by fear? Or is it more a feeling of *uneasiness* that is elicited when confronted with cues that have been associated with the training of the avoidance response? For example, on a Sidman avoidance schedule as well as in shuttle-boxes, animal responses are distributed in time. Is the *fear* of electric shock ever present during a one-hour session, day in and day out? Or is it more likely that rats, dogs, and humans are merely wary and uneasy when faced with cues that predict aversive consequences unless they do something? Is *fear* reduced with each response, or is it likely that responding becomes more automatic, and animals are less conscious of the response-shock contingency?

The Kamin, Brimer, and Black (1963) Experiment.   An experiment by Kamin, Brimer, and Black (1963) provides some insight into these complicated issues. Rats were first trained to bar press for food, and then were put into a shuttle-box where a tone S^d set the occasion for shuttle-avoidance behavior. Different groups were trained to four criterion levels of experience in avoiding electric shock in the presence of the tone. That is, the four groups successfully avoided shock on 1, 3, 9, or 27 consecutive trials. All rats were then returned to the Skinner Box, where they continued bar pressing for food. The tone was sounded while they bar pressed, and the effect this tone had on their response rate was measured. Kamin et al. (1963) found that following shuttle-aversion training, the tone produced different levels of suppressed responding in each group. The groups that reached the shuttle-avoidance criterion of being successful on three and nine consecutive shock avoidance trials apparently were more fearful of the tone to which they had been conditioned (i.e., the tone suppressed more responding than in the one-trial group). Those rats with extensive experience on the shuttle-avoidance task, who in the presence of the tone reached the criterion of 27 consecutive avoidance responses, however, showed a very different pattern. The somewhat surprising finding was that the tone did *not* suppress lever-pressing responses in this group.

Vigilance Replaces Fear.   One interpretation of this experiment is that fear *diminishes* with increasing experience (and increasing success) in successfully making avoidance responses. We humans have no way of knowing if these rats were fearful or merely "uneasy." Because their avoidance behavior was maintained at a high level of proficiency, we know they were *motivated* to respond even though they were independently assessed as being less fearful (see Mineka, 1979, for a discussion of the independence of fear measures and avoidance responding). Humans monitoring radar screens in submarines and in air control terminals report high levels of *vigilance,* and autonomic nervous system measures tell us they are physiologically aroused. But until and unless there is an emergency (a particularly configured pattern on the radar screen), fear is *not* ever present during these stressful avoidance tasks. As a final consideration, review the continuous and discrete avoidance tasks required of chimpanzees in Box 7.2. Note that while maintaining a relatively high rate of lever pressing in the presence of the red S^d, one-second duration discrete avoidance visual and auditory stimuli were presented. These stimuli elicited successful avoidance responses within a fraction of a second of their onset. Again, a state of vigilance rather than fear better characterizes the mental state of these monkeys (and of humans playing Nintendo®).

Cognitive Analysis of Avoidance Behavior

Of the following two possibilities, which is more likely? Is the behavior of "playing Nintendo®" maintained more by positive or by negative reinforcement contingencies? That is, is the attraction of playing games reinforcing because skilled responses produce positive consequences, or because skilled responses prevent disaster? For example, in playing a melody on the piano, depressing middle C on the keyboard is reinforced by the sound of middle C at the right time and in the right sequence in relation to other sounds. Responding to middle C when middle C is called for is positively reinforcing. Is it not also the case that the very same response is reinforcing because making the response *avoids* violating the expectation that the note should be there? That is, responses to middle C avoid disharmony and prevent violation of the expected tempo.

Do animals develop *expectations* about the occurrence and nonoccurrence of events, and can they become more vigilant? Apparently so. Characterizing an animal's avoidance behavior in these terms provides a cognitive perspective to questions inherent in avoidance behavior (see Seligman & Johnston, 1973). For example, consider again Sidman's unsignaled avoidance task. Responding by rats to avoid shock has been demonstrated even when time cues predicting the shock-shock and response-shock interval were masked (Herrnstein & Hineline, 1966; Herrnstein, 1969). Instead of fear reduction, these researchers argued, rats merely learn that a contingency exists between their responses and shock reduction. Sometimes called a *one-factor theory of avoidance,* this theory stresses that rats are sensitive to rates of shock, and their lever-pressing patterns change in response to the shock schedule. While the simplicity of this one-factor theory is appealing, a criticism is that it does not adequately address *why* the rat responds to avoid shock in the first place. Merely detecting a response-shock reduction contingency is not adequate *motivation* for a rat to bother to respond.

Persistence of Avoidance Responses

The foregoing analysis helps us understand why avoidance responding is so slow to extinguish. Each avoidance response is at one and the same time *being reinforced* and *not being punished.* First, *a response is reinforced because it produces the desired outcome* (avoiding shock; avoiding falling on the ski slopes; avoiding an F on a test; avoiding hitting keyboard D when you wanted C; avoiding GAME OVER on the video screen, etc.). In addition, *the response prevents an undesirable, punishing outcome* (electric shock, falling, failing, fumbling, choking, etc.). Second, a response is reinforced because *not responding* is punished. In learning avoidance responses, humans and animals are punished for not responding appropriately. Hitting keyboard D instead of C is punishing to an ear expecting C. As is falling, failing, fumbling, choking, etc.

Avoidance responses extinguish slowly, therefore, because the consequence of responding is reinforcement, and the consequence of not responding is punishment.

Interim Summary

1. Negative reinforcement is a process in which a response that is instrumental in either escaping or avoiding an aversive event is strengthened. A negative reinforcer is operationally defined as an event that when escaped from or avoided increases the rate of the preceding response.
2. In an *escape procedure,* a response is instrumental in removing or terminating an aversive stimulus; opening an umbrella in a torrential downpour is an example.
3. In an *avoidance procedure,* a response is instrumental in preventing, or avoiding, an aversive stimulus; opening an umbrella *before* walking out into a rainstorm is an example.
4. Common laboratory investigations of negative reinforcement include *continuous,* or *free-operant, avoidance (Sidman avoidance)* or *discrete avoidance* tasks. These tasks may be either *signaled* or *unsignaled.*

5. On a Sidman avoidance task an animal must respond on a lever repeatedly to delay (avoid) an electric foot shock. If this free-operant avoidance task is unsignaled, both the lever (and other stimuli within the Skinner Box) and time cues act as discriminative stimuli that control the response rate.

6. Skilled human behavior is maintained by negative reinforcement. Examples include piano playing, operating word processors and automobiles, and following directions in filling out forms.

7. The two-process theory of avoidance was first proposed by Mowrer (1947). Pavlovian-conditioned emotional behavior and instrumentally conditioned motor (skeletal) responses underlie two-factor theory.

8. Vigilance rather than fear seems to better characterize long-term avoidance behavior of both infrahumans and humans.

9. Avoidance responses are highly resistant to extinction because these responses have been reinforced in two different ways.

V. Punishment

Anyone who has ever received a speeding ticket can appreciate the complexity of emotional responses accompanying *punishment*. First, a sinking feeling when you notice the flashing blue lights in your rear-view mirror. Not quite fear, perhaps, unless there is an open container of alcohol in the car, or your probationary period from the last ticket has not yet expired. But confusion and anxiety as you anticipate the unknown? Yes. The fear may soon give way to denial and anger as you review the unjust contingencies you have been subjected to. (No way I could have been going that fast. Why didn't you ticket the one that had just passed me? Lousy cops should be out catching the *real* criminals. Cruel and unusual punishment because this is going to cost me far more than it should. I drive fast, but safely. Etc. Etc.)

Applying an Aversive Stimulus.   The preceding scenario is an example of punishment because—as indicated in the top right hand cell of Figure 7.2—a response (speeding) has produced an aversive consequence (a ticket and a fine). Response tendencies that diminish because they produce aversive consequences define the process of *punishment*. Does getting a speeding ticket result in less speeding? Not necessarily. We will consider the *effectiveness* of punishment later.

Withholding a Positive Stimulus.   Let us take another example. Your exam is returned and a "67" is scrawled by your name. You vaguely remember that you had two other exams on that day, and instead of studying all the material in the assigned chapters, you only read the chapter outlines. But the "67" still gives you a sinking feeling, followed perhaps by confusion, anger, resignation, etc. One way of analyzing this complex behavioral sequence is to point out that you were punished for studying too little. The "67" is punishing only in reference to a "97," which you would have earned if you had read all of the assigned material. Your response (reading only the *Chapter Summaries*) was punished by not earning a good grade.

Referring again to Figure 7.2, the bottom right cell describes the punishment contingency of a response not producing an expected reward. By way of summary, the process of punishment can be effected by either applying a response-contingent aversive stimulus, or by withholding an expected positive stimulus.[6]

What Is Punishing?

Innate, or Primary, Punishers.   What Thorndike labeled as "annoyers," Skinner simply described as aversive, or punishing, stimuli. For humans and most other animals, common aversive stimuli include cold, heat, hunger and thirst, loud noises, and a host of environmental stimuli that can cause pain, nausea, illness, etc. A stimulus that is inherently aversive is called a **primary punisher.** The pain induced by spanking a child is an example of a "physical," or a primary, punisher.

Acquired, or Secondary, Punishers.   Neutral stimuli can also acquire secondary punishing properties through association with these primary aversive stimuli. In one method described earlier, rats heard a neutral tone followed by a painful electric shock. In this *conditioned suppression* procedure, we hypothesized, the tone had two effects. The tone acted to suppress lever pressing, and it also caused emotional responses not unlike those you feel when you see lights flashing on a police car. Punishing properties of stimuli, then, can both come from innate predispositions and be acquired through conditioning. The latter describes a **secondary punisher.** "Spanking" (physical pain) is a *primary* punisher, whereas "scolding" ("psychological pain") is a *secondary* punisher. Another term for "psychological pain" is *learned* pain.

[6]Punishment is a singular process described by two procedures. Some theorists use the term "positive punishment" to describe responses that produce an aversive consequence (i.e., speeding followed by a ticket) and "negative punishment" to describe responses that do not produce expected rewards (i.e., getting a grade of "67" rather than an "A" or "B"). The adjectives "positive" and "negative" are confusing in this context and will not be used here. ("Positive punishment" is another oxymoron, and "negative punishment" is redundant.)

Combining Punishments. Secondary punishers include social disapproval, ridicule, and other violated expectancies. Punishments are often combined. For example, having your phone service disconnected due to late payment combines two kinds of punishment. Disconnection violates your expectancies and deprives you of convenience (*removes* you from Thorndike's pleasing state of affairs), *and* it costs you a penalty to reconnect (*applies* a punishing stimulus). A penalty is defined as "an imposed punishment for violating a rule." Penalties in our culture run the gamut from a yellow hanky thrown for being offside, to expulsion from school for low grades, to fines, to capital punishment—loss of life.

Separating Innate from Acquired Punishers. Characterizing punishment as innate or acquired can be difficult. Consider, for example, the punishing effects of isolation. Solitary confinement in prison is considered to be one of the worst punishments a human can experience. Why is isolation considered to be so punishing? One might argue that mammals are by nature gregarious, or that they have a freedom reflex (Pavlov). Or you might argue that a human acquires expectancies of social contact during a lifetime, and that isolation violates these learned expectancies. Both are reasonable explanations.

Another example of the difficulty of separating innate and acquired aspects of punishment can be found in how we use language. Consider the parent who uses abusive language to control a child's behavior. The abusive language may acquire some of its punishing properties by being paired with physical punishment. But, because loud noise by itself is punishing, innate aspects of abusive language cannot be ruled out. (Men are often accused of arguing unfairly because their voices are typically louder and arguably more innately punishing than women's voices.) Certainly the secondary punishing properties of abusive language are confounded by a "scolding" or "bullying" delivery.

Reviewing the Nature and Procedures of Punishment. Before considering whether punishment is effective in controlling behavior, let us briefly summarize and review what we have learned to this point by having you sort the following examples of punishment into four categories: the punishment is either (a) innate or (b) acquired, and is produced by either (c) applying a negative stimulus or (d) withholding an expected positive stimulus.[7]

---

[7](1) acquired, withhold; (2) innate, withhold; (3) innate, apply; (4) acquired, withhold; (5) mixed, withhold; (6) mixed, withhold; (7) mixed, applied; (8) innate, applied; (9) acquired, applied.

1. Having one's driver's license revoked following a serious driving infraction
2. Not feeding a hungry baby
3. Spanking a crying baby
4. Removing a hockey player to the penalty box for fighting
5. Confining a child to her room for lying
6. Reducing the rank or salary of an employee for incompetent behavior
7. Making a child sit quietly in a classroom that is 90 degrees Fahrenheit
8. Getting sick after eating a meal
9. Quietly informing your lover you have found another

How Effective Is Punishment?

On the basis of only a few observations, both Thorndike (1932) and Skinner (1953) independently decided that punishment was relatively ineffective in controlling behavior. Given the general perception that punishment can have long-lasting effects, it is especially ironic that Skinner concluded that, relative to the way in which reinforcement permanently changed behavior, the effects of punishment were only temporary. During the past 40 years, however, new observations have led behavioral scientists to different conclusions; namely, that under the right conditions, punishment can have specific, and permanent, effects on behavior. Let us first look at factors we now know are important in punishment, and then return to evaluate Skinner's position.

Rules of Punishment

In Chapter 4 we summarized many observations about the determinants of Pavlovian conditioning by specifying five rules that govern the acquisition of conditioned responses. Here we will also organize conclusions from many different experiments that have investigated the effect of punishment on behavior. A comparison of the rules of punishment with the rules of conditioning is presented in Table 7.1.

Punishment Is Associative. A quick comparison of the rules governing the effectiveness of Pavlovian conditioning (including both acquisition and resistance to extinction measures; see Chapter 4) with those of punishment reveals a considerable degree of overlap. Both punishment training and Pavlovian conditioning are in part determined (a) by the intensity of the US or the punisher; (b) by the number of conditioning trials; (c) by the interval of time between the response and the punisher (or the CS and the US); and (d) by the sequence (response → punisher, or CS → US).

TABLE 7.1 A Comparison of Five Rules of Pavlovian Conditioning with Four Rules of Punishment

Pavlovian Conditioning	Punishment
1. US intensity rule: *More intense USs yield better conditioning.*	1. Punishment intensity rule: *More intense punishers produce better conditioning.*
2. Number of trials rule: *More CS-US trials yield better conditioning.*	2. Number of trials rule: *More response-punishment trials produce better conditioning; Qualify: Intensity of punishment must be relatively high.*
3. CS-US interval rule: *Shorter CS-US intervals yield better conditioning.*	3. Response-to-punishment interval rule: *Shorter response-to- punishment intervals produce better conditioning.*
4. CS-US sequencing rule: *CS-US sequences yield excitatory conditioning; US-CS sequences typically produce inhibitory conditioning.*	4. Response-punishment sequencing rule: *Response-contingent punishment produces better conditioning than noncontingent punishment. A punishment-response sequence defines an escape paradigm.*
5. CS intensity rule: *More intense CSs yield better conditioning.*	5. *No comparable finding; no relationship between response strength (effort?) and effect of punishment.*

Other Common Associative Features. In addition to the similarities in Table 7.1, both punishment procedures and Pavlovian conditioning procedures share the common effects of extinction, latent inhibition, generalization, etc. From these observations we can tentatively conclude that punishment is an associative process. Under many circumstances punishment experiments yield outcomes similar to those of classically and reinforcement-based learning.

Punishment Intensity

The effect of punishment on responses is *directly related to the intensity of the pain-inducing stimulus.* Because it is easy both to quantify and control, electric shock is used in many animal experiments. Severity of electric shock affects how rats run in the alley of a maze (Karsh, 1962) or bar press in a Skinner Box (Storms, Boroczi, & Broen, 1962). Intensity of electric shock also affects how quickly humans learn to not open a cigarette case—when they are punished for opening it (Powell & Azrin, 1968). Other commonly used punishing stimuli are aversive chemicals and toxins, which, by their sickness-inducing properties, punish eating, drinking, and other consummatory responses. The familiar dose-response curves of nausea-inducing drugs accurately predict their punishing effects, for example, on suppressing the drinking of saccharin solution (Gamzu, 1977). Predictably, rats do not run as fast or lever press or lick as often and humans become leery of opening a cigarette case when they have been shocked for doing so. Animals learn more or less rapidly depending upon shock intensity, level of poisoning, and intensity of other punishment treatments.

Skinner's Failed Punishment Experiment.   Let us reexamine Skinner's (1953) mistaken conclusion about the effects of punishment. In one experiment, he used a low-intensity aversive stimulus—a spring-loaded lever that "slapped" the rat as it lever pressed for food (Skinner, 1938). After "punishing" lever-pressing responses with this slapping device, Skinner first demonstrated response suppression for a short period of time, and then watched the response rate recover in extinction. Because responding recovered to baseline levels relatively quickly under these conditions, Skinner reasoned that punishment was ineffective in permanently altering behavior. As we saw in the preceding section, however, a punishment must be sufficiently intense "to work." From other experiments with other punishers, we now know that rats can be permanently trained to not lever press by consistently applying an intense punishing stimulus. A simple conclusion is, then, that Skinner's "slapping" stimulus was too weak. His conclusion regarding punishment is suspect for an additional reason—namely, that extinction has the same effect on *reinforced behavior* as he observed for the "slapped" lever pressing. Responses diminish in extinction following both reinforcement and punishment procedures. A more parsimonious conclusion is that punished behavior is neither more nor less permanent than food-based behavioral change when intensities of stimuli are equated.

Does Low-Intensity Punishment Habituate?   Azrin, Holz, and Hake (1963) reported another interesting finding relating shock intensity and lever pressing. If the intensity of the punishing stimulus is low on the first few trials, the cumulative effect of numerous trials is less than it is in Pavlovian- or reinforcement-based conditioning. Initial trials with low-intensity punishment have the effect of *diminishing* the punishing properties of later trials using higher-intensity aversive stimuli (Azrin et al., 1963). Again, the animals act as if they become immunized against the effects of electric shock in that higher shock intensity is ineffective in punishing behavior.

Performance Masks Punishment Effects.   An alternative explanation is that hunger-motivated lever pressing is sufficiently strong to mask the effects of punished responding. The question then becomes one of performance rather than learning. A human example illustrates this point quite well. Both children and adults can train themselves to self-administer insulin by painfully sticking a needle into their thigh muscle. "Needle-sticking" behavior should diminish because the response produces immediate pain. Out of necessity, however, some people stick themselves daily over many years. Following a surgery, an elderly acquaintance of mine hired a home nurse. The nurse now afforded the opportunity of having someone else administer his daily insulin, and, not surprisingly, he was more than content to let the nurse do the honors. Why? The needle-stick had been self-punishing over many years, and the response was clearly aversive to my friend. Performing the response, however, had been a necessity that did not allow the aversive learning to show. Recall, again, that hunger-motivated rats will *not* respond to low-intensity shock. If they had the alternative of not being hungry, the punishing properties of low-intensity shock would no doubt suppress a lever-pressing response. The point is that the *performance level* of a response is not always a reliable indicator that a response has (or has not) been learned.

Trials Effect

When an aversive stimulus is of sufficient intensity, punishment shows a *trials effect: The more frequently that responses are punished, the lower is the subsequent response rate.* A common way of measuring the effects of punishment is to shock the lever-pressing responses of an animal working on a food-based schedule of reinforcement. Each response followed by shock is a trial. Using a moderately high-intensity shock, if every response in a work session is punished, rats stop bar pressing altogether. By contrast, rats shocked on every one-hundredth or five-hundredth response merely slow their rate of response. The rate of response is proportional to the number of punished responses (Azrin et al., 1963).

Results of Continued Punishment Training.   Once animals have learned the response-punishment contingency, their long-term behavior may change as they continue to be shocked. For high-intensity shocks, responses may remain suppressed indefinitely. For low-intensity aversive stimuli, the punishment may lose its effectiveness altogether; under these conditions the response rate has been demonstrated to recover even to its preshock level (Camp, Raymond, & Church, 1967). Low-intensity painful stimuli habituate, and as a result responses are not as effectively punished by the shock. Such habituation seems to act as if it "immunizes" the animal against experiencing higher levels of pain.

Response-to-Punishment Interval Rule

Earlier we argued that a "67" grade on a test paper punished the reading of Chapter Summaries in lieu of studying the text more thoroughly. It was also suggested that a "67" exam score might not change studying behavior, in the same way that a traffic ticket often is ineffective in slowing down drivers. One reason why a "67" might be ineffective in changing this student's behavior is that it was delivered three weeks after the response. In this example, many nonspecific responses are being punished by a secondary punisher delivered three weeks too late!

The foregoing example not withstanding, punishment *is* an adaptive process that changes behavior. Punishment no less than reinforcement guides behavior by selecting from alternative responses those that produce the most pleasure and/or avoid the most pain. The CNS is designed to accomplish this task optimally under certain conditions. For example, some pain fibers are especially fast conducting. Both bee stings and touching a hot curling iron produce rapid reflexive responses and equally rapid association formation. A key to effective punishment is to mimic the reflexive S-R action of the nervous system by rapidly applying an aversive stimulus to the desired response. *The shorter the response-to-punishment interval, the more effective is the punishment treatment.* The adverse effects of delaying the punishing properties of electric shock following a lever-pressing response are detailed in Box 7.3.

Response-to-Punishment Contingency

A "67" on a test paper delivered *three weeks* after the examination is arguably noncontingent. Such treatment resembles the noncontingent punishment group described in Box 7.3. The noncontingent group violates the response-to-punishment *sequence* common to the other treatment groups (groups that in turn varied only by the response-to-punishment *interval*).

Why did we see a suppression of responses by this noncontingent punishment group? First, a few lever-pressing responses might have been paired with punishment in the same way that a *truly random control group* produces chance pairings. Second, we can speculate about nonassociative punishment effects, or better, punishment effects attributed to associations of aversive stimuli with the *context* in which they occurred rather than with specific responses. A general wariness about the testing environment might develop, which in turn

BOX 7.3

Catch Him in the Act

Gary Larson's cartoon captures the behavioral law relating to the ineffectiveness of delayed punishment. The effects of delaying the interval of time between a response and an electric shock are clearly seen in an experiment by Camp, Raymond, and Church (1967). The response-to-shock delays were 2.0, 7.5, and 30.0 seconds, and the results of these three groups were compared with a zero-second-delay group (i.e., immediate punishment), a noncontingent-punishment group (group NC), and an unshocked control group. Note that immediate shock is best, both in faster acquisition

(asymptotic during the second training session) and in maintaining suppressed responding for the duration of the experiment. Note also that 2.0- and 7.5-second delays yield better suppression of responses than 30-second delays.

The *noncontingent punishment* group was shocked during the session, but not when it lever pressed. Note both the initial suppression and the long-term "dampening" effects on behavior of this group, relative to the control group. Apparently the Skinner Box environment was more aversive for group NC than for the control group.

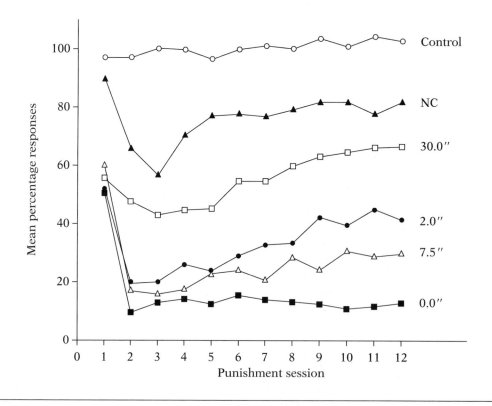

BOX 7.3

Continued

"Harold! The dog's trying to blow up the house again! Catch him in the act or he'll never learn."

would affect the *performance* of the learned response. Is it possible that a general disdain for school in part reflects noncontingent punishment far removed from specific performances? Whether the response in question is lever pressing or writing the answer to a question, an immediate response-punishment contingency is the most effective way in which to change the desired response.

Another way to analyze the sequencing effects of aversive stimulation is to note that by definition, punishment only works in one direction. If an aversive stimulus *precedes* a response, and the response terminates that stimulus, the procedure is defined as escape, as indicated in Figure 7.2. Responding *increases* following escape training procedures.

Latent Inhibition of Punishment

Recall that prior exposure to a CS or a US makes these stimuli familiar, and that familiar stimuli do not condition as readily as novel stimuli. The phenomenon is known as *latent inhibition* (see p. 171). One explanation for the finding that a low-intensity punisher "habituates" and is no longer effective in controlling behavior is that punishers can also be latently inhibited. A number of laboratory demonstrations using a variety of stimuli have shown this to be the case. For example, shock is not as effective in punishing bar pressing when rats are familiar with it. In addition, a prior history with lithium makes it less effective in punishing saccharin drinking (Suarez & Barker, 1976). Punishers, then, can be latently inhibited in the same manner as CSs and USs.

Theories of Punishment

As was noted in Figures 7.1 and 7.2, Thorndike's "theory" of punishment is part of the law of effect—a recognition that animals have innate tendencies to seek out pleasure and to avoid pain. Thorndike's theory of punishment, then, is an adaptive/evolutionary one. Skinner's "atheoretical" description of the effects of punishing stimuli on responding provides our contemporary *behavioral definition* rather than a theory of punishment.

In this section we look at one other theory of punishment; namely, the **two-factor theory of punishment** of Mowrer (1947, 1960), as elaborated by Dinsmoor (1954, 1977). As previously noted, Mowrer's theory of avoidance posited that learning proceeded in two stages: First, a fear response is conditioned classically; then an avoidance response is learned by reducing the fear response. Mowrer's punishment theory is similar. Cues in the environment, including the stimuli produced by the animals while responding, are classically (S-S) conditioned to the aversive punishing stimulus. In psychological terms, rats and humans fear or are wary of situations in which punishment has previously been meted out. Rats and humans can escape from their fear by engaging in some other behavior than the responses that have been punished (Dinsmoor, 1954). Humans often change study habits that produce punishing consequences, and, when faced with stimuli predicting punishment, rats suppress lever pressing (measured) presumably by engaging in other behaviors (unmeasured).

Applying Punishment

> "Beat me, beat me!" said the *masochist*.
> "No!" said the *sadist*.

We began this chapter by raising questions about *acquired motivation*. We now have several conceptual tools that may allow us to shed light on the intriguing bit of human behavior captured by the verbal interchange of these two maladjusted individuals. What reinforcement contingencies maintain the quite different roles that pain plays in the lives of the sadist and masochist?

Sadists.   The sadist we can dispose of quickly. Both sharp tongues and the playground bully's fists produce small victories in complex social interactions. Children reared in competitive environments are rewarded for being aggressively stronger, faster, and smarter, and along other dimensions by which individual differences can vary. Behavior learned in competition does not always translate well in social interactions calling for cooperation. "Winners" deliver the punishment to "losers." In social interactions, the sadist becomes a *discriminative stimulus* predicting punishment, and most humans will both be wary of and will suppress ongoing behavior in the sadist's presence.

Masochists.   The masochist's motivation is far more intriguing, because the following simple question cannot be easily answered: How can pain become reinforcing? How do people apparently learn to use pain to give themselves pleasure?[8] Several psychologists have attempted to model this behavior using laboratory animals, and they

---

[8]Recognize that theories of reinforcement and punishment demand that masochistic behavior be reinforcing. If masochism were punishing, our theory predicts it would not exist because the masochistic responses would be consistently punished, and thereby suppressed.

have been surprisingly successful. Assuming that a low-intensity punisher can be used to signal as well as to punish, Holz and Azrin (1961) first trained pigeons to peck a key on a VI schedule for food. With the VI schedule still in effect, each pecking response was then punished with mild electric shock. The result was to halve the rate of key pecking. These food-reinforced sessions in which each peck was also punished alternated with nonpunished, non–food-reinforced sessions. From the hungry pigeon's perspective, no cues other than electric shock predicted when food was available. Therefore, the pigeon had to engage in "masochistic" behavior (self-induced pain) in order to find out if food was available. Pain now acts as an S^d that signals the presence of food. The pigeons eventually learned to continue pecking for food only if their key pecks were punished, and to stop pecking if key pecking was not punished! Punished key pecking served as the S^d for food reinforcement.

Pain as an S^d for Pleasure.   Is it possible that masochists *also* learn to use pain as an S^d for pleasure? Another clever animal experiment suggests this might be the case. First, rats were taught to run quickly down an electrified runway to a nonelectrified goal box. In this *escape* procedure, the rats are reinforced by the termination of electric shock (cf. Figure 7.2, lower left cell). After learning this response, the rats were divided into two groups: For half the shock was turned off; and for the other half the section of the runway nearest the goal box remained electrified. You be the rat. What would you do under these circumstances? Let us first consider the extinction group. What would you do upon encountering a nonelectrified runway? For the first few trials you might run quickly even though you were not being shocked. The experimenter interprets your running speed to be a measure of *resistance-to-extinction* of the learned escape response. The more slowly you run, the more your learned escape response has extinguished. Eventually you might learn, as the rats did in this group, that you could take your time getting to the goal box, there to be removed and returned to your home cage.

What about the group encountering the electrified runway near the goal box? One might argue that the electric shock punishes entry into both the last part of the alley and the goal box. Since punished responses normally decrease in frequency, you might predict that rats would stay in the first part of the alley, where they are not punished. The interesting finding in this situation is that punishment *increases* the speed of running relative to the nonshocked rats (Brown & Cunningham, 1981). By not entering the last part of the alley, the animal could escape shock altogether; apparently, however, the shock acts as a signal that the escape contingency is still in effect.

Rather than freeze (for which there is no penalty), they run in pain through the electrified portion into the goal box.

Abusive Relationships. Perhaps like these rats, masochists seek out punishment that when terminated is reinforcing. In other words, pain may become an S^d that is reinforced by its termination. For example, after being beaten by their abusive husbands, many women leave them only to cyclically return to them. Such behavior appears to be maladaptive, and these women are often criticized for intentionally putting themselves in harm's way. What is maintaining their behavior? A number of reinforcement and punishment contingencies can be identified. In addition to financial pressures of "going it alone" and learned social pressures "to keep the family together," such women often have a learning history that includes feelings of affection for the husband. In addition, beatings also have signal value other than the pain induced. In abusive relationships, beatings are often followed by pleasurable sexual relationships with the same man who a few minutes earlier was inflicting pain. In these situations, then, pain signals are reinforced in two ways: first, by their cessation, and second, by pleasurable sensations of sex. It is no wonder that often the cycle continues.

Interim Summary

1. Punishment is a process by which the application of an aversive stimulus decreases the frequency of response that precedes the aversive stimulus.
2. Punishment is associative. Punishment is affected by latent inhibition, extinction, generalization, etc.
3. The process of punishment is most effective when the punisher is intense, when the response-punishment interval is minimal, and when the response-punisher contingency is not degraded.
4. Noncontingent effects of punishment include a general response suppression. The response suppression may be due to the associative conditioning of aversive stimuli with environmental cues, so that an adverse emotional state causes a performance decrement.
5. The effects of punishment are likely due to two processes: emotional conditioning of environmental cues, and relief from aversive emotional states by making responses that minimize or remove these cues.
6. Masochistic behavior can be understood by recognizing that the cessation of pain is reinforcing; that the presence of pain becomes positive in that it signals that relief from pain is imminent; and that putting oneself into painful situations often reflects a past reinforcement history of pleasure derived from pain cessation.

VI.   Integration of Theories: Reinforcement and Punishment; Pavlovian and Instrumental Conditioning

We began this chapter by reviewing the major learning theories. Each theorist suggested that a symmetry of sorts existed for the processes of reinforcement and punishment. For B. F. Skinner and E. L. Thorndike, however, punishment effects were construed to be *not* equivalent to reinforcement effects. Research conducted since they wrote about these issues, reviewed in the foregoing, found that to the extent that a symmetry exists, it holds for a limited upper range of punishment intensities. Generally speaking, however, as summarized in Figure 7.2, punishment can be conceptualized as a mirror-image reversal of the associative process of reinforcement. Reinforcement increases, and punishment decreases, behavioral responses.

Similarities of Pavlovian and Instrumental Conditioning

Throughout this text parallels have been drawn between instrumental and Pavlovian conditioning as well as between the reinforcing and punishing effects of stimuli. In the interest of simplifying thousands of experiments in Pavlovian conditioning and instrumental learning, and risking oversimplification in the process, Figure 7.6 attempts to summarize and integrate these two systems.

Note that the 2 × 2 matrix in Figure 7.6 incorporates some of the notation used earlier in Figure 7.2. The matrix summarizes the associative effect of either (a) introducing or removing (b) pleasing or annoying stimuli, (c) contingent upon either a response or another stimulus. The four possible outcomes are to either increase (positive and negative reinforcement) or decrease (punishment) the frequency of the preceding response.

Minimizing Differences in S-S and R-S Contingencies

The key to integrating Pavlov's system with the instrumental system is provided by notation to the immediate left of the matrix; namely, "the experimenter or a response" *introduces* or removes (a pleasing stimulus, S^+, or an annoying stimulus, S^-). The "experimenter" introduces an *unconditioned stimulus*, and a "response" introduces a *reinforcer*. The terminology is different, but in both instances the animal is delivered a pleasing stimulus (S^+). The present schema minimizes the traditional distinction between stimulus-stimulus (S-S) and response-stimulus (R-S) contingencies.

Pleasing stimulus (S^+)	Annoying stimulus (S^-)
The Experimenter or a Response **Introduces:**	(1) Name: *Positive Reinforcement* (2) Effect: ↑ response rate (3) UR to S^+ → "pleasure" (4) CS^+ or S^d → "hope"	(1) Name: *Punishment* (2) Effect: ↓ response rate (3) UR to S^- → "pain" (4) CS^+ or S^d → "fear"
The Experimenter or a Response **Removes:**	(1) Name: *Punishment* (2) Effect: ↓ response rate (3) Absence of S^+ when expected → "confirmed disappointment" (4) CS^+ or S^d → "disappointment"	(1) Name: *Negative Reinforcement* (2) Effect: ↑ response rate (3) Absence of S^- when expected → "relief" (4) S^d → "fear" or "vigilance"

FIGURE 7.6   Comparison of Classical and Instrumental Conditioning

Summary of sequence of events in both classical and instrumental conditioning, including (1) the name of the procedure; (2) the effect on ongoing behavior; (3) the psychological consequences of the procedures; and (4) expectancies in the presence of stimuli that signal the various procedures.

Moving inside the matrix, each of the four possible outcomes (1) has a name—*positive reinforcement* and *negative reinforcement,* and two different ways to *punish* behavior. Each process (2) either increases or decreases response rate, presumably because of (3) affective responses to the stimuli. Further integration of Pavlovian and instrumental conditioning is indicated by (4) in each cell of the matrix—the stimulus contexts in which the four procedures occur. As pointed out in earlier sections, learning occurs within stimulus contexts that set the occasions for responses to be either rewarded or punished. Examples from this chapter include "red lights" (S^ds) that come to control the behavior of both a monkey lever pressing to avoid shock and also a human applying brakes to avoid collisions at intersections. By way of comparison, in Pavlov's experiments dogs can be trained to salivate in the presence of a circle (CS^+) and to not respond to an ellipse (CS^-). The point is that in both systems responses come to be controlled by stimulus cues.

Unmeasured Emotional Responses.   These stimulus cues come to control affective (emotional) responses in both systems. Presumably dogs are *disappointed* (bottom left cell) when an ellipse predicts no food, and rats are *disappointed* when their lever-pressing responses do not produce food as expected. These emotional responses are seldom measured in learning situations; rather, in the black box behaviorist tradition, emotional responses are ignored. Recognizing that emotional responses probably accompany *all* learning situations, however, aids our understanding of an animal's learned behavior (Mowrer, 1960). Stimulus cues that have been associated with food or with shock set up expectations—*hope* that food is forthcoming, and *fear* of impending shock. When expectations are not met, animals are *disappointed* and *relieved*, respectively.

Continuing our analysis of (4) in the lower left cell, we note that CS^- and S^Δ designate stimulus cues that set the occasion for the absence or removal of a reinforcing stimulus. Following training, emotional responses elicited by CS^+ and S^d cues have been labeled *disappointment*.

Interim Summary

Having compared S-S and R-S conditioning paradigms, the overwhelming impression is that their similarities outweigh their differences. From the animal's perspective, distinctive stimuli can be readily associated with good and bad outcomes. To the extent animals respond in the presence of these stimuli, their responses—and those of humans—tend to be understandable within an adaptive/evolutionary framework. Learned emotional responses are seldom measured in animal learning experiments. To ignore the cognitive/affective dimension of animal learning for the sole purpose of maintaining the integrity of a descriptive behaviorism, however, seems counterproductive at our present stage of theory development.

Summary

1. Traditional theoretical conceptions of reinforcement and punishment were proposed by Pavlov, Thorndike, Skinner, and Hull. Their terminology and methods of studying the two categories of reinforcing and punishing stimuli were varied. Pavlov identified appetitive and defensive reflexes and conditioning; Thorndikean satisfiers and annoyers "stamped in" behavior; and maintaining homeostatic balance was seen to be reinforcing in Hull's approach. All three recognized the adaptive/evolutionary significance of two classes of positive and negative stimuli having opposite effects on behavior.

2. By contrast, in B. F. Skinner's descriptive behaviorism, reinforcement is defined as the process of strengthening, and punishment as the process of weakening, responses.

3. Clark L. Hull initially proposed a formal drive reduction theory of behavior, later modified to a drive-stimulus reduction theory. Recognizing that physiological needs induced drives, he proposed to replace an S-R model of behavior with an S-O-R model. Organismic variables such as hunger determined the manner in which instrumental responses could be learned.

4. Reinforcers can be viewed as "pleasing events" or as the opportunity to "engage in pleasing behaviors." Based upon studies using electrical stimulation of the brain (ESB), many such operationally defined reinforcers have been found to have a common brain basis.

5. Latent learning is the term Tolman used to account for the fact that food reinforcement was not necessary for maze learning. Our current understanding of latent learning is that hungry rats in mazes engage in species-typical foraging behavior; rats learn where food isn't as well as where food is.

6. Escaping or avoiding aversive events is negatively reinforcing. Responses that either terminate aversive events or are instrumental in avoiding aversive events increase in frequency through the process of negative reinforcement. Accelerating to avoid an automobile collision is an example of a behavior maintained by negative reinforcement.

7. Mowrer (1947) proposed that avoidance responses were learned by two processes—classically conditioned emotional responses, followed by instrumentally conditioned motor responses. Following conditioning, vigilance or fear responses to cues associated with the aversive stimulation are highly resistant to extinction.

8. Punishment is a process that results in lower rates of the response with which the punishing stimulus is associated. Punishment is affected by latent inhibition, extinction, generalization, intensity of punisher, short response-to-punishment intervals, and the number of punishment trials.

9. A general decrement in overall performance following punishment is likely due to the conditioning of contextual cues with the punishing stimuli. The decrement is presumably due to a spread of negative affect, in the same way that food-reinforced contexts acquire secondary reinforcing properties.

10. Masochistic behavior is maintained by two sources of reinforcement: in the context of pain, the pleasure of relief from pain; and the use of pain to signal that its termination will shortly follow.

11. Parallels were drawn (Figure 7.6) between the use of pleasurable and aversive stimuli in two types of conditioning. Much evidence suggests that similar processes underlay S-S and R-S conditioning. It is most certainly the case that common affective responses are conditioned in all combinations of Pavlovian and instrumental reinforcement and punishment procedures.

Discussion Questions

1. It has been commonly observed that only when sick do we become aware of how good we normally feel when healthy. That is, when healthy, most of us would not describe our everyday lives as being *pleasurable,* because a state of pleasure is subjectively better than "normal." Tasty foods and jokes induce plea-sure over and above our normal well-being. With this in mind, how would you answer the following question: Is pleasure the opposite of pain?

2. Is punishment the opposite of reinforcement?

3. Can you recapitulate the argument that Skinner's definition of a reinforcer, and of the process of reinforcement, is circular? One way out of the circle is to note that reinforcing events are more often than not *transituational*. That is, reinforcers will "work" in a variety of situations. Do observations of the effects of ESB and addictive drugs on the MFB constitute further evidence of the transituational nature of reinforcers?

4. Why is "kissing" not considered to be a *drive-reducing* reinforcer? Why is "kissing" reinforcing in some contexts but not in others?

5. Most parents attempt to use the secondary punishing properties of language to control their children's behavior. "No" (sometimes accompanied by a spanking hand) is understood by most English-speaking 18-month-olds. Under what conditions will the word "no" alone become a punishing stimulus? Why does "no" not work for some parents?

6. Gauging the appropriate intensity of secondary punishment is highly problematical. An interaction I had with a four-year-old daughter made me acutely aware of my overreliance on (and the ineffectiveness of) parental scolding and bullying. My goal was to "teach" her to say "please" and "thank you." My method was to constantly scold her for omissions and to reinforce her (praise her) for correct language usage. Leaving a restaurant one evening (after having scolded her during the meal) we happened upon a window display of sides of beef hanging in a butcher's shop. Curious as to what a four-year-old thought about the display, I asked her why she thought they were hanging there.

"Because they didn't say please?" she offered.

What have you learned about the nature of punishment that makes her response understandable? Why should parents use punishment more sparingly than most of us do? Assuming that you will want your children to say "please" and "thank you," what reinforcement (and punishment?) contingencies will *you* use?

7. High-school coaches and aerobic instructors alike talk about "no pain, no gain." The long-distance runner is exhorted to "push through the pain barrier." How is the way that athletes "use pain" to perform better similar to the way that a person in an abusive relationship "uses pain" to achieve pleasure? How is it different?

8. Many skiers look for increasingly difficult downhill runs, perhaps to experience the pleasure of conquering fear as well as to experience the exhilaration of speed and control. Many skiers also think that falling down is a signal that they are sufficiently challenging themselves, and that only through such challenges will they become better skiers. Why is "no pain, no gain" too simple to account for a skier's motivation?

9. What motivates you to study for your exams? Why do so many people watch so much television? Can you identify positive and/or negative reinforcement contingencies for each behavior?

Glossary

Acquired Incentives Stimuli paired with innate incentives such as food and water become *acquired incentives* in Hull's system (and are *secondary reinforcers* in Skinner's system).

Acquired Motivation Behavior motivated

by secondary reinforcers. (Primary reinforcers provide innate motivation.)

Avoidance Procedure Any procedure in which an animal's instrumental response prevents an aversive consequence. Example: A lever press prevents, or avoids, delivery of electric shock.

Behavioral Contrast A contrast procedure that demonstrates that reinforcement/punishment effects are determined in part by the immediate context in which these stimuli are delivered and the animal's prior history with other reinforcers/punishers. (Also known as *incentive contrast;* see *negative contrast*).

Discrete Avoidance A procedure in which a stimulus sets the occasion for an avoidance response, which, when emitted, delays or prevents an aversive stimulus.

Discrete Trial A stimulus is presented to an animal for a specified period of time, during which a particular instrumental response (or set of responses) is required for task completion.

Drive Reduction Theory (Hull) When behavior is instrumental in fulfilling specific *needs* (i.e., restores an organism to homeostatic balance) the drive is said to be *reduced. Drive reduction* reinforces the instrumental behavior in Clark L. Hull's theory.

Drive States (Hull) Food and water deprivation sets up conditions of specific physiological needs, which are translated into motivated behavior called *drive states.*

Drive-Stimulus Reduction The theory that stimulus properties of incentives, and not the necessity of meeting physiological needs, are sufficient to reduce drive states.

Drive Theory See *drive reduction theory.*

Electrical Stimulation of the Brain (ESB) Passing minute amounts of electric current through an implanted electrode to specific areas of the brain can act as a reinforcer. Experimental animals will press a lever to self-administer ESB.

Escape Procedure A procedure in which an animal makes an instrumental response that has the effect of terminating an aversive stimulus.

Incentive Motivation Motivation to behave that can be attributed to the quality and amount of a reinforcer. The reinforcer is said to act as an *incentive.*

Latent Learning (Tolman) Learning that is alleged to occur in the absence of specific food rewards.

Negative Contrast After experiencing both a small and a large reward, their comparison makes the perception of the smaller reward more negative than it would be in the absence of the contrast. See also *behavioral contrast.*

Negative Reinforcement Responses that are instrumental in preventing or avoiding an aversive stimulus *increase* in frequency by the process called *negative reinforcement.* (Cf. *punishment,* a procedure in which responses that produce an aversive stimulus lead to a *decrease* in frequency of the response.)

Premack Principle David Premack's proposal that the more probable of two responses would always reinforce the less probable response, and never vice versa.

Primary Punisher A stimulus that is inherently aversive.

Punisher Any stimulus whose application acts to decrease the rate of emission of the preceding response is defined to be a punisher.

Punishment The process by which an aversive stimulus acts to decrease the rate of the response to which it is applied.

Secondary Punisher Stimuli that acquire punishing properties through a conditioning procedure. Example: The word "no." (Cf. secondary reinforcement.)

Shuttle-Avoidance Avoidance conditioning in a shuttle-box in which the terminal behavior is to "shuttle" between two compartments, thereby avoiding electric shock.

Shuttle-Box An apparatus in which animals can be conditioned to *escape* and/or *avoid* electric shock by jumping across a barrier dividing the two compartments of the shuttle-box.

Sidman Avoidance Murray Sidman designed this negative reinforcement procedure in which the lever in a Skinner Box is the only signal that electric shock can be delayed/avoided by continuously lever pressing.

S-O-R Theory (Hull) A neobehaviorist, S-R theory in which intervening variables, specifically *organismic* variables such as thirst and hunger, are considered in the functional relationship between stimulus and response variables.

Two-Factor Theory (Mowrer) A theory proposing that two factors underlying avoidance behavior are Pavlovian-conditioned emotional behavior and instrumentally conditioned motor (muscle) responses.

Two-Factor Theory of Punishment A theory that punishment learning is accomplished in two stages; i.e., a fear response is first conditioned classically, and then an avoidance response reduces the fear response.

8

Applications of Learning

I. Introduction

To this point both the systematics and theories of "animal learning" and "animal behavior" have been presented. At opportune times throughout the text application of these findings to human learning and behavior have been noted. We have primarily focused, however, upon how relatively simple reflexes are modified and how new ways of simple responding are acquired.

Note in Table 4.1 (p. 108) that some of the listed "reflexes" are in fact complicated, highly integrated response systems—immune system functioning, ingestional behavior, and responses to drugs are three examples. In these three examples, immunologists, nutritionists, and pharmacologists, respectively, are the acknowledged experts. In what ways can learning theory be applied to help us understand these complicated physiological systems? A brief overview of issues raised in this chapter follows.

Role of Behavior in Physiology

Drugs.   Drugs act upon humans and infrahumans alike. Using animal models of drug effects for several decades, pharmacologists identified both physical addiction and tolerance properties of certain drugs. But pharmacologists cannot tell us why humans abuse drugs while infrahumans, for the most part, do not. By applying Pavlovian conditioning theory to the study of drug effects during the past two decades, behavioral scientists have provided insight into both drug-taking behavior and drug tolerance.

Foods. Also using animal models, nutritionists and dieticians have learned a great deal about foods and their ingestional consequences. These experts are less informed about when, what, and why people select certain foods and drinks. Why, for example, do some people overeat and others undereat to the detriment of their health? Do they learn this, or are these disorders physiological in origin? A quick comparison of the cuisines of different cultures attests to the idiosyncratic food choices that humans can *learn* during their life-times. We will see that the application of learning theory using animal models aids our understanding of human eating and drinking behavior.

Health. In our culture physicians are entrusted to apply their knowledge of anatomy, physiology, pharmacology, etc., in providing health care for people who become ill. The very existence of the concept of *mental health* and the field of **behavioral medicine** attests to the fact that "health" encompasses both physiology *and* behavior. Behavioral medicine is an interdisciplinary field concerned with the etiology of illness and wellness, preventative medicine, biofeedback and other forms of psychophysiology, treatment and rehabilitation strategies, etc. (Schwartz & Weiss, 1978). Learning theory also aids our understanding of health issues by spanning the behavioral gap between "physical" and "mental" realms. In the last part of this chapter we will analyze the role of learning in issues of *behavioral medicine.*

Analysis of Complex Behavior

Two problems have been identified that need a closer look. First, we know that simple reflexes and simple motor responses are easily conditioned. How does learning affect more complex physiological functioning? How can learning affect, for example, the immune system? Second, humans behave in ways that seem to involve conscious choice; they select certain foods, drinks, drugs, etc. Does human consciousness, human language, and so-called voluntary behavior (a) make our reliance upon animal models of learning and behavior suspect and (b) demand more sophisticated learning theories than those based upon simple association.

We begin by analyzing the last question first: Given similarities in human and infrahuman physiology and behavior, what inferences can we make regarding differences in mind and consciousness?

II. Humans and Infrahumans: A Comparison of Physiology, Behavior, and Mind

Geneticists posit the continuity of all life forms through evolutionary processes (Chapter 2), and within this framework behavioral scientists have developed a conception that general processes of learning exist across vertebrates (Chapters 3–7). A common vertebrate physiology reflects our continuous genetic history. Most people in our culture readily accept the fact that a comparative mammalian physiology exists—that lungs are lungs, lymphatic systems, immune systems, and the physiology of digestion work in about the same way, and bacterial infections are the scourge of humans and animals alike.

Continuous Brains, Discontinuous Minds?

Moreover, our culture generally acknowledges that research in animal physiology directly underlies our knowledge of human physiology, of human disease states, and of medical practice. Most people would even agree that brain structures of humans and animals are related. Nonetheless, brain *functioning* of infrahuman animals is thought by many to be somehow discontinuous with that of humans.

Corticalization and Emergence.   Noting that the human brain has both phylogenetically newer and older areas, those invested in discontinuity might argue that the old parts of the brain are continuous with infrahumans, but not the more recently evolved areas. For example, changes in behavior that come about through "general process learning theory" may be mediated by primitive parts of the brain (cf. Herrick's *vertebrate plan*; MacLean's *triune brain* in Figure 2.6, p. 62). S-S and R-S learning may be general to all vertebrates—but apply least of all to highly corticalized humans. Perhaps corticalization permits some kind of "cognitive override," if you will; it allows the emergence of voluntary behavior, language, and the ability to choose from among alternatives rather than merely responding reflexively to environmental stimuli. These arguments have merit and deserve our serious consideration.

Consciousness as a Species-Specific Behavior.   In what other ways can we think about human uniqueness? Taking our cues from classical ethologists, we might raise the question of *species-specific behaviors* of humans. For example, we might note that humans have *minds*, which allow conscious reflection upon, among other things, the differences between other animals and ourselves.[1] Our human *language* allows us to think, to compare other animals with ourselves, and to comment upon the differences we see among us. Among the major apparent differences are the very language and cognitive processes that permit us an awareness of these differences!

Based upon these observations, rightly or wrongly we can entertain the proposition that human cognitive properties allow us to transcend the animal (infrahuman) mind, thereby making us different from all other species. Framing the question one last time, does human language and human cognition allow us to get beyond the simple models of conditioning? We will return to this topic at length in Chapter 10. Suffice it to say here that an emerging understanding of human brain functioning and human consciousness is that different parts of the brain contribute different components of learning, of memory, of consciousness, and of awareness.

The issue of the role of consciousness in conditioning has been raised, and we need a rule of thumb to help us decide when behavioral changes in humans are due to "simple" conditioning procedures, and when they are due to the exercise of higher levels of consciousness. One such rule follows.

The Law of Parsimony

There is no escaping human uniqueness, and this text would not be credible if the complexities of the human mind were forced into the simple conceptual box labeled "general process learning theory." Having stated this position, however, a research strategy suggests itself. Let us resort to complex explanations only if simple explanations will not suffice. This excellent, well-exploited heuristic goes by several names—*Occam's Razor,* (Lloyd) *Morgan's Canon,* or yet more simply, the **law of parsimony.**

What are *parsimonious* explanations of behavior? Those which assert simple rather than complex processes. Consider this example: You observe a young lady drinking from a water fountain. Is she likely to be exerting free will, by consciously, after some reflection, *voluntarily choosing* to drink water? Or can her behavior be better understood as a *conditioned reflex,* intimately tied to unconscious homeostatic mechanisms of meeting water needs? Does she consciously decide, after reflection, how much water she needs to slake her thirst, or does she mindlessly take a few swallows and continue on her way. Perhaps both views are partially correct. Recognize, however, that the latter explana-

---

[1]See Ludvigson (1989) for a brief history of how psychologists have wrestled with human/animal issues of mind during this century. A more detailed treatment of comparative human and animal mind can be found in Boakes (1984).

tion is the more parsimonious. By hypothesizing that her behavior in general resembles that of most other vertebrates—animals to which we would *not* attribute higher-order cognitive processes—scientists can bring to their investigation and understanding of her behavior a wealth of infrahuman research findings.

Voluntary and Involuntary Behavior

Two distinctions have traditionally been made regarding the concepts of **voluntary behavior** and **involuntary behavior.** One is that humans alone are capable of voluntary behavior—the human/infrahuman distinction alluded to in the foregoing. The second is that there are voluntary and involuntary aspects of human behavior; walking and talking are examples of voluntary behavior, and digestion, breathing, and the regulation of fluids are examples of involuntary behavior. Let us look more closely at these distinctions.

The CNS and ANS.   Historically, the central nervous system (CNS) was conceptualized as functioning to control voluntary behavior, while the autonomic nervous system (ANS) controlled involuntary behavior. Even into the 1960s this partitioning of behavior permeated learning theory. B. F. Skinner among others had proposed that S-S conditioning was CNS mediated, and R-S conditioning was CNS mediated (Skinner, 1938). That is, responses by skeletal muscles (such as those used in running a maze, or pressing a lever, or talking), controlled by the CNS, could be conditioned by reinforcement and punishment. By contrast, salivation was ANS controlled, and Pavlovian conditioning (Skinner used the term *respondant conditioning*) was presumed to be controlled by the brain's involuntary functioning.

Experiments by Neil Miller and Associates.   Several researchers set out to test the foregoing relegation of two types of conditioning to different parts of the nervous system. The question asked? Is it possible to get *voluntary* control over autonomic nervous system functioning (which was assumed to function involuntarily)? One assumption made in setting up the research protocol was that skeletal muscles (controlled by the CNS) would have to made nonfunctional to rule out their inadvertent effect on the ANS. Therefore, laboratory rats were totally paralyzed with curare (d-tubocurarine) and put on artificial respiration for the duration of the experimental procedure (Miller & Banuazizi, 1968). Passing a minute amount of electricity through an electrode implanted in a *pleasure center* of the hypothalamus was used to as a *reinforcer.* Delivery of the reinforcer was made contingent upon slight changes in the rat's heart rate. As can be seen in Figure 8.1, heart rate was effectively controlled by the ESB rein-

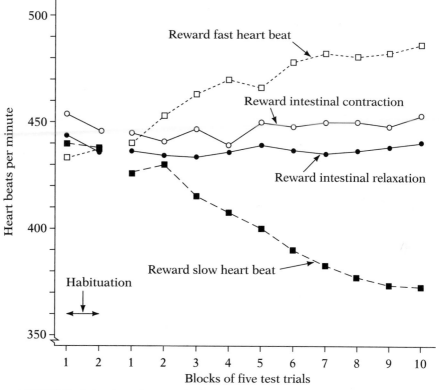

FIGURE 8.1 Conditioning Heart Rate

Using ESB to reinforce slightly increasing (top dashed line) or slightly decreasing (bottom dashed line) changes in heart rate elevates or lowers heart rate throughout a 50-trial period of time. A control group in which ESB-reinforced intestinal contraction or relaxation had no effect on heart rate is also presented. The control group allows us to conclude that the pleasant sensation of ESB by itself does not systematically increase or decrease heart rate. (From Miller & Banuazizi, 1968.)

forcement (Miller & Banuazizi, 1968). Miller and his colleagues concluded that voluntary control over involuntary brain functioning was possible.[2] As we will see, that the immune system can be conditioned further blurs the distinction between voluntary and involuntary functions of the brain.

[2]The experiment is technically difficult to accomplish, and several attempts to replicate this experiment have been unsuccessful. In light of other demonstrations and experiments in this chapter, however, the conclusion that voluntary control can be achieved over certain aspects of involuntary brain functioning seems irrefutable.

Thought question 1: What is the difference between demonstrations of one's heart racing because of revolving blue and white lights in the rear-view mirror, and heart-rate increases in rats reinforced for doing so?

Thought question 2: What are the implications of Miller's demonstration experiment for *behavioral medicine* (i.e., medicine based upon behavioral manipulation rather than drugs or surgery)? We will return to this question in the concluding section of this chapter.

Are the CNS and ANS Conceptually Different?

Distinctions made between S-S and R-S conditioning in previous chapters may allow you to provide several answers to the first thought question that has been posed. The truth of the matter is that behavioral scientists are currently less interested in S-S and R-S distinctions than they once were. Similarities in the presumed processes underlying "both" kinds of learning have been detailed (e.g., Bindra, 1972), and there is now evidence of remarkable interactions among what were once thought to be relatively isolated physiological systems. So, the second thought question is of greater interest. What physiological systems, and in which ways, can be controlled by the environment? If, as was alluded to, the immune system can be affected by Pavlovian conditioning, distinctions between the ANS and CNS, and between S-S and R-S conditioning become less important.

Studies of neuroendocrine, immune system, CNS, and ANS functioning in the past decade have led to a new integration and redefinition of these systems (Booth & Ashbridge, 1992). Evidence from a wide variety of studies (Husband, 1992) now attests to the fact that these systems are interconnected: One such holistic configuration is diagrammed in Figure 8.2.

Conclusions? (a) The central and autonomic nervous systems are more interconnected than they are conceptually separate. (b) Distinctions between voluntary and involuntary behavior have become blurred. (c) S-S and R-S differences, to the extent they exist, have little basis in brain organization.

Looking Ahead

Mind and behavior are integral to the interconnected functioning of these physiological systems. In the remainder of this chapter we will explore research and theory underlying behavioral medicine and other applications of learning relative to physiological functioning. How do physiology and behavior interrelate? Which physiological systems can be conditioned, and a related question, is there any physiological system that *cannot* be conditioned? Is human consciousness a factor?

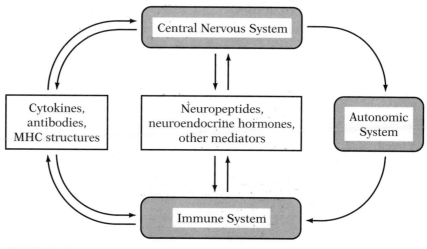

FIGURE 8.2

A schematic representation of the interactions of the CNS, ANS, and the immune and neuroendocrine systems. (From Booth & Ashbridge, 1992.)

A brief listing of what *can* be conditioned follows:

- Various components of the *immune system*
- Temperature, reactivity, pain *(ANS)* when drugs are used as unconditioned stimuli
- Drug tolerance
- Physiology relating to sensory and postingestive homeostatic mechanisms concerned with feeding behavior
- Physiology relating to sickness and wellness behavior
- Physiology of behavior relating to sexual functioning
- Components of both the CNS and ANS relating to emotional responses (including neurosis, learned helplessness, phobias, PTSD, etc.).

This is an impressive list. We begin our analysis of conditioning complex physiological systems by examining psychosomatic interactions.

III.   Psychosomatic Interactions

In a very real sense Pavlov (1927) began the experimental study of *psychosomatic interactions* (psych = mind; soma = body) with his simple demonstrations of psychic secretions at the turn of the century. The perception of a ringing bell affected the body's saliva flow. He could not have foreseen that Pavlovian conditioning would become the primary research methodology for contemporary studies of behavioral medicine.

Let us take as an example of a psychosomatic interaction the following bit of intriguing human behavior. By applying research findings and theories you have been exposed to in preceding chapters, try to hypothesize what is going on as you read this vignette:

> A hypnotist and his subject, both males, performed this demonstration on "live" television. A hypnotic trance is induced, and then deepened. After sufficient preparation, the hypnotist shows the audience a piece of chalk, tells the subject "I'm now going to burn you with a lighted cigarette," and then places the chalk on an exposed forearm. The subject's arm jerks away (conditioned withdrawal reflex?). The hypnotist asks "did it hurt?" The subject replies, "yes," that it did.

The camera focuses upon the arm. First there is a reddening of the skin where the chalk had been placed, and, within minutes, a blister appears.[3]

The "Blister Reflex."   How can the blister be explained? We could focus upon the "hypnotic state," or perhaps posit subconscious (or unconscious) mechanisms. Perhaps "cognitive" processes mediated the behavior. By contrast, a more parsimonious Pavlovian might begin by asking how "normal" blisters are formed. Referring back to Table 4.1, might not we consider blister formation to be a form of reflex?

US = heat
UR = blister

Physiology of Blisters

Capillaries become increasingly permeable when skin is heated (the eliciting stimulus), and plasma loss produces the localized edema called a blister (the reflexive response). Might blister formation in the absence of heat be considered a *conditioned reflex?* If so, how was it conditioned? The student might want to stop and construct a possible conditioning scenario that likely preceded the televised demonstration.

Analysis of Blisters as CRs.   If the phenomenon in question is a conditioned response, what might the CS or CS-complex be? Three possible CSs are (a) the chalk, (b) touching the forearm, and (c) the hypnotist's words. The placement of the chalk on the forearm in-

---

[3]I saw this demonstration on "The Paul Coates Show," truly "live" television, without interruptions or gimmicks, in the early 1950s in Los Angeles.

formed the brain where to place the blister. The operative CS, however, was the word "burn." Had the hypnotist done everything the same, except to substitute a different word in place of "burn" (such as, "I'm now going to *murph* you with a lighted cigarette"), it is unlikely that the blister would have formed.

Pavlov's Second Signal System.   Given the foregoing analysis, what the television camera did not show were the "conditioning trials" preceding the demonstration. More than likely the subject had previously experienced burns (including cigarette burns) and consequent blister formation. Most humans have had such experiences. Is it likely that the word "burn" functions as a CS in this and other situations? Yes. As we saw in an earlier section, Pavlov's (1927) analysis of the *second signal system* detailed how our language can be considered the "signal of signals," a representation of reality one level removed from incoming first-order sensory "signals." To the extent that language is learned, many of our nouns and verbs have been *associated* with objects and actions in the environment. A lighted cigarette is an object that burns. Apparently the words signaled the reflex, thereby eliciting blister formation.

Conditioning of Psychosomatic Disorders

Does the foregoing conditioning analysis completely explain the phenomenon in question? No. Too many questions remain. Blisters and warts can apparently be conditioned in a hypnotic state (Spanos & Chaves, 1989), whereas other demonstrations of conditioning occur during "normal" consciousness.[4] While normal conditioning can be accomplished with almost all conscious vertebrates, estimates are that probably only 10 to 30 percent of adult humans could make conditioned blisters (Hilgard, 1979). Another argument against a general process learning theory account of the blister phenomenon is that similar demonstrations involving infrahumans have not been reported.

If one maintains that *only* humans can make conditioned blisters, because humans alone have higher cognitive processes, however, the *law of parsimony* would be violated. Rather, we should ask if evidence exists that complex physiological responses can be conditioned in humans and animals. The answer to this question is a resounding yes, and, presumably, by similar processes. Does conditioning provide a good model for **psychosomatic disorders** in general? Again the answer is yes, as we will see throughout the chapter.

---

[4]While nonhypnotized subjects in theory could produce conditioned blistering, I am not aware of controlled demonstrations to this effect (however, see the related example of "hive" formation in this chapter).

Interim Summary

1. Behavior affects physiology as readily as physiology affects behavior.
2. The distinction between voluntary and involuntary physiological systems, between voluntary and involuntary behavior, and between S-S and R-S conditioning becomes clouded when one considers their many interactions.
3. Heart rate and other aspects of the cardiovascular system regulated by both the CNS and ANS can be conditioned.
4. Due to their interactions, the CNS, ANS, immune system, and other physiological systems are now better conceptualized as an interdependent, integrated holistic system.
5. Behavior mediated by the CNS, ANS, and immune system provides the basis for psychosomatic interactions.
6. Blisters can be conditioned.
7. Pavlovian conditioning is a primary source of psychosomatic disorders, and one of the primary research methodologies of contemporary behavioral medicine.

IV.   The Immune System and Psychoneuroimmunology

As suggested by Figure 8.2, the term **psychoneuroimmunology** refers to the research field that has gathered evidence of the interconnectedness of the immune system, brain, and behavior. Before examining this evidence, let us first look at how the immune system is believed to function "alone."

Immune System Functioning

The function of the *immune system* in mammals is to resist toxins and infectious organisms that might cause damage to tissues and organs. *Acquired immunity* describes the process whereby antibodies and sensitized lymphocytes (white blood cells) destroy invading organisms and toxins.

T-lymphocytes are an integral component of the immune system. Present at birth, T-lymphocytes directly bind to the membranes of invading cells (such as a cancer cell, or a heart transplant cell) and release both *lysomal enzymes,* which directly attack the cell's integrity, and a *macrophage chemotaxic factor,* which attracts other killer cells to the site.

Conditioning the Immune System: T-lymphocytes

Robert Ader and his associates demonstrated that the number of T-lymphocytes present in rats could be manipulated by a simple conditioning experiment (Ader, 1985). First, they injected rats with a drug called Cytoxan® (the US) and the next day recorded a reduced T-lymphocyte count (the UR). Cytoxan® is a radiomimetic drug known generically as cyclophosphamide. It is routinely used in chemotherapy to suppress immune system functioning, including the lowering of T-lymphocyte production.

Conditioned Immunosuppression.   Ader and associates then conditioned the rats by allowing them to drink a saccharin solution (the CS), followed by the Cytoxan® injection (the US). After several trials, one per day, they recorded the number of T-lymphocytes when the rats drank saccharin in the absence of the drug (i.e., an extinction test). This treatment reduced the number of the T-lymphocytes relative to control animals that received saccharin and Cytoxan® noncontingently.

The reduction of T-lymphocytes following a conditioning procedure is called **conditioned immunosuppression.** Presumably the saccharin had become associated with the drugs, and components of the immune system responded to the saccharin flavor in the same way they had to the drug.

Conditioned Facilitation of Immune Response.   Ader's demonstration of conditioned immunosuppression was the first of many investigations in a research area now called psychoneuroimmunology. **Conditioned facilitation** of the immune response has since been reported, using exteroceptive stimuli as CSs (Gorczynski, Macrae, & Kennedy, 1982; Bovbjerg, Cohen, & Ader, 1987; Krank & MacQueen 1988). In research by Krank & MacQueen (1988), for example, *increases* in antibody production resulted when animals were injected with cyclophosphamide while drinking water in a distinctive environment (a novel room in which 80-dB music was played). After these pairings, mice exposed to the room and music alone produced higher levels of antibodies compared with groups of mice in which there was no prior pairing of stimuli. Possible reasons for the differences between this study and Ader's finding of *suppression* of antibodies are discussed later (see *compensatory conditioning*).

Importance of Psychoneuroimmunology.   Why is psychoneuroimmunology important? These experiments demonstrate that elements of the immune system can be "tricked" into functioning in the absence of stimuli that normally trigger them. We should not be surprised by these findings; in Chapter 4 we learned that a dog's salivary response could also be brought under the control of an arbitrary stimulus, such as a bell. The present findings are more important. Salivation and changes in salivation via conditioning have implications for the preliminary stages of digestion. By contrast, the integrity of the immune system is vitally important for optimal functioning of all physiological systems and behavior, and, therefore, it is of critical importance for health and longevity.

Thoughts Affect Immune Systems. That the immune system can be conditioned raises the distinct possibility that words, thoughts, beliefs, and other cognitive stimuli acting as CSs can become associated with immune system functioning. What do you think? Can thought processes, such as the perception of stressors, affect your health? Several studies using both rats and humans provide supportive evidence. For example, the immune systems of rats given the opportunity to escape the stress of electric shock have been found to be normal in comparison with immunosuppressed rats unable to escape the same shocks (Laudenslager, Ryan, Drugan, Hyson, & Maier, 1983). The *perception* of the stressor, and not the stressor alone, produced these changes in the immune system.

Levels of IgA (immunoglobin A1, an antibody that protects the upper respiratory tract from infection) were compared in dental students before, during, and after final exams. The IgA levels were lower during the exams, reflecting a somewhat compromised immune system (Jemmott & Magloire, 1988). Personality variabilities have also been found to affect immune function. Both perceived stress and immunosuppression during test taking were found to differ as a function of students' personality profiles (Jemmott et al., 1990).

There is evidence, then, that the perception of stressors can affect one's immune system, and by extrapolation, one's health.

Conditioning the Immune System: Asthma

Nine million Americans suffer from a baffling condition called asthma. Although these people come from every walk of life, and range in age from infants to the very old, they have one thing in common—difficulty in breathing, alternatively described as "hungry for air."

The sign in the allergist's office summarizes what the allergy sufferer already knows: Asthma attacks occur under a variety of conditions (see Figure 8.3). Another way of saying this is that the same amount of external stimulus (cedar pollen, for example) does not always produce an identical asthmatic response, as would be the case if asthma were a simple reflex. Let us look more closely at this psychobiological condition.

Environment	Provides antigen (allergen)
	Provides irritant (harsh, dry, cold)
Exertion	Causes irritation of mucous membranes
Emotion	Always heightens symptoms with any combination of the preceding, or may induce asthma even in the absence of the foregoing factors

FIGURE 8.3   The Rule of E's

The *Rule of E's* summarizes three of the most important variables that contribute to asthma attacks.

Physiology of Asthma.   Asthma is a type of allergy involving yet another component of the immune system. In normal people, certain stimuli that invade the body, called *antigens,* activate immune responses. The presence of large quantities of *reagins,* or sensitizing antibodies, causes some individuals to overreact to certain types of antigens, known as *allergens.* When this occurs in allergic or asthmatic individuals, an allergic response called an *allergen-reagin reaction* takes place.

Serious health problems may ensue from such overly sensitive immune systems, and asthma can be thought of as a disorder involving overly sensitive airways. Allergen-reagin reactions involve attaching antibodies to, and thereby damaging, cells throughout the body. If a sufficient number of cells are damaged in this *anaphylactoid* reaction, death can ensue.

The allergen-reagin reaction can therefore be construed as a US-UR reflex. Is it possible to condition an asthmatic reaction? That is, can asthmatic and allergic responses be brought under the control of neutral stimuli? A related question is the role emotion plays in the Rule of E's. How can emotion be a facilitating factor in this reflex? Let us first look at asthma in animals.

Asthma in Guinea Pigs

Guinea pigs have overly sensitive airways, making them good animal subjects upon which to do asthma research. Guinea pigs can be made asthmatic pharmacologically by first injecting them with a foreign protein, such as egg albumin. Their immune system responds by making sensitizing antibodies (allergens) to the invading protein. Upon subsequent encounters with the allergen, an allergen-reagin reaction occurs in the bronchioles of the lungs. There, mast cells release a *slow-reacting substance of anaphylaxis* causing the bronchial smooth muscle to spasm, and breathing difficulties ensue. The response of the guinea pig following one sensitizing treatment is so severe that unless a vasoconstrictor (such as Isuprel®) is immediately administered, the guinea pig will die.

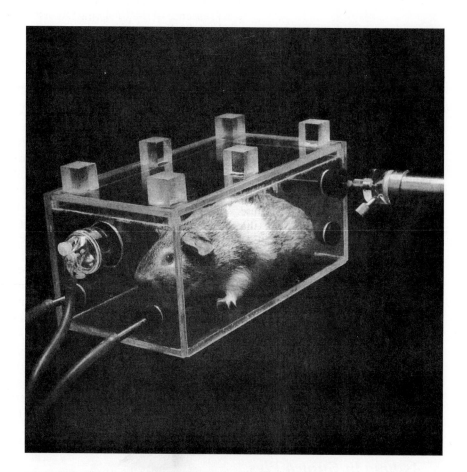

FIGURE 8.4 Conditioning Asthma in Guinea Pigs

Whole-body plethysomograms (breathing records) were recorded from fluctuations in air pressure within a sealed Plexiglas chamber. The guinea pig shown weighs about 850 grams, compared with laboratory rats that weight about 350–400 grams. The nebulizer is attached at the back of the box. (From Justeson et al., 1970.)

Conditioning Asthma in Guinea Pigs. Asthma in guinea pigs has
been conditioned (Justesen, Braun, Garrison, & Pendleton, 1970).
Following the foregoing sensitizing treatment, which makes the
guinea pig asthmatic, breathing is measured by pressure transducers
in a sealed environment (see Figure 8.4). Recordings are made of
slight changes in air pressure as the animal breathes normally, and
again as breathing is disrupted (the UR) when aerosol egg albumin
(the US) is administered into the air stream serving the chamber (see
below).

A hissing nebulizer squirts the egg albumin into the air stream,
allowing the US to be administered to the guinea pig in an aerosol. A
conditioning trial consists of the hissing sound (the CS), the aerosol
egg albumin (the US), disrupted breathing (the UR), and, finally, recovery as aerosol Isuprel® is administered, returning the animal's
breathing to baseline levels. In the research by Justesen et al. (1970),
all guinea pigs showed conditioned disruptions in breathing to the
sound of the nebulizer alone after 6–12 trials.

Such demonstrations of conditioned asthma raise several important issues. Would it be possible, for example, to maximize conditioning (more trials, more salient CSs, etc.) and fatally disrupt breathing

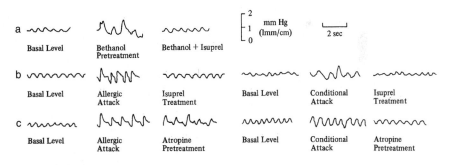

FIGURE 8.4 *(continued)*

Breathing records for several conditions are shown. The left-hand
portion of the upper, middle, and lower records ("a," "b," and "c,"
respectively) shows the basal, or control, level breathing pattern.
Record "b" shows the breathing described in the text in which
aerosol egg albumin causes the "Allergic Attack." Isuprel® returns
breathing to control levels. The conditioned allergic response (labeled "Conditional Attack") shows disrupted breathing caused by
sounding the nebulizer alone. In record "c" atropine is used in place
of Isuprel®. (From Justesen et al., 1970.)

using only a CS? Another experiment: Could one train a discrimination between the aerosol egg albumin and aerosol Isuprel® such that the CSs associated with the latter could be shown to relieve breathing disruptions to the former?

Conditioning Asthma in Humans. The behavioral conditioning of allergic reactions such as asthma has also been reported in humans. In a design similar to the guinea pig study just noted, for example, two allergic individuals were first exposed to allergens when using a breathing apparatus. After several trials, they produced allergic symptoms when asked to use the breathing apparatus alone, in the absence of allergens. Within the clinical literature on asthma treatment are numerous reports of psychosomatic (i.e., conditioned) components in how asthma is expressed. Included is an allergic reaction to an artificial rose in a patient allergic to roses (reported by Gauci, Husband, & King, 1992).

Allergic rhinitis (hay fever) can be conditioned in humans, using both mast-cell mediators and a "subjective symptom score" as dependent variables (Gauci et al., 1992). In this research, a number of asthma suffers were recruited to participate in a study concerned with "alternative" treatments for hay fever and allergic rhinitis. Divided into three groups, they were given water, a "medicine" (actually an inert soft drink), or nothing. Each treatment was conceptualized as the "conditioned stimulus," and immediately thereafter each subject was challenged with an allergen. Both "subject symptom scores" (a self-report measure) and mast-cell activity were measured. Two days later, the procedure was repeated without administering the allergen. These researchers reported that the "medicine" treatment diminished mast-cell activity relative to the other two groups. They hypothesized that subject *expectations* regarding treatment was an important confounding variable in this study, and that the "medicine" had exerted placebo properties. Their results suggested to these researchers that the entire experimental treatment had CS properties, and that one-trial conditioning had been effected.

Asthma and Emotionality. In addition to conditioned allergic reactions, asthma sufferers are also provided excellent opportunities for a variety of conditioning situations. Have you ever had your breathing forcibly disrupted for any length of time? Without special training most people panic. That suffocation produces such extreme emotional responses is adaptive; oxygen is our most critical homeostatic need, and its availability demands our immediate attention. The point is that the emotional components of allergic responses are also excellent USs, available for conditioning to a variety of environmental cues. It is no wonder that allergists have long recognized the inherent circularity of this condition; emotion causes the asthma causes the emotion, etc. (see Figure 8.3).

Risking anthropomorphism, we can posit that it is likely that guinea pigs also suffer emotional responses as they gasp for air. The stimuli attendant with these emotional responses are readily available to enter into association with the nebulizer concurrently with disruptions in breathing. After several pairings, the sound of the nebulizer would produce a "panic" response, further disrupting normal breathing.

In any case, both the Justesen et al. (1970) and Gauci et al. (1992) experiments provide compelling demonstrations of human psychophysiological (cf. psychosomatic) disorders. And, as we will see in a later section, human food allergies are also subject to conditioning.

Conditioning the Immune System: Hives

Urticaria is an immune system response commonly known as *hives*. Though not well understood, hives result when antigens enter specific skin areas and cause histamine release, producing a localized response. Among other actions, histamine produces a local vascular dilation and capillary permeability, within a few minutes causing a "red flare" and swelling (a hive), respectively.

Many individuals produce hives in situations where the antigen is either not present or is present but not causing a reaction. Consider the following example:

> A woman in her mid-thirties appears stressed by the presence of visiting in-laws. After several hours she is overheard telling her husband that she must get away from his family or she will "go crazy." A few minutes later the first hive appears on her arm. She retires to her bedroom, saying she will be okay "if left alone." Within the next 15 minutes, several six-inch diameter, one-half-inch raised welts appear on her arms, legs, and torso. An hour later all hives had disappeared without leaving a mark.[5]

It is tempting to speculate that the presence of in-laws acted as proximal conditioned stimuli, setting the occasion for the somatized stress response. It is likely that histamine was released locally as a conditioned rather than as an unconditioned response. Another example: "Blushing" is caused by localized vasodilation of the face and neck, most noticeably the cheeks.

Which particular conditioned stimuli control your "blushing reflex"? Certain people? Certain words?

---

[5]Personal observation by the author.

Interim Summary

1. The *immune system's* function in mammals is to resist toxins and infectious organisms. For example, *T-lymphocytes* attack and ultimately destroy invading cells.
2. Psychoneuroimmunology is a research area that integrates physiology and behavior. Pavlovian conditioning is the primary methodology used in psychoneuroimmunology.
3. The immune system can be conditioned to respond to previously neutral stimuli. Rats drink flavors followed by toxins that suppress immune functioning. Ultimately, *conditioned immunosuppression* results when these rats merely taste the flavors—a conditioned response. Conditioned *immunofacilitation* has also been demonstrated.
4. The perception, or interpretation, of stressors has been demonstrated to have immune system consequences in rats and humans.
5. A common disorder of the immune system that often has a behavioral component in its etiology is asthma.
6. Asthma has been classically conditioned in guinea pigs and humans. The emotional consequences of disrupted breathing are potential USs available for association with environmental cues.
7. Blushing and hives can be interpreted as highly individualized conditioned responses.

V.   Drugs, Drug Effects, and Conditioned Drug Effects

Drugs as Stimuli

That stimuli can be conceptually grouped into simple and complex categories was proposed in Chapter 4. Short duration, pure tones and lights were characterized as "simple" CSs. Simple stimuli are experienced simply—they produce definable afferent neuronal responses of limited duration that project to primary sensory areas of the brain. By contrast, Pavlov's USs ("biologically meaningful stimuli") are more complex stimuli, evoking motivational and emotional responses from more diverse areas of the brain.

Drugs as USs.   Drug stimuli belong to the latter category. Drugs not only have sensory properties, but each drug also has one or more sites of action—systemically, and often also involving specific brain sites. The pharmacological effects of a drug constitute its unconditioned stimulus properties.

Drug Overdoses. Given the complexity of drugs as stimuli, should we anticipate that conditioning using drugs as USs will differ from salivary conditioning in dogs? Surprisingly, simple associative models work quite well. Consider the following case history of a drug overdose:

> An elderly man in the terminal stages of cancer, suffering intense, chronic pain, was being maintained on a high dosage of morphine. Bedridden, the patient was administered the morphine on a strict schedule by a relative. On one occasion the relative was late, and the patient crawled into the next room where he administered the drug to himself. Though the drug dosage was equivalent to what he had been receiving, the patient died of an "overdose." (Siegel, Hinson, Krank, & McCully, 1982)

How can this be? How can the same dosage of a drug have two different effects? Fortunately, experimental work has been accomplished in this area that provides a conceptual framework to help us understand how a "normal" drug dosage can sometimes be an "overdose." The process is not unlike that of a drug dosage *losing* its effectiveness with repeated usage. Let us first look at various aspects of drugs and drug-taking behavior, and then we will return to questions of "overdosing."

Drug-Taking Behavior

On the surface, taking drugs seems to be an example of a voluntary behavior. Addictive drugs, however, are often craved, and both food and drug cravings can be analyzed as resulting from physiological need states. After a thorough literature review, Tiffany (1990) concluded that drug-seeking behavior of habitual drug users may largely be determined by "automatic" (read involuntary) processes, rather than as the result of conscious processes.

Drugs are powerful unconditioned stimuli, and addictive drugs are potent reinforcers. Each drug-taking episode can be considered a conditioning trial in which environmental stimuli (CSs) are paired with drug effects (USs). Each drug-taking episode is also one in which drug-taking behaviors may be *reinforced or punished* by the drug's effects.

As is the case with many other stimuli used in conditioning, both the effectiveness and the associability of drugs change with repeated trials. The reduced effectiveness of drugs repeatedly taken, called *drug tolerance*, is especially true of "addictive drugs." An excellent example of an addictive drug that loses its effectiveness over time is morphine.

Drugs as USs: Conditioning and Drug Tolerance

Morphine. Morphine is an alkaloid derivative of opium primarily used at analgesic (pain relieving) dosages in humans. Its central nervous system effects are that complex endogenous opioid receptors (such as endorphins) are activated by morphine, producing a number of changes in brain functioning and concomitant physiological systems. Among the easily measured "unconditioned responses" to morphine are respiratory depression (at high doses), and analgesia, euphoria, and increased body temperature (at moderate doses).

Simple Conditioning with Morphine. Pavlov (1927) reported some of the first conditioning experiments using injections of morphine and other drugs in dogs. The contextual cues attendant with morphine injection, including the appearance of the white-coated researcher who injected the animal, eventually became CSs that produced druglike responses in the absence of morphine administration (see Box 8.1).

Pavlov's observations of conditioning using morphine as a US and sights and sounds as CSs produced results similar to his other preparations. But we now know that "drug effects" are more complicated than his simple picture suggests. Consider the following questions about tolerance.

BOX 8.1

Conditioning Drug Responses in Dogs

"It is well known that the first effect of a hypodermic injection of morphine is to produce nausea with profuse secretion of saliva, followed by vomiting, and then profound sleep.

. . . when the injections were repeated regularly . . . after five or six days the preliminaries of injection were in themselves sufficient to produce all these symptoms—nausea, secretion of saliva, vomiting and sleep.

. . . in the most striking cases all the symptoms could be produced by the dogs simply seeing the experimenter. Where such a stimulus was insufficient, it was necessary to open the box containing the syringe, to crop the fur over a small area of skin and wipe with alcohol, and perhaps even to inject some harmless fluid before the symptoms could be obtained. The greater number of previous injections of morphine the less preparation had to be performed in order to evoke a reaction simulating that produced by the drug" (Pavlov, 1927, pp. 35–36).

Pharmacological and Behavioral Tolerance

Tolerance is typically defined as a reduction in the intensity of the effect of a dose of a drug over repeated trials. Tolerance has been likened to habituation (Baker & Tiffany, 1985). Another way of assessing tolerance is to note the increasing requirement of a larger dose to achieve the same level of drug effect over trials.

Mechanisms of tolerance vary from drug to drug. For example, *metabolic tolerance* to the daily ingestion of alcohol is characterized by compensatory changes in biochemicals (such as increased levels of alcohol dehydrogenase) that inactivate (metabolize) the drug. Because it is metabolized, less of the drug is available to reach receptor sites in the brain. *Physiological tolerance* to alcohol occurs when the presumed receptive sites on (as yet unspecified) neurons change, so that the effects of the drug at these sites are reduced.[6] These and other biological mechanisms for other drugs characterize the many ways in which **pharmacological tolerance** for a drug is effected.

It is also the case that in addition to the development of pharmacological tolerance over trials, animals experience a **behavioral tolerance,** which helps them cope with drug effects on sensory and motor components of behavior. For example, given enough trials in a drug state, rats under the influence of alcohol can learn to balance better while traversing a narrow ledge (Wenger, Tiffany, Bombardier, Nicholls, & Woods, 1981). This sensory-motor adjustment is a form of behavioral tolerance. Indeed, demonstrations of tolerance to stimuli other than drugs suggest there may be generalizable homeostatic adjustments to repetitive stimuli. For example, tolerance develops to a variety of physical circumstances such as heat, cold, delivery of electric shocks, exercise (cf. training effect), and even to the effects of brain lesions. A general question, then, is the extent to which organisms can learn to tolerate, or adjust to, repetitive stimuli.

A Pavlovian Conditioning Analysis
of Morphine Tolerance

How much tolerance can a person develop to morphine? A great deal. An initial dose of 100–200 mg produces sedation and respiratory depression to the point of death. After repeated administrations, tolerant subjects can take 20–40 times this dosage (as much as 4.0 gm) without adverse effect (Baker & Tiffany, 1985).

---

[6]"Physiological tolerance" is far more complicated than indicated here. In addition to changes in receptor number and receptor sensitivity, probably there are changes in intracellular second-messenger systems to which opiate receptors couple.

We are now ready to consider an elegant demonstration of how drug tolerance for morphine can be partitioned into *behavioral* and *pharmacological* components. Siegel (1975, 1977) began by injecting rats with 5.0 mg/kg morphine sulfate subcutaneously (under the skin) on a daily basis. This dosage of morphine produced several unconditioned responses: increased body temperature (hyperthermia), decreased heart rate (bradycardia), and decreased sensitivity to pain (analgesia). Drug administration took place in a room in which 60-dB

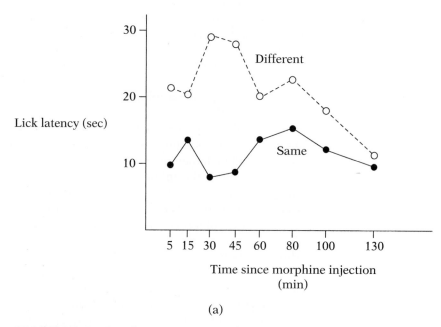

(a)

FIGURE 8.5 Conditioning Pain and Temperature Responses

(a) Rats without morphine will immediately withdraw and lick their paw when it is placed upon a hot plate. Morphine's effect reduces their sensitivity to pain, and they may wait 20–30 seconds before removing their paw from the hot surface. Rats repeatedly injected with morphine, however, show different pain responses depending upon whether they are in a *familiar* or *novel* environment. Morphine tolerance is induced over several days in the *same* environment. Morphine loses its pain-killing effectiveness as is evidenced by rats withdrawing their paw from a hot surface and licking it within about 10 seconds. The same rats injected with the same dose of morphine, when tested in a different environment, however, do not experience as much pain: They leave their paws on the hot surface 2–3 times as long. (After Siegel, 1977.)

white noise (the sound made when parents "shush" a small child) provided a constant background. This "distinctive environment," we will see, provided the contextual cues that eventually controlled some of the responses to the morphine.

Effects of Environment on Tolerance. As tolerance to the morphine accrued (about six days), each injection produced less analgesia and less hyperthermia. The question Siegel wanted to answer was how much of the reduction in analgesia and hyperthermia was due to decreases in the drug's pharmacological action, and how much was due to behavioral tolerance. To find out he interrupted the schedule of drug administration by taking the rats to yet another room having different background cues. The morphine administered in this new environment again became effective; i.e., the morphine

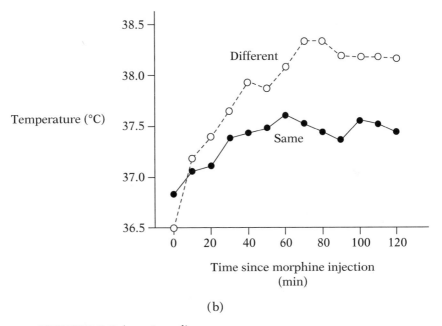

(b)

FIGURE 8.5 *(continued)*

(b) Same rats, same conditions as described in (a). Administered morphine normally increases body temperature. After morphine tolerance occurs, the drug no longer warms the body. This effect, however, is also dependent upon the environment in which the morphine is administered. Not only does morphine block pain better in a *different* environment, it also warms the body more than the same dosage in a *same* environment. (After Siegel, 1977.)

again warmed the animals and produced a renewed analgesic effect (see Figure 8.5).

Conditioned Compensatory Responses. Siegel concluded that the environmental context of the "familiar" room (in which the rats had been injected with morphine) had become conditioned; the rat's tolerance to the morphine in part was due to being administered the drug *in this environment*. The *familiar environment,* Siegel reasoned, contained CSs that had come to control **conditioned compensatory responses.** How so? The rats normal physiology allows homeostatic mechanisms to counteract the effects of drugs; i.e., cooling to counteract the warming effects of morphine; increasing heart rate (tachycardia) to counteract the bradycardia produced by morphine; and an increased sensitivity to pain to counteract the analgesia produced by morphine.

Siegel concluded that the previously neutral stimuli present during drug administration became conditioned stimuli and as such were important components in the development of drug tolerance. He bolstered his arguments concerning the associative nature of tolerance by demonstrating (a) that placebo sessions (contextual cues without morphine administration—i.e., extinction trials) would extinguish the environmental component of acquired tolerance, and (b) that placebo sessions prior to conditioning acted to retard the acquisition of tolerance (cf. latent inhibition). Table 8.1 summarizes Siegel's method demonstrating conditioned morphine tolerance.

Returning to the case study of apparent morphine overdose, taking the drug in a novel environment (self-administered in a different room) bypassed the familiar environmental stimuli that would have elicited the conditioned compensatory responses. The effectiveness of the high dosage of morphine was thereby increased, unfortunately, to a fatal level.

Conditioning Withdrawal Responses in Humans

Other drug-conditioning phenomena have been demonstrated in humans. Addicts volunteered to be studied during drug withdrawal in methadone-maintenance programs (O'Brien, 1975). In one study the drug naloxone (which mimics heroin withdrawal effects) was paired with a tone/odor-conditioned stimulus complex. Naloxone by itself produces a host of effects, including subjective components (craving, nausea, and cramps); behavioral components (blinking, yawning, restlessness); and ANS components (decreased skin temperature, increased heart rate, tears from the eyes). After 7 to 10 trials the CS complex reliably produced conditioned responses similar to the naloxone treatment.

TABLE 8.1   Conditioning Morphine Tolerance

Stage of Experiment	*Treatment Group*	*Control Group*
Training phase	Days 1–6: Morphine in familiar environment	Days 1–6: Morphine in familiar environment
Testing phase	Day 7: Morphine in *different* environment	Day 7: Morphine in *familiar* environment
Results	Day 7: Reduction in morphine tolerance: more hyperthermia, more analgesia relative to control group	Day 7: Morphine *tolerance:* reduced warming; loss of morphine's analgesic effects
Analysis	Contextual cues of familiar environment are *absent;* no conditioned compensatory responses; no homeostatic adjustments to counteract morphine's pharmacological effects	Contextual cues of familiar environment produced *conditioned compensatory responses;* i.e., homeostatic cooling and homeostatic hyperalgesia which counteract morphine's pharmacological effects

Street addicts coming into the treatment centers carry their drug-conditioning history with them. When asked to perform a "cook-up" ritual under laboratory conditions, the detoxified addicts' pupils dilate and skin temperature decreases prior to any drug action (O'Brien, Testa, Ternes, & Greenstein, 1978). The conditioned stimuli controlling the response is a complex of the sight of a bag of heroin, the odor of the cooker, and anticipation of shooting up. Such "naturalistic" stimuli easily become conditioned stimuli (Ternes, O'Brien, Grabowski, Wellerstein, & Jordan-Hays, 1980).

Drugs as USs: Conditioning Alcohol Tolerance

Most of the readers of this text are neither heroin addicts nor morphine users. If it turns out that conditioned compensatory responses are specific to conditioning with opiates, application to humans, while interesting, is limited. Research by Le, Poulos, and Cappell (1979) is important in extending the generality of Siegel's framework to a commonly used drug with pharmacological action quite different from the opiates. Their research, and that of others in this area, now provides a conditioning model of alcohol tolerance that has important treatment implications (Melchior & Tabakoff, 1984).

Among its more interesting pharmacological actions, ethyl alcohol has a cooling effect on the body.[7] Le et al. (1979) injected rats ip (intraperitoneal) with 2.5 g/kg for nine trials in a distinctive environment. When first administered, this dosage produces substantial motor impairment and drops the body temperature from 98.6 to about 95 degrees Fahrenheit. The change in the hypothermic unconditioned response over nine alcohol treatments (one every other day) is noted in Figure 8.6.

When on the tenth day alcohol was administered in the rat's home cage rather than in the distinctive (familiar) environment, the cooling effect again reappeared. Le et al. (1979) interpreted this finding within Siegel's framework: conditioned *hyperthermic* compensatory responses were interfering with the normal pharmacological action of ethanol. With respect to the development of alcohol tolerance, environmental cues were controlling at least a portion of the temperature UR to alcohol, and therefore not all of the observed tolerance could be due to loss of pharmacological action at a receptor site.

Conditioning Temperature Changes. Because body temperature itself is a factor in how well the immune system functions, there is increasing interest in demonstrating that body temperature changes can also be conditioned (Bull, Brown, King, Husband, & Pfister, 1992). Novel-flavored fluids are paired with either pyretics or antipyretics, and conditioned temperature changes on the order of magnitude reported by Le et al. (1979) to ethanol are observed (Bull, Brown, King, & Husband, 1991). Body temperature, therefore, can be conditioned by a variety of mechanisms.

Drug Craving. Humans are creatures of habit, and for obvious reasons it is important to understand habitual alcohol-drinking behavior. When people are asked why they drink alcohol, many simply respond "I crave it." Others drink alcohol but do not report consciously "craving" it (Kassel & Shiffman, 1992).

Le et al. (1979) speculated that periodic drinking in familiar environments would produce both time and place cues for the conditioned compensatory responses, including hyperthermia. They further reasoned that a slight warming effect could provide the somatic basis for the "psychological craving" for alcohol. Treatment of alco-

[7]Saint Bernards carrying brandy kegs provide a substance to stranded mountaineers that may burn the throat and stomach (and thereby arouse the reticular activating system). Nevertheless, the end result is to further cool the body—unless the person has an extensive history with ethanol consumption in cold climates—see text.

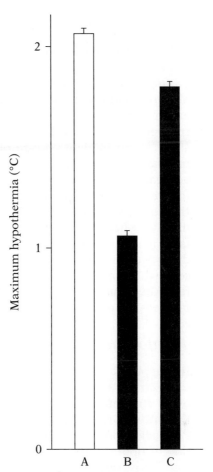

FIGURE 8.6   Alcohol, Tolerance, and Body Temperature

Rats injected with alcohol experience a rather profound hypothermia. Condition "A" shows a 2 degree Centigrade drop in body temperature following a 2.5 gm/kg ip injection of ethanol (dropping the rat's body temperature to approximately 95–96 degrees Fahrenheit). After nine such injections, the body temperature of alcohol-tolerant rats does not decrease as much (Condition "B") unless the rat is injected in a novel environment (Condition "C"). See text for further details of this *conditioned compensatory response.* (After Le et al., 1979.)

holism should take into effect this learning component, including the extinction of conditioned compensatory responses, along with alcohol abstinence (Melchior & Tabakoff, 1984).

Familiar versus Novel Places.   The finding that both morphine and alcohol tolerance are determined in part by whether they are experienced in novel or familiar places raises questions about other environmentally sensitive conditioning phenomena. For example, *food allergies* occur in eight percent of children, yet the role of environment in *conditioning allergic responses* to flavors of foods has never been investigated. In a recent report of 13 children who had life-threatening food allergy incidents, five of the six fatal cases occurred outside of the home, whereas the remaining seven nonfatal reactions occurred in private homes (Sampson, Mendelson, & Rosen, 1992). Of the nonfatal reactions to foods, two of the children who came closest to dying were visiting in other people's homes. The report focused on somewhat longer delays in the administration of epinephrine in the fatal versus nonfatal incidents; however, the role of environment cannot be ruled out.

Drugs as USs: Reinforcing Properties

In Chapter 7 we saw evidence of the tremendous reinforcing effects of electrical stimulation of the so-called *pleasure centers* in, among other dopamine-releasing sites, the *medial forebrain bundle (MFB)* of the brain. Given the limited availability of ESB, and cognizant of Premack's conception that the value of a reinforcer changes as a function of opportunities to engage in behaviors that produce it, what is *your* "most reinforcing stimulus"?

One candidate is crack cocaine (Flynn, 1991). Money (secondary reinforcer) and crack (primary reinforcer) command and control the behaviors that produce the intense reinforcing effect reported by those who use the drug. Some human lives are totally rearranged to provide the opportunity for the next hit . . . including the bypassing of food and sex. Seldom do reinforcers exert quite the total control that this drug does, presenting major difficulties for those wishing to apply some form of remedial therapy. Indeed, chemical dependency on a gamut of drugs of abuse, including alcohol, presents major challenges to health care. By one analysis, alcohol is addictive because it produces both positive reinforcement (a slight euphoria, presumably caused by the release of dopamine) as well as negative reinforcement (i.e., alcohol reduces the discomfort of anxiety). This one-two punch makes it difficult for many people to resist (Carlson, 1992).

Thought question: Can you apply *Premackian reinforcement* to come up with a more powerful reinforcer than crack cocaine? If not, what is the prognosis for behavioral treatment of those chemically dependent on (and highly reinforced by) crack?

Interim Summary

1. A drug's pharmacological effects are its unconditioned stimulus properties.
2. Drug-taking behavior is influenced by both the pharmacological properties of the drug and the conditioned responses to the environment in which the drug effects were experienced.
3. Early experiments with morphine demonstrated that conditioned stimuli could produce morphinelike effects in an animal.
4. Morphine tolerance is due both to the waning of the drug's effects (*pharmacological tolerance,* presumably adaptations in tissue) and to *behavioral tolerance,* the *conditioned compensatory responses* investigated by Siegel (1977).
5. Conditioned compensatory responses are understood as homeostatic adjustments elicited by drug-predictive environmental cues. When rats and humans experience the drug in a novel environment (which does not contain drug-predictive cues), tolerance disappears and the drug again becomes effective.
6. Siegel's conditioning model of drug tolerance for morphine has been successfully extended to ethyl alcohol.
7. Drugs affect the immune system, and the foregoing drug tolerance conditioning models have had the effect of providing some heuristic models for research in conditioning body temperature changes.
8. Cocaine and other drugs have reinforcing properties that can come to control behavior. Alcohol has both positive and negative reinforcing properties.

VI.   Conditioning Ingestional Behavior

During the past century hundreds of researchers have been drawn to the study of ingestive behaviors—that is, to the study of eating and drinking. Why? Because foods and fluids, more tangible than the air we breathe, sustain life. Ingestive behaviors in part define the ethologists' concern with *consummatory* behaviors, those behaviors essential for survival. For other researchers eating and drinking are among life's great pleasures; perhaps they are drawn to the study of what makes us feel good. Eating and drinking help define our social interactions—indeed, help define the world's cultures.

Selected areas of the diverse eating and drinking research interests can be found in Table 8.2. Of the 942 feeding-related articles Weingarten (1990) surveyed, only five percent are concerned with

TABLE 8.2 Classification of Feeding-Related Articles by Topic for the Years 1980–1988 Inclusive

Journal	Neural Controls	Peptides	Pharmacological/ Hormonal Controls	Glucostatic Controls	Palatability	Learning and Experience	Unclassified[a]	Total
Physiology & Behavior	110	112	81	63	56	27	180	629
Appetite	32	15	23	12	50	10	81	223
JCPP/Behavioral Neuroscience	33	5	13	1	8	11	19	90
Total	175	132	117	76	114	48	280	942
Percentage	19	14	12	8	12	5	30	

[a]Unclassified denotes that the article did not conform to any of the other categories.
From Weingarten (1990).

the role of environment—that is, of learning and experience. Note that the overwhelming majority of articles are physiological in nature. One could get the mistaken impression from this analysis that eating and drinking behavior are primarily governed by innate factors.

Nothing could be further from the truth. Pavlov began with digestion and ended up founding a major area within psychology. As noted by a number of investigators, and as stated succinctly by Elliot Stellar of the University of Pennsylvania, in no other area of human experience do we see quite so clearly the interplay of genes and environment, of physiology and behavior:

> Biological factors . . . individual experience . . . [and] cultural factors . . . work together to determine the food choices an individual makes at any instant. This interaction of factors is accomplished through the brain, which is the final common path for all behavior. (Stellar, 1982, pp. xi–xii)

In this section a brief overview of the determinants of eating and drinking behavior will be sketched, with an emphasis upon Pavlovian conditioning. The interested reader is directed to Logue (1991) and Capaldi and Powley (1990) for more extensive overviews of an enormous and growing behavioral literature.

Chemical Sensitivity and the Evolution of Feeding Niches

Membranes evolved having properties that allowed them to be selectively sensitive to their interface with the environment. And in meeting the challenge of efficiently securing palatable foods and avoiding toxins, our taste and smell receptors evolved in ways that took advantage of this sensitivity (Pfaffman, 1959; Young, 1966; Beidler, 1982). Hence, newborn humans display innate preference for sweet and innate dislike of bitter substances.

Receptor-Driven Feeding of Simple Animals.   Unlike those found on flies, however, human receptors do not determine appetite. Earlier in the text (p. 28) we looked at an example of a relatively simple behavioral system that is "receptor driven"—specifically, we saw that a house fly reflexively lowers its proboscis to feed when taste receptors on its legs are stimulated (Dethier, 1978). Other animals also occupy relatively more circumscribed feeding niches than do humans, i.e., carnivores and herbivores, to name but two well-known relatively restricted feeding niches. As will be discovered shortly, it is with omnivory that eating and drinking become dicey.

Eating Behaviors and Biocultural Evolution

Specific brain structures as well as taste and olfactory receptor tissue have evolved in humans and other animals. An ability to monitor food value once it is past the peripheral sensing receptors is also part of our physiology; homeostatic mechanisms are as much a product of evolution as bitter and sweet receptors.

A few examples of how human ingestive behaviors may have evolved reveal both the complexities of what, how, and why we eat, as well as to serve notice as to the limitations of a purely physiological approach.

Corn.   Noting that the quality of the digestible protein in corn is increased if, during food preparation, the corn is treated with an alkali solution, Katz (1982) inquired as to why some American Indian cultures treated their corn with alkali and others did not. He found that those who *did* treat their corn with alkali both grew more corn and ate more of it than did those not using the alkali treatment. Katz reasoned that the alkali food preparation method increased the nutritional value of the corn, which in turn influenced how corn was incorporated into the diet.

Two points are stressed: (a) The determinants of corn selection (or other food selection) involve more than its taste and smell, and (b) somehow, for unknown reasons, certain American Indians *learned* to treat corn with alkali, recognized (?) the value of this treatment in the course of a lifetime, and transmitted the acquired information to the next generation.

Fava Beans, Bitter Manioc, and Soybeans.   Katz (1982) accomplished similar studies of African tribes eating Fava beans, bitter manioc, and soybeans. He noted that cultural transformations of foods often enhanced adaptive fitness. For example, when bitter manioc (a tuber) is prepared in a certain way, the food offers increased protection against *sickle cell anemia*. Food preparation that enhances adaptive fitness often becomes part of the culture, a process that Katz (1975) labeled **biocultural evolution.**

Similar work on the relationship of those African tribes which historically use cow's milk, and the prevalence or absence of lactose insufficiency was reported by Simoons (1973). He theorizes that the consumption of particular types of food and not others over time may have led to divergence of human populations. Katz and Simoons view both the choice of food for consumption and methods of food preparation as an evolutionary interface; those people who do this more successfully than others enjoy a reproductive advantage.

Origin of Cuisines.   What humans learn about foods during their lifetimes is important. Such learning complements the functioning of taste and smell receptors as well as innately organized homeostatic regulatory processes. Furthermore, the cross-generational transmission of food information is the basis for the origin of the world's various cuisines.

Thought question: What do you know about the origins of food choices within your particular ethnic cuisine?

Specific Hungers

Evolution aside for the moment, individuals survive by eating foods selected from their local environments several times each day. The task is not particularly easy even with a full complement of evolved food selection mechanisms and a supportive culture. Some insight into the complexity of this process can be gained by examining a case history. Box 8.2 illustrates how one particular child with faulty physiology learned to eat and drink.

What is remarkable about this example is that it points out the redundant physiological systems we have (a) for recognizing salt and water in both the internal and external environment and (b) for regulating their intake. We have **specific hungers** for salt and water. Why are salt and water considered to be special cases? For many reasons. Both are essential to survival in the short term. Animals can survive only a few days without fluid replenishment, and, as we saw in the case of D.W., salt is also a critical need.

Special Nature of Salt and Water.   Another indication of the "special" nature of salt and water is that every language around the globe has words for these nutrients. By contrast, no language (other than the language of science) has a word for "thiamine," "magnesium," "selenium," and other vitamins and minerals (including the words "vitamins" and "minerals"!). Salt joins sweet, bitter, and sour as one of the four "basic tastes," which, along with water, are presumably mediated by evolved receptors sensitive to substances with these tastes.

Specific hungers are mediated by peripheral receptors (CNS), neuroendocrine systems, and homeostatic mechanisms of the ANS. These interrelated systems comprise the innate equipment that allows us to regulate calories, electrolytes, minerals, and other specific nutrients. We will not cover these systems here. Rather, we will continue our focus upon the role learning plays in modifying and directing our innately organized eating and drinking behaviors.

BOX 8.2

Salt Craving and Personality Development: A Mystery Story

A baby known to us only by his initials, D. W., was born in the mid-1930s near Baltimore. What happened to him in his short lifetime contains the drama of a good mystery as well as an introduction into the complexities of appetite.

Sickly from birth, D. W. would drink milk only when mixed with water. He regurgitated most "solid" foods. A watery, salted gruel barely kept him alive. At about 18 months of age, physically and mentally slowed by dietary deficiencies, he began to say a few words—among them were "Ma-ma," "Wa-wa," and "Salt!" His mother described D. W.'s behavior at this time:

> As soon as he knew what the word "water" meant, he would cry for it every time he heard the word mentioned. And when he saw the river or the ocean, he always thought he had to have some to drink. We were finally able to explain to him that it wasn't drinking water.

And then he discovered the salt shaker.

> He poured some out and ate it by dipping his finger in it. After this he wouldn't eat any food without having the salt, too. . . . He really cried for it and acted like he had to have it . . . practically everything he liked real well was salty, such as crackers, pretzels, potato chips, olives, pickles, fresh fish, salt mackerel, crisp bacon, and most fruits and vegetables if I added more salt.

Between 1 and 3 years old, D. W.'s obsession with salt and water found him looking at pictures of lakes in magazines for hours. During playtime he made imaginary meals, which he always liberally "salted."

His parents obviously knew D. W.'s abnormal cravings were peculiar. But they must have been horrified when he then developed a truly freakish problem. The tiny child became virilized—he began growing pubic hair and an adult-sized penis. He was referred to Dr. Lawson Wilkins, the founder of pediatric endocrinology at Johns Hopkins School of Medicine. D. W. was admitted to a large children's ward and put on the standard hospital diet, presumably restricting access to salt and water. He died seven days after admission.

The child's death would be unnoted and unremarkable at the time were it not for Curt Richter, a scientist at Johns Hopkins University who had spent the latter part of the 1930s investigating how and why laboratory rats ate what they ate and drank what they drank. In the course of his experiments on appetite he had removed their adrenal glands. He found rats invariably died within a few days. If he gave them extra salt and ad lib water, however, they lived quite normally (Richter, 1936).

Richter heard about the boy in the hospital who craved salt. He contacted Wilkins and proposed that D. W.'s unusual salt craving suggested problems with his adrenal glands. Richter and Wilkins performed an autopsy and found an adrenal tumor (Wilkins & Richter, 1940). They correctly suspected that the tumor had been responsible for two separate disorders. Too much androgen had produced virilization, and too little aldosterone had caused overexcretion of salt in the child's urine. Salt and water restriction in the hospital presumably killed him. The child's obsession with salt and water had helped him survive for over three years—a remarkable example of the interplay of physiological regulation and the behavioral selection of essential nutrients in a preverbal child.

Carnivores, Herbivores, and Omnivores

The Omnivore's Paradox. As is the case with carnivores, herbivores, and all other living creatures, omnivores must secure from the environment those nutrients essential for survival. On the surface omnivory appears to be an ideal solution in meeting these needs; if plant sources dry up, eat meat (too bad, herbivores). If rabbits and small rodents disappear, eat plants (sorry, carnivores). The paradox facing the omnivore, however, is that this more open eating strategy increases our risk of making mistakes. If *everything* is fair game, recognize that *everything* includes toxic plants, *salmonella,* environmentally contaminated shellfish, etc. By being less specialized, a wide open system contains fewer safeguards. That is why omnivory, beneficial during famine, can also be detrimental to health and well-being. The foregoing cost-benefit analysis has been called the **omnivore's paradox** (Rozin & Kalat, 1971).

Interaction of Innately Organized and Learned Eating and Drinking Behaviors

As we saw in a previous chapter, one innately organized behavior that helps us resolve the omnivore's paradox is food *neophobia*—a wariness concerning new foods. Are there other adaptive behavioral strategies that function to aid in food selection? In Box 8.3 we examine the eating behavior of another child, named Jane. We assume that she has had less opportunity to *learn* to select foods than those humans who have eaten thousands of meals over several years. Her experiences allow us to see what innately predisposed behaviors she brings to this task. Some questions to keep in mind: What is the role of caretakers in Jane's culture? How well could she accomplish her food selection task without the help of adult caretakers?

Open Feeding Systems of Young Humans

What lessons can we learn from Jane B.'s case history of early omnivory?

1. In large measure, choices expressed by very young humans seem to be determined primarily by the *flavors* of food and drink. Preference for sweet may lead to the selection of (overall) less nutritious foods. A reinforcer is not choosy about the behavior it reinforces. (See the discussion by Pliner, Herman, & Polivy, 1990).

BOX 8.3

And This Is Normal?

Unlike D. W.'s earliest eating experiences (Box 8.2), Jane B. was a perfectly normal infant. She nursed healthily at mama's breast for one year and maintained an optimal growth curve; her physical and psychological development were textbook normal.

"Omnivory" begins with selecting choices from alternative foods as well as learning when, what, and where to eat. For example, at about ten months Jane B. was offered apple juice from a nursing bottle, and she drank avidly. On her first birthday she abruptly refused breast milk and all other animal milk offered her. (Mother was devastated.) Jane B. drank apple juice for the next eight to nine years of her life, and then other sweetened drinks; at age eleven she continues to reject milk but still loves her mother.

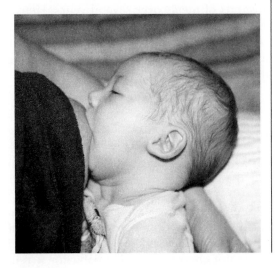

What did Jane B. learn from her first omnivorous (open) encounter? Did she learn that the sight of a baby bottle (CS) contained a very sweet fluid (US) that she could drink more rapidly than nursing from a breast? That is, was the sweeter, more rapidly attained apple juice a more potent reinforcer that shaped her preference over breast milk? In this particular instance, was the apple flavor and rapid glucose repletion more reinforcing than the overall more nutritious but less sweet, less rapidly digested milk? (These questions are not easily answered. See Weiffenbach, 1977.)

During the second year of her life Jane B. ate bread, fruit, ice cream, Jello®, some vegetables, and most anything sweet. No meat, poultry, or fish, and rarely cheese. She was avid about her likes and dislikes; she has always seemed to know exactly what and when she wanted to eat, and exactly what and when she did not want to eat. Familiar, not novel, foods were the rule. Two examples: From sixteen months to about two years of age she ate an egg and toast for every breakfast, seven days a week. One day she abruptly stopped eating eggs, and to the present day does not eat eggs (she prefers to not eat any breakfast). At age six she could not get enough of McDonald's Chicken McNuggets®; then as abruptly she rejected them. Any food item offered her that is either new, or that she no longer likes, is treated as poison, and the caretaker regarded as a probable assassin.

BOX 8.3

Continued

Jane B. has always had a wide variety of foods from which she was allowed to choose with few restrictions. In a busy household during her first four to five

years she ate pretty much on her own schedule, with only a nod to that of her family. While at grandmother's she was allowed to eat in the middle of the night if she woke up and was hungry. Grandmother's philosophy was to let her eat whatever she wanted, in whatever amount, around the clock (in a laboratory setting this is known as an *ad libitum*, or *ad lib*, feeding schedule—cf. *liberty*).

Bright, alert, and happy, at age 11 Jane B. is average in size (slightly thin) and above average in intellectual achievement. (Apparently her brain did manage to get enough protein during development, a constant source of worry for her parents.) Other than normal childhood diseases and accidents, her health appears to be near optimal. Congratulations, parents, for providing adequate genes, and an adequate environment.

---

2. Food *neophobia* (translated as finickyness) describes the overall pattern of eating among young humans. Moreover, the highly conservative food selections made by children belie labeling them "omnivorous."

3. Although the foods offered Jane B. were culturally determined, her selections were highly idiosyncratic. She seems to have learned from direct experience that "if it looks like A, then it tastes/smells like B." And "B," how it tastes and smells, *not* the caretaker's admonitions, guided her ingestive behavior.

4. Selecting one food and eating it nearly exclusively, and then abruptly switching, has been described as a "feeding jag" (Davis, 1939). We will discuss "feeding jags" as an adaptive specialization of eating in the next section. In her classical *cafeteria feeding studies*, Davis (1928, 1939) also concluded that *ad libitum* selections of type and amount of food could be as readily accomplished by rug rats as by adult caretakers.

5. Advice for new parents: (a) Prepare to worry about your child's nutrition (worrying about your child's nutrition is adaptive and contributes to your *inclusive fitness)*; (b) provide many alternative foods (some of them nutritious) from which your child can choose; (c) put the poisons out of reach; (d) get real laid back; and (e) get out of the way.

Learning About Foods; Eating and Becoming Ill

In Chapters 4 and 5 we used the phenomena of *conditioned taste aversions* to investigate and illuminate general properties of association formation. We saw that conditioned taste aversions decreased the preference for flavored foods and fluids, thereby influencing future food choices. For this reason, obviously, such conditioned aversions play a role in what animals eat and drink. In this section we shift our focus from general associative mechanisms to the specifics of how learning determines food choices.

The Role of Sickness in Learning to Recognize Nutrients. Paul Rozin and his colleagues posed research questions about specific hungers other than those for salt and water (Rodgers & Rozin, 1966; Rozin, 1967). Identifying, ingesting, and regulating salt, they reasoned, must be performed differently from the way animals locate other nutrients—thiamine, for example. Why? Because animals have not evolved taste receptors sensitive to approximately 100 other vitamins, minerals, and essential nutrients. These trace elements are typically masked within food complexes, and as such they are not consciously recognizable.

How Is Thiamine Recognized? Rozin and colleagues set out to determine how a trace element such as thiamine is recognized in diets. That is, how do animals know which foods contain thiamine if the latter cannot be detected by peripheral receptors? Recognize that this is not an academic question. On the contrary, the answer to this question would go a long way toward helping us understand how Jane B. managed to survive and thrive the first 11 years of life—by selecting the right foods, in the right amounts, and at the right times, from a variety of food sources.

Rats eating a diet lacking thiamine become *thiamine deficient*.[8] They lose appetite and weight, their coat does not shine, and they will die unless they replace the thiamine they lack. If given thiamine in a saccharin-flavored solution, they will avidly drink it, ingest the thi-

---

[8]The acute condition of thiamine deficiency in humans is called *Beri Beri*—a continuing problem in third world countries.

amine, and recover from the deficiency state. They tend to like the saccharin better than control rats, presumably because of the positive association of the flavor with recovery from sickness (Garcia, Ervin, Yorke, & Koelling, 1967). Other experiments have revealed that the analysis of increasing a flavor's preference by its association with recovery from deficiency is more complicated than suggested by Garcia et al. (1967). Zahorik, Mair, and Pies (1974) ran additional control groups that allowed Zahorik (1977) to analyze the problem as follows:

1. Animals learn to dislike the flavor of the thiamine deficient diet (i.e., the illness state of thiamine deficiency conditions a taste aversion to the *familiar–deficient* diet).
2. The *familiar–deficient* diet having become aversive, hungry rats overcome their innate *neophobia* and choose an alternative diet. If the alternative diet is familiar (and safe—*not* associated with thiamine deficiency), it is selected over a novel diet. Rats will select a novel diet in preference to a *familiar–deficient* diet.
3. Recovery from deficiency after eating a novel-flavored diet (which contains thiamine) increases the preference for that novel flavor. This *conditioned preference* is greater than controls who like the flavor merely because it has become familiar—*preference due to familiarity.*

It is to conditioned dietary preferences that we now turn.

Learning About Foods; Food as Reinforcers and Punishers

In the preceding examples we noted that salt detection differed from that of thiamine detection; we are conscious of salt on our tongue, but the taste of thiamine is not recognized in food. Thiamine is "recognized" by deficiency and recovery states caused by the flavored foods that alternatively lack and contain the substance, respectively.

Hedonic Conditioning.   What an interesting system! The possibility is raised that many dozens of nutrients are "unconsciously" regulated by an associative mechanism. Flavors of foods (of which we are presumably conscious) are associated with repletion of nutrients (of which we are unaware). Booth (1982) has called this regulation of nutrient selection by the association of flavored foods with their postingestional consequences **hedonic conditioning** (cf. hedonism). In his schema, following every meal flavors of foods consumed during that meal are hedonically adjusted according to their nutritional effects. If the consequences are positive (i.e., reinforcing), we increase our preference for the items most recently eaten. If the consequences are negative (i.e., punishing, such as when deficiency states are induced), we are less likely to continue eating those particular flavored foods.

Recall that rats prefer *familiar safe* diets to *novel* diets. A child's feeding jags (Davis, 1939) are followed by abrupt switches to new foods. Such switches may reflect the formation of conditioned aversions to a familiar–deficient diet. In the case history described in Box 8.3, Jane B.'s abrupt rejection of eggs may have reflected a shift to meet nutritional needs.

Generality of Conditioned Flavor Preferences.   Are changes in preference for flavored foods and beverages restricted to recovery from a thiamine deficiency state? No. The phenomenon is quite general. Increased preference for flavors has been associated with *protein replacement* (Baker, Booth, Duggan, & Gibson, 1987), *calories* (Bolles, Hayward, & Crandall, 1981; Mehiel & Bolles, 1984; Capaldi, Campbell, Sheffer, & Bradford, 1987); *recovery from gastrointestinal sickness* (Green & Garcia, 1971; Barker & Weaver, 1991); *ethanol (beer, spirits, etc.)* (Sherman, Hickis, Rice, Rusiniak, & Garcia, 1983; Deems, Oetting, Sherman, & Garcia, 1986); and a *physiological state accompanying low food deprivation* (Capaldi & Myers, 1982; Campbell, Capaldi, & Myers, 1987). Excellent evidence exists, then, to support Booth's notion of *hedonic conditioning*. The reader is referred to Capaldi and Powley (1990) for an overview.

Interim Summary

1. Eating and drinking behaviors are best understood as an interplay of genes and environment, of physiology and behavior.
2. In addition to taste and olfactory receptors that allow the location of foodstuffs in the environment, homeostatic mechanisms have evolved to regulate essential nutrients.
3. The concept of *biocultural evolution* views the food selection and food preparation process as evolutionary determinants. Feeding behaviors that are adaptive are selected for because they enhance inclusive fitness. What humans learn about foods during their lifetime and transmit to their offspring complements (a) basic taste and smell receptors and (b) homeostatic regulatory processes.
4. Salt and water are examples of *specific hungers*. Both peripheral receptors and homeostatic mechanisms have evolved to recognize and regulate these critically essential nutrients.
5. Human are omnivores. The *omnivore's paradox* is that their relatively more open feeding system allows them a diverse range of potential foods, but increases the risks of ingesting toxins.

6. Children often display profound food preferences, food *neophobias*, and prolonged *feeding jags*. They also manage to self-select foods without adverse consequences.

7. General associative mechanisms complement innately organized eating and drinking behavior. Essential nutrients such as thiamine seem to be regulated by learning which flavors produce postingestional deficiency or recovery states.

8. The punishing and reinforcing properties of foods experienced postingestionally, called *hedonic conditioning,* appear to complement innate flavor preferences in determining food selections.

VII. Role of Conditioning in Behavioral Disorders and Behavioral Therapy

By the mid-1970s a growing number of health care professionals were advocating major revisions in the basic way physicians and patients alike viewed issues of health (Knowles, 1977). A **biopsychosocial model** of health was proposed as the most meaningful alternative to an outmoded **biomedical model.** The coup was bloodless. Cultural practices, learned behavior, and genetically determined anatomy and physiology are now viewed as interlocking determinants of an individual's health. Figure 8.2 is one version of the contemporary understanding of the determinants of health.

Earlier in this chapter we reviewed strong evidence attesting to the power of the associative conditioning of immune system responses. We also saw that both the perception of pain and a drug's effectiveness could be markedly influenced by learning experiences. Finally, the open feeding systems of omnivores allow not only ingestional errors such as poisoning and nutritional deficiency, but also the possibility of eating disorders in the form of clinical obesity, anorexia nervosa, and bulimia. Clinical obesity, anorexia nervosa, and bulimia are three examples of disorders whose etiology and treatment fall within the purview of *behavioral medicine*. In this section we will review several conditioning examples that have implications for health, and then look ahead to the promising integration offered by behavioral medicine.

Animal Models of Neurosis and Conditioned Fear

Experimental Neurosis.   Remember Pavlov's experiment in Chapter 4 in which he conditioned a dog to discriminate between a circle and an ellipse (see Figure 4.12)? When the ellipse became too similar to the circle, the discrimination broke down, and, as was noted at that time, so did the dog. The biting and snarling behavior exhibited when the discrimination was further tested—when the dog continued to be pushed and challenged beyond its perceptual capacities—indicated to Pavlov a strong link between the dog's personal experience and its mental health. His dog's behavior changed for several weeks and extended beyond the immediate testing situation into other aspects of its life. Pavlov labeled the phenomenon **experimental neurosis.** He thought his model had direct parallels with some examples of human neurotic behavior.

What do you think? Can you relate Pavlov's findings to what you know about human responses to stressful situations? When faced with deciding how to split your study time the night before three tests, are there emotional consequences? Pavlov noted individual differences in how dogs responded to training. Do you know your limits?

Conditioning Emotional Responses in Humans.   In Chapter 4 we discussed *conditioned suppression*, perhaps the most widely used method of investigating associative processes. Recall that when a tone or light (CS) is repeatedly paired with electric shock (US), the neutral stimulus takes on shocklike properties. Rats, dogs, and humans respond fearfully in the presence of the formerly neutral stimulus (see also Box 4.1, p. 125). Such conditioned fear responses are presumed to be the basis for both phobias and anxiety. Why posit learning, as opposed to innately predisposed behavioral patterns? Because both phobias and anxiety are highly idiosyncratic among individuals, and classical conditioning continues to be the best way to account for their origins (Davey, 1992). Let us look at a historical example.

Watson and "Little Albert."   John B. Watson asserted that human behavior could be controlled by reinforcing and punishing stimuli (see Box 6.3, p. 227). His infamous experiments on "Little Albert" bear directly upon questions of emotional health and well-being, the etiology of phobias, and related issues in behavioral medicine. Assuming that humans innately have three basic emotions—fear, rage, and love—upon which all other behaviors are based, Watson and Rayner (1920) conditioned a fear response in an eleven-month-old child named Albert. Their point was to demonstrate that innate fears could be arbitrarily attached to any neutral stimulus, the result being a maladaptive phobic response. On numerous occasions in his laboratory, Watson showed Albert a white rat (CS) and paired it with a very loud clanging noise (US). Albert soon responded in the presence of the white rat in the same way he responded to the loud noise; he startled, cried, and initiated escape responses.

Given the wealth of findings from general process learning, it should come as no surprise that Watson's "attachment" of fear responses through conditioning was found to *generalize* to other furry objects presented Albert, including an inanimate fur coat and a Santa Claus mask. Indeed, the whole gamut of related associative phenomena might have been used to analyze the extent of Albert's emotional conditioning. Perhaps fortunately, Albert was removed from Watson's and Rayner's care before treatment of this phobia could be initiated. They were prepared to present the fear-inducing white rat and stimulate Albert's genitals at the same time so as to attach pleasurable feelings to the rat (Watson & Rayner, 1920).

Anyone care to predict another likely outcome? We will look at more reasonable treatment strategies in the last section of this chapter.

Posttraumatic Stress Disorder and Learned Helplessness

Ample evidence attests to the positive health outcomes of many of life's experiences. In a very real sense the status of our health "when things go right" provides the control condition by which to gauge compromised health caused when bad things happen to people. For example, the health we enjoy due to the foods we normally eat may only become appreciated during times of malaise caused by famine or poisoning. Pain makes us appreciate its absence. Likewise, the role that catastrophe, trauma, and Thorndike's annoyers (i.e., loud clangs, mild electric shock, and gastrointestinal distress) play in our health gets our attention precisely because so often the behavioral consequences of these events are unusually unpleasant and long lasting.

Posttraumatic stress disorder (PTSD) sometimes results in individuals who experience intense aversive stimuli. The human response to overwhelming events that occur during war, and as a result of rape, child abuse, and natural disasters (fires, hurricanes, etc.), is often severe and unique enough to be categorized as a disorder in the DSM-III-R (*Diagnostic and Statistical Manual of Mental Disorders, Third Edition, Revised; American Psychiatric Assn.*).

The incidence of PTSD in the general population is estimated to be as high as 9.2 percent (Breslau, Davis, Andreski, & Peterson, 1991), compared with estimates of drug abuse (5.9 percent) and depression (8.3 percent) (Solomon, Gerrity, & Muff, 1992). Box 8.4 highlights one individual who still suffers from PTSD decades after the trauma was experienced.

Other humans have suffered similar trauma and returned to full functioning within months. Why after the passage of many years does this otherwise talented, intelligent individual continue to suffer debilitating nightmares, continue to reexperience the trauma of war via memories and flashbacks, and continue to be severely hyperreactive (for example, put his fist through a wall in response to a minor hassle)? Some forms of PTSD are considered to be associative, i.e., a spe-

BOX 8.4

A Day to Relive the Rest of Your Life

"Thwack-thwack-thwack-thwack."

The relentless roar of the Medevac's blades drowned out all but the staccato bursts of automatic weapons fire punctuated by confused shouting, screams, and cries. The firefight had turned disastrous. A few retreating soldiers were alternatively dragging their wounded to the chopper, then briefly standing to return fire from the sweltering clearing back into the dark jungle canopy.

"Thwack-thwack-thwack-thwack."

A young marine manned the machine gun mounted on the chopper. He provided continuous cover for the retreating Americans by sweeping an arc of bullets just over their heads toward the advancing ARVN regulars. The intense fear, anger, and excitement of combat. And then, to his horror, he watched his bullets decapitate one of his comrades.

He continued firing, screaming, cursing . . .

"Thwack-thwack-thwack-thwack."

---

cial type of conditioned emotional response (Kolb, 1984). The distinctive sounds of a helicopter, for example, may elicit intense conditioned fear responses. The "conditioned response," however, may be of such intensity that the person reports reliving or reexperiencing the original event. No other examples of conditioned responses having this characteristic come to mind.

Other features of the disorder (explosive outbursts, atypical dreams, hyperirritability, and startle reflex) seem to be better described in terms of *sensitization*. One prominent researcher (van der Kolk, 1987) invokes Pavlov's notion of an innate reflexive response, or defensive reaction, to environmental threat. Reflexes, however, typically are adaptive; they promote inclusive fitness. By contrast, the PTSD response pattern would appear to be maladaptive. The interested reader is referred to van der Kolk (1987) for an in-depth analysis of this fascinating disorder.

Learned helplessness is another apparently maladaptive behavior pattern, described by Seligman and Maier (1967). In research using dozens of dogs, they found that following administration of intense electric shocks, two of every three dogs failed to respond adaptively thereafter. In Chapter 3 it was argued that intense electric shocks should *sensitize* the dogs, making them tend to respond to future electric shocks even more vigorously. Following Seligman's treatment, though, dogs described as helpless are immobile; in the presence of shock, though unrestrained, they whine and defecate but do not try to escape the shock by moving away. This *reduction* in responsiveness is opposite to some PTSD behavior just described—namely, explosive outbursts, hyperirritability, and startle reflex. It *is* characteristic of other PTSD victims whose response to rape, for example, is sometimes characterized by immobility, passivity, helplessness, and dissociative memory (Burgess & Holstrom, 1979). Why the responses to intense aversive stimuli are so unpredictable is unknown.

Learned Helplessness in Humans. The findings of the learned helplessness research with dogs and rats have been applied to humans (Seligman, 1975). In his earliest formulation Seligman identified three consequences of learned helpless training in humans: namely, *motivational, cognitive,* and *emotional* deficits. The motivational deficit is characterized by performance changes not unlike those seen in dogs. Whereas dogs will not bother to get off the grid floor to avoid electric shock, a human might not get out of bed for several days. Along with this reduction in a human's behavioral response is his or her *cognitive* interpretation that "responding is futile." Finally, *emotional* distress accompanies both the performance decrements and cognitive ideation. People who perceive themselves as helpless and depressed simply feel bad.

Critics of Seligman's (1975) theory pointed out that not all people who are subjected to uncontrollable events suffer these three deficits (Buchwald, Coyne, & Cole, 1978). For example, some individuals continue to live relatively normal lives even after having found out that they have a terminal illness with only months to live. Nevertheless, learned helplessness theory does fit the response patterns of many individuals, and it continues to receive serious attention in psychophysiological theories of stress and other psychosomatic disorders. For example, withdrawal and concomitant depression are common responses seen in college students who fail the first test, study hard for the second one, and then fail it. In this example, which response(s) is withdrawn in the face of what "uncontrollable events"?[9]

Eating Disorders: Anorexia Nervosa, Bulimia, and Obesity

Earlier in this chapter evidence was offered supporting two views of human ingestional behavior; i.e., that it is both innately organized and culturally determined (i.e., learned). The prevalence of eating disorders in our culture is hard evidence for ingestional *plasticity.* Some individuals learn to override the multiply redundant homeostatic

[9]Studying and class attendance, because neither response seems to affect the grades earned on tests.

mechanisms that are designed to preclude disorders such as anorexia nervosa and bulimia.

Failures of Primary Reinforcers and Punishers. Because the topic is highly visible, very few readers are unaware of the prevalence of eating disorders in our culture. The etiology of *anorexia nervosa* and *bulimia* is unknown, and because of a paucity of animal models for these disorders, they will likely remain a mystery for some time. That these disorders are due to maladaptive learned behavior is assumed (Hsu, 1990). The sequences of conditioning experiences underlying such learning have never been described, however. In both instances *secondary reinforcers* seem to be maintaining these behaviors. Primary reinforcers (i.e., alleviating hunger in anorexia nervosa) and normally punishing stimuli (vomiting in bulimia) no longer function to reinforce and punish behavior, respectively. Alternatively, the learned (mis)perception of thinness serves to act as a reinforcing stimulus maintaining the maladaptive eating behaviors.

Pain as Reinforcement. Under the slogan "no pain, no gain" athletes use the response-produced stimuli of exertion and pain to motivate yet greater pain-producing exertion. Such behavior is not considered maladaptive. Rather, the more bench press repetitions, or miles run, the greater the pleasure of attaining personal goals.

The intense motivation of the anorexic to stay thin appears to be achieved in a similar manner. *Not* responding to the hunger pains (normally unpleasant, and simply alleviated) to achieve the goal of thinness becomes highly reinforcing. The trick of the masochist is to perceive normally painful stimuli as pleasurable; then the *law of effect* continues to work as predicted. Though maladaptive, anorexia nervosa and bulimia should not be considered as exceptions to the law of effect. Rather, hunger and pain become discriminative stimuli to *not* eat. Furthermore, the ingestion of tasty food sets the occasion for vomiting in the bulimic, and it serves as highly effective punishment for the anorexic.

Obesity. Merely overweight, or obese? Obesity has been defined as being 40 percent or more above the ideal weight as determined by Metropolitan (standard) weight charts (Bray, 1976). And, although classified as an eating disorder, and typically included in the same discussions with anorexia nervosa and bulimia, obesity is both more familiar and better understood than the "thin" disorders. One difference is that being overweight is not nearly as life threatening as anorexia nervosa. At 20 percent above average weight, only very slight increases in morbidity and mortality exist. At 40 percent above average, however, overweight men are two and a half times more likely to die from all causes (Van Itallie, 1979).

Food as Reinforcer.   Clearly the role of learning in creating obesity is different from the other two eating disorders in that tasty foods reinforce the behavior of eating tasty foods. As in any other situation, reinforcement increases the frequency of the preceding behavior. A simple view of obesity, then, is one in which normal homeostatic control mechanisms are overridden by the reinforcing power of tasty foods. Animal models support this theory. Rats allowed a frequently changing diet of bananas, chocolate, chocolate chip cookies, cheese, fat, marshmallows, peanut butter, sweetened condensed milk, and salami gained 269 percent more weight than controls eating lab chow (Sclafani & Springer, 1976). Furthermore, sugar and fat mixed together produced greater weight gains than diets of sugar, or fat, or lab chow alone (Lucas & Sclafani, 1990).

The animal model just described does not begin to account for the individual differences observed among humans. Although there is some evidence (Jirik-Babb & Katz, 1988) that bulimics and anorexics are *less* sensitive to tastes (and, arguably, are less reinforced for eating tasty food) and that flavors are *more* reinforcing for the obese (Schiffman, 1983), these disorders are presumably under more complex stimulus control than merely the taste of foods. Both self-perception and learned social roles are precipitating conditions, and changing maladaptive cognitive and emotional variables are common therapeutic goals in dealing with these disorders.

Let us turn to behavioral therapy.

Behavioral Therapies

Behavioral therapy (and cognitive behavior therapy) is among the most successful of the various psychotherapies used to effect changes in maladaptive cognitive and emotional behaviors. The fact that the various techniques now used in behavioral therapy were developed using Pavlovian conditioning models is reflected in their earliest descriptions; i.e., *conditioned reflex therapy* (Salter, 1949) and the *conditioning therapies* (Wolpe, Salter, & Reyna, 1964). Likewise, one of the more important methodologies used in therapy, **behavior modification,** is a direct application of Skinner's operant conditioning by employing extinction procedures and the systematic application of reinforcers and punishers to change target behaviors.

Systematic Desensitization.   Suppose during his thirties "Little Albert" had presented himself to a psychotherapist for treatment due to an inordinate fear of animals—especially dogs—that interfered with his job as a letter carrier. During an interview with his patient, the therapist attempts to determine the boundaries of Albert's phobia. All animals? Furry animals? Large or small animals? Neither knowing nor especially caring about the reasons underlying the phobia, the behavioral therapist tries to *target* the specific behavior in question, and to get some idea of the extent of the *generalization gradient* around the target behavior

Albert's therapist would probably have decided to employ a common behavioral technique called *systematic desensitization.* Systematic desensitization involves first extinguishing fear responses to stimuli far removed from the target, then systematically approaching the sensitive target behavior in small steps, allowing responses to extinguish at each step. For example, while in a relaxed state the therapist might ask Albert to visualize an elephant sleeping safely behind bars in a zoo. Assuming that Albert showed no fear responses (ANS activity—altered breathing, sweating, nausea) to this image, the therapist might direct Albert to visualize the animal awakening, beginning to move, getting to its feet, etc. A next step might be to ask Albert to visualize the cage bars being removed, or to have him visually walk to another cage containing a furry animal such as a lion.

The fear responses evoked by these images are allowed to extinguish in the safety of the therapist's office. Assuming that the target response to be alleviated is *fear in the presence of dogs,* the therapist is little by little incorporating more of the distinguishing characteristics of dogs in situations that have caused the patient's past fear responses. *Say the word "dog"* (Allow Extinction of Conditioned Fear Response—AECFR). *Imagine the dog barking* (AECFR). *See the stuffed toy dog* (AECFR). *Approach the stuffed toy dog* (AECFR). *Touch the stuffed toy dog* (AECFR). *See the live dog from a distance* (AECFR). *Approach the live dog* (AECFR). *Touch the live dog* (AECFR). *Walk the neighborhood* (AECFR).

Biofeedback. **Biofeedback** refers to a procedure in which a patient (or experimental subject) is provided "feedback" regarding unconscious physiological processes. For example, even though alpha waves (8–13 cycles per second) are frequently produced by the human brain, we are not normally aware of this or any other pattern of brainwaves. Biofeedback equipment can be programmed to monitor a particular waveform, and to signal the subject by beeping when the waveform occurs. When patients are then asked to "make it beep" by outputting alpha, they can do so "voluntarily" even though, when asked, they report "I don't know how I'm doing it." In and of itself, this demonstration indicates that conscious control can be exerted over involuntary processes. From a training perspective, the target waveform can be considered an operant response, and the beeper a secondary reinforcer via verbal instructions. (A therapist, for example, might say "good" when the patient is successfully producing alpha; the beeper is associated with "good.") That the reinforcement procedure is effective is evidenced by the increased frequency of outputting alpha.

In addition to changes in brainwaves, other physiological responses that can be manipulated by biofeedback reinforcement procedures are muscle tension, skin temperature, blood pressure, heart rate, gastric motility, and skin conductance. That such physiological changes can be accomplished in the laboratory is not in question. The usefulness of biofeedback as behavioral therapy, however, is controversial. For example, comparison of biofeedback with relaxation training for headache pain (Blanchard, Andrasik, Ahles, Teders, & O'Keefe, 1980) and for control of blood pressure (Blanchard & Epstein, 1977) has led some researchers to question its practical clinical usefulness. Relaxation training appears to be equally effective, and it does not require the expensive instrumentation used in biofeedback.

Analysis of Biofeedback Efficiency.   Given that biofeedback training is a form of operant conditioning, and that operant conditioning has proven to be a highly effective way to train instrumental responses, we might ask why biofeedback is not a more effective therapeutic procedure. In the first place, biofeedback uses a rather weak secondary reinforcer to effect permanent psychophysiological changes. Recall that in a biofeedback situation the reinforcement procedure of verbal praise ("good") follows the target psychophysiological response. Pavlov's *second signal system* describes how verbal praise (the word "good") attains its reinforcing value due to second-order conditioning. The beeper sound is then paired with "good"; any reinforcing value of the beeper is attained by conditioning of the third order. Indeed, outside of the biofeedback situation it is unlikely that the beeper would have any reinforcing value at all. Secondly, outside of a one-hour training session once or twice weekly, the conditioned change in the target psychophysiological response is "in extinction." Since these target responses are for the most part not consciously experienced, there is no awareness of the response-outcome contingency. The conditioned response can therefore extinguish without the person realizing that it is. To summarize, it is highly likely that the therapeutic goals of biofeedback are not being realized because of less than optimal operant conditioning methods during acquisition, and due to simple extinction of the conditioned response.

Diverse Applications of Behavioral Therapy.   Controversy over the long-term effectiveness of biofeedback aside for the moment, in general terms the treatment of phobias and other psychophysiological disorders involving the ANS using behavioral modification techniques is highly effective. Outcome studies generally indicate the long-term remediation of symptoms, with little recidivism. That behavioral therapies can be as effective as invasive biomedical therapies (such as drugs and surgery) has been demonstrated for such disorders as low back pain (Heinrich, Cohen, Naliboff, Collins, & Bonebakker, 1985; Fordyce, Brockway, Bergman, & Spengler, 1986); survival time in terminal cancer (Grossarth-Maticek & Eysenck, 1989); pain management (Turk, Meichenbaum, & Genest, 1983); and enuresis (Kimmel & Kimmel, 1970). Box 8.5 shows how behavioral therapy can be used as an alternative to biomedical therapy.

BOX 8.5

Bladder Control: Surgery or Behavioral Modification?

What was merely an embarrassment to the five-year-old was perceived as a major problem to mom. Every day, a half dozen or more wet underpants accumulated in the laundry, testimony to a weak external sphincter connecting the child's bladder with her urethra. Her incontinence occurred while playing, when excited at her dance competitions, and if she waited too long between voidings.

Though behavioral modification is now recognized as a treatment of choice for this condition (Philips, Fenster, & Samson, 1988), 20 years ago "exploratory" surgery was recommended. When no pathology was detected, physically "stretching" the urethra, it was alleged, would subsequently allow for more voluntary control over urination.

After consulting with a pediatric urologist, and rejecting the suggestion of performing this invasive procedure under general anesthesia, her parents initiated a "home" behavioral modification program instead. In a busy household, the first two

steps in her program were combined and accomplished at the same time; that is, determining how many times each day the

BOX 8.5

Continued

five-year-old urinated (determining her *baseline of bladder voiding*) and simultaneously increasing her sensitivity to the cues attendant with urination. The latter is especially difficult, because even adults suffering from *female urethral syndrome* report few prevoiding sensations (Bernstein, Philips, Linden, & Fenster, 1992). The child was asked to make a mark on "her chart" by the toilet each time she urinated. Her behavioral treatment was both simple and noninvasive. If, when she went to urinate, she discovered dry underpants, she was asked to place a gold stick-on star on her chart. If she discovered wet underpants, she merely changed herself and put an "x" on the chart instead of the star. At the end of each day she received a dime for each star. The dependent variables, then, were *frequency of micturition,* and *daily count of wet underpants.*

From Chapter 6 we can identify the relevant components of this behavior modification program. Her *baseline,* or *operant level,* of micturition was determined by the first day's count of stars and "x's." Discovering wet underpants (a) increased her awareness of the problem behavior to be changed and (b) helped focus her attention on subtle prevoiding sensations. The foregoing intervention consisted of several forms of *reinforced* and *punished* behaviors using the following stimuli:

Primary reinforcers

- (a) Parental attention and interest (and the absence of parental concern and disappointment) and (b) the comfort of dry underpants

Secondary reinforcers

- Gold stars, dimes, and words of praise

Punishers

- Discomfort of wet underpants and loss of expected gold stars and dimes

What was the success of this program? The short-term and long-term outcome was mixed. The frequency of "wet pants" went down rapidly within the first few days. Among the behaviors that had been reinforced was "spending more time on the toilet," and in part the decreased frequency of "wet pants" can be attributed to the fact that she wore them less and sat on the toilet more. Increasing her frequency of attempted bladder voidings was a desirable outcome, because it helped her focus on the attendant sensations preceding micturition, and also because frequent bladder emptying is healthier than prolonged urine retention. In addition, the five-year-old's successes gave her a sense of personal control. As time passed, she was encouraged to regard occasional incontinence as "accidents." That is, her parents communicated to her that her self-worth would not be measured by absolute continence, and that more girls than boys had this problem because of different plumbing.

Her "occasional" problem persisted, however, and at age 13 she exercised her option (as an adult responsible for her own health) to have the exploratory surgery previously described. Six months post-surgery she reported no changes— that is, on certain occasions of intense

BOX 8.5

Continued

physical activity and/or excitement she continued to lose voluntary control in retaining her urine. In discussing this problem with her female friends, similar outcomes following their surgeries were reported.

Given the baseline degree of incontinence in this five-year-old, behavioral therapy was effective in changing her behavior without general anesthesia, surgery, or drugs. The secondary gains of enhanced self-esteem and personal control have no counterpart in traditional biomedical approaches. The interested reader is referred to Philips et al. (1988).

Evaluating Behavioral Therapy. How effective is behavioral therapy? We saw in the foregoing that phobias are successfully treated. Some problem behaviors are more resistant to therapeutic intervention than others, however. For example, programs to change drinking alcohol, smoking tobacco, and weight control behaviors have follow-up success rates of only 20 to 30 percent (Kaplan, 1984). Extrapolation of laboratory results using short-term behavior change in laboratory animals to lifelong habits of humans is problematic. Adult humans in therapy must overcome literally years of reinforced trials, and neither therapists nor patients should expect one-hour weekly sessions to reverse these lifetime habits. Such cautions, however, are tempered by the observation that both behavior therapy and *cognitive behavior therapy* are the most efficacious of the various types of psychotherapy. For example, for treating PTSD, better outcomes result from behavioral techniques than the use of drugs or other forms of therapy (Solomon et al., 1992).

Interim Summary

1. A *biopsychosocial* model of health has replaced a strictly *biomedical* model.
2. Pavlov and others have investigated animal models of neurosis in laboratory settings.
3. Conditioning emotional responses such as fear and anxiety is easily accomplished in humans and other animals.
4. Posttraumatic stress disorder (PTSD) and learned helplessness occasionally result from intense aversive stimulation. These disorders can be analyzed from both associative and nonassociative perspectives.

5. Eating disorders such as anorexia nervosa, bulimia, and obesity are maladaptive but are explainable by the application of the law of effect. In obesity, the reinforcing effects of palatable foods override homeostatic regulatory mechanisms. In the "thin" disorders, secondary reinforcing effects of "perceived image" override the primary reinforcers of palatable foods.

6. *Behavioral therapies* (or conditioning therapies) are effective and noninvasive methods used in *behavioral medicine*. In *behavior modification*, problem behaviors are identified and modified by the systematic application of reinforcers and punishers, by systematic desensitization, and by biofeedback.

Summary

1. Learning theory can be applied to analyze the interaction of physiology and behavior. Animal models of drug-taking behavior, ingestional behavior, and immune system functioning provide insight into complex human behavior in these realms.

2. Historical distinctions tying instrumental conditioning to central nervous system functioning, and Pavlovian conditioning to the ANS have broken down for two reasons: general agreement that common processes underlie S-S and R-S conditioning, and demonstrated interactions of CNS, ANS, and endocrine and immune system functioning.

3. Psychosomatic (cf. psychophysiological) disorders have their origin in Pavlovian conditioning. Apparently any physiological reflex can be conditioned—including blisters. Words/beliefs often function as conditioned stimuli that control responses.

4. Psychoneuroimmunology defines a research area in which immune system functioning can come under the control of previously neutral stimuli. Both immunosuppression and immunofacilitation of T-lymphocytes can be conditioned. Psychoneuroimmunology provides the mechanism by which thoughts can have an effect on immune system functioning.

5. Drugs such as morphine and ethyl alcohol can function as unconditioned stimuli. By entering into association with environmental cues, the pharmacological effects of drugs can be enhanced or reduced by environmental cues. In this way drug tolerance can be understood as a conditioned response, rather than merely being a pharmacological phenomenon. Drugs can also function as reinforcers that increase drug-taking behavior.

6. Ingestional behavior reflects evolutionary predispositions in the form of innate flavor receptors and homeostatic regulatory mechanisms. The latter include innate recognition of certain foodstuffs like salt and water, called specific hungers, and specialized eating behaviors such as "feeding jags" and neophobia.

7. Ingestional behavior also has plastic components, including the conditioning of flavor aversions and flavor preferences. More subtle conditioning based upon application of the law of effect, called hedonic conditioning, is a mechanism that regulates and readjusts food preferences based upon each meal's postingestive consequences.

8. Behavioral disorders including phobias and other conditioned fear responses are understood in terms of laboratory models initially developed by Pavlov ("experimental neurosis") and John B. Watson (who conditioned "Little Albert"). PTSD is a more serious disorder resulting from intense aversive experiences that seems to have both associative and nonassociative components. Disorders of eating behavior (anorexia nervosa, bulimia, and obesity) are also learned.

9. Behavioral therapies, including behavioral modification, extinguish as well as reinforce (or punish) target behaviors to effect the desired behavioral change. Behavioral medicine employs a variety of animal-based methodologies as therapeutic alternatives to invasive procedures such as drugs and surgery.

Discussion Questions

1. Charged with buying illegal amounts of Valium, a 24-year-old college student from Austin, Texas, spent almost 10 months in a prison in Reynosa, Mexico, surviving there without her asthma medication. Two hours after her release in September 1992, she suffered an asthma attack while her parents drove her across the border into southern Texas. A lifelong asthma sufferer, she died a few hours later in an American hospital. Can you think of some reasons why her attack might have been so severe the day she reentered the United States?

2. Ted drinks five beers at a party, while his twin brother Ned consumes the same amount of alcohol "bar hopping." Given equal histories with alcohol (and, hence, equivalent amounts of alcohol tolerance), which twin would you predict would be the most wasted after five drinks? Why? Under what conditions might they be similarly affected?

3. *Dorland's Illustrated Medical Dictionary, 25th Edition,* (1974; W. B. Saunders Press) defines **pica** as "a craving for unnatural articles of food; a depraved appetite, as seen in hysteria, pregnancy, and in malnourished children." What reasons can you come up with for changes in appetite in these three categories of "abnormality"?

4. Is conscious awareness necessary for a person to exhibit voluntary behavior? Must a person be "aware" of the response being made for that response to be reinforced? Must a rat be aware of its lymphocytes for them to decrease or increase in number, depending upon whether the rat tastes saccharin following a conditioning episode? Must a preverbal human be "aware" of the relationship of his or her responses to the reinforcing or punishing stimulus that changes those responses?

5. *Pseudocyesis* is a psychosomatic condition more commonly known as "false pregnancy." In addition to cessation of the menstrual cycle, some females experience breast swelling, morning sickness, pica, and, as the ninth month approaches, the appearance of *colostrum* (a clear, sweet fluid that precedes breast milk), the onset of labor, and dilation of the cervix in preparation for "delivery." In pseudocyesis there is no fetus. Women who experience the most symptoms previously have had a child or have read about the sequences of symptoms. Most

such women "want" to be pregnant and grieve when they find out they have merely experienced some of the signs of pregnancy. Can you make the case that pregnancy is an elaborate nine-month "reflex" and that pseudocyesis is a conditioned reflex?

6. Any analysis of pseudocyesis would employ the concept of "expectancy" (no pun intended). A woman "expects" she might be pregnant and "expects" what changes will occur in her body. Can animals have "expectancies"? Does Pavlov's dog expect food when the bell rings? Where do our expectancies come from?

7. Finding yourself in a biofeedback situation, you are faced with an hour of "making the beeper come on." At the end of the hour, you are informed that you kept the beeper on for a total of 5 minutes out of the 60 you were in the chair. The next session, the therapist reminds you of your previous performance and suggests you try to keep the beeper on for a few more minutes. Now imagine an alternative biofeedback session—one in which you accumulate points that can be traded in for money. For the sake of the argument, let us say $5 for every minute you keep the beeper on. Would you perform better the first session? The second and third sessions? Would you be more likely to output the target response outside of the biofeedback session given money rather than hearing a beeper sound during training? Before we write off biofeedback as a bad therapeutic procedure, wouldn't you like to see it tried under some conditions other than "keeping the beeper on"?

Glossary

Behavioral Medicine An interdisciplinary field concerned with the etiology of illness and wellness, preventative medicine, biofeedback and other forms of psychophysiology, and treatment and rehabilitation strategies.

Behavioral Therapy Any psychotherapeutic procedure involving the systematic application of reinforcers or punishers, or the implementation of extinction or other classical or operant procedures, known to be effective in effecting behavioral change.

Behavioral Tolerance That portion of total drug tolerance that can be attributed to learned, or environmental, variables, as opposed to pharmacodynamic variables.

Behavior Modification The systematic application of reinforcers, punishers, extinction, and other classical and operant conditioning procedures to change target behaviors.

Biocultural Evolution The process by which the selection, preparation, and consumption of particular types of food by some individuals gives them a reproductive advantage, which, over time, has probably led to the divergence of human populations. (Proposed by S. Katz.)

Biofeedback A procedure used in both research and therapy in which a human subject is made aware of and can gain voluntary control over his or her involuntary processes (such as brainwaves, heart rate, skin conductance, etc.) through differential reinforcement.

Biomedical Model The traditional approach to health care that, in emphasizing anatomy and physiology, assumes that almost all illness can be attributed to a specific pathogen or specific biochemical malfunction.

Biopsychosocial Model   An approach to health care that attempts to integrate cultural, social, psychological, and behavioral approaches with the traditional biomedical model.

Compensatory Responses   See *conditioned compensatory responses.*

Conditioned Compensatory Responses (Siegel)   In pairings of environmental stimuli with certain drug USs, the form of the conditioned response is opposite to the normal drug response. Example: Morphine causes hyperthermia, and CSs paired with morphine often produce hypothermic responses, possibly as compensation in achieving homeostasis.

Conditioned Facilitation   Pavlovian conditioning experiments in which the end result is to *increase* antibody production in the immune system.

Conditioned Immunosuppression   Pavlovian conditioning experiments in which the end result is to decrease antibody production in the immune system.

Experimental Neurosis (Pavlov)   The end result of a conditioning experiment in which an animal is required to perform beyond its capacity to discriminate between two similar stimuli. The animal becomes emotionally distraught and refuses to participate further in the experiment.

Hedonic Conditioning   A theory proposed by David Booth to account for meal-to-meal changes in particular foods selected based upon the positive or negative postingestional consequences of previous selections. Tastes and textures are CSs that become associated with postingestional consequences (USs).

Involuntary Behavior   Physiology and behavior under the control of the autonomic nervous system. Unintentional, unwillful behavior. (cf. *reflex, voluntary behavior.*)

Law of Parsimony   The strategy of explaining phenomena in terms of simple, rather than by appealing to complex, mechanisms and/or processes. (Also known as Occam's Razor or Morgan's Canon.)

Omnivore's Paradox   Omnivores eat a wide variety of food sources, thereby enhancing fitness during famine. Paradoxically, eating from a wide variety of food sources also increases their risk of poisoning, thereby *diminishing* fitness. (Paradox posed by Paul Rozin.)

Pharmacological Tolerance   That portion of total drug tolerance which can be attributed to pharmacodynamic properties of drugs.

Pica   Unusual appetite or craving for "unnatural" foodstuffs, such as chalk or clay.

Posttraumatic Stress Disorder (PTSD) PTSD is a disorder characterized by one or more of the following symptoms: intense fear, feelings of helplessness, and recurrent intrusive memories/dreams, whose etiology is thought to be caused by an unusual, markedly distressing event such as rape, battle fatigue, etc.

Psychoneuroimmunology   The field of research attempting to describe and integrate the interconnectedness of the immune system, the central and autonomic nervous systems, and behavior.

Psychosomatic Disorders   Disorders of anatomy and/or physiology that can be attributed in part to psychological or behavioral variables.

Specific Hungers   The translation of physiological needs into cravings and hungers for specific, identifiable nutrients. Examples are cravings for salt and water.

Tolerance   Changes in the effectiveness of drugs taken repeatedly, as measured by the necessity to increase a drug dosage to get the same effect, or as measured by the decreased effectiveness of a given drug dosage taken repeatedly.

Voluntary Behavior   Physiology and behavior under the control of the central nervous system. Intentional, willful behavior. (cf. *reflex, involuntary behavior.*)

9

Choice Behavior

I. Introduction

Decisions, decisions. Two tests tomorrow—do I study psychology or Spanish? Gaining weight—should I eat dessert or not? Call Margaret or mom first? Watch my favorite program on television or listen to my newest CD? Study now, or sleep and get up early tomorrow? Sleep in, or make my 9:00 class? Blue jeans or slacks? Getting serious—should I get married, or not?

Daily, hourly, and by the minute people engage in decision making. Making choices of one kind or another is characteristic of all animal life. As an animal you make the basic decision to move, to engage in voluntary behavior, or not. So the simplest voluntary responses of animals involve choice. What is known about this process? How do we make choices? How do we choose from among alternatives? Are there rules, or laws, governing our behavior? For example, are we born knowing how to make the best decisions, or do we merely make the best decisions we are capable of? Are our decisions the product of past reinforcement history—do we choose (as was suggested in Chapters 6–7) merely on the basis of maximizing reinforcement? Or are our choices guided by a wisdom of our species; animals that consistently make bad choices more than likely do not thrive. Let us begin by looking at some "simple" choices people make.

Choice Behavior and Economics

How people make choices is of as much interest to the marketing divisions of businesses around the world as it is to philosophers and psychologists. When more people choose to buy widgets than whatnots (or Japanese rather than American automobiles), investors will line up behind the former. The task of the marketing divisions of companies making whatnots and American-made cars is to influence the decisions of purchasers to buy *their* products. Notice in this example that neither the purchaser nor the marketer much cares whether humans are *free* to *choose* from among alternatives. Philosophical positions of determinism versus free will do not allow us to predict how individuals make choices. Here we are interested in choice behavior, not the philosophy of choice. The question of widgets or whatnots focuses our observations: (a) that selecting one object rather than another from the environment is a common human behavior; and (b) that choices are influenced by environment.

Evaluating Decision Making

Assume that widgets are better made than whatnots. Will everyone choose widgets? Highly unlikely. This question goes to the heart of individual differences in choice behavior; there are no simple answers as to why people make the choices they do. All humans make questionable decisions at one time or another. Indeed, some of us are more notorious than others for the consistency of our bad judgment. For example, what are some circumstances in which whatnots rather than widgets might be purchased? You might decide that even if whatnots are not made quite as well, they are made sufficiently well for your purposes; whatnots are available nearby, and widgets are across town; whatnots are $1 cheaper; whatnots are a more pleasing shade of purple; they are out of widgets, and you want one or the other right now; no one in your family would be caught dead buying a widget; your ex-boyfriend flaunts his widget, and you can't wait to buy a whatnot out of spite, etc.

Value. One word can be used to summarize the reasons people choose between widgets or whatnots, namely the object's **value.** The value of whatnots in this example was determined by *aesthetics* (how it looked—the color purple), how useful it was (its *utility*), how much it cost, how near it was *(availability),* and the individual's *perception* of its worth *(perceived utility).* Note that almost all these variables can be subsumed under the rubric of perceived *utility*—cost and time and esthetics and buying to spite someone all vary as a function of how an individual perceives the choice. To give you a flavor of the complexity of this situation, let us note just a few of the choice determinants in this example: A $1 difference in purchase price is *everything* to a person with only a few dollars to his or her name, and *nothing* to a millionaire, and *something* to the rest of us, depending upon how near to payday it is. Likewise, taking a half-hour drive across town to buy a widget rather than a whatnot is nothing to a person with plenty of free time and an automobile at his or her disposal, and everything to someone with no time to spare. (Let us not even consider the cost of gasoline to make that drive, relative to what you "save.") The color purple? Wonderful, or unimportant, unless you have a conditioned emotional response to that particular shade.

Limitations of Theory. Now, the astute reader should have antennae out. If we cannot predict something as unimportant as whether a person will buy a widget or a whatnot, we are not going to be able to do a very good job either predicting or advising on the choice of a career, or a marriage partner, or the advantages of renting versus buying your own home. This being the case, perhaps we should fold our tent, and cut to Chapter 10, because in reality the analysis of choice behavior is even more complex than choosing between two items that are matched on most dimensions, such as whatnots and widgets. As is the case with all such human enigmas, we have more than one model, more than one law, and many observations about choice behavior for which we have neither models nor laws.

Chapter Preview

However deficient our state of knowledge is, the issue of choice behavior is too important to ignore. From health decisions at the personal level, to political decisions at the social level, and to environmental decisions at the world level, good and bad choices are made daily. In this chapter we begin our inquiry into the origins of choice behavior with an overview of utility theory. Can we mathematically model the factors leading to choice decisions? From utility theory we turn to an in-depth examination of a model of choice based upon adaptive-evolutionary considerations. Is there a genetic basis for making decisions? We then turn to a variety of animal models of choice behavior and examine several interesting laws that have come from laboratory experimentation. Can we design meaningful animal models to help us predict the choices that humans make? In the last section, we will attempt to apply what we have learned to your situation. Can we use our theories to help train people to make better decisions, in their personal life, in educational settings, and in behavioral therapy? We begin with utility theory.

II.   Utility Theory

Assume that an eccentric uncle has died. His will is being read, and you are to be a beneficiary. Among the conditions of his will are that you have to make a choice from the following two alternatives: (a) You can choose to receive $3000 outright, or (b) you can gamble to win $4000 by spinning a "wheel-of-inherited-fortune." There are 10 slots on which the wheel can land. Eight of the ten slots will earn you $4000, and two of the slots read "$0." You are assured that the game is not fixed, and that the two probabilities are correct: $3000 with the probability of 1.0; $4000 with a probability of 0.8. What do you choose to do? When a study outlining this proposition was conducted in the late 1970s, over 80 percent of the people responded that they would take the $3000; only 20 percent were willing to gamble at even these high (80 percent chance of winning) odds (Kahneman & Tversky, 1979). I would be very surprised if the findings would be any different today; the old axiom to the effect that a bird in the hand is worth two in the bush is a timeless, accurate prediction concerning human behavior. But why do people make this choice?

Expected Utility

A model that came to be known as **expected utility** was proposed in the eighteenth century by Bernoulli, a mathematician who described, among other functions, probabilities associated with gambling. In this century his work was incorporated into both economic gaming theory (von Neuman & Morganstern, 1944) and *decision theory* (French, 1986). Bernoulli's analysis of humans making decisions that did not match the odds of winning bets was that people preferred to focus upon the risk of losing and the *perceived value* of the money involved, rather than on winning and the absolute value of the money involved.

In some ways the concept of expected *utility* is similar to the findings of traditional *psychophysics* formulated by the nineteenth-century German mathematician (and early psychologist) Gustav Fechner. Recall that the study of psychophysics described the mathematical relationship of the responses of the senses to the physical stimulus energy in the environment. "Brightness" and "loudness," for example, are psychological terms referring to (and mapping) the intensity of visual and auditory stimuli, respectively. Likewise, the expected utility, or expected gain, from a decision made about money is a psychological function related to the real-world value of money. Assume that such decisions must be made repeatedly about a given wager (X). Equation (9.1) describes this relationship mathematically. Note that the perceived, or expected, utility (EU) of a quantity of money (X) is a function of expected gain (G), the mean value of X (μ_X), and the standard deviation of X (σ_X^2):

$$EU(X) = G(\mu_X, \sigma_X^2). \tag{9.1}$$

The important thing to remember about this equation is that human and animal judgments about gains (G) in money, or food, or anything of value depend in part upon how much money we are talking about (i.e., μ_X), and how variable the amount is (i.e., σ_X^2). In a wager, the risk of losing is worth taking only under certain conditions.

Economics of Choice in Animals

Equation (9.1) has been used to analyze decisions people and animals make relating to their perception of the real world. As stated earlier, because most humans are risk averse, their *expected utilities* do not match the actual values of their transactions. That is, *because* humans are risk averse, they do not maximize the gains available to them. What their expected utility *does* reflect are the multitudinous psychological variables that govern their decisions: Buying a whatnot because an ex-boyfriend has a widget is one example. For this reason, a number of researchers have decided to investigate choice behavior in infrahumans. Presumably the learned psychological complexity that motivates animals is less than is found in humans. In the next section, we begin with a "simple" model of the choice behavior of honeybees. The question raised by Real's (1991) investigation seems simple enough: What is the biological and evolutionary basis of expected utility?

III. Adaptive-Evolutionary Considerations in Choice Behavior

Yes, honeybees. Your presumed question as to the ecological validity of studying the behavior of honeybees as a model for human choice behavior is a legitimate one. Having raised questions regarding the extrapolation of research results from animals to humans throughout the text, I would be remiss to not comment here about the use of honeybees as a model of choice behavior. First, Real's (1991) investigation of choice behavior in honeybees succeeds at several levels; he does not conceptualize his research regarding how bees make decisions to be an exact model of how humans make choices. Second, the abilities of bees are quite remarkable (see Box 9.1), and their decision making is orderly with respect to the expected utility model that has been described. Finally, some remarkable consistencies of choice behavior exist whether bees, rats, pigeons, or humans are studied. Let us take an in-depth look, then, at what decisions bees are capable of. (The superskeptical among you might want to take an extended look at Box 9.1 before proceeding. Call it consciousness raising, or whatever. I think that you will find that these insect brains are not what you thought they were.)

Foraging in Honeybees

What kinds of decisions do foraging honeybees make? Simply put, bees must determine which nearby flowers contain the most nectar. Energy is expended in foraging, and the return (gain in nectar) must always be balanced against this energy loss. Leslie Real (1991) studied how bees adjust their behavior (make their next decision about which flowers to visit) as a function of the reinforcement value of previously visited flowers. His method is to allow wild bumblebees to search a large, netted enclosure in which artificial cardboard flowers of different colors can be "sampled." Let us look at the details.

Colored Flowers Predict Reinforcement. In the middle of each cardboard flower is a well containing a specified amount and concentration of diluted honey ("nectar"). That bees rapidly associate the color of the flower with the nectar has long been known. That is, bees learn to return to the flowers of the color that have the most nectar. In one experiment Real allowed single bees to visit a patch

BOX 9.1

Are Bee Brains Smart Enough to Make Decisions?

Sejnowski and Churchland (1992a,b) are intrigued by the parallels of both organization and performance of computers and living brains. An excerpt from their article "Bee Smart," which appeared in the computer magazine BYTE follows:

"Start by contrasting what a small honeybee can do with tasks that today's most powerful computers can't do, and add the fact that a honeybee's brain has only about one million neurons versus the human brain's 100 billion neurons. Then consider the following information:

Energy efficiency. A honeybee's brain dissipates less than 10 microwatts (10^{-6}). It is superior by about seven orders of magnitude to the most efficient of today's manufactured computers.

Speed. A honeybee's brain, roughly and conservatively, performs at about 10 TFLOPS (10,000 GFLOPS). The most powerful of today's computers approach speeds of only 10 GFLOPS (i.e., 1 billion operations per second).

Behavioral abilities. Honeybees harvest nectar from flowers and bring it back to the hive. They maximize foraging benefits and minimize foraging costs—for example, by recognizing high nectar sites and remembering which flowers they have already visited.

Honeybees can see, smell, fly, walk, and maintain balance. They can navigate long distances and predict changes in nectar location. They communicate the location of nectar sources to worker bees in the hive; they recognize intruders and attack; they remove garbage and dead bees from the hive; and, when the hive becomes crowded, a sub population will swarm in search of a new home.

Autonomy and self-reliance. Honeybees manage these activities entirely on their own without any help from superior beings. By contrast, a supercomputer needs the constant care of a cadre of maintainers and programmers.

Size. A honeybee's brain takes up only a few cubic millimeters of space. It is a marvel of miniaturization. You cannot reach all the way around a supercomputer.

From this comparison, it seems we have a ways to go in allowing computers to perform some of the simpler things in life. Nature and its creatures are models for ways in which to improve our computing devices." (From Sejnowski & Churchland, 1992, p. 142)

---

containing 100 blue and 100 yellow flowers, randomly spaced. All of the blue flowers contained 2 µl (microliters) of nectar, and one-third of the yellow flowers contained 6 µl nectar (the remaining two-thirds of the yellow flowers had no nectar). A foraging bee, by Real's analysis, could therefore sample each color equally often and receive an average 2 µl nectar per trip. (Six microliters divided across visits to three yellow flowers equals an average of two microliters per visit.)

Remember, however, the "bird in the hand" concept. Even though bees choosing blue flowers will never experience the 6-µl nectar jackpot of some yellow flowers, the blue flowers always have some nectar. What is your prediction of what bees would do in Real's experiment?

Bees Avoid Risk, Favor Consistency.   Figure 9.1 shows the results of this experiment (using the average performance of five bees) after allowing these bees a 40-visit foraging bout. We presume that the bees learned what the reinforcement contingencies were during these first 40 visits. Over the first 16 trials (see Figure 9.1) bees chose to visit the 2-µl rewarded blue flowers approximately 84 percent of the time. On trials 17–31, the colors of the flowers were reversed; now yellow flowers always contained 2 µl of nectar, one-third of the blue flowers had 6 µl, and two-thirds contained nothing. The solid line after trial 17 shows a major reversal of preference mirroring the switch in reinforcement contingencies; now only about 23 percent of the visits were made to blue flowers.

Computing Risky Choices

How good are bees at adjusting their behavior as a function of even more subtle changes in reinforcement contingencies? That is, what if the problem were not quite so simple as having bees decide between consistent reinforcement and low-probability reinforcement? In another experiment Leslie Real continued to reinforce blue flowers with 2 µl nectar; but now one-third of the yellow flowers had 5 µl nectar, and the remaining two-thirds of the yellow flowers had 0.5 µl. In this case, choosing yellow or blue flowers will continue to provide equivalent amounts of nectar over the long run (i.e., the reinforcement contingencies of blue and yellow flowers are equal). And *all* choices will be reinforced. Again, for bees, the expected utility of these two conditions are *not* equivalent: Apparently bees (and probably humans in a similar situation) prefer the less risky proposition of consistent reward. The dashed lines in Figure 9.1 indicate that the consistently reinforced blue flowers on trials 1–16 were visited 62 percent of the time, and following a color switch the now consistently reinforced yellow flowers were visited approximately 63 percent of the time. Real (1991) speculates that because the variance in expected reward was narrower in the second experiment (5 vs. 0.5 µl compared with 6 vs. 0.0 µl in the first experiment), the bees' preference for consistently rewarded colors was commensurably less in the second experiment (62 vs. 84 percent in the first experiment).

Raising the Stakes.   Let us return to our initial gamble to better compare what bees do relative to humans. Few of us would turn down $3000 cash for an 80 percent chance at $4000. Let us up the

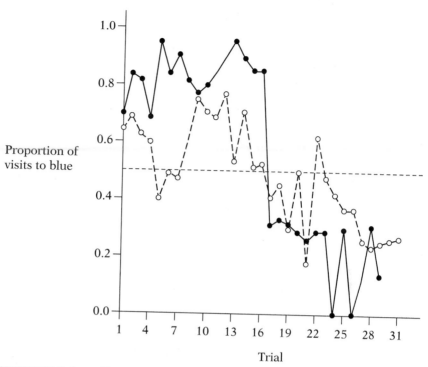

FIGURE 9.1 Efficiency in Time and Effort

Two separate experiments are plotted in the figure. The solid line shows that bees prefer blue to yellow flowers when blue flowers are consistently paired with 2 µl nectar and only one-third of the yellow flowers are reinforced (with 6 µl nectar); the remaining two-thirds have no nectar. After 16 trials, the reinforcement contingencies of the blue and yellow colors are switched, and bees continue to prefer the consistently reinforced color.

The dashed lines are the results of a second experiment in which blue flowers continued to be reinforced with 2 µl nectar, one-third of the yellow flowers are reinforced with 5 µl nectar, and two-thirds of the yellow flowers with 0.5 µl. The consistently reinforced blue flowers on trials 1–16 (dashed lines) were visited 62 percent of the time. Following a color switch (trials 17–31), visits to blue flowers dropped to 27 percent. (From Real, 1991.)

ante. Would you take $3000 cash, or an 80 percent chance at $10,000? Or $100,000? Or $1,000,000? An 80 percent probability means that four times out of five you are going to win the bet: Try getting those odds from Las Vegas for *any* athletic contest! The point is that the expected utility function (Eq. 9.1) predicts that risk taking will increase—that uncertainty can be compensated for—by increasing expectation. The prediction is that bees (and humans) will take more risks for greater-than-average expected rewards. In a second experiment (see Figure 9.1), Real (1991) covaried the probability of finding a reward with the size of the reward, and he found just that—greater risk taking. As predicted in our human example, he reported a linear relationship connecting risk taking and reward size; specifically, he concluded from his studies that uncertainty can be compensated for by increasing the amount of the expected reward.

Maximizing Energy Gain

At several places in the text (typically within an adaptive-evolutionary context) reference has been made to the concept of "maximizing reinforcement opportunities." Never well specified, the general idea being proposed was that behavior is neither trivial nor random. To behave entails costs. To "behave" means to "expend energy." The Brelands' pigs and raccoons (Chapter 6) that engaged in behaviors that delayed reinforcement (i.e., "washing" or "rooting" tokens, rather than trading them for food) were viewed as "maladaptive." Likewise, choosing larger rewards over smaller ones is viewed as adaptive. Why? Because of an implicit awareness that energy well expended is more adaptive than energy wasted. Engaging in behavior incurs an (energy) cost, and the benefit should at a minimum be equal to that cost.

Biomechanics of Utility

As you might expect from reading about bees in Box 9.1, expected utility theory can be profitably applied to the problems faced by bees in meeting energy needs (Harder & Real, 1987). Indeed, bees maximize their net energy gain by the decisions they make about which flowers to visit during foraging. Equation (9.2) is introduced with the following caution: The student is not expected to either memorize or solve it (unless your prof. wants you to, in which case I sincerely apologize). Rather, the equation is introduced for two reasons: First, to draw parallels with Hull's formidable equation (Eq. 7.1, p. 293), which attempted to predict the likelihood of occurrence of a learned response based upon both physiology and learned performance; and second, to address risk aversion (a psychological construct) by examining niche behaviors.

Equation 9.2 (from Real, 1991) predicts that the rate of net energy uptake (E) for each flower visited by a bee is equal to

$$E = \frac{epSV - W(K_p(T_a + V/I) + K_f T_f)}{T_f + T_a + V/I} \tag{9.2}$$

in which e = the energy content of the "nectar" (15.48 joules/mg sucrose); p = the nectar density (mg/μl); S = nectar concentration; V =

nectar volume; W = the bee's mass in grams; K_p and K_f = the energy costs of probing and flying, respectively; T_f = flight time between flowers; T_a = total time at a flower; and I = ingestion time, in seconds.

Equation (9.2) predicts that the costs associated with foraging are real, and further, that because of these costs, the rate of energy intake is a decelerating rather than a linear function of nectar volume (Harder & Real, 1987). Such a function predicts that smaller, consistent rewards are more energy efficient than foraging for larger, but more variable rewards. (Going to a yellow flower that has little or no nectar is a high energy cost.) At least in this simple animal, a cognitive function called "choosing" can be modeled and predicted merely by measuring simple biomechanical factors of energy expenditure and energy intake! *Choosing* is in quotation marks here, because the term implies a level of consciousness that bees and other infrahumans likely do not share with humans. Bees, and birds in the following example, presumably respond to the results of a concluded foraging experience and adjust their foraging behavior involuntarily; that is, without being aware of what they are doing.

Take one last look at Eq. (9.2). Would you say that the science of behavioral analysis has been successful in delving into the *black box*? Certainly the analytical model proposed by Clark Hull, which was maligned in his lifetime, was on the right track.

So Much for Bees. How Do Birds Do It?

The question of animal awareness aside for the moment, effectively "choosing" from among foraging alternatives has Darwinian, life and death, implications. When foraging involves the feeding of hungry offspring, the importance of making good decisions is paramount. To take but one example, the manner in which mountain chickadees (*Parus gambeli*), located in the mountains of northern California, go about poking insects into voracious mouths in their nests has recently been reported by Grundel (1992). His results can be summarized in the form of "decision trees" regarding whether to return to a previous foraging location, and what type of prey to take from there. In essence, his findings parallel what we now know about the decisions bees make in foraging.

Beginning with a successful foraging expedition, and having fed their offspring, chickadees typically adopt a *win-stay* strategy. (If prey is found, i.e., *win*, then *stay* with that location.) But not always. Grundel found that the proximity of the foraging location to the nest was important. If it took too long to get there on the previous flight, the chickadee would shift to another location. The operative rule was that if the time to get there was approximately 30 percent longer than the shortest successful foraging distance, the chickadee was unlikely to return, even though prey was found at the more distant site—a *win-shift* strategy.

Once at a site, which prey do I take? Grundel reported three rules that account for most of the variance he observed in chickadee foraging patterns. The best predictor was quantity of prey; chickadees appear to take whatever size insect that was available in the largest numbers. In other words, quantity of insects was a better predictor of prey selection than *size* of prey, the second best predictor. Confounding both of these observations, Grundel (1992) noticed a trend that if the foraging time was sufficiently short (i.e., if the location was a very short distance from the nest), chickadees would be even less selective of prey and would be more likely to select "the same as last time." These strategies, presumably inborn response tendencies honed by experience, serve both bees and birds, and they do not seem to be unreasonable for humans.

IV.   The Matching Law

You are a hungry pigeon trapped in a Skinner Box in Richard Herrnstein's laboratory. Two keys in front of you seem to have something to do with food, because you have learned to peck at the red key on the left-hand side and the white key on the right-hand side, and the grain hopper has sometimes magically appeared. Now, however, you find you must peck more often, and yet you receive less food. If you were able to understand English, you might have heard a lab assistant mumble something about putting you on a *partial schedule of reinforcement*. And if you could read, you might notice that one of the tapes used to schedule your reinforcement on the left-hand key is labeled VI-135, and the schedule of reinforcement on the right-hand key is a VI-270 seconds. These are lean schedules; you are only reinforced for pecking on these keys, on the average, every two minutes (plus) and every four and a half minutes. Both tapes run simultaneously, and both reinforcement schedules are independent of each other. Such schedules are called **concurrent schedules** of reinforcement.

Question: How would you distribute your responses? As a hungry bee would, in a way that *minimizes risk?* Recall that bees distributed more than 80 percent of their responses to the color of flower that was consistently reinforced (and less than 20 percent of their responses to a color that was not consistently reinforced). Or would you distribute your responses in a way that *maximizes reinforcement?*

The Matching Law in Pigeons

Herrnstein (1961) found that pigeons made twice as many responses to the VI-135 as they did to the VI-270. That is, they matched their responses to the available reinforcement. In a one-hour work session,

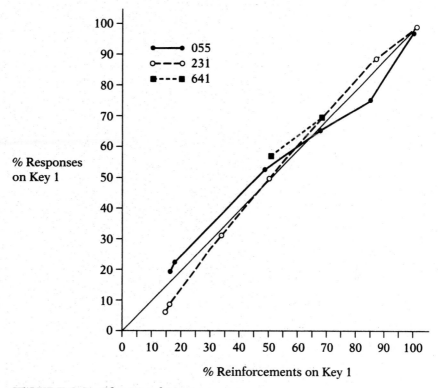

FIGURE 9.2   The Matching Law

A perfect match between percent responses and ratio of reinforcements is indicated by the diagonal line. Depicted are the performances of three birds on several different concurrent schedules (see text). These behavioral data match the predicted line, the basis for what Herrnstein (1961) has called the *matching law*.

for example, pigeons working on the VI-135 averaged approximately 3100 responses to earn 27 positive reinforcers, and concurrently responded approximately 1600 times on the VI-270, earning 13 reinforcers. Herrnstein then continued working his pigeons on different combinations of concurrent VI schedules to see if the percentage of key-pecking responses would consistently match the ratio of available reinforcement on each schedule. As can be seen in Figure 9.2, pigeons match their responses to available reinforcement almost flawlessly—a behavioral regularity called the **matching law.**

The relationship of responses made and reinforcement earned is mathematically described by the equation (Baum, 1974)

$$\frac{R_A}{R_B} = b\left(\frac{r_A}{r_B}\right)^a. \tag{9.3}$$

R_A and R_B refer to the *rates* of responding on keys A and B (i.e., the left and right keys, respectively), and r_A and r_B refer to the rates of reinforcement on those keys. When the value of the exponent a is equal to 1.0, the matching law entails: Responses perfectly match available reinforcement. (The variable b can be used to weight non-matched response topographies, or nonmatched reinforcers.)

Although the derivation of the matching law from the expected utility function expressed in Eq. (9.1) is beyond the scope of this text, these two functions are related. The regularity (low variability) of Herrnstein's data is reminiscent of Real's bee foraging data (see Figure 9.1). Accuracy of prediction of behavior is high for both the bees and pigeons under the circumstances of these experiments. How do we know this? Because the observed functions lie very close to their predicted values. There are circumstances in which pigeons do not match responses to reinforcements. By way of illustrating these exceptions consider the following scenario.

Undermatching

You talk on the phone with your two best friends several times daily. Assume that they both work odd hours and make other phone calls, and that the longer you delay your calls to each of them, the higher the probability is that each of them will be home to take your call. Friend A is home more than Friend B, and the probability of Friend A answering when you call is twice that of Friend B. Not surprisingly, you match these reinforcement contingencies by calling Friend A twice as often as Friend B. Your phone calling/hit rate would fall along the diagonal in Figure 9.2.

Undermatching Phone Calls.   Further assume that over a period of time, you consistently call Friend A first, thereby introducing a delay in calling Friend B. Your strategy thereby *increases* the likelihood of being reinforced when you call Friend B. Under these conditions your phone-calling responses would no longer match the reinforcement contingencies of getting through; by delaying, you increased your hit rate for Friend B. Reinforcement theory predicts that you would increase the rate of making phone calls to Friend B relative to Friend A. If in fact you respond by calling Friend B more than predicted by the matching law, you are **undermatching** the predicted 2:1 ratio of phone calls. That is, by calling Friend B more, your ratio might come closer to a 50-50 match (i.e., 1:1), undermatching the predicted 2:1 ratio. Such undermatching has been observed under a variety of conditions, and several alternative explanations for under-matching have been proposed (Baum, 1974, 1979; Myers & Myers, 1977).

Changeover Delays. The hit rates for phone calls to Friend A and Friend B are similar to pigeons pecking on key A and key B for food reinforcement in Herrnstein's (1961) experiment. Recall that key A was reinforced twice as often as key B (VI-135 vs. VI-270). In fact, Herrnstein's pigeons initially *undermatched* by getting more rein-forcements/peck on the VI-270 than predicted by the matching law. Why? First, they learned that key A delivered the most reinforcement. Then, by primarily responding to key A (VI-135) for a long period of time, key B (VI-270) was more likely to deliver reinforcement on the pigeon's first peck on key B. These changeover responses would have the highest probability of being reinforced of any responses in the session. To keep this from happening, Herrnstein introduced a **changeover delay (COD)** to separate the two components of the con-current schedules. Whenever a pigeon switched from the left to right, or from the right to left key, no reinforcement was available for 1.5 seconds. Herrnstein viewed this 1.5-second changeover delay as a punishment contingency for "switching" (see also Davison, 1991). An-other view is that the COD differentially punished switching from key A to key B and made the animal respond with a few more pecks on key B than it normally would have. Without the *COD*, a pigeon could even better maximize reinforcement on the VI-270 by virtually ignor-ing it and only minimally responding on it.

Melioration

A more recent interpretation of matching and undermatching has been proposed by Herrnstein and Vaughan (1980) and by Vaughan (1981, 1985). Their analysis of pigeons responding on concurrent schedules is that the pigeon's response strategy is continually chang-ing within a session. After gaining experience with the two VI sched-ules, within each session a pigeon will shift from one key to the other, always attempting to meliorate, or maximize, local (moment to moment) changes in available reinforcement. The difference in the **melioration** position from that of *matching* is that the latter term better describes an overall (read daily) maximizing strategy, whereas melioration places more emphasis upon a pigeon's short-term memory, and upon key-to-key shifts depending upon the most recently obtained reinforcement. The issue of molar versus molecu-lar strategies is far from settled (see Williams, 1991). Bees, it is ar-gued, are short-term energy maximizers, perhaps due to constraints upon their memory systems that do not allow them to keep a daily running total of the results of their choices (Real, 1991). By contrast, humans have both excellent short-term and long-term memories. You are likely to remember that Friend B answered the phone each of the last three times you called, and at the same time know that in the long run of events Friend A is usually easier to contact.

Overmatching

Recall the rats that had electrodes implanted in their brains and that had learned to bar press for ESB. Anderson et al. (1992) reported that when these hungry rats were allowed sequential access to either food or ESB reinforcement, after experience with both schedules they quit responding for food entirely. He called the phenomenon absolute *negative contrast*, a special case of *incentive contrast.* In general, when rewards of different value are repeatedly experienced, the better one becomes even better, and by comparison the lesser one sinks even further in value (see Flaherty, 1991). Similar behavior observed on concurrent schedules of reinforcement has been called **overmatching.** In overmatching, a rat or pigeon spends too much time responding on the better of the two VI schedules; it does not distribute enough responses to the less reinforced lever to match the available reinforcement. In one study, for example, switching between levers was punished by electric shock, and pigeons restricted a higher proportion of their responses (than predicted by matching theory) to the richer schedule—hence, *overmatching* (Todorov, 1971). (Recall that the COD also acted as a punisher; yet it improved the match between responses and available reinforcement on two VI schedules.) The increment of food available on the lesser VI schedule apparently did not offset the painful cost of switching. Another way of interpreting this phenomenon is that the introduction of shock magnified the contrast between the two schedules.

Overmatching in Play. Have you ever watched two young children playing with toys? During a play session, both children will play with a variety of toys. Each toy has a particular value, as reflected by the amount of time a child plays with it. It is often the case that in the midst of plenty both will zero in on one particular toy—Toy X. If Child A then asserts ownership of Toy X, a wary game of who plays with what ensues. The cost of choosing Toy X by Child B now includes the penalty of being harassed for attempting to play with it. One outcome is that when Toy X now becomes available (when Child A shifts interest to other toys), Child B is less likely to choose it. The reinforcement is now available, but Child B does not respond commensurately with its availability—behavior similar to pigeons who overmatch on concurrent schedules.

Matching Law in an Ecological Niche

Regularities of behavior are indicative of adaptive-evolutionary mechanisms; i.e., of responses that fit (match) the environment. Perhaps this is the reason that the way pigeons behave on concurrent schedules is not especially surprising; indeed, the matching law has an intuitive ring to it. Two common colloquialisms are "dogs [or people] respond to the way they are treated" and "hard work will be rewarded." Both sayings suggest that behavioral responses match (agree with) the reinforcement and punishment contingencies that have shaped, and that maintain, behavior. We are puzzled by misbehaving pigs and raccoons precisely because for the most part our personal behavioral experiences conform closely to the matching law.

Searching and Working for Food. George Collier (1983) expanded upon the empirical evidence demonstrating that behavior often matches available reinforcement. He built a controlled ecological system for rats in which he could more precisely measure the relationship of energy expended in work ("pumping iron") and energy attained through such work (i.e., food). Rats were trained to press one lever (called the "search bar"), and they were reinforced by the onset of S^d's that signaled additional work requirements. Energy expended in "work" was varied on each lever by adjusting both the weight and the number of repetitions of the lever press. If an S^d associated with an additional low-work requirement was illuminated (an FR-10 with little added weight, for example), the rat could complete the work requirement and then eat. Other S^d's, however, required more repetitions at higher weights. The experimenter chose the various work schedules that the rats had to complete for their food reinforcement. Rats could choose *not* to work on a particular schedule with a high energy requirement by returning to the "search bar." There the rat could complete an additional work assignment and search for other S^d's that required less work.

(Note that like Real's (1991) foraging bees, the energy these rats expended shopping around for an easier schedule on the search bar (cf. *procurement costs*) is "real" energy that must be made up. That is, searching for an easier job takes time and energy, and these costs must at some point be recovered.)

What did Collier find? Rats entered into a trade-off between minimizing search time by working on high–energy-expending schedules and increasing search time if the costs were *too* high. That is, if the energy costs associated with pumping iron were too high, rats would spend more time searching for a low–energy-expending schedule leading to food. As has been found with other species, then, given a variety of options, rats are able to adjust their work schedules in a way that maximizes calories from food relative to calories expended in earning it.

V.   Self-Control

Put yourself in the following two situations:

Scenario A.   You have stopped in the middle of a hectic day to have a bite of lunch, and you are reviewing your schedule. You have a psychology exam tomorrow that *must* be studied for. At that moment your best friend calls and begs you to go to the movies that night. The film you have been dying to see is playing that night, and you are now torn between two alternatives: Go to the movie, or study for your exam. You tell your friend that you have to study. Your friend counters that you can study before and after the show, but you are skeptical; you have been down that road before. After another 15 minutes of agonizing indecision, you say no. You reluctantly choose to study.

Scenario B.   You have a psychology exam tomorrow that *must* be studied for. You finish a bite to eat, and at 7 P.M. you open your book. At that moment your best friend calls and begs you to go to the film. It starts at 7:20. You have been dying to see this movie, and you are now torn between two alternatives: Go to the movie, or study for your exam. You tell your friend that you have to study. Your friend counters that you can study after the show. You have a moment of self-doubt. Your friend says "let's get going or we'll be late." You look at your watch, at your psychology textbook, and hear yourself say "okay." You can always study after the show.

Immediate and Delayed Gratification.   Which scenario is more likely? If you answer that both choices are likely, what are the circumstances that account for these two different courses of action? Assume that studying for the exam was a better decision: Is it the case that we make better decisions earlier in the day (i.e., noon as opposed to suppertime)? It is likely that you were more tired when the decision was made to go to the show. Do people consistently make bad decisions when they are tired? Not too likely. What we can agree upon is that the decision to go to the show was made more impulsively. Deciding upon a moment's notice allows less time for reflecting upon the consequences of one's actions. We can also make a value judgment. Deciding to go to the show rather than study showed a lack of self-control. Let us begin with this issue.

Immediate Gratification and Self-Control

One very useful application of animal research on choice behavior is in the area of **self-control**. *Self-control* is defined as the ability to delay immediate gratification, usually with the goal of attaining a larger reinforcer at a later time. Achieving self-control is viewed as a defining feature of *civilized* behavior. Certainly self-control is conceptualized as being learned; the selfish behavior of infants and small children is accepted as normal. Should a student fail to graduate from school due to bad decisions about when and how much to study, a counselor would likely label the person (and the behavior) immature.

The Sins of Immediate Pleasure.   Other decisions we make daily reflect a conflict between achieving an immediate (proximal) pleasure at the expense of a delayed (distal) reinforcer. Many decisions that affect a person's health fall into these categories. Choosing to drink alcohol may lead to immediate pleasure at the expense of incurring less favorable, more distal outcomes (such as automobile injuries and hangovers). Choosing not to drink produces the greater pleasure of not being hurt and not having a hangover. The same can be said for impulsive sexual encounters, which may lead to unwanted pregnancies and diseases. Likewise, choosing not to smoke (proximal) increases longevity (distal). Choosing not to eat the double banana fudge sundae (proximal) allows for the reinforcement of reduced obesity/increased longevity (distal). In this section we will explore what is known about how self-control is trained in both animals and humans.

Training Self-Control in Pigeons

Hungry again, you find yourself in a Skinner Box. One peck at key A raises the grain hopper immediately, allowing you to feed a short while. One peck at key B raises the grain hopper for a longer period of time, allowing you to eat more food—but a four-second delay has been imposed between your pecking response and food availability. Your choices are, then, a small immediate reward versus a large delayed reward (see Figure 9.3a). You more often than not choose the key producing the immediate small reward. (Why should I delay gratification? I'm only a bird!)

Time Delays and Self-Control.   Rachlin and Green (1972) then tried to train *self-control* in these pigeons by increasing the time interval between "making the choice" and "receiving the reinforcement" (see Figure 9.3b). Using a *concurrent chain* procedure, a single response to key A put the pigeon into a second schedule, an FR-10 on key A. Likewise, a response to key B put the pigeon in a FR-10 on key B. Com-

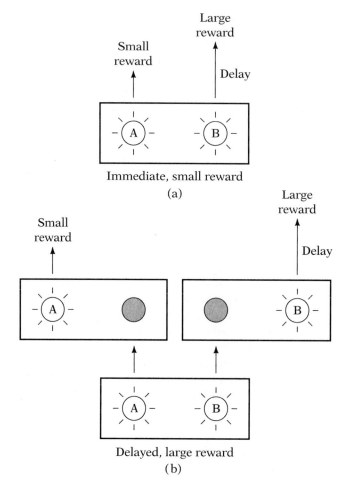

FIGURE 9.3 Teaching Patience to Pigeons

In (a) pigeons are first taught that their choice of the left or right key produces respectively either a small reward immediately or a larger reward after a delay. After this training (b), responding to key A leads to an FR-10 requirement (on key A), followed by a small reinforcement delivered immediately. Responding to key B leads to an FR-10 requirement, followed by a four-second delay, followed by a larger reinforcer. Pigeons choose the small reward in the procedure in (a), and the larger reward in the procedure in (b).

pleting the 10 pecks on key A produced the small immediate reward; completing the 10 pecks on key B produced a four-second delay and then the large (delayed) reward. Under these circumstances, pigeons began to peck key B, leading to the large delayed reward. They delayed immediate gratification, overcame their impulsive behavior, and (to the extent a pigeon can be a "self") they exhibited self-control. Why? Alexandra Logue (1988) argues that these results, and the results of many other experiments using both humans and animals, can be interpreted as shifts in reward value over time. Let us analyze her reasoning.

Self-Control, Immediate Gratification, and Expected Utility

Figure 9.4 shows the relationship of the value of a reward (i.e., its expected utility) as a function of the time prior to experiencing the reward. Note that if a choice between a large and small reward is made just prior to the small reward becoming available (i.e., point T_1 on the time line), the reward value of the small reward is greater than the reward value of the large reward. As we saw in Eqs. (9.1) and (9.2), expected utility theory describes the relative value of rewards. The value of an item or action is in part determined by its ready availability; for example, your inheritance is of limited value if you cannot get to it for 30 years. "A bird in the hand is worth two in the bush" is as much

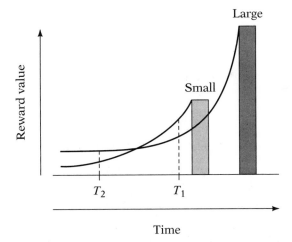

FIGURE 9.4   Expected Value of Large and Small Rewards

A reward's expected utility changes as a function of time. The value of a reward increases as the experience of the reward approaches. At time T_2, the expected values of two rewards are more in synchrony with their actual values. At time T_1, the expected value of the small reward exceeds the expected value of the large reward, because the small reward is imminent. Choices for small rewards made at time T_1 reflect the fulfilling of immediate gratification, while those made for large rewards at time T_2 reflect self-control.

a statement about *time* (now versus the future) as it is about certainty and uncertainty.

Do you want to go to the show, or do you want to study? The relative value of studying versus going to the show varies as a function of when the question is asked and when the decision is made. If, for example, the question is posed and the decision is made at time T_2 (hours, weeks, or days before the event), the relative values of Activity A (two hours' pleasure enjoying a movie) versus Activity B (studying to pass a class, earn a degree, etc.) can be more fairly weighed.[1] If, however, the question is posed at time T_1, the immediate anticipation of Activity A may outweigh that of Activity B. The moral of the story is to decide with your children in early December, and not on Christmas Eve, that their presents will be opened on the morning of December 25.

Training Self-Control in Children

Earlier it was asserted that learning self-control is culturally based. Several studies have demonstrated that children learn to tolerate delays, and thereby to make better choices. For example, children six and older select large delayed rewards from two alternatives, while the four-year-old typically chooses smaller, immediate rewards (Sonuga-Barke, Lea, & Webley, 1989). In another study, impulsive children were first allowed direct, immediate experience with both small and large rewards. A delay interval was gradually lengthened for access to the larger reward, while the smaller reward continued to be immediately available. Several hyperactive children learned to choose the larger, delayed reward with this training, thereby demonstrating increased self-control (Schwitzer & Sulzer-Azaroff, 1988). Finally, children have been found to model on adults who verbalize the benefits of delayed rewards as being "worth the wait" (Mischel, 1966). It is likely that other children model on impulsive parents with less desirable results.

VI.   Labor, Leisure, and Wages

How much is one's labor worth? The answer lies somewhere between what the worker thinks is fair and what the boss thinks is adequate. Is there any evidence that the matching law applies to the work output of laborers and the money expended by owners? That is, do peo-

---

[1]Note in the time prior to T_2 in Figure 9.4 that the expected reward values are in agreement with the "real" values of small and large rewards. This may not always be the case in real life, where often there exist disagreements about the relative values of events and activities.

ple work harder if they are paid more? Economists have analyzed this problem and have modeled this relationship as a **labor supply curve,** one version of which is depicted in Figure 9.5. Let us analyze this function, and then see if human economics conforms to the matching law studied in animals.

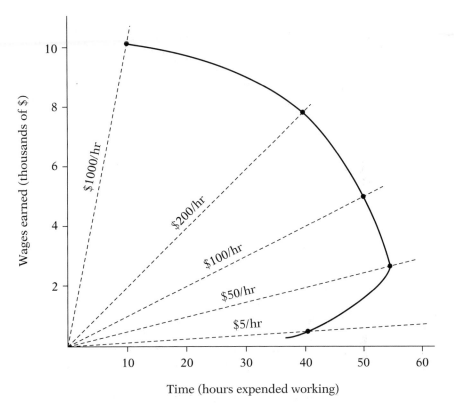

FIGURE 9.5   A Labor Supply Curve

Wages earned (in thousands of dollars) is plotted as a function of "hours expended working" for wage rates between $5 and $1000 per hour. For the medium and high wage rates, people work to maximize total wages earned (i.e., at lower wage rates they work longer to increase their total wages toward—but in general not reaching—the level of those earned by people with a higher hourly wage). However, at the lowest wage rate, individuals appear to "give up" and no longer work as hard. At this lowest wage rate of $5 per hour, the tiny increment in wages attainable by additional work is apparently not worth the expended energy. The reversal in the function at this lowest wage level gives the standard labor supply curve its "backward bending" character—presumably reflecting a work-leisure trade-off.

Working for Wages.   Note in Figure 9.5 that a person making $1000 per hour works less (fewer hours) to earn a relatively high wage.[2] By contrast, a person making $200 per hour must work more hours to earn less money. This relationship holds for the intermediate wage levels: The trend in Figure 9.5 is that an individual's effort (hours worked) attempts to maximize total wages earned. Such are the workings of a free enterprise economy, and most readers are familiar with this reality. As the wage rate drops even more precipitously, however, to $5 per hour, an interesting thing happens: Most individuals no longer work longer hours to make more money. The relatively flat slope of the $5 per hour wage rate in Figure 9.5 indicates that little is gained in wages even when many more hours are worked. In the vernacular, "the juice isn't worth the squeeze" (i.e., the extra money is not worth the effort).

Labor Supply Curves and the Matching Law.   Is this "backward bending" curve in Figure 9.5 indicative of a breakdown in the matching law? Probably not. Among the differences between our animal models and the human experience is that (at least in some experiments) animals are very hungry and their work efforts result directly in eating and alleviating hunger. Humans earn wages that are traded for other amenities of life as well as for food.

The Labor-Leisure Trade-Off.   Look again at the idealized performance depicted in Figure 9.5. It shows the behavior of individuals working during typical 40-hour-plus work weeks. Even working 40 hours per week, humans have much discretionary time in which to spend the wages they have accrued. Leisure time is valuable; much of the wage not spent on meeting energy needs (food) and in meeting other consummatory response needs (clothing, shelter, family needs, etc.) is spent on leisure. Not working costs, and it is considered worth the cost by many humans. One interpretation of the $5 per hour wage earner who limits total work is that this individual's leisure time has become more valuable relative to the benefits of working. Once basic energy needs are met, humans have earned the choice of not working.

We have no animal model for the work-leisure trade-off, other than to note that when work requirements get too high for the payoff (i.e., when it appears that the juice isn't worth the squeeze), having met their energy needs animals will also quit responding for "discretionary" pleasure. For example, rats love sucrose solutions and will work (press a lever) for the sweet taste. (Assume here that the rat's energy needs have been met independently of this sucrose option.) What

---

[2]The figure is hypothetical. Several possible salaries earned and hours worked by some individuals participating in the American economy in the early 1990s have been adjusted to match an idealized standard labor supply curve.

happens if you continue to increase the number of lever presses a rat must make just for the taste of sucrose? Given the option of not doing anything, or working hard for a brief pleasure, rats eventually chose to do nothing (Kelsey & Allison, 1976), and likewise, pigeons will quit rather than work hard for nominal rewards (Green, Kagel, & Battalio, 1987). Not unlike the $5 wage earner, these animals chose to work less with two consequent results: (a) they did without the few extra reinforcements they might have earned; and (b) they were reinforced for doing nothing (leisure) as opposed to expending energy on work.

Summary

1. Humans and animals engage in decision making throughout their lifetimes. Choices are influenced by feedback from the environment.

2. People and animals decide between two or more alternatives based upon the perceived value of alternatives. Value is determined by esthetics, utility, cost, availability, and perception of worth. Together these factors comprise the expected utility of an item.

3. Choice behavior can be understood within an adaptive-evolutionary context. Choices among food alternatives are seen as adaptive when they maximize energy attained (food) for energy expended (foraging, work).

4. Bees choose among alternatives in a way that avoids risk and favors consistency. Humans and other animals do likewise.

5. Initially measured in pigeons working on VI-VI concurrent schedules of reinforcement, the matching law describes a form of choice behavior in which responses match the available reinforcement. For example, if one component of the concurrent schedule makes available three times the reinforcement compared with the other, pigeons make three times as many responses, matching the schedule.

6. Undermatching is likely to occur when the passage of time obscures or distorts the reinforcement contingencies of the leanest of the concurrent VI schedules. In undermatching, proportionately more responses are made to the lean schedule. The insertion of changeover delays in the concurrent schedules corrects for undermatching.

7. Melioration describes attempts by experienced animals to maximize reinforcement on two keys by paying attention to the most recently obtained patterns of reinforcement. Overmatching refers to pigeons on concurrent schedules that by spending a disproportionate amount of time on the rich VI component underrespond on the lean VI component. Theoretical accounts of both melioration and overmatching disagree on whether molecular (short-term effects) or molar (long-term maximization) factors better account for the phenomena.

8. Animals have been trained to choose between receiving either immediate or delayed reinforcement. Choosing delayed reinforcement demonstrates self-control.

9. The preference of both humans and animals for immediate gratification obtained by choosing small rewards (relative to selecting larger rewards that are delayed) can be accounted for by expected utility theory. Expected utility theory takes into account the relative value of immediate and delayed reinforcers. Expected utility theory predicts that choices between two alternatives will vary as a function of time preceding the experiencing of the reinforcers.

10. When labor supply curves are compared with the matching law, breakdowns in matching occur for the lowest level of earned wages. Leisure has value, and expending energy to work must be balanced against the costs of leisure. Matching laws predict the behavior of hungry birds better than they predict the behavior of humans motivated by nonhunger variables.

Discussion Questions

1. A friend of mine is about to buy an off-road vehicle. Living in a small town with a single dealership, he compares vehicles and prices available in a large town 100 miles away. He has one decision to make from three choices: (a) He can order his choice of model and features from the factory, deliverable after 30 days; (b) He can buy outright a locally available vehicle that he likes—except for an automatic transmission (he prefers a manual transmission); or (c) He can buy the model he wants with a manual transmission from the town 100 miles away. He is leaning toward buying the car locally. Why? Can you explain his decision by reference to Figure 9.4?

2. What are the meanings of the following sayings? Are they descriptive of human behavior? What theories help account for them?
   (a) "Beggars can't be choosers."
   (b) "I've saved the best for last."
   (c) "Let me sleep on it, and I'll give you my decision tomorrow."
   (d) "Never go grocery shopping when you are hungry."

3. What different food choices might you make from a menu as compared with a cafeteria line? In addition to the obvious benefits of seeing your choices rather than imagining them (i.e., remembering them from a menu), what is the role of *time* in both scenarios? Can you use the role time plays, as displayed in Figure 9.4, to make the case that from the standpoint of health and nutrition, better overall choices will be made from the menu?

4. Compare and contrast the choice to *elope* or to have a *long engagement*.

5. Based upon what you have read, do all humans make *rational* decisions, and all animals *impulsive* decisions? What is a rational decision? Is the matching law observed by pigeons evidence for their rationality? Why or why not?

6. What are the implications of our ability to write equations that model our choice behavior, on one hand, and our concept of *free will* on the other? Are the choices of chronically hungry people more predictable than the choices of the affluent? For example, are we truly free to select whichever foods we want, or do our choices vary if we scavenge from a dumpster, or order from a cafeteria line or from a menu? Are hunger level, food cost, prior learning (expectations), etc. relevant to questions of free will? It is your choice whether to answer this question or not.

7. A nephew sheepishly explained to me that he dropped out of school for a year to work at a ski resort. Analyze his decision in terms of the trade-off between leisure time and work time. What is he maximizing?

8. The NCAA has ruled that an athlete transferring to a new school is typically ineligible to play the first year. What is

the purpose of this rule? Does this rule have the same effect as the *changeover delay* that prevents pigeons from undermatching?

9. Note that the labor supply curve in Figure 9.5 is for wages paid. What is the difference between a salary and a wage? How do employer's expectations differ for those employees paid wages and those paid salaries? From the employees' perspective, are there different expectations regarding leisure while on the job?

10. Why is "impulse control" training an important aspect of child rearing in most (all?) of the world's cultures?

Glossary

Changeover Delay (COD) In a *concurrent schedule* procedure, a brief period of time during which reinforcement is not available immediately following a switch, or changeover, from one reinforcement schedule to the other.

Concurrent Schedules A training procedure in which two or more reinforcement schedules run simultaneously and independently of each other, and a subject can respond on either. Used in the measurement of choice behavior.

Expected Utility The expected gain from a decision made about a wager or transaction involving money or another tangible valuable.

Labor Supply Curve A "backward bending" curve that deviates from the *matching law*, reflecting a breakdown in the general rule that effort will increase indefinitely to match available reinforcement.

Matching Law (Herrnstein) When an animal is given two response alternatives, a monotonic functional relationship is typically found between the rate of responding and available reinforcement: Responses typically match available reinforcement.

Melioration On concurrent reinforcement schedules, pigeons behave in ways that maximize local (moment to moment) changes, the result of which is to take advantage of available reinforcement. Specifically, *melioration* describes shifting to the opposite key shortly after being reinforced.

Overmatching Relative to the *matching law*, the rate of responding to the more rewarding schedule is found to be *more* than, or over, that predicted given the amount of available reinforcement. (Cf. *matching law.*)

Self-Control The ability to delay immediate gratification, usually with the goal of attaining a larger reinforcer at a later time.

Undermatching Relative to the *matching law*, the rate of responding to the more rewarding schedule is found to be *less* than, or under, that predicted given the amount of available reinforcement. (Cf. *matching law.*)

Value The relative worth, merit, or importance of an object or activity, based upon *esthetics, cost, availability, perceived utility,* and other properties.

10

Conceptual Learning, Thinking, Language, and Culture

I.   Introduction

We have come full circle. To this point we have studied common processes of learning in animals, and through the use of animal models we have been successful in achieving a better understanding of human behavior. In this chapter we return to themes and issues set forth in Chapter 1. Among these issues is the extent to which relatively simple models of association formation can account for what appear to be *qualitative* differences between the human mind and the minds of animals. There is little disagreement, for example, that animals and human infants (and adult humans) can be conditioned. Insights attained through the application of conditioning enhance our understanding of health issues, eating behaviors, emotional behavior, behavioral control, etc.

Now we turn to the study of conceptual learning, thinking, and language. Can we continue to extrapolate findings from animals to humans as we conduct research into conceptual learning and other forms of complex learning? Animals and human infants cannot talk. Are they *conscious*? Can they *think*? Or, because only humans think and talk, are thinking and talking *prerequisites* for complex learning? If so, then animal models become irrelevant, and our study of thinking, language, and complex learning should be restricted to human adults.

In this chapter we study *conceptual learning, thinking,* and *language,* recognizing that these properties of mind generate behaviors that raise yet other questions—about the nature of *consciousness* and of *intelligence.* Our cultural knowledge leads us to assume that language, intelligence, thinking, and consciousness *go together*—for example, that you cannot be intelligent if you are not conscious; and that conceptual thinking is impossible without language. Given that these terms are typically defined in reference to, and are characteristic of, adult humans, what does it mean to ask whether animals have **cognitive processes?** What is the nature of *animal* thinking, *animal* language, and *animal* intelligence?

Can animals think? Are animals conscious? What are their language capabilities? How different *are* humans from other primates? Does humans' use of language and other highly developed cognitive abilities require extension and further revision of the simple associative frameworks we have studied? For example, does language so change the nature of human thought and behavior that simple associative frameworks become irrelevant? Is a human, then, the only animal who can form concepts, who can think, and who is truly conscious?

Comparing Human and Animal Consciousness. These are not easy questions, and not everyone agrees on what constitutes evidence bearing on their answers. Some answers may surprise you. For example, it was just suggested that only humans can think conceptually, presumably because we have language, which allows us the conscious ability to talk about concepts as well as to each other. As can be seen in Focus on Research 10.1, however, Larry Weiskrantz and other respected neuroscientists are of the opinion that even in the absence of language, some higher animals are every bit as conscious as humans.

Weiskrantz's position on the question of human and animal consciousness is controversial (see also Weiskrantz, 1988). Most of the issues dealt with in this chapter are controversial. Why? Because the issues in this chapter help us to define human nature and our place in the universe. Each of us has a conception of who and what we are and of our place in the universe, and most of us become uncomfortable when our closeness to nonhuman animals is so baldly made apparent. In this chapter the intent is not to make monkeys of us all, but rather to inquire into the rudiments of our human nature. Why is it, for example, that only humans enjoy culture? How can we gain insight into what makes us so different from other animals? It is a reasonable strategy to study other animals as well as humans to find out, and researchers in the field of *comparative animal cognition* do just that.

Dr. Larry Weiskrantz

Do Animals Think?

Dr. Larry Weiskrantz, Department of Experimental Psychology, University of Oxford, Oxford, England

"All multi-cellular animals show changes in behavior as a result of experience—from habituation in the simpler organisms to complex forms of learning and memory in mammals. It cannot be this capacity to learn, per se, that distinguishes animals from humans. The challenging difference concerns the issue of animal *thought*. Undoubtedly thought is immensely enriched by language, but the question is whether it absolutely *requires* language. Many philosophers, from Locke in 1690 to Wittgenstein in 1922, have been resolutely unwilling to make concessions to non-verbal animals in this regard, largely on *a priori* grounds. That language is not essential for complex cognitive skills is clear even at the human level: severely aphasic patients can score highly on IQ tests like Raven's Matrices (Kertesz, 1988; Newcombe, 1987), and preverbal infants can segment and categorize their causal world (Spelke, 1988; Leslie, 1988). Therefore, there is no logical necessity to deprive animals of advanced mental skills because they lack language. Many impressive demonstrations have been reported, such as the ability of the chimpanzee to perform arithmetical addition or ratios (Premack, 1988), of rats to show "intentional" behavior (Dickinson, 1985; 1988), and the spatial cognitive abilities of a number of animals (Thinus-Blanc, 1988). (For examples and a review of 'thought without language' in both animals and humans, cf. Weiskrantz, 1988.)

"But complex cognition, it might be argued, is not the same as having mental imagery. What about animals' images and imaginings? There are a number of approaches to this question. Detailed analysis of S-S classical conditioning suggests a control of behavior by representations of absent events, which have been interpreted as being 'imagined' (cf. review by Holland, 1990). Secondly, evidence of deception by primates leads to the suggestion that they have 'theories of other minds,' i.e., imagine what the consequence of their behavior will be, based on their beliefs about other's belief (Woodruff & Premack, 1979). Finally, human neuropsychology has revealed a large number of residual cognitive capacities caused by brain damage of which the patient is 'unconscious' or 'unaware,' capacities sometimes called 'implicit processes.' One can consider comparable cognitive dissociations in animals based upon homologous brain systems. It may be possible to study the difference between 'conscious' (explicit) and 'thoughtless' (implicit) performance in animals (cf. Weiskrantz, 1986; Miller & Rugg, 1992)."

To better frame such issues as conceptual thinking and talking, let us begin by examining the following two behavioral vignettes.

Vignette 1: Human Language Acquisition

"Pup-pee" was the sound my daughter Jane made at 17 months of age when together we turned the pages of her picture book of animals. A "pup-pee" was any picture of a cow, horse, dog, and, for a while, even an elephant. As she rapidly acquired words during the next year, each incorrect label of "puppy" was replaced by the appropriate word: i.e., "cow," "horse," and "dog." Yet later, she learned to discriminate a rhinoceros from an elephant, and, with apparent ease, she correctly applied the verbal label "dog" to both real dogs and pictures of dogs. "Puppy" ultimately was a term restricted to small, young, dogs with puppylike characteristics.

How did Jane do this? Did she "learn" to say these words? Or as America's foremost linguist, Noam Chomsky (1980), argues, did she use an innate, species-specific, language-acquisition device—a process, Chomsky asserts, that does not resemble learning at all? For Chomsky, the associative processes of learning discussed in this text are meaningless and irrelevant to *all* questions of human language.

Associative Processes in Language Acquisition. There is no doubt that humans share with infrahumans associative processes, and that meaningful behavioral change can result in all animals due to such shared processes. Contrary to Chomsky's assertions that language is not learned, *naming* objects resembles other instances of associative conditioning that we have studied throughout this text. Pavlov's *second signal system* is a parsimonious description of how humans are conditioned to apply arbitrary names to objects in the environment; how the sounds of words can become CSs for objects; how conditioned responses (such as saying "pup-pee") can *generalize* along any of a number of stimulus dimensions to similar objects in the environment; and how, with further training, *discriminations* between words can be learned. Following *discrimination training,* specific responses are consistently associated with specific stimuli. Obviously, human language is far more complicated than learning what is and is not a puppy. And human language is not restricted to naming objects; indeed, Chomsky would likely assert that "naming" is a trivial component of language. Behavioral scientists would argue, however, that "naming" is a highly functional building block upon which more complex aspects of language are built, including both syntax and semantics (e.g., Skinner, 1957; Stemmer, 1989). That particular issue aside for the moment, from Jane's puppy example we can see that associative processes play some part in the language acquisition process, a "middle of the road" position adopted by a number of researchers who have addressed this complex issue (i.e., Pinker, 1991). As we will see in a later section, reinforcement and punishment also play a major role in the *expression* of language once it has been acquired.

Vignette 2: Concept Formation in Animals

Earlier we learned that monkeys and chimpanzees will make key-pressing responses for food reinforcement. In one experiment (Koestler & Barker, 1965), a display of visual stimuli such as those seen in Figure 10.1 were presented to a chimpanzee, and a response to the one shape that was unlike the other two shapes (e.g., the triangle in the apparatus in Problem 1) was reinforced with food. A response to either of the same shapes (i.e., either of the circles) was not reinforced. All responses terminated the visual display for 10 seconds. On the following discrete training trial, a new stimulus array was presented: Both the *position* of the odd stimulus was altered (i.e., placed in the left, center, or right position) and/or an entirely new stimulus display was introduced. For example, Problem 6 in the table of stimulus sequences in Figure 10.1 presents two squares and a triangle. With extensive training, eight chimpanzees were able to pick the odd stimulus from these 18 arrays with an average efficiency of 60–70 percent (33 percent = chance performance). One way to think about this task is that the *odd* stimulus was an S^d, and the two identical stimuli were S^Δ's. Using these two-dimensional representational stimuli, the chimpanzees seem to have learned the concept of **oddity.** Let us further analyze this problem.

Animals Can Think.   It seems to be apparent from this example that nonhuman animals are capable of *concept formation*, arguably a form of *thinking*. If so, then nonhuman animals are not doomed to be the machinelike automatons envisioned by Descartes, forever restricted to behavior generated by the lowest level of conditioned reflex. Anthropomorphic speculation is always risky; however, in the example given, following extensive training, chimpanzees (and other animals in other experiments to be discussed later) seem to "get the idea" of a pattern of responding, rather than performing a conditioned reflex to a particular stimulus element. In a later section, we shall return to the question of the concept of oddity and look at an alternative explanation for these animals' performance.

Searching for Human Capabilities in Animals.   One path to understanding what it is that discriminates the human mind from the minds of other animals is to see what we can and what other animals cannot accomplish. Even if some animals are capable of forming simple concepts, the fact remains that we are qualitatively superior to all other animals in the realm of language and thinking. To take another

Problem no.	Symbol on display		
	1	2	3
1	○	△	○
2	△	△	○
3	○	○	□
4	△	○	○
5	△	○	△
6	□	□	△
7	○	□	□
8	△	□	□
9	△	△	□
10	□	○	□
11	□	△	△
12	○	□	○
13	○	○	△
14	○	△	△
15	△	□	△
16	□	○	○
17	□	△	□
18	□	□	○

FIGURE 10.1   Oddity Problems

The sequence of oddity problems used by Koestler and Barker (1965). Symbols were projected on back-lit keys. Each display would terminate if the chimp hit any key, or would time out if the chimp failed to respond within 10 seconds. Responding to the correct key was reinforced with a banana-flavored pellet. Correct responses advanced the display to the next problem; incorrect responses re-presented the display until the chimp got it right.

example, we will see that, after extensive, painstaking training, chimpanzees may exhibit some language capabilities—but nothing resembling the ability of a three-year-old human with little formal training.

Why study animals? Because we have so little insight into human complexity. It is human nature to talk, and yet the process of acquiring speech and generating language remains an enigma. Possessing analytical skills that far exceed those of other animals, we are puzzled over how we do it, and why they cannot. Recognizing at the outset that no other animal has even the rudiments of what we humans call *culture,* nevertheless we shall seek clues to human uniqueness in the behavior of our smaller-brained animal cousins. Before further addressing the complexities of thinking and language, let us begin at the beginning by asking how nonhuman animals learn about simple patterns in time and space.

II. Learning About Patterns in Time and Space

Learning about concepts and rules involves learning about relationships. Even a seemingly simple concept such as "odd and even" appears to be difficult for chimpanzees. Let us begin by analyzing how humans and animals learn about simpler relationships. Among the simplest of relationships that animals learn is that events are distributed in *time*, and that events can occur in *patterns*.

Timing Behavior in Animals

In previous chapters we have marveled at the ability of animals to "keep track of time." Beyond speculating that their time perception likely differs from that of humans, we know very little about other animals' psychological appreciation of time. There is no disagreement that the rats, monkeys, and pigeons we have studied have the ability to use the passage of time as a discriminative stimulus to control the patterning of their responses. For example, monkeys on DRL schedules of reinforcement can *withhold* lever-press responding for a specified duration of time within margins measured in *hundredths* of a second (see Box 6.5, p. 249). Their behavior is evidence that monkeys have an excellent sense of *timing*. And rats and pigeons as well as monkeys and chimpanzees can be trained to make panel-push or lever-press responses within seconds of the onset of a stimulus to avoid an electric shock or to secure food (see Box 7.2, p. 315).

Indeed, the very basis of conditioning is predicated upon the animal's ability to discriminate the time relationships of stimuli and responses. Only a fraction of a second differentiates *forward* from *trace*, or *backward*, conditioning; yet, as we saw in Chapters 4 and 5, such differences are critical in determining both the amount and nature of the resulting association.

A number of models of timing behavior in animals have been proposed (see Roberts, 1981; Gibbon & Church, 1984). But at present the existence of a central nervous system mechanism (a biological "clock") that would mediate precise timing behaviors is only speculative. All we can say is that an animal's sensitivity to time attests to the precision of sensory and motor nerve conduction velocities measured in fractions of a second, and to the overall adaptive functioning of a nervous system whose very survival is dependent upon such exquisite time-keeping functions.

Counting Behavior in Animals

When information provided the animal by the environment concerns the *number* of events rather than the *duration* of events in a given period of time, *counting* rather than *timing* behavior is described (Meck & Church, 1983).

Counting behavior can be considered to be another example of preconceptual pattern learning. Children learn to count, initially from 1 to 10, and then, with conceptual training, to identify odd and even numbers, to learn the "times tables," prime numbers, etc. Counting is, therefore, a precursor to each human's mathematical abilities. While recognizing that the term "mathematics" is seldom used in reference to infrahuman capabilities, it is not unreasonable to inquire into the abilities of animals to quantify; i.e., is the ability to *count* restricted to humans?

Counting and Rhythmic Timing. That counting and timing behavior are related is evidenced by musical abilities of humans; the timed beats of varying duration can be considered a form of rhythmic counting. An example of similar behavior in Rhesus monkeys has been previously described (Box 6.5, p. 249). Recall that these monkeys were reinforced with a sugar pellet for *withholding* responses for 15 seconds before striking a lever. One animal's incredible timing accuracy (responses were repeatedly within hundredths of a second of the target time) was apparently achieved by a sequenced pattern resembling rhythmic counting. After making a reinforced response, this seated monkey would exhibit the following sequence of behaviors: (a) she rhythmically chewed the pellet for a few seconds; (b) she began to sway from side to side, metronome-like, for the next few seconds; (c) still swaying, with her left hand she began to rhythmically tap the upper center section of the performance panel positioned in front of her; (d) as the end of the 15-second interval approached, with exaggerated intensity her sway switched from side-to-side to front-to-back, and her tapping speeded up to about two taps per second; (e) finally, with her right hand she deftly slapped the appropriate lever located on the lower left-hand portion of the performance panel. She would then pick up her sucrose pellet and begin the sequenced pattern again, her interresponse latencies not varying by more than a fraction of a second (Barker, 1968).

Was this monkey *counting?* I think the answer is yes, unless counting is restricted to a human verbal behavior. If a human were instructed to repeatedly make a chalk mark on a blackboard every 15 seconds, a rhythmic motion that resembled the monkey's behavior (probably accompanied by rhythmic sub-vocalization) would likely occur. Counting appears to be one of the simplest possible timed patterns.

Counting, Timing, Attention, and Memory

Counting and timing behaviors require the animal to *pay attention* to what it is doing. The monkey's rhythmic counting and precisely timed lever-pressing response are a reflection of the animal's *memory* for what it has previously learned. In a sense, each timed response matches the monkey's memory of how much time had passed from the last response. Using the terms *attention* and *memory* is a departure from the descriptive language used to this point to account for animal learning and animal behavior. As discussed earlier, we have attempted to apply *Morgan's Canon* whenever possible. Working within the rigorous methodologies afforded by Skinner's descriptive behaviorism, a great deal of learned human and animal behavior has been accounted for without formally acknowledging the cognitive processes of *paying attention,* of *remembering,* and of *memory.* To the extent these cognitive terms and constructs help us both to explain patterned and other complex animal behavior, and to bridge the gap with behaviors that humans engage in, these terms will be used with caution in discussions of complex behavior throughout this chapter. A brief history of why we use different language to account for human and animal behavior can be found in Box 10.1.

Serial Pattern Learning in Animals

In addition to counting and timing, quite a lot of research has been directed toward understanding how sensitive animals are to serial patterns. Again, this research is best understood within the frameworks of both *animal memory* for patterns and simple *rule learning.* Given a series of items to remember, which patterns presented them can rats and pigeons recognize (i.e., *remember*) and use to solve problems?

Serial Pattern Methodology. The methodology used by Stewart Hulse and his graduate students illustrates how rats can learn serial patterns. Given that hungry rats will run faster or slower in a runway depending upon whether they receive food or not, Hulse (1978) measured the running speed of rats rewarded with a *monotonic series* of reinforcer amounts. Over five successive trial runs, one group of rats found consistently decreasing amounts of pellets of food in the goal box—14, 7, 3, 1, and finally zero pellets. This same sequence was re-

BOX 10.1

A Brief History of Cognitive Science

Introducing cognitive terms into a text-book on animal learning forces us to acknowledge the historical gap between animal *learning* and human *cognition* and *memory*. Recall that in formulating behaviorism, both John B. Watson and B. F. Skinner were reacting against "soft" conceptions of mind. Confident that the human *mind* could not be investigated scientifically, they opted for experimental analyses of *behavior*. Rejecting *mind* properties that could not be operationally defined, they implicitly accepted the Darwinian notion of continuity among animals and adopted instead animal models of behavior. To this behavioral framework, both adaptive-evolutionary theory and the findings of contemporary neuroscience have been incorporated. This textbook is written from within such a perspective.

In the 1950s and 1960s, another epistemology developed outside the behaviorist framework. *Cognitive psychologists* focused their study exclusively upon humans, and they developed their own language and methodologies (see Gardner, 1985, for an excellent history and review). And during the past 40 years, a very interesting pattern has developed. Cognitive psychologists have conducted research, written books, and published articles in journals that dealt with properties of mind *exclusively human*—including learning, intelligence, memory, attention, cognition, language, problem solving, thinking, etc. During the same time period, *comparative psychologists* and other behavioral scientists conducted research, wrote books, and published articles in journals that dealt with properties of mind almost as *exclusively non-human*. For the most part their focus has been on animal learning and behavior.

Many textbooks written in the 1970s, for example, reflected this strange dichotomy. Several had titles like *Learning and Memory* and were written in a fairly standardized format: The first part of these books dealt with animal learning, and the last half with human memory and cognition (e.g., Tarpy & Mayer, 1978; J. Hall, 1982; see also Schwartz & Reisberg, 1991). With exceptions (e.g., Dennett, 1983; Griffin, 1985; Weiskrantz, 1988) few contemporary theorists attempt to bridge the conceptual gaps created by these different philosophical approaches, different research methods, and different terminology.

I wish I could reassure the reader that this issue has been resolved, or that it will be at some time in the near future. But the conduct of science is a slow, very human endeavor, and scientists, their thinking constrained by empirical observations, are conservative. Some researchers *are* bridging the gap by using animals to study parallel problems in human memory (for example, Kesner, 1990). At the same time, however, behaviorists continue to decry the cognitive psychologists' plethora of "mind" terms and hypothetical constructs devoid of empirical reference (Malone, 1982; Wright & Watkins, 1987). Lewontin (1981), for example, argues for "replacing the clockwork mind with something less silly. Updating the metaphor by changing clocks into computers has got us nowhere." Ironically, rapid advances in the study of the central nervous system by behavioral neuroscientists may *shape* both disciplines, forcing them to pay more attention to each other.

peated (five runs × five sequences of reinforcements each day). Eventually these rats were found to run more slowly on those trials that ended in an empty goal box. Note that the only way the rats could *know* that there would be no food in the goal box (as evidenced by their slow rate of running) was that they had learned the sequence of the serial pattern of reinforcement. For this reason, the phenomenon is called **serial pattern learning.**

Cued Counting.   What was the pattern learned in this task? Several analyses are possible. The most parsimonious argument is that these rats may be doing something akin to rhythmic counting. That is, they may have learned the simple rule that they would not be reinforced on every fifth run down the runway. Count to four, pause, count to four, pause, *cha-cha-cha.* If this were the case, then *any* sequence of four reinforced trials preceding a nonreinforced trial would suffice. Or are *some* serial patterns more easily learned than others? Hulse compared the performance of rats on the monotonic series just described with another group of rats that successively found 14, 1, 3, 7, and 0 pellets in the goal box. The same training conditions were used; however, notice that the sequence of pellets was *not* monotonic (the amounts did not consistently decrease). After training, however, these rats *also* learned to slow down on the fifth run, although (a) they took more trials to learn the pattern, and (b) they did not ever slow down as much on the fifth, nonreinforced trial as did the group with the monotonic pattern. We can conclude that rats learned the *pattern* of reinforcement, and the decreasing monotonic series was a more effective cue than the nonmonotonic sequence of 14, 1, 3, 7, and 0 pellets.

Phasing Cues Improve Performance.   What else do we know about serial pattern learning? Other researchers have reported that eliminating the delay between the end of one series (i.e., 0 pellets) and the beginning of the next series (i.e., 14 pellets) makes the pattern unlearnable. Apparently, without the pause in the series, the individual elements of the "pattern" become one long sequence with (to the rat) no discernible elements. The time delay between each repeating series is conceptualized as a *phasing cue*, which serves to demarcate each series (Fountain, Henne, & Hulse, 1984). These investigators also found that a series longer than five elements can be effectively learned by rats if *phasing cues* are introduced, which effectively break the long series into a sequence of shorter elements. Their finding parallels our understanding of how humans reduce long serial patterns into shorter ones, such as telephone numbers (817/829-1979), social security numbers (123-45-6789), and the like.[1]

---

[1]The phenomenon of grouping elements into smaller units is called *chunking.* The phone number is for the post office in Elm Mott, Texas.

Interim Summary

Rats are apparently capable of learning to respond to patterns of stimuli grouped together in time. The task is probably best conceptualized as one in which various cues allow the rat to memorize short repeating patterns, separated from each other by discrete periods of time. For reasons that are at present not understood, monotonic series cues (which are orderly for humans) produce better serial learning performance than nonmonotonic cues in rats. Rats are apparently able to detect the pattern of monotonicity and use it in addition to a serial pattern of reinforcement.

Maze Learning in Animals

The learning of serial patterns as demonstrated by Hulse and his colleagues is in some ways similar to how a rat learns to find its way through a maze. For example, the running speed of rats changes as they learn the particular pattern of the maze in which they are placed. Note the two different patterns of mazes in Figure 10.2. One, the eight-arm radial maze, has a central start box and any of the eight arms can be baited with food and used as a goal box. A traditional maze has a start box and paths containing a number of *choice points* leading to either *cul-de-sacs* or the shortest path to the *goal box*. After many trials in the traditional maze, appropriately patterned responses occur; the rat eliminates blind alleys and wrong turns, allowing rapid entry into the goal box. Let us analyze experiments conducted in these two types of mazes, and then compare maze learning with the serial pattern learning described by Hulse.

How Rats Learn Mazes

A traditional type maze (see Figure 10.2a) was used by Tolman and Honzik (1930a). On successive trials, rats typically run faster and make fewer errors at the choice points on their way to food reinforcement in the goal box. For this reason, much early attention was directed to the rat's performance at these choice points. Among the questions raised were, for example, whether rats make more errors in the first or last part of the maze; whether they learned a *sequence* of left and right turns in an associative manner, and/or whether they *memorized*, or learned, to map the maze. It is beyond the scope of this book to summarize the 90-plus years of research devoted to how rats learn mazes.[2] But for present purposes, let us briefly look at the three questions raised.

[2]Small (1901) built a rat-sized replica of the high-hedged human maze located in the gardens of Henry VIII's Hampton Court Palace and was the first psychologist to study the rat's maze-learning abilities. Having been hopelessly lost in the Hampton Court Maze on several occasions (trials), I find it incredible that Small's rats ever found their way out.

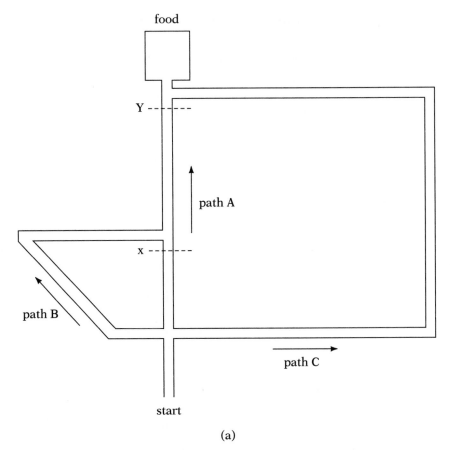

(a)

FIGURE 10.2 Rats in Mazes

(a) The plan of Tolman and Honzik's (1930) "insight" maze. Note that path A is the shortest one unless blocked at point X or point Y. With both blocks in place, path C, the longest route, is the only way to get to the food in the goal box.

In Early Trials, Do Rats Learn the First or Last Part of the Maze?
Rats eliminate errors nearest the goal box, and only after many trials do they successfully make appropriate left and right turns in the early part of the maze (Hull, 1932). Hull described this in terms of the principle of *delay of reinforcement;* the responses at the end of a series of responses are closest to the reinforcing stimulus. Furthermore, Hull (1943) hypothesized that rats learn the maze from back to front by a conditioning process. By his analysis, stimuli encountered upon entry into the goal box are paired with food reinforcement. Fractional

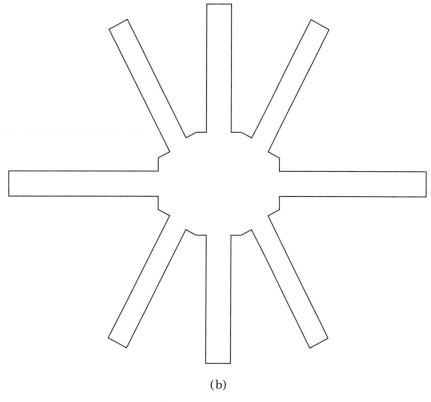

(b)

FIGURE 10.2   *Continued*

(b) Olton's eight-arm radial maze (Olton & Saumelson, 1976). Rats are placed in the center and are free to enter any of the eight arms at any time. None or all of the eight arms may contain food; hungry rats will systematically forage all eight arms, seldom repeating those previously visited.

traces of even earlier stimuli in the maze are *also* conditioned; these stimuli in turn become secondary reinforcers for the earliest responses in the maze. In Hull's system of terminology and notation, these stimuli are called **fractional anticipatory goal responses (r_Gs).** So, to the second question of whether rats learn a *sequence* of left and right turns in an associative fashion, Hull's answer would be a resounding yes. Stimuli comprising each choice point (the shape, color, smell, vestibular and somesthetic cues, orientation of the maze in the room, etc.) are reinforced by secondary reinforcement and eventually by primary reinforcement in the goal box.

Role of r_Gs's in Serial Pattern Learning.   Recall that Hulse's rats learned a serial pattern of reinforcement. After four straight reinforced trials, they learned to run slower on a fifth trial that was never food reinforced. One hypothesis is that rats *connect* the individual elements of this sequence into a *pattern*. The rat uses each reinforced trial as a discriminative stimulus for the next trial. That is, each trial is part of a pattern of trials; each trial has distinctive stimulus properties that signal the rat where it is in the pattern. The patterned sequence of four reinforced trials signals a fifth, nonreinforced trial, in a manner similar to the patterned sequence of left and right turns that signal reinforcement in a goal box.[3] The interested reader is directed to Capaldi and Miller (1988) and Capaldi, Verry, Nawrocki, and Miller (1984) for further analysis and discussion of this hypothesis.

Cognitive Maps of Mazes.   Tolman provided another hypothesis concerning the way rats learn the pattern of a maze; rats make a **cognitive map** of the maze. Tolman was well aware that the term *cognitive map* represented a departure from the connectionist model of association formation. That is, rather than learning a maze dumb-dumb fashion through a trial and error sequence of reinforced and nonreinforced responses, Tolman assumed that a rat "got the idea" of where, in two-dimensional space, *I am located, of where food is located, and of the shortest path connecting me to the food.*

Tolman and Honzik's (1930a) Experiment.   What is the evidence for cognitive maps? Look again at the maze in Figure 10.2a, and notice that "X" and "Y" represent blockades of passages in the maze. Using an analysis of *learning by association*, rats encountering these blocked passages could not make the appropriate instrumental responses leading to reinforcement, and, therefore, they could learn nothing directly about path A (i.e., the straight path from the *starting place* to the *food box*). Indeed, with the passage blocked at two places, Tolman's rats had no alternative but to learn to take the long route (path C) through the maze. When the blockades were then removed, however, the rats quickly took the shortcut, path A. They had never before been food reinforced for taking path A. They had no direct experience with path A. How did they know about the shorter path? Tolman argued that the rats could do this only if they had a *mental representation* of the maze's configuration. The rat's *memory* for the overall pattern of the maze, apparently attained even in the absence of direct experience, allowed the rat, given the opportunity, to efficiently solve the maze.

---

[3]Note that this analysis can likewise be applied to the learning of a long musical piece in which one sequence of finger placements and sounds signals the next sequence of finger placements and sounds, etc.

Spatial Memory in Mazes and Other Environments

Whether or not we buy into Tolman's "mentalistic" terminology, his analysis of this problem in terms of the acquisition of *spatial memory* is probably correct. Bowe (1984) argues that psychologists have long ignored the ability of animals to learn about *spatial relationships,* focusing instead upon *time relationships.* Work with traditional mazes and many experiments using the eight-arm maze (Olton, Collison, & Werz, 1977; see Figure 10.2b) now lead us to believe that rats are expert in the domain of spatial relationships. Why? Presumably because their search for food in a spatial domain uses innately determined **foraging patterns** (Haig, Rawlings, Olton, Mead, & Taylor, 1983). For example, rats first become familiar with the eight-arm pattern of this type of maze by finding food placed in one or more of its "arms." After training, when placed in the start box, rats conduct systematic searches of the eight arms of the maze. Defining an error as reentry of an arm previously searched for food, *rats seldom make errors* under these conditions. On a given series of trials, they enter each arm in turn; even if a previously visited arm is rebaited, or if shaving lotion is used to mask *trail cues* (Olton & Samuelson, 1976). Note that rebaiting the arm with food should provide usable odor cues; since rats do not reenter these arms, odor cues apparently do not play a role in their search pattern. If not food odor, what *does* determine their search pattern? If rats are allowed to visit a few arms and then are removed while the entire maze is rotated 45 degrees, they will go to the previously visited arms in new locations. That is, they seem to be responding almost exclusively in terms of spatial cues and not to characteristics of individual arms of the maze.

Foraging Behavior of Other Animals.   Rats are not the only animals who bring innately determined patterns of behavior to their task of securing food from the environment. Pigeons (Olson & Maki, 1983), marsh tits (Shettleworth & Krebs, 1982), and chimpanzees (Menzel, 1978) join humans in their ability to conduct patterned searches, the result of which is to rapidly locate and remember where food is located in three-dimensional space. Menzel's (1978) chimpanzee experiment is reminiscent of Tolman and Honzik's (1930) blockaded maze experiment. Chimps were carried around an acre of rough outdoor terrain and were allowed to watch as fruits and vegetables were "hidden" at 18 different locations. A short time later, they were turned loose from a central location. Not surprisingly, without hesitation the chimps went by the shortest paths to their most preferred foods (sweet fruits), then systematically collected the remaining vegetables from all 18 sites. In making few errors, each acted as if it had memorized the area through which it conducted a patterned search.

Interim Summary

1. The cognitive abilities of animals are often studied within two separate domains; i.e., (infrahuman) animal learning and human cognitive psychology.

2. Two quite different types of terminology are used in these two fields. *Animal learning* uses a *descriptive behaviorism* terminology, which has two effects: It tends to (over)explain complex processes using a simple associative framework, and in doing so it probably oversimplifies the cognitive abilities of humans. *Cognitive psychology* uses a plethora of cognitive terms, not always operationally defined, many of which are a priori restricted to humans, and in doing so it probably underestimates cognitive processes in animals.

3. Among the simplest of complex behaviors are timing and rhythmic counting. Many animals are highly sensitive to the passage of time.

4. One form of counting is evidenced by the fact that rats can learn *serial patterns* of events distributed in time and can break down long serial patterns into shorter ones by the use of *phasing cues.*

5. Many animals have been demonstrated to have excellent memories for spatial events. Not only can rats learn to negotiate mazes without errors, they also form *cognitive maps* of the areas they are traversing. Some response tendencies at choice points in mazes can be accounted for by Hull's principle of *fractional anticipatory goal responses.*

6. The readiness with which different species of animals learn complex spatial patterns is highly suggestive of an innately *prepared* form of learning. By this analysis, species-specific innate foraging behaviors locate food via patterned searches rather than a random, trial and error approach. Locating food both stops the search and reinforces the pattern; searching continues on nonreinforced trials.

III. Learning About Rules and Concepts

One of the two behavioral vignettes introducing this chapter described the behavior of chimpanzees who apparently had learned a *general rule* governing the oddity task they were confronted with—i.e., they appeared to learn to select the *odd* stimulus of three stimuli presented on a display panel (see Figure 10.1). In some ways this "oddity" configuration is similar to the mazes and patterned reinforcement sequences described in the preceding section. Each oddity problem has a pattern, and the animal's task is to learn the pattern.

Both the oddity task and the animal's behavior differ, however, in that the "pattern" these primates had to learn changed from trial to trial. In the other examples, both the maze pattern and Hulse's reinforcement pattern remained fixed from trial to trial over many sessions. And unlike maze learning, chimpanzees and other animals do not bring innately predisposed foraging strategies to the solution of an oddity problem. Rather, the food hopper is in a fixed position, and animals must learn to solve symbolic problems unrelated to the location of food in space. Symbolic conceptual learning, then, is a different task, presumably a more complex form of learning. Let us take a closer look at the oddity task.

Associative Conditioning, Memorization, or Conceptual Learning?

Note in Figure 10.1 the various positions that triangles, circles, and squares can assume in the oddity problem. Recall that responding to a square in the center position, for example, was sometimes reinforced and sometimes punished. The same was true for a triangle, circle, or square in any position. Throughout the 18 presentations of stimuli in every session, responding to the triangle (S^d) when it appeared with either two squares or two circles was reinforced on each of six occasions and in each of three positions. During the same session, responding to any of the 12 triangles when they were S^Δ's did *not* produce reinforcement. The animals learned to respond to a particular stimulus only when it was positioned in a particular array with other stimuli.

How did chimpanzees accomplish this task? Is it a case of "simple" differential conditioning of a relatively large number of S^d's and S^Δ's? Given the limited number of stimulus arrays (18 in total; see Figure 10.1), following extensive conditioning perhaps they *memorized* which response went with each array. (A human analogy would be the rote memorization of the "times tables.") Or did the animals truly learn to respond to the *odd* stimulus in each array? (A human analogy would be using rules to memorize the times tables—such as "anything multiplied by five ends in zero or five"; "any number multiplied by an even number ends in an even number," etc.) Recognize that the latter alternative is typically what is meant by *conceptual learning;* the former can be considered a repertoire of conditioned responses. Note also that when humans memorize the times tables, both kinds of learning are presumably involved.

Memory Capacity versus General Rule Learning? How can we decide whether the chimpanzees who were able to solve this oddity task memorized particular stimulus configurations or learned a general rule? Unfortunately, for reasons that will soon become apparent, in these experiments we *cannot* decide between these two alternatives. We require at least two kinds of information to help us decide: First, we need information regarding the abilities of nonhuman primates and other animals to memorize (to learn to recognize) a large number of stimulus arrays. Can chimpanzees memorize the correct response to the 18 stimulus arrays depicted in Figure 10.1 without having developed a *concept* of oddity? Second, we need a methodology that allows us to bypass specific memories for previously learned items. We need a task that requires the animal to select novel (untrained) stimuli using a general rule rather than relying upon conditioned responses to particular stimuli that had been reinforced. Let us first look at evidence that chimpanzees can memorize a large number of complex stimulus arrays.

Match-to-Sample

Figure 10.3a depicts "Minnie," a chimpanzee making a conditioned response on a **match-to-sample** task. In this experiment, Don Farrar (1967) trained Minnie and two other chimpanzees to perform at better than 90 percent accuracy. A work session consisted of presenting the chimp a sequence of the 24 different problems, each involving a different stimulus array (see Figure 10.3b). Each problem began with the appearance of a single visual stimulus displayed on a back-lit key located above four similar side-by-side keys. This stimulus, called the *sample,* was displayed for three seconds. The sample was varied in shape and/or color (e.g., a *blue circle*). After the three-second display of the sample, four back-lit keys located below the sample were also illuminated, displaying stimuli varying in color and shape (see Figure 10.3c). The chimpanzee's task was to survey the four keys and to locate and push the one key on which the symbol matched the sample above—hence, *match-to-sample.* For example, the sample stimulus displayed for three seconds in Problem 15 (see Figure 10.3b) was a *plus sign* (+). After three seconds, the sample (+) remained illuminated and the four-stimulus display of a *red circle*, a *minus sign* (-), (+), and a *square* was lit for 10 seconds. The chimp was reinforced by delivery of a banana pellet for pressing the key displaying the (+), in the third position. If the wrong stimulus was selected, the display would terminate without food, and the same problem (beginning with the sample) would be presented until a correct response was made.

After learning this task (which required hundreds of trials; see the following discussion), the procedure was slightly changed. The sample was illuminated for three seconds and *terminated* at the onset of the four-stimulus array. Technically, this procedure is called a **delayed match-to-sample** (with a zero-second delay). Using delayed match-to-sample (especially with longer delays), the animal must remember what the stimulus was and select its match from memory.

FIGURE 10.3 Minnie and the Story of Picture Memory

(a) Chimpanzee #46 ("Minnie") is seen performing on the *match-to-sample* task described in the text. Note the large size of the equipment used to measure responses and to control timing and stimulus configurations in the precomputer era comprising the early 1960s. Minnie continues to live in New Mexico. Now in her mid-thirties, she has successfully borne and raised 15 chimpanzees in captivity. A good mother, she remains a joy to all humans who ever had the pleasure of working with her.

Serendipity. The three chimpanzees in Farrar's study learned this task and performed at high levels of proficiency. Minnie, for example, achieved perfect scores (144 correct/144 problems per day) on 5 of 10 test days; the occasional "misses" appeared to be due to lack of

Problem no.	Pictures				Correct position
	Lever no. 1	Lever no. 2	Lever no. 3	Lever no. 4	
1	+	(G)	|	×	4
2	△	−	□	◎	2
3	(G)	(W)	+	×	3
4	(B)	−	(R)	□	1
5	(G)	△	−	×	2
6	+	×	(R)	(B)	4
7	|	(G)	(W)	△	3
8	|	(G)	−	◎	1
9	+	◎	(OR)	×	3
10	△	□	|	×	2
11	(W)	◎	(B)	|	4
12	◎	(OR)	□	−	1
13	(OR)	(W)	−	(G)	1
14	×	□	(OR)	(R)	2
15	(R)	−	+	□	3
16	△	(G)	|	(R)	4
17	×	□	◎	(B)	3
18	(B)	|	×	−	4
19	(B)	+	□	−	1
20	+	(G)	|	(B)	2
21	×	(W)	−	(B)	2
22	△	×	(G)	(R)	1
23	□	(B)	×	|	3
24	△	−	□	(R)	4

FIGURE 10.3 *Continued*

(b) Table of the 24 problems in Farrar's (1967) study of picture memory. Letters on symbols indicate color (W = white, R = red, etc.). Note that Problem 2 (*triangle, horizontal line, square,* and *circle*) is displayed on the performance panel in Minnie's cage in Figure 10.3c.

FIGURE 10.3 *Continued*

(c) Minnie saw this problem when Farrar began removing stimulus elements from the picture (see text). Pressing the panel with the circle displayed would be reinforced. Amazingly, Minnie could consistently solve this problem even if, for example, neither the horizontal bar nor the circle were illuminated.

attention and to problems timing out before responses were made. Minnie's and the two other chimpanzees' 10-day average accuracy was 99.3, 95.4, and 93.7 percent, respectively. Farrar had noted that Minnie's lack of attention to the display panel did not seem to impede her performance. On several occasions she did not look at the three-second sample stimulus, but when the four-stimulus display was illuminated, she nevertheless made the correct response.[4] One day a technician noticed that the light bulb used to illuminate the sample stimulus was burned out. He checked each of the three animals' records for that day and found that none of the three had suffered any performance decrement.

[4]Farrar, 1992, personal communication.

Picture Memory.   Farrar concluded that each stimulus arrangement comprised a *picture,* and that the chimps had memorized each of the 24 different pictures in Figure 10.3(b)—a phenomenon he called **picture memory.** But note that each picture, while distinctive, has common elements. For example, a green circle appears on 9 of the 24 pictures, but it is reinforced only on Problem 20. On the seven occasions in which a red circle is part of the picture, it is reinforced twice in position 4 and is not reinforced on five other occasions (including twice in position 4, twice in position 3, and once in the first position). What aspect of each picture, then, is controlling the animal's response?

Randomizing the Serial Position Pattern.   Intrigued, Farrar (1967) ran a series of experiments to attempt to determine how these chimpanzees were solving the problem in the absence of a sample. Leaving the sample light off, he first randomized the order of the sequence of presentation of the 24 pictures. The chimps' performance did not change. Farrar concluded that the chimps had not solved the problem by responding based upon the serial presentation of the 24 pictures. That is, the chimps had apparently *not* learned the sequence—"on trial 1, far right key; on trial 2, second from the left," etc.

Removing Elements of Each Picture.   In subsequent daily tests (again with the sample light off), Farrar (1967) systematically eliminated one or two of the distractor symbols in each of the 24 pictures. The deleted stimulus elements appeared as blank (unlit) response keys (see example with all stimulus keys lit, Figure 10.3c). Only one of the three chimps suffered any change in performance (i.e., 85 percent rather than 95 percent accuracy) even when *half the picture* (i.e., *two of the four distractor stimuli,* or S^{Δ}'s) *was eliminated.* For example, in Problem 10 (see Figure 10.3b) the triangle and the (X) were removed, and only the square and the vertical slash appeared. Having never seen this picture before, and in the absence of a sample, the chimps nevertheless picked the square, the S^d previously associated with reinforcement. Apparently, Farrar concluded, merely the presence of the S^d in a particular position along with at least one other stimulus element was enough of the picture for the animal to solve the problem.

What Is the S^d in "Degraded" Pictures?   Farrar then gambled ingeniously. What if the consistently rewarded stimulus in each picture does *not* by itself constitute the S^d, he wondered? What would happen if instead of removing two of the three S^{Δ}'s from each picture, he removed the S^d and one S^{Δ}? How would the animals respond in the absence of the correct stimulus element? On each of the next two days all three chimpanzees were presented with pictures that contained only 50 percent of the elements they originally had been trained with. On the first day, one each of 12 S^d's and S^Δ's were deleted from half the pictures; two S^Δ's were deleted from each of the other 12 pictures. The second day was like the first except that Farrar deleted different S^d's and S^Δ's. Recall that these deleted stimulus elements appeared as blank (unlit) response keys, and if the blank key was in the position that an S^d usually occupied, responding to the blank key would be reinforced.

The performance of the three chimps deteriorated but, again, far less than one might assume. Assuming that the animals would continue to respond to blank keys (which they did), their chance performance, or guessing, on this problem can be computed to have an expected efficiency of 25 percent. (Given four keys, the chimps had a one in four chance of being reinforced on each trial.) The three chimps' performance on the first test day with S^d's missing was 49.3, 57.6, and 50.0 percent, and on the second day, with a different set of S^d's removed was 68.1, 72.9, and 62.5 percent, respectively. Farrar speculated that the improvement on the second day represented relearning of a new picture, a picture in which the blank keys effectively served as stimulus elements. Unfortunately, training was disrupted at this point, and terminal performance on such highly degraded pictures was not realized.

Learning About Pictures, or Learning Concepts?

What have we learned? Or better, what have these animals learned? This extended section on *picture memory* was introduced to answer a specific question about the memory capabilities of chimpanzees for this type of problem. Specifically, we wanted to know if chimpanzees were capable of *memorizing* which response went with each of the 18 oddity problems displayed in Figure 10.1, or, alternatively, if they learned a *general rule* (i.e., if they learned to respond to the *odd* stimulus in each array). From Farrar's experiment we know that chimpanzees are capable of memorizing at least 24 pictures—each of which has more pictorial elements than the three-symbol oddity problem. And so it is possible that in the behavioral vignette opening this chapter, chimpanzees did *not* learn the concept of oddity—rather, they might have learned to make specific conditioned responses to 18 different pictures. Although supporting records do not exist, the chimpanzees' performance in Koestler and Barker's (1965) study was low (60–70 percent efficiency) because they consistently missed *particular* problems: Errors were not randomly distributed throughout the set of 18 problems. Their pattern of performance suggests *picture memory* rather than a *concept of oddity*.

Indeed, Farrar's (1967) study of picture memory raises problems for all "concept formation" methodologies that use a relatively small number of items. Memorization precedes, and perhaps precludes, rule learning in these tasks. Given the apparently excellent memory of chimpanzees for pictures, we are faced with devising a task that requires an animal to select a novel stimulus using a general rule rather than relying upon conditioned responses to particular stimuli. And Harry Harlow (1949) already had showed us how to do just that.

Learning a Win-Stay, Lose-Shift Strategy

Harlow's task was simpler than the oddity task we have described. His monkey-training apparatus is depicted in Figure 10.4a. The experimenter lowers a screen so that the Rhesus monkey cannot watch where food is hidden in either of two food cups located beneath two objects arranged on a tray. (The stimulus objects were small toys and other novelty items purchased from the local variety store.) One of the items is designated as the "correct" choice for six consecutive trials (i.e., the reward is hidden beneath it), and the position of the "correct" item is determined by a randomization scheme. The monkey has a 50 percent chance of being right on each trial. It can maximize reinforcement by a **win-stay, lose-shift** strategy, as follows.

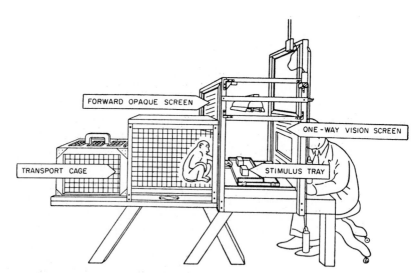

FIGURE 10.4   Learning to Learn

(a) An apparatus called the WGTA (*Wisconsin General Test Apparatus*) placed an experimenter across from a monkey. A series of screens could be raised and lowered, allowing the experimenter, out of view of the monkey, to "bait" the correct food cup over which a stimulus object was placed. Once in place, the monkey's screen could be raised, allowing it to respond to the testing situation (see text for further details).

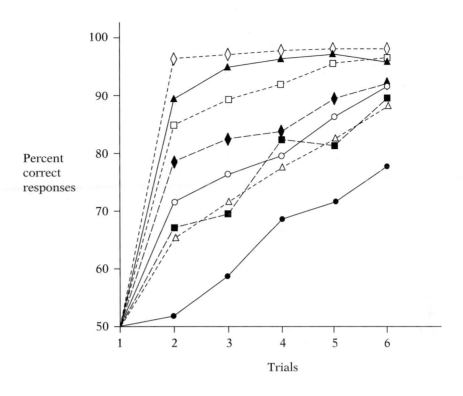

Discriminations		Discriminations
● —— ● 1–8		◆ - - - - ◆ 1–100
△ - - - - - △ 9–16		□ - - - - - □ 101–200
■ - - - - ■ 17–24		▲ —— ▲ 201–256
○ —— ○ 25–32		◇ - - - - - ◇ 257–312

(b)

FIGURE 10.4 *Continued*

(b) Harlow's (1949) *learning set* data, which shows the acquisition of a *win-stay, lose-shift* strategy over several hundred trials. Each learning set consists of six consecutive trials in which two objects were presented to a monkey, one of which is arbitrarily and consistently rewarded if the monkey chooses it rather than the other. Mean percent correct responses are plotted for the first eight problems the monkeys encountered, then the next eight (i.e., 9–16), the next eight (17–24), and so on. The data are then regrouped and plotted in blocks of 100 problems (i.e., 1–100, 101–200, etc.). Note the performance for problems 257–312; after this number of trials the *win-stay, lose-shift* strategy has been almost perfectly learned, as evidenced by 97 percent correct performance on the second trial.

Let a red block be the correct stimulus, and a thimble the incorrect stimulus. If the monkey selects the red block on the first trial, it will be rewarded (i.e., "win"), and on the next trial with the same pair of stimuli, it will continue to be reinforced for selecting the red block (i.e., for "staying" with the red block). Selecting the thimble is never reinforced. After six trials, the monkey is confronted with two new objects, one of which is reinforced, the other not. Note that the sooner this rule is learned (i.e., "if reinforced, stay with that choice; if not reinforced, shift to the other choice"), the more reinforcements will be attained. Harlow found that after having six trials with each of eight pairs of objects, monkeys averaged about 75 percent correct responses on their sixth trial with the eighth pair (see Figure 10.4b). He concluded that monkeys were capable of learning a *win-stay, lose-shift* rule.

Learning Sets, or Learning to Learn

As Harlow's monkeys continued their training with new objects (i.e., trained beyond the first eight pairs of objects), another phenomenon emerged. They got better at the task. To perform at only 75 percent efficiency on the sixth trial of a two-choice task means that during these first eight successive pairs of objects, the monkeys required several trials to learn to *stay* (if reinforced) and several trials to learn to *shift* (if punished). These monkeys apparently were learning anew the solution to each novel problem within the six training trials. Once each monkey had mastered this concept, however, and had learned a *strategy*, it no longer needed six trials to learn the correct response. Rather than having to be differentially conditioned to each new S^d and S^Δ, these monkeys applied a *general rule* to each new set of paired objects. Harlow described this as **learning to learn.**

Our attention, therefore, shifts to the animal's behavior on the *second* trial. Figure 10.4(b) shows how these monkeys continued to improve their performance, so that after 100 or so sets of six trials (with two new objects in each set), they began to stay or shift on the second trial of the six-trial set. That is, with each new pair, they did not have to learn the strategy anew; rather they had only to implement a strategy (apply a rule) already learned. Harlow called this task a **learning set.** The monkeys, he reasoned, had *learned how to learn* novel *learning sets.* After 250-plus trials, the monkeys were about 98 percent accurate on the second through sixth trials with each newly introduced pair of stimuli.

Comparison of Learning Set Performance Across Species

The simplicity of Harlow's method allowed for the comparison of *learning set formation* across different species. Figure 10.5 is a composite of studies conducted by different researchers and plotted by

Warren (1965). Data on children aged two to five years reported by Harlow (1949) have been added to Warren's (1965) figure. As can be seen, rats and squirrels seem to be pretty much incapable of learning a win-stay, lose-shift strategy; squirrel monkeys, marmosets, and cats are somewhat better after 1000 problems (six trials per problem); Harlow's Rhesus monkeys do well after several hundred trials; and human children learn the most rapidly of all animals tested. While some of the children (presumably the older ones) were 85 percent accurate in less than 20 trials, their group means nevertheless showed a typical negatively accelerated learning curve. In this study, then, young humans also had to learn a rule before they could apply it with a high degree of accuracy. The process by which they learned this rule is presumably similar to the process by which Rhesus monkeys

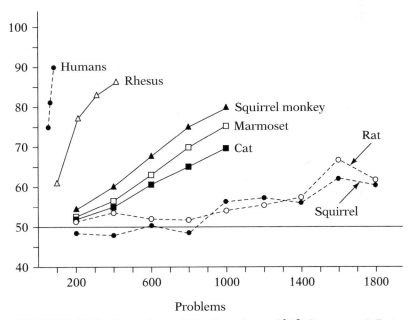

FIGURE 10.5   Learning a Win-Stay, Lose-Shift Strategy: A Between-Species Comparison

The percent correct responses on trial 2 is plotted as a function of the number of problems encountered in *learning set* training. Note that after 1000 trials rats and squirrels finally begin to perform slightly better than chance. Rhesus monkeys clearly outperform cats and squirrel monkeys (from Warren, 1965). The data from children aged two to five years (Harlow, 1949) have been added to Warren's (1965) comparative data.

and other animals learned. Only humans are smarter—they learned much more quickly.

New Stimulus Test in Both Match-to-Sample and the Oddity Problem

The importance of Harlow's "learning to learn" demonstration is that it clearly shows that animals can learn to apply a rule to solve a novel problem. By contrast, using the discrete number of both oddity and match-to-sample problems described earlier, the ability of monkeys and chimpanzees to solve novel problems was not tested. Is there *other* evidence that monkeys can learn concepts of match-to-sample and oddity by applying a general rule to novel items? The short answer is yes. After extensive training, Capuchin and squirrel monkeys (both are New World monkeys) can solve oddity problems with novel items on the first trial (Thomas & Boyd, 1973). Capuchin monkeys are also capable of learning to apply a rule to solve a simplified version of the match-to-sample task. In this task, a sample stimulus such as a square is illuminated, and next to it an identical square and a "different" stimulus are presented. The monkey is reinforced for matching two identical stimuli. After approximately 1000–1500 trials, monkeys are able to correctly match a novel sample with a high level of efficiency (D'Amato, Salmon, & Colombo, 1985). Had the chimpanzees who had learned the 18-array oddity task (Figure 10.1) and the 24-array match-to-sample task (Figure 10.3b) been given *new stimulus* tests, based upon these results with monkeys, it is likely that chimpanzees could have learned to perform a *new stimulus* test as well as monkeys.

Transitive Inference Reasoning by Chimpanzees

If *a* is greater than *b,* and *b* is greater than *c,* is *a* greater than *c?* Most (but not all) schoolchildren can answer this riddle. We call the ability of those who can solve this problem **transitive inferential reasoning.** Can chimpanzees *reason* in this way? If, after having learned that $a > b$ and that $b > c$, a chimp can answer, "yes, *a* is greater than *c,*" without ever having been reinforced for choosing $a > c$, we have evidence of reasoning, and we have also satisfied the requirement of a *new stimulus* test.

Sadie, Luvie, and Jessie. Some evidence exists that with difficulty some (but not all) chimpanzees can be trained to solve this problem (Gillan, 1981, 1983). The method was simple. On a given trial two of five different containers were presented to the animal; choosing the "correct" one was reinforced with a preferred food. The five containers each had a distinctively colored lid by which the chimp could tell one from the other. The rules governing reinforcement were that for every pair, one color was consistently "greater than" the other color. For example, in a green vs. blue pairing, green was reinforced; in a red vs. green pairing, red was reinforced. After extensive training, a novel question could then be asked of the animal: Which do you choose from a red vs. blue pairing? Those chimps consistently choosing red over blue provided evidence for *transitive inferential reasoning.* Gillan reports that after extensive training, Sadie performed at 89 percent accuracy, and Luvie and Jessie were 72 percent and 69 percent accurate (50 percent = chance performance). Chimpanzees, then, are marginally capable of learning a series of specific relationships taken two at a time and, by extrapolation, applying these learned rules to construct a larger pattern of relationships. This ability of chimps albeit halting and puny, resembles the transitive inferential reasoning abilities of most children.

Pigeons Can Learn the Concept of Sameness

Note in Figure 10.5 the marginal performance of rats and squirrels on a *learning set* problem. Are the foregoing conceptual abilities of rule learning (such as *win-stay, lose-shift; oddity;* and *match-to-sample*) restricted to primates? The answer is a qualified "no." Pigeons, for example, cannot perform oddity tasks, but how they learn concepts has been extensively studied, with surprising results. In a **sameness task,** for example, pictures of objects are sequentially presented to pigeons. Following this series, a final picture is presented that either was or was not in the series (i.e., *same* or *different,* respectively). Pigeons are apparently able to remember a series of pictures seen on only one previous occasion, because they can solve this problem for food reinforcement by responding to one key if this final picture is the same, and to another key if this picture is different from all those in the preceding series (Wright, Santiago, Sands, & Urcuioli, 1984).

Natural Concepts in Pigeons

The abilities of pigeons to extract information from complex pictures of natural environments is truly remarkable. In a series of experiments by Herrnstein and his colleagues (reviewed by Herrnstein, 1984), pigeons were trained to respond to photographs in a way that indicated they recognized such **natural concepts** as trees, people, and other "open-ended" categories. For example, pigeons who pecked at slides of pictures (projected onto keys in the Skinner Box) containing trees (S^d's) were reinforced, while pigeons pecking at slides *not* containing trees (S^Δ's) were not reinforced (Herrnstein, Loveland, &

Cable, 1976). The pigeons learned this discrimination to a discrete set of stimuli, and the concept generalized to new pictures. Herrnstein et al. (1976) also were successful in training pigeons to discriminate photos of a particular person (S^d) from photos of other people (S^{Δ}'s). This discrimination was learned even when similar clothing was worn by the target and the distractors. This is surprising? Shouldn't clothing be as discriminative a stimulus as facial features, hair, and whatever other human attributes controlled the response?

Abstracting Taxonomic Classifications.   How are pigeons able to learn this difficult discrimination? Even though pigeons are unable to learn to solve oddity problems, and physical dissimilarity of the pictures alone cannot account for what is learned about them, Roitblat (1987, p. 307) argues that pigeons are apparently capable of learning "relatively abstract *taxonomic classifications*" of objects. Another mystery surrounding the pigeon's ability to abstract a rule from highly ambiguous information is that fewer trials are needed relative to the number of trials chimpanzees and monkeys require to learn oddity and match-to-sample tasks. Let us examine this issue more closely.

Number of Trials in Learning Abstract Concepts

Fifteen hundred trials? Why does it take monkeys and chimpanzees so many trials to learn seemingly simple rules? Learning strategies such as win-stay, lose-shift, and abstract concepts such as oddity, match-to-sample, and inferential reasoning tasks are difficult for chimpanzees, where difficulty is operationally defined as the number of trials to criterion. In the absence of language, it is apparent that animals learn strategies and rules via basic associative processes. After many hundreds of consistently reinforced responses to stimuli with specifiable characteristics, they begrudgingly acquire a response strategy that allows them to solve new problems. No "*Eureka!*" experience. No "A-ha" phenomenon. Nothing that resembles what humans typically mean when they use the term *insight*. Rather, the cognitive processes these animals display after extensive training appear to have been learned by differentially reinforced responding. "Rules" governing the selection of specific reinforced choices are learned slowly, and they appear to be applied to untrained stimulus objects without keen insight. Indeed, it was argued that chimpanzees working oddity and match-to-sample problems seem to prefer to memorize pictures rather than to learn rules.

Pigeons Prepared to Learn Natural Concepts?   In this regard, as noted before, pigeons remain a mystery. Granted that pigeons also learn the S^d-S^{Δ} discrimination in an associative manner, they seem, however, to be prepared (in an adaptive-evolutionary sense) to learn some discriminations more easily than others. What is the evidence for *prepared* learning by pigeons? Learning natural concepts requires fewer trials than learning a complex visual discrimination without such taxonomic features. For example, Herrnstein and de Villiers (1980) reported that "fish slides" are more easily discriminated from "non-fish slides" than a control condition in which one set of slides is arbitrarily grouped as S^d's and another set as S^Δ's. More rapid acquisition of natural concepts (i.e., fish, people, trees) is taken as evidence for *prepared learning* as discussed in Chapters 5 and 6. For unknown reasons, pigeons have preferences for some pictures over others, and they seem to use a taxonomic grouping rule without extensive training.

In addition, after learning a set of fish pictures, a *new* fish picture tends to be also be treated as an S^d on the pigeon's first encounter with that picture. Reinforcement of a particular picture is not necessary for it to be included in a category. Pigeons learn faster than monkeys that, after learning either win-stay, lose-switch strategies (Harlow, 1949) or an oddity concept (Thomas & Boyd, 1973), are able to respond meaningfully to novel stimuli. The pigeon's task may be easier, however; recall that pigeons are *unable* to learn to solve oddity problems (Roitblat, 1987). Perhaps we have underestimated just how difficult the oddity task is to learn.

Primates Contraprepared to Learn Concepts?

Given that small-brained pigeons can learn natural concepts, what can be said of the pitiful efforts of larger-brained primates who require trials numbering in the thousands? Normally, monkeys and chimpanzees never encounter match-to-sample, oddity problems, and other conceptual tasks as presented them in human laboratories. So, from an adaptive-evolutionary perspective, we are asking them to do something other than what their brains were designed to do. Having trained many chimpanzees to solve such conceptual problems, allow me to observe that their task-solving behavior often brought to mind that of children—and of mentally retarded and otherwise brain-impaired human adults, and of college professors and students—who are confronted with a very difficult problem to solve. Chimpanzees often vocalized their frustration, anger, and sadness when they failed, and they exhibited happiness when they succeeded. And, like many bright schoolchildren I know, on many occasions chimpanzees also expressed disdain and disinterest for the task at hand.

Do All Humans Form Concepts? The latter point is not unimportant. Conceptual learning does not come easily to all children, nor, for that matter, to all adults. College-educated students find some concepts easy to understand, and yet others, impossible. How many trials? After how many years of formal instruction in school do we continue to find "bright, mature adults," who, in the words of Diamond (1988, p. 337), continue to "show the same dumb behaviours seen in infants—e.g., failure to show transfer of training, absence of systematic hypothesis testing or planning, rigidity, and perseveration"?

An alternative view of the relatively poor performance of primates compared with pigeons on concept-learning tasks is that primates bring to these tasks more hypotheses or strategies that must be discarded. Their poor performance might be viewed as resulting from their relatively greater cognitive resources. Though possible, I find this alternative unlikely. Humans are considered intelligent in no small measure because they rapidly learn response-reinforcement relationships. Why other primates do so poorly is a mystery.

Some forms of conceptual learning, then, seem to be acquired by trial and error rather than by "insight." Our association models *are* relevant to accounts of conceptual learning. But, you may argue, we have yet to consider language. What is the role of language in abstract thinking processes? Let us now turn to language, something that humans in fact do better than animals.

Interim Summary

1. Primates (humans, monkeys, and chimpanzees) are able to learn simple concepts and form general rules to solve such problems as match-to-sample and oddity. Chimpanzees can be trained to reason. Rats and pigeons are incapable of forming the concept of *oddity*.
2. After many hundreds of training trials, chimpanzees are able to form memories of pictures. They can respond in meaningful ways when the pictures are highly degraded, even to the point of continuing to respond in the absence of the discriminative stimulus element.
3. Given a two-choice task, a variety of animals (including children, pigeons, and rats) can learn a win-stay, lose-shift rule that can then be applied to successfully solve novel problems.
4. Pigeons are capable of extracting a surprising amount of information from pictures presented to them in the laboratory. Pigeons can remember whether they have (or have not) seen a particular picture from a series of pictures presented earlier. They are also capable of learning so-called *natural concepts*, taxonomically grouping trees, fish, humans, etc., and responding to new examples by including them in the correct categories.
5. The large number of trials required to learn even the simplest of concepts suggests that primates, including humans, are *not* evolutionarily prepared to think conceptually. The fact remains that humans can outperform all other animals on every conceptual task devised.

IV. Communication, and Animal "Language"

Thinking Without Language

In Focus on Research 10.1, Larry Weiskrantz presented convincing arguments that language is *not* essential for complex cognitive skills in animals or in humans. Evidence for this assertion? Severely aphasic (non–language-using) patients often score highly on nonverbal IQ tests. Another important consideration is that preverbal infants "can sometimes apprehend the unity, the boundaries, the persistence, and the identity of objects," thereby presumably displaying conceptual knowledge of the world (Spelke, 1988, p. 180). Humans think in language, but humans also "think" musically, mathematically, visually, gastronomically, athletically, etc. In addition, as we learned in the preceding section, nonverbal animals are capable of learning simple rules, strategies, and concepts that arguably constitute evidence for simple *thinking*.

Nevertheless, language usage is considered by many scientists and philosophers to be *the* distinctive, defining characteristic of *Homo sapiens*. What species-specific capability is universally recognized as quintessentially human? Language. What do humans use language to do, and to do better than any other animal? To think abstractly. So the question entertained in this section is not whether animals can think without language (cf. Weiskrantz, 1988) but rather, what does language *add* to thinking processes?

Framing the Arguments. The strategy for tackling these difficult issues will proceed along several venues. First, we will consider evidence as to whether animals other than humans (a) display rudimentary communication skills/language; (b) can be trained to manipulate "words" in the form of symbols that stand for agents, actions, and objects; and (c) having learned symbolic communication skills, can appropriately and spontaneously use this artificial language as humans use *their* language. In a later section on human language, we will explore the role that associative learning plays in both the acquisition and usage of language; namely, do simple laws of association help us understand human language, or can language only be understood by reference to higher—specifically human—cognitive functioning? As we explore human language, inevitably we return to questions of thinking and of human consciousness. Let us begin with animal communication and animal language.

What Is Animal "Language"?

Are humans the only animals capable of learning language? Before examining the evidence for language capabilities among animals, the semantic problem of "what constitutes language" seemingly must be addressed. But the problem of "what constitutes language" is so thorny that for present purposes we shall merely look at what some investigators *think* is evidence for language capabilities in animals. As the argument develops, it is hoped that you will begin to have a better understanding of just how marvelous your language behavior is.

Communication

A traditional approach to these complex questions is to distinguish between animal *communication* and animal *language.* Many animals "communicate" with each other (i.e., with conspecifics—members of the same species), among other ways, by pheromones, by visual displays, and by vocalizations. Recognize that these types of "communications" involve both the production and reception of signals, typically meaningful only to conspecifics. Such communications seem to have similar functions to that of human language.

But are these signals language? While modifiable by experience, such animal communications are considered to be reflexively tied to specific eliciting conditions in the environment. By contrast, human language is typically viewed as being less reflexive and more *intentional.* Humans, the argument goes, *know* what they are talking about, and animals do not.

Vervet Monkeys.   Perhaps the most intriguing example of animal communication is some clever research on vervet monkeys first reported by Seyfarth, Cheney, and Marler (1980). Vervet monkeys make what are called *alarm calls* in the presence of predators. These investigators recorded the alarm calls and systematically observed the various reactions of the monkeys when (in the absence of predators) particular calls were replayed from carefully hidden speakers. Seyfarth et al. found evidence of a primitive form of language; one of the alarm calls caused the monkeys to look up (for predatory eagles), another to look around on the ground (for pythons), and yet another call to take to the trees (to escape leopards). Infant vervet monkeys vocalized these alarm calls imperfectly, but improved with age and experience.

Intentionality.   What are we to make of vervet monkey alarm calls? Are they words? Does a monkey making an alarm call *intend* to warn others, or is the sight of a predator merely acting as a *sign-releasing stimulus* that triggers a *fixed action pattern (FAP)* consisting of both a particular vocalization and attendant movement response? Dennett (1983) argues in favor of *intentionality* in vervet monkey calls and in other forms of animal communication. He cites Seyfarth et al.'s

(1980) observation that when alone (out of the hearing range of other monkeys), on seeing a leopard a vervet monkey will silently climb to safety rather than vocalize an alarm call. By this analysis, the vocalization response to seeing a leopard is not reflexive (involuntary); rather, alarm calls are *intended* (voluntary) to warn other nearby members of predators.

Origins of Animal Communication.   Not all behavioral scientists who study comparative animal cognition agree with Dennett's (1983) analysis. Monkeys may or may not be that smart. Others would like to see evidence of intentionality independent of their innate vocalization FAP; for example, shaking a branch, throwing something, etc. What is unarguably clear from this example of vervet monkey behavior, however, is that primates other than humans use vocalized signals to communicate with each other. Our special interest in asking these questions about *primate* communication is an acknowledgment of both our genetic relatedness and our curiosity regarding the *origins* of human language. In the movie *Quest for Fire,* primitive hominids are characterized as having limited language capabilities—simple words and phrases directly related to meeting survival needs. It is assumed that human language evolved, presumably from simple to complex, but no evidence of such transformation exists. Because language does not fossilize, we have no record of the origins of language. When we ask questions about early hominid capabilities, we are restricted to studies of extant primates.

Brain Basis of Communication and Language.   Among the many features shared by all primates are patterns of brain organization. One attempt to probe the origins of human language is to compare the organization of the human brain—especially the language areas—with that of other living primates. As can be seen in Focus on Research 10.2, Peter MacNeilage and his students have come to some interesting conclusions about the relationship of right- and left-handedness, and the left and right hemispheres of the brain, to the origins of language.

Bridging the Language Gap.   Not matter how close the brain organization of other primates resembles that of humans, we are left with the fact that humans speak and animals do not. If only animals could talk, we might know more about their *intentions* as well as other aspects of their psychological experience. The Seyfarth et al. (1980) research strategy was to eavesdrop on what vervet monkeys were saying in their ecological niche, and then by analyzing their behavioral responses to interpret what the vocalizations meant. We leave this area of research in animal communication to look at the results of a

FOCUS ON RESEARCH 10.2

Dr. Peter MacNeilage

Evolution of Higher Human Functions

Dr. Peter MacNeilage, Department of Linguistics and Psychology, University of Texas at Austin

"The classical Darwinian view of the evolution of all important properties of life forms is one of descent with modification. However, the typical approach to the evolution of higher human functions such as language and skilled handedness is an *anthropocentric* one, emphasizing human *uniqueness*. Most common right handedness is thought to have first evolved with the construction and use of tools by hominids living about two and a half million years ago; the associated left hemisphere brain specialization was later used for speech.

"Evidence is accumulating for a radically different view more in accord with Neodarwinism. Judging from living prosimians (e.g., *bush babies*), a *right* hemisphere visuospatiomotor specialization associated with left handedness for predatory reaching and eating insects and small animals may have evolved in the earliest primates—about fifty-million years ago. At the same time, a complementary left hemisphere postural control specialization (i.e., for hanging onto tree branches) developed. Evidence for right handed manipulation in monkeys and apes suggests that the fine control capabilities of the right hand evolved from the left hemisphere postural control specialization. Evidence of a left hemisphere specialization for vocal communication in monkeys suggests that *prior to language origins,* the postural demands of communication in trees might have led to a specialization of the postural control hemisphere for production of communicative gestures."

different research strategy. What happens if researchers try to teach animals an artificial, symbolic language? Since untrained animals do not understand human language, and we likewise struggle with theirs, why not try to develop a common, simplified, symbolic language? In doing this we remove the animal from its ecological niche and ask it to do the "unnatural" task of communicating on human terms. We will first look at research with porpoises and dolphins, and then we will return to primates.

Porpoises and Dolphins

As was alluded to in the previous section, many animals, porpoises and dolphins included, vocalize amongst themselves in their natural habitats. Presumably because of these abilities, and their apparent eagerness to both interact and communicate with humans (Lilly, 1961), a number of dolphins have been subjected to intensive symbolic language training regimens. Here we will concentrate on research by Louis Herman and his associates, and another research program headed by Ronald Schusterman. Although both use similar training methods, and get similar results, their various interpretations of the language capabilities of dolphins differ markedly, along the behavioral-cognitive split alluded to in Box 10.1. The issues raised by these two interpretations will reemerge in a later discussion of what both chimpanzees and humans "mean" when they use "language."

What Can Dolphins Learn About Symbols? If you have ever had the good fortune of watching a trained dolphin perform, you probably wondered how the dolphin was able to respond to a series of verbal and hand-signal commands. Did the porpoise really *understand* the signaled instructions to fetch the red ball and shoot the ball at the basket on the *right-hand side* of the pool? Herman, Richards, and Wolz (1984) consider that Ake, a bottlenose dolphin, after learning such a task, has a "tacit knowledge of syntactic rules," allowing the animals to comprehend three- to five-word "sentences." Each "sentence" learned by the dolphin had three essential components, hand-signaled in sequence: the (direct) *object* (i.e., the "basket on the right-hand side of the pool"); the *action* (i.e., "fetch"); and the *agent* (i.e., "red ball"). Both the color of the objects and the positions (right, left) were modifiers that required Ake to select from alternatives. Herman et al. (1984) consider the "sentence" components to be "words" and, further, that "dolphins are sensitive to the semantic and syntactic features of the sentences we construct in those languages, because their responses covary with variations in those features" (Herman, 1989, p. 46).

Language, or Rule Learning? While acknowledging the complexity of the tasks Ake was able to learn, other researchers disagree with Herman's (1989) linguistic analysis. For example, Schusterman and Gisner (1988, 1989) have trained both dolphins and sea lions using the same techniques, and with the same results reported by Herman. Invoking *Morgan's Canon*, however, they argue that animals are performing conditioned responses, not understanding language. They see the animal's task as a *conditional sequential discrimination* problem, involving three categories of signs, and using two rules:

1. **If** an OBJECT is designated by one, two, or three signs (an OBJECT sign and up to two modifiers), **then** perform the designated ACTION to that object.

2. **If** two OBJECTS are designated (again, by one to three signs each) and the ACTION is *FETCH*, **then** take the second designated object to the first (Schusterman & Gisner, 1988, p. 346).

Analysis of "Language-Trained" Dolphins.   Which analysis is correct? In this text we have consistently taken the position that given two accounts, the more parsimonious explanation is to be preferred. In doing so we run the risk of underattributing complexity of thought that may in fact accompany the dolphins' performance. Let us here, then, simply emphasize what can be agreed upon. There is no disagreement that these dolphins' trained behaviors required many hundreds of trials using both Pavlovian and Skinnerian techniques. Nothing emerged from the system that was not put into it. Following this elaborate training, we have no window into the dolphin's mind. We do not know (to paraphrase Dennett, 1983, p. 344) what dolphins *know*, what they *want*, what they *understand*, and what they *mean*. Other aspects of human language, including such possibilities as irony, metaphor, storytelling, confabulation, etc. (ibid., p. 347), did not emerge, nor could they have, given the primitive language components provided the dolphins. In this regard, the more parsimonious behavioral account is probably closer to the truth of the matter. Rather than language comprehension, their behavior is better construed as a further example of the ability of animals to learn complex rules. For example, their "if *x*, then *y*" rule is similar to the win-stay, lose-shift response strategy described earlier. Indeed, previously considered examples of how S^d's can come to control the behavior of rats and pigeons in *multiple* and *chained* schedules of reinforcement approach the complexity of these dolphins' behavior.

Language Studies with the Common Chimpanzee (**Pan troglodytes**)

Donald, Gua, and Viki.   Winthrop Kellogg's interest in both porpoise and chimpanzee behavior resulted in two classic publications—*Porpoises and Sonar* in 1961, and *The Ape and the Child* in 1933. In both books he addressed questions of comparative cognition: Can these animals communicate with humans, and can we use their vocalizations as a window into animal consciousness?[5] Kellogg was

---

[5]A staunch behaviorist, Kellogg would not have used terminology referring to "consciousness."

among the first of many researchers in this century who systematically attempted to break the communication barrier with chimpanzees (Benjamin & Bruce, 1982). *The Ape and the Child* chronicled Luella and Winthrop Kellogg's nine-month experiment of raising an infant chimp named Gua along with their 10-month old child, Donald, in their home environment. Among their research objectives, simply stated, was whether humanlike behavior would emerge if a chimp was raised in a human environment. One finding, simply stated, is that not only did Gua remain mute, he seemed to have a retarding effect on Donald's acquisition of language (Benjamin & Bruce, 1982). Other efforts (Hayes & Hayes, 1951) over several years time to teach a chimpanzee named Viki to talk proved equally ineffective. Conclusion? The common chimpanzee, **Pan troglodytes,** is unable to talk to us.

Washoe, Nim, and Koko.   Though unquestionably fascinating, the Kelloggs' and Hayes' failure to communicate with their chimps speaks more to these investigators' methodological limitations than to the chimpanzees' lack of capacity for language. Both attempted to use the chimpanzees' innate vocalizations, but chimps rarely make humanlike sounds. Allen and Beatrice Gardner provided a solution to this problem by training a chimpanzee named Washoe to sign using *ASL*, or American Sign Language (Gardner & Gardner, 1971). Using both food and praise as reinforcers, they reported that Washoe learned well over 100 signed words. Terrace (1979) also trained Nim Chimpsky (cf. Noam Chomsky) in ASL, but contrary to the Gardners' conclusions about Washoe's language capabilities, Terrace was struck more by the differences between humans and chimps. He cites (a) the intensity of training effort required for even the simplest of words with his chimp, relative to the little effort expended on humans; (b) the lack of either spontaneity or creativity in language use when not prompted by the experimenter; and (c) evidence that the chimp echoed back the same "multi-word" sentences *as trained* rather than as novel combinations of signs. Although not all primate researchers agree with Terrace, similar criticism has been made of the language skills of a lowland gorilla named Koko following ASL training (Patterson & Linden, 1981). Terrace's assessment, you might note, is similar to that of Schusterman and Gisner (1989), who concluded that after extensive training dolphins exhibited conditioned responses rather than "language." This question can be alternatively framed as one of whether animal language is ever proactive (i.e., generative) or always is merely reactive (elicited after training). Humans definitely exhibit proactive as well as reactive language.

Sara and Lana.   Two other methodological attempts to talk to chimpanzees were independently implemented in the 1970s by David

Premack and by Duane Rumbaugh and their respective collaborators. In both methods, chimps were trained to associate artificial symbols with actions and objects using food reinforcement. For example, Premack and Premack (1972) trained a chimp named Sara to associate uniquely shaped plastic tokens with particular *agents, actions,* and *objects* (cf. Ake's dolphin "language"). Sara was taught to first "read" and then to physically arrange a three-token sequence, for example, standing for "Sara," "take," and "apple." After several years training, the Premacks reported that Sara eventually learned to use the *agent-action-object* format to create unique "sentences" never before reinforced.

Chimpanzee-Computer Interactions. The method designed by Duane Rumbaugh and colleagues to train Lana (Rumbaugh & Gill, 1976; Rumbaugh, 1977), while not conceptually different from Sara's training, involved building a chimp-computer-human interface. A control panel contained keys with illuminated geometric symbols (called lexigrams), each lexigram standing for an object, agent, or action. The lexigrams could be activated by the experimenter, either requesting or instructing Lana to respond. Lana in turn could communicate by pressing a sequence of keys. If the sequence of lexigrams was correct, she received food reinforcement.

Sherman and Austin. A more sophisticated computer-controlled interface continues to be used in modified form at the *Language Research Center* in Georgia (e.g., Savage-Rumbaugh, McDonald, Sevcik, Hopkins, & Rubert, 1986). Sue Savage-Rumbaugh and her colleagues trained the chimps Sherman and Austin during the 1970s using a combination of lexigrams, ASL, and real-world objects, and they reported results that exceeded previous efforts with other chimps. Specifically, Sherman and Austin could (a) sort and categorize both objects and lexigrams on the first trial of a blind test; (b) carry out commands in the absence of seeing the object (i.e., go into a different room and bring back a designated object); and (c) make statements (arrange lexigrams) about future actions (Savage-Rumbaugh, 1987).

Is There a Message in the Medium? A concern of all animal language researchers has been that the various means of communication afforded chimpanzees—ASL, plastic tokens, and computer interfaces—are artificial and highly limiting. An analogy would be to take a young child into a laboratory, give her a saxophone, and measure how well she "uses language" by which notes she plays on certain occasions, whether she plays it spontaneously, tries to get other children to play it, etc. Her language abilities under these conditions would likely be found wanting. Both vocalization and signing are the preferred patterns of language in humans. What is the preferred pattern of communication in chimpanzees? Let us look at another species of chimpanzee.

Language Studies with the Pygmy Chimpanzee (Pan paniscus)

Just when many comparative psychologists thought that the animal language story had become pretty uninteresting, fortuitous observations of the behavior of a young pygmy chimpanzee named Kanzi breathed in new life (Savage-Rumbaugh et al., 1986; see Figure 10.6). Pygmy chimpanzees are known as *bonobos,* and their scientific name is **Pan paniscus.** A half-century of intensive effort had produced

FIGURE 10.6

Dr. Sue Savage-Rumbaugh with Kanzi, an adult bonobo chimpanzee (*Pan paniscus*), at the Language Research Center, Georgia State University.

rather meager language results in the common chimpanzee, *Pan troglodytes*. The training gains were hard to attain and easy to lose. Two possibilities suggested themselves; either these chimps were not especially interested in talking with humans, or they were incapable of entering the conversation. Scientists have argued over whether signing ASL and manipulating artificial symbols are merely conditioned responses or are true attempts at symbolic communication. For many psychologists, the chimpanzees' performance was so minimal that it really did not matter who won the argument.

Kanzi. Kanzi's behavior was a different matter. Without formal training—from merely watching other chimps and humans interact—Kanzi learned more language than any other chimpanzee. And though his accent is still thick, he also seems to have learned a bit of English. Let us look at the details.

From six months of age Kanzi found himself in the artificial language environment of his mother, Matata, who was a subject learning lexigrams on a keyboard. One year later Kanzi began to show interest in the symbols; without prodding or training he quickly learned to respond to lexigrams on the keyboard. At no time, according to Savage-Rumbaugh et al. (1986), was Kanzi food rewarded for the appropriate use of a symbol. Part of his training took place on a 55-acre forest. At three years of age, Kanzi had learned the location of food stashes throughout the forest, and he was able to "select each location by pointing to either a photograph or a lexigram" and then proceed "to guide the experimenter to the location of the food he had selected." This behavior both confirms previous reports of chimpanzee foraging abilities (i.e., Menzel, 1978) and signals *intentionality* of a planned behavior (some of the locations were 30 minutes distant from where Kanzi initially signaled).

Over the years Kanzi's comprehension of English has continued to increase. Recently, Kanzi's language skills were compared with those of a two-year-old human child (Savage-Rumbaugh et al., 1993). In a test of 660 human-chimp interactions, and in comparison with an equal number of human-child interactions conducted in a manner as similar as possible, Kanzi was found to understand more English than did the child. Language production was a different matter, as the child's spoken language was decidedly better than the chimp's attempts.

Having said this, perhaps the most interesting finding of Savage-Rumbaugh's research with Kanzi is his apparent attempt to vocalize/talk to humans. Although both species of chimpanzees are said to lack the ability to form consonants, Savage-Rumbaugh and her colleagues are nevertheless convinced that Kanzi, a bonobo chimp, engages in intentional vocal efforts—"answering, disagreeing, or expressing emotion" (Savage-Rumbaugh et al., 1986). This behavior is totally lacking in the common chimpanzee, *Pan troglodytes*. Kanzi has spoken and used appropriately the English words "bunny," "good," "groom," "sweet potato," and "tomato," and he has used appropriately words that "sound like" lettuce, orange drink, raisins, carrot (all foods); as well as yes, there, knife, snake, hot, oil, paint, get it, and others (Savage-Rumbaugh et al., 1993). Apparently, *Pan paniscus* does not suffer to the same extent the vocalization disabilities of *Pan troglodytes*.

Analysis of Kanzi's Language Abilities.   What can be concluded from this study of Kanzi? I believe that Savage-Rumbaugh and her colleagues are correct in their analysis that *Pan paniscus*, the pygmy chimp, qualitatively differs in language ability from *Pan troglodytes*, the common chimp. One has more of a species-specific propensity for language than the other, the same argument, we will see in the next section, that is proposed to account for the qualitative differences between human and nonhuman forms of communication. The crucial difference appears to be that "someone's home" in the pygmy chimp's head; when Savage-Rumbaugh talks about differences in these chimpanzees' receptive language, she is positing that pygmy chimps "listen" and that common chimps, for the most part, do not. She also suggests that language *receptivity* precedes language *productivity*, and that "when an ape can, simply by virtue of human rearing, begin to comprehend human speech, the power of culture learning looms very large indeed" (Savage-Rumbaugh et al., 1986, p. 231). I would add the coda that a *talking* chimpanzee far exceeds the expectations of any other species. At the risk of being overly dramatic, Savage-Rumbaugh's interactions with Kanzi may be considered the most successful attempt yet in establishing contact with another species.

Interim Summary

1. Animal communication can be meaningfully distinguished from animal "language." A number of animals innately vocalize and otherwise signal conspecifics in meaningful ways. In addition, some animals have been taught to associate artificial symbols with objects and behaviors, and occasionally engage in languagelike behavior.
2. Among the issues raised by the question of animal language is the difficult question of *intentionality*. For example, vervet monkeys make predator alerting vocalizations, which can be analyzed as an involuntary (reflexive) species-specific behavior or as an intentional (voluntary) act.
3. Porpoises and dolphins learn to use artificial signals to perform relatively complex acts. While some theorists talk about their accomplishments in terms of their having learned a simple *grammar*, others view their behavior as the application of learned rules.

4. *Homo sapiens'* most recent common ancestor, the common chimpanzee (*Pan troglodytes*) has been the subject of numerous language investigations during this century. While these chimpanzees for the most part do not vocalize "words," they do learn to use American Sign Language (e.g., Washoe), plastic tokens (e.g., Nim), and other artificial symbols (e.g., Lana, Sherman, and Austin) to engage in meaningful languagelike behavior with their human caretakers.

5. The most promising nonhuman candidate to exhibit language abilities is a pygmy chimpanzee (*Pan paniscus*). According to Savage-Rumbaugh, Kanzi's speech comprehension and vocalizations are qualitatively different from the common chimpanzee. Nevertheless, even pygmy chimpanzees have meager language abilities relative to humans.

V. Language and Thinking

We have some tentative answers to questions raised earlier in this chapter. Animals can think, but they cannot talk. Animals are conscious, but arguably *not* in the same way as humans. Monkeys and chimpanzees can learn relatively complex rules and concepts much more easily than other mammals, and humans require fewer trials to learn even higher order concepts. No surprises here.

What makes us different? Certainly language defines us, but other areas of our brain also make us different. No other animal composes music, records it symbolically, builds the instruments on which to play it, nor invests the time and effort necessary to accomplish a virtuoso performance. No other animal comes anywhere near the accomplishments of humans in the arts, in mathematics, in cooking, in literature, in athletics, or in science and technology.

What makes us different? Certainly our brain is different. But what is the role of experience in the development of human thought? What is the role of language in thought? Is it the case, as Benjamin Whorf (1956) hypothesized, that our language both *allows* us to think and directly determines the *nature* of our thought? Or, as Weiskrantz (1988) speculated, are thinking and language better conceptualized independently? It is to these issues we turn.

A Long-Running Nature-Nurture Argument

For most every instance of behavior described in this text we have been able to identify both heritable and learned components. There is no reason to expect that human thought and language behavior should be analyzed otherwise. Here we will first examine the amazing development of language abilities in children, and then the positions of the main players on both the nature side of the argument (i.e., that language is a *species-specific behavior*) and on the nurture side (i.e., that language is shaped and molded as a function of experience). The intensity with which these respective positions on language acquisition are held affords us the rare opportunity of declaring both sides wrong at the outset. That is, neither of the protagonists, nativist Noam Chomsky or environmentalist B. F. Skinner, nor their adherents can alone account for all the known facts of human language. That this argument has gone on for over 30 years with both sides asserting the supremacy of their philosophical positions is testimony to the tenaciousness of both ego and theory in science. What are they arguing about?

Prelanguage Communication in Humans

Crying as an FAP.   Human infants vocalize distress cries at birth. As is the case with other animals, such crying is adaptive. Vocalizations alert and sensitize caretakers to action—typically to alleviate hunger, uncomfortable temperature, and other discomforts. Such crying can be characterized as a species-specific behavior, with each species having a particular pattern of both sound production and reception. More specifically, crying can be analyzed as a fixed action pattern (FAP).[6]

Crying as an Instrumental Behavior.   Crying behavior can be reinforced or punished; that is, infants (especially older, more experienced infants) are afforded the opportunity of crying *instrumentally*. Caretakers adopt various strategies to deal with instrumental crying behavior; for example, if, after a feeding and a diaper change, the infant continues to cry, a parent might decide to let the infant "cry itself out."[7] In this behavioral contingency, the child is not "picked up" when it cries. As is the case with all learned behaviors, instrumental crying extinguishes in the absence of reinforcement. Alternatively, at Grandma's the child might be reinforced for instrumental crying by being held and rocked through the night. The frequency of an infant's vocalizations, then, can be manipulated by reinforcement and punishment contingencies. Infants cry innately; the environment acts to modify even the earliest of such vocalizations.

Cooing and Babbling

The first noncrying sounds made by infants appear within a few months of being born. Because deaf children make these *cooing* and *babbling* sounds, there is no argument that they are innately deter-

---

[6]You may want to review the criteria Moltz (1963) proposed for a behavioral sequence to be considered an FAP (Chapter 2).

[7]The author is describing, not prescribing, this approach to parenting.

mined. By about one year of age (Weir, 1966), hearing babies begin to produce "intonal patterns" that resemble the sound characteristics of the caretaker's language (i.e., English, or Spanish, or Vietnamese, etc.). Once again, this innate behavior is modified by the child's immediate environment.

Caretakers cross-culturally interact with infants by talking back to them as they make their endearing sounds. Such adult verbal behavior is also likely to have a genetic basis. "Language impoverished" environments are those that provide both less modeling of the target language and less reinforcement (paying attention, smiling, cuddling, etc.) for the *babbling* behavior. The large individual differences seen in adult human language behavior likely have their origins (at least in part) as a result of these earliest interactions (see the discussion that follows).

First Words

Although infants are highly variable in their "time-to-first-word," at about one year of age the average child begins to speak the language he or she has been hearing. The first words are usually names for objects encountered in their environment—"mama" and "milk"—and for actions—such as "get" and "go." Known variously as the **one-word utterance stage,** or as *holophrastic speech,* adults judge the meaning of these single words by the context in which they are delivered. For example, sitting in a high chair and reaching for her cup, a child might say "wa-wa"—short for "I'm thirsty, I want some water." Later, "wa-wa" might be playfully splashed (and drank) during an evening bath. Parents typically have no problems either understanding or meeting the needs expressed by such utterances. Again, the child learns to use these first words instrumentally. How such words are reinforced (or extinguished, or punished) thereafter influences their frequency of usage.

Analysis of "First Words"

Where do these first words come from? How and why are they produced? Theories abound. Let us join the argument by reviewing both cognitive and behavioral theories.

Cognitive Theory.   For Noam Chomsky (1965, 1975)—who, incidentally, is far more interested in the grammar revealed in the next, two-word utterance, stage—a child's first words reflect nothing more than the operation of an innate **Language Acquisition Device, or LAD.** For the same reason that children begin to babble, they are evolutionarily prepared to speak their first word. The infant's task is to "map" each new word onto a previously acquired concept (Levine & Carey, 1982). For example, according to this cognitive view, an infant must have acquired a (preverbal) concept of *mama* before being able to *map* the word "mama" onto her. Language acquisition is preceded by and predicated upon these innate cognitive categories. (Note: Cognitivists assume that these preverbal cognitive categories are not learned. What would John Locke have thought about this assertion?)

The Behaviorist's View.   It goes without saying that postulating the existence of "innate cognitive structures" prior to language acquisition is anathema to any behaviorist. For B. F. Skinner (1957), first words, like babbling sounds, are best described as *emitted operants.* Skinner is less concerned about where the words come from than in how they can be manipulated—reinforced and punished—once they are spoken.

An offshoot of Skinner's behavioral position that *does* address the origin of first words is that they appear as a result of "generalized imitation" and subsequently are maintained by conditioned reinforcement (Baer & Sherman, 1964; Kymissis & Poulson, 1990). In this analysis, imitation is itself viewed as an innate behavior that, when combined with reinforcement, produces the first French or Japanese word. Contemporary behaviorists referring to an *innate* mechanism of imitation? An interesting development!

Two Words, and the Beginning of a Grammar

Telegraphic speech is the term used to define the next stage of language output, during which, at around a year and a half, children begin to string together two words (Bloom, 1970). That the two words are not randomly stuck together is indicated by the fact that grammatical conventions of the parent language are observed. For example, a child will say in English, "get cookie," and not "cookie get."

It is also the case that the child's *receptive language* is better at the one- and two-word utterance stage than is the child's *productive language*. As every parent knows, preverbal children understand more than they can say. Even though parents simplify their language appropriately to the age of the child, from the child's perspective parental language usage extends beyond the child's productive language capability. (Recall Savage-Rumbaugh et al.'s (1986) observation that the pygmy chimpanzee Kanzi had far more receptive than productive language.)

Universal Grammar.   In his earliest writings, Chomsky was struck by the appearance of this two-word utterance stage in cultures around the world; he postulated the existence of an innate **universal**

grammar to account for these observations. In no meaningful way, he reasoned, could *learning* account for this time-locked appearance of patterned communication by 18-month-olds. His theoretical position resembles a *doctrine of innate ideas*, as revealed in the following quotation taken from an interview:

> I'm not . . . convinced that there ever is going to be such a thing as a theory of learning. . . . I see what we call learning as one kind of growth. You know we don't learn to grow arms. We also don't learn to have language in any very interesting sense. What happens is that systems that are sort of pre-formed in a certain fashion, or pre-adapted to certain consequences will interact with the environment in such a way as to sharpen them by filling in blanks, and you develop a system. . . . We can hardly fail to be struck by the fact that so-called "learning theory" has been pursued for seventy or eighty years, and is so limited in its results—very little has come out of it. (Noam Chomsky, in Beckwith & Rispoli, p. 195)

From Two to Thousands of Words

As remarkable as the language acquisition process is up to 18 months of age (by which time the average child speaks about 25 words), a virtual word explosion occurs during the next few years. By age six, an average child's lexicon contains more than 15,000 words (Medin & Ross, 1990). Long before that, by about age three and a half, a child has acquired the grammar and speech patterns (if not the working vocabulary) of the parents' language.

How can this happen? Parents spend less, not more, time eliciting and shaping language behavior after age three. Can the rapid growth of words, and the grammar adopted by the child, be considered innate, or rather accounted for by environmental processes of imitated, reinforced, and punished verbal exchanges? Behaviorally oriented researchers decided to find out (Brown & Hanlon, 1970). They went into homes and recorded parent-child verbal interactions. They concluded that middle-class parents do *not* consistently reinforce proper grammatical conventions. For example, a toddler whose mother was brushing her hair said, "her curl my hair" and was immediately reinforced by mom, saying, "that's right, darling." By contrast, a grammatically correct comment by the child to the effect that "Walt Disney comes on Tuesday" was punished with "No it doesn't, it comes on Thursday." Roger Brown and his colleagues concluded that the "truth value" of the utterance, i.e., the semantic meaning rather than grammar, was being reinforced. Note also in this example that the parents' "words" (having presumably acquired secondary reinforcing and punishing properties) by themselves shape the child's language behavior.

The Role of Culture in Language Acquisition

Brown and Hanlon (1970) rediscovered what we all suspected: i.e., that children apparently grow up in less than optimal language environments. Yet many (but not all) children nevertheless acquire the major grammatical features of their parents' language. Does that mean that Chomsky's theory of universal grammar is correct? Further, is his assertion that learning plays no role in language acquisition a reasonable one?

Associative Learning of the Lexicon.   Not everyone agrees with Chomsky. For example, Stemmer (1989) makes a convincing case that empiricist theories better account for the data of language acquisition than cognitive theories. In particular, he rejects the cognitivists' claims that a child innately maps language onto objects in the environment. Mapping, Stemmer reasons, is nothing more than what Pavlov described in terms of the *pairing of stimuli.* Stemmer reasons that children, not unlike Pavlov's dogs, have an *inductive capacity;* after pairing neutral stimuli (words) with known objects, the child can then meaningfully respond to (i.e., induce) "new" objects as long as they are within the *generalization gradient.* The (mis)application of the term "ma-ma" in reference to *daddy,* for example, can be interpreted as an example of the Pavlovian phenomenon of generalization. With further conditioned discrimination trials, the appropriate response can be consistently paired with the appropriate stimulus (i.e., the word "mama" becomes associated with *mama;* "papa" with *papa,* etc.). Stemmer's analysis of language acquisition is a logical extension of Pavlov's *second signal system.* The role of generalization and the learning of discriminations enable an individual (human or animal) to learn *perceptual concepts.* An elaboration of this theory can be found in G. Hall (1991).

Parents Simplify Language.   In what other ways do we see the environment entering into the acquisition and usage of language? We have already noted that parents simplify and structure language at the one- and two-word utterance stages. Young children, after all, often do not know what adults are talking about. The fact of the matter is that children enjoy many years of a structured, simplified, interactive language environment before being gradually incorporated into the realm of adult language.[8] (It will be argued later that language usage and thinking are substantially changed when the child learns to read.)

---

[8]A conservative estimate is that during the first five years of life, 10,000 hours of time are spent "practicing speaking" (Anderson, 1990).

Attaching Emotion to Words, and Vice Versa.   Emotions, objects, and words are embedded in the experience of life. The language structure provided by parents includes the attachment of emotion, through emotional conditioning, to words and phrases. To say that the word "mama," for example, is associated (or "mapped") with the object *mama* is an oversimplification. *Mama* is a composite of pleasure. *Mama* is the *feel good* of our earliest experiences: of food in the stomach, of warmth, of familiar smells and tastes; of physical contact. *Mama* is the emotional contract against fear, the dark, the unknown, and Binky's nightmare closet. *Mama* is symbolic of the lifelong quest for self-understanding that begins with coping when she is not there. Throughout a lifetime, each experience with *mama* continues the growth of the associative framework of the word, person, and emotional attachment. And then there is *papa,* and other moving animals, including siblings and pets. Language is only a small part of the experience of living. "Experiencing" other living beings includes unique sensations and emotions as well as the attachment of a language that refers to them.

Unique Emotional Attachments to Words.   Remember D. W., the three-year-old who survived as long as his mother allowed him to eat salt and drink water around the clock (Box 8.2, p. 376)? Do you suspect that satisfying physiological needs produced emotional attachments to salt and to water, and that the words "salt" and "water" became conditioned stimuli that gave D. W. pleasure? That meeting unusual needs attaches special meaning to some words is not the point. Rather, each of us lives in a unique flux; we share a common language, but the meanings of words reflect idiosyncratic learning histories.

Consider another, more common, example. A newly married couple finds themselves arguing about each other's families. One says, "I don't want anything to do with *family.*" The other says, "*Family* is very important to me." They are both using the same word, but their experience with the meaning of that word and the emotions attached to the word are very different.

Language Meaning in Context.   Do all of us learn the same meaning of even simple words such as "yes" and "no"? Or do we learn *conditional* "yes's" and "no's"? Arguments for a *universal grammar* ignore the subtleties and idiosyncrasies of language learning and language usage experienced by everyone who learns to speak. For example, strict parents attach strong emotions to *yes* and *no,* to *right* and *wrong.* Less strict parents use *yes* and *no* in a looser fashion. Recall the verbal interchanges of Joey and his mother in the grocery store (summarized in Table 6.1, p. 262). "No" never meant more than "maybe"; Joey had learned that with enough verbal persistence (a behavior that had been consistently reinforced), the "no you can't" would soon become "oh, all right, but this is the last time." Few question that the *meaning* of words is conditioned; reconditioning the meaning of words is one goal of psychotherapy (Staats & Staats, 1957). Many demonstrations of classical and operant conditioning of language meaning have been reported (for example, see Cicero & Tryon, 1989). In summary, postulating a universal grammar does not tell us much at all about *what* will be verbalized *when,* what such verbalizations *mean,* nor why the same words mean different things to different people.

Language Growth or Language Learning?

Chomsky (1980) conceptualizes the environment as a *triggering* and *shaping* instrument that determines the manner in which language grows. An analogy is that acorns do not *learn* to be oaks, but rather *grow* into oaks; likewise, language growth is viewed as a genetic unfolding shaped by environment (Pateman, 1985). Perhaps, then, in seeking to determine language behavior, we are merely arguing over the relative roles of environment and genetics—an argument that we have encountered so often in analyses of other areas of animal learning.

Continuing the Case for Learning.   But surely Chomsky underestimates the role of environment. In the first place, as Skinner (1957) pointed out, language *behavior* is not synonymous with linguistic *structure.* Postulating a universal grammar and noting similarities across the world's different languages accounts more for the form than the function of language. Where do we see the influence of environment? Examples abound. Chinese is not French, and the differences between these and hundreds of other languages are *environmentally* determined. In addition, language *fails to develop* in language-deficient environments (Curtiss, 1977). The tremendous variation in language acquisition and usage both within and across cultures can be tied directly to environmental experiences. For example, postulating a universal grammar does not address the enormous individual differences we find in spoken vocabulary—estimates of which range from a few thousand words in some individuals to tens of thousands of words in others. It is likely that profound individual differences in thought and consciousness accompany such vocabulary differences. Let us take a brief look at where all these words come from, and then consider the significance of individual differences for a theory of language behavior.

The Role of Reading in Language Behavior

While it can be argued that the acquisition of words and of grammar reflects a relatively *prepared* form of learning (albeit slow and highly practiced—see Footnote 8, p. 479), schoolchildren around the world proclaim that learning to read and write is *contraprepared*—so painfully slow and difficult that after 12 years of formal schooling, some reported high school illiteracy estimates are as high as 25 percent (Weaver, 1993). Learning to read requires thousands of hours of exposure to the printed word; indeed, those children who will become the best readers have an estimated 1500 hours of print exposure prior to formal schooling in the form of parental reading. Such effort is reminiscent of our primate relatives who also require thousands of trials to learn to use artificial symbols both to communicate and to solve problems.

Associative Theory and Reading.   Both Pavlovian and instrumental versions of associative theory account very well for how a child (or an adult) learns to read. Beginning with a formal analysis of the process, letters are CSs with phonemic signaling properties (e.g., the symbolic letter "D" is pronounced "dee"). The child learns to make sight-sound associations. (The process is obviously more complex than this simple associative analysis suggests in that the *kinesthetic cues* of vocal cords, tongue, and air passage also become associated with the *sight* and *sound* of the letter.) The parent correctly vocalizes (models) each letter; correct vocalizations by the child are shaped by successive approximation.

Conditioning Emotional and Performance Factors.   More is going on in this parent-child reading interaction, however, than merely "learning letters." In reading to the child, parents direct attention to visual features of letters (and colors and pictures) in special books for children. With practice, the mechanics of holding the book and of turning pages become automatic. Attention spans are systematically lengthened (shaped) as children first experience and then demand longer reading periods; the child develops expectations about the amount of information per unit time that can be processed. (By contrast, shorter attention spans are conditioned by television programmers. In reading, but not in watching television, the child can control the pace of behavioral engagement, and hence, the flow of information.) The value of books and of reading is further conditioned by parental attention, physical contact, pleasing sights, sounds, and odors, etc.[9] Such early emotional conditioning might account for lifelong emotional attachment to books by some people, such as librarians and others who *love* both libraries and the smell of books, and who consider books as "best friends." Note that these

---

[9]A Jewish custom is to give candy to children during their first encounters with books. In an even older custom, infants were allowed to taste a drop of honey from a book cover, thereby conditioning a love of books by their pleasurable association with a sweet taste.

positive preverbal, pre-reading conditioning factors are accomplished prior to other considerations—such as the reinforcing properties of concepts and ideas contained in the print.

Reading, Literacy, and Intelligence.   What is the outcome of these thousands of hours of exposure to the printed word? Nothing less than qualitative differences in the use of language for those who read versus those who do not. Consider the following facts: An excellent reader in the fifth grade is encountering millions of words each year (Anderson, Wilson, & Fielding, 1988).[10] And even after controlling for differences in nonverbal cognitive ability (differences that are considerable), a recent study reports that mere exposure to large numbers of words enhances the "verbal intelligence" of college students (Stanovich & Cunningham, 1992). One important finding in this latter study was that the *quality* of reading material was a less important factor than the *quantity* of reading. Conclusion? Read a lot of whatever you want, and your overall cognitive abilities will be enhanced.

Interim Summary

1. Human language behavior can be analyzed within the same nature-nurture framework as are other instances of human and animal behavior.
2. Crying, babbling, and cooing behaviors have both innate and instrumental components.
3. Cross-culturally there exists a normal progression (a systematic growth resembling an "unfolding") of babbling, first word, and one- and two-word utterance stages, and the growth of vocabulary.
4. Nativists such as Noam Chomsky describe language growth in terms of an innately disposed *universal grammar* that grows as a result of a genetically determined *language acquisition device.*
5. Environmentalists such as B. F. Skinner analyze the role environment plays in shaping language behavior, emphasizing the cultural and individual variability in language behavior, the crucial role played by parents, and the thousands of hours of language environment in which children learn about language, including the attachment of emotional meaning to words.
6. Individual differences in language behavior are accentuated by different reading abilities. Learning to read is painstakingly slow, suggesting that humans are not genetically predisposed to learn artificial symbols for the language they speak.

---

[10]At the time of this writing my daughter Jane is an avid reader in the fifth grade. Doubting this statistic, Jane and I used several methods to estimate her "word exposure," and we arrived at approximately five to nine million words per year.

7. Reading leads to literacy. The absolute amount of print exposure (reading environment) is a contributing factor in verbal behavior and verbal intelligence.

VI. Language, Thought, and Culture

As we near the end of our inquiry into human and animal behavior, important questions have yet to be addressed. Among these are the nature of human and animal intelligence, and a more satisfactory comparison of human and animal consciousness. In earlier chapters we were content to seek out and focus upon those processes of learning that are common to all animals, and to otherwise catalogue and compare a number of species-typical behaviors. In this chapter we have also noted common properties of conceptual learning and thinking. In examining the communicative abilities of other animals, we speculated about the precursors of human language and wondered what, if anything, other animals *know* and *think* about the world. My hope is that through these comparisons with other animals, you have shared with me wonderment and marvel at the accomplishments of humans as reflected by our culture. Let us inquire further into the origins and nature of human intelligence and culture.

Human Culture, but Not Animal Culture

Human culture differentiates us from other animals both because of our unique language behavior and, using language, by our transmission of one generation's accomplishments to the next. Since no other animal engages in either behavior, no other animal has culture.

For thousands of generations, human thought and culture were transmitted by oral history. More recently (i.e., for the past several thousand years), written records in the form of books have bypassed the bottleneck imposed by slow, restrictive oral history traditions. A working assumption is that *written* history has allowed the tremendous explosion in knowledge and culture humans have entertained during the past few thousand years.

Written Language and Human Culture. From a comparative perspective, then, it is reasonable to assume that human language preceded and allowed the development of important aspects of human thought—and that language as a species-specific behavior remains the most important difference separating humans from other animals. Moreover, with written language we see opening an enormous chasm among members of the human species—those who *learn* to read and write, and those who do not. As we saw earlier, reading is a

better predictor of an individual's thought and consciousness—and a better indicant of human potential—than merely having learned a language via a universal grammar. And in the same way that mere print exposure to words during a lifetime enhances an individual's "verbal intelligence" (Stanovich & Cunningham, 1992), the transmission of knowledge across generations via print (and now other media) determines a culture's literacy. All cultures have language, but all cultures are not uniformly literate.

Language and Intelligence

Through traditions of written language, human cultures have developed in the past several hundred years new ways of thinking—about ourselves, and about the universe. Science, technology, and other defining characteristics of Western culture, for example, are much more the product of written than of spoken language. All cultures may acquire language in the same way (i.e., as described by Chomsky), but some cultures enjoy literacy, and the science and technology such literacy affords, while others do not. Another way of saying this is that human intelligence is a product and reflection of the content, rather than the form, of language.

Human versus Animal Intelligence. Questions regarding the multifaceted nature of human intelligence are beyond the scope of this text. Note, however, in Figure 10.7 that literate people score higher on tests of intelligence than the nonliterate, and that nonlanguage skills (mechanical reasoning and quantitative skills) play a lesser role than language skills. Indeed, to the extent that animal and human intelligence can be compared, of the seven components of intelligence graphed in Figure 10.7, only on one of the "lowest" predictors of intelligence, that of "spatial reasoning," would animals score any points. Conclusion? Human intelligence is both language and literacy driven.

Learning, Reading, Intelligence, and Culture

Learning to read and write, and not language per se, plays a critical role in the level of measured intelligence a person can achieve. It is for this reason that Chomsky's assertion to the effect that learning plays no meaningful role in human behavior is so baffling. What is the counterpoint? First, that language behavior affords humans a unique place in the animal world. Second, that reading and writing allow some fortunate humans (and cultures) to achieve a qualitatively higher level of discourse—of conceptual thinking, of realized consciousness, of intelligence—than that enjoyed by speaking, but

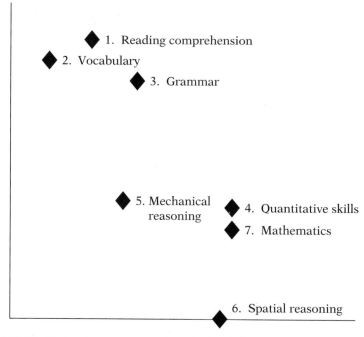

FIGURE 10.7   Comparative Intelligence Tests

The intercorrelations of seven subtests (named in the figure) of a human general intelligence test were factor analyzed and then plotted (on arbitrary coordinates) in such a way that the distance among the tests reflects their degree of relatedness. In this plot, three "intelligence factors" visually emerge; a linguistic factor, a reasoning factor, and a spatial factor (Anderson, 1990, p. 438). Notice that *grammar* is only one component, and a lesser one, of "linguistic ability" in comparison with *vocabulary* and *reading comprehension* components. Note also that "linguistic ability" is a larger component of human intelligence than "reasoning ability" (quantitative, mechanical, and mathematical skills). Finally, only in measurements of spatial reasoning and simple "quantitative skills" (such as counting) could infrahuman intelligence even be compared with that of humans.

illiterate humans. And, finally, since reading and writing—literacy—are *learned,* and learned only by tremendous effort within a supportive environment, contrary to Chomsky's view, *the role of learning and environment is paramount in determining human intelligence and human culture.*

Human culture is learned, not innately determined.

Summary

1. Conceptual learning, thinking, and language can be studied from within a comparative perspective. Insight can be attained into the human mind: (a) by comparing what we can and other animals cannot do; and (b) by examining the respective roles of genetics and environment as determinants of conceptual learning, thinking, and language.

2. Evidence from a variety of experiments leads to the conclusion that the categories of conceptual learning, of reasoning, of thinking, and of language: (a) can be differentiated from one another; and (b) are not exclusive properties of the human mind.

3. An array of evidence leads us to the conclusion that animals can think: Rats and other animals can (a) count; (b) keep track of time; (c) solve serial pattern problems; and (d) memorize complex maze patterns (cf. cognitive maps).

4. A variety of animals have been trained to apply rules and concepts to solve learning set problems (win-stay, lose-shift strategy), match-to-sample and delayed match-to-sample, oddity and sameness, etc. Even though they require many hundreds of trials, monkeys and chimpanzees learn these problems better than other infrahumans. Pigeons learn sameness and natural concepts tasks in surprisingly few trials, but they cannot solve oddity problems.

5. While a number of animals show communication patterns in the real world (some even resembling primitive language), the results of having animals learn symbolic language in laboratories have been discouraging. Among the issues related to animal "language" are questions of intentionality, of spontaneity (proactive rather than reactive use of "language"), and of cost versus benefit (so little animal language resulting from intensive training efforts).

6. Despite numerous efforts to engage porpoises and chimpanzees in symbolic conversation throughout this century, in the realm of language humans remain in a class by themselves. The most encouraging findings have come from work with Kanzi, a pygmy chimpanzee (*Pan paniscus*) who differs from other chimpanzees in that: (a) he voluntarily enters the conversation as opposed to being trained into it; (b) he seems interested in learning about humans and their language; and (c) he attempts to vocalize language as humans do.

7. While humans' rapid acquisition of language can be construed as species specific, language behavior is readily modifiable by environment. Language behavior, not unlike other behavior, then, is best understood as resulting from both hereditary and environmental constraints.

8. Individual differences in language usage (including *which* language is spoken) vary along dimensions of receptivity (understanding what you hear), of speaking, of reading, of writing, of size of vocabulary, of meaning of words, etc. Such individual differences are best accounted for by traditional theories of learning by association rather than by innate language mechanisms.

9. Reading and writing are acquired even more slowly than speaking, and likewise they are best understood from within a framework of learning by association; i.e., of contingencies of reinforcement and punishment applied to language behavior.

10. Language behavior is facilitated by reading and writing. Both literacy and the "verbal intelligence" it spawns differentiate the thinking and consciousness of both individuals and cultures.

Discussion Questions

1. Recall the monkeys that were conditioned to time their lever-pressing responses. One became so accurate that her interresponse interval never varied by more than a few hundredths of a second. Humans have a great sense of timing, as attested to by such skilled performances as hitting a curve ball or playing the piano. Could you ever train *yourself,* however, to do as well as this monkey on her task—i.e., hit a lever every 15 seconds for five minutes, and never vary the response interval by more than a few *hundredths* of a second? Under what conditions could you do this? Would you concentrate, or try to "get in a zone"? Would it help or hurt your performance if $100 rode on every response, or if you received a rather severe electric shock if your responses varied too much? Is it possible that monkeys are able to do this task so well because they *do not* think as much, or as well, as you?

2. I have often wondered what animals think when you give them a problem that can only be solved by application of a *rule.* Their bewilderment reminds me of my own at a recent party in which a guy played a game of *mime:* He modeled a series of different movements (simple dance steps, pulling his ears, patting his arms, etc.) and asked us to find the one thing in common he did on each different occasion. As person after person was able to solve the puzzle by applying the discovered rule, those of us who could not figure out the pattern became increasingly uncomfortable. It turned out that the only thing that was common to the series of different movements he made was that he cleared his throat before each one. So easy when you know what the rule is. . . . In your own experi-

ence, which *rules* have you found more or less difficult to learn? Can you verbalize *rules* you learned in algebra or trigonometry? Were your "a-ha" experiences better characterized as having been attained by trial and error, or by a "cognitive process" called *insight?* (Or, after reading this chapter, do you suspect that these terms are not mutually exclusive?)

3. Relevant to the preceding question, are you of the opinion that human language so changes the nature of human thought and behavior that simple associative frameworks become irrelevant? Alternatively, can you use the concepts of reinforcement and punishment to help you account for your rule learning in Spanish 101, math, computer science, etc.?

4. Assume that you have been taken to an extraterrestrial's laboratory, where you were handed a saxophone. What would you do? What would you think? Under such circumstances, would you even make the assumption that the sax was to be used to communicate? Maybe it was intended as a cup to drink from, or the closest thing to a toilet the extraterrestrial could come up with. If you did assume that the extraterrestrial was trying to communicate with you, what assumptions, given the saxophone's characteristics, would you make about the nature of "its" language. Pity the poor chimpanzee!

5. Roger Brown and his colleagues studied how parents reinforced and punished their children's language behavior. Their conclusion was that correct grammar was less important to parents than how well the child's language accurately reflected what was going on around them. These researchers pointed out the irony

of children being consistently reinforced for telling the truth, but who then lie so much as adults. Can you identify the contingencies of reinforcement and punishment that maintain confabulation, lying, and other deceptive language practices? That is, under what conditions is lying reinforced, and when is it punished? What are "white lies"? Does a *universal grammar* predict *white lies?*

6. Given the finding that children who have their nose in a book most of the time do better in school, score higher on intelligence tests, and are generally smarter than their less scholarly contemporaries throughout a lifetime, how are *you* going to raise your own children? Do you suppose that the world's best artists, musicians, and athletes spend disproportionate amounts of time doing something other than reading as a child? What are *your* values? What do you want for your child? Are you up to the task of helping your child "choose" his or her ultimate direction in life by providing the appropriate early environment? Or are you content to hand them the remote control, and let them choose their own channel? Decisions, decisions! Have a good life.

Glossary

Cognitive Map (Tolman) The hypothesis that some animals (including rats) can form memories of where they are located relative to a food source, and even without direct experience of the route, "know" the shortest path connecting them with the food.

Cognitive Processes Psychological processes of perceiving, thinking, knowing, remembering, etc.

Delayed Match-to-Sample A task measuring learning and memory processes that involves briefly presenting a target stimulus (i.e., the stimulus to be remembered), and after a delay again presenting the target with a number of distractor stimuli. The animal is reinforced for selecting the target from the distractors, thereby *matching the sample.*

Foraging Patterns Innately disposed behavior that results in the conduct of patterned searches and remembering where food is located in three-dimensional space.

Fractional Anticipatory Goal Responses (r_Gs) (Hull) The theory that stimuli encountered in the pathway prior to entry into the goal box are reinforced, and in turn become secondary reinforcers for even earlier responses in the maze. This theory allows a single reinforcer to connect complex sequences of behavior.

Language Acquisition Device (LAD) (Chomsky) A proposed species-specific brain mechanism (or series of mechanisms) that allows a human child to rapidly acquire language once triggered by a minimal language environment.

Learning Set (Harlow) A learning procedure in which two stimuli are presented to an animal for a set of six consecutive trials. Selecting one, arbitrarily designated as the "correct" choice, is reinforced. After completing many sets of such problems, animals learn a win-stay, lose-shift strategy and are able to consistently respond correctly on the first opportunity. (See *win-stay, lose-shift; learning to learn.*)

Learning to Learn (Harlow) The term Harlow used to describe the ability of animals to slowly learn a *general rule* that could then be applied to rapidly solve new problem sets. (See *win-stay, lose-shift; learning sets.*)

Match-to-Sample See *delayed match-to-sample.* The difference between the two procedures is that in match-to-sample the target stimulus does not terminate prior to presentation of the target plus distractors.

Natural Concepts A term used to describe the ability of pigeons to extract information from complex pictures of natural environments and to respond in a way that indicates they recognize trees, people, and other "open-ended" categories.

Oddity A learning task in which an animal must pick the "odd" stimulus from a three-stimulus array in which two stimuli are identical.

One-Word Utterance Stage The first words spoken in any language, typically referring to names for objects encountered in their environment such as "mama" and "milk" and for actions such as "get" and "go." (Also known as holophrastic speech.)

Pan paniscus The *bonobo* chimpanzee, sometimes referred to as the *pygmy chimp.* (Cf. the common chimpanzee, *Pan troglodytes.*)

Pan troglodytes The common chimpanzee. (Cf. the pygmy chimpanzee, *Pan paniscus.*)

Picture Memory (Farrar) The term Farrar used to describe the performance of his chimpanzee, Minnie, in which 24 pictures with common elements were memorized and apparently not learned by applying a general rule.

Sameness Task A learning task in which pictures of objects are sequentially presented to pigeons. A final picture is presented that either was or was not in the series (i.e., *same* or *different,* respectively). Pigeons solve this problem for food reinforcement by responding to one key if the same, and to another key if different.

Serial Pattern Learning A learning task in which rats are exposed to and learn a sequence of patterns of reinforcement (or nonreinforcement) in the goal box over a succession of trials.

Telegraphic Speech The term used to define the stage of language when, at the age of about one and a half years, children begin to string together two words in a grammatically meaningful fashion.

Transitive Inferential Reasoning A problem of the following type: "If *a* is greater than *b*, and *b* is greater than *c*, is *a* greater than *c*?"; its solution is indicative of reasoning ability and a knowledge of relationships that extends beyond immediate experience.

Universal Grammar (Chomsky) A theoretical position initially formulated by Noam Chomsky that postulates the existence of innate structures underlying the rapid acquisition and output of grammatically correct language, and that denies any role for Pavlovian and instrumental conditioning processes.

Win-Stay, Lose-Shift (Harlow) A strategy animals are capable of learning. When presented with repeated opportunities to solve a two-choice discrimination problem in which one of the choices is consistently rewarded, reinforcement can be maximized by adopting the two-part rule: (a) to continue selecting the reinforced choice (i.e., win-stay); and (b) to shift to the alternative choice when not reinforced (i.e., lose-shift). (See *learning set; learning to learn.*)

Glossary

Acquired Incentives Stimuli paired with innate incentives such as food and water become *acquired incentives* in Hull's system (and are *secondary reinforcers* in Skinner's system).

Acquired Motivation Behavior motivated by secondary reinforcers. (Primary reinforcers provide innate motivation.)

Adaptation Any characteristic that improves an organism's chances of transmitting its genes to the next generation.

Adaptive Describing a characteristic or behavior that enhances survival.

Animal Model The use of animals in research that bears upon the human condition. Example: An animal model of alcohol addiction.

Annoyers Thorndike's law of effect proposed that when unpleasant stimuli, which he called *annoyers*, followed a response, the response would less likely be made thereafter (cf. *punisher*).

Antecedent Condition In a causal relationship, that condition which precedes, and causes an event to occur.

Appetitive Conditioning (Pavlov) Food-based Pavlovian (classical) conditioning (cf. appetite).

Association The relationship (connection, union) that results when two or more stimuli are paired together in time.

Associationism Basic learning defined as the association of two or more sensory experiences. (Cf. *association;* association formation.)

Automaintenance Pigeons that have a history of being fed in the presence of a lighted key will unnecessarily peck at the light even though their pecking response has no effect on when food is made available. The maintenance of pigeons continuing to respond under these conditions is called *automaintenance.*

Autoshaping An untrained pigeon is placed in a Skinner Box, and food is presented in the presence of a lighted key. Without specific training, the bird will begin to peck at the lighted key, a procedure (and phenomenon) called *autoshaping* (and also called *sign tracking*).

Aversive Conditioning Conditioning experiments using aversive unconditioned stimuli (as opposed to an appetitive food stimulus). Three contemporary *aversive* conditioning procedures are eye-blink conditioning, conditioned suppression, and taste aversion conditioning, employing aversive air puffs to the eye, electric shock, and toxins, respectively.

Avoidance Procedure Any procedure in which an animal's instrumental response prevents an aversive consequence. Example: A lever press prevents, or avoids, delivery of electric shock.

Backward Conditioning (Pavlov) A conditioning procedure in which the onset of the unconditioned stimulus precedes the onset of the conditioned stimulus. Both inhibitory conditioning (often) and excitatory conditioning (rarely) can result from backwards pairings of US and CS. (Also referred to as a *negative contingency* between the CS and the US.)

Baseline The preexperimental, or normal level of a measured response. The baseline often constitutes the control condition to which the effects of an experimental treatment are compared.

Behavior The way in which an animal acts or responds within the environment.

Behavioral Contrast A contrast procedure that demonstrates that reinforcement/punishment effects are determined in part by the immediate context in which these stimuli are delivered and the animal's prior history with other reinforcers/punishers. (Also known as *incentive contrast;* see *negative contrast*).

Behavioral Control The past and present reinforcement and punishment contingencies that determine the expression of a behavior.

Behavioral Ecology The study of interrelationships among organisms and their environments focusing upon the development of survival behaviors—feeding, reproduction, social organization, etc.

Behavioral Genetics The study of the interaction of environment and patterns of inheritance in expressed behavior.

Behavioral Medicine An interdisciplinary field concerned with the etiology of illness and wellness, preventative medicine, biofeedback and other forms of psychophysiology, and treatment and rehabilitation strategies.

Behavioral Therapy Any psychotherapeutic procedure involving the systematic application of reinforcers or punishers, or the implementation of extinction or other classical or operant procedures, known to be effective in effecting behavioral change.

Behavioral Tolerance That portion of total drug tolerance that can be attributed to learned, or environmental, variables, as opposed to pharmacodynamic variables.

Behaviorism A philosophical position that ignores genetic influences and espouses an extreme environmental determinism. The assertion that human and animal behavior is directly, inevitably determined and controlled by the reinforcing and punishing contingencies of the local environment. (John B. Watson and B. F. Skinner are two famous proponents of behaviorism.)

Behavior Modification The systematic application of reinforcers, punishers, extinction, and other classical and operant conditioning procedures to change target behaviors.

Behavior Theory An analysis of the way in which animals act or respond within environments; the theory that encompasses the interplay of behavior, genes, and environment.

Between-Groups Design The design of an experiment in which the effect of manipulating an independent variable (i.e., the treatment group) is compared with a control group not exposed to the independent variable. (Cf. *within-groups design*.)

Biocultural Evolution The process by which the selection, preparation, and consumption of particular types of food by some individuals gives them a reproductive advantage, which, over time, has probably led to the divergence of human populations. (Proposed by S. Katz.)

Biofeedback A procedure used in both research and therapy in which a human subject is made aware of and can gain voluntary control over his or her involuntary processes (such as brainwaves, heart rate, skin conductance, etc.) through differential reinforcement.

Biological Determinism The philosophical position that behavior is caused by the immutable action of genes. (Cf. *environmental determinism*.)

Biomedical Model The traditional approach to health care that, in emphasizing anatomy and physiology, assumes that almost all illness can be attributed to a specific pathogen or specific biochemical malfunction.

Biopsychosocial Model An approach to health care that attempts to integrate cultural, social, psychological, and behavioral approaches with the traditional biomedical model.

Black Box A model of investigating causal relations that focuses upon the relationship of input to output variables, and that ignores intervening variables hidden within the "black box."

Blocking When, following conditioning to CS_1, CS_1 is then put into a compound with CS_2, attempts to condition CS_2 in the compound fail. The phenomenon is called *blocking* (or, sometimes, "Kamin blocking" after the researcher who designed the procedure and described the phenomenon). One hypothesis is that CS_2 is blocked because it is a *redundant* stimulus; i.e., not useful in predicting the occurrence of the US.

Causality The relationship of cause and effect. A goal of science is to investigate *why* events occur, on the assumption that nothing can happen without a cause.

CER See *conditioned emotional response.*

Chained Operants A behavioral sequence analyzed in terms of a succession of discriminative stimuli that set the occasions for operant responses, eventually leading to reinforcement. (Cf. *stimulus-response chains.*)

Changeover Delay (COD) In a *concurrent schedule* procedure, a brief period of time during which reinforcement is not available immediately following a switch, or changeover, from one reinforcement schedule to the other.

Chimpanzee See *Pan paniscus* and *Pan troglodytes.*

Classical Conditioning See *Pavlovian conditioning.*

COD See *changeover delay.*

Cognition The acts of perceiving, thinking, knowing, and remembering.

Cognitive Map (Tolman) The hypothesis that some animals (including rats) can form memories of where they are located relative to a food source, and even without direct experience of the route, "know" the shortest path connecting them with the food.

Cognitive Processes Psychological processes of perceiving, thinking, knowing, remembering, etc.

Comparative Psychology The study of animal behavior, stressing both similarities and species-specific differences.

Compensatory Responses See *conditioned compensatory responses.*

Concurrent Schedules A training procedure in which two or more reinforcement schedules run simultaneously and independently of each other, and a subject can respond on either. Used in the measurement of choice behavior.

Conditioned Compensatory Responses (Siegel) In pairings of environmental stimuli with certain drug USs, the form of the conditioned response is opposite to the normal drug response. Example: Morphine causes hyperthmia, and CSs paired with morphine often produce hypothermic responses, possibly as compensation in achieving homeostasis.

Conditioned Discrimination A procedure used to train an animal to discriminate and respond differently to two different stimuli. One stimulus (CS^+) is reliably paired with an unconditioned stimulus, and on alternating trials, another stimulus (CS) is *not* paired with the US. The animal learns to respond to CS^+ and to not respond to CS^- thereby demonstrating that it can *discriminate* one from the other. (Cf. *generalization*, in which an animal responds in a *similar* manner to different stimuli.)

Conditioned Emotional Response (CER) The outcome of an experimental treatment in which emotional responses are conditioned to neutral (non–emotion-inducing) stimuli. (Cf. fear conditioning; *conditioned suppression.*)

Conditioned Excitor A descriptive term for the CS after it has been conditioned in a forward, or excitatory, manner. The CS acquires excitatory properties; for example, the excitor can be used "as a US" in higher-order conditioning.

Conditioned Facilitation Pavlovian conditioning experiments in which the end result is to *increase* antibody production in the immune system.

Conditioned Immunosuppression Pavlovian conditioning experiments in which the end result is to decrease antibody production in the immune system.

Conditioned Inhibition The usual result of "backward" procedures (cf. *negative contingency*), conditioned inhibition is the opposite of conditioned excitation. Example: If *fear* is the conditioned (excitatory) response, *safety*, or *elation*, is the conditioned inhibitory response.

Conditioned Inhibitor A descriptive term for the CS after it has been conditioned in a backward, or inhibitory, manner. The CS acquires inhibitory properties; for example, the inhibitor can retard the conditioning of another stimulus.

Conditioned Reflex See *conditioned response*.

Conditioned Response (CR) (cf. Pavlov's conditioned reflex). Following pairings of a neutral stimulus (i.e., the CS) with an unconditioned stimulus, a new response, called a *conditioned response*, is learned to CS. Salivation to the sound of a bell is an example of a conditioned response.

Conditioned Stimulus (CS) (Pavlov) Following pairings with an unconditioned stimulus (i.e., food), a stimulus such as the sound of a bell can come to control a new response such as salivation. The bell's sound is initially "neutral"—it doesn't make the animal salivate. The bell is called a *conditioned stimulus* when, after conditioning with food, the animal salivates to the sound of the bell.

Conditioned Suppression A laboratory technique used to measure aversive (fear) conditioning. A neutral stimulus is paired with electric shock while an animal is lever pressing for food. Following tone-shock conditioning, the tone disrupts (suppresses) lever pressing, allowing the experimenter to easily quantify the amount of fear conditioning the animal has experienced. (Cf. *conditioned emotional response*.)

Confounded Variables Changes in a dependent variable may be mistakenly attributed to the independent variable under study and may be really due to other (*confound-*

ing) variables. Example: The study of how a drug affects activity may be *confounded* by normal changes in activity during a 24-hour cycle.

Connectionism See *associationism*.

Consummatory Behaviors (Ethology) Innate, genetically determined "survival" behaviors, including *fixed action patterns*, which determine species-specific patterns of feeding, courting, reproduction, social interactions, etc.

Context The immediate environment, background, attendant circumstances, or conditions in which an event is measured.

Contiguity Theory of Association The theory that stimulus-stimulus associations occur because the animal perceives the two stimuli close together (cf. contiguous) in time.

Contingency Theory of Association The theory that stimulus-stimulus associations occur because the animal perceives the relationship, or pattern, or sequence, of one stimulus preceding and *signaling* the occurrence of a second stimulus.

Continuity of Species (Darwin) The theory that all living organisms are evolutionary adaptations of earlier life forms and, therefore, are all genetically related.

Continuous Reinforcement (CRF) A schedule of reinforcement in which each emitted response produces a positive reinforcement. (Cf. *schedules of reinforcement*.)

Contraprepared The opposite of a prepared, or easily conditioned, response. When associations between two stimuli, or a stimulus and a response, require many trials to learn, an animal is said to be *contraprepared* for association.

Control Group A comparison group for a treatment group. In an experiment, a group of subjects exposed to all conditions that the treatment group experiences, but *not* to the independent variable.

CR See *conditioned response*.

CRF See *continuous reinforcement*.

Critical Period (Ethology) A specific time period (usually early in an animal's development) when an animal is particularly sensitive to certain features in the environment. Exposure to such *sign stimuli* "releases" genetically determined behavioral responses. (Cf. *imprinting; sign stimulus.*)

CS   See *conditioned stimulus.*

CS⁺ and CS⁻ Trials   In a conditioned discrimination procedure, an animal is taught to discriminate between two different CSs by pairing one with food (called *CS⁺ trials*) and the other CS without food (called *CS⁻ trials*). Following training, the animal responds in extinction to CS⁺ but not to CS⁻. CS⁺ trials yield excitatory conditioning, and CS⁻ trials, inhibitory conditioning.

CS Preexposure Effect   Preexposed, or familiar, conditioned stimuli require more trials to become associated with a given US than do novel conditioned stimuli. The reduced associability of familiar stimuli is also known as *latent inhibition.*

CS-US Interval   During conditioning, the CS and the US are related to each other by time. By convention, the *CS-US interval* is measured from the onset of the conditioned stimulus to the onset of the unconditioned stimulus. (Also called the *interstimulus interval.*)

Cumulative Record   A visual record of responses and reinforcement patterns in time generated by an ink-writing instrument called a *cumulative recorder.*

Darwinian Evolution   See *evolution.*

Defense Conditioning (Pavlov)   In contrast to his food-based appetitive conditioning experiments, Pavlov used the term *defense conditioning* to describe experiments that used aversive unconditioned stimuli (i.e., sour solutions placed on the tongue; electric shock to condition a leg-withdrawal reflex, etc.). Experiments using aversive USs are now referred to as *aversive conditioning.*

Delayed Match-to-Sample   A task measuring learning and memory processes that involves briefly presenting a target stimulus (i.e., the stimulus to be remembered), and after a delay again presenting the target with a number of distractor stimuli. The animal is reinforced for selecting the target from the distractors, thereby *matching the sample.*

Dependent Variable   In an experiment, the treatment effects of an independent variable are measured by measuring changes in the *dependent variable.* In the behavioral sciences, most dependent variables are changes in behavior. Example: A drug (independent variable) *caused* increased activity (dependent variable).

Determinism   In psychobiology, the philosophical position that behavior is caused by the joint actions of genes (i.e., biological determinism) and environmental influences (i.e., environmental determinism). (See also *biological determinism; environmental determinism.*)

Differential Reinforcement of High Rates (DRH)   A schedule of reinforcement designed to reinforce bursts of operant responding. (Example: The tenth response within a five-second time period would be reinforced.)

Differential Reinforcement of Low Rates (DRL)   A schedule of reinforcement designed to reinforce timed pauses between operant responses. (Example: The first response after five seconds of nonresponding would be reinforced.)

Discrete Avoidance   A procedure in which a stimulus sets the occasion for an avoidance response, which, when emitted, delays or prevents an aversive stimulus.

Discrete Trial   A stimulus is presented to an animal for a specified period of time, during which a particular instrumental response (or set of responses) is required for task completion.

Discriminated Operant   A particular operant response under stimulus control. (Example: Removing the wrapper [S^d] from a stick of gum [reinforcer].)

Discriminative Stimulus (S^d)   A stimulus that signals that a particular response-reinforcement contingency is in effect, therefore setting occasions during which operant responses become highly probable.

Disinhibition (Pavlov)   An extraneous stimulus that disrupts the ongoing effects of an inhibitory stimulus, typically allowing a release of excitation, is called a *disinhibiting* *stimulus,* and the process is called *disinhibition.* Example: the effect of a loud noise on a drowsy state.

Dizygotic   Developed from two zygotes; fraternal, or two-egg, twins. Dizygotic twins have different genotypes.

DNA (Deoxyribonucleic Acid)   A complex molecule that composes the chromosomes and is the primary genetic material in (most) organisms.

Dominance-Contiguity Theory   See *Razran's dominance-contiguity theory.*

DRH   See differential reinforcement of high rates.

Drive Reduction Theory (Hull)   When behavior is instrumental in fulfilling specific needs (i.e., restores an organism to homeostatic balance) the drive is said to be reduced. Drive reduction reinforces the instrumental behavior in Clark L. Hull's theory.

Drive States (Hull)   Food and water deprivation sets up conditions of specific physiological needs, which are translated into motivated behavior called *drive states.*

Drive-Stimulus Reduction   The theory that stimulus properties of incentives, and not the necessity of meeting physiological needs, are sufficient to reduce drive states.

Drive Theory   See *drive reduction theory.*

DRL   See *differential reinforcement of low rates.*

Ecological Niche   The place of an animal or plant in nature; the interrelatedness of plants and animals with their local environments.

Ecological Validity   In animal experiments, requiring an animal to learn a task that is likely to be encountered in the real world. Learning about foods is an *ecologically valid* task; learning to maintain balance on a hind paw while inebriated is of questionable ecological validity.

Electrical Stimulation of the Brain (ESB)   Passing minute amounts of electric current through an implanted electrode to specific areas of the brain can act as a reinforcer. Experimental animals will press a lever to self-administer ESB.

Elicited Behavior   Reflexive, or otherwise innately organized behavior, sometimes characterized as *involuntary* behavior (cf. Skinner's distinction of *elicited* and *emitted* behavior).

Embedded Conditioning   A variation of simultaneous conditioning in which the onset and offset of either the CS or US occurs during (i.e., *embedded in the middle of*) presentation of the other element. Embedded conditioning situations often involve the pairing of long-duration stimuli, such as flavors experienced during meals, sensory events during drug effects, etc.

Emitted Behavior   Instrumental responses, sometimes characterized as *voluntary* behavior, that are not readily tied to specific eliciting stimuli (cf. Skinner's distinction of *elicited* and *emitted* behavior).

Empiricism   The primary method (and philosophy) of *observation* and *experimentation* that distinguishes science from other ways humans can get knowledge about the world. (Cf. "intuitionism," which has no real-world referents.)

Environment   The sum total of conditions and influences affecting the growth and development of living things, including air, water, soil, other plants and animals, etc.

Environmental Determinism   The philosophical position that behavior is caused (determined) by environmental influences. (Cf. *behaviorism; biological determinism.*)

Escape Procedure   A procedure in which an animal makes an instrumental response that has the effect of terminating an aversive stimulus.

Evolution   Changes taking place in the genetic makeup of populations. *Darwinian,* or neo-*Darwinian, evolution* is a complex theory (comprised of many subtheories) proposed to account for the history of life on earth.

Excitatory Conditioning (Pavlov)   "Normal" forward conditioning in which a CS is paired with a US, and the conditioned response resembles the unconditioned response.

Expected Utility   The expected gain from a decision made about a wager or transaction involving money or another tangible valuable.

Experimental Extinction See *extinction*.

Experimental Neurosis (Pavlov) The end result of a conditioning experiment in which an animal is required to perform beyond its capacity to discriminate between two similar stimuli. The animal becomes emotionally distraught and refuses to participate further in the experiment.

External Inhibition (Pavlov) Temporarily disrupting the ongoing process of conditioned excitation by introducing an extraneous stimulus. The extraneous stimulus acts as a distractor, a temporary inhibitory stimulus.

Extinction (or **Experimental Extinction**) (Pavlov) Following conditioning, when the CS continues to be presented without the US, the conditioned response diminishes. The conditioned response is said to *extinguish*, and the procedure is called *extinction*, or *experimental extinction*. When, after instrumental conditioning, a response is no longer reinforced or punished, the response tends to *extinguish* to its preconditioning, or baseline, level. This treatment is also called extinction.

Extinction Curve (or **Extinction Gradient**) During extinction, a plot of the magnitude of the conditioned response as a function of extinction trials is called an *extinction curve* (or *extinction gradient*). In a typical extinction curve, response magnitude diminishes to preconditioning levels.

Extrapolation The real-world application of experimental results found in field and laboratory experimentation (typically conducted with animals) to the human condition.

FAP See *fixed action pattern*.

FI See *fixed-interval schedule*.

Fixed Action Pattern (FAP) (Ethology) A fixed series of movements ordered in time and space and triggered by an environmental stimulus. FAPs are species-typical, and once initiated, proceed through sequence to completion.

Fixed-Interval (FI) Schedule A schedule of reinforcement in which an animal is reinforced for its first response following a specified *time interval* from the preceding reinforcer.

Fixed-Ratio (FR) Schedule A schedule of reinforcement in which reinforcement is contingent upon the completion of a fixed number of operant responses.

Foraging Patterns Innately disposed behavior that results in the conduct of patterned searches and remembering where food is located in three-dimensional space.

Forward Conditioning (Pavlov) In forward conditioning the CS onset precedes the US onset, and both stimuli overlap somewhat in time. Forward conditioning is the most common form of "normal" excitatory conditioning; an example is a bell CS followed immediately by a food US.

FR See *fixed-ratio schedule*.

Fractional anticipatory goal responses (rGs) (Hull) The theory that stimuli encountered in the pathway prior to entry into the goal box are reinforced, and in turn become secondary reinforcers for even earlier responses in the maze. This theory allows a single reinforcer to connect complex sequences of behavior.

Free Operant An easy, repeatable operant response, such as a lever press. (Contrast with tasks requiring *discrete trials*.)

Frequency (*associative theory*) The observation that associations are strengthened through repetition; that the number of times two stimuli occur together, or a response is reinforced, strengthens their respective association.

Frustration Theory (Amsel) Following a history of continuous reinforcement, the theory that an extinction procedure produces a state of negative emotions such as frustration.

Functional Relationship An orderly relationship existing between stimulus and response. Example: Higher drug doses cause higher levels of activity.

Gene Comprised of DNA (deoxyribonucleic acid), a gene is a part of a chromosome that, during the reproductive process, influences the inheritance and development of characteristics in the offspring.

Generalization The tendency of animals to both perceive (*stimulus generalization*) and to respond (*response generalization*) in a similar manner to stimuli that share common properties.

General Process Learning Theory The theory that common anatomical and physiological features among animals (i.e., genetic similarity producing similar brains, immune systems, digestive systems, etc.) provide the mechanisms by which animals perceive, associate, and learn to respond in similar ways.

Genetics The study of patterns of heredity and variations in plants and animals.

Genotype The genetic constitution of an individual organism.

Habituation The reduced responsiveness of an organism to repeated stimulation.

Habituation Control Group A nonassociative control group that is presented only the CS during conditioning. The manner in which this group responds to the CS following conditioning provides a basis for comparison with the association formed in a CS-US treatment group.

Hedonic Conditioning A theory proposed by David Booth to account for meal-to-meal changes in particular foods selected based upon the positive or negative postingestional consequences of previous selections. Tastes and textures are CSs that become associated with postingestional consequences (USs).

Hedonism A philosophical position to the effect that the sole motivation of humans and other animals is to seek pleasure and to avoid pain.

Heredity The genetic transmission of characteristics from one generation to the next.

Heritability The fraction of the total phenotypic variance that is accounted for by genetic variation.

Higher-Order Conditioning (Pavlov) The process by which an arbitrary (conditioned) stimulus (CS_1) acquires unconditioned stimulus properties. CS_1 is first paired with a US. Following conditioning, CS_1 is then paired with yet another arbitrary stimulus (CS_2). CS_2 acquires US properties through the process called *higher-order conditioning*. (See also *second-order conditioning*.)

Hypothesis A hunch, or idea, or theory that is formally tested in an experiment.

Hypothetical Construct The conceptualization of an alleged process of the mind to account for various aspects of personality, memory, motivation, perception, intelligence, etc. (Cf. *intervening variable*.)

Imprinting (Ethology) A genetically programmed aspect of behavior change involving the rapid development of a response to a specific stimulus at a particular stage of development. (Cf. *critical period; innate releasing mechanism*.)

Incentive Motivation Motivation to behave that can be attributed to the quality and amount of a reinforcer. The reinforcer is said to act as an *incentive*.

Independent Variable In an experiment, the experimenter manipulates the *independent variable* (a stimulus condition) to see how it affects the dependent variable. The independent variable is seen as the cause, and the effect is how it changes the dependent variable. Example: A drug (independent variable) *caused* increased activity (dependent variable).

Induction Method An excitatory stimulus (such as a tone) is paired with shock. When another stimulus (such as a light) is paired with the tone, and the pair is not shocked, the tone "induces" the light to become an inhibitory, or "safe," stimulus. The procedure is called the *induction method* of conditioned inhibition.

Inhibition of Delay (Pavlov) The passage of time can produce an inhibitory process. Responding is suppressed, or inhibited, during the first part of regularly spaced intervals. An extraneous stimulus can disinhibit this *inhibition of delay*.

Innate Releasing Mechanism (IRM) (Ethology) A postulated neural mechanism that, when stimulated by a *sign-releasing stimulus*, triggers an innately organized motor program. (Cf. *critical period; sign stimulus*.)

Instinct Innately organized behavior.

Instinctive Drift (Breland) The theory that arbitrarily established responses erode (drift) in the face of more innately organized (instinctive) behavior.

Instrumental Conditioning See *instrumental learning.*

Instrumental Learning (Thorndike) Acquiring and modifying so-called "voluntary," emitted, or otherwise nonreflexive behavior by the application of reinforcers or punishers. (Cf. *Pavlovian conditioning; operant conditioning.*)

Instrumental Response Voluntary, nonreflexive responses that act upon the environment in a meaningful, or instrumental, fashion.

Intensity (*associative theory*) The observation that the association of two stimuli is influenced by the intensity with which the stimuli are perceived. More intense stimuli are more associable. (Cf. *law of strength.*)

Intermittent Reinforcement See *partial reinforcement.*

Internal Inhibition (Pavlov) A term Pavlov used to account for the loss of a conditioned response during an extinction procedure. Spontaneous recovery was interpreted by Pavlov as evidence for an active process of *internal* inhibition (i.e., within the dog), as opposed to the disruptive effects of an *external* inhibitor (i.e., a stimulus occurring external to the dog).

Interstimulus Interval See *CS-US interval.*

Intertrial Interval The elapsed time between conditioning trials in a conditioning experiment.

Intervening Variable Processes of the mind, such as learning, memory, motivation, etc., are such variables, inferred from observations of behavior. When "learning," for example, is operationally defined and studied by experimentation, it is conceptualized as an *intervening variable* that bridges the gap between measurable *stimulus* and *response variables*. (Cf. *hypothetical construct.*)

Introspection Looking within. Analyzing the "contents" of mind by verbal descriptions of perceptions, thoughts, memories, etc.

Involuntary Behavior Physiology and behavior under the control of the autonomic nervous system. Unintentional, unwillful behavior. (Cf. reflex, *voluntary behavior.*)

Labor Supply Curve A "backward bending" curve that deviates from the *matching law*, reflecting a breakdown in the general rule that effort will increase indefinitely to match available reinforcement.

LAD See *Language Acquisition Device.*

Lamarckian Evolution The theory that genetic changes in populations (i.e., evolution) can occur through the inheritance of characters acquired during a lifetime.

Language Acquisition Device (LAD) (Chomsky) A proposed species-specific brain mechanism (or series of mechanisms) that allows a human child to rapidly acquire language once triggered by a minimal language environment.

Latent Inhibition Preexposed, or familiar, conditioned stimuli require more trials to become associated with a given US than do novel conditioned stimuli. A preexposed CS thus is said to be *latently inhibited.* Reduced associability of familiar stimuli is also known as the *CS-preexposure effect.*

Latent Learning (Tolman) Learning that is alleged to occur in the absence of specific food rewards.

Law of Effect (Thorndike) An elementary principle, postulated by Thorndike to govern *all* behavior, which simply states that a response that is followed by a pleasant consequence will tend to be repeated and a response followed by an unpleasant consequence will tend to decrease in frequency.

Law of Parsimony The strategy of explaining phenomena in terms of simple, rather than by appealing to complex, mechanisms and/or processes. (Also known as *Occam's Razor* or *Morgan's Canon.*)

Law of Strength (Pavlov) Three interrelated factors that account for the *strength* (or magnitude) of a conditioned response are the intensity of the CS, the intensity of the US, and a close interstimulus interval between the CS and US.

Learned Helplessness The results of a *learned helplessness treatment* in which an animal is prevented from escaping intensely painful stimuli. Subsequently, the animal fails to respond in an adaptive fashion by escaping a painful experience when allowed the opportunity. The animal is said to have *learned* to be *helpless.*

Learning   A relatively permanent change in observable behavior that results from experience within the environment.

Learning-Performance Distinction   The difference between what is actually measured (performance) and that which is inferred from the performance (learning).

Learning Set (Harlow)   A learning procedure in which two stimuli are presented to an animal for a set of six consecutive trials. Selecting one, arbitrarily designated as the "correct" choice, is reinforced. After completing many sets of such problems, animals learn a win-stay, lose-shift strategy and are able to consistently respond correctly on the first opportunity. (See *win-stay, lose-shift; learning to learn.*)

Learning Theory   The proposition that a limited number of general principles of learning can account for much of the observed variability in animal behavior.

Learning to Learn (Harlow)   The term Harlow used to describe the ability of animals to slowly learn a *general rule* that could then be applied to rapidly solve new problem sets. (See *win-stay, lose-shift; learning set.*)

Long-Term   Potentiation   (LTP)   Neurons rapidly stimulated for a brief time show *potentiation* (increased responsiveness) lasting for days and even weeks. LTP may mediate associative effects between neurons.

LTP   See *long-term potentiation.*

Magazine Training   An initial stage of operant conditioning in which approaches to the food cup (or magazine) are *reinforced* when the animal finds food there, and somewhat later, when the sound of the food delivery mechanism becomes associated with food delivery.

Match-to-Sample   See   *delayed   match-to-sample.*   The difference between the two procedures is that in match-to-sample the target stimulus does not terminate prior to presentation of the target plus distractors.

Matching Law (Herrnstein)   When an animal is given two response alternatives, a mono-

tonic functional relationship is typically found between the rate of responding and available reinforcement: Responses typically match available reinforcement.

Melioration   On   concurrent   reinforcement schedules, pigeons behave in ways that maximize local (moment to moment) changes, the result of which is to take advantage of available reinforcement. Specifically, *melioration* describes shifting to the opposite key shortly after being reinforced.

Molar Level   In research, investigations of the behavior of whole, intact organisms. (Contrast with *molecular level.*)

Molecular Level   In research, investigations of behavior by determining which parts of the brain (anatomy) or which biochemicals are involved concomitant with the behavior. (Contrast with *molar level.*)

Monozygotic   Developed from a single zygote; identical, or one-egg, twins. Monozygotic twins have identical genotypes.

Natural Concepts   A term used to describe the ability of pigeons to extract information from complex pictures of natural environments and to respond in a way that indicates they recognize trees, people, and other "open-ended" categories.

Natural Selection (Darwin)   An aspect of the theory of evolution that stresses the reproductive advantage of certain offspring suited to their environment over others not suited. Darwin argued that environment (i.e., nature) selects those individuals who will reproduce the next generation depending upon their relative fitness. Animals not able to overcome these *selection pressures* drop out of the gene pool. (Cf. *selective pressure.*)

Negative Contingency   A   backward   pairing sets up a *negative contingency* of CS and US. By contrast, a forward pairing sets up a positive contingency. Negative contingencies often result in the formation of conditioned inhibition, rarely in conditioned excitation.

Negative Contrast   After experiencing both a small and a large reward, their comparison makes the perception of the smaller reward more negative than it would be in the absence of the contrast. See also *behavioral contrast.*

Negative Discriminative Stimulus (S$^\Delta$) A stimulus that signals that response-food contingencies are *not* in effect. Responding in the presence of this stimulus is not reinforced.

Negative Reinforcement Responses that are instrumental in preventing or avoiding an aversive stimulus *increase* in frequency by the process called *negative reinforcement.* (Cf. *punishment,* a procedure in which responses that produce an aversive stimulus lead to a *decrease* in frequency of the response.)

Neo-Darwinian Evolution See *evolution.*

Neophobia A behavioral tendency to approach new objects cautiously (literally, *fear of the new*). When applied to rats and humans responding to unfamiliar foods, their innate feeding tendencies are to cautiously approach and sniff before tasting, to be generally finicky.

Neuroethology The study of the relationship between the nervous system and consummatory behaviors.

Nonassociative Learning Relatively permanent changes in behavior that result from an animal experiencing a particular stimulus. *Sensitization* and *habituation* are two examples. (Cf. associative learning.)

Null Hypothesis In an experiment, a researcher compares the results of a treatment condition with a control group. The *null hypothesis* is that there are no differences between these two groups. Rejecting the null hypothesis (using a statistical analysis) leads to the conclusion that the two groups in fact differ, and that the treatment effect caused this difference.

Oddity A learning task in which an animal must pick the "odd" stimulus from a three-stimulus array in which two stimuli are identical.

Omnivore's Paradox Omnivores eat from a wide variety of food sources, thereby *enhancing* fitness during famine. Paradoxically, eating from a wide variety of food sources also increases their risk of poisoning, thereby *diminishing* fitness. (Paradox posed by Paul Rozin.)

One-Word Utterance Stage The first words spoken in any language, typically referring to names for objects encountered in their environment such as "mama" and "milk" and for actions such as "get" and "go." (Also known as holophrastic speech.)

Ontogenetic History A history of an animal's entire development—from fertilization through death.

Operant (or Operant Response) (Skinner) A designated response, such as a lever press, that effectively *operates* upon the environment. (Cf. *instrumental response.*)

Operant Conditioning (Skinner) A variant of instrumental conditioning defined by B. F. Skinner. (See *instrumental conditioning.*)

Operant Level (Skinner) An existing baseline rate of a response as measured prior to the administration of reinforcement and punishment contingencies (cf. *baseline* or *free-operant level*).

Operational Definition A definition of a term or concept that refers to the operations that measure the presumptive process. Example: Intelligence is that which IQ tests measure.

Orienting Reflex (Pavlov) When a CS such as a tone is first sounded, a dog will prick up its ears and turn its head, locating the source of the sound. Pavlov labeled this response an *orienting reflex.*

Overmatching Relative to the *matching law,* the rate of responding to the more rewarding schedule is found to be *more* than, or over, that predicted given the amount of available reinforcement. (Cf. *matching law.*)

Overshadowing When two CSs are conditioned at the same time, the usual result is that one CS acquires more associative strength than the other. This result is called *overshadowing,* in which one CS is said to overshadow the other CS.

Pan paniscus The *bonobo* chimpanzee, sometimes referred to as the *pygmy chimp.* (Cf. the common chimpanzee, *Pan troglodytes.*)

Pan troglodytes The common chimpanzee. (Cf. the pygmy chimpanzee, *Pan paniscus.*)

Parameter In an experiment, the various levels that an independent variable can assume are referred to as the *parameters* of that variable. Example: The parameters of a drug treatment are low, medium, and high dosages.

Partial Reinforcement Any reinforcement situation other than continuous reinforcement. Also called *intermittent reinforcement.*

Partial Reinforcement Effect (PRE) The tendency for animals maintained on partial reinforcement schedules to be highly resistant to extinction.

Pavlovian Conditioning An experimental procedure in which a basic *reflex,* consisting of an *unconditioned stimulus* (*US*) and an *unconditioned response* (*UR*), is paired in time with a neutral stimulus (called the *conditioned stimulus, CS*). After several pairings, the CS by itself can elicit components of the original reflex, called the *conditioned response* (*CR*). (Also called *conditioning; classical conditioning; excitatory conditioning.*)

Peak Shift Following S^d/S^Δ discrimination training of two wavelengths, the peak response of the generalization gradient to the target S^d is shifted in a direction opposite to (away from) the S^Δ wavelength.

Pharmacological Tolerance That portion of total drug tolerance that can be attributed to pharmacodynamic properties of drugs.

Phenotype The physical expression of features in an individual animal that results from the interaction of its genotype with the environment.

Phylogenetic History The entire evolutionary history of a specific taxonomic group of organisms. Collectively, the natural history of life on earth.

Pica Unusual appetite or craving for "unnatural" foodstuffs, such as chalk or clay.

Picture Memory (Farrar) The term Farrar used to describe the performance of his chimpanzee, Minnie, in which 24 pictures with common elements were memorized and apparently *not* learned by applying a general rule.

Positive Reinforcement The process by which the application of a reinforcer contingent upon a desired response increases the frequency of that response.

Positive Reinforcer Any stimulus (such as food) delivered to an animal immediately following a designated response that leads to an increase in the frequency of that response is called a positive reinforcer. (Cf. Thorndike's "*satisfiers.*")

Postreinforcement Pause A break in responding following delivery of a reinforcer. Longer pauses are seen for higher FR schedules than for lower FR schedules (i.e., for FR-100 vs. FR-10), and very *short* postreinforcement pauses are typically found using VI and VR schedules of reinforcement.

Posttraumatic Stress Disorder (PTSD) PTSD is a disorder characterized by one or more of the following symptoms: intense fear, feelings of helplessness, and recurrent intrusive memories/dreams, whose etiology is thought to be caused by an unusual, markedly distressing event such as rape, battle fatigue, etc.

Potentiation When a flavor stimulus (CS_1) is simultaneously conditioned with any other conditioned stimulus (i.e., CS_2), CS_2 is conditioned better than it would have been if merely conditioned by itself. The flavor stimulus is said to *potentiate* the conditioning of CS_2.

PRE See *partial reinforcement effect.*

Premack Principle David Premack's proposal that the more probable of two responses would always reinforce the less probable response, and never vice versa.

Preparedness The argument that animals are (evolutionarily) prepared to readily make associations between certain stimuli, and between some stimuli and certain responses, because such rapid learning enhances fitness.

Primary Punisher A stimulus that is inherently aversive.

Pseudoconditioning See *sensitization control group.*

Psychic Secretion (Pavlov) Pavlov's term for salivation attributable to psychological factors—the dog's thoughts, memories, expectations, prior learning, etc.—rather than due to a physiological reflex.

Psychobiology An interdisciplinary approach to questions of physiology, learning, and behavior that draws upon and attempts to integrate observations and experiments in, among other sciences, psychology, ethology, physiology, and genetics.

Psychoneuroimmunology The field of research attempting to describe and integrate the interconnectedness of the immune system, the central and autonomic nervous systems, and behavior.

Psychosomatic Disorders Disorders of anatomy and/or physiology that can be attributed in part to psychological or behavioral variables.

Punisher Any stimulus whose application acts to decrease the rate of emission of the preceding response is defined to be a punisher.

Punishment The process by which an aversive stimulus acts to decrease the rate of the response to which it is applied.

R-S Conditioning In instrumental conditioning, a response is required prior to presentation of a food stimulus. Hence, instrumental conditioning is sometimes referred to as response-stimulus, or *R-S conditioning*. (Contrast with *S-S* or *Pavlovian conditioning*.)

Random Control Group A nonassociative control group in which the CS and US are both presented separately, never together, in time.

Rattus Norvegicus (Norway rat) The genus and species designation for the wild Norway rat, whose descendants are the most commonly used laboratory rat.

Razran's Dominance-Contiguity Theory A modification of Pavlov's basic theory of conditioning that (a) focused upon the associability of an animal's *responses* to CSs and USs, rather than the stimuli; (b) stressed the role of contiguity over contingency; and (c) postulated that the second of two stimulus events must "dominate" the first for association to occur.

Reductionism Explaining a phenomenon by reference to a more molecular analysis (i.e., a biochemical level) is to *reduce* the level of

analysis—hence, *reductionism*. Reductionism is the primary means of scientific explanation.

Reflex An innate, involuntarily response an animal makes to a specific stimulus in the environment. Iris closure in response to sudden bright light is an example.

Reification Asserting the existence of a presumptive process independent of evidence for that process. Example: Intelligence is *there*, awaiting its measurement.

Reinforcement See *positive reinforcement* and *negative reinforcement*.

Reproduction The behavioral and physiological means by which animals produce offspring.

Rescorla–Wagner Model Rescorla and Wagner modeled the growth of association during conditioning (a) by quantifying the effects of using stimuli of different novelty and salience; (b) by predicting and quantifying the greater growth of associative potential in early training trials; and (c) by predicting and quantifying the effects of extinction and blocking procedures.

Resistance-to-Extinction The number of extinction trials necessary for a conditioned response to extinguish; an indirect measure of the amount of conditioning that has occurred. Greater *resistance-to-extinction* is found following many conditioning trials compared with a few conditioning trials in Pavlovian conditioning, and following partial rather than continuous reinforcement in instrumental conditioning.

Response Contingency In instrumental conditioning, making a reinforcer or punisher contingent upon a specified response. No such requirement exists for Pavlovian conditioning.

Response Variable The measured response in a behavioral experiment is called the *response variable*. (In chemistry, the "response variable" is typically called a *reaction*.) In the behavioral sciences, the response variable is typically some measure of behavioral change.

Retardation Test A procedure that allows indirect measurement of conditioned inhibition. A stimulus is first made a conditioned inhibitor, and it is then conditioned as an excitor. The acquisition of conditioned excitation is retarded when a conditioned inhibitor is used, relative to a neutral stimulus.

Reward See *positive reinforcement; satisfiers.*

r_Gs See *fractional anticipatory goal responses.*

Salience A descriptive (not explanatory) term, the salience of a stimulus refers to its relative associability. More salient stimuli are more easily conditioned.

Salivary Reflex Food placed on a dog's tongue elicits reflexive salivation.

Sameness Task A learning task in which pictures of objects are sequentially presented to pigeons. A final picture is presented that either was or was not in the series (i.e., *same* or *different*, respectively). Pigeons solve this problem for food reinforcement by responding to one key if the same, and to another key if different.

Satisfiers Thorndike's *law of effect* proposed that if pleasant stimuli, which he called satisfiers, followed a response, the response would more likely to occur thereafter. (Cf. *positive reinforcer.*)

Schedules of Reinforcement The experimenter specifies rules that govern the relationship of reinforcing events to an animal's responses. Example: In *continuous reinforcement* the rule is that each response is reinforced. Other schedules include fixed ratios, variable intervals, etc.

S^Δ See *negative discriminative stimulus.*

S^d See *discriminative stimulus.*

Second-Order Conditioning (Pavlov) The first step, and the lowest level, of higher-order conditioning. After CS_1 has been paired with a US, CS_1 is then paired with CS_2—called conditioning of the second order. CS_2 acquires US properties through the process called higher-order conditioning.

Secondary Punisher Stimuli that acquire punishing properties through a conditioning procedure. Example: The word "no." (Cf. secondary reinforcement.)

Secondary Reinforcers Neutral stimuli that acquire reinforcing properties via the process of higher-order conditioning are called *secondary,* or conditioned, reinforcers. An example is money.

Second Signal System (Pavlov) Words are arbitrary auditory (i.e., spoken) and visual (i.e., written) signals that are associated with real-world sensory impressions, such as "red sun" and "cold water." *Red sun* and *cold water* are the first signals of the real world. Words are symbols that represent these raw sensory experiences. Words are one level of abstraction removed from the world they represent—in Pavlov's terms, words are the signal of signals; hence, the *second signal system.*

Selective Pressure Any feature of an environment that allows one phenotype to have reproductive advantage over another.

Self-Control The ability to delay immediate gratification, usually with the goal of attaining a larger reinforcer at a later time.

Sensitive Period See *critical period.*

Sensitization If, after experiencing a stimulus, an animal tends to become *more* activated when the stimulus is presented again, the animal is said to be *sensitized.* This increased responsiveness, or *sensitization,* is considered to be a form of nonassociative learning.

Sensitization Control Group A nonassociative control group exposed only to the US during conditioning. The manner in which this group responds to the CS following conditioning provides a basis for comparison with the association formed in a CS-US treatment group. The *sensitization* control group is sometimes called a *pseudoconditioning* control.

Sensory Preconditioning A method used to measure CS-CS associations. In the first step, two conditioned stimuli (CS_1 and CS_2) are repeatedly paired together. CS_1 is then conditioned to a US, after which CS_2 is tested as if it had been conditioned. In sensory preconditioning, CS_2 shows (indirect) evidence of conditioning through its prior association with CS_1.

Serial Pattern Learning A learning task in which rats are exposed to and learn a sequence of patterns of reinforcement (or nonreinforcement) in the goal box over a succession of trials.

Shaping A training system that involves the selective reinforcement of responses that approximate the target behavior. The process by which increasingly stringent response requirements are placed on the animal, eventuating in reinforcement only for successful completion of the target response (i.e., a lever press), is called *shaping by successive approximation.*

Sherringtonian Reflex A reflex characterized by an identifiable *sensory neuron* synapsing upon an identifiable *interneuron* and *motor neuron.*

Shuttle-Avoidance Avoidance conditioning in a *shuttle-box* in which the terminal behavior is to "shuttle" between two compartments, thereby avoiding electric shock.

Shuttle-Box An apparatus in which animals can be conditioned to *escape* and/or *avoid* electric shock by jumping across a barrier dividing the two compartments of the shuttle-box.

Sidman Avoidance Murray Sidman designed this negative reinforcement procedure in which the lever in a Skinner Box is the only signal that electric shock can be delayed/avoided by continuous lever pressing.

Sign Stimulus (Ethology) A specific environmental stimulus that triggers innately organized behaviors. (Cf. *fixed action pattern; innate releasing mechanism.*)

Sign Tracking See *autoshaping.*

Similarity (*associative theory*) The associability of two stimuli is strengthened if they are in some way *similar* to each other or if they are perceived as "belonging" together. (Cf. *preparedness.*)

Simultaneous Conditioning (Pavlov) The CS and US have identical onsets, durations, and offsets in simultaneous conditioning. Very little conditioning results in these trials.

Single-Stimulus Effect (*associative theory*) Behavioral change due to the action of a single stimulus, as opposed to the association of two or more stimuli. (See *nonassociative learning; sensitization; habituation.*)

Skinner Box An experimental environment consisting of a small box containing one or more (a) levers or response keys, (b) lights/speakers, and (c) feeding/watering devices used in animal learning experiments (named for B. F. Skinner).

Sociobiology The study of the genetic determinants of social behavior.

S-O-R Theory (Hull) A neobehaviorist, S-R theory in which intervening variables, specifically *organismic* variables such as thirst and hunger, are considered in the functional relationship between stimulus and response variables.

Species-Specific Behaviors Innate perceptual and response patterns typical of a species.

Species-Specific Defense Reaction (SSDR) An innately organized hierarchy of defense behaviors elicited by signals indicating potential danger.

Specific Hungers The translation of physiological needs into cravings and hungers for specific, identifiable nutrients. Examples are cravings for salt and water.

Spontaneous Recovery (Pavlov) The reappearance of a higher level of conditioned response following a delay in the extinction process.

S-S Conditioning In Pavlovian conditioning, a stimulus is paired with another stimulus (such as food). Hence, Pavlovian conditioning is sometimes referred to as stimulus-stimulus, or S-S *conditioning.* (Contrast with *R-S* or *instrumental conditioning.*)

SSDR See *species-specific defense reaction.*

Stimulus Control Trained humans and animals that reliably make operant responses in the presence of S^d's and do *not* respond in the presence of S^Δ's are said to be under *stimulus control.*

Stimulus Generalization See *generalization.*

Stimulus Generalization Gradient Following training to a target stimulus, a pattern of responses to similar stimuli, in which more responses are made to the most similar, and the fewest responses are made to stimuli most different from the target.

Stimulus-Response Chains The theory that in learning to perform a sequence of responses (such as left and right turns in a maze), each response may acquire stimulus properties that cue the next response. (Cf. *chained operants.*)

Stimulus Specificity in Conditioning Genetically determined (prepared) brain structures allow rapid learning of certain (specific) stimuli, and make the learning of other associations more difficult. Example: Garcia's telereceptor-cutaneous and gustatory-visceral conditioning systems. (Cf. *preparedness.*)

Stimulus Substitution (Pavlov) The theory that in the course of conditioning, animals come to consider the conditioned stimulus to be a "substitute" for the unconditioned stimulus. (Example: Chimpanzees who hoard tokens associated with prior food reinforcement.)

Stimulus Variable The experimental manipulation imposed on a subject in an experiment is the *stimulus variable,* or independent variable. Stimulus variables impinge upon animals, causing responses (see *black box*).

Successive Approximation See *shaping.*

Summation Test A procedure that allows indirect measurement of conditioned inhibition. Following conditioning of CS_2 (a conditioned inhibitor) and CS_1 (a conditioned excitor), when presented together in extinction CS_1 and CS_2 will algebraically combine, or sum, such that both the excitatory and inhibitory response are lessened.

Target Response The instrumental or operant response that, when executed, is reinforced.

Taste Aversion Conditioning A method of studying aversive Pavlovian conditioning in which rats are allowed to drink a flavored solution (the CS) and then are made sick by giving them an illness-inducing toxin (the US). Conditioned taste aversions to the target flavor result from one or a few pairings.

Telegraphic Speech The term used to define the stage of language when, at the age of about one and a half years, children begin to string together two words in a grammatically meaningful fashion.

Temporal Conditioning (Pavlov) A variation of conditioning in which dogs are presented food at regular intervals. After many such trials, salivation is found to occur just prior to food administration. Pavlov interpreted these results by postulating that the inter-food time interval had acquired conditioned stimulus properties, and that the salivation was a conditioned response.

Temporal Contiguity (*associative theory*) Two or more events closely related together in time are said to be temporally contiguous. (See *contiguity theory of association.*)

Thorndikean Conditioning See *instrumental learning.*

Thorndikean Learning See *instrumental learning.*

Tolerance Changes in the effectiveness of drugs taken repeatedly, as measured by the necessity to increase a drug dosage to get the same effect, or as measured by the decreased effectiveness of a given drug dosage taken repeatedly.

Trace Conditioning (Pavlov) *Trace conditioning* is a special example of forward conditioning in which both the CS onset and *offset* precede the US onset. Historically, the term "trace" refers to a hypothetical memory trace that remains after the termination of the stimulus.

Transitive Inferential Reasoning A problem of the following type: "If *a* is greater than *b*, and *b* is greater than *c*, is *a* greater than *c*?"; its solution is indicative of reasoning ability and a knowledge of relationships that extends beyond immediate experience.

Treatment Group In all experiments the experimental manipulation is called the *treatment*, and the group of subjects that receive the experimental manipulation—the independent variable—is called the treatment group.

Trial A *trial* consists of a CS-US pairing, or, in instrumental conditioning, a response or set of responses terminating in reinforcement or punishment.

Tropism A differential growth movement in a plant away from or toward a directional stimulus.

Two-Factor Theory (Mowrer) A theory proposing that two factors underlying avoidance behavior are Pavlovian-conditioned emotional behavior and instrumentally conditioned motor (muscle) responses.

Two-Factor Theory of Punishment A theory that punishment learning is accomplished in two stages; i.e., a fear response is first conditioned classically, and then an avoidance response reduces the fear response.

Unconditioned Response (UR) (Pavlov) The reflexive response to an unconditioned stimulus (the US). Salivation is the unconditioned response to food.

Unconditioned Stimulus (US) (Pavlov) A stimulus that innately, involuntarily, elicits a reflexive response (i.e., the UR). Food is an unconditioned stimulus that elicits reflexive salivation.

Undermatching Relative to the *matching law*, the rate of responding to the more rewarding schedule is found to be *less* than, or under, that predicted given the amount of available reinforcement. (Cf. *matching law*.)

Universal Grammar (Chomsky) A theoretical position initially formulated by Noam Chomsky that postulates the existence of innate structures underlying the rapid acquisition and output of grammatically correct language, and that denies any role for Pavlovian and instrumental conditioning processes.

Unprepared The theory that while some learning is *prepared* (i.e., learned in one or only a few trials), and other learning is *contraprepared* to be associated (i.e., many, many trials to learn); yet other stimuli and responses are *unprepared*, i.e., are relatively neutral in their associability (requiring an intermediate number of trials).

UR See *unconditioned response.*

US See *unconditioned stimulus.*

US Preexposure Effect Preexposed, or familiar, unconditioned stimuli require more trials to become associated with a given CS than do novel unconditioned stimuli. (Cf. *CS preexposure effect.*) Example: Exposing an animal to an electric shock before conditioning makes the electric shock a less effective unconditioned stimulus.

Value The relative worth, merit, or importance of an object or activity, based upon *esthetics, cost, availability, perceived utility,* and other properties.

Variability (Darwin) An aspect of the theory of evolution that describes the role played by the wide range of genetic variation (i.e., variability) within a species. Genetic variance is the raw material upon which natural selection works. (Cf. *natural selection; selective pressure.*)

Variable-Interval (VI) Schedule A schedule of reinforcement in which an animal is reinforced for its first response following a *variable interval* of time from the preceding reinforcer. Example: An animal on a VI-60 is reinforced at varying time periods averaging 60 seconds from the preceding reinforcement.

Variable-Ratio (VR) Schedule A schedule of reinforcement in which delivery of a reinforcer is contingent upon the completion of a variable number of operant responses from the preceding reinforcement. Example: An animal responding on a VR-10 is reinforced for different numbers of responses, their average being 10.

Vertebrate Plan The observed similarities in brain structure among all vertebrates, characterized by their common bilaterality, cranial nerves, thalamus, medulla, etc.

VI See *variable-interval schedule.*

Voluntary Behavior Physiology and behavior under the control of the central nervous system. Intentional, willful behavior. (Cf. reflex, *involuntary behavior.*)

VR See *variable-ratio schedule.*

Win-Stay, Lose-Shift (Harlow) A strategy animals are capable of learning. When presented with repeated opportunities to solve a two-choice discrimination problem in which one of the choices is consistently rewarded, reinforcement can be maximized by adopting the two-part rule: (a) to continue selecting the reinforced choice (i.e., win-stay); and (b) to shift to the alternative choice when not reinforced (i.e., lose-shift). (See *learning set; learning to learn.*)

Within-Groups Design The design of an experiment in which a pretreatment measure of the dependent variable is compared with a posttreatment measure *in the same subjects*. (Cf. *between-groups design.*)

Working Hypothesis A simple statement of what is expected to happen in an experiment. Example: A low dose of drug X will have less effect on activity than a high dose of drug X.

Written History The transmission of cultural knowledge; a cumulative record of the ontogenetic histories of many individuals that provides the basis for *civilization*, which is an invention unique to *Homo sapiens*.

References

Ader, R. (1985). Conditioned taste aversions and immunopharmacology. *Annals of the New York Academy of Sciences, 443*, 293–307.

Ader, R., & Cohen, N. (1982). Behaviorally conditioned immunosuppression and murine systemic lupus erythematosus. *Science, 215*, 1534–1536.

Ader, R., Cohen, N., & Bovbjerg, D. (1982). Conditioned suppression of humoral immunity in the rat. *Journal of Comparative & Physiological Psychology, 96*, 517–521.

Amsel, A. (1958). The role of frustrative non-reward in partial reinforcement and discrimination learning. *Psychological Review, 69*, 306–328.

Anderson, C. D., Ferland, R. J., & Williams, M. D. (1992). Negative contrast associated with reinforcing stimulation of the brain. *Society for Neuroscience Abstracts, 18*, 874.

Anderson, J. R. (1990). *Cognitive psychology and its implications*. New York: Freeman.

Anderson, R. C., Wilson, P. T., & Fielding, L. G. (1988). Growth in reading and how children spend their time outside of school. *Reading Research Quarterly, 23*, 285–303.

Annau, Z., & Kamin, L. J. (1961). The conditioned emotional response as a function of intensity of the US. *Journal of Comparative & Physiological Psychology, 54*, 428–432.

Archer, T., & Sjoden, P. O. (1982). Higher-order conditioning and sensory preconditioning of a taste aversion with an exteroceptive CS1. *Quarterly Journal of Experimental Psychology, 34B*, 1–17.

Ayllon, T., & Azrin, N. (1968). *The token-economy: A motivational system for therapy and rehabilitation*. New York: Appleton-Century-Crofts.

Azrin, N. H., & Holz, W. C. (1966). Punishment. In W. K. Honig (Ed.), *Operant behavior: Areas of research and application*. New York: Appleton-Century-Crofts.

Azrin, N. H., Holz, W. C., & Hake, D. F. (1963). Fixed-ratio punishment. *Journal of the Experimental Analysis of Behavior, 6*, 141–148.

Azrin, N. H., Hutchinson, R. R., & Hake, D. F. (1966). Extinction-induced aggression. *Journal of the Experimental Analysis of Behavior, 9*, 191–204.

Baer, D. M., & Sherman, J. A. (1964). Reinforcement control of generalized imitation in young children. *Journal of Experimental Child Psychology, 1*, 37–49.

Baker, A. G., & Baker, P. A. (1985). Does inhibition differ from excitation: Proactive interference, contextual conditioning, and extinction. In R. R. Miller & N. E. Spear (Eds.), *Information processing in animals: Conditioned inhibition*. Hillsdale, NJ: Erlbaum.

Baker, A. G., & Mackintosh, N. J. (1977). Excitatory and inhibitory conditioning following uncorrelated presentations of CS and UCS. *Animal Learning & Behavior, 5*, 315–319.

Baker, A. G., & Mercier, P. (1982). Extinction of the context and latent inhibition. *Learning & Motivation, 13*, 391–416.

Baker, A. G., Mercier, P., Gabel, J., & Baker, P. A. (1981). Contextual conditioning and the US preexposure effect in conditioned fear. *Jour-*

nal of Experimental Psychology: Animal Behavior Processes, 7, 109–128.

Baker, A. G., Singh, M., & Bindra, D. (1985). Some effects of contextual conditioning and US predictability on Pavlovian conditioning. In P. Balsam & A. Tomie (Eds.), *Context and learning.* Hillsdale, NJ: Erlbaum.

Baker, B. J., Booth, D. A., Duggan, J. P., & Gibson, E. L. (1987). Protein appetite demonstrated: Learned specificity of protein-cue preference to protein need in adult rats. *Nutrition Research, 7,* 481–487,

Baker, T. B., & Tiffany, S. T. (1985). Morphine tolerance as habituation. *Psychological Review, 92,* 78–108.

Bandura, A. (1977). *Social learning theory.* Englewood Cliffs, NJ: Prentice-Hall.

Barash, D. (1979). *The whisperings within: Evolution and the origin of human nature.* New York: Harper & Row.

Barash, D. (1982). *Sociobiology and behavior* (2nd ed.). New York: Elsevier.

Barker, L. M. (1968). *Effects of [classified drug] on aversive and appetitively motivated behavior of Rhesus monkeys in aeronautical simulation studies* (Unpublished Technical Report). Holloman AFB, NM: 6571st Aeromedical Research Laboratory, USAF.

Barker, L. M., Best, M. R., & Domjan, M. (Eds.). (1977). *Learning mechanisms in food selection.* Waco, TX: Baylor University Press.

Barker, L. M., & Smith, J. C. (1974). A comparison of taste aversions induced by radiation and lithium chloride in CS-US and US-CS paradigms. *Journal of Comparative & Physiological Psychology, 87,* 644–654.

Barker, L. M., Suarez, E. R., & Grey, D. (1974). Backward conditioning of taste aversions in rats using cyclophosphamide as the US. *Physiological Psychology, 2,* 117–119.

Barker, L. M., & Weaver, C. A. (1991). Conditioning flavor preferences in rats: Dissecting the "Medicine Effect." *Learning & Motivation, 22,* 311–328.

Barnett, S. A. (1981). *Modern ethology.* New York: Oxford University Press.

Baum, W. M. (1974). On two types of deviation from the matching law: Bias and undermatching. *Journal of the Experimental Analysis of Behavior, 22,* 231–242.

Baum, W. M. (1979). Matching, undermatching, and overmatching in studies of choice. *Journal of the Experimental Analysis of Behavior, 32,* 269–281.

Baum, W. M. (1981). Optimization and the matching law as accounts of instrumental behavior. *Journal of the Experimental Analysis of Behavior, 36,* 387–403.

Beach, F. (1950). The Snark was a Boojum. *American Psychologist, 5,* 115–124.

Beckwith, R., & Rispoli, M. (1986). Aspects of a theory of mind: An interview with Noam Chomsky. *New Ideas in Psychology, 4,* 187–202.

Beidler, L. M. (1982). Biological basis of food selection. In L. M. Barker (Ed.), *The psychobiology of human food selection.* Westport, CT: AVI Publishing.

Benedict, J. O., & Ayres, J. J. B. (1972). Factors affecting conditioning in the truly random control procedure in the rat. *Journal of Comparative & Physiological Psychology, 78,* 323–330.

Benjamin, L. T., & Bruce, D. (1982). From bottle-fed chimp to bottlenose dolphin: A contemporary appraisal of Winthrop Kellogg. *The Psychological Record, 32,* 461–482.

Bernstein, A. M., Philips, H. C., Linden, W., & Fenster, H. A. (1992). Psychophysiological evaluation of female urethral syndrome: Evidence for a muscular abnormality. *Journal of Behavioral Medicine, 15,* 299–312.

Bernstein, I. L. (1978). Learned taste aversions in children receiving chemotherapy. *Science, 200,* 1302–1303.

Bernstein, I. L., & Borson, S. (1986). Learned food aversion: A component of anorexia syndromes. *Psychological Review, 93,* 462–472.

Bernstein, I. L., & Webster, M. M. (1980). Learned taste aversions in humans. *Physiology & Behavior, 25,* 363–366.

Best, M. R. (1975). Conditioned and latent inhibition in taste-aversion learning: Clarifying the role of learned safety. *Journal of Experimental Psychology: Animal Behavior Processes, 1,* 97–113.

Best, M. R., & Barker, L. (1977). The nature of "learned safety" and its role in the delay of reinforcement gradient. In L. M. Barker,

M. R. Best, & M. Domjan (Eds.), *Learning mechanisms in food selection*. Waco, TX: Baylor University Press.

Best, M. R., Brown, E. R., & Sowell, M. K. (1984). Taste mediated potentiation of non-ingestional stimuli in rats. *Learning & Motivation, 15*, 244–258.

Best, M. R., & Gemberling, G. A. (1977). The role of short-term processes in the CS preexposure effect and the delay of reinforcement gradient in long-delay taste-aversion learning. *Journal of Experimental Psychology: Animal Behavior Processes, 3*, 253–263.

Best, M. R., & Meacham, C. L. (1986). The effects of stimulus preexposure on taste mediated environmental conditioning: Potentiation and overshadowing. *Animal Learning & Behavior, 14*, 1–5.

Best, P. J., Best, M. R., & Henggeler, S. (1977). The contribution of environmental non-ingestive cues in conditioning with aversive internal consequences. In L. M. Barker, M. R. Best, & M. Domjan (Eds.), *Learning mechanisms in food selection*. Waco, TX: Baylor University Press.

Best, P. J., Best, M. R., & Mickley, G. A. (1973). Conditioned aversion to distinct environmental stimuli resulting from gastrointestinal distress. *Journal of Comparative & Physiological Psychology, 85*, 250–257.

Bindra, D. (1972). A unified account of classical conditioning and operant training. In A. H. Black & W. F. Prokasy (Eds.), *Classical conditioning II: Current research and theory*. New York: Appleton-Century-Crofts.

Bitterman, M. E. (1975). The comparative analysis of learning. *Science, 188*, 699–709.

Black, A. H. (1971). Autonomic aversive conditioning in infrahuman subjects. In F. R. Brush (Ed.), *Aversive conditioning and learning*. New York: Academic Press.

Blanchard, E. B., Andrasik, F., Ahles, T. A., Teders, S. J., & O'Keefe, D. (1980). Migraine and tension headache: A meta-analytic review. *Behavior Therapy, 11*, 613–631.

Blanchard, E. B., & Epstein, L. H. (1977). The clinical usefulness of biofeedback. In M. Hersen, R. M. Eisler, & P. M. Miller (Eds.), *Progress in behavior modification* (Vol. 4). New York: Academic Press.

Bliss, T. V. P., & Lomo, T. (1973). Long-lasting potentiation of synaptic transmission in the dentate area of the anaesthetized rabbit following stimulation of the perforant path. *Journal of Physiology (London), 232*, 331–356.

Bloom, L. (1970). *Language development: Form and function in emerging grammars*. Cambridge, MA: MIT Press.

Boakes, R. A. (1984). *From Darwin to behaviourism*. Cambridge: Cambridge University Press.

Boakes, R. A., & Halliday, M. S. (Eds.). (1972). *Inhibition and learning*. London: Academic Press.

Boice, R. (1973). Domestication. *Psychological Bulletin, 80*, 215–230.

Boice, R. (1977). Burrows of wild and albino rats: Effects of domestication, outdoor raising, age, experience, and maternal state. *Journal of Comparative & Physiological Psychology, 91*, 649–661.

Boice, R. (1981). Behavioral comparability of wild and domesticated rats. *Behavior Genetics, 11*, 545–553.

Boland, F. J., Mellor, C. S., & Revusky, S. (1978). Chemical aversion treatment of alcoholism: Lithium as the aversive agent. *Behaviour Research & Therapy, 16*, 401–409.

Bolles, R. C. (1970). Species-specific defense reactions and avoidance learning. *Psychological Review, 71*, 32–48.

Bolles, R. C. (1971). Species-specific defense reactions. In F. R. Brush (Ed.), *Aversive conditioning and learning*. New York: Academic Press.

Bolles, R. C. (1972). The avoidance learning problem. In G. H. Bower (Ed.), *The psychology of learning and motivation* (Vol. 6). New York: Academic Press.

Bolles, R. C. (1991). *The hedonics of taste*. Hillsdale, NJ: Lawrence Erlbaum Associates.

Bolles, R. C., Hayward, L., & Crandall, C. (1981). Conditioned taste preferences based on caloric density. *Journal of Experimental Psychology: Animal Behavior Processes, 7*, 59–69.

Booth, D. A. (1982). How nutritional effects of foods can influence people's dietary choices. In L. M. Barker (Ed.), *The psychobiology of human food selection*. Westport, CT: AVI Publishing.

Booth, R. J., & Ashbridge, K. R. (1992). Implications of psychoimmunology for models of the immune system. In A. J. Husband (Ed.), *Behavior and immunity*. London: CRC Press.

Bouchard, T. J., Lykken, D. R., McGue, M., Segal, N. L., & Tellegen, A. (1990). Sources of human psychological differences: The Minnesota study of twins reared apart. *Science, 250*, 223–228.

Bouton, M. E. (1984). Differential control by context in the inflation and reinstatement paradigms. *Journal of Experimental Psychology: Animal Behavior Processes, 10*, 56–74.

Bouton, M. E. (1991). Context and retrieval in extinction and in other examples of interference in simple associative learning. In L. Dachowski & C. F. Flaherty (Eds.), *Current topics in animal learning*. Hillsdale, NJ: Erlbaum.

Bouton, M. E., Dunlap, C. M., & Swartzentruber, D. (1987). Potentiation of taste by another taste during compound aversion learning. *Animal Learning & Behavior, 15*, 433–438.

Bouton, M. E., & Swartzentruber, D. (1986). Analysis of the associative and occasion-setting properties of contexts participating in a Pavlovian discrimination. *Journal of Experimental Psychology: Animal Behavior Processes, 12*, 333–350.

Bovbjerg, D., Cohen, N., & Ader, R. (1987). Behaviorally conditioned enhancement of delayed-type hypersensitivity in the mouse. *Brain Behavior Immunology, 1*, 64.

Bowe, C. A. (1984). Spatial relations in animal learning and behavior. *The Psychological Record, 34*, 181–209.

Bower, G. H., & Hilgard, E. R. (1981) *Theories of learning* (5th ed.). Englewood Cliffs, NJ: Prentice-Hall.

Bray, G. A. (1976). *The obese patient*. Philadelphia: Saunders.

Breland, K., & Breland, M. (1961). The misbehavior of organisms. *American Psychologist, 16*, 681–684.

Breslau, N., Davis, G. C., Andreski, P., & Peterson, E. (1991). Traumatic events and post-traumatic stress disorder in an urban population of young adults. *Archives of General Psychiatry, 40*, 216–222.

Brett, L. P., Hankins, W. G., & Garcia, J. (1976). Prey-lithium aversions III: Buteo hawks. *Behavioral Biology, 17*, 87–98.

Brown, J. S., & Cunningham, C. L. (1981). The paradox of persisting self-punitive behavior. *Neuroscience & Biobehavioral Reviews, 5*, 343–354.

Brown, P. L., & Jenkins, H. M. (1968). Autoshaping the pigeon's key peck. *Jounal of the Experimental Analysis of Behavior, 11*, 1–8.

Brown, R., & Hanlon, C. (1970). Derivational complexity and the order of acquisition of speech. In R. Brown (Ed.), *Psycholinguistics*. New York: Free Press.

Buchwald, A. M., Coyne, J. C., & Cole, C. S. (1978). A critical evaluation of the learned helplessness model of depression. *Journal of Abnormal Psychology, 87*, 180–193.

Buckley, K. W. (1989). *Mechanical man: John Broadus Watson and the beginnings of behaviorism*. New York: Guilford Press.

Bull, D. F., Brown, R., King, M. G., & Husband, A. J. (1991). Modulation of body temperature through taste aversion conditioning. *Physiology & Behavior, 49*, 1229–1233.

Bull, D. F., Brown, R., King, M. G., Husband, A. J., & Pfister, H. P. (1992). Thermoregulation: Modulation of body termperature through behavioral conditioning. In A. J. Husband (Ed.), *Behavior and immunity*. London: CRC Press.

Bull, J. A., III, & Overmier, J. B. (1968). Additive and subtractive properties of excitation and inhibition. *Journal of Comparative & Physiological Psychology, 66*, 511–514.

Burgess, A. W., & Holstrom, E. (1979). Adaptive strategies in recovery from rape. *American Journal of Psychiatry, 136*, 1278–1282.

Caggiula, A. R., & Hoebel, B. G. (1966). "Copulation-reward" site in the posterior hypothalamus. *Science, 153*, 1284–1285.

Camp, D. S., Raymond, G. A., & Church, R. M. (1967). Response suppression as a function of the schedule of punishment. *Psychonomic Science, 5*, 23–24.

Campbell, D. H., Capaldi, E. D., & Myers, D. E. (1987). Conditioned flavor preferences as a function of deprivation level: Preferences or aversions? *Animal Learning & Behavior, 15*, 193–200.

Capaldi, E. D., Campbell, D. H., Sheffer, J. D., & Bradford, J. P. (1987). Conditioned flavor preferences based on delayed caloric consequences. *Journal of Experimental Psychology: Animal Behavior Processes, 13,* 150–155.

Capaldi, E. D., & Myers, D. E. (1982). Taste preferences as a function of food deprivation during original taste exposure. *Animal Learning & Behavior, 10,* 211–219.

Capaldi, E. D., & Powley, T. L. (Eds.). (1990). *Taste, experience, and feeding.* Washington, DC: American Psychological Society.

Capaldi, E. J., & Miller, D. J. (1988). Counting in rats: Its functional significance and the independent cognitive processes that constitute it. *Journal of Experimental Psychology: Animal Behavior Processes, 14,* 3–17.

Capaldi, E. J., & Molina, P. (1979). Element discriminability as a determinant of serial pattern learning. *Animal Learning & Behavior, 7,* 318–322.

Capaldi, E. J., Verry, D. R., Nawrocki, T. M., & Miller, D. J. (1984). Serial learning interim association, phrasing cues, interference, overshadowing, chunking, memory, and extinction. *Animal Learning & Behavior, 12,* 7–20.

Carew, T. J., Hawkins, R. D., & Kandel, E. (1983). Differential classical conditioning of a defensive withdrawal reflex in *Aplysia californica. Science, 219,* 397–400.

Carlson, N. R. (1992). *Foundations of physiological psychology* (2nd ed.). Boston: Allyn & Bacon.

Chambers, K. C. (1990). A neural model for conditioned taste aversions. *Annual Review of Neuroscience, 13,* 373–385.

Chomsky, N. (1965). *Aspects of the theory of syntax.* Cambridge, MA: MIT Press.

Chomsky, N. (1972). *Language and mind.* New York: Harcourt Brace Jovanovich.

Chomsky, N. (1975). *Reflections on language.* New York: Pantheon.

Chomsky, N. (1980). *Rules and representations.* New York: Columbia University Press.

Church, R. M., Wooten, C. L., & Matthews, T. J. (1970). Discriminative punishment and the conditioned emotional response. *Learning & Motivation, 1,* 1–17.

Cicero, S. D., & Tryon, W. W. (1989). Classical conditioning of meaning—II. A replication of triplet associative extension. *Journal of Behavioral Therapy & Experimental Psychiatry, 20,* 197–202.

Coleman, S. R., & Gormezano, I. (1979). Classical conditioning and the "Law of Effect": Historical and empirical assessment. *Behaviorism, 7,* 1–33.

Collier, G. (1983). Life in a closed economy: The ecology of learning and motivation. In M. D. Zeiler & P. Harzem (Eds.), *Advances in analysis of behavior: Vol. 3. Biological factors in learning.* Chichester, England: Wiley.

Collier, G., Hirsch, E., & Hamlin, P. H. (1972). The ecological determinants of reinforcement in the rat. *Physiology & Behavior, 9,* 705–716.

Corballis, M. C. (1989). Laterality and human evolution. *Psychological Review, 96,* 494–505.

Corballis, M. C. (1991). *The lopsided ape.* Oxford, England: Oxford University Press.

Curtiss, S. (1977). *Genie: A psycholinguistic study of a modern day wild child.* New York: Academic Press.

D'Amato, M. R., Salmon, D. P., & Colombo, M. (1985). Extent and limits of the matching concept in monkeys *(Cebus apella). Journal of Experimental Psychology: Animal Behavior Processes, 11,* 35–51.

D'Amato, M. R., & Schiff, E. (1964). Further studies of overlearning and position reversal learning. *Psychological Reports, 14,* 380–382.

Dantzer, R., Arnone, M., & Mormede, P. (1980). Effect of frustration on behavior and plasma corticosteroid levels in pigs. *Physiology & Behavior, 24,* 1–4.

Dantzer, R., & Kelley, K. W. (1989). Stress and immunity: An integrated view of relationships between the brain and the immune system. *Life Sciences, 44,* 1995–2008.

Darwin, C. (1859/1962). *The origin of species.* New York: Collier Books.

Darwin, C. (1871). *The descent of man and selection in relation to sex.* London: John Murray.

Darwin, C. (1872/1965). *The expression of emotions in man and animals.* Chicago: University of Chicago Press.

Davey, G. C. L. (1992). Classical conditioning and the acquisiton of human fears and phobias: A review and synthesis of the literature. *Advances in Behavior Research & Therapy, 14,* 29–66.

Davis, C. M. (1928). Self-selection of diet by newly weaned infants. *American Journal of Diseases of Children, 36*, 651–659.

Davis, C. M. (1939). The results of self-selection of diets by young children. *The Canadian Medical Association Journal, 41*, 257–261.

Davis, M. (1974). Sensitization of the rat startle response by noise. *Journal of Comparative & Physiological Psychology, 87*, 571–581.

Davis, M., & File, S. E. (1984). Intrinsic and extrinsic mechanisms of habituation and sensitization: Implications for the design and analysis of experiments. In H. V. S. Peeke & L. Petrinovich (Eds.), *Habituation, sensitization, and behavior*. New York: Academic Press.

Davison, M. (1991). Choice, changeover, and travel: A quantitative model. *Journal of the Experimental Analysis of Behavior, 55*, 47–61.

Dawkins, R. (1976). *The selfish gene*. London: Oxford University Press.

Deems, D. A., Oetting, R. L., Sherman, J. E., & Garcia, J. (1986). Hungry, but not thirsty, rats prefer flavors paired with ethanol. *Physiology & Behavior, 36*, 141–144.

Dennett, D. C. (1975). Why the law of effect will not go away. *Journal of the Theory of Social Behavior, 5*, 169–187.

Dennett, D. C. (1983). Intentional systems in cognitive ethology: The "Panglossian paradigm" defended. *The Behavioral & Brain Sciences, 6*, 343–355.

Dess, N. K. (1991). Ingestion and emotional health. *Human Nature, 2*, 235–269.

Dess, N. K., & Soltysik, S. S. (1989). Ontogeny of conditioned inhibition of conditioned respiratory suppression in kittens. *Developmental Psychobiology, 22*, 257–259.

Dess, N. K., & Soltysik, S. S. (1993). Associative properties of a conditioned inhibitor as a function of age in kittens. *Animal Learning & Behavior, 21*, 138–144.

Dethier, V. G. (1978). Other tastes, other worlds. *Science, 201*, 224–228.

Deutsch, R. (1974). Conditioned hypoglycemia: A mechanism for saccharin-induced sensitivity to insulin in the rat. *Journal of Comparative & Physiological Psychology, 86*, 350–358.

Dews, P. B. (1958). Studies on behavior. IV: Stimulant actions of methamphetamine. *Journal of Pharmacology & Experimental Therapeutics, 122*, 137–147.

Diamond, A. (1988). Differences between adult and infant cognition: Is the crucial variable presence or absence of language? In L. Weiskrantz (Ed.), *Thought without language*. Oxford, England: Clarendon Press.

Dickinson, A. (1985). Actions and habits: The development of behavioural autonomy. *Philosophical Transactions of the Royal Society (London), B308*, 67–78.

Dickinson, A. (1988). Intentionality in animal conditioning. In L. Weiskrantz (Ed.), *Thought without language*. Oxford, England: Clarendon Press.

Dinsmore, J. A. (1954). Punishment I. The avoidance hypothesis. *Psychological Review, 61*, 34–46.

Dinsmore, J. A. (1977). Escape, avoidance, punishment: Where do we stand? *Journal of the Experimental Analysis of Behavior, 28*, 83–95.

Domjan, M. (1977). Attenuation and enhancement of neophobia for edible substances. In L. M. Barker, M. R. Best, & M. Domjan, (Eds.), *Learning mechanisms in food selection*. Waco, TX: Baylor University Press.

Domjan, M. (1983). Biological constraints on instrumental and classical conditioning: Implications for general process theory. In G. H. Bower (Ed.), *The psychology of learning and motivation* (Vol. 17). New York: Academic Press.

Domjan, M. (1987a). Animal learning comes of age. *American Psychologist, 42*, 556–564.

Domjan, M. (1987b). Comparative psychology and the study of animal learning. *Journal of Comparative Psychology, 101*, 237–241.

Domjan, M., & Burkhard, B. (1988) *The principles of learning and behavior*. Belmont, CA: Brooks/Cole.

Domjan, M., & Wilson, N. E. (1972). Specificity of cue to consequence in aversion learning in the rat. *Psychonomic Science, 26*, 143–145.

Durlach, P. J., & Rescorla, R. A. (1980). Potentiation rather than overshadowing in flavor-aversion learning: An analysis in terms of within-compound associations. *Journal of Experimental Psychology: Animal Behavior Processes, 6,* 175–187.

Eibl-Eibesfeldt, I. (1975). *Ethology: The biology of behavior* (2nd ed.). New York: Holt, Rinehart & Winston.

Eikelboom, R., & Stewart, J. (1982). Conditioning of drug-induced physiological responses. *Psychological Review, 89,* 507–528.

Emmelkamp, P. M. G. (1982). *Phobic and obsessive-compulsive disorders: Theory, research, and practice.* New York: Plenum.

Estes, W. K., & Skinner, B. F. (1941). Some quantitative properties of anxiety. *Journal of Experimental Psychology, 29,* 390–400.

Falk, J. L. (1961). Production of polydipsia in normal rats by an intermittent food schedule. *Science, 133,* 195–196.

Farrar, D. (1967). Picture memory in the chimpanzee. *Perceptual & Motor Skills, 25,* 305–315.

Fisher, J., & Hinde, R. A. (1949). The opening of milk bottles by birds. *British Birds, 42,* 347–358.

Flaherty, C. F. (1982). Incentive contrast: A review of behavioral changes following shifts in reward. *Animal Learning & Behavior, 10,* 409–440.

Flaherty, C. F. (1991). Incentive contrast and selected models of anxiety. In L. Dachowski & C. F. Flaherty (Eds.), *Current topics in animal learning.* Hillsdale, NJ: Erlbaum.

Flynn, J. C. (1991). *Cocaine.* New York: Birch Lane Press.

Fountain, S. B., Henne, D. R., & Hulse, S. H. (1984). Phasing cues and hierarchical organization in serial pattern learning by rats. *Journal of Experimental Psychology: Animal Behavior Processes, 10,* 30–45.

Fordyce, W. E., Brockway, J. A., Bergman, J. A., & Spengler, D. (1986). Acute back pain: A control group comparison of behavioral vs. traditional management methods. *Journal of Behavioral Medicine, 9,* 127–140.

French, S. (1986). *Decision theory.* New York: Halstead Press.

Freud, S. (1930/1961). *Civilization and its discontents.* New York: Norton.

Galef, B. G. (1984). Reciprocal heuristics: A discussion of the relationship of the study of learned behavior in laboratory and field. *Learning & Motivation, 15,* 479–493.

Gamzu, E. (1977). The multifaceted nature of taste-aversion-inducing agents: Is there a single common factor? In L. M. Barker, M. R. Best, & M. Domjan (Eds.), *Learning mechanisms in food selection.* Waco, TX: Baylor University Press.

Gamzu, E., & Schwartz, B. (1973). The maintenance of key pecking by stimulus-contingent and response-independent food presentation. *Journal of the Experimantal Analysis of Behavior, 19,* 65–72.

Gamzu, E., Vincent, G., & Boff, E. (1985). A pharmacological perspective on drugs used in establishing conditioned food aversions. *Annals of the New York Academy of Sciences, 443,* 231–249.

Gamzu, E., & Williams, D. R. (1971). Classical conditioning of a complex skeletal act. *Science, 171,* 923–925.

Gamzu, E., & Williams, D. R. (1973). Associative factors underlying the pigeon's key pecking in autoshaping procedures. *Journal of the Experimental Analysis of Behavior, 19,* 225–232.

Gantt, W. H. (1966). Conditional or conditioned, reflex or response? *Conditioned Reflex, 1,* 69–74.

Garb, J. J., & Stunkard, A. J. (1974). Taste aversions in man. *American Journal of Psychiatry, 131,* 1204–1207.

Garcia, J., Ervin, F. R., & Koelling, R. A. (1966). Learning with prolonged delay of reinforcement. *Psychonomic Science, 5,* 121–122.

Garcia, J., Ervin, F. R., Yorke, C. H., & Koelling, R. A. (1967). Conditioning with delayed vitamin injections, *Science, 155,* 716–718.

Garcia, J., Hankins, W. G., & Rusiniak, K. W. (1974). Behavioral regulation of the milieu interne in man and rat. *Science, 185,* 824–831.

Garcia, J., Kimeldorf, D. J., & Koelling, R. A. (1955). Conditioned aversion to saccharin resulting from exposure to gamma radiation. *Science, 122,* 157–158.

Garcia, J., & Koelling, R. A. (1966). Relation of cue to consequence in avoidance learning. *Psychonomic Science, 4,* 123–124.

Gardner, B. R., & Gardner, R. A. (1971). Two-way communication with an infant chimpanzee. In A. M. Schrier & F. Stollnitz (Eds.), *Behavior of nonhuman primates* (Vol. 4). New York: Academic Press.

Gardner, H. (1985). *The mind's new science: A history of the cognitive revolution.* New York: Basic Books.

Gauci, M., Husband, A. J., & King, M. G. (1992). Conditioned allergic rhinitis: A model for central nervous system and immune system interaction in IgE-mediated allergic reactions. In A. J. Husband (Ed.), *Behavior and immunity.* London: CRC Press.

Gibbon, J., & Church, R. M. (1984). Sources of variance in information processing theory of timing. In H. L. Roitblat, T. G. Bever, & H. S. Terrace (Eds.), *Animal cognition.* Hillsdale, NJ: Erlbaum.

Gillan, D. J. (1981). Reasoning in the chimpanzee: II. Transitive inference. *Journal of Experimental Psychology: Animal Behavior Processes, 7,* 150–164.

Gillan, D. J. (1983). Inferences and the acquisition of knowledge by chimpanzees. In M. L. Commons, R. J. Herrnstein, & A. R. Wagner (Eds.), *Quantitative analyses of behavior: Vol. 4. Discrimination processes.* Cambridge, MA: Ballinger.

Gillan, D. J., Premack, D., & Woodruff, G. (1981). Reasoning in the chimpanzee. I. Analogical reasoning. *Journal of Experimental Psychology: Animal Behavior Processes, 7,* 1–17.

Goddard, M. E., & Beilharz, R. G. (1983). Genetics of traits which determine the suitability of dogs as guide-dogs for the blind. *Applied Animal Ethology, 9,* 299–315.

Gorczynski, R. M., Macrae, S., & Kennedy, M. (1982). Conditoned immune response associated with allogeneic skin grafts in mice. *Journal of Immunology, 129,* 704.

Gormezano, I., Kehoe, E. J., & Marshall, B. S. (1983). Twenty years of classical conditioning research with the rabbit. In J. M. Prague & A. N. Epstein (Eds.), *Progress in psychobiology and physiological psychology* (Vol. 10). New York: Academic Press.

Gormezano, I., & Tait, R.W. (1976). The Pavlovian analysis of instrumental conditoning.

The Pavlovian Journal of Biological Science, 11, 37–55.

Gottlieb, G. (1984). Evolutionary trends and evolutionary origins: Relevance to theory in comparative psychology. *Psychological Review, 91,* 448–456.

Gould, J. L., & Marler, P. (1987, January). Learning by instinct. *Scientific American, 256,* 74–85.

Gould, S. J. (1989). *Wonderful life: The burgess shale and the nature of history.* New York: W. W. Norton.

Gould, S. J., & Lewontin, R. C. (1979). Spandrals of San Marco and the Panglossian paradigm: A critique of the adaptionist program. *Proceedings of the Royal Society of Britain, 205,* 581–598.

Gratton, A. P., & Wise, R. A. (1988). Comparisons of connectivity and conduction velocities for medial forebrain bundle fibers subserving stimulation-induced feeding and brain stimulation reward. *Brain Research, 438,* 264–270.

Gray, J. A. B. (1964). *Pavlov's Typology.* New York: Pergamon Press.

Green, K. F., & Garcia, J. (1971). Recuperation from illness: Flavor enhancement for rats. *Science, 173,* 749–751.

Green, L., Kagel, J. H., & Battalio, R. C. (1987). Consumption-leisure tradeoffs in pigeons: Effects of changing marginal wage rates by varying amount of reinforcement. *Journal of the Experimental Analysis of Behavior, 47,* 17–28.

Griffin, D. R. (1985). Animal consciousness. *Neuroscience & Biobehavioral Reviews, 9,* 615–622.

Grossarth-Maticek, R., & Eysenck, H. J. (1989). Length of survival and lymphocyte percentage in women with mammary cancer as a function of psychotherapy. *Psychological Reports, 65,* 315–321.

Grundel, R. (1992). How the mountain chickadee procures more food in less time for its nestlings. *Behavioral Ecology & Sociobiology, 31,* 291–300.

Guttman, N., & Kalish, H. I. (1956). Discriminability and stimulus generalization. *Journal of Experimental Psychology, 51,* 79–88.

Haig, K. A., Rawlins, J. N. P., Olton, D. S., Mead, A., & Taylor, B. (1983). Food searching strategies of rats: Variables affecting the relative strength of stay and shift strategies. *Journal of Experimental Psychology: Animal Behavior Processes, 9,* 337–348.

Hake, D. F., & Azrin, N. H. (1965). Conditioned punishment. *Journal of the Experimental Analysis of Behavior, 8,* 279–293.

Hall, G. (1991). *Perceptual and associative learning.* Oxford: Clarendon Press.

Hall, J. F. (1982). *An invitation to learning and memory.* Boston: Allyn & Bacon.

Hallam, S. C., Matzel, L. D., Sloat, J. S., & Miller, R. R. (1990). Excitation and inhibition as a function of posttraining extinction of the excitatory cue used in Pavlovian inhibition training. *Learning & Motivation, 21,* 59–84.

Halliday, T. R., & Slater, P. J. B. (Eds.). (1983). *Animal behavior: Vol 3. Genes, development, and learning.* New York: W. H. Freeman.

Hanson, H. M. (1959). Effects of discrimination training on stimulus generalization. *Journal of Experimental Psychology, 58,* 321–333.

Harder, L. D., & Real, L. A. (1987). Why are bumble bees risk averse? *Ecology, 68*(4), 1104–1108.

Harlow, H. F. (1949). The formation of learning sets. *Psychological Review, 56,* 51–65.

Harlow, H. F. (1969). Age-mate or peer affectional system. In D. S. Lehrman, R. H. Hinde, & E. Shaw (Eds.), *Advances in the study of behavior* (Vol. 2). New York: Academic Press.

Harriman, A. E. (1955). The effect of a preoperative preference for sugar over salt upon compensatory salt selection by adrenalectomized rats. *Journal of Nutrition, 57,* 271–276.

Hartman, T. F., & Grant, D. A. (1960). Effect of intermittent reinforcement on acquisition, extinction, and spontaneous recovery of the conditioned eyelid response. *Journal of Experimental Psychology, 60,* 89–96.

Hayes, C. (1951). *The ape in our house.* New York: Harper & Row.

Hearst, E. (1972). Some persistent problems in the analysis of conditioned inhibition. In R. A. Boakes & M. S. Halliday (Eds.), *Inhibition and learning.* London: Academic Press.

Hearst, E., & Jenkins, H. M. (1974). *Sign-tracking: The stimulus-reinforcer relation and directed action.* Austin, TX: Psychonomic Society.

Heath, R. G. (1963). Electrical self-stimulation of the brain in man. *American Journal of Psychiatry, 120,* 571–577.

Hedges, S. B., Kuman, S., Tamura, K., & Stoneking, M. (1991). Human origins and analysis of mitochondrial DNA sequences. *Science, 255,* 737–739.

Heinrich, R. L., Cohen, M. J., Naliboff, B. C., Collins, G. A., & Bonebakker, A. D. (1985). Comparing physical and behavioral therapy for chronic low back pain on physical abilities, psychological distress, and patients' perceptions. *Journal of Behavioral Medicine, 8,* 61–78.

Herman, L. M. (1989). In which procrustean bed does the sea lion sleep tonight? *Psychological Record, 39,* 19–50.

Herman, L. M., Richards, D. G., & Wolz, J. P. (1984). Comprehension of sentences by bottlenosed dolphins. *Cognition, 16,* 129–219.

Herrick, C. J. (1948). *The brain of the tiger salamander.* Chicago: University of Chicago Press.

Herrnstein, R. J. (1961). Relative and absolute strength of response as a function of frequency of reinforcement. *Journal of the Experimental Analysis of Behavior, 4,* 267–272.

Herrnstein, R. J. (1969). Method and theory in the study of avoidance. *Psychological Review, 76,* 49–69.

Herrnstein, R. J. (1970). On the law of effect. *Journal of the Experimental Analysis of Behavior, 13,* 243–266.

Herrnstein, R. J. (1984). Objects, categories, and discriminative stimuli. In H. L. Roitblat, T. G. Bever, & H. S. Terrace (Eds.), *Animal cognition.* Hillsdale, NJ: Erlbaum.

Herrnstein, R. J., & Hineline, P. N. (1966). Negative reinforcement as shock frequency reduction. *Journal of the Experimental Analysis of Behavior, 9,* 421–430.

Herrnstein, R. J., Loveland, D. H., & Cable, C. (1976). Natural concepts in pigeons. *Journal of Experimental Psychology: Animal Behavior Processes, 2,* 285–301.

Herrnstein, R. J., & Vaughan, W., Jr. (1980). Melioration and behavioral allocation. In J. E. R. Staddon (Ed.), *Limits to action*. New York: Academic Press.

Heth, C. D. (1976). Simultaneous and backward fear conditioning as a function of number of CS-UCS pairings. *Journal of Experimental Psychology: Animal Behavior Processes, 2*, 117–129.

Hilgard, J. R. (1979). *Personality and hypnosis: A study of imaginative involvement* (2nd ed.). Chicago: University of Chicago Press.

Hinde, R. A. (1981). Biological approaches to the study of learning: Does Johnston provide a new alternative? *Behavior & Brain, 4*, 146–147.

Hodos, W., & Campbell, C. B. G. (1969). Scala Naturae: Why there is no theory in comparative psychology. *Psychological Review, 76*, 337–350.

Hogan, J. (1973). How young chicks learn to recognize food. In R. A. Hinde & J. Stevenson-Hinde (Eds.), *Constraints on learning*. London: Academic Press.

Hogan, J. (1977). The ontogeny of food preferences in chicks and other animals. In L. M. Barker, M. R. Best, & M. Domjan (Eds.), *Learning mechanisms in food selection*. Waco, TX: Baylor University Press.

Holland, P. C. (1990). Event representation in Pavlovian conditioning: Image and action. *Cognition, 37*, 105–131.

Holz, W. C., & Azrin, N. H. (1961). Discriminative properties of punishment. *Journal of the Experimental Analysis of Behavior, 4*, 225–232.

Honig, W. K., Boneau, C. A., Burstein, K. R., & Pennypacker, H. S. (1963). Positive and negative generalization gradients obtained under equivalent training conditions. *Journal of Comparative & Physiological Psychology, 56*, 111–115.

Honig, W. K., & James, P. H. R. (Eds.). (1971). *Animal memory*. New York: Academic Press.

Hsu, L. K. G. (1990). *Eating disorders*. New York: Guilford Press.

Hull, C. L. (1932). The goal gradient hypothesis and maze learning. *Psychological Review, 39*, 25–43.

Hull, C. L. (1943). Principles of behavior. New York: Appleton.

Hull, C. L. (1952). *A behavior system*. New Haven: Yale University Press.

Hulse, S. H. (1978). Cognitive structure and serial pattern learning by animals. In S. H. Hulse, H. F. Fowler, & W. K. Honig (Eds.), *Cognitive processes in animal behavior*. Hillsdale, NJ: Erlbaum.

Hursh, S. R., Navarick, D. J., & Fantino, E. (1974). "Automaintenance": The role of reinforcement. *Journal of the Experimental Analysis of Behavior, 21*, 117–124.

Husband, A. J. (Ed.). (1992). *Behavior and immunity*. London: CRC Press.

Jaynes, J. (1969). The historical origins of "ethology" and "comparative psychology." *Animal Behavior, 17*, 601–606.

Jemmott, J. B., III, Hellman, C., McClelland, D. C., Locke, S. E., Kraus, L., Williams, R. M., & Valeri, C. R. (1990). Motivational syndromes associated with natural killer cell activity. *Journal of Behavioral Medicine, 13*, 53–73.

Jemmott, J. B., III, & Magloire, K. (1988). Academic stress, social support, and secretory immunoglobulin A. *Journal of Personality & Social Psychology, 55*, 803–810.

Jenkins, H. M., & Moore, B. R. (1973). The form of the autoshaped response with food or water reinforcers. *Journal of the Experimental Analysis of Behavior, 20*, 163–181.

Jirik-Babb, P., & Katz, J. L. (1988). Impairment of taste perception in anorexia nervosa and bulimia. *International Journal of Eating Disorders, 7*, 353–360.

Justesen, D. R., Braun, E. W., Garrison, R. G., & Pendleton, R. B. (1970). Pharmacological differentiation of allergic and classically conditioned asthma in the guinea pig. *Science, 170*, 864–866.

Kagel, J. H., Rachlin, H., Green, L., Battalio, R. C., Basmann, R. L., & Klemm, W. R. (1975). Experimental studies of consumer demand behavior using laboratory animals. *Economic Inquiry, 13*, 22–38.

Kahneman, D., & Tversky, A. (1979). Prospect theory: An analysis of decision under risk. *Econometrica, 47*, 263–291.

Kalat, J. (1977). Status of "learned-safety" or "learned noncorrelation" as a mechanism in taste aversion learning. In L. M. Barker, M. R. Best, & M. Domjan (Eds.), *Learning mechanisms in food selection*. Waco, TX: Baylor University Press.

Kalat, J. W. (1984). *Biological psychology*. Belmont, CA: Wadsworth.

Kamin, L. J. (1965). Temporal and intensity characteristics of conditioned stimulus. In W. F. Prodasy (Ed.), *Classical conditioning*. New York: Appleton-Century-Crofts.

Kamin, L. J. (1968). "Attention-like" processes in classical conditioning. In M. R. Jones (Ed.), *Miami symposium on the prediction of behavior: Aversive stimulation*. Miami: University of Miami Press.

Kamin, L. J. (1969). Predictability, surprise, attention, and conditioning. In B. A. Campbell, & R. M. Church (Eds.), *Punishment and aversive behavior*. New York: Appleton-Century-Crofts.

Kamin, L. J., & Brimer, C. J. (1963). The effects of intensity of conditioned and unconditioned stimuli on a conditioned emotional response. *Canadian Journal of Psychology, 17*, 194–200.

Kamin, L. J., Brimer, C. J., & Black, A. H. (1963). Conditioned suppression as a monitor of fear of the CS in the course of avoidance training. *Journal of Comparative and Physiological Psychology, 56*, 497–501.

Kandel, E. R., & Schwartz, J. H. (1982). Molecular biology of learning: Modulation of transmitter release. *Science, 218*, 433–443.

Kaplan, R. M. (1984). The connection between clinical health promotion and health status. *American Psychologist, 39*, 755–765.

Karsh, E. B. (1962). Effects of number of rewarded trials and intensity of punishment on running speed. *Journal of Comparative & Physiological Psychology, 55*, 44–51.

Kassel, J. D., & Shiffman, S. (1992). What can hunger teach us about drug craving? A comparative analysis of the two constructs. *Advances in Behavioral Research & Therapy, 14*, 141–167.

Katz, S. (Ed.). (1975). *Biological anthropology: Selected readings from Scientific American*. San Francisco: W. H. Freeman.

Katz, S. (1982). Food, behavior, and biocultural evolution. In L. M. Barker (Ed.), *The psychobiology of human food selection*. Westport, CT: AVI Publishing.

Kellogg, W. N. (1961). *Porpoises and sonar*. Chicago: University of Chicago Press.

Kellogg, W. N., & Kellogg, L. A. (1933). *The ape and the child*. New York: Whittlesey House (McGraw-Hill).

Kelsey, J. E., & Allison, J. (1976). Fixed-ratio lever pressing by VMH rats: Work vs. accessibility of sucrose reward. *Physiology & Behavior, 17*, 749–754.

Kelso, S. R., Ganong, A. H., & Brown, T. H. (1986). Hebbian synapses in hippocampus. *Proceedings of the National Academy of Sciences USA, 83*, 5326–5330.

Kertesz, A. (1988). Cognitive function in severe aphasia. In L. Weiskrantz (Ed.), *Thought without language*. Oxford, England: Clarendon Press.

Kesner, R. P. (1990). New approaches to the study of comparative cognition. In National Institute on Drug Abuse, *Alcohol, drug abuse, and mental health administration* (pp. 22–36). Washington, DC: U.S. Department of Health and Human Services.

Kimble, G. A. (1992). *A modest proposal for a minor revolution in the language of psychology*. Paper presented at the 4th annual meeting of the American Psychological Society, San Diego, CA.

Kimmel, H. D., & Kimmel, E. (1970). An instrumental conditioning method for the treatment of enuresis. *Journal of Behavior Therapy & Experimental Psychiatry, 1*, 121–123.

Klopf, A. H. (1988). A neuronal model of classical conditioning. *Psychobiology, 16*, 85–125.

Knowles, J. H. (1977). The responsibility of the individual. In J. H. Knowles (Ed.), *Doing better and feeling worse: Health in the United States*. New York: W. W. Norton.

Koestler, F. G., & Barker, L. M. (1965). *The effect on the chimpanzee of rapid decompression to a near vacuum* (Contractor Report No. NASA CR-329). Washington, DC: NASA.

Kolb, L. (1984). The posttraumatic stress disorders of combat: A subgroup with a conditonal emotional response. *Military Medicine,*

149, 237–243. (As cited in van der Kolk, B. S. (1987). *Psychological trauma.* Washington, DC: American Psychiatric Press.)

Krane, R. V., & Wagner, A. R. (1975). Taste aversion learning with a delayed shock US: Implications for the "generality of the laws of learning." *Journal of Comparative & Physiological Psychology, 88,* 882–889.

Krank, M. D., & MacQueen, G. M. (1988). Conditioned compensatory responses elicited by environmental signals for cyclophosphamide-induced suppression of antibody production in mice. *Psychobiology, 16,* 229–235.

Kymissis, E., & Poulson, C. L. (1990). The history of imitation in learning theory: The language acquisition process. *Journal of the Experimental Analysis of Behavior, 54,* 113–127.

Laudenslager, M. L., Ryan, S. M., Drugan, R. C., Hyson, R. L., & Maier, S. E. (1983). Coping and immunosuppression: Inescapable but not escapable shock suppresses lymphocyte proliferation. *Science, 221,* 568–570.

Le, A. D., Poulos, C. X., & Cappell, H. (1979). Conditioned tolerance to the hypothermic effect of ethyl alcohol. *Science, 206,* 1109–1110.

Lehner, G. F. J. (1941). A study of the extinction of unconditioned reflexes. *Journal of Experimental Psychology, 29,* 435–456.

Leslie, A. L. (1988). The necessity of illusion: Perception and thought in infancy. In L. Weiskrantz (Ed.), *Thought without language.* Oxford, England: Clarendon Press.

Lett, B. T. (1980). Taste potentiates color-sickness associations in pigeons and quail. *Animal Learning & Behavior, 8,* 193–198.

Levine, S. C., & Carey, S. (1982). Up front: The acquisition of a concept and a word. *Journal of Child Language, 9,* 645–657.

Levis, D. J. (1976). Learned helplessness: A reply and alternative S-R interpretation. *Journal of Experimental Psychology: General, 104,* 47–65.

Lewontin, R. C. (1977). The selfish gene. *Nature, 267,* 202.

Lewontin, R. (1981, October 22). [Review of Gould's *The mismeasure of man*]. *New York Review of Books,* pp. 12–16. (As quoted in Dennett, D. C. (1983). Intentional systems in

cognitive ethology: The "Panglossian paradigm" defended (p. 355). *The Behavioral & Brain Sciences, 6,* 343–390.)

Lewontin, R. C. (1983). Gene, organism, and environment. In D. S. Bendell (Ed.), *Evolution from molecules to men.* Cambridge, UK: Cambridge University Press.

Lilly, J. C. (1961). *Man and dolphin.* New York: Doubleday.

Lockard, R. B. (1969) The albino rat–a defensible choice or a bad habit? *American Psychologist, 23,* 734–742.

Locke, J. (1690). An essay concerning human understanding. (Reprinted in E. Sprague & P. W. Taylor (Eds.) (1959). *Knowledge and value.* New York: Harcourt, Brace.)

Loehlin, J. C., Willerman, L., & Horn, J. M. (1988). Human behavioral genetics. *Annual Review of Psychology, 39,* 101–133.

Logue, A. W. (1985). Conditioned food aversion learning in humans. *Annals of the New York Academy of Sciences, 443,* 316–329.

Logue, A. W. (1988). Research on self-control: An integrating framework. *Behavioral & Brain Sciences, 11,* 665–709.

Logue, A. W. (1991). *The psychology of eating and drinking* (2nd ed.). New York: W. H. Freeman.

LoLordo, V. M. (1979). Selective associations. In A. Dickinson & R. A. Boakes (Eds.), *Mechanisms of learning and motivation.* Hillsdale, NJ: Erlbaum.

Lorenz, K. (1935). Der Kumpan in der Umwelt des Vogels; die Artgenosse als auslosende Moment sozialer Verhaltungswiesen. *Journal fur Ornithologie, 83,* 137–213. (As cited in Hess, E. H. (1973). *Imprinting.* New York: Van Nostrand.)

Lorenz, K., & Tinbergen, N. (1938). Taxis und instinkthandlung in der eirollbewegung der graugans. *Zeitschrift fur Tierpsychologie, 2,* 1–29. (As cited in Eibl-Eibesfeldt, I. (1975). *Ethology, the biology of behavior* (2nd ed.). New York: Holt, Rinehart & Winston.)

Lubow, R. E. (1989). *Latent inhibition and conditioned attention theory.* Cambridge, England: Cambridge University Press.

Lubow, R. E., & Moore, A. U. (1959). Latent inhibition: The effect of nonreinforced preexposure to the conditioned stimulus. *Journal of Comparative & Physiological Psychology, 52,* 415–419.

Lucas, F., & Sclafani, A. (1990). Hyperphagia in rats produced by a mixture of fats and sugar. *Physiology & Behavior, 47,* 51–55.

Ludvigson, H. W. (1989). *Commentary: The dilemma of mind and the quest for understanding in comparative psychology.* Paper presented at the Annual Meeting of the Southwestern Comparative Psychological Association, San Antonio, TX.

Mackenzie, S. A., Oltenacu, E. A. B., & Houpt, K. A. (1986). Canine behavioral genetics–A review. *Applied Animal Behavior Science, 15,* 365–393.

Mackintosh, N. J. (1983). *Conditioning and associative learning.* New York: Oxford University Press.

MacLean, P. D. (1970). The limbic brain in relation to the psychoses. In P. Black (Ed.), *Physiological correlates of emotion.* New York: Academic Press.

MacLean, P. D. (1977). The triune brain in conflict. *Psychotherapy & Psychosomatics, 28,* 207–220.

MacNeilage, P. F. (1991). The postural origins theory of neurobiological asymmetries in primates. In N. Krasnegor, D. Rumbaugh, M. Studdert-Kennedy, & R. Schiefelbusch (Eds.), *The biological foundations of language development.* Hillsdale, NJ: Erlbaum.

Maier, S. F., & Jackson, R. L. (1979). Learned helplessness: All of us were right (and wrong): Inescapable shock has multiple effects. In G. H. Bower (Ed.), *The psychology of learning and motivation* (Vol. 13). New York: Academic Press.

Malone, J. C. (1982). The second offspring of general process learning theory: Overt behavior as the ambassador of the mind. *Journal of the Experimental Analysis of Behavior, 38,* 205–209.

Marler, P., & Peters, S. (1988). Sensitive periods for song acquisition from tape recordings and live tutors in the swamp sparrow, *melospiza georgiana. Ethology, 77,* 76–84.

Mayr, E. (1991). *One long argument: Charles Darwin and the genesis of modern evolutionary theory.* Cambridge, MA: Harvard University Press.

McCormick, D. A., & Thompson, R. F. (1984). Cerebellum: Essential involvement in the classically conditioned eyelid response. *Science, 223,* 296–299.

Meachum, C. L., & Bernstein, I. L. (1990). Conditioned responses to a taste CS paired with LiCl administration. *Behavioral Neuroscience, 104,* 711–715.

Meck, W. H., & Church, R. M. (1983). A mode control model of counting and timing processes. *Journal of Experimental Psychology: Animal Behavior Processes, 9,* 320–334.

Medin, D. L., & Ross, B. H. (1990). *Cognitive psychology.* Austin, TX: Harcourt Brace Jovanovich.

Mehiel, R., & Bolles, R. C. (1984). Learned flavor preferences based on caloric outcome. *Animal Learning & Behavior, 12,* 421–427.

Melchior, C. L., & Tabakoff, B. (1984). A conditioning model of alcohol tolerance. In M. Galanter (Ed.), *Recent developments in alcoholism* (Vol. 2). New York: Plenum Press.

Melzac, R. (1990, February). The tragedy of needless pain. *Scientific American, 262,* pp. 27–33.

Menzel, E. W. (1978). Cognitive mapping in chimpanzees. In S. H. Hulse, H. F. Fowler, & W. K. Honig (Eds.), *Cognitive processes in animal behavior.* Hillsdale, NJ: Erlbaum.

Miller, A. D., & Rugg, M. D. (Eds.). (1992). *The neuro-psychology of consciousness.* London: Academic Press.

Miller, N. E. (1969). Learning of visceral and glandular responses. *Science, 163,* 434–445.

Miller, N. E., & Banuazizi, A. (1968). Instrumental learning by curarized rats of a specific visceral response, intestinal or cardiac. *Journal of Comparative & Physiologial Psychology, 65,* 1–7.

Miller, R. R., & Matzel, L. D. (1988). The comparator hypothesis: A response rule for the expression of associations. In G. H. Bower (Ed.), *The psychology of learning and motivation.* Orlando, FL: Academic Press.

Miller, R. R., & Matzel, L. D. (1989). Contingency and relative associative strength. In S. B. Klein & R. R. Mowrer (Eds.), *Contem-*

porary learning theories: Pavlovian condition-ing and the status of learning theory. Hills-dale, NJ: Erlbaum.

Miller, R. R., & Schactman, T. R. (1985). Condi-tioning context as an associative baseline: Implications for response generation and the nature of conditioned inhibition. In R. R. Miller & N. E. Spear (Eds.), *Informa-tion processing in animals: Conditioned inhi-bition.* Hillsdale, NJ: Erlbaum.

Milner, P. M. (1976). Theories of reinforcement, drive, and motivation. In L. L. Iverson & S. H. Snyder (Eds.), *Handbook of psy-chopharmacology* (Vol. 7). New York: Plenum Press.

Mineka, S. (1979). The role of fear in theories of avoidance learning, flooding, and extinction. *Psychological Bulletin, 86,* 985–1010.

Mischel, W. (1966). Theory and research on the antecedents of self-imposed delay of reward. *Progress in Experimental Personality Re-search, 3,* 85–132.

Mitchell, D. (1976). Experiments on neophobia in wild and laboratory rats: A reevaluation. *Journal of Comparative & Physiological Psy-chology, 90,* 190–197.

Moltz, H. (1963). Imprinting: An epigenetic ap-proach. *Psychological Review, 70,* 123–138.

Monroe, B., & Barker, L. M. (1979). A contin-gency analysis of taste aversion condition-ing. *Animal Learning & Behavior, 7,* 141–143.

Morgan, C. L. (1903). *An introduction to compar-ative psychology.* New York: Scribner.

Mowrer, O. H. (1947). On the dual nature of learning: A reinterpretation of "condition-ing" and "problem solving." *Harvard Educa-tional Review, 17,* 102–148.

Mowrer, O. H. (1960). *Learning theory and be-havior.* New York: Wiley.

Mowrer, O. H., & Lamoreaux, R. R. (1942). Avoidance behavior and signal duration: A study of secondary motivation and reward. *Psychological Monographs, 54* (Whole No. 247).

Myers, D. L., & Myers, L. E. (1977). Under-matching: A reappraisal of performance on concurrent variable-interval schedules of re-inforcement. *Journal of the Experimental Analysis of Behavior, 25,* 203–214.

Newcombe, F. (1987). Psychometric and behav-ioral evidence: Scope, limitations, and eco-logical validity. In H. S. Levin, J. Grafman, & H. M. Eisenberg (Eds.), *Neurobehavioral recovery from head injury.* Oxford, England: Oxford University Press.

Nottebohm, F. (1980). Testosterone triggers growth of brain vocal control nuclei in adult female canaries. *Brain Research, 189,* 429–436.

O'Brien, C. P. (1975). Experimental analysis of con-ditioning factors in human narcotic addic-tion. *Pharmacological Reviews, 27,* 533–543.

O'Brien, C. P., Testa, T., Ternes, J. W., & Green-stein, R. (1978). Conditioning effects of nar-cotics in humans. In *Behavioral tolerance* (Research Monograph No. 18, pp. 67–71). Washington, DC: NIDA.

Olds, J. (1962). Hypothalamic substrates of re-ward. *Psychological Review, 42,* 554–604.

Olds, J., & Milner, P. (1954). Positive reinforce-ment produced by electrical stimulation of septal area and other regions of the rat brain. *Journal of Comparative & Physiologi-cal Psychology, 47,* 419–427.

Olson, D. J., & Maki, W. S. (1983). Characteris-tics of spatial memory in pigeons. *Journal of Experimental Psychology: Animal Behavior Processes, 9,* 266–280.

Olton, D. S. (1979). Mazes, maps, and memory. *American Psychologist, 34,* 583–596.

Olton, D. S., Collison, C., & Werz, M. A. (1977). Spatial memory and radial arm maze per-formance of rats. *Learning & Motivation, 8,* 289–314.

Olton, D. S., & Samuelson, R. J. (1976). Remem-brance of places passed: Spatial memory in rats. *Journal of Experimental Psychology: An-imal Behavior Processes, 2,* 97–116.

Pateman, T. (1985). From nativism to sociolin-guistics: Integrating a theory of language growth with a theory of speech practices. *Journal of the Theory of Social Behavior, 15,* 38–58.

Patterson, F., & Linden, E. (1981). *The education of Koko.* New York: Holt, Rinehart & Winston.

Pavlov, I. (1927/1960). *Conditioned reflexes.* New York: Dover. (First published, 1927, Oxford University Press.)

Peeke, H. V. S., & Petrinovich, L. (Eds.). (1984). *Habituation, sensitization, and behavior.* New York: Academic Press.

Pfaffman, C. (1959). The sense of taste. In J. Field (Ed.), *Handbook of physiology. Neurophysiology* (Vol. 1). Washington, DC: American Physiological Society.

Pfaffman, C. (1960). The pleasures of sensation. *Psychological Review, 67,* 253–268.

Philips, H. C., Fenster, H., & Samson, D. (1988). An effective treatment for voiding dysfuntion: A control treatment trial. *Journal of Behavioral Modification, 15,* 45–63.

Phillips, A. G., & Fibiger, H. C. (1989). Neuroanatomical bases of intracranial self-stimulation: Untangling the Gordian Knot. In J. M. Liebman & S. J. Cooper (Eds.), *The neuropharmacological basis of reward* (pp. 66–105). Oxford, England: Clarendon Press.

Pinel, J. P. J. (1993). *Biopsychology.* Boston: Allyn & Bacon.

Pinker, S. (1991). Rules of language. *Science, 253,* 530–535.

Pliner, P., Herman, P. C., & Polivy, J. (1990). Palatability as a determinant of eating: Finickiness as a function of taste, hunger, and the prospect of good food. In E. D. Capaldi & T. L. Powley (Eds.), *Taste, experience, and feeding.* Washington, DC: American Psychological Society.

Plomin, R. (1990). The role of inheritance in behavior. *Science, 248,* 223–228.

Powell, J., & Azrin, N. (1968). The effects of shock as a punisher for cigarette smoking. *Journal of Applied Behavior Analysis, 1,* 63–71.

Premack, A. J. & Premack, D. (1972, October). Teaching language to an ape. *Scientific American, 227,* 92–99.

Premack, D. (1962). Reversibility of the reinforcement relation. *Science, 136,* 255–257.

Premack, D. (1965). Reinforcement theory. In D. Levine (Ed.), *Nebraska symposium on motivation* (Vol. 13, pp. 123–180). Lincoln: University of Nebraska Press.

Premack, D. (1971). Language in chimpanzee? *Science, 142,* 808–822.

Premack, D. (1976). *Intelligence in ape and man.* Hillsdale, NJ: Erlbaum.

Premack, D. (1988). Minds with and without language. In L. Weiskrantz (Ed.), *Thought without language.* Oxford, England: Clarendon Press.

Rachlin, H. C., & Green, L. (1972). Commitment, choice, and self-control. *Journal of the Experimental Analysis of Behavior, 17,* 15–22.

Randich, A., & LoLordo, V. M. (1979). Preconditioning exposure to the unconditioned stimulus affects the acquisition of the conditioned emotional response. *Learning & Motivation, 10,* 245–275.

Razran, G. (1957). The dominance-contiguity theory of the acquisition of classical conditioning. *Psychological Bulletin, 54,* 1–46.

Razran, G. (1971). *Mind in evolution.* Boston: Houghton Mifflin.

Real, L. A. (1991). Animal choice behavior and the evolution of cognitive architecture. *Science, 253,* 980–986.

Rescorla, R. A. (1967). Pavlovian conditioning and its proper control procedures. *Psychological Review, 74,* 71–80.

Rescorla, R. A. (1968). Probability of shock in the presence and absence of CS in fear conditioning. *Journal of Comparative & Physiological Psychology, 66,* 1–5.

Rescorla, R. A. (1969). Pavlovian conditioned inhibition. *Psychological Bulletin, 72,* 77–94.

Rescorla, R. A. (1971). Summation and retardation tests of latent inhibition. *Journal of Comparative & Physiological Psychology, 75,* 77–81.

Rescorla, R. A. (1985). Conditioned inhibition and facilitation. In R. R. Miller & N. E. Spear (Eds.), *Information processing in animals: Conditioned inhibition.* Hillsdale, NJ: Erlbaum.

Rescorla, R. A. (1990a). The role of information about the response-outcome relation in instrumental discrimination learning. *Journal of Experimental Psychology: Animal Behavior Processes, 16,* 262–270.

Rescorla, R. A. (1990b). Evidence for an association between the discriminative stimulus and the response outcome association in instrumental learning. *Journal of Experimental Psychology: Animal Behavior Processes, 16,* 326–334.

Rescorla, R. A., & Wagner, A. R. (1972). A theory of Pavlovian conditioning: Variations in the effectiveness of reinforcement and nonreinforcement. In A. H. Black & W. F. Prokasy (Eds.), *Classical conditioning II: Current research and theory.* New York: Appleton-Century-Crofts.

Richter, C. P. (1936). Increased salt appetite in adrenalectomized rats. *American Journal of Physiology, 115,* 155–161.

Richter, C. P. (1942). Total self-regulatory functions in animals and human beings. *Harvey Lectures, 38,* 63–103.

Richter, C. P. (1958). Rats, man, and the welfare state. *American Psychologist, 13,* 1–17.

Riley, A., & Tuck, D. L. (1985) Conditioned taste aversions: A behavioral index of toxicity. *Annals of the New York Academy of Sciences, 443,* 272–292.

Roberts, S. (1981). Isolation of an internal clock. *Journal of Experimental Psychology: Animal Behavior Processes, 7,* 242–268.

Rodgers, W., & Rozin, P. (1966). Novel food preferences in thiamine deficient rats. *Journal of Comparative & Physiological Psychology, 61,* 1–4.

Roitblat, H. L. (1987). *Introduction to comparative cognition.* New York: Freeman.

Romanes, G. (1884). *Animal intelligence.* New York: Appleton.

Routtenberg, A., & Lindy, J. (1965). Effects of the availability of rewarding septal and hypothalamic stimulation on bar pressing for food under conditions of deprivation. *Journal of Comparative & Physiological Psychology, 60,* 158–161.

Rozin, P. (1967). Thiamine specific hunger. In C. F. Code (Ed.), *Handbook of physiology (Section 6): Alimentary canal (Vol. 1): Control of food and water intake.* Washington, DC: American Physiological Society.

Rozin, P., & Kalat, J. W. (1971). Specific hungers and poison avoidance as adaptive specializations of learning. *Psychological Review, 78,* 459–486.

Rumbaugh, D. M. (Ed.). (1977). *Language learning by a chimpanzee: The LANA project.* New York: Academic Press.

Rumbaugh, D. M., & Gill, R. V. (1976). The mastery of language-type skills by the chimpanzee (*Pan*). *Annals of the New York Academy of Sciences, 280,* 562–578.

Rzoska, J. (1953). Bait-shyness: A study in rat behavior. *The British Journal of Animal Behavior, 1,* 128–135.

Sagan, C. (1977). *The dragons of Eden: Speculations on the evolution of human intelligence.* New York: Random House.

Salter, A. (1949). *Conditioned reflex therapy.* New York: Farrar, Straus.

Sampson, H. A., Mendelson, L., & Rosen, J. P. (1992). Fatal and near fatal anaphylaxis reactions to food in children and adolescents. *Journal of the American Medical Association, 327,* 380–384.

Savage-Rumbaugh, S. (1987). Communication, symbolic communication, and language: Reply to Seidenberg and Petitto. *Journal of Experimental Psychology: General, 116,* 288–292.

Savage-Rumbaugh, S., McDonald, K., Sevcik, R. A., Hopkins, W. D., & Rubert, E. (1986). Spontaneous symbol acquisition and communicative use by pygmy chimpanzees (*Pan paniscus*). *Journal of Experimental Psychology: General, 115,* 211–235.

Savage-Rumbaugh, S., Murphy, J., Sevcik, R. A., Brakke, K. E., Williams, S. L., & Rumbaugh, D. M. (1993). *Language comprehension in ape and child* (Monographs, Serial No. 233, Vol. 58(3–4), pp. 30–170). Chicago: Society for Research in Child Development.

Schiffman, S. S. (1983). Taste and smell in disease. *New England Journal of Medicine, 308,* 1337–1342.

Schneiderman, N., Fuentes, I., & Gormezano, I. (1962). Acquisition and extinction of the classically conditioned eyelid response in the albino rabbit. *Science, 136,* 650–652.

Schusterman, R. J., & Gisner, R. (1988). Artificial language comprehension in dolphins and sea lions: The essential cognitive skills. *Psychological Record, 38,* 311–348.

Schusterman, R. J., & Gisner, R. (1989). Please parse the sentence: Animal cognition in the procrustean bed of linguistics. *Psychological Record, 39,* 3–18.

Schwartz, B., & Reisberg, D. (1991). *Learning and memory.* New York: W. W. Norton.

Schwartz, B., & Williams, D.R. (1972). The role of the response-reinforcer contingency in negative automaintenance. *Journal of the Experimental Analysis of Behavior, 17,* 351–357.

Schwartz, G. E. & Weiss, S. M. (1978). Behavioral medicine revisited: An amended definition. *Journal of Behavioral Medicine, 1,* 249–251.

Schwitzer, J. B., & Sulzer-Azaroff, B. (1988). Self-control: Teaching tolerance for delay in impulsive children. *Journal of the Experimental Analysis of Behavior, 50,* 173–186.

Sclafani, A., & Springer, D. (1976). Dietary obesity in adult rats: Similarities to hypothalamic and human obesity. *Physiology & Behavior, 17,* 461–471.

Sears, L. L., & Steinmetz, J. E. (1991). Dorsal accessory inferior olive activity diminishes during acquisition of the rabbit classically conditioned eyelid response. *Brain Research, 545,* 114–122.

Sejnowski, T. J., & Churchland, P. S. (1992a). *The computational brain.* Cambridge, MA: MIT Press.

Sejnowski, T. J., & Churchland, P. S. (1992b). Silicon brains. *BYTE, 17*(10), 137–146.

Seligman, M. E. P. (1970). On the generality of the laws of learning. *Psychological Review, 77,* 406–418.

Seligman, M. E. P. (1975). *Helplessness: On depression, development, and death.* San Francisco: Freeman.

Seligman, M. E. P., & Johnston, J. C. (1973). A cognitive theory of avoidance learning. In F. J. McGuigan & D. B. Lumsden (Eds.), *Contemporary approaches to conditioning and learning.* Washington, DC: Winston-Wiley.

Seligman, M. E. P., & Maier, S. F. (1967). Failure to escape traumatic shock. *Journal of Experimental Psychology, 74,* 1–9.

Seligman, M. E. P., & Weiss, J. (1980). Coping behavior: Learned helplessness, physiological activity, and learned inactivity. *Behavior Research & Therapy, 18,* 459–512.

Seyfarth, R. M., Cheney, D. L., & Marler, P. (1980). Vervet monkey responses to three different alarm calls. Evidence of predator classification and semantic communication. *Science, 210,* 801–803.

Sheffield, F. D., & Roby, T. B. (1950). Reward value of a non-nutritive sweet taste. *Journal of Comparative & Physiological Psychology, 43,* 471–481.

Sheffield, F. D., Roby, T. B., & Campbell, B. A. (1954). Drive reduction versus consummatory behavior as determinants of reinforcement. *Journal of Comparative & Physiological Psychology, 47,* 349–354.

Sheffield, F. D., Wulff, J. J., & Backer, R. (1951). Reward value of copulation without sex-drive reduction. *Journal of Comparative & Physiological Psychology, 44,* 3–8.

Sherman, J. E., Hickis, C. F., Rice, A. G., Rusiniak, K. W., & Garcia, J. (1983). Preferences and aversions for stimuli paired with ethanol in hungry rats. *Animal Learning & Behavior, 11,* 101–106.

Sherrington, C. S. (1906). *Integrative action of the nervous system.* New York: Scribner.

Shettleworth, S. J. (1975). Reinforcement and the organization of behavior in golden hamsters: Hunger, environment, and food reinforcement. *Journal of Experimental Psychology: Animal Behavior Processes, 1,* 56–87.

Shettleworth, S. J., & Krebs, J. R. (1982). How marsh tits find their hoards: The roles of site preference and spatial memory. *Journal of Experimental Psychology: Animal Behavior Processes, 8,* 342–353.

Shumake, S. A., Thompson, R. D., & Caudill, C. J. (1971). Taste preference behavior of laboratory versus wild Norway rats. *Journal of Comparative & Physiological Psychology, 77,* 480–494.

Sidman, M. (1953). Avoidance conditioning with brief shock and no exteroceptive warning signal. *Science, 118,* 157–158.

Siegel, S. (1975). Evidence from rats that morphine tolerance is a learned response. *Journal of Comparative & Physiological Psychology, 89,* 498–506.

Siegel, S. (1977). Morphine tolerance acquisition as an associative process. *Journal of Experimental Psychology: Animal Behavior Processes, 3,* 1–13.

Siegel, S. (1983). Classical conditioning, drug tolerance, and drug dependence. In Y. Israel, F. B. Glaser, H. Kalant, R. E. Popham, W. Schmidt, & R. G. Smart (Eds.), *Research advances in alcohol and drug problems* (Vol. 7). New York: Plenum.

Siegel, S., Hinson, R. E., Krank, M. D., & McCully, J. (1982). Heroin "overdose" death: Contribution of drug-associated environmental cues. *Science, 216,* 436–437.

Simoons, F. J. (1973). New light on ethnic differences in adult lactose intolerance. *American Journal of Digestive Disorders, 18,* 595–611.

Skinner, B. F. (1938). *The behavior of organisms.* Englewood Cliffs, NJ: Prentice-Hall.

Skinner, B. F. (1948) *Walden two.* New York: Macmillan.

Skinner, B. F. (1950). Are theories of learning necessary? *Psychological Review, 57,* 193–216.

Skinner, B. F. (1953). *Science and human behavior.* New York: Macmillan.

Skinner, B. F. (1957). *Verbal behavior.* New York: Appleton.

Skinner, B. F. (1959). A case history in scientific method. In S. Koch (Ed.), *Psychology: A study of a science.* New York: McGraw-Hill.

Skinner, B. F. (1963). Behaviorism at fifty. *Science, 140,* 951–958

Skinner, B. F. (1966). The phylogeny and ontogeny of behavior. *Science, 153,* 1204–1213.

Skinner, B. F. (1971). *Beyond freedom and dignity.* New York: Knopf.

Skinner, B. F. (1989). The origins of cognitive thought. *American Psychologist, 44,* 13–18.

Small, W. S. (1901). An experimental study of the mental processes of the rat. *American Journal of Psychology, 12,* 206–239.

Smith, J. C., & Roll, D.L. (1967). Trace conditioning with x-rays as the unconditioned stimulus. *Psychonomic Science, 9,* 11–12.

Solomon, P. R., Brennan, G., & Moore, J. W. (1974). Latent inhibition of rabbits' nicitating membrane response as a function of CS intensity. *Bulletin of the Psychonomic Society, 4,* 445.

Solomon, R. L. (1977). An opponent-process theory of motivation: V. Affective dynamics of eating. In L. M. Barker, M. R. Best, & M. Domjan (Eds.), *Learning mechanisms in food selection.* Waco, TX: Baylor University Press.

Solomon, R. L. (1980). The opponent-process theory of acquired motivation: The costs of pleasure and the benefits of pain. *American Psychologist, 35,* 691–712.

Solomon, R. L., & Corbit, J. D. (1974). An opponent-process theory of motivation: I. The temporal dynamics of affect. *Psychological Review, 81,* 19–145.

Solomon, R. L., & Wynne, L. C. (1953). Traumatic avoidance learning: Acquisition in normal dogs. *Psychological Monographs, 67* (Whole No. 354).

Solomon, S. D., Gerrity, E. T., & Muff, A. M. (1992). Efficacy of treatments for posttraumatic stress disorder: An empirical review. *Journal of the American Medical Association, 268,* 633–638.

Sonuga-Barke, E. J., Lea, S. & Webley, P. (1989). The development of adaptive choice in a self-control paradigm. *Journal of the Experimental Analysis of Behavior, 51,* 77–85.

Spanos, N. P., & Chaves, J. F. (Eds.). (1989). *Hypnosis: The cognitive-behavioral perspective.* Buffalo, NY: Prometheus Books.

Spelke, E. S. (1988). The origins of physical knowledge. In L. Weiskrantz (Ed.), *Thought without language.* Oxford, England: Clarendon Press.

Spetch, M. L., Wilkie, D. M., & Pinel, J. P. (1981). Backward conditioning: A reevaluation of the empirical evidence. *Psychological Bulletin, 89,* 163–175.

Staats, C. K., & Staats, A. W. (1957). Meaning established by classical conditioning. *Journal of Experimental Psychology, 54,* 74–80.

Staddon, J. E. R. (1971). The "superstition" experiment: A reexamination of its implications for the principles of adaptive behavior. *Psychology Review, 78,* 3–43.

Stanovich, K. E., & Cunningham, A. E. (1992). Studying the consequences of literacy within a literate society: The cognitive correlates of print exposure. *Memory & Cognition, 20,* 51–68.

Stein, L. (1969). Chemistry of purposive behavior. In J. T. Tapp (Ed.), *Reinforcement and behavior.* New York: Academic Press.

Stellar, E. (1982). Preface. In L. M. Barker (Ed.), *The psychobiology of human food selection.* Westport, CT: AVI Publishing.

Stemmer, N. (1989). The acquisition of the ostensive lexicon: The superiority of empiricist over cognitive theories. *Behaviorism, 17,* 41–61.

Stoddart, D. M. (1990). *The scented ape: The biology and culture of human odour.* Cambridge: Cambridge University Press.

Storms, L. H., Boroczi, G., & Broen, W. E. (1962). Punishment inhibits an instrumental response in hooded rats. *Science, 135,* 1133–1134.

Stringer, C. B., & Andrews, P. (1988). Genetic and fossil evidence for the origin of modern humans. *Science, 239,* 1263–1268.

Suarez, E. M., & Barker, L. M. (1976). Effects of water deprivation and prior lithium chloride exposure in conditioning taste aversions. *Physiology & Behavior, 17,* 555–559.

Tarpy, R. M., & Mayer, R. E. (1978). *Foundations of learning and memory.* Glenview, IL: Scott, Foresman.

Ternes, J. W., O'Brien, C. P., Grabowski, J., Wellerstein, J., & Jordan-Hays, J. (1980). Conditioning drug responses to naturalistic stimuli. In *Problems of drug dependence 1979* (Research Monograph No. 27, pp. 67–71). Washington, DC: NIDA.

Terrace, H. S. (1979). *Nim.* New York: Alfred A. Knopf.

Terrace, H. S. (1984). Animal cognition. In H. L. Roitblat, T. G. Bever, & H. S. Terrace (Eds.), *Animal cognition.* Hillsdale, NJ: Erlbaum.

Terry, W. S., & Wagner, A. R. (1975). Short-term memory for "surprising" versus "expected" unconditioned stimuli in Pavlovian conditioning. *Journal of Experimental Psychology: Animal Behavior Processes, 1,* 122–133.

Theios, J., Lynch, A. D., & Lowe, W. F. (1966). Differential effects of shock intensity on one-way and shuttle-avoidance conditioning. *Journal of Experimental Psychology, 72,* 294–299.

Thellier, M., Desbiez, M. O., Champagnat, T., & Kergosien, Y. (1982). Do memory processes occur also in plants? *Physiologia Plantarum, 56,* 281–284.

Thinus-Blanc, C. (1988). Animal spatial cognition. In L. Weiskrantz (Ed.), *Thought without language.* Oxford, England: Clarendon Press.

Thomas, R. K., & Boyd, M. G. (1973). A comparison of *Cebus albifrons* and *Saimiri sciureus* on oddity performance. *Animal Learning & Behavior, 5,* 151–153.

Thompson, R. F. (1986). The neurobiology of learning and memory. *Science, 233,* 941–947.

Thompson, R. F., & Spencer, W. A. (1966). Habituation: A model phenomenon for the study of neuronal substrates of behavior. *Psychological Review, 73,* 16–43.

Thorndike, E. L. (1898). Animal intelligence: An experimental study of the associative processes in animals. *Psychological Review Monograph Supplement, 2,* 1–109.

Thorndike, E. L. (1932). *Fundamentals of learning.* New York: Teachers College, Columbia University.

Tiffany, S. T. (1990). A cognitive model of drug urges and drug use behavior: The role of automatic and non-automatic processes. *Psychological Review, 97,* 147–168.

Timberlake, W. (1984). Behavior regulation and learned performance: Some misapprehensions and disagreements. *Journal of the Experimental Analysis of Behavior, 41,* 355–375.

Timberlake, W., & Grant, D. S. (1975). Autoshaping in rats to the presentation of another rat predicting food. *Science, 190,* 690–692.

Timberlake, W., Wahl, G., & King, D. (1982). Stimulus and response contingencies in the misbehavior of rats. *Journal of Experimental Psychology: Animal Behavior Processes, 8,* 62–85.

Tinbergen, N. (1951). *The study of instinct.* Oxford, England: Clarendon Press.

Todorov, J. C. (1971). Concurrent performances: Effect of punishment contingent on the switching response. *Journal of the Experimental Analysis of Behavior, 16,* 51–62.

Tolman, E. C. (1932). *Purposive behavior in animals and men.* New York: Appleton-Century-Crofts.

Tolman, E. C. (1938). The determiners of behavior at a choice point. *Psychological Review, 45,* 1–41.

Tolman, E. C., & Honzik, C. H. (1930a). "Insight" in rats. *University of California Publications in Psychology, 4,* 215–232.

Tolman, E. C., & Honzik, C. H. (1930b). Degrees of hunger; reward and non-reward; and maze learning in rats. *University of California Publications in Psychology, 4,* 241–256.

Turk, D. C., Meichenbaum, D., & Genest, M. (1983). *Pain and behavioral medicine: A cognitive behavioral perspective.* New York: Guilford Press.

Valenstein, E. S., Cox, V. C., & Kakolewski, J. W. (1967). Polydipsia elicited by the synergistic action of a saccharin and glucose solution. *Science, 157,* 552–554.

van der Kolk, B. S. (1987). *Psychological trauma.* Washington, DC: American Psychiatric Press.

Van Itallie, T. B. (1979). Adverse effects on health and longevity. *American Journal of Clinical Nutrition, 32,* 2723–2733.

Vaughan, W., Jr. (1981). Melioration, matching, and maximizing. *Journal of the Experimental Analysis of Behavior, 36,* 141–149.

Vaughan, W., Jr. (1985). Choice: A local analysis. *Journal of the Experimental Analysis of Behavior, 43,* 383–405.

Vigilant, L., Stoneking, M., Harpending, H., Hawkes, K., & Wilson, A. C. (1991). African populations and the evolution of human mitochondrial DNA. *Science, 253,* 1503–1507.

von Neuman, J., & Morganstern, O. (1944). *Theory of games and economic behavior.* Princeton, NJ: Princeton University Press.

Wagner, A. R. (1976). Priming in STM: An information processing mechanism for self-generated and retrieval-generated depression in performance. In T. J. Tighe & R. N. Leaton (Eds.), *Habituation: Perspectives from child development, animal behavior, and neurophysiology.* Hillsdale, NJ: Erlbaum.

Wagner, A. R., & Rescorla, R. A. (1972). Inhibition in Pavlovian conditioning: Application of a theory. In R. A. Boakes & M. S. Halliday (Eds.), *Inhibition and learning.* London: Academic Press.

Warren, J. M. (1965). Primate learning in comparative perspective. In A. M. Schrier, H. F. Harlow, & F. Stollnitz (Eds.), *Behavior of non-human primates* (Vol. 1). New York: Academic Press.

Washburn, M. F. (1908). *The animal mind: A textbook of comparative psychology.* New York: Macmillan.

Washburn, S. L., & Moore, R. (1974). *Ape into man.* Boston: Little, Brown.

Watson, J. B. (1913). Psychology as the behaviorist views it. *Psychological Review, 20,* 158–177.

Watson, J. B. (1919). *Psychology from the standpoint of a behaviorist.* Philadelphia: Lippincott.

Watson, J. B. (1924). *Behaviorism.* New York: Norton.

Watson, J. B., & Rayner, R. (1920). Conditioned emotional reactions. *Journal of Experimental Psychology, 3,* 1–14.

Weaver, C. A. (in press). The psychology of reading. In *The Encyclopedia of Human Behavior.* San Diego: Academic Press.

Weiffenbach, J. M. (Ed.). (1977). *Taste and development: The genesis of sweet preference* (Publication No. (NIH) 77-1068). Bethesda, MD: DHEW.

Weingarten, H. P. (1990). Learning, homeostasis, and the control of feeding behavior. In E. D. Capaldi & T. L. Powley (Eds.), *Taste, experience, and feeding.* Washington, DC: American Psychological Society.

Weir, R. H. (1966). Some questions on the child's learning of phonology. In F. Smith & G. A. Miller (Eds.), *The genesis of language.* Cambridge, MA: MIT Press.

Weiskrantz, L. (1986). *Blindsight: A case study and implications.* New York: Oxford University Press.

Weiskrantz, L. (Ed.). (1988). *Thought without language.* Oxford, England: Clarendon Press.

Wenger, J. R., Tiffany, T. M., Bombardier, C., Nicholls, K., & Woods, S. C. (1981). Ethanol tolerance in the rat is learned. *Science, 213,* 575–577.

West, M. S., & King, A. P. (1980). Enriching cowbird song by social deprivation. *Journal of Comparative Psychology, 94,* 263–270.

Whorf, B. (1956). *Language, thought, and reality.* Cambridge, MA: MIT Press.

Wickler, W. (1973). Ethological analysis of convergent adaptation. *Annals of the New York Academy of Science, 223,* 65–82.

Wilcoxson, H. C., Dragoin, W. B., & Kral, P. A. (1971). Illness-induced aversions in rats and quail: Relative salience of visual and gustatory cues. *Science, 171,* 826–828.

Wilkins, L., & Richter, C. P. (1940). A great craving for salt by a child with a corticoadrenal insufficiency. *Journal of the American Medical Association, 114,* 866–868.

Williams, B. A. (1991). Choice as a function of local versus molar reinforcement contingencies. *Journal of the Experimental Analysis of Behavior, 56,* 455–473.

Williams, D. R., & Williams, H. (1969). Automaintenance in the pigeon: Sustained pecking despite contingent non-reinforcement. *Journal of the Experimental Analysis of Behavior, 12,* 511–520.

Wilson, E. O. (1975). *Sociobiology: The new synthesis.* Cambridge, MA: Harvard University Press.

Wolfe, J. B. (1934). Effectiveness of token rewards for chimpanzees. *Comparative Psychology Monographs, 12*(5) (Serial No. 60).

Wolpe, J., Salter, A., & Reyna, L. J. (1964). *The conditioning therapies.* New York: Holt, Rinehart & Winston.

Woodruff, G., & Premack, D. (1979). Intentional communication in the chimpanzee: The development of deception. *Cognition, 7,* 333–362.

Wright, A. A., Santiago, H. C., Sands, S. F., & Urcuioli, P. J. (1984). Pigeon and monkey serial probe recognition: Acquisition, strategies, and serial position effects. In H. L. Roitblat, T. G. Bever, & H. S. Terrace (Eds.), *Animal cognition.* Hillsdale, NJ: Erlbaum.

Wright, A. A., & Watkins, M. J. (1987). Animal learning and memory and their relation to human learning and memory. *Learning & Motivation, 18,* 131–146.

Young, P. T. (1966). Hedonic organization and regulation of behavior. *Psychological Review, 73,* 59–86.

Zahorik, D., & Bean, C. A. (1975). Resistance of "recovery" flavors to later association with illness. *Bulletin of the Psychonomic Society, 6,* 309–312.

Zahorik, D. (1977). Associative and non-associative factors in learned food preferences. In L. M. Barker, M. R. Best, & M. Domjan (Eds.), *Learning mechanisms in food selection.* Waco, TX: Baylor University Press.

Zahorik, D., Mair, S. F., & Pies, R. W. (1974). Preferences for tastes paired with recovery from thiamine deficiency in rats. *Journal of Comparative & Physiological Psychology, 87,* 1083–1091.

Acknowledgments

P. 27, Fig. 2.2 and P. 36, Fig. 2.4 (a) from Robert A. Wallace, *Animal Behavior: Its Development, Ecology, and Evolution.* Santa Monica, CA: Goodyear Publishing Company.

P. 37, Fig. 2.4(b) from Strickberger, M. W. (1990). *Evolution,* Fig. 19.2 Copyright © 1990 by Jones and Bartlett Publishers, Boston. Reprinted by permission. Adapted from Schultz, A. H., 1933. Die körperproportionen der erwachsenen catarrhinen Primaten, mit spezieller Berücksichtigung der Menschenaffen. *Anthropol. Anz., 10,* 154–185.

P. 47, Box 2.6 from Eibl-Eibesfeld, I., *Ethology: The Biology of Behavior,* Fig. 3.1. Copyright © 1967 by R. Piper & Co. Verlag, Munich. Reprinted by permission from the English translation of Eibl-Eibesfeld, I. *Grundriß der vergleichenden Verhaltensforschung: Etho logie* by permission of R. Piper & Co. Verlag.

P. 51, Table 2.1 from Goddard, M. E. & Beilharz, R. G. (1993). Genetics of traits which determine the suitability of dogs as guide-dogs for the blind, Table 1. *Applied Animal Ethology, 9,* 299–315. Reprinted by permission of Elsevier Science Publishers BV.

P. 122, Fig. 4.6 from *The Principles of Learning and Behavior,* 2nd ed., by M. Domjan and B. Burkhard. Belmont, CA: Brooks-Cole Publishing Co., 1986, p. 46. Copyright © 1986, 1982 by Wadsworth, Inc. Reprinted by permission of Brooks-Cole Publishing Co., Pacific Grove, CA 93590.

P. 123, Fig. 4.7(a) from Schneiderman, N., Fuentes, I., & Gormezano, I. (1962). Acquisition and extinction of the classically conditioned eyelid response in the albino rabbit. *Science, 136,* 650–652. Copyright 1962 by the A.A.A.S. Reprinted by permission of the American Association for the Advancement of Science.

P. 126, Fig. 4.8(a) from Kamin, L. J. & Brimer, C. J. (1963). The effects of intensity of conditioned and unconditioned stimuli on a conditioned emotional response, Figure 1. *Canadian Journal of Psychology, 17,* 194–200. Reprinted by permission. Figure 4.8(b) from Kamin, L. J. (1965). Temporal and intensity characteristics of the conditioned stimulus. In Prokasy, W. F., editor. (1965). *Classical Conditioning.* New York: Appleton-Century-Crofts, 1965. Reprinted by permission.

P. 206, Fig. 5.13 from Garcia, J., Hankins, W. G., & Rusiniak, K. W. (1974). Behavioral regulation of the milieu interne in man and rat. *Science, 185,* 824–831.

531

University of California Publications in Psychology, 4, 215–232. Copyright 1930 by the University of California Press. Reprinted by permission of the University of California Press. P. 443, Fig. 10.2(b) from Olton, D. S. & Samuelson, R. J. (1976). Remembrance of places past: spatial memory in rats. *Journal of Experimental Psychology: Animal Behavior Processes, 2*, 97–116. Copyright 1976 by the American Psychological Association. Reprinted by premission.

Pp. 449–451, Fig. 10.3 from Farrar, D. N. (1967). Picture memory in the chimpanzee. *Perceptual and Motor Skills, 25*, 303–315. © *Perceptual and Motor Skills,* 1967. Reproduced with permission of author and publisher.

P. 457, Fig. 10.5 from Warren, J. M. (1965). Primate learning in comparative perspective, Figure 4. In Schrier, A. M., Harlow, H. F., & Stollnitz, F., editors. *Behavior of Nonhuman Primates.* New York: Academic Press. Reprinted by permission of Academic Press, Orlando, FL.

P. 486, Fig. 10.7 from *Cognitive Psychology and its Implications*, by J. R. Anderson. Copyright © 1980, 1985, 1990 by W. H. Freeman. Reprinted by permission.

Photo Credits

Pp. 24, 125, 315, 449, and 451 courtesy of United States Air Force; p. 24 used by permission of Don Van Piper and USAF; p. 30, courtesy of National Portrait Gallery, London, England; p. 41, courtesy of Dr. Stephen Jay Gould and Harvard University; p. 45, Thomas McAvoy/Life Magazine, © Time Warner; p. 53, courtesy of Dr. Nancy K. Dess; pp. 112 and 223, Bettmann Archive; p. 127, courtesy of Prof. Ilene Bernstein; p. 147, courtesy of Prof. Robert A. Rescorla; p. 184, courtesy of Dr. Michael Best; p. 227, courtesy of Dr. Charles Brewer; p. 232, Nina Leen/Life Magazine, © Time Warner; pp. 377, 378, and 392 courtesy of the author; p. 432, courtesy of Dr. Larry Weiskrantz; p. 466, courtesy of Dr. Peter MacNeilage; p. 471, courtesy of Dr. Sue Savage-Rumbaugh.

Name Index

I1

Subject Index